Introduction to
Early Childhood Education

3rd Edition

Introduction to Early Childhood Education

3rd Edition

Eva Essa

University of Nevada-Reno

Delmar Publishers

an International Thomson Publishing company I(T)P®

Albany • Bonn • Boston • Cincinnati • Detroit • London • Madrid
Melbourne • Mexico City • New York • Pacific Grove • Paris • San Francisco
Singapore • Tokyo • Toronto • Washington

NOTICE TO THE READER

Cover Design: The Drawing Board

Delmar Staff:
Publisher: William Brottmiller
Administrative Editor: Jay Whitney
Acquisitions Editor: Erin O'Connor Traylor
Production Coordinator: James Zayicek
Art and Design Coordinator: Timothy J. Conners
Editorial Assistant: Mara Berman
Marketing Manager: Nicole Benson

Printed in the United States of America

For more information contact:

Delmar Publishers
3 Columbia Circle, Box 15015
Albany, New York 12212-5015

International Thomson Publishing Europe
Berkshire House
168-173 High Holborn
London, WC1V 7AA
United Kingdom

Nelson ITP Australia
102 Dodds Street
South Melbourne
Victoria 3205, Australia

Nelson Canada
1120 Birchmount Road
Scarborough, Ontario
M1K 5G4, Canada

International Thomson Editores
Seneca 53
Colonia Polanco
11560 Mexico D. F. Mexico

International Thomson Publishing GmbH
Königswinterer Strasse 418
53227 Bonn
Germany

International Thomson Publishing Asia
60 Albert Street
#15-01 Albert Complex
Singapore 189969

International Thomson Publishing—Japan
Hirakawacho Kyowa Building, 3F
2-2-1 Hirakawacho Chiyoda-ku
Tokyo 102, Japan

1 2 3 4 5 6 7 8 9 10 XXX 03 02 01 00 99 98

Library of Congress Cataloging-in-Publication Data

Essa, Eva.
Introduction to early childhood education instructor's annotated edition / Eva Essa. — 3rd ed.
p. cm.
Includes bibliographical references and index.
ISBN 0–7668–0048–2
1. Early childhood education—United States. 2. Early childhood educators—Training of—United States. I. Title.
LB1139.25.E87 1999
372.21'0973—dc21 98–13673
CIP

Brief Contents

Preface

Chapter Contents

Part III The *Why* of Early Childhood Education

Chapter 5: Rationale Supporting Early Childhood Education 103

Chapter 6: Goals, Objectives, and Evaluation 141

Part IV The *Where* of Early Childhood Education

Part V The *How* of Early Childhood Education—Curriculum

Chapter 9: Creative Development Through the Curriculum 219

Chapter 10: Physical Development Through the Curriculum 249

Chapter 11: Cognitive Development Through the Curriculum 279

Part VI The *How* of Early Childhood Education—Guidance

Preface

DEAR STUDENTS:

With this book, you are embarking on a fascinating journey. The field of early childhood education is a rich and rewarding endeavor for a dedicated person, like yourself, whose aim is to make a difference by working with young children. By the end of the course for which you are reading this book, you will be much more knowledgeable about young children, the many components of high-quality early childhood programs, and the role of the professional early childhood educator. What can you expect as you read on?

Who is this Book for?

This text is intended for current or future professionals who want to learn more about early childhood education. This field encompasses work with children from infancy through age eight. Thus, included in the book is information about infant and toddler programs, programs for preschool-aged children, and before- and after-school programs for young school-aged children. Most obviously this book is for those who teach and care for young children. But it is also relevant for those who work in other capacities in early childhood education programs—administrators, parent education and involvement coordinators, curriculum coordinators, staff training consultants, and others.

Philosophy

This text adheres to the underlying philosophy that the early childhood educator's most important task is to provide a program that is sensitive to and supports the development of young children. Only in a child-centered program, in which children are allowed to make choices, the guidelines are clear and logical, activities are planned to meet the needs of the individual children in the group, and adults are consistent and loving, will children flourish. A good early childhood experience can contribute immeasurably to helping children become responsible people who care about and show concern for others. This philosophy is reflected throughout the book, in all chapters and on all topics.

Content

This book is divided into 6 parts and further subdivided into 16 chapters. The purpose of these six parts is to answer the questions, "**What** is early childhood education?" "**Who** are the people involved in early childhood education?" "**Why** is early childhood education important?" "**Where** is early childhood education carried out?" and "**How** is early childhood education implemented?" These questions are important ones as you gain insight into all aspects of early childhood education.

Within the 16 chapters you will learn more about the scope of early childhood education and why it is needed (Chapter 1); the children, families and teachers involved in early childhood education (Chapters 2 to 4); the history leading up to the field today, the theoretic rationale supporting it, and how theory is translated into specific types of programs (Chapter 5); the relevance of goals, objectives, and evaluating progress toward meeting these (Chapter 6); the importance of the physical environment as the setting of early childhood education programs (Chapter 7); scheduling for and planning the curriculum (Chapter 8); contents of the curriculum as it supports children's creative, physical, cognitive, language, and social development (Chapters 9 to 13); guiding children through daily routines and in group activities (Chapter 14); guiding individual children's social behaviors, including handling problem behaviors (Chapter 15); and helping children cope with stress in their lives (Chapter 16). These chapters will help you learn a great deal of information about the basic components of early childhood education and working with young children.

Features of this Book

As you begin to use this text, you will appreciate some of its features, which are designed to help you learn the material as thoroughly and efficiently as possible. As you browse through the book, you will note that its page format is set up with the text on the inside two-thirds of each page and marginal notations on the remaining one-third. Pay close attention to the outside section of each page, for there are the features that will be of most help to you. You will find three specific types of information here.

Definitions: Important definitions of concepts introduced in the book are placed in the outer margin. When you see a new term discussed in the text, it will be highlighted in blue and then defined nearby in the margin. This will help reinforce concepts and help you more easily learn some of the important terminology used in the field of early childhood education. It is also helpful for you to know that all definitions appear again, in alphabetical order, at the back of the book in the **Glossary.**

Key Points: Also in the margin is, in effect, an outline of the major points of the book. At the beginning of sections and important subsections you will find a one- or two-sentence summary statement about the key point of that section.

Key Questions: Finally, some important questions are posed in the margin to help you consider the information you are reading and to further explore its relevance. Some of the key questions suggest activities that will help you learn more about the topic. Your instructor may also suggest activities related to the Key Questions.

From Theory and Research to Practice

Like most fields, early childhood education is built on theoretical ideas and concepts and on research that give it a strong and cohesive foundation. In Chapter 5 several key theories are introduced. Throughout the book, these are referred to, with particular emphasis on making them relevant to work with young children. In addition, relevant research studies are cited throughout the text to provide scientific validity to many of the practices and ideas of early childhood education.

To help make theoretical and research information meaningful, actual examples of young children and their teachers are frequently provided. These examples help make the contents of the book, especially theoretical and research information, take on meaning and come alive. As you read through the book and continue to come across names such as Piaget, Erikson, and Vygotsky, these influential people and their ideas will become familiar to you. They are important allies in an introduction to early childhood education because their contributions provide such valuable insights to our understanding of children.

Boxes

Each chapter contains two special features or boxes. One of these, "A Closer Look," offers in-depth information about a topic of importance. Some of the featured items in "A Closer Look" review recent research studies that broaden our understanding of the field of early childhood education and of young children; others examine professional position statements about topics of importance. The second special feature is called "Experiences" and focuses on individuals who work in the field of early childhood education. These first-hand narratives provide insight into what makes working with young children meaningful to professionals.

Working with Parents

Within each chapter you will find a section that focuses on one of the important tasks of early childhood teachers—communicating, coordinating, and working with parents. These sections tie the topic of each chapter to the needs and interest of parents. These features appear in addition to Chapter 3, which focuses specifically on families of young children. Parents and other family members are a vital and integral part of early childhood programs, and the focus on working with families in each chapter is intended to help highlight and strengthen this element.

I wish you success as a student in this early childhood education course and as a future or current professional in the field. It is a field that is important and exciting, one that has much potential for growth. In your role as an early childhood professional, you can contribute a great deal to young children, their families, and the profession. Best of luck!

Eva L. Essa
Reno, Nevada

Acknowledgments

Many people have continued to be supportive, facilitating the great commitments of time, energy, and resources that are needed in an undertaking such as the writing and revision of *Introduction to Early Childhood Education.* I would like to gratefully acknowledge their assistance, for without them the original book, the second edition, and this third edition would not have been possible. Good friends and colleagues such as Joanne Everts, Jane Hogue, Richard Kettring, Geoffrey Leigh, Yvonne Lineau, Sally Kees Martin, Leigh Ann Maxwell, Colleen Murray, Sue Oriard, Tina Springmeyer, Sherry Waugh, and many others have offered wonderful ideas and great support. I am particularly grateful to Margie Lawlor, for her insightful review of the first edition, and Dr. Alice Honig of Syracuse University, for her helpful comments and suggestions.

Special thanks are due the reviewers of the manuscript:

Andrew Carroll, Ed.D.
Georgia Southwestern College
Americus, GA

Janet E. Fish, Ed.D.
California State University, Northridge
Northridge, CA

Teresa C. Hopkins, Ph.D.
Germanna Community College
Locust Grove, VA

James Kerr, Ph.D.
Edward Waters College
Jacksonville, FL

Judy Lindman
Rochester Community & Technical College
Rochester, MN

Terry Oliver
Technical College of the Lowcountry
Beaufort, SC

Barbara P. Shelton, Ed.D.
Villa Julie College
Stevenson, MD

Nancy Winter
Greenfield Community College
Greenfield, MA

Stacey York
Minneapolis Community & Technical College
Minneapolis, MN

I am also grateful to Melissa Burnham, whose assistance through careful research and insightful comments was instrumental in development of the section, "Who's Who in Early Childhood Education?" found in Chapter 5.

Another person who deserves special appreciation is my editor, Jay Whitney, of Delmar Publishers. His prodding to meet the needs of early childhood education students more fully, his knowledge about early childhood education training programs, and his many wonderful ideas have helped considerably in shaping this book.

DEDICATION

Uncountable thanks go to my husband, Ahmed Essa, whose encouragement, ideas, and steadfast support keep me going. To him, and to my daughter, Fiona, and my son, Eugene, I dedicate this third edition of *Introduction to Early Childhood Education.*

part I

The What of Early Childhood Education

Each section of this book focuses on a different aspect of early childhood education, beginning with defining just *what* this field is. Part I addresses the *what* of early childhood education.

chapter 1

The Scope of and Need for Early Childhood Education

Early childhood education—This is the profession you are exploring through this text and the course in which you are enrolled. Just what is this field? What does it encompass? What does it involve? Why is it important? What is its place in today's society? What is its future? There is so much to discuss about early childhood education, so much to share. As you begin learning about this field of study, the answers to some of these questions will gain greater significance and become more focused. This chapter presents an overview of the field of early childhood education.

THE GROWTH OF EARLY CHILDHOOD EDUCATION

Although the importance and value of education in the early years of life have been acknowledged for more than 2,000 years (Carter, 1987), relatively recent factors have brought early childhood education to the forefront of public awareness. Fundamental changes in the economy, family life, public awareness, and public support have had a profound effect on early childhood education. You have undoubtedly seen the recent newspaper headlines and national magazine covers that have directed a spotlight on child care. Much of their focus has been on changes in family life that have brought about the need for child care outside the home. These changes include many complex factors such as a rising cost of living, an increased number of dual-income families, an increase in single-parent families, an increased number of teenage parents, greater mobility as families move more readily to different parts of the country, and a decrease in the impact of the extended family.

Early childhood education—Term encompassing developmentally appropriate programs that serve children from birth through age eight: a field of study that trains students to work effectively with young children.

The needs of working families are not the only reason early childhood has been in the public focus. Over the past quarter century, the success of publicly funded programs such as Head Start has shown us that high-quality early educational intervention can combat poverty and dysfunction. There has also been increased attention to the needs of special populations of young children and how to bring them into the the mainstream of society; for instance, children who are handicapped, abused, or culturally different.

Finally, many professionals are outspoken and eloquent advocates for the rights of children.

Changes in Family Life

Increasing numbers of women are entering the work force. Almost 60 percent of mothers of preschoolers now work and require child care for their youngsters.

"Typical" family life has changed considerably since the end of World War II. Demographic information indicates that increasing numbers of women are entering the work force. No longer do most mothers stay at home to rear their young children. Economic necessity forces many families to rely on two paychecks because one simply does not provide for all of their financial needs. In other families, both parents work because of the desire for personal and professional development rather than from economic exigency.

Whereas in 1950 only 12 percent of mothers of children under six worked, that number has risen to almost 60 percent (Children's Defense Fund, 1991; Lerner & Abrams, 1994) and is projected to continue to rise to about two-thirds (Hofferth, 1989; Hofferth & Phillips, 1987). This growth in the number of families in which both parents work has dramatically increased the need for child care.

There are significantly more single parents today than ever before, mostly because of the increase in divorce. These parents need care for their children while they work.

Another family change that has affected the demand for child care is the increase in the number of single parents. The majority of single-parent families are created through divorce. Couples today are far more apt to divorce than in the past—about $2^1/_2$ times as likely in the 1980s than in the 1960s, and about four times as likely as in the 1930s. The divorced single parent who now has custody of the children is probably the mother. Not only will she experience a significant decrease in income and standard of living, but she will also, most likely, have to work (or work longer hours) to support the family. Of course, to work outside the home, the single parent needs to find appropriate child care. In addition to the increased number of families headed by a divorced single parent is a growing number of never-married parents,

Today, an increasing number of women in their childbearing years are in the work force. It is estimated that almost 60 percent of mothers of young children work, requiring some form of child care for their children. What will the percentage of working mothers be as we enter a new century? Experts predict a continuing rise.

some still finishing their high school education. Today, far more teenage mothers opt to keep their babies than in past years. They also need child care while they are at school or work.

A third change in family life is the increasing mobility of many of today's families. Work demands cause some families to move away from relatives who might otherwise provide support. Family mobility, involving only the small **nuclear family,** has contributed to the declining influence of the **extended family,** that network of relatives such as grandparents, uncles and aunts, or adult brothers and sisters beyond the immediate family.

Families today move more than families did in the past. Mobility takes them away from relatives who might have been available to provide child care while the parents work.

Nuclear family—The smallest family unit made up of a couple or one or two parents with child(ren).

Extended family—Family members beyond the immediate nuclear family; for instance, aunts and uncles, grandparents, or cousins.

The most prevalent form of child care has always been that provided by a relative. One reason is that many parents seem more comfortable leaving a young child with a relative than with a stranger. In addition, relatives may charge little or no money for taking care of the child, making this a financially attractive alternative. Although relatives continue to provide the most widely used form of child care, that rate has been decreasing. From the 1960s to the 1980s, the rate of preschool child care provided by a relative dropped from almost two-thirds to less than one-half of the total number of children in care (Wash & Brand, 1990). This change in family support is another reason for the increased demand for outside child care.

Changes such as increasing numbers of dual-income families and single-parent families, and a decline in the impact of the extended family, have dramatically raised the demand for child care and brought early childhood education to the forefront of public attention. "Child care is now as essential to family life as the automobile or the refrigerator. . . . [T]he majority of families, including those with infants, require child care to support parental employment" (Scarr, Phillips, & McCartney, 1990, p. 26).

Benefits of Early Childhood Education

The need of working parents for child care makes early childhood education a topic of national prominence, but this is not the only reason for its increasing importance. On a parallel though separate track, there has been extensive discussion and research about the benefits of early education for special populations of children and families. Thus, children from low-income families, children with disabilities, and children at risk for other reasons have been enrolled in publicly funded programs. Since the mid-1960s, federal, state, and local support has increased as a result of mounting evidence that high-quality early childhood programs can and do make a long-term difference that carries into adulthood. Researchers have concluded that good early childhood programs not only improve the lives of the children and families involved but also result in substantial economic benefits for society. Although early intervention programs are expensive, their cost is more than recovered in subsequent years through greater schooling success, decreased need for special education, lowered delinquency and arrest rates, and decreased welfare dependence (Berrueta-Clement, Schweinhart, Barnett, Epstein, & Weikart, 1984). We will discuss more specific aspects of some of this research in Chapter 5.

Research has shown that good early childhood education programs have a lasting effect on children from disadvantaged backgrounds.

Investment in early intervention programs has substantial social and financial benefits for society.

Research has shown that programs such as Head Start offer many positive benefits for children from low-income families.

Child Advocacy

Many professionals participate in child advocacy, bringing to public and legislative attention the needs of children and families in poverty as well as the need for affordable child care for families with moderate incomes.

KEY QUESTION #1

If you were given "three wishes" to bring about changes for young children and their families, what would they be? Share these with others in your class. From a combined list, develop several child and family issues that you think child advocates might address.

Child advocacy—Political and legislative activism by professionals to urge change in social policies affecting children.

A third factor that has brought early childhood education into the public consciousness is the urgency with which many professionals view the plight of increasing numbers of children and families. Of particular concern are the many families that face abject poverty, lacking the most basic necessities. Yet the social problems reach beyond the needs of the poor, to working parents with moderate incomes who are beset by the scarcity of affordable, high-quality care. Dr. T. Berry Brazelton (1990), a well-known pediatrician and child advocate, concludes that America is failing its children because they are subject to more deprivations than any other segment of society. As the poorest group in America, 20 to 25 percent of children live in poverty.

In its 1990 report card, the Children's Defense Fund considers that "as the wealthiest nation on earth and the standard-bearer of Democracy, we have an 'A' capacity to care for our children but an 'F' *performance* on many key indicators of child well-being. By every measure, the U.S. performance is unsatisfactory" (p. 5).

Organizations such as the Children's Defense Fund and the National Association for the Education of Young Children actively advocate children's rights. Their frequent lobbying for children's rights through **child advocacy** in the nation's capital has promoted legislation related to child care, mandatory education for children with disabilities, Head Start, health care for poor children, and other vital services. It was largely through their efforts that the ABC bill (Act for Better Child Care) was developed and presented to Congress in the late 1980s. In its 1990 session, Congress finally passed a child care bill that succeeded to a large extent because of the relentless effort of thousands of early childhood professionals and other advocates who inundated members of Congress with letters, visits, and phone calls (Mann, 1991). This legislation, however, achieved only part of what was originally envisioned by those who advocated it. Far more needs to be done.

The needs of children and families have become political concerns. They have come to the attention of both political leaders and the public through the astute efforts of those dedicated to advocating the rights of children, including early childhood professionals. But there is a continuing need to promote a common concern for the welfare of all children. Based on current trends, researchers predict that the problems facing children and families will intensify, the gap between the well-to-do and the poor will widen, and the number of children who grow up in poverty will increase (Halpern, 1987).

WHAT IS INCLUDED IN EARLY CHILDHOOD EDUCATION?

We have looked at some of the concerns that have made early childhood education, as one aspect of the needs and welfare of young children, a current issue. But early childhood education is a broad term and includes a variety of approaches and programs. We will now examine some of the ways in which this term is used and some of the classifications into which programs can be grouped.

Early childhood education programs can be defined by their purpose. The main purpose of many programs is child care. The goal of others is enrichment. A third category includes programs whose main aim is compensation for some lack in the children's backgrounds.

Purpose of Programs

We have already touched on some basic differences in programs that stem from their underlying thrust. The major purpose of many programs is to care for children while their parents work. The rapid rise in recent years in the numbers of children in full-day care, either in child care centers or in family child care homes, has paralleled the increasing prevalence of working mothers. The primary goal of child care programs is to provide safe and nurturing care in a developmentally appropriate setting for children.

Enrichment is a second aim, prevalent particularly in part-time preschools. Such programs usually include specific activities to enhance socialization, cognitive skills, or overall development of young children. The underlying notion is that children will benefit from experiences that they may not receive at home; for instance, participating in group activities, playing with a group of age-mates, or learning specific concepts from specially trained teachers.

A recent phenomenon that has proliferated is **hothousing**, an apt term that has become popular. Hothousing is aimed at accelerating some aspect of young children's development and is of considerable

KEY QUESTION #2

Visit an early childhood program in your community and share this information with other members of your class who have visited different programs. Classify the programs according to their characteristics; for instance, purpose, setting, ages of children served, and source of support. Does your community have a variety of programs? Which types of programs predominate? What family needs are met by these programs?

Hothousing—Term taken from horticulture in which plant growth is speeded up by forced fertilization, heat, and light; refers to accelerated learning programs for young children.

Many young children are cared for in family child care homes rather than in center-based care facilities. Typically, family child care homes have children of various ages, spanning infancy through the preschool years.

concern to many early childhood professionals (Gallagher & Coche, 1987; Hills, 1987; Sigel, 1987). It differs from enrichment by the nature of its activities and by its lack of developmental appropriateness. Such programs are generally designed to meet the expectations of "upwardly mobile 'yuppie' parents, who want designer diapers and designer degrees in Greek, Suzuki, and computer programming for their infants" (Clarke-Stewart, 1988, p. 147).

A third major purpose, found particularly in publicly funded programs, is compensation. Compensatory programs aim to make up for some lack in children's backgrounds. The basic philosophy of programs such as Head Start is to provide experiences that will help children enter the mainstream of society more successfully. Such experiences include a range of services, encompassing early childhood education, health and dental care, nutrition, and parent education.

These categories, although descriptive of some underlying differences among programs, are not mutually exclusive. Few child care centers are concerned with only the physical well-being and care of children. Most also provide enriching experiences that further children's development. At the same time, preschool programs have to be concerned with appropriate nurture and safety while the children are in their care. Similarly, compensatory programs are also concerned with enriching experiences and caring for children, whereas child care or preschool programs may serve to compensate for something lacking in the backgrounds of some of the children.

Program Settings

Family child care homes—Care for a relatively small number of children in a family home that has been licensed or registered for that purpose.

Programs are either home-based, such as family child care homes, or center-based, located in a school facility and usually serving large groups of children.

Programs for young children can be divided into home-based and center-based settings. In the United States, when all ages of children are considered, the largest number are cared for in **family child care homes.** Infants and toddlers in particular are cared for in such homes (Hofferth & Phillips, 1987) because parents of very young children seem to prefer a more intimate, homelike setting. Most states require licensing or registration of family child care homes, although it is estimated that a great majority of homes are unlicensed (Halpern, 1987).

About 33 percent of families with mothers in the work force use family child care. Twenty percent are providers who are not related to the child, whereas 13 percent are relatives (Galinsky, Howes, Kontos, Shinn, 1994). In the first extensive study of family child care settings, Galinsky and her colleagues (1994) found that many of the homes were less than adequate. Only 9 percent of the homes studied were rated as good, 35 percent were rated as inadequate, and the remaining 56 percent were considered custodial, neither good nor "growth-enhancing." The study also found a clear relationship between program quality and children's development.

Center-based programs—A program for young children located in a school setting, usually including larger groups of children than are found in home-based programs.

Center-based programs are located in early childhood centers and usually include larger groups of children than do home-based programs. Center-based programs represent the greatest increase in the types of programs offered in the United States. In the 1960s only about 6 percent of young children were cared for in centers, but that number increased to 28 percent by the 1990s (Galinsky et al., 1994). At the same time, the number of preschoolers cared for in family child care homes decreased slightly, while the percentage of those cared for by a relative dropped considerably (Wash & Brand, 1990).

Ages of Children

Another way early childhood programs can be grouped is by the age of the children. The classification of early childhood spans birth to age eight, which includes infants, toddlers, preschoolers, kindergartners, and children in the primary grades. Needless to say, working parents need care for children of varying ages.

Programs are specially designed for children of varying ages, such as toddlers, preschoolers, and school-aged children.

Infants and Toddlers. One of the most dramatic increases in recent years has been in infant and toddler programs. In fact, center-based care for infants and toddlers represents the fastest growing type of program today (Howes, 1987). The majority of children under age three are cared for in family child care homes or by a relative; however, almost 7 percent of infants and 14 percent of toddlers were in center-based infant/toddler programs in the mid-1980s (Hofferth & Phillips, 1987). Across the country, child care centers have been converting part of their facilities to care for infants and toddlers, and many states have incorporated new sections in licensing standards to consider the special needs of this youngest segment of the population.

Not all infant/toddler programs fall under the rubric of child care, however. A number of compensatory programs enroll children from infancy, starting with early parent-child education as a way of intervening in the poverty cycle.

Preschoolers. The largest segment of children in early childhood programs are preschool-aged, including youngsters from two or three years of age until they begin formal schooling. Some programs consider the preschool period as beginning at age three; others enroll children once they are out of diapers.

Programs for this age group include a wide variety of options. The majority of preschoolers are in all-day programs that provide care while their parents work. Some children attend part-day preschool or nursery school programs for social and educational enrichment. We

Center-based infant and toddler programs are one of the fastest growing types of programs today.

will examine more specific components or developmentally appropriate practice for preschoolers in the remaining chapters.

Kindergarten and Primary Children. Many definitions of early childhood include children up to age eight. Thus, directions for curriculum, teaching strategies, and the environment in kindergartens and primary classrooms derive from what is known about the development and mode of learning of young, school-aged children.

Integrated curriculum—A program that focuses on all aspects of children's development, not just cognitive development.

Developmentally appropriate practice for this age group, just as for earlier ages, involves an integrated approach. **Integrated curriculum** acknowledges the importance of all aspects of human development—social, emotional, physical, cognitive, language, and creative—rather than focusing primarily on the cognitive. It also involves learning experiences that promote all aspects of development rather than separating the day into discrete times, such as for math, reading, physical education, or social studies. Through the use of learning centers (to be discussed in Chapter 7) and themes (Chapter 8), such subjects are fully integrated and considered an inseparable part of each other (Bredekamp, 1987).

Centers that serve school-aged children before and after school are an alternative to leaving these children, termed latch-key children, alone at home.

Before- and After-School Care. Young school-aged children whose parents work full time also require care when they are not in school. This is often provided through before- and after-school programs and full-day holiday and summer care. Such programs generally focus on recreation rather than education, particularly self-directed and self-initiated activities, since the children spend the bulk of their day in school (Alexander, 1986).

Latch-key children or **Self-care children**—School-aged children who, after school, return to an empty home because their parents are at work.

While many young children are enrolled in such programs, millions of others, labeled **latch-key** or **self-care children,** return to an empty home after school. Concerns about the safety, vulnerability, and lack of judgment of young school-aged children have prompted an increase in before- and after-school programs. Relatively little research, however, has been carried out to measure the long-term effects of various arrangements for the school-aged children of working parents (Powell, 1987a).

Sources of Support for Programs

Yet another way of grouping early childhood programs is by the base of their support, especially financial. Many early childhood programs are privately owned, for-profit businesses, whereas others are not-for-profit enterprises operated through public funds or sponsored by an agency or church. A growing number of early childhood programs are also supported by employers.

The majority of early childhood programs are privately owned and operated for profit. Among these, the number of child care chains has increased dramatically over the past three decades, particularly in metropolitan areas.

For-Profit Programs. About 60 percent of all child care programs are operated for profit, either as a single, independently owned business or as part of a regional or national chain (Wash & Brand, 1990). This is a rapidly rising figure, and it is expected to continue to increase. For many years, the majority of child care in most American communities was provided by local owners who operated one or two centers. Over the past three decades, however, child care chains, which

Franchised child care centers are one of the fastest growing providers of child care for children of working parents. KinderCare is the largest of these chains with well over 1,000 KinderCare Centers, most in urban areas.

have experienced tremendous growth—increasing by as much as a thousandfold—have moved into virtually every metropolitan area (Neugebauer, 1988). The expansion of large child care chains appears to be slowing down in the 1990s, partly because so many new centers opened during the previous decade (Neugebauer, 1991). Child care chains are big business! Some even sell stock that is traded on the New York Stock Exchange, deal in mergers and takeovers, and utilize sophisticated marketing strategies.

Not-for-Profit Programs. In for-profit early childhood programs, what is left over after expenses are paid is considered profit, which goes back to the owner or stockholders. In not-for-profit programs, such monies are incorporated back into the program or are returned to the sponsoring agency. Not-for-profit centers gain that status through incorporation or sponsorship from an entity that is itself not operated for profit. Churches are the most common sponsors of early childhood programs, and other groups, such as YMCAs, YWCAs, city recreation departments, hospitals, colleges, and universities, also are frequent sponsors.

Religious houses of worship are the most common sponsors of not-for-profit programs, although other organizations and agencies also sponsor early childhood programs.

Many religiously sponsored programs came into existence in the 1970s and 1980s. Often, religious buildings included nursery, preschool, or recreational rooms that were used primarily on the day of worship. As the need for child care for working parents became a more pressing social concern, many religious groups responded to that need by opening their facilities during the week. Some such programs are affiliated with and incorporate their religion, but many are secular.

A unique form of not-for-profit early childhood program is the **parent-cooperative.** Parent-cooperatives, usually part-day preschool programs, are based on a staffing structure that includes a paid professional head teacher and a rotating staff of parents. As part of enrolling their children in the program, parents are required to assist a specified number of days in the classroom. This arrangement serves both a staffing and a parent education function. With increasing numbers of parents entering the work force full time, however, fewer parents have the time to participate in cooperative programs. The popularity of cooperatives, which was high in earlier decades, has waned

Parent-cooperative—A program staffed by one professional teacher and a rotating staff of parents.

considerably, and many communities today do not have such programs available at all.

Another rapidly growing type of early childhood program is sponsored or supported by an employer for the children of employees. Child care as a work benefit has proved to increase worker productivity and loyalty.

Employer-Supported Programs. One of the fastest growing groups with a stake in early childhood programs are employers. Many companies have found that their interest in the needs and concerns of parent-employees has resulted in a more productive and stable work force. For the working parents of young children, work and family are not separable and, in fact, often overlap. Child care, in particular, is not just a family issue but also a concern to employers. Employees with young children, compared to other workers, more often are late for work, leave work early, miss work altogether, and deal with personal issues while at work. When employers support child care in some way, the result is lower absenteeism, greater stability and loyalty, better morale, decreased stress, and less distraction among their employees (Fernandez, 1986).

There are many ways in which employers can support their workers' child care needs. Some large companies have created child care centers in or near the place of work. In some instances, several employers band together in supporting a child care center that meets the joint needs of their employees. Another way in which employers help their workers is through arrangements with community child care centers; for instance, through a voucher system or direct subsidies. Such an arrangement can ensure that employees are given priority when child care openings are available.

Other employers provide referral services to help match the employee's need with available resources in the community. Some companies have helped develop and train a community network of family child care homes to meet their workers' needs. A growing trend among employers is to provide more responsive scheduling options; for instance, job sharing or flex-time. Child care is increasingly becoming a benefits option as companies allow their employees to select from a menu rather than providing a common benefits package for all. Some companies, recognizing the significant problem posed by children who are mildly ill, have begun to explore sick-child care options (Friedman, 1989; NAEYC Information Service, 1990).

Although a growing number of companies are getting involved, it is estimated that only about 10 percent of the nation's large employers and less than 1 percent of all employers are providing any type of child care assistance (Friedman, 1989). Yet recent surveys have shown that many companies are considering work/family programs in their future plans, including various child care assistance options (Galinsky, 1989).

Early childhood programs affiliated with institutions of higher learning provide training for students, and child care for student-parents, faculty, and staff.

University- and College-Affiliated Programs. A sizable group of early childhood programs is linked to higher education. The institution in which you are enrolled may, in fact, have such a program. Some are specifically laboratory or training programs that support student practicum and provide subjects for research; others serve primarily as campus child care centers for the young children of students, staff, and faculty. The trend in the 1980s and 1990s is for campus programs to combine these two functions, offering child care to the campus community while utilizing the children and families for practicum

EXPERIENCES

chapter 1

JANE, Child Care Resource Center Director

Meeting Many Needs

Finding affordable, quality child care is difficult for many parents, especially parents with infants and toddlers. My job is to help them in this quest. Our resource center is supported by local business and the university, which contract with us to help parents find affordable, high-quality care. We do this through two separate but complementary components of our program.

One major element of our resource center is to recruit family home care providers. Some are already in the business, while others are new providers. We screen applicants carefully to ensure that our philosophy and practices are compatible. We provide training, ongoing support, start-up funds for licensing fees and equipment, and monitoring to the providers. In exchange, those invited to become part of our network make a commitment to give priority to children whose parents come to the resource center. Our main goal is to expand the selection of high-quality home care programs, particularly ones that care for infants and toddlers. One way for us to validate quality is to encourage the caregivers in our network to apply for home child care accreditation, which many pursue.

The second element of our center is to help parents find a good match to meet their child care needs. We keep track of all available child care openings in the community so that we can inform parents of various options. Part of our service to parents is to help them identify elements of quality in child care programs. We try to educate and sensitize parents to what they should look for in seeking a high-quality program for their young children through brochures, checklists, videos, and conversations with staff. Some children of university families are placed in the university's child care facility; other children are placed in one of the network homes; still others find what they need in a community facility.

We monitor information about the various available options for child care and match these to what parents need; the age of the child, the location and distance between home and work, cost, and type of program are some of the considerations we put into the equation. In addition, we try to impact the community by recruiting and training new home care providers so that the choices for high-quality care are increased.

A combination of employer support and trained professionals can make a difference in a community, as this child care resource center has shown. Increasingly, families, employers, and professionals are finding innovative ways of meeting the needs of children, parents, child care providers, and the community.

experiences

and research purposes (Everts, Essa, Cheney, & McKee, 1993; Herr & Zimmerman, 1989).

Such programs are operated either as a campuswide venture or are affiliated with a specific department or unit; for instance, early childhood education, child development, home economics, or psychology. Because of the involvement of professional educators, campus programs are generally high quality, incorporating what has been learned about young children and early childhood programs through research, theory, and professional practice.

Publicly Supported Programs. Another significant supporter of early childhood programs is the public sector, whether it is the federal government or state and local agencies. Head Start is probably the best known federally supported program. In addition, Federal Social Services Block Grant (Title XX) funds allow states to provide child care support for low-income working parents, parents who participate in training or educational programs, teenage parents, and children who are placed under some form of protective services. There are also federally subsidized early childhood programs at the more than 400 U.S. military bases around the world (Wash & Brand, 1990). We will discuss two types of publicly supported programs, Head Start and public school preschools, in more detail.

Head Start is the largest publicly supported early childhood program, providing educational, nutritional, health, and parent support to enrolled children and families.

Head Start. In 1964, in response to a growing concern about the perceived handicap with which many children from poverty environments entered elementary school, Project Head Start was initiated. The goal of Head Start was to help break the poverty cycle by providing children and their families with a comprehensive program that would help meet some of their needs. Today, there are Head Start programs in every state and territory, in rural and urban sectors, on American Indian reservations, and in migrant areas. Head Start serves close to half a million preschoolers; it is estimated that this figure represents only about 20 percent of the eligible children in the country. Altogether, more than 11 million youngsters and their families have been involved in Head Start since its inception.

Although Head Start is an education program aimed at providing a high-quality early childhood experience for three-to five-year-olds, it

Almost half a million children are served every year through Head Start programs, but it is estimated that this program serves only about one-fifth of those children eligible.

also encompasses several other components. An important element is the provision of health care through medical, dental, nutritional, and mental health services for all of its children. This recognizes that children who are hungry or ill cannot learn. All children receive medical and dental examinations, immunizations, a minimum of one hot meal and a snack each day, and the services of a mental health specialist if needed.

KEY QUESTION #3

Visit a local Head Start program. What benefits do you see for the children? Talk to a staff member and find out what services are provided for the children and their families.

Parenting education and parent involvement are also integral elements of Head Start. Many parents have found employment through the program because it gives them priority for any available nonprofessional Head Start jobs. Another component involves social services for families to provide assistance, information about community resources, referrals, and crisis intervention. Finally, Head Start also serves children with special needs, following the congressional mandate that at least 10 percent of its children must be handicapped (Head Start, 1990).

Public School Involvement. A relatively recent development in early childhood program sponsorship is the involvement of public schools. A few states have provided services to young children below kindergarten age for a number of years, and more public schools are considering extending their programs to preschoolers. By the late 1980s, over half of the states had appropriated monies for prekindergarten programs (Mitchell & Modigliani, 1989); others have placed early childhood high on their agendas. In another way, public schools have, for many years, provided early childhood centers as part of high school or vocational training programs.

Increasing numbers of school districts across the country are offering programs for preschoolers, particularly for those considered at risk for school failure.

Although many early childhood educators feel that public school involvement is a natural and inevitable step, some persistent issues surround this move. One of the most serious concerns is that prekindergarten programs in public schools will focus on school readiness rather than on developmental appropriateness, simply offering a downward extension of the kindergarten and first grade curriculum and methods (Elkind, 1988; Morado, 1986).

A recent study of public school prekindergartens provides support that such fears may, in many instances, be legitimate. "We saw some wonderful programs, full of child-centered and interesting activities. Others were rigid and boring. Still others sounded good on paper, but observations revealed that classroom practice in no way resembled written philosophy" (Mitchell & Modigliani, 1989, p. 57). The authors of this report go on to say, however, that their finding of a mix of good and inappropriate practice in public school programs was not so different from what they saw in community-based early childhood programs.

Public school sponsorship of early childhood programs is, of course, subject to the same limited supply of money that constrains other publicly supported programs. Typically, therefore, existing programs serve a limited group of children. In most states, such programs give priority to children who are considered at risk for school failure. Some states specify low-income children, while others indicate that participants have to be Head Start eligible. This focus on poor children or children at risk to a large measure responds to the 80 percent of children who are eligible for Head Start but are not included in that program. Some states provide programs for three- as well as four-year-olds, although the majority are structured to serve only fours. In a few states, prekindergarten programs are designed for children who come from non-English-speaking families. Educators, however, are calling for a broader constituency in public school early childhood programs, one that includes all children rather than only a limited group (Day, 1988).

DEFINING QUALITY IN EARLY CHILDHOOD PROGRAMS

Up to this point, we have discussed early childhood programs in fairly concrete, descriptive terms, looking at characteristics by which programs can be grouped. Programs can and should also be examined in terms of how they best meet the needs and consider the well-being of children. Such considerations are related to quality.

Current research is, in fact, focusing on identifying factors that create good early childhood programming for young children. The old questions about whether child care is good or bad for children or what type of care is best are now obsolete; today's research questions seek to find out how to make child care better for young children (Phillips, 1987). Current research is attempting to provide empirical support for the reasons commonly cited as indicators of good programs. The emerging picture tells us that quality in child care is not dependent on single, separable factors but is a result of the presence of and interaction among a variety of complex elements (Clarke-Stewart, 1987a).

Child-Adult Ratio

When an adult is in charge of too many children, the behaviors of both the children and adults are adversely affected by this high child-adult ratio.

It has generally been assumed that when caregivers are responsible for large numbers of children, the quality of care is adversely affected. A number of studies have addressed this assumption and found that the ratio significantly affects children's behavior and child-adult interaction (Phillips & Howes, 1987; Howes, 1997).

For instance, when there are larger numbers of children per adult, there is less verbal interaction among adults and children than

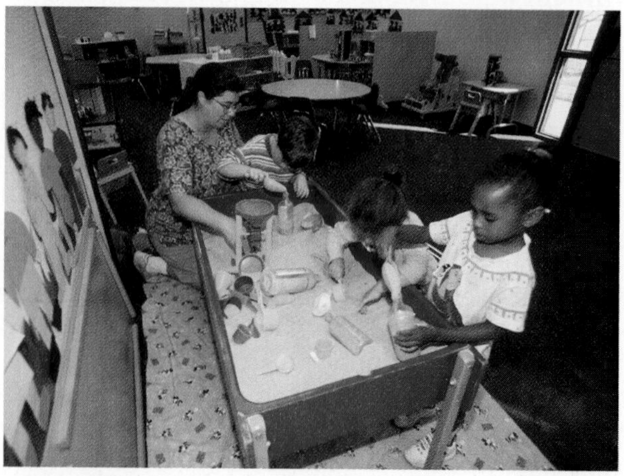

An optimal ratio of adults to children is one indicator of quality in early childhood programs. A low ratio facilitates interaction and allows for more individualized attention to each child. According to research and the advice of experts, what is an appropriate ratio for young children? What other factors are important in determining an appropriate ratio?

when the **child-adult ratio** is lower. Conversations are brief and routine and contain more prohibitions (Smith & Connolly, 1981). A significant factor in providing quality care has to do with giving children individualized attention, confirming their unique identity and worth as individuals. When an adult is responsible for a large number of children, that adult is less able to provide such attention and is more concerned instead with controlling and managing the group.

Child-adult ratio—The number of children for whom an adult is responsible, calculated by dividing the total number of adults into the total number of children.

What is an appropriate child-adult ratio? There is no definitive answer, although the literature does provide some suggested guidelines. For instance, the National Association for the Education of Young Children suggests a ratio of 3 to 1 for infants, 6 to 1 for toddlers, 8 to 1 for three-year-olds, 10 to 1 for four- and five-year-olds, and 15 to 18 to 1 for children in the primary grades (Bredekamp, 1987).

Keep in mind, however, that child-adult ratio is one variable that interacts with other factors, such as group size and teacher qualifications. For instance, in France, child-adult ratios are considerably higher than in the United States, but French preschool teachers are highly trained, adequately paid, and accorded greater status and respect than their American counterparts (Howes & Marx, 1992). "We should avoid blanket statements about high child-adult ratios being good and low ratios being bad until we check out the *limits* beyond which a low ratio is bad and the *outcome* for which a high ratio is good" (Clarke-Stewart, 1987a, p. 114).

Group Size

In the late 1970s, the large-scale National Day Care Study (Roupp, Travers, Glantz & Coelen, 1979) published its findings. These indicated that group size was one of two consistently important variables that define quality of care for young children. In smaller groups, adults and children interacted more; children were more cooperative, innovative, and verbal; and they earned better scores on cognitive and language tests. Another study found more elaborate play, including more pretend play, among children in smaller rather than larger groups (Bruner, 1980). One recent study summarized that with a moderate number of children in a group, children seem to demonstrate greater social competence (Clarke-Stewart, 1987b). When caregivers are in charge of large groups of children, on the other hand, they tend to be less responsive to the children and provide less social stimulation (Howes, 1983).

Research has shown that a moderate group size results in children who are more socially and intellectually competent than those who spend their day in large groups.

Ideal group size cannot really be defined because other variables, including the parameters of the physical environment, need to be considered. The National Association for the Education of Young Children provides some guidelines for group size (Bredekamp, 1987). For very young preschoolers, the association recommends no more than 12 children per group; a maximum group size of 20 children is recommended for four-and five-year-olds.

Mixed-Age Grouping

Only in relatively recent times has our society stratified children into narrow groups defined by age, particularly in the educational context. "Although humans are not usually born in litters, we seem to insist that they be that they be educated in them" (Katz, Evangelou, & Hartman, 1990, p. viii). Many theorists and researchers have expressed concern about the increasing separation of people into age-segregated groups in education, housing, recreation, work, and other aspects of life (Bronfenbrenner, 1971). It is more natural, they say, that people of all ages interact and share various aspects of their lives. Throughout history, socialization was facilitated because people of all ages learned from and helped each other.

Grouping children of varying ages together has benefits in many development areas for both younger and older children.

Mixed-age grouping—Programs in which children of different ages—for instance, three- to six-year-olds—are together in one class.

Early childhood education programs are also often segregated into narrow, homogeneous age groups, with the three-year-olds in one class, four-year-olds across the hall in another, and the mature five-year-olds in their own environment. But many educators suggest that heterogeneous or **mixed-age grouping** will benefit both younger and older children. Positive social behaviors such as sharing, turn taking, and helpfulness are encouraged in mixed-age groups. Similarly, older children have more opportunities to practice leadership skills, and young children become involved in more complex forms of pretend play. Children also appear to reap cognitive benefits from mixed-age grouping (Katz et al., 1990).

Both younger and older children benefit from mixed-age grouping, as in this class, which enrolls children between the ages of three and six.

As we have already mentioned, quality in early childhood programs depends on many factors. There are certainly many outstanding, high-quality programs in which children are grouped by narrow age criteria; other equally good programs utilize a mixed-age model. Nonetheless, research suggests that children receive some unique benefits from being placed in groups that contain a wider age-range of children. For this reason, mixed-age grouping is included as a criterion of quality.

Developmental Appropriateness of the Program

High-quality programs have developmentally appropriate expectations and activities, and do not push children into inappropriate, accelerated activities.

Child development theory and research have given us a good understanding of what young children are like and under what conditions they thrive and learn best. From such information, we are able to plan environments, develop activities, and set expectations that are congruent with children's needs and characteristics (Bredekamp, 1987). Throughout this book—particularly Chapter 7, which considers how to structure an appropriate environment; Chapters 8 through 11, which examine how various components of the curriculum reinforce development; and Chapters 15 through 17, in which we consider guidance principles—we will focus on developmentally appropriate practice.

In recent years, there has been increasing concern that public education is not adequately preparing children for the challenges of the future. This concern has been accompanied by a push to return to "the basics" in education. Some have interpreted this to include young children, with the idea that an earlier introduction to academics will result in better prepared and educated children.

As we will consider in various contexts in this book, early childhood professionals and researchers have expressed grave apprehensions about this trend, aptly termed hothousing, which pushes preschoolers into inappropriate tasks for which they are not develop-

A Closer Look

Quality, Compensation, and Affordability

"The ability of many early childhood programs to provide high-quality services is in jeopardy because they lack sufficient resources to fully cover the costs of quality. As a result, the development and well-being of millions of children may be at risk" (NAEYC, 1995). These words capture the essence of NAEYC's position statement, revised in 1995, on quality, compensation, and affordability. It brings together the three interrelated elements that keep early childhood education from reaching its potential. Recommendations and goals for achieving higher quality, equitable compensation, and affordable access are outlined in the position statement.

Considerable research has recently underscored the wide range in quality of programs for young children. For instance, review A CLOSER LOOK in chapter 3 for a dicussion of the *Cost, Quality, and Child Outcomes in Child Care Centers* report (Helburn et al., 1995), which found that only a small percentage of early childhood programs meet standards of excellence and that the majority are mediocre or less in quality. Poor quality programs place children at risk in all areas of development.

Research has also demonstrated that children's development is supported by professionals who are specifically educated in early childhood education. Yet those who work with young children are not adequately compensated for their work. The average salary of those who work with young children is considerably less than the pay received by others with comparable training. As a result, there is a high rate of turnover in early childhood programs (Whitebook, Howes, & Phillips, 1993), a factor which further compromises the well-being of children who need consistency and stability in their lives.

The third interrelated element is affordability of child care, particularly for low income families. There is considerable inequity in the percentage of salary that families spend for child care. Families with low income spend 25% or more of that income on child care, compared to the 6 to 8% spent by families in median to higher income brackets. Affordable access to child care is estimated to keep many low-income mothers from the work force or from educational pursuits.

Recognition of the seriousness of this "trilemma" has led to active and aggressive measures by NAEYC and other committed organizations and individuals who are concerned about the welfare of young children. For instance, efforts such as the **Worthy Wage Campaign** have been designed to educate decision-makers and the public to help improve the salaries and benefits earned by early childhood professionals. But considerably more work is needed before the goals of NAEYC's position statement on quality, compensation, and affordability are met.

a closer look

Warm, responsive interaction among adults and children is an important element in defining quality in early childhood programs.

mentally ready (Gallagher & Coche, 1987). Young children can learn a lot of material in a mechanistic, rote manner, but if these experiences are meaningless, such information has little relevance (Sigel, 1987). Thus, for an early childhood program to meet quality criteria, it must respect the emerging abilities of young children without imposing inappropriate expectations.

Child-Adult Interaction

Frequent and responsive interaction between adults and children is a necessity in high-quality programs.

Although many factors contribute to the quality of an early childhood program, perhaps the most important factor on which quality depends is the interaction between the adults and the children. In a good program, adults are involved with children, they are nurturing and responsive, there is ample verbal exchange, and interactions aim to teach, not just to control (Clarke-Stewart, 1987a). A wonderful physical facility, an exemplary child-adult ratio, and a favorable group size would all be negated by uncaring and unresponsive child-adult interaction. It is, after all, the teachers who determine the tone and the character—in effect, the quality—of a program.

Staff Qualifications

Research shows that teachers with specific early childhood training are important in a high-quality program.

Research has given us some indication about teachers who are most likely to provide a high-quality early childhood program. Earlier we discussed how the National Day Care Study (Roupp et al., 1979) found group size to be one of two important quality variables. The other significant variable that emerged from this study was the importance of a staff with specific training in early childhood education and development. Such teachers engaged in more interactions with the children, and the children showed greater social and cognitive abilities compared to those whose teachers lacked such training. These findings, particularly in relation to children's more advanced cognitive and language ability, have been supported in other research (Clarke-Stewart, 1987a; Clarke-Stewart & Gruber, 1984; Howes, 1983). In addition, teachers with early childhood training were rated as more positive and less punitive, employing a less authoritarian style of interaction with the children (Arnett, 1987).

Staff Consistency

A serious concern among professionals and parents alike is the high rate of staff turnover in early childhood programs, estimated at 41 percent per year in a recent national study (Whitebook, Howes, & Phillips, 1989). Many young children spend the bulk of their waking hours in child care, with adults other than their parents. One important task of the early years is forming a secure attachment relationship to adults. Although primary attachment is with parents, research has shown that young children certainly do become attached to their caregivers. But when children lose an adult with whom they have formed such an attachment, the loss can be profound (Phillips & Howes, 1987).

Staff consistency is important, because high staff turnover has a negative impact on young children.

One study found that there is less child-adult interaction in centers with a high teacher-turnover rate (Phillips, Scarr & McCartney, 1987). This is not surprising when interaction is dependent in part on establishing a relationship, something that takes time to develop. Another study (Howes & Hamilton, 1993) found toddlers who experienced changes in their primary teachers were more aggressive as four-year-olds. This research supports the importance of a stable, secure relationship between young children and their caregivers.

Respect and Concern for Staff

As we have discussed, a nurturing, well-trained, and consistent staff is important to a quality program, but a reciprocal concern for the well-being of the staff also is needed. Working with young children is a demanding, challenging job. Thus, it is in the best interests of the children, the families, and the employer if staff members receive appropriate pay and benefits, and work in a satisfying environment. In such a setting, the needs of the staff are seriously considered, an atmosphere of camaraderie is fostered, autonomy is encouraged in planning an appropriate program for the children, and the physical environment includes space for adults (Jorde-Bloom, 1988a). Chapter 4 will discuss some of the parameters and issues associated with providing such an environment for the staff.

A good staff, which provides an appropriate program for young children, has to be respected and nurtured.

Physical Environment

Even though we will discuss the physical environment of the early childhood program in greater detail in Chapter 7, it is necessary to note here that the physical facility is another important factor that contributes to program quality. According to research, children demonstrate higher cognitive skill levels and greater social competence in schools that are safe and orderly, contain a wide variety of stimulating equipment and materials, and are organized into learning centers on the basis of similar materials and activities when compared to children in programs that lack these features (Clarke-Stewart, 1987b).

A physical environment that is child-centered, organized, and stimulating is integral to the overall quality of a program.

A child-oriented environment and family involvement also contribute to the quality of a program.

A child-oriented environment conveys to children that this place is meant for them. There are interesting and worthwhile things to do in a child-oriented environment because it was designed with the characteristics, ages, and abilities of the children in mind. A child-centered environment also requires fewer restrictions and prohibitions because it was fashioned specifically for children. This contributes toward a positive and pleasant atmosphere. In short, a good environment conveys to children that this is a good place to be, that people here care about them, that they are able to satisfy their desire to learn and their innate curiosity, and that it is safe to try without fear of failure.

Family Involvement

With increasing numbers of children spending many hours per day in child care, parents and teachers are, more than ever, partners in many aspects of child rearing and socialization. Studies have shown that the children benefit when parents and the early childhood staff share a common commitment to the best interests of the children, communicate openly, and have mutual respect. On the other hand, if there is a lack of communication so that parents do not know what happened at school and teachers are not informed of significant events in the child's home life, there is lack of continuity for the child. In Chapter 3 we will explore this homeschool link in much greater detail.

Quality as a Combination of Factors

KEY QUESTION #4

Suppose you were asked by the parent of a young child, "How do I find a good child care program?" What would you answer? How can you help a parent recognize quality indicators?

For the purposes of discussion, we have isolated a number of components that contribute to quality early childhood programming, including child-adult ratio, group size, mixed-age grouping, developmental appropriateness of the program, child-adult interaction, staff qualifications, staff consistency, concern for staff, the physical environment, and family involvement. It is important to keep in mind, however, that quality can best be understood and studied as a combination of components (Phillips, 1987). As you further your understanding and knowledge of the field of early childhood education, remember that quality is not defined by a single factor but depends on the complex interaction of a variety of elements in which you, as an early childhood professional, play a key role.

THE FUTURE OF EARLY CHILDHOOD EDUCATION

Up to this point, we have examined social forces that have helped to shape the field of early childhood education, looked at the multifaceted descriptors that define the field today, and examined some qualitative aspects of programs for young children. As we move into the twenty-first century, we can look back and unravel some of the factors that have shaped the field as it exists today.

But what lies ahead? Are there more changes in store? Will unresolved social issues be addressed? Will early childhood education become an important force in considering these issues? Lacking the aid of a crystal ball, we might, nonetheless, try to predict what lies ahead by extrapolating from current trends.

KEY QUESTION #5

Projections for the future, as we have discussed, indicate an increased need for good early childhood programs. What changes do you think are needed to bring about improvements for children and for early childhood professionals?

Economic and social factors point to a continued growing need for early childhood education. These include an expected increase in the number of women in the work force, an increase in the number of children in poverty, and greater employer sponsorship of child care.

- From all economic and social indications, it is reasonable to expect that a high percentage of families will continue to have two parents in the work force. Thus, while they are at work, dual-income families, along with working single parents, will continue to need care for their young children.
- At the same time, the increase in the percentage of women in the childbearing years has slowed down in the late 1990s. Nonetheless, the number of children potentially requiring child care in the year 2000 will be higher than in the middle to late 1990s (Wash & Brand, 1990).
- Employment opportunities in early childhood education will continue to increase. Bureau of Labor Statistics projections indicate that employment in the child care field will increase faster than for all other occupations through the year 2005 (Bureau of Labor Statistics, 1996).
- The number of young children who live in poverty is also expected to increase (Halpern, 1987; Wash & Brand, 1990). Federal funding for programs such as Head Start, and local and state allocations to serve children at risk, are likely to increase, along with programs and job opportunities for teachers of young children.
- Employer involvement in child care sponsorship has been one of the fastest growing trends during the past decade. This interest is likely to increase as employers recognize the need to provide child care benefits for parent-employees to help maintain a productive work force. A shift in type of program sponsorship, along with new job opportunities, is likely to accompany such a trend.
- All indications are that the number of positions for early childhood professionals will continue to rise because of the ongoing need of families for child care, welfare reform creating a larger work force, projected expansion in publicly funded programs for children at risk, and increasing numbers of employer-sponsored

The need for qualified early childhood educators will increase.

programs. Yet there are and will continue to be grave concerns about the stability of the early childhood work force. In no other industry is there such a high turnover of employees as in child care.

- As we have discussed, stability of staff is an important element in the quality of early childhood programs because children's trust and attachment to the adults in their lives depends on that stability. As a result, there has been increasing concern about the interplay between the needs of children for quality care, the needs of parents for affordable child care, and the needs of early childhood professionals for appropriate compensation and status (Willer, 1987). This concern, expressed both from within and from outside the early childhood profession, will continue to be articulated. We can expect greater focus on and increasing public awareness of this issue in the future.

The early childhood profession will continue to address issues related to quality care and the needs of staff.

- As issues related to early care and education continue to occupy public attention, it becomes more and more apparent that our country lacks a cohesive and consolidated social policy within which to consider child and family matters. For instance, a wide variety of agencies initiate, license, administer, and evaluate varying programs for children and families, often relying on disparate philosophies, approaches, and regulations. But, at the same time, because of increased public attention, there also seems to be greater willingness to address such issues with more depth, integration, and forethought. Sharon Kagan (1990), in her examination of legislation in this field, came to the following conclusion:

  > A review of [such] bills . . . indicates that there is a clear and pervasive realization that grave injustices exist, and that structural changes in our ways of doing business have never been more necessary. Recognizing the severity of the fragmentation among systems, nearly every bill, ranging from large federal to small municipal initiatives, including those that foster single sector delivery systems (e.g., the schools), calls for the establishment of inter-agency and or multi-disciplinary committees to facilitate cross-sector planning and program implementation. (p. 15)

  It can be expected, therefore, that efforts to coordinate early childhood policies and approaches will continue in the future.

- Publicly funded programs for young children, including many Head Start and kindergarten programs, often are operated only part-day. Such scheduling is problematic for working parents who need full-day care for their children. This conflict may prevent youngsters, who would potentially benefit, from participating in such programs (Washington & Oyemade, 1985). Because limited funding is the major stumbling block to extending these programs to meet working parents' needs, this issue will continue to be raised.

- Within the early childhood profession, there is a continued focus on the pluralistic nature of our society and the shrinking world in which children are growing up. Many early childhood programs can be expected to focus more than ever on curriculum based on nonbias and inclusion of children and families from different cultural, ethnic, and economic backgrounds, as well as children with disabilities. We will explore this topic in more detail in Chapter 13.

- Finally, because of recent legislation ensuring that young children with disabilities are included in early education, there will be continued efforts to integrate them into programs with children who do not have disabilities. As we will see in the next chapter, such inclusive programs benefit everyone involved.

SUMMARY

1. A number of social factors have contributed to the expansion of early childhood programs and brought early childhood education into the public consciousness. These include:
   A. Changes in family life such as an increased number of two-earner families and single parents
   B. Growing evidence of the benefits of early education for children from poverty, children with disabilities, and other children at risk
   C. Child advocacy, which has helped bring the needs of young children and their families to public and legislative prominence
2. There is considerable diversity in the types of early childhood programs with variations according to:
   A. Purpose of programs
   B. Program settings
   C. Ages of the children
   D. Sources of funding support
3. A most important factor in describing early childhood programs is quality. The following elements contribute to the quality of early childhood programs:
   A. Child-adult ratio
   B. Group size
   C. Mixed-age grouping
   D. Developmental appropriateness of the program
   E. Quality of adult-child interaction
   F. Staff qualification
   G. Staff consistency
   H. Respect and concern for the staff
   I. Quality of the physical environment
   J. Family involvement
   K. Quality as a combination of factors
4. There are trends and projections that suggest what the future holds for early childhood education.

KEY TERMS LIST

center-based programs
child-adult ratio
child advocacy
early childhood education
extended family
family child care homes
hothousing
integrated curriculum
latch-key or self-care children
mixed-age grouping
nuclear family
parent-cooperative
self-care children

part II

two

The Who of Early Childhood Education

Early childhood education is made up of different people. In Part II we will explore the *who* of this field by examining the characteristics and needs of three groups—children, families, and teachers.

chapter 2

The Children

At the heart of early childhood education are young children. All the topics we will discuss in ensuing chapters are aimed at gaining a better understanding of children and how, together with their families, we can best meet their needs. Although our focus will be on children, it is always important to keep in mind that they must never be seen in isolation, but rather as part of a family system that provides context and identity through its lifestyle, culture, heritage, and traditions. In this chapter we will take a closer look at children.

CHILDREN—SIMILARITIES

Children are generally wonderfully engaging and winning, in part because of the freshness with which they approach all experiences. Most children possess a sense of trust that the world and the people in it are friendly and kind, and they will tackle that world with joy and enthusiasm. The amount of information that children learn in the first few years of life is unparalleled in later learning. At no other time in life will there be such zest and liveliness toward acquiring skills and knowledge.

Our task in working with young children is to provide an environment in which this enthusiasm is nurtured and sustained rather than subdued or even destroyed. Young children are eager to learn, but such eagerness can be battered down if they are frequently overwhelmed by developmentally inappropriate experiences. This is an awesome responsibility on the shoulders of early childhood educators, which can be met through careful and sensitive study and understanding of the characteristics and needs of young children.

The early childhood educator's understanding of child development is vital in providing a supportive and developmentally appropriate program for young children.

KEY QUESTION #1

Observe several children of the same age. These might be children you work with and know well or children that you are observing for the first time. What traits do they share? How are they similar? Can you draw some conclusions about children of that particular age?

Age-Related Commonalities Among Children

Although children are each unique, they nonetheless have much in common. All children share the need for nurturing and trustworthy adults, for stability and security, for increasing autonomy, for a sense of competence and self-worth. Similarly, there are common attributes and skills that characterize children at different ages during the early years. In the course of normal development, children reach developmental milestones in a fairly predictable manner and within a reasonable time range (Allen & Marotz, 1994). Following is a brief overview of some developmental characteristics of infants, one-, two-, three-, four-, five-, and six- to eight-year olds.

Infants rapidly gain skills in all areas of development, relying on information about the world from movement and their senses. They acquire strong attachments to significant adults in their lives; stable, consistent, and loving care are vital for babies.

Infants. The first year of life is very crucial in establishing a foundation for all areas of development. Astounding changes mark the first year; within that time newborns, whose existence is totally dependent on adults, become mobile, communicating 12-month-olds. Professionals who care for infants need a sound understanding of the developmental changes that take place during infancy.

Newborns' earliest movements are reflexive, but they quickly develop into more purposeful activity. In addition, their senses operate remarkably well, providing a wealth of valuable information about this new world into which they have been thrust. By the middle of the first year, babies are reaching for and grasping objects, rolling over, and sitting up with support. During the latter half of the year, infants master the pincer grasp (holding objects with thumb and forefinger), crawling, pulling themselves upright, and perhaps walking alone. Through increasing skill in motor activity and use of all the senses, children learn about and make sense of the world.

Socially, infants signal their recognition of significant people, especially parents and caregivers. This burgeoning affinity shifts from following with the eyes to smiling and later to crawling after adults. By the end of the first year, babies show strong attachment to parents and caregivers and may show considerable fear or reluctance toward strangers. Infants are amazingly adept at communicating and demon-

Children's enthusiasm and eagerness to learn must be nurtured through a supportive environment and by sensitive teachers who understand their development.

strate increasing understanding of language. They "converse" with adults through babbling and jabbering long before they can produce recognizable words. First words also appear by the end of the first year, usually relevant to social relationships, especially, "ma-ma" and "da-da" (Allen & Marotz, 1994; Gonzales-Mena & Eyer, 1989; Wilson, 1995).

Infants need responsive adults who recognize and meet their individual needs in a consistent, nurturing, respectful manner. Caregivers of infants must be extremely sensitive to the importance of establishing a stable relationship through which trust and security are established. They provide daily routines that are tailored to each child's individual rhythm and needs for care, food, sleep, play, and social interaction. Later, when babies begin to be mobile, caregivers must provide appropriate space for crawling and beginning walking. There must be interesting things to explore, yet it must also be safe and hygienic (Bredekamp & Copple, 1997).

One-Year-Olds. Toddlers, as one-year-olds are also called, have access to an expanding world of wonders to be explored. They gain increasing skills in moving through this world, starting with a lurching, wobbly gait when they first begin to walk and quickly refining their walk so by the end of the second year it is quite smooth and steady and includes running, walking backwards, and negotiating stairs. Soon they also begin to combine their newly developed locomotion skill with pushing and pulling objects. They are adept at picking up objects and, with great glee, also love to drop or throw them. Their increasing control over their finger muscles can be seen in their participation at meal times; they enjoy self-feeding finger foods, wielding a spoon, and drinking from a cup, though these endeavors are not always negotiated successfully. They become more independent, wanting to do many things for themselves.

One-year-olds' rapidly growing mobility, coupled with their expanding desire for independence and their curiosity about everything around them, lead them to become avid explorers of their environment. Their growing mastery of language and new ability to mentally represent objects and experiences help them move beyond the here-and-now experiences of infancy.

Language blossoms during the second year, becoming increasingly more intelligible and varied. Vocabulary grows from a few words to an impressive mastery of up to 300 words, and single words soon become two-word sentences. During the second half of the second year, toddlers gain the ability to internally represent objects and events. This is often seen in play, when they imitate the actions of others, engage in simple make-believe play, or dress up. Toddlers have great interest in other children, but their play is characteristically parallel rather than interactive. They focus on their own wants and needs and are not yet able to place these in the context of other children's wants and needs. Perhaps the greatest challenge for toddlers is the need to reconcile their continuing desire for closeness to their caregivers and their growing need for independence (Allen & Marotz, 1994; Gonzalez-Mena & Eyer, 1989; Honig, 1993; Wilson, 1995).

Caregivers of one-year-olds must continue to provide a safe, consistent, sensitive, loving, and supportive environment. The interactions, conversations, and give-and-take play between caregivers and children contribute immensely to toddlers' development. Caregivers must also be constantly vigilant because toddlers are very curious about everything around them and have very little awareness of safety. The daily schedule provided for one-year-olds is still dictated by individual rhythms and needs, but toddlers begin to exhibit greater similarity in their daily patterns; thus, caregivers may be able to schedule meals and naps for the group, while still remaining sensitive to individual differences (Bredekamp & Copple, 1997).

Two-year-olds, in transition from babyhood to childhood, quickly master many skills. Their growing independence and assertiveness are both a source of enjoyment and a challenge for adults.

Two-Year-Olds. Some early childhood programs incorporate two-year-olds, especially older ones, into preschool groups, whereas others place twos into a separate toddler category. Twos are in a transitional stage, making the move from babyhood to childhood. They are in the process of acquiring and enthusiastically using many new skills, particularly the two that most visibly mark the distinction between baby and child—language and motor control.

During this year, most children increasingly gain body control, in their more self-assured walking and running that has lost its baby stagger, and in their new-found finger control that allows them to put together simple puzzles or paint with a brush. At the same time, they experience tremendous language growth. Their growing vocabulary, sentence length, and grammatical forms open up all sorts of possibilities because of this increased communication competence. Self-help skills are also improving, including the achievement of toilet training for the majority of children during this year. Just as important as learning motor, language, and self-help skills is the process of gaining independence through this mastery.

Two-year-olds undertake many activities for their sheer enjoyment rather than to reach a goal. Running is pleasurable in itself rather than a means of getting somewhere fast; painting means involvement in a sensory process rather than an interest in producing a picture. Activities are also undertaken with enormous enthusiasm. Twos wholeheartedly throw themselves into activities, whether painting, squishing play dough, pouring sand and water, or reading books. They particularly enjoy sensory experiences, using touch, taste, and smell, as well as sight and sound. Two-year-olds are notorious for their desire to repeat, using newfound skills over and over again. This desire is normal and should be encouraged, for it builds competence and allows children to fully assimilate skills before moving on to new ones.

Two-year-olds, in transition from babyhood to childhood, are just beginning to master many skills. These are particularly noticeable in the language and motor areas.

Two-year-olds are just beginning to gain some social skills, although association with peers is more characterized by playing side by side than by interacting. They are generally not involved in cooperation and sharing. In fact, young twos, with their limited self-control, may well express their growing independence and self-assertiveness by grabbing a desired toy from a peer or by throwing a tantrum. Tantrums, in fact, are common among twos, reflecting, for instance, their limited verbal skills, which are not yet adequately able to express what they want. They are also not adept at delaying gratification; they do not have the ability to wait for something they want "right now" (Allen & Marotz, 1994; Ames, Gillespie, Haines, & Ilg, 1980; Bredekamp & Copple, 1997).

Teachers of two-year-olds need to provide a supportive, consistent, and safe environment in which rapidly growing skills can be practiced and mastered. Frequent and enthusiastic praise conveys that adults value the acquisition of skills. Gentle guidance acknowledges children's growing sense of self while helping them develop self-control in relation to others (Bredekamp & Copple, 1997).

By age three, children are much more adept in motor, self-help, and language skills and are becoming more socially aware of peers. They enjoy helping and pleasing adults.

Three-Year-Olds. Three year-olds have truly left babyhood behind, not only in appearance—with the loss of baby fat—but also in added skills. Increased balance and control are evident in large motor, fine motor, and self-help areas. Threes like to use their new skills by being helpful and wanting to please adults. Their added competence does not mean, however, that they won't occasionally have accidents or revert to earlier behaviors when upset. Overall, however, their characteristic way of responding to school experiences is with enthusiasm and enjoyment.

By three, children's speech is intelligible most of the time and consists of longer sentences. Language becomes much more of a social and cognitive tool. Three-year-olds engage in more extensive conversations, talking *with* and not just *to* people, and answer as well as ask questions. In fact, three-year-olds are usually full of questions, constantly asking Why? or What for? or How come? Vocabulary continues to increase dramatically, and grammar becomes more accurate.

This greater language facility helps increase peer interaction among this age group. Three-year-olds are much more socially aware than younger children, and their make-believe play, which began in the previous year by imitating simple personal and home routines, at times includes two or three children. Short-lived friendships begin to form, and children will play with each other as well as near each other. Social problem-solving skills are just beginning to emerge. With guidance, threes may share and take turns, but they still find such behaviors difficult (Allen & Marotz, 1994; Ames et al., 1980).

Three-year-olds' budding skills allow them to enjoy an ever-widening array of activities and peer interactions.

Teachers of three-year-olds need to respect the growing skills and competencies of their charges without forgetting just how recently they acquired them. It is important to maintain patience and good humor, remembering that the enthusiasm with which threes use these skills is not always matched by accuracy and speed. Because three-year-olds enjoy helping as well as practicing self-help skills, such behaviors should be promoted and valued. The emerging social skills of three-year-olds should be encouraged in an atmosphere in which social exploration is safe and where playing alone or not having to give up a favorite toy is also acceptable (Bredekamp & Copple, 1997).

Four-year-olds have achieved considerable mastery in their motor and language abilities. They tend to be quite self-confident, often boasting or showing off. Social play is an important part of their lives.

Four-Year-Olds. Four-year-olds have achieved a maturity and competence in motor and language development that leads them to assume a general air of security and confidence, sometimes bordering on cockiness. "Children test limits in order to practice self-confidence and firm up a growing need for independence" (Allen & Marotz, 1994, p. 97).

Fours seem to be in perpetual motion, throwing themselves whole-heartedly into activities. They have mastered the basics of movement and now eagerly embellish on these. Climbing, pedaling, pumping on a swing, jumping over or off objects, easily avoiding obstacles when running, all contribute to greater flexibility and exploration in play. Four-year-olds like to try and to show off with physical stunts. Improved muscle coordination is also evident in more controlled use of the fingers, such as in buttoning, drawing, and cutting with scissors. In addition, many self-care activities have become routines rather than challenges, as they were at earlier ages.

If increased competence leads to noticeable embellishments in motor activities, this is even more evident in the language area. By age four, most children's language usage has become remarkably sophisticated and skilled. This accomplishment seems to invite new uses for language beyond communication. Fours love to play with language, using it to brag, engage in bathroom talk, swear, tell tall tales, and make up silly rhymes. Four-year-olds are even more persistent than threes in asking questions.

For four-year-olds, peers have become very important. Play is a social activity more often than not, although fours enjoy solitary activities at times as well. Taking turns and sharing become much easier because four-year-olds begin to understand the reciprocal benefits of cooperation. Their imaginative variations of movement and language skills extend into group play, which is usually highly creative and ingenious, touched by their sense of humor.

Teachers of four-year-olds need to provide an environment in which children have many opportunities for interactions with each

Four-year-olds need a stimulating environment in which to channel their abundant energy and curiosity.

other, with adults, and with a wide selection of appropriate and stimulating materials. Because of their heightened social involvements, fours need consistent, positive guidance to help them develop emerging social skills, for instance, in sharing, resolving conflicts, and negotiating (Allen & Marotz, 1994; Ames et al., 1980; Bredekamp & Copple, 1997).

Five-Year-Olds. Fives are much more self-contained and controlled, replacing some of their earlier exuberant behaviors with a calmer, more mature approach. They are competent and reliable, taking responsibility seriously. They seem to be able to judge their own abilities more accurately than at earlier ages, and they respond accordingly.

Five-year-olds, compared to their younger peers, are much more mature, controlled, and responsible. Many skills have been refined so that at this age children are more interested in projects and activities that result in products.

Five-year-olds' motor activities seem more poised, their movement more restrained and precise than ever before. There is also greater interest in fine motor activities as children have gained many skills in accurate cutting, gluing, drawing, and beginning writing. This interest is spurred by the new desire to "make something" rather than merely to paint, cut, or manipulate the play dough for the sheer enjoyment of these activities. Five-year-olds' self-reliance extends to assuming considerable responsibility for self-care as well.

Language has also reached a height of maturity for fives, exhibited through a vocabulary that contains thousands of words, complex and compound sentence structures, variety and accuracy in grammatical forms, and good articulation. Language increasingly reflects interest in and contact with a broadening world outside the child's intimate family, school, and neighborhood experiences. The social sphere of five-year-olds revolves around special friendships, which take on more importance. By five, children are quite adept at sharing toys, taking turns, and playing cooperatively. Their group play is usually quite elaborate and imaginative, and it can take up long periods of time (Allen & Marotz, 1994; Ames et al., 1980).

Teachers of five-year-olds, after providing a stimulating learning environment and setting reasonable limits, can expect this age group to take on considerable responsibility for maintaining and regulating a smoothly functioning program. Fives need to be given many

For five-year-olds, prolonged activity involvement and completion of projects become particularly important. These five-year-olds had an end product in mind when they began working with the art media.

opportunities to explore their world in depth and assimilate what they learn through multiple experiences. One way in which children can discuss, plan, and carry out ideas stimulated by their experiences is through group projects (Katz & Chard, 1989).

Six- to eight-year-olds in before- and after-school programs are very independent, though they still need support and structure provided by caring adults. Their mental abilities allow them to think much more logically and take into consideration the viewpoint of others, which becomes an important factor in their more involved peer relations.

Six- to Eight-Year-Olds. Before- and after-school programs are designed primarily for young elementary school children of working parents. The children in such programs have remarkably mature skills in all areas of development. Physically, they show well-developed and refined motor skills. Their thinking has become much more logical and systematic than it had been during the preschool years, and they are able to recognize and take into consideration the viewpoint of others. The language of school-aged children is impressively adultlike, and they love to use these language skills.

Six- to eight-year-olds exercise considerable independence and are able to follow rules and standards without the need for constant monitoring; yet they certainly still have need for the nurturance and security of caring adults. They also have need for the world of peers, within which they often form close friendships. Such friendships are, in most instances, with same-sex peers. For school-aged children, play is still a most important activity. It is more complex and organized than at earlier ages, incorporating both formal and informal games with rules. At this age, children enjoy projects they can initiate, implement, and carry through to completion, exercising their sense of industry.

The child with good self-esteem has confidence in his ability to succeed and master his environment. What elements of the early childhood environment and what teacher behaviors support and nurture a child's growing sense of who he is and what he can do?

Adults who work with six- to eight-year-olds in before- and after-school programs must provide a safe, nurturing climate. Caregivers should provide materials appropriate for the expanding interests of this group and allow children enough independence to pursue these in their own way. At the same time, adults should be available as a resource and to provide guidance and limits. Particularly after school, children also need opportunities to expend energy through large motor activity and games, which adults can arrange (Allen & Marotz, 1994; Click, 1994; Seligson & Allenson, 1993).

Positive self-esteem is a need shared by all children and is fostered by adults who convey to children that they are competent and worthwhile.

Self-Esteem

Self-concept—Perceptions and feelings children may have about themselves, gathered largely from how the important people in their world respond to them.

Self-esteem—Children's evaluation of their worth in positive or negative terms.

One commonality shared by all children is the need to feel good about themselves. Young children are beginning to form a **self-concept,** perceptions and feelings about themselves gathered largely from how the important people in their world respond to them. One aspect of self-concept is **self-esteem,** children's evaluation of their worth in positive or negative terms (Essa & Rogers, 1992; Marshall, 1989; Samuels, 1977). Such evaluation can tell children that they are competent, worthwhile, and effective or, on the other hand, incapable, unlikable, and powerless. It is particularly noteworthy that children who feel good about themselves seem to be more friendly and helpful toward peers (Marshall, 1989).

Children's perceived competence reflects their belief in their own ability to be successful; such self-confidence contributes to positive self-esteem.

A healthy self-concept is vital to all areas of a child's development. Although readiness in the natural progression of development is triggered internally and furthered by appropriate external stimuli, successful mastery of new learning also depends on a child's feelings of competence and ability to meet new challenges. **Perceived competence** reflects the child's belief in his or her ability to succeed in a given task (Marshall, 1989). Successful experiences result in self-confidence that, in turn, boosts self-esteem. Thus, many appropriate yet challenging experiences help the child feel successful, confident, and capable (Essa & Rogers, 1992).

Perceived competence—Children's belief in their ability to succeed in a given task.

The child needs to feel competent and able to face challenges as well as have a sense of **personal control**—the feeling of having the power to make things happen or stop things from happening. When children generally feel that what happens to them is completely out of their hands, particularly if what happens is not always in their best interest, they cannot develop this sense of control and will tend to see themselves as helpless and ineffective. All children need opportunities to make appropriate choices and exercise autonomy to begin to develop the perception that they have control, which also contributes to their emerging sense of responsibility for their own actions (Marshall, 1989).

Personal control—The feeling that a person has the power to make things happen.

KEY QUESTION #2

As you observe children, identify a child who appears to be self-confident. How does the child express this confidence? Do you see a difference between this child and another who seems less assured?

Children who have a sense of personal control and a feeling that they can make things happen see themselves as effective, which also contributes to self-esteem.

The early years are crucial in the development of self-concept, since it forms and stabilizes early in life and becomes increasingly resistant to change (Samuels, 1977). Above all, children's positive concepts of themselves reflect healthy parent-child relationships that are founded on love, trust, and consistency. When early childhood teachers enter young children's lives, they also contribute to the formation of that concept.

At the same time, if a child comes to school with a history of abuse or neglect, the teacher's contribution of offsetting negative experiences can help nurture self-esteem. Teachers strengthen children's positive self-esteem if they are sensitive to each child as an individual and to the needs of children for affection, nurture, care, and feelings of competence. Thus, teachers who understand children, know their characteristics, respond to them, and know how to challenge them in a supportive manner contribute to this positive sense of self. In essence, everything the early childhood teacher does has an impact on children's self-concept.

Play

Another commonality among all children is the need for play, which serves as a means of learning about and making sense of the world. But more than that, play is essential to all aspects of children's development. "It is an activity which is concerned with the whole of his being, not with just one small part of him, and to deny him the right to play is to deny him the right to live and grow" (Cass, 1973, p. 11). Play promotes mastery as children practice skills; it furthers cognitive development as thinking abilities are stretched; it involves langauge, encouraging new uses; it involves physical activity; it helps children work through emotions; its inventive nature makes it creative; it is often a socializing event; beyond all that, however, it provides a way for children to assimilate and integrate their life experiences. In no way is play a trivial pursuit, but rather it is a serious undertaking necessary to healthy development for all children (Almy, Monighan, Scales, & Van Hoorn, 1984).

Play provides many opportunities for children to practice skills, stetch thinking abilities, work through emotions, socialize, and be creative.

KEY QUESTION #3

Observe a group of young children at play. Look for examples of the various types of play discussed in this chapter. Do you see a relationship between age and type of play?

Children often engage in solitary play, playing alone and not involved in the activities of peers.

Play can be categorized by its social (six stages) or its cognitive (four stages) characteristics.

Stages of Play. Play has been of interest to child researchers for many years. Mildred Parten (1932) provided one of the landmark studies, still considered valid today (Sponseller, 1982), in which young children's social play was categorized. She found an age-related progression in five types of play. Although children at later ages engage in earlier forms of play, their play is typically more complex than it was when they were younger. Parten's six categories of social play are listed and explained in Figure 2-1.

Other researchers have viewed play from a different perspective. For instance, Sara Smilansky (1968) proposed play categories based on children's increasing cognitive abilities and measured by how children use play materials. This view is complementary to Parten's classifications because it focuses on a different aspect of play. Smilansky's categories are shown in Figure 2-1.

It is important for teachers to be aware of the different types of play and to recognize that children develop increasing social and cognitive skills as they progress. In particular, this awareness helps set appropriate expectations for young children. For instance, infants need appropriate objects, space, and time for observation, manipulation, and exploration, which helps them learn about the properties of their en-

The play of these children, engaged in similar activities but not really interacting with each other, can be described as parallel.

FIGURE 2-1 Stages of Play

Parten's Categories of Social Play

Types of Play	**Definition**	**Example**
Unoccupied behavior	The child moves about the classroom going from one area to another, observing but not getting involved.	*Sebastian wanders to the blocks and watches several children work together on a structure. After a few seconds he looks around, then walks over to the art table, where he looks at the finger painting materials briefly but does not indicate a desire to paint. He continues to wander, going from area to area, watching but not participating.*
Solitary play	The child plays alone, uninvolved with other children nearby. Children at all ages engage in this type of play, although older children's solitary play is more complex (Amy et al., 1984; Rubin, 1977).	*Lorraine works diligently at building a sand mountain, not looking at or speaking with the children who are involved in other activities around her.*
Onlooker play	Quite common among two-year-olds, a child stands nearby watching others at play, without joining in.	*Rajeef stands just outside the dramatic play area and watches a group of children participate in doctor play, using various medical props.*
Parallel play	Children use similar materials or toys in similar ways but do not interact with each other.	*Kalie alternates red and blue Legos on a form board while Terrance, sitting next to her, uses Legos to build a tall structure. They seem influenced by each other's activity but do not talk to each other or suggest joining materials.*
Associative play	Increasingly evident as preschoolers get older, children interact and even share some of their materials, but they are not engaged in a common activity.	*Several children are in the block area working on a common structure. Jolynne runs a car through an arch she has built at one side of the structure; Arlen keeps adding blocks to the top, saying, "This is the lookout tower," while Akira surrounds the structure with a "fence."*
Cooperative play	Typical of older preschoolers, is the most social form of play and involves children playing together in a shared activity.	*On arriving at school one day, the children find an empty appliance box in their classroom. At first they climb in and out of the box, but then a few of them start talking about what it might be used for. Jointly they decide to make it into a house, and their discussion turns to how this could be accomplished. While continuing to discuss the project, they also begin the task of transforming the box, cutting, painting, and decorating to reach their common goal. It takes several days, but the children together create a house.*

Smilansky's Categories of Cognitive Play

Types of Play	**Definition**	**Example**
Functional play	Characteristic of infants' and toddlers' repetitive, motor play used to explore what objects are like and what can be done with them.	*Clark picks up a block, turns it, and looks at it from all sides. He bangs it on the floor, then picks up another block with his left hand and bangs the two blocks together. He alternates striking the blocks against each other and on the floor.*
Constructive play	Involves creating something with the play objects.	*Clark uses blocks to construct a tower. His activity now has a purpose.*
Dramatic play	The child uses a play object to substitute for something imaginary.	*Clark takes four blocks, puts one on each of four plates placed around the table, and says, "Here is your toast for breakfast."*
Games with rules	Involve accepted, prearranged rules in play. This stage is more typical of older children.	*In kindergarten, Clark and a group of peers play the game "Blockhead," agreeing on the game's rules.*

vironment. Toddlers need the kind of toys and props that help them use and integrate their growing ability to mentally represent experiences. Preschoolers need sizable blocks of time to engage in self-selected play and many open-ended materials that lend themselves to exploration and mastery (for instance, play dough, blocks, sand and water, Legos). In addition, time, space, and materials that lend

Although these boys are engaged in the same activity and are sharing some of the materials, they are still working on separate projects, as is typical in associative play.

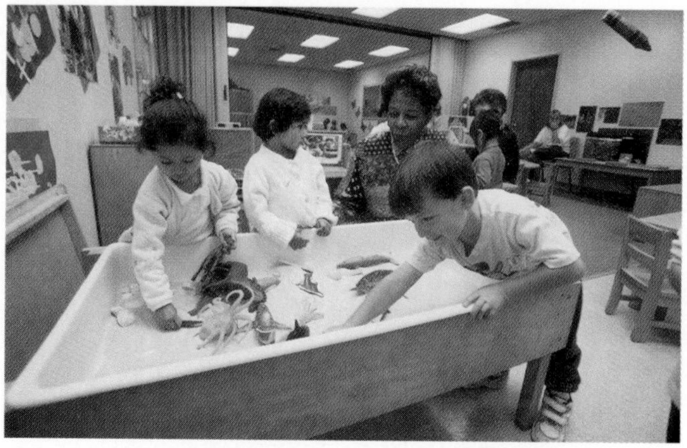

These children have worked together at the sand table to build a zoo for their animals. Their play can be described as cooperative.

themselves to social play should always be available, including dolls, dress-up clothes, and blocks. School-aged children, while appreciating such open-ended materials, also enjoy some simple organized games with rules. It is important, however, to avoid highly competitive activities, which only foster resentment and ill-will. We will discuss an alternative, cooperative games, in Chapter 13.

CHILDREN—DIFFERENCES

KEY QUESTION #4

Think about the same children you observed earlier for KEY QUESTION #1 and describe what makes each of them unique. How do they differ? Do you have any indications about what factors underlie these differences?

Children have many characteristics in common and certainly share basic needs for affection, acceptance, consistency, respect, and appropriate challenges, yet there are many variations among children. The "profiles" of young children presented earlier reflect many common characteristics of these ages, but they will rarely describe any one child. While falling within the normal range of development, each child possesses a unique blend of attributes that makes him or her one of a kind.

Although children of the same age share many characteristics, there is also a wide range of differences among them. These children all are four years old, but, as you can see, there is a great variation in their physical makeup. What are some factors that contribute to physical and personality differences in children?

Children's differences reflect both inborn and external factors that have molded who they are. Some children are born with an easygoing **temperament;** for instance, they have a moderate activity level, predictable schedule of sleeping and eating, and a positive attitude toward and curiosity in new experiences. Other children have more difficult temperaments and, for example, are more irritable, unpredictable, and more difficult to calm down (Thomas, Chess, & Birch, 1968). Although children are born with such temperamental characteristics, these gradually tend to affect the adults around them so that parents and teachers may begin to think of children as "difficult" or "easy" and expect and reinforce their behavioral traits. In turn, then, adults' perceptions of children contribute to children's self-perceptions.

Temperament—Children's inborn characteristics, such as regularity, adaptability, and disposition, that affect behavior.

Children have inborn temperaments that contribute to individual differences. Some children are predisposed to be easygoing, whereas others tend to be basically difficult.

Children's individuality is also shaped by the cultural, ethnic, religious, and economic background of the family. It is important that early childhood teachers and caregivers be sensitive to family diversity and genuinely value different cultures and backgrounds. Children mirror their primary environment—their home and family—as, of course, they should. If teachers, whether consciously or unconsciously, denigrate what children experience and learn at home, they will convey that the family, including the child, is in some way inferior and undesirable. What a detrimental impact this would have on children's self-concept!

Children's uniqueness also derives from the cultural, ethnic, religious, or economic background of their families.

CHILDREN WITH SPECIAL NEEDS

Children with developmental delays accomplish tasks at an age older than their peers, whereas the development of children with impairments is in some way different, not just slower.

Some children are born with or acquire conditions that place them outside the typical range of development for their age. They might have a **developmental delay,** meaning that they accomplish tasks in one or more developmental areas at a considerably later age than their peers. Some children are considered **at risk** for delay, with a significant probability that problems will occur because of adverse environmental factors such as poverty or low birth weight. With appropriate help, children who have developmental delays may well catch up to age norms. Other children may have a **deficit or impairment,** indicating development that is in some way different (not just slower) from that of most children. Children with hearing or visual deficits, mental retardation, or motor disabilities are part of this category.

Developmental delay—A child's development in one or more areas occurring at an age significantly later than that of peers.

At-risk children—Because of adverse environmental factors—for instance, poverty or low birth weight—children considered at risk for developmental delay.

Deficit or impairment—A problem in development, usually organic, resulting in below-normal performance.

It has become more and more evident that children with special needs benefit from early intervention. In fact, the importance of providing services as early as possible has been underscored by national policies that mandate such services for young children who have special needs. In 1975, Public Law 94-142 (Education for All Handicapped Children Act) was passed to ensure a "free and appropriate public education" for all handicapped children between the ages of 3 and 21. A decade later, in 1986, PL 99-457 (the Education of the Handicapped Act Amendments) added provisions for children from birth to age 5. Specifically, what is referred to as Part H of this law addresses the needs of disabled infants and toddlers. It calls for services to children under 3 who are experiencing or are at risk for developmental delays and requires an **individualized family service plan (IFSP)** for the child and family, developed by a transdisciplinary team. Both of these laws came into being because of the commitment, dedication, and hard

Individualized Family Service Plan (IFSP)—Required by the 1986 Education of the Handicapped Act Amendments for handicapped children under the age of three and their families; the IFSP, often developed by a transdisciplinary team that includes the parents, determines goals and objectives that build on the strengths of the child and family.

Legislation mandates services for infants, toddlers, and preschoolers with special needs.

work of parents and professionals whose advocacy eventually led to legal remedies for the plight of disabled children who too often were excluded from the educational system (Deiner, 1993).

Inclusion

Least restrictive environment– A provision of Public Law 94-142 that handicapped children be placed in a program as close as possible to a setting designed for children without disabilities, while being able to meet each child's special needs.

Many early childhood programs integrate children with special needs. Such inclusion, when carefully planned, provides benefits for all involved.

KEY QUESTION #5

If you are able, observe an early childhood program in which a child with special needs is integrated. Observe and talk to one of the teachers. What special accommodations have been made for this child? How does the child interact with the other children in the class? How is the child's independence encouraged? Does the child participate in a few, some, or all activities?

One of the provisions of PL 94-142 is that disabled children be placed in the **least restrictive environment.** This means they should be placed in programs that are as close as possible to settings designed for nondisabled children, while remaining appropriate for their unique needs (Spodek & Saracho, 1994). This concept has led to the expansion of inclusion, the integration of children with special needs into regular programs. Inclusion is certainly not new, having informally been part of many early childhood programs throughout this century and more formally incorporated over the past several decades into Head Start programs (Hanson & Lynch, 1989). It is also important to recognize that inclusion may not be the best alternative for all disabled children; thus, a decision to integrate a child with special needs into a regular classroom should be made only after careful consideration.

An inclusive program is founded on the premise that young children, whether disabled or not, are much more similar than different (Wilderstrom, 1986). Children with special needs can benefit from a good inclusion program by experiencing success in a variety of developmentally appropriate activities, through contact with age-mates who can be both models and friends, and by exposure to the many opportunities for informal incidental learning that take place in all early childhood programs (Deiner, 1993). At the same time, children without disabilities benefit from inclusion by learning that children who are in some way different from them nonetheless have far more commonalities than differences (Karnes & Lee, 1979). An increasing number of young children with disabilities are enrolled in early childhood programs (Wolery et al., 1993).

Although inclusion has many potential benefits, the benefits do not happen automatically. In other words, inclusion does not simply mean enrolling children with special needs in an early childhood program. Careful planning, preparation, modification, evaluation, and support are necessary for successful inclusion. Early childhood teachers, because they know a great deal about children and how best to work with them, have many skills needed for working with children with disabilities as well.

But placement of children with special needs in their classes also involves learning some additional skills. It often means having to acquire and use new teaching strategies, new terminology, and different evaluation tools. It also involves working with a wider range of professionals (for instance, speech and physical therapists or psychologists) and more focused involvement with parents. In addition, early childhood teachers may find themselves with unexpectedly strong emotional reactions such as pity for the child, anger that the child has to suffer, fear of the disability, or self-doubt in their own abilities, which they must face and resolve.

One of the keys to successful inclusion is to view each child, whether disabled or not, as an individual with unique characteristics,

Many children with mild or moderate disabilities are effectively included in early childhood programs. The teacher may work individually with the child in some activities, but the child is a part of the large group in most aspects of the program.

strengths, and needs. This involves an attitude that sees *a child,* not a child with Down syndrome or a child who is blind or a child who stutters. For example, Ted may have Down syndrome but he loves to paint, enjoys listening to stories at group time, and gives terrific hugs. Similarly, Noni's visual impairment does not diminish her enjoyment of the sand table, her budding friendship with Connie, or her ability to make others laugh through her language play. And Manuel, while often tripping over words, can throw and catch a ball accurately. Many times he is the one who notices a colorful butterfly passing or the first buds of spring, and he has a totally winning smile. Working with a group of children means recognizing, encouraging, and building on each child's strengths. In this way, children's self-concept and self-assurance are boosted so they can meet the challenges posed by their disabilities.

Characteristics of Children With Special Needs

It is beyond the scope of this text to discuss in depth such topics as characteristics of children with special needs, appropriate teaching methods, testing and assessment tools, and the unique needs of the parents of children with disabilities. Considerable training is necessary to fully master the skills and information of the relatively new field of early childhood special education. This field combines and integrates the traditional skills of teachers of young children with the specialized expertise of special educators, therapists, and medical personnel.

Most early childhood teachers, however, will inevitably find themselves in one or both of the following situations:

- One or more children with special needs will be included in their class, or
- They will have concerns about a child who seems to experience consistent difficulties in one or more areas of development.

In the former case, it is important that teachers work with parents and specialists to make the inclusion experience successful. In the

EXPERIENCES chapter 2

Diana, Head Teacher, Class of Three-Year-Olds

You Be the Doctor

Arianne was one of several children with special needs included in our classroom. Arianne's language and social development were both delayed. When she started school, she was very shy and quiet, rarely talking, and then only in a whisper. Most of Arianne's time was spent in unoccupied or onlooker behavior, and only if a teacher was directly involved would she engage in solitary play. Group times seemed very uncomfortable for her. Yet, it was important that she develop a sense of group belonging to facilitate both social and language development.

After several unsuccessful months of trying various strategies to encourage greater participation, we decided to try an intervention based on encouraging social pretend play, with adult support as needed. Arianne had developed a special affinity to one adult, Teacher Pam, and she was the one who took on the role of facilitator in the pretend play scenarios. We developed several themes, with appropriate props, based on Arianne's and the other children's common life experiences. These themes included taking care of babies, cooking, visits to the doctor, and grocery shopping.

At the beginning, we found that Arianne would be interested for a while, but gradually slip away as the other children took over the activity. For instance, when we made cookies, she readily joined the activity, but left when several other children became involved with great animation. Thus, for the next scenario, a doctor theme, Teacher Pam made sure that Arianne had an important role and that particularly competent peers were invited to participate. With verbal cues and support from Teacher Pam, Arianne, as the doctor, took center stage in the role play.

Teacher Pam, for instance, said, "Michael, you look sick. Come and lie down so Doctor Arianne can take care of you."

When Michael readily joined in the activity, Teacher Pam gave Arianne specific directions on how to treat Michael and gave her constant reinforcement about her role as doctor and about her attempts at speech. Later, Pam suggested a reversal of roles, and an enthusiastic Arianne became the patient while another child was the doctor.

Gradually, Arianne's social participation and language usage increased. Through other social pretend play themes, she more readily joined in the play, choosing her own roles, although Teacher Pam was still available to engage her and help her find the words for those roles. Adult support and reinforcement became more subtle as Arianne became more involved and assertive in participating in play. By the end of the year, Arianne was far less an onlooker than a participant, spent longer time periods engaged in play, sought out peers on her own as play partners, and became much more verbal with teachers and children.

Most children enter social play spontaneously, but some need the gentle support of an adult to help them become a part of play. Often success in social play, as in Arianne's case, can pave the way for the confidence to master other skills.

latter instance, teachers concerned about a child's functioning need to document their concerns and discuss them with the parents, as well as offer some concrete suggestions, for instance, how to begin the referral process so the child is seen by an appropriate specialist. (We will examine methods of observation and assessment in more detail in Chapter 6.) For both of these reasons, it is important that teachers of young children have some basic information about the characteristics of children with special needs.

Children with Physical Disabilities. Children can experience a wide range of motor limitations, from being slightly clumsy to having virtually no muscular control. The causes of such disabilities can stem from orthopedic problems, genetic defects, brain dysfunctions, or central nervous system damage. One of the most common motor impairments is cerebral palsy, a central nervous system dysfunction that can cause children to be uncoordinated and awkward or can leave them totally helpless. Children with cerebral palsy often have problems in other areas of development, but the fact that a child is severely impaired physically does not mean that he or she is necessarily mentally impaired.

Motor problems can range from slight awkwardness to complete helplessness. Special equipment, careful classroom arrangement, and adaptation of activities allow children with motor disabilities to be included.

Some motor problems can be corrected surgically or with orthopedic aids such as casts, many others can be improved through systematic physical therapy. For some children, improved functioning can be facilitated through adaptive equipment, for instance, a special chair that supports weak muscles, or a wheeled board on which the child can scoot to get around. Generally, specialists make determinations about corrective measures, although early childhood teachers will be able to carry out special procedures or help children adapt to new equipment. It is important to help children feel as independent and involved as possible. Some ways of encouraging independence and involvement include placing materials within their reach, keeping paths accessible to children in wheelchairs or using crutches, and adapting ongoing activities to facilitate as much participation as possible (Cook, Tessier, & Armbruster, 1987).

Children with Cognitive Disabilities. When children's intellectual abilities lag significantly behind their chronological age, they are considered to have special intellectual needs (Deiner, 1993). Intellectual functioning is conventionally measured through IQ tests (see Chapter 6 for a fuller discussion), which indicate whether a child's score falls within the average range or is above or below average. Fifty percent of all Americans fall within the average range.

Children with cognitive disabilities, who are classified as slow learners or educable mentally retarded, can benefit from inclusive programs.

About 16 percent are considered **slow learners,** having some mild delays manifest by such indicators as late talking and walking and general immaturity. Another 7 percent fall into the **educable mentally retarded** group, with noticeable delays in most areas of development (percentages based on Wechsler, 1944). Both slow learners and educable mentally retarded children are often integrated into regular early childhood programs. Children classified as more seriously involved—for instance, the trainable or severely or profoundly retarded—are generally placed into programs specifically designed for

Slow learner—A child with mild cognitive delay and general immaturity.

Educable mentally retarded—A child who has noticeable delays in most areas of development, including cognitive, but can function quite well in a regular early childhood program.

A Closer Look

Children in Jeopardy

Many young children today come to early childhood programs with a fate over which they had neither choice nor say. Innumerable numbers of children have had their futures limited because of prenatal exposure to drugs, alcohol, or diseases such as AIDS. It is estimated that well over a million babies are born each year having been exposed to illicit drugs or to legal drugs such as alcohol and nicotine (Brady, 1994). Their circumstances often require that early childhood teachers take special safeguards or use strategies to help these children flourish in the early childhood environment.

In recent years, considerable media attention has focused on children prenatally exposed to such drugs as crack or cocaine. When drug-exposed children enter an early childhood program, they often need additional attention and supervision because many, though certainly not all, have developmental delays, are impulsive, fail to understand cause and effect, display out-of-control behavior, and have unpredictable mood swings which can result in aggressive outbursts. The stability and support provided by a high-quality early childhood program has proven effective for many drug-exposed young children. A responsive caregiver seems to be the most important factor in the lives of such vulnerable children (Zuckerman, 1991) because many have the added burden of an unstable home life; the early childhood program can meet this need for some children.

Awareness has also been raised about the effects of alcohol on unborn children. **Fetal alcohol syndrome (FAS)** and the less severe manifestation, **fetal alcohol effects (FAE)**, can result in behaviors such as impulsivity, hyperactivity, poor attention span, poor judgment, and difficulty in remaining on task (Rice, 1992). The most effective environment for children with FAS or FAE seems to be one that is structured and predictable. Consistency can help FAS and FAE children learn the parameters of environment more effectively.

Another contemporary special group of young children is those who were prenatally exposed to the HIV infection. Children with HIV and AIDS may well be enrolled in early childhood programs, and those who work with them need to understand the characteristics of their illness, how it is transmitted, and precautions that need to be taken, particularly since there are many misconceptions about AIDS. It is important that Universal Precautions, usually spelled out by local or state health codes, are taken. These dictate that blood and other body fluids be handled by someone wearing latex (e.g., disposable) gloves, that materials that come in contact with such fluids and materials used to handle them be disposed in a childproof container with a plastic liner, and that spillages are cleaned immediately with a disinfectant (Kelker, Hecimovic, & LeRoy, 1994). Taking such precautions are adequate to prevent transmission of the virus. Wadsworth and Knight (1996) also note that children with the AIDS virus may have damage to the central nervous system that can affect their senses, cognitive and motor abilities, and language development. Young children with AIDS or HIV need the sensitivity and care that a high-quality early childhood program can provide.

One caution must be mentioned. While there are some general characteristics that describe many children who were prenatally exposed to drugs, alcohol, or the HIV virus, each child's history, personality, behavior pattern, and development are unique. Thus, like with any child, the individuality of that child is what is most precious and important.

their needs. In public schools, these children may be integrated into regular programs at lunch or recess times or during art or music activities.

Children with cognitive deficits seem to have problems with memory and attention (Fallen & Umansky, 1985). This has implications for expectations and for strategies used by the teacher. For instance, providing ample opportunity for repetition, many activities that use more than one sensory modality, numerous motor activities that reinforce concepts with action, and an environment that is not overly stimulating and distracting can help children with cognitive deficits focus on activities. Because children with cognitive deficits are usually less mature than their peers, they may need help in joining in the social play of the class. The teacher's assistance can be helpful by modeling appropriate social behaviors to the child and by encouraging other children to be accepting.

Fetal Alcohol Syndrome (FAS)—Irreversible birth abnormalities resulting from mother's heavy alcohol consumption during pregnancy. Children are usually retarded and hyperactive, and may have small head size, and various limb or face abnormalities.

Fatal Alcohol Effect (FAE)—Not as serious or noticeable as fetal alcohol syndrome, FAE, nonetheless, can leave children at a disadvantage in ability to learn and reach optimal development.

Children with Learning Disabilities. The term learning disability can have many meanings. Such disabilities affect basic learning processes and may be seen in young children who have problems listening, thinking, or speaking; in school-aged children, learning disabilities become more apparent when children have difficulties with reading, writing, and math. Children with learning disabilities are of average or above-average intelligence; their problem seems to be one of processing information. They often also have problems with motor control, particularly balance, coordination, body image, awareness of space, and directionality (Fallen & Umansky, 1985).

Learning disabilities affect basic learning processes. Attention deficit disorder (ADD) and attention deficit hyperactivity disorder (ADHD) are sometimes associated with learning disabilities.

Sometimes, though not always, learning disabilities occur in conjunction with **attention deficit disorder (ADD)** or **attention deficit hyperactivity disorder (ADHD)**. It is important not to confuse the normal activity and exuberance of young children with ADHD. A child who is truly hyperactive—with a very short attention span, undue restlessness, poor impulse control, inability to concentrate, and great distractibility—needs medical help. Various treatments, particularly psychoactive drugs, have helped many children gain better control over their behavior; however, there is considerable concern in the medical community about the long-term effects of such medications (Weiss & Hechtman, 1986). Be aware that drugs do not cure ADHD but can help children manage their behavior more effectively (Deiner, 1993). Medication is effective for over 70% of children (Landau & McAninch, 1993).

Attention deficit disorder (ADD)—Difficulty in concentration on an activity or subject for more than a few moments at a time.

Attention deficit hyperactivity disorder (ADHD)—Manifested by short attention span, restlessness, poor impulse control, distractibility, and inability to concentrate.

If a child in your class has been medically diagnosed as having ADHD and is now taking medication, it is important that you carefully observe how the medication affects the child and report this to the parents. Particularly for children who spend many hours a day in a child care setting, the teacher's reports can be invaluable. We will discuss various methods of observation, which can help you in this task, in Chapter 6.

Children with Visual Impairments. There are varying degrees of visual impairment, with complete sightlessness as the most extreme. However, many children who are considered to be visually impaired are able to see imperfectly, less clearly than a normal person.

Children with mild or moderate visual problems can function well in a regular early childhood program. Children with severe visual impairments will need considerable special assistance.

Many visual impairments can be corrected or reduced through corrective lenses.

Some visual impairments, especially if they are caused by a defect of the eye, can be corrected or reduced through surgery or corrective lenses. Others, particularly those stemming from brain or optic nerve damage, are most likely not correctable (Deiner, 1993).

Children with severe visual impairments are usually identified at an early age. Many children with less serious problems, however, may go undiagnosed, because most children do not routinely see an ophthalmologist and are simply not aware that something is wrong. It is important to look for signs of potential visual problems. Eyes that are frequently red or watery, have discharge, develop styes, or seem uncoordinated should be checked.

Some behavioral signs may also warn of possible visual problems. These include frequently rubbing the eyes, tilting the head, continually blinking, frowning, squinting, or complaining about headaches or dizziness. It is also important to observe a child carefully who persists in holding a book too close or too far, over- or underestimates distances when putting together manipulative toys, loses interest in activities such as group book reading (if this inattentiveness is unusual in other activities), or can't recognize familiar people from a distance. Any of these signs, particularly if they occur in combination with others, are reasons to discuss your concern with the parents.

If a child with a severe visual disability is enrolled in your class, there are some approaches you can use to maximize involvement and learning. As with any sensory deficiency, it is important that acuity in the other senses be heightened to help the child learn about the world; thus, the senses of hearing and touch become particularly important. Every new word or concept should be associated with touch. Allow plenty of time for tactile exploration of new objects, particularly relating parts to the whole in more complex items (for instance, pegboard and pegs). Encourage the child to engage in physical activity and talk about what he is doing. Also discuss what you and the other children are doing as it happens. The environment should be free of clutter so the visually impaired child can get around without danger of tripping over an unexpected obstacle. All the children in the class can help maintain an orderly environment. Use auditory and tactile cues to help the child identify various areas of the room (the bubbling sound of the aquarium to identify the science area, for instance). A specialist who works with visually impaired children can be a great resource in finding ways to make the child as independent and involved as possible (Cook et al., 1987; Deiner, 1993).

Children with mild or moderate hearing problems can function well in a regular early childhood program. Children with severe hearing impairments will need considerable special assistance, usually including special equipment.

Children with Hearing Impairments. Hearing is very much tied to communication because children learn to understand and talk by listening to and imitating others. Thus, a child with a hearing impairment usually experiences problems in language learning as well. Because language is also a primary tool in acquiring concepts about the world, a child whose language is limited by hearing loss may also experience cognitive problems. Severity of hearing loss, anywhere on the continuum from mild to profound, will affect the corrective measures as well as the strategies a teacher might use. Some children benefit from hearing aids, which amplify sounds. Others are helped to learn a combination of methods, for instance, sign language, using whatever hearing capacity they might have, and speech reading skills as part of a **total communication approach.**

Total communication approach—Used with hearing impaired children, utilizing a combination of methods such as sign language, speech reading, and hearing aids.

Some children with mild hearing loss may not have been identified as having a problem. In addition, ear infections can affect hearing; thus, some children are at risk of losing some of their hearing capacity. Be alert to signs of potential problems. If a child frequently requests that you repeat, often seems not to hear when you speak to her, is inattentive or baffled at group times that require listening, or shows indications that her ears hurt, there may be cause for concern. Plan to observe such signs more specifically and then share your observations with the parents.

If a child with an identified hearing disability is enrolled in your class, the audiologist or speech therapist can provide guidelines for adapting the program to maximize learning, possibly including some of the suggestions listed here. Before talking to a hearing impaired child, make sure that you have the child's attention and wait for eye contact. While talking, always face the child, preferably at eye level, and don't cover your mouth. Whenever appropriate, use body language to augment your words. Also reduce background noise as much as possible to help the child focus on relevant sounds. Enrich the visual environment of the class by adding as many visual aids as possible; for instance, pictures of the day's routine activities and pictorial labels of classroom materials. If the child is learning sign language, try to learn as many of the signs as possible and help the other children in the class learn some as well (Deiner, 1993).

Children with Communication Impairments. Language is a complex process (we will discuss it in more detail in Chapter 12) that depends on a number of interrelated factors. It involves the ability to hear, understand, process information, speak, and articulate sounds so they can be understood by others. Problems in communication can stem from a variety of causes. For instance, a child's language learning might be delayed because of inadequate language stimulation in early life; poor communication could be a symptom of problems synthesizing information in a meaningful way; or poor articulation might be caused by a malformation in the structure of the mouth. If, compared to agemates, a child in your class is particularly difficult to understand, has difficulty understanding what you say, or consistently refuses to talk, there may be a language or speech disability that should be discussed with the parents.

The early childhood program can provide a language-rich environment for a child with a communication impairment.

Coordination with the speech therapist can ensure that what is accomplished in therapy is augmented in the early childhood setting. In addition, a stimulating, consistent, and language-rich environment can encourage the child to use language. Structure activities that will result in success to build the child's sense of confidence. Encourage the child to participate in social activities by encouraging all forms of communication, even if it is nonverbal. When appropriate, create a need for speech, for instance, by "misunderstanding" the child's request made through gestures. Particularly if the child does not talk, maintain relevant commentary. If the child does talk, be a patient listener, giving your undivided attention. Never criticize the child's incorrect speech, or lack of speech, but praise appropriate speech when it occurs.

Communication may also be problematic if a child has little or no command of the English language. A child learning English as a second language does not, however, have a language deficit, because the child most likely is fluent in the family's language. Strategies for helping children become bilingual communicators are discussed in detail in Chapter 12.

Although display of some behavior problems is normal for young children, some have emotional deficits that require special attention.

Children with Emotional or Behavioral Deficits. As an early childhood teacher, you will inevitably be around children whose behavior is at times out of control. Most children will respond negatively to some circumstances or provocations, such as hitting out, using aggressive language, or being destructive. Such occasional behavior is normal and can be dealt with by using suitable guidance techniques. All children need positive guidance to help them gradually develop self-control and acquire appropriate social skills and attitudes toward other people. Because guidance is such an integral part of working with young children, we will devote two chapters to various aspects of guidance, including dealing with problem behaviors (see Chapters 14 and 15).

Autism—A socioemotional disorder of unknown origin in which the child's social, language, and other behaviors are inappropriate, often bizarre.

A small percentage of children have much more severe problems that require intensive therapeutic intervention. One such condition is **autism,** a social-emotional condition of unknown origin in which the child shows inappropriate, even bizarre, behaviors. It is not likely that a severely autistic child would be enrolled in an integrated classroom. However, if a child in your class seems particularly distant from or oblivious of others in the class, seems out of touch or disinterested in what is going on, generally reacts with inappropriate emotions or shows no emotion, frequently engages in self-stimulating behaviors, or repeats words rather than responding to them, talk with the parents and urge them to seek a professional diagnosis and help (Deiner, 1993).

Children who suffer from chronic or long-term illnesses also have special needs.

Children with Health Problems. A range of chronic, long-term health conditions can cause various problems for children. In addition to the physical symptoms of the illness, which are often painful, children with health problems are frequently subjected to scary medical treatment and hospitalizations, may well be excluded from participating in some activities, can be beset by anxiety and fears, and are absent from school more than other children. Thus, children with health impairments need special consideration, not only to ensure that their medical needs are met but also to help them cope as effectively as possible with their illnesses.

Children can be beset by numerous health impairments, too numerous to review here. If a child in your class has been diagnosed as having a chronic health problem, it is important to gather information about the illness. Parents, doctors, and therapists will be the best sources of information because they can give you not only general information about the illness but information about the child's specific needs as well. Another source is literature prepared by support or informational organizations related to specific illnesses (for instance, the American Diabetes Association or the Asthma and Allergy Foundation of America). Be particularly aware of preventive measures that need to be taken, for instance, medication or periods of rest. If there is the possibility that the child may suffer an attack, as may happen with asthma or epilepsy, know what steps should be taken. If appropriate, at least one member of the staff should be trained in emergency procedures related to the child's condition.

It is also important to know what information the child has been given about the condition. What you say to the child should agree with what the parents or other professionals have told the child. In addition, an open atmosphere allows the child, as well as other children, to discuss fears, concerns, or questions. If a child is frequently absent from school, take steps to ensure that the child continues to feel part of the class. Involve other children in sending get-well messages or telephoning the child (if appropriate), visit the child at home or in the hospital, and send school activities that can be done at home (Deiner, 1993).

Gifted Children. Recently there has been increasing attention paid to the special needs of another group, those considered **gifted children.** As you read the word "gifted," you can probably conjure up an image of a child you have come across, one who, in some ways, seemed precocious and talented. Although we often can think of some characteristics of giftedness in specific children, it is much more difficult to define this word because different people have different concepts of its meaning. A broad definition of giftedness would include children whose performance is significantly above average in intellectual and creative areas. At the same time, it is also important to acknowledge that some children have the potential for outstanding performance that may only emerge from a supportive atmosphere.

Gifted children—Children who perform significantly above average in intellectual and creative areas.

Another group with special needs are gifted children, who perform above average in intellectual and creative areas. Such children need a stimulating and challenging environment.

Children may show a number of traits and abilities that provide clues to their giftedness. They are often precocious in various developmental areas, particularly in language. They may have an unusually large and advanced vocabulary; employ it appropriately in conversation on a wide variety of topics; use language in humorous and creative ways by making up elaborate stories, rhymes, and songs; and often begin to read and write earlier than their peers. Giftedness can also be seen in problem-solving ability as children like to play with ideas, come up with unusual solutions, and see more than one viewpoint. They are generally observant, catch on quickly to new concepts, and have a longer than average attention span (Deiner, 1993; Roedell, Jackson, & Robinson, 1980). Children displaying such traits usually score significantly above average on intelligence tests, which is one (though certainly not the only) measure of giftedness.

Some children's gift is seen through special talent in art, music, or another creative area in which they are particularly advanced. One such child, three-year-old Karen, continued to astound teachers as she drew careful renditions of objects in her environment. On the playground Karen often lay on her stomach on the grass to observe bugs, which she then drew with meticulous detail.

Because gifted children often catch on quickly, they need a wide variety of challenging and rewarding experiences that help them develop positive attitudes about school and learning. At the same time, it is important to keep in mind that gifted young children are, although advanced in some areas, still preschoolers with the social and emotional needs of those in their age group. Sensitive guidance can help them develop a good sense of self, recognition of individual differences and strengths, and appropriate social interaction skills. The interests of gifted children are similar to those of their age-mates, although they may want to learn more about a topic or delve into it in more depth. Thus, it is important to provide a variety of activities that allow children to enjoy involvement at different levels. At the same time, all of the children will benefit from exposure to novel, diverse, and enriching activities through classroom materials, books, field trips, and class guests (Wolfe, 1989).

WORKING WITH PARENTS OF SPECIAL CHILDREN

Families of children with disabilities also have some special needs that the early childhood program can help meet.

All parents need support, understanding, and reassurance, something that is particularly true of parents with children who have special needs. In addition to dealing with the common multifaceted aspects of parenting, parents of young children with disabilities often also experience greater emotional, financial, and physical strains. When a disabled child is involved in an early childhood program, it is particularly important that open and accepting communication be established between parents and teachers.

Teachers need to be sensitive to the various reactions that parents of children with disabilities may experience. Often parents feel a sense of grief for losing the "ideal" child they had been expecting before its birth. This grief can turn to anger, which parents might direct at themselves, the child, a doctor, or another professional who can be "blamed" for the disability. Some parents cope with their child's disability by denying that there is a problem, and they may, in fact, continue to seek out different professionals in hopes of finding the one who will tell them that the child's situation is normal or that he or she will soon "catch up." Parents may also experience guilt about something they perceive they had done wrong, perhaps before the child was even born. Gradually most parents come to accept the child's disability and view it from a more realistic perspective, although it is normal for them to continue to feel grief, anger, or guilt at times (Gargiulo, 1985). Parents whose children are enrolled in your program may experience some of these feelings. It is important to acknowledge and accept their reactions by listening, providing practical advice, and offering information on community resources that can be of help.

Only relatively recently has the importance of the family in the lives of young children with special needs been legally acknowledged. Both Public Laws 94-142 and 99-457 are very specific in outlining the rights and roles of parents in determining the kinds of educational and therapeutic services their children will receive in programs in which public funding is provided for young children with disabilities. Specifically, these laws outline guidelines for development of an **Individualized Education Plan (IEP)** for preschoolers and an Individualized Family Service Plan (IFSP) for children under the age of three. Both processes require thorough involvement of parents and teachers.

Individualized Education Plan (IEP)—Mandated by Public Law 94-142, such a plan must be designed for each child with disabilities and must involve parents as well as teachers and other appropriate professionals.

In addition to such legally mandated involvement of parents of children with disabilities, parents should be included and supported in many other ways. Exchange of relevant information between teachers and parents will help both better understand and work with the child. The school's philosophy of focusing on commonalities rather than differences among children should also provide support for parents. Sometimes parents of children with special needs are so centered on the disability that they do not see other aspects of the child's development with a clear perspective; parents can be helped to see just how similar their child is to other children. By recognizing the unique strengths and needs of each family, teachers can be the best possible resource by listening sensitively and openly, offering practical recommendations and support, and helping to maximize each child's potential.

SUMMARY

1. Young children are alike in three common areas:
   A. "Profiles" that identify typical traits shared by the majority of children of different ages
   B. The need of all children for positive self-esteem
   C. The need of all children for play as a way of learning about the world
2. Factors that contribute to the wonderful diversity among children include inborn traits and external factors.
3. Some children have specific, special needs that make them unique. The early childhood program can help meet the needs of special children by:
   A. The inclusion of disabled and nondisabled children into the same program
   B. Recognizing characteristics of children with motor, cognitive, learning, visual, hearing, communication, emotional, and health problems, as well as gifted children

KEY TERMS LIST

at-risk children
attention deficit hyperactivity disorder (ADHD)
attention deficit disorder (ADD)
autism
deficit or impairment
developmental delay
educable mentally retarded
fetal alcohol effect (FAE)
fetal alcohol syndrome (FAS)
gifted children
individualized education plan (IEP)
individualized family service plan (IFSP)
least restrictive environment
perceived competence
personal control
self-concept
self-esteem
slow learner
temperament
total communication approach

chapter 3

The Families

As we discussed in the last chapter, children are central in early childhood education. Families have to be considered equally important, however, in part because children are integral members of their family systems, and, conversely, family values and culture are an inseparable part of children. Families are also at the core of early childhood education because the early childhood staff shares with families the responsibility for socializing young children. It is important to provide for children a sense of continuity between home and school experiences, which can best be assured through a carefully fostered partnership between the family and the early childhood program (Powell, 1989). That effort will be the focus of this chapter.

A THEORETICAL PERSPECTIVE

Throughout this book, we will review a variety of theories to help you understand more clearly the many aspects of children's development and behavior. It is equally important to understand family functioning from a theoretical perspective. **Family systems theory** provides a useful approach to understanding the family as an ever-developing and changing social unit in which members constantly have to accommodate and adapt to each other's demands as well as to demands from outside the family. This theory provides a dynamic rather than static view of how families function.

From the perspective of family systems theory, the influence that family members have on each other is not one-way but rather interactive and reciprocal. Furthermore, it is impossible to understand the family by gaining an understanding of its individual members because there is more to the family that the "sum of its parts." It is necessary to view its interaction patterns and the unspoken "rules" that govern the members' behaviors. Healthy families work well together,

Family systems theory—A view of the family as an ever-developing and changing social unit in which members constantly accommodate and adapt to each other's demands as well as to outside demands.

Microsystem—According to family systems theory, that part of the environment that most immediately affects a person, such as the family, school, or workplace.

Mesosystem—According to family systems theory, the linkages between the family and the immediate neighborhood and community.

Exosystem—According to family systems theory, that part of the environment that includes the broader components of the community that affect the functioning of the family, such as governmental agencies or mass media.

Macrosystem—According to family systems theory, the broadest part of the environment, which includes the cultural, political, and economic forces that affect families.

Family systems theory views the family as a dynamic, constantly changing system that interacts with other systems, for instance, those within the community.

communicate often, are able to make effective decisions, and can handle change. In addition, understanding the family means looking at its functioning within the larger context, for instance, the extended family, the community, and the neighborhood. The early childhood center becomes part of that larger context in which families function (Bronfenbrenner, 1986; Walker & Crocker, 1988).

Each individual's development occurs in a broader ecological context, within different but overlapping systems. The **microsystem** is the most immediate system that affects the individual; it includes the family, classroom, or workplace. These components of the microsystem are linked together in the **mesosystem** through such relationships as parent-teacher interaction or employment practices that affect the family (for instance, employer-supported child care or paid maternity leave).

The **exosystem** includes broader components of the neighborhood and community that affect the functioning of the family, for example, governmental agencies or mass media. Finally, the broadest system to affect families is the **macrosystem,** which includes cultural, political, and economic forces (Bronfenbrenner & Crouter, 1983). From such an ecological perspective, the child and family are seen more clearly as part of and affected by many other systems, each of which influences their development and functioning.

Viewing children and families as parts of various systems helps us avoid seeking simple explanations and acknowledge the complex interactions that often underlie children's and parents' behaviors. We must take time to look at the many factors affecting behavior before jumping to conclusions. It is also important to recognize that family and school interact to affect children's development in myriad possible directions (Goelman, 1988). This perspective makes good communication between home and school an imperative, not a choice. Finally, a systems approach helps us see the interrelatedness of all aspects of children's lives. We simply cannot assume that the child's home exists in one isolated "compartment," while the school is in another. In the same way, we cannot presume the families' lives can be segmented into isolated facets.

THE CHANGING AMERICAN FAMILY

The family is and always has been the most important element in most children's lives. The family is where children experience the emotional and physical care and sustenance vital to their well-being. But the family has no simple definition or boundaries. Whereas several decades ago many young children might have been part of a "traditional" family—working father, housewife mother, and two or three children—today's youngsters live in any of a wide variety of family configurations (Fraser, 1989). Douglas Powell (1989) summarized this change well in a monograph on families and early childhood programs, published by the National Association for the Education of Young Children:

> Early childhood educators increasingly serve families characterized by single-parent households, cultural diversity and ethnic minority status, dual-worker or dual-career lifestyles, reconstituted ("blended") family arrangements, struggles

with real or perceived economic pressures, and geographic mobility that decreases access to support traditionally available from extended family members. (p. 15)

Family Forms

There is no simple or single definition of the family because families come in many forms.

KEY QUESTION #1

Think of your own family history. How has your family changed over the past two (or three or four) generations? Consider maternal employment, divorce, closeness to extended family, and other factors. Compare your family with that of other members of your class.

A family may be made up of one parent and one child, or it may be part of an extended family of grandparents, uncles, aunts, cousins, and many other relatives who are in frequent, close contact. Families may have one, two, or more parents; these may be the biological parents, stepparents, adoptive parents, or emotionally rather than legally related care-givers. A single parent may have never been married or be divorced, separated, or widowed; as part of this group, an increasing number of young children live with single fathers (Briggs & Walters, 1985).

If a family has undergone a divorce, children may live with the same single or remarried parent all of the time, many alternate between two parents who have joint custody, or may see one parent for brief times during weekends or holidays. For some children, grandparents or other relatives take on the function of parents. Some divorced parents find alternate living arrangements, perhaps moving back with their own parents, sharing housing with another adult or single parent, or joining in a group housing arrangement. Because of divorce and remarriage, today's children may also acquire various natural and adoptive brothers and sisters, as well as half-siblings, step-siblings, or unrelated "siblings" in less formal family arrangements.

Whatever the family form, a wide range of people can make up children's network of significant family members, as defined by emotional as well as legal ties. It is necessary, as a teacher of young children, that you also consider and acknowledge these persons as part of a child's family. Anyone who is important in the child's mind should be considered as important by you as well.

It is also important to be aware of legal restrictions that might affect children's relationships with adults in their lives. During some divorce proceedings, one parent may file a restraining order against the other, legally limiting or forbidding contact with the child. Although

In two-earner families, parents often share child care responsibilities.

such situations are usually upsetting, it is necessary to be aware of and make appropriate provisions for complying with any legal action. Keep in mind that the majority of children who are kidnapped are taken by a divorced parent who does not have custody of the child (Sheldon, 1983). Having a release form on file at the school is one important way of ensuring that only authorized persons pick up the child.

Families also differ based on economic, racial, cultural, ethnic, religious, language, and geographic factors.

Other Family Variations

Not only is there great variation in family form and composition, but other characteristics differentiate families as well. Some of these include economic, racial, cultural, ethnic, religious, language, and geographic factors, and the sexual orientation of the parents. Such elements can not only affect family customs and traditions, but also reflect deeper meanings, for instance, defining values and relationships (Jenkins, 1987). In some cases, a family's uniqueness includes a mixture of cultures, religions, races, or generations. A teacher can learn about characteristics of various cultural, racial, or religious groups by reading, but it is very important to avoid making large-scale generalizations about a family based on group traits. Families are complex, and only through genuine interest can a teacher get to know them well. Effective and frequent communication helps the teacher become aware of family attributes that can affect the child and family as participants in the early childhood program. (Note that in Chapter 13 we will discuss some guidelines for promoting understanding of cultural and ethnic variations in children and families; in Chapter 12 we will consider some issues in working with children and families who are bilingual or do not speak English at all.)

Increasing numbers of families from varied cultural and ethnic backgrounds enroll their children in early childhood programs. In fact, it is estimated that by the year 2000 over one-third of children in the United States will be from nonwhite, non-Anglo groups (Leister, 1993). It is, therefore, particularly important for teachers to be sensitive to differences in values, cultural expectations, and child-rearing practices. Effective communication is especially important to help both

Families vary widely, something to which the early childhood teacher must be sensitive. Differences in culture, ethnicity, race, religion, language, and family composition are contributing factors. How can you, as the teacher of a diverse group of children, get to know the families and their values?

parents and teachers achieve mutual understanding and appreciation, which, in turn, will help provide a consistent and positive experience for the children.

Families in Poverty

An estimated one-fifth of American children and one-fourth of preschool-aged children grow up in poverty.

Today, increased numbers of children grow up in poverty. The estimated 20 percent of American children living in poverty includes 39.9 percent of black, 40.3 percent of Hispanic, and 16.3 percent of white children (Children's Defense Fund, 1998). This means that one-fifth of American children live in families that suffer such severe financial strains that they cannot meet their basic needs (Chafel, 1990). The poverty rate for children under six is even higher, with one-fourth of that group living in poverty (Kids Count Data Book, 1996). A different way of underscoring this circumstance comes from a survey of eight industrialized nations, in which the United States had the highest child poverty rate; in fact, American children were two or three times more likely to be poor than children in the other countries studied (Children's Defense Fund, 1990).

Historically, many early childhood education efforts have been aimed at helping economically disadvantaged families, with Head Start as the most extensive of such antipoverty endeavors. While such programs initially focused almost exclusively on the children, more recently they have emphasized providing strong support to families as well. This includes information and education, concrete assistance (for instance, providing transportation), and emotional support (Weiss, 1987). Careful research has shown that high-quality early childhood programs, particularly those in which family support has been included, have a dramatic effect, not only in terms of children's later school achievement, but also on their families (Chafel, 1990; Seitz, Rosenbaum, & Apfel, 1985; Zigler & Freedman, 1987).

The end of the twentieth century has brought another element into the picture of child care, families, and families in poverty. The Welfare Reform Act of 1996, formally called the Personal Responsibility and Work Opportunity Reconciliation Act, has set the expectation that recipients will receive welfare support for a limited time only and then must become employed. Since many welfare recipients have young children, the child care system has to absorb additional children as these parents enter the work force (Gnezda, 1996). The implications of this act are further discussed in Chapter 16.

THE NEEDS OF FAMILIES

One of the most important needs of working parents is for high-quality, reliable care for their young children.

The fact that a child is enrolled in an early childhood program indicates that the family has a need that the program is able to meet. The most common and certainly the most obvious family need is provision of child care while the parents are at work. The proliferation of child care centers and family child care homes over the past three decades has been in response to the dramatic increase in the number of working, single-parent, and two-earner-parent families.

But beyond the overall need for responsible and knowledgeable adults to provide care for children while their parents work, families have other needs that the early childhood center can help meet. Some of these needs concern helping the parents, as individuals, meet the demands of their multiple roles. Others revolve around coordination of home and school routines and practices. One note to keep in mind: Although it is an ideal to consider that early childhood teachers can meet everyone's needs—children's parents', co-workers'—sometimes this is just not possible in actuality. Setting realistic goals within the particular work setting can help establish priorities. There are other community services that may provide for other needs.

Parenthood

Many parents are part of Erikson's stage of generativity, in which care and nurture of children is important.

Generativity—According to Erik Erikson, the stage of human development in which the mature adult focuses on the care and nurture of the young.

KEY QUESTION #2

Sometimes the needs of families conflict with those of the program. Which elements of the early childhood program could pose a potential conflict? How might these be resolved? Read "Ethics Case Studies: The Working Mother" in *Young Children*, November 1987, page 16, for insight into the suggestions of professionals to resolve such a conflict.

Nurturing stage—Stage of parenting defined by Ellen Galinsky into which the parents of an infant fit, as they form an attachment with and integrate the new baby into the family.

We typically view parenthood from the perspective of children's development and how parents facilitate, support, and promote it. Rarely is parenthood seen from the viewpoint of parents and their needs. Erik Erikson (1963), whose theory of human development was one of the first to span adulthood as well as childhood, considers that the most important need of the mature adult in the stage of **generativity** is to care for and nurture others. The tasks of this stage are often carried out in parenthood, through which the adult is concerned with meeting the needs of the next generation. Implied in this process is growth of the adult as an individual that is separate from the nurturance extended to children. This acknowledgment of adulthood as a period of continued development has been advanced in recent years by other writers (for instance, Gould, 1978; Levinson, 1978; Sheehy, 1976).

Parenthood as a distinct process has also been examined in greater depth. Ellen Galinsky (1981), after intensive research and interviews with scores of individuals, suggests that parents change and develop in their roles just as children do, by moving through six stages of parenthood. Each stage involves issues to be faced and a crisis that the parent has to resolve successfully. For instance, the parents of an infant are in the **nurturing stage,** forming a strong attachment with and integrating this newest family member into their lives. Parents of

Parents also go through defined stages of parenting; for instance, explaining and clarifying the world to their children.

toddlers and younger preschoolers, find themselves enmeshed in the **authority stage,** defining rules and their own roles. Toward the end of the preschool years, parents enter the **interpretive stage** in which they are confronted with the task of explaining and clarifying the world to their children.

Authority stage—Stage of parenting defined by Ellen Galinsky typifying parents of young preschoolers who are defining rules as well as their own parenting role.

Interpretive stage—Stage of parenting defined by Ellen Galinsky typifying the parent of an older preschooler or school-aged child who faces the task of explaining and clarifying the world to the child.

Galinsky is particularly concerned with the "images" that parents create, images of what they expect the child to be like before it is born, images of how they and their children will act and interact, or images of the loving relationship they expect. These images, especially what they wish to recreate or what they would like to change, emerge from parents' past experiences. Often, however, images and reality are different. Growth occurs when parents modify images so they become more consistent with reality or adjust their behavior to come closer to the image.

Galinsky emphasizes throughout her book that parents frequently feel their responses and emotions are unique, unaware that other parents also encounter them. Yet, as she points out, during each of the stages of parenthood, parents face predictable issues and strong emotions. It helps parents to discuss and recognize their shared experiences as well as to have opportunities to observe the behaviors of others' children. It is also helpful when professionals explain common reactions and feelings, for instance, to a child's first day of school. In working with children, then, it is very important to acknowledge that parents undergo personal development that parallels their children's growth but that has separate issues and conflicts that need to be resolved.

Galinsky identifies stages of parenthood that are distinct from but overlap with their children's stages of development.

Empowerment

When parents feel confident and competent in their abilities as mothers and fathers as well as members of the larger community, their children benefit. Unfortunately, some parents feel that they are powerless in controlling what happens to them and to their children. An important role that early childhood programs can serve for families is to promote **empowerment,** a sense of control or power over events in their lives. This is particularly important as families deal with a variety of agencies and professionals, for instance, school, welfare, and political systems.

A goal of some early childhood programs is to promote empowerment of the parents, to help them achieve a sense of control over their lives.

Empowerment—Helping parents gain a sense of control over events in their lives.

Parental empowerment has been a direct aim or an unexpected outcome in some programs designed for low-income families (Cochran, 1988; Ramey, Dorvall, & Baker-Ward, 1983; Seitz et al., 1985). As cited in one report of such a program, "Intangible but crucial shifts in attitude took place in parents who were often severely demoralized at the start" (Nauta & Hewett, 1988, p. 401). Parents began to see that they could have an impact. Professionals can use a wide variety of techniques to help parents attain this sense of control, including approaches described in a number of excellent publications, such as Alice Honig's *Parent Involvement in Early Childhood Education* (1979).

One of the forces behind the concept of parental empowerment has been the move toward viewing parents and teachers as equals. Not too many years ago, the pervasive attitude was that professionals were experts, whereas parents were the passive recipients of their expertise

(Powell, 1989). Such a view does not provide parents with the security that they know their child best and that they should be full participants in any decisions that affect the child. Parents need to be treated with respect, their opinions should be solicited and taken seriously, and they must be integrally involved in decisions about the child. In addition, when early childhood professionals give parents child development information, parents have tools with which to make informed decisions about their children's needs. Thus, involving, consulting with, and providing relevant education for parents can have a far-reaching impact by helping parents recognize their own importance and competence (Swick, 1994).

Coordinating Family Needs and the Program

Coordinating the needs of parents with the needs of children and the program can be a challenge for early childhood teachers.

Helping parents reach their potential as effective adults may be a goal in some programs that work extensively with families, particularly those from impoverished backgrounds. In all early childhood programs, there are additional points of contact between parents and teachers, at times revolving around seemingly mundane matters, but nonetheless important. A flexible, good-humored attitude can help establish and maintain positive home-school relationships.

Parents' busy lives, or unforeseen events, are sometimes at odds with the schedule and routine of the early childhood center. For instance, one mother expressed concern that the center's afternoon snack, provided at 3:30, was served too late and that the child was not interested in dinner at 5:30. Another parent preferred that her child not take a nap at school, because when he slept during the day, he was just not ready to sleep at home until quite late in the evening. Other problems may keep a parent from arriving until after the center has closed, for instance, car trouble, a traffic snarl, or unexpected overtime at work.

All of these situations can cause conflict but also provide an opportunity to evaluate what is best for the child, the parents, the other children, and the teachers. Sometimes such predicaments can be resolved fairly easily, but there are times when the needs of the child, the parent, or the school directly conflict. There is no simple answer, for instance, to weighing whether a child should take a nap, particularly

Viewing parents and teachers as equals, each contributing relevant information and expertise, helps empower parents.

EXPERIENCES

chapter 3

LEE, Parent Program Coordinator

Busy Parents

Today's moms and dads are doing it all: they work, they go to school, they maintain a home, many are partners in a marriage, and, of course, they are parents. Times have definitely changed. Parents just have less time than their counterparts of two decades ago, so our entire approach to involving parents in their children's child care program has had to be modified.

Actually, the great majority of what might be considered parent education, as well as communication between parents and teachers and parents and parents, happens before and after school. The informal networking that goes on at those times covers a lot of ground. But there are times when it is more fruitful to reach a large group of parents rather than to talk to many parents about the same topic individually. What we have found is that there are certain "burning" issues that come up at certain times of the year, issues about which a number of parents need information.

Our most successful group parent functions have revolved around such issues. So, when we consider having a parent meeting, the first prerequisite is the relevance of the topic to a sizeable group of parents. Once we have identified such a topic, we work with three other elements: time, food, and child care. We talk to parents to find out when the most convenient time for such a meeting would be. Almost always, parents want to meet about the time the center closes, so they don't have to come back in the evening. It is also helpful for us to serve a substantial snack. Food is a great way of enticing people to an extracurricular function. Finally, we always provide child care so parents don't have to worry about having to get a baby sitter or dealing with their children while trying to listen to the topic under discussion.

One of the most popular parent meeting topics, year after year, has to do with transitions. Parents whose children are moving from our center to kindergarten or first grade, whose children are moving from our infant and toddler program to a preschool class, or whose children are moving into our kindergarten class have many questions. Major changes such as these often raise doubts and anxieties. So, we share information about how within-center changes are made, and we invite public school representatives to discuss the transition to public kindergarten or first grade. Parents have opportunities to ask questions and often misconceptions are clarified. We generally hold our transition meeting in April.

Earlier in the year we also hold a meeting to discuss assessment of children. Parents are very interested in knowing how we evaluate their children and what we do with the information. We share with parents our philosophy and show them examples of the kinds of information we seek. Since we use a portfolio approach to keeping records about the children, parents are generally reassured when they recognize that we use an individualized method that does not "compare" children to each other. A group meeting to discuss general information is then followed by opportunities for parents to speak briefly with their child's teacher and set appointments for more in-depth conferences.

Parents, teachers, and other staff members of child care programs are busy people. Finding the most relevant topics and most appealing methods to bring these people together takes some ingenuity, but successful parent functions can be rewarding for all those who are involved.

experiences

when he appears to need it, or not take a nap because a delayed evening bedtime keeps his mother from getting the sleep she needs. Teachers must carefully weigh their own professional judgment of what is best for the child and take into account the child's need for sleep, the potential effect of being sleepy and cranky on the ability to function well at school, and the fact that the child would be treated differently from the other children by not napping (Ethics Commission, 1987). One way of resolving such conflicts—whether it is a matter of discussing naps, snacks, or pick-up time—is communication, our next topic.

COMMUNICATING WITH FAMILIES

Effective home-school communication is important to parents, teachers, and children.

Effective, positive communication with families is vital to providing a consistent and congruent experience for young children, but there is no simple formula for assuring that such contact does indeed take place. Each family is unique and brings to the early childhood program distinctive strengths and needs. Just as the teacher deals with each child as a unique individual by employing a variety of teaching and guidance methods, so must a flexible approach be maintained in communicating with families to meet their individual requirements.

There are many bits of information that need to be shared by teachers and the family. For instance, both sides will benefit from mutually discussing the child. In addition, there is often more general information about various aspects of the program that must be shared with families. The type of information to be conveyed often determines the communication method used. Communication, as we will discuss, can be carried out using both individual and group methods. Most early childhood centers utilize a combination of these approaches.

Individual Methods of Communicating with Families

The best way to get to know each family is through individual interaction and contact. Informally, such contact can take place daily, for instance, when children are dropped off and picked up from school. More formally, scheduled conferences between teacher and parents or other family members provide an avenue for exchange of information.

Parents and teachers often use the beginning and end of the day as a time for brief, informal communication.

KEY QUESTION #3

Visit an early childhood program. What evidence of communication with parents do you see? Look at bulletin boards, notes, pictures, and other written material. What kind of interaction do you notice between parents and teachers? What "messages" about the school's concern for parents do parents get from this communication?

Informal Contact with Families. At the beginning and end of each day, at least one teacher should be available to exchange a few words with family members who drop off or pick up their children. Such informal interactions can make teachers more sensitive to the needs of children and families, can establish a mutual trust, can convey a feeling of caring and interest to parents, and can heighten parents' involvement in the program. "By being open, receptive, and chatty, teachers encourage parent interest and commitment" (Reiber & Embry, 1983, p. 162).

Daily informal contact between teachers and parents is important for another reason when very young children are concerned. "During the time the parent is away, the infant is busily going about the business of growing up. Each new achievement . . . should be shared with parents" (Wilson, 1995, p. 90). In addition to being given information about the child's achievements and activities, parents of infants also must be kept informed about their children's routine activities, such as eating, sleeping, and toileting. A consistent form, which caregivers fill out throughout each day, can help parents see at a glance what the child's day was like.

Because frequent school-family contacts are important, it makes sense to structure the schedule so that staff are free to participate in such exchanges (Tizard, Mortimer, & Burchell, 1981). Informal dialogues at the start and end of the day tend to be the most pervasive form of family involvement in early childhood programs (Gestwicki, 1992), especially those primarily involving working parents. In programs where children arrive by bus or come in car pools, the teacher needs to make an extra effort to maintain contact with parents, for instance, through notes or telephone calls (Gestwicki, 1992).

Another informal means of contact with parents is through occasional telephone calls. These provide a comfortable way of talking to parents, particularly if the calls are made often enough so they do not signal "a problem." Some schools send home "happy notes," brief, personalized notes that share with the parents something positive that happened during the day (Bundy, 1991).

Formal Contact With Families. Informal daily contacts between teachers and family members can create a mutually respectful and nonintimidating atmosphere. When teachers and parents feel comfortable with each other, communication will more likely be honest. In addition to such day-to-day encounters, more formal opportunities should be structured, when a sizable block of uninterrupted time is set aside for in-depth discussion. Such formal contacts can take the form of a parent-teacher conference or a home visit.

More formal parent-teacher communication takes place through parent conferences and home visits. Both should be planned to facilitate a positive exchange of information.

A **parent-teacher conference** is a regularly scheduled meeting that can satisfy different objectives. It can focus on getting acquainted; sharing information about the child and presenting a "progress report"; or, at the initiation of either teacher or parents, solving problems or discussing specific issues (Bullock, 1986; Reiber & Embry, 1983). Conferences often have negative connotations for the participants, who

Parent-teacher conference—A one-on-one interaction between the teacher and the child's parent(s).

Regularly scheduled conferences, where teachers and parents share information and insights, should be positive and affirming.

may view them as a time to share complaints and problems, even as a "last resort" when all else fails. But routinely scheduled conferences should be positive, affirming, and supportive.

A conference should never be an impromptu event. The teacher needs to be well prepared ahead of time, reviewing relevant information and thinking about how best to present it. In fact, preparing for conferences should be an ongoing process, beginning when the child first enters the program (Bjorklund & Burger, 1987). It is helpful if the teacher is ready with some anecdotes to support what the parents are told as well as to convey to them that the teacher knows the child well. It is also important to think through what questions to ask of the parents to help the teacher better understand and work with the child.

At the same time, the teacher should facilitate a relaxed and easy forum for conversation. Sometimes sharing something with the parents—for instance, a picture painted by the child or a favorite recipe for play dough—contributes toward creating a positive atmosphere.

Home visit—A one-on-one interaction between the teacher and the parent(s) of the child that takes place in the child's home.

Another type of formal individual contact between teachers and family is a **home visit.** Home visits share some of the same objectives and procedures with parent-teacher conferences, but they contribute some added benefits as well. A teacher who visits a family at home conveys a sense of caring and interest in the child's world beyond the classroom. Children are usually delighted to introduce their room, toys, pets, and siblings to the teacher and are made to feel very special that the teacher is visiting them at home. Parents can observe firsthand the interaction between the child and the teacher and may become more relaxed with the teacher who has shown this special interest. In addition, teachers can observe firsthand the family's home environment and parent-child interactions as a way of better understanding the child's behavior. In some instances, especially once a sense of trust has been established, home visits can become an extremely important source of support, for instance, for teen-aged parents.

Although there are very important benefits in conducting home visits, they are also quite time consuming and may (though certainly not inevitably) intimidate the parents. A teacher's commitment to learning as much as possible about the children in the class and their families has to be weighed against the investment of time involved in home visits and the parents' potential anxiety (Gestwicki, 1992).

There are some strategies that can help when problems arise between parents and teachers.

When Problems Come up Between Parents and Teachers. Ideally, parents and teachers cooperate fully to provide congruent, positive experiences for children at home and at school. Unfortunately, there are times when this ideal is not always realized. In fact, parent-teacher disharmony is quite common (Galinsky, 1990). Parents and teachers may disagree, particularly when they feel rushed and tired or when they are preoccupied with other aspects of their lives. In addition, both may harbor some unacknowledged negative feelings, for instance, disapproval of working mothers, jealousy or competition for the child's affection, or criticism of the other's child guidance approach (Galinsky, 1988; Galinsky, 1990). Although the child is the common bond between parents and teachers, there are many other factors that affect their moods and impinge on their interactions. The job stress ex-

Parents and teachers may, at times, disagree. Communication to help each other see the others' point of view can help ease such tensions.

perienced by parents as well as by teachers can certainly spill over into the brief contact between them as children are dropped off or picked up at school during what Ellen Galinsky calls the "arsenic hour" (1988).

Galinsky (1988) offers some concrete suggestions for working more effectively with parents. She suggests that when teachers become upset with parents, it is often because teachers' underlying expectations are somehow not realized; teachers need to examine whether what they expect is realistic or not. Similarly, teachers should scrutinize their attitudes toward the parents, looking for hidden resentments or prejudices. Teachers also need to make an effort to see the situations from the parents' point of view, asking themselves how they might feel if they were in the parents' shoes.

It can be very helpful to teachers to develop a support system, whether within their own program or even outside of it, that allows them to express and explore their feelings in an accepting and safe atmosphere. Teachers must also recognize and convey to parents the limits of their role. This includes being familiar with community resources to which parents can be referred when a problem is beyond the scope of the teacher's role and expertise.

There is no simple formula for effective parent-teacher communication. The parent-teacher relationship is founded on trust and respect that grow out of many small but significant daily contacts. Greeting parents by name; sharing brief, positive anecdotes about their children; writing personalized notes; making phone calls to parents the teacher does not see often; and being sensitive to parents' needs all contribute to a good relationship (Morgan, 1989).

Group Methods of Communicating with Families

Effective methods of communicating with groups of parents include newsletters, memos, bulletin boards, and group meetings.

In addition to personalized, individual contact between parents and teachers, early childhood programs generally also utilize other communication methods for getting information to the parents as a group. These methods can serve a functional purpose, for instance, to let parents know that the school will be closed the day after Thanksgiving. They may also take on an educational role, for example, to give parents

KEY QUESTION #4

Ask several parents whose children are enrolled in an early childhood program about their contacts with the teachers and the program. What is their overall attitude about contact between home and school? Do they feel it is important or not important . . . positive or negative . . . present or absent . . . supportive or lacking in support? What do they expect from the teachers? Do they feel communication between parents and teachers is important for their children?

insight into an aspect of child development. We will review three such methods—written communiques, bulletin boards, and meetings.

Written Communiques. Newsletters, memos, or other written material can be an effective way of getting information to all families. It is, of course, important to match written information to the reading abilities of the parents. If many or all of the families in the program are non-English-speaking, for instance, communiques should be written in the parents' primary language.

It is also important that all such materials be neat, attractive, and accurately written. A sloppy, misspelled, and ungrammatical letter conveys that the message is probably not very important and that the teacher does not care enough about the families to produce a thoughtful document. Today, many schools have access to a computer, which makes it simpler than ever to compose attractively arranged letters or newsletters, to check the grammar and spelling, and to incorporate graphics.

Many programs produce a regular newsletter that may contain announcements, news of what the teachers have planned for the upcoming time period, new policies, relevant community information, child development research summaries, columns by local experts, and other information of interest to families. A newsletter is only effective if it is read. Thus, its length, the information included, and the writing style need to be carefully considered.

Another form of written communication that can convey a great deal of information to parents is a school handbook, which parents are given when they enroll their children in the early childhood program. Such a handbook should contain relevant information about school policies and procedures, fees, hours of operation, holidays, sick child care, birthday routines, and other important matters. At the same time, it should include a clearly articulated statement of the school's philosophy (Bundy, 1991).

Bulletin Boards. Bulletin boards can be a useful means of conveying information, or they can be a cluttered mass of overlaid memos that no one bothers to look at. To be effective, a bulletin board should be attractively laid out, its contents need to be current, and posted items should not compete with each other for attention. Furthermore, if family members know that only current and important items will be posted on a specific bulletin board, they are more likely to pay attention to it.

Bulletin boards can be used for a variety of purposes. They can be informative, for instance, letting parents know that the children will be taking a field trip the following week or that a child in the group has the chicken pox. Many centers include a notice of the day's activities on a bulletin board, which lets parents know the highlights of their child's day. Bulletin boards can also be educational, conveying relevant information in a way that appeals to those who look at it.

At one center, for instance, the teachers wanted to follow up on comments from several parents that their children were just scribbling rather than drawing something recognizable. The teachers wanted to help parents understand that children's art follows a developmental

A bulletin board can be an effective way of conveying information to parents as a group. This bulletin board, for instance, is organized and the information is current. What other methods can help ensure good communication with parents?

pattern. They matted selections of the children's pictures, arranged them attractively on bulletin boards organized by the children's ages, and interspersed the pictures with quotes from experts on children's art. The pictures supported the quotations, thus conveying the messages that children gradually move toward representational art and that there are common steps children go through in their development of art. Many parents commented on how helpful they found this bulletin board message. It proved to be a most effective teaching tool!

Meetings and Other Group Functions. Group gatherings can provide another effective way of reaching family members. Such functions can take the form of meetings, the traditional forum for formal parent education, or they can be social. In addition, parent discussion groups may be part of the early childhood program. When planning any kind of group function, however, keep in mind that family members are busy people who will weigh the benefits of attending a school program against other demands on their time. In fact, for some parents the pressure of one more thing to do might be so stressful that it would outweigh the advantages of the program. Because each family's needs are different, the early childhood program must facilitate communication with parents in many different ways and be prepared to individualize ways of meeting these needs.

If the director and staff feel that parent meetings can serve a positive function in meeting the needs of some of the families, they must ensure that what they plan will interest potential participants. One way to assess what might be relevant to parents is to conduct an interest survey. A brief form can solicit preferences about topic choices, time and day, and type of meeting (see Figure 3-1 for a sample form). If the teachers or the director plan parent functions without input from the parents, these functions may well fail to match the interest of the parents and result in very low attendance (Gestwicki, 1992). Also, parents are often more likely to come to a meeting if a meal or snack is included and if child care is provided. On the other hand, keep in mind that if children have already spent 9 or 10 hours at the center, adding 2 evening hours may be more than is reasonable.

FIGURE 3-1 Parent interest survey

Dear Parents:

We would like to plan some family events for this year and want your suggestions. Please help us by sharing your preferences about the following:

(Please rate these as follows: A = yes, definitely interested; B = moderately interested; C = not at all interested.)

1. **Type of event:**
    - _____ Parent meeting on a specific topic (topic choice below)
    - _____ Parent discussion groups on specific topics
    - _____ Family social function (picnic, dinner, party, etc.)
    - _____ Fund-raiser to benefit your child's class
2. **Topic choice** (for meetings or discussion groups):

_____ Child behavior/guidance	_____ Television
_____ Child nutrition	_____ Good toys for children
_____ Learning to read	_____ Balancing family/work
_____ Self-esteem	_____ Working mothers
_____ What happens at school?	_____ Child development
_____ ____________________	_____ ____________________

3. **Best day** (circle your choices): M T W Th F Sa
4. **Best time:**

_____ Lunch time	_____ Afternoons
_____ After work	_____ 7:30-9:00 p.m.

5. **Other matters:** Will your attendance be influenced by

_____ Provision of child care	_____ Provision of meals/snack

Thank you for your help!

Parent get-togethers may focus on having a speaker with expertise on a topic of common interest, or they may revolve around discussion led by a facilitator. It is important to remember that parents' shared experiences are a valuable source of information and support (Kelly, 1981). Thus, if the main part of the program includes a speaker, time should also be allocated for discussion.

One particularly enjoyable way of presenting some topics is to illustrate them with slides or videotapes taken of the children at the school. Such subjects as children's play, social development, or developmentally appropriate toys can be enhanced with such visuals. In addition to gaining insight into an aspect of their children's development, parents will feel great pride in seeing their youngsters depicted on the screen.

Small groups are generally more effective than large groups in facilitating participation (Gestwicki, 1992). A common interest can also encourage a more intimate atmosphere for a meeting, for instance, involving parents whose children will enter kindergarten, or moving from the infant room to the toddler program the following year, or just the parents of children in one class rather than those from the entire early childhood center.

Some centers generate considerable enthusiasm for social events during which parents and teachers have the opportunity to exchange information in a relaxed atmosphere. These can include holiday parties, meals, or an open house, and they can involve all family members. One university program sponsored a potluck dinner for families, staff, and student teachers each semester. Prearranged seating assured that students sat with the families of children they were observing. This event attracted almost all of the families and proved to be enjoyable as well as valuable for all involved.

FAMILY INVOLVEMENT

Family involvement in the early childhood program has positive benefits for children, families, and the school.

We have been discussing various ways in which communication between teachers and families can be maintained. However this communication takes place, it implies involvement on the part of the family. Let's look at family involvement in more detail now.

Family involvement in the early childhood program is a multifacted concept, embracing a wide range of options and levels. It can mean, on the one hand, that parents and other family members are passive recipients of information; parents may be more intensely engaged by serving as volunteers in the program; or, at an even more complex level of involvement, they can be participants in the decision-making process of the program (Honig, 1979). Whatever the level, however, ample research has shown that such involvement has positive benefits for children as well as for families (Becher, 1986; Powell, 1989).

Family involvement—The commitment of parents to the early childhood program through a wide variety of options.

KEY QUESTION #5

How can parental involvement benefit the early childhood program? List some concrete ways in which parents might contribute to the program.

There is a reciprocal relationship between the family and the early childhood program, each providing support and help to the other as they are able. Family involvement will vary according to each family's ability to contribute and to its needs. Some families invest a great deal of their time and energy in the program, whereas others need all their resources to cope with the stresses they face. Some families support the program by participating in and contributing time to various school activities; others seek support from the program in facing their personal strains. The early childhood staff must be flexible to be able to recognize each family's capabilities and needs and to set expectations or provide support accordingly.

Families can be involved in their children's programs in many ways. We will look at some of these; specifically, family members as resources, as volunteers in the classroom, and as decision makers.

Families as Resources

Family members may serve as resources to the program by contributing special talents, interests, and abilities; as volunteers, or as members of a policy board, in a decision-making capacity.

Family members have many talents and abilities to contribute to the program. Many early childhood programs invite parents or relatives to participate on occasions when their job skills, hobbies, or other special expertise can augment and enrich the curriculum. For instance, a teacher may invite Ronnie's mother, who is a dentist, to help the children understand the importance of good dental hygiene and care; the teacher may take the children to visit the bakery owned by Annie Lee's uncle, because the class is discussing foods; she can ask Junior's father to show the children how he makes pottery; or she may invite Ivan's mother and new baby brother when the class talks about babies and growing up. All family members—parents, siblings, grandparents,

Family members other than parents can also share their special interest or talents with children in the early childhood program. The children were fascinated with the big camera brought in by this photographer, who is the uncle of one of the children.

other relatives, even pets—can be considered part of the program, extending its resource base.

Family members can also help out with maintenance and construction tasks that are part of the program. In some schools, parents routinely take home the dress-up clothes and other classroom items to wash or clean. In others, regularly scheduled clean-up days bring teachers and family members to school on specified weekends to deep clean the facility, materials, and equipment. Family members with carpentry skills may construct or repair equipment. Others may develop learning materials and games at home that will expand the activity options available to the children.

There are other ways in which family members can serve as program resources. For instance, they can help orient new families to the early childhood program, serve as role models, and provide support to other families. Their suggestions and ideas can enrich the program. Family members can also be extremely effective in providing local and state support for legislation that affects children and families. They can help provide program visibility in the community if the school is seeking outside funding. Family support can be a potent force in maintaining a high-quality early childhood program.

Family Members in the Classroom

Family members may also volunteer as teacher aides. Programs such as parent-cooperative preschools require parent involvement. Some Head Start programs have also required that parents spend time in the classroom, although forced participation can be counterproductive (Honig, 1979). In most programs, particularly child care centers, parents participate occasionally or not at all because parents are usually working while their children are at school. Some teachers relish such involvement; others feel skeptical and reluctant, fearing a clash with the parents' childrearing practices, feeling stress about being under constant observation, or worrying that the children will get overexcited (Gestwicki, 1992).

Having parents in the classroom can have many benefits for children, parents, and teachers. Children can benefit from having their parents participate in the classroom, feeling pride and a sense of security as they see their parents and teachers working together (Gestwicki, 1992). For parents, such firsthand experience can provide insight into how their children spend their time at school, a basis for observing their own children in relation to age-mates, and a chance to note guidance techniques used by teachers. Teachers can benefit from the support parents offer, the added pair of hands that can allow expanded activity possibilities, and the opportunity to gain insight into parent-child interactions (Gestwicki, 1992).

Family Members as Decision Makers

Some programs ask parents to serve on an advisory or policy board. Head Start and other federally funded programs, for instance, invite parents to participate in parent advisory councils, as outlined by federal regulations. Many not-for-profit child care or preschool centers also require a governing board of which parents are members. Effective decision-making boards can promote a true partnership between families and the school program (Dunst & Trivette, 1988), providing support for the school, empowerment of parents, and increased mutual understanding.

PARENT EDUCATION

Parent education can take many forms to meet the many different needs of families.

Parent education—Programs aimed at enhancing parent-child relations and improving parenting competence.

All forms of family involvement potentially serve an educational function, as parents have the chance to gain insights into their children's development and the school's program. Often, however, early childhood programs provide specific **parent education** aimed at enhancing parent-child relations and improving parenting competence. Given the numbers of children who grow up in abusive homes, and in abject poverty, some professionals even consider that high-quality parent education programs should be mandatory to prevent needless impairment of children through abuse, neglect, and deprivation (Anastasiow, 1988). Evaluation of many parent education programs aimed at economically disadvantaged families has indicated that such programs can be very effective, although much still remains to be learned through systematic research (Clarke-Stewart, 1983; Powell, 1986). In addition, there is limited evidence that parent education enhances the parenting skills of middle class families as well (Harris & Larsen, 1989).

The scope of parent education programs is not easy to capture in a single definition because there is great diversity in the field. Douglas Powell (1986) spells out some of the contrasts in parent education:

> Some programs focus on family-community relations while others teach parents how to stimulate a child's cognitive development. Some programs prescribe specific skills and styles in relating to young children while other programs help parents determine what is best for them. Some programs are designed primarily to disseminate child development information to parents while others attempt to foster supportive relationships among program participants. Some programs are highly structured while others let parents select activities they wish to pursue. In some programs the staff serve as child development experts while other programs adhere to a self-help model with staff in nondirective facilitator roles. There are important differences in the use of professionals, assistants or

A Closer Look

What Do We Know About the Quality of Child Care?

The *Cost, Quality, and Child Outcomes in Child Care Centers* report (Helburn et al., 1995) paints a bleak picture of child care in America today. The results of this large-scale study indicate that the quality of most centers is poor to mediocre and quality is even lower in infant/toddler centers. Very few centers were considered to be excellent, with 24 percent of preschool and 8 percent of infant/toddler programs receiving such a rating. At the other end of the scale, 10 percent of preschool and 40 percent of infant/toddler programs were rated as less than minimal.

The authors of the study found these results disturbing enough to conclude that quality in most American child care centers is sufficiently poor to affect young children's emotional and cognitive development. Regardless of their family backgrounds, children in lower-quality child care were found to be less competent in social ability, language, and other developmentally related skills than those in higher-quality programs. The difference was even more marked for children already at risk.

This study confirmed many previous studies' findings about the variables that contribute to quality in child care, many of which we examined in Chapter 1. The most significant factor was higher adult-child ratios. Also important was the staff's education level, especially specialized training. In addition, the prior experience of the administrator and teachers' wages were correlated with quality. Interestingly, states with higher licensing standards had fewer poor-quality centers.

One of the most provocative findings of this research is that, while such a high percentage of programs was rated by professionals as being mediocre or poor, 90 percent of parents considered their children's centers to be very good. This is clearly an overestimation of quality on the part of parents. What might be the reason for this discrepancy? The researchers speculate that one reason is the difficulty of monitoring a child care program because parents have relatively little opportunity to observe in the facility. Another reason may be that some parents have never seen high-quality child care and thus have no basis for comparison. Parents may also feel they have no choice; therefore, it is easier for them to consider that their children are cared for appropriately. Because this study found little difference in the cost between high- and low-quality child care, the researchers conclude that parents simply are not demanding quality, although they state that quality in their children's care is important to them.

This study underscores a number of important issues. Good child care is not easily available to most families; thus, a majority of children are getting less than adequate care. Adverse outcomes are associated with this poor quality care, which puts the future of America's children, indeed the future of the country, in jeopardy. The nation must make a strong commitment so all children and their families have access to quality child care. This commitment involves educating parents to help them both understand and demand appropriate quality for their children. You, as an early childhood educator, can be a force in ensuring that the children you work with experience a quality program, and you can help educate parents about what quality means.

volunteers, program length (weeks versus years), and program setting (group- versus home-based). (p. 47)

Although parent education can take many forms, parent get-togethers or meetings are one frequently used forum. The content of such programs can vary widely, determined by parent interest and need. Christine Cataldo, in her book *Parent Education for Early Childhood* (1987), suggests a wide variety of subjects. Popular topics often revolve around children's development, including characteristics and common problems of various ages. Other topics can focus on various aspects of caring for children, for instance, nutrition, health and fitness, self-care and protection, and selecting child care services. Family composition, challenges, and crises offer many program possibilities as well. Children's play and appropriate toys provide other topic choices of interest to parents. In addition, most parents are concerned with issues related to children's behavior, discipline, guidance, fears, sexual development and interest, personality development, and self-esteem. Finally, the family's involvement in and promotion of children's education includes many areas of interest to parents.

Programs can be presented by the early childhood staff based on their own expertise, or by local resource persons. It is important that presenters be well informed on the topic chosen and that they provide accurate information. In addition, a variety of packaged parent education materials are also available. Such packages may include extensive manuals and provide the facilitator with all the necessary resources to conduct the program. Two popular examples of such parent education programs that focus on development of child guidance skills are Parent Effectiveness Training (PET) (Gordon, 1976) and Systematic Training for Effective Parenting (STEP) (Dinkmeyer & McKay, 1976).

SUMMARY

1. Family systems theory is a way of viewing the family as a dynamic unit.
2. The American family has undergone many changes recently. Consider some of these changes by looking at the following:
   A. Variety in family forms
   B. Other factors that contribute to family diversity
   C. Families in poverty
3. Families have specific needs that the early childhood program can address. Consider issues related to family needs, including:
   A. The needs of adults in a unique stage of development, separate from their children's development
   B. The need to feel empowered, in control of their lives
   C. Coordination of the needs of the family with the early childhood program

4. Two-way communication between families and the early childhood program is an important element in providing consistency for children. Consider the following methods of communicating with parents:
   A. Communicating with individual parents informally, on a day-to-day basis, and formally, through conferences and home visits
   B. Communicating with groups of parents, through written communiques, bulletin boards, and meetings
5. Families can be involved in the early childhood program in a number of ways—as resources, in the classroom, and as decision makers.
6. One function of the early childhood program is parent education, which can take a variety of forms.

KEY TERMS LIST

authority stage
empowerment
exosystem
family involvement
family systems theory
generativity
home visit
interpretive stage
macrosystem
mesosystem
microsystem
nurturing stage
parent education
parent-teacher conference

chapter 4

The Teachers/ Caregivers

This chapter will focus on you . . . you as an individual, you as a teacher or caregiver, you as a member of a profession. However, everything discussed in this book is relevant to you as a teacher. You are the one who integrates knowledge about the development of children, about the importance of families, about creating a healthy and stimulating environment, about child-sensitive curriculum planning, and about appropriate and nurturing guidance to provide the best possible care and education for young children. Thus, in this chapter we will explore important aspects of teaching and the profession of early childhood education.

THE EARLY CHILDHOOD TEACHER AND CAREGIVER

Before beginning a discussion of early childhood teachers, it is important to make some distinctions in terminology. Unfortunately, no universally accepted categories and titles define those who work with young children, although some have been proposed, as we will discuss later. Often labels conjure up stereotypes and do not reflect different educational and experiential backgrounds found in the field (Phillips & Whitebook, 1986).

Throughout this book the terms **early childhood teacher** and **early childhood educator** will be used synonymously. Other terms are also applied to those who work with young children, particularly **caregiver** and **child care worker.** Traditionally, the distinction has been made that a caregiver—for instance, someone who works in a child care center—cares for the physical and emotional needs of infants, toddlers, or children whereas the teacher serves an educational function. "However, this distinction is not a particularly clear one, for the line between education and nurture in the early years is not a distinct one" (Spodek & Saracho, 1982, p. 401).

Early childhood teacher or **Early childhood educator**—A specifically trained professional who works with children from infancy to age eight.

Caregiver or **Child care worker**—Term traditionally used to describe a person who works in a child care setting.

A professional early childhood teacher is distinguished by professionalism, knowledge and standards, judgment, and ability to translate theoretical information into practical application.

Certainly the early childhood teacher "cares for" and the caregiver "teaches" young children. Which teacher has not tied shoelaces, wiped noses, or dried tears? And which caregiver has not helped children learn how to zip a coat, assemble a puzzle, or share the tricycle? Teaching and caregiving functions seem not only inherent but also integrally related in both roles to the point where a distinction is impossible to make (Willer, 1990).

Lilian Katz (1972) has, in fact, included these among the four roles she delineates as functions of teachers of young children: caretaking, providing emotional support and guidance, instructing, and facilitating. The caregiving role, similar in many ways to the role of the mother, diminishes as the child gets older (Katz, 1980).

The distinction between the teacher and the caregiver, then, is more than a general description of what they do, for their roles certainly overlap. What does distinguish teachers, according to Katz (1984b), is their professionalism, the way they use their knowledge and standards of performance. Teachers possess advanced knowledge in child development and early childhood education that they apply when they have to make judgments and decisions on a moment-by-moment basis. At the same time, they also share with other professionals a commitment to maintaining the high standards set by the profession through its organizations. But there really is no simple or single definition of a good teacher of young children. In a summary of six in-depth interviews that searched for a definition of "the good preschool teacher," Ayers (1989) concludes that there is "a kaleidoscope of possibility, for there are endless good preschool teachers" (p. 141).

Qualities of the Good Early Childhood Teacher

If asked what qualities a good teacher of young children possesses, most of us would come up with an intuitive list of characteristics such as warmth, sensitivity, energy, sense of humor, flexibility, or patience. Empirical research, however, is not particularly clear-cut in showing a consistent relationship between teacher effectiveness and personal qualities. This is partly due to problems in the methodology of such research, inconsistency in what is being measured, difficulty in distinguishing between teaching style and teaching techniques, and even lack of agreement about what constitutes "good" teaching (Feeney & Chun, 1985; Katz, 1984a).

Some clues about what makes a good teacher of young children can be gleaned from early childhood educators and researchers based on their experience and insight. Millie Almy (1975) lists some attributes dictated by "common sense," including patience, warmth, nurturance, and energy. She also describes maturity, openness to new ideas, and tolerance for a certain amount of ambiguity as necessary qualities. In addition, she finds it particularly important that the early childhood teacher be able to move easily between the concrete level of thinking of the child and the abstract level of the adult, at which theoretical information is translated into appropriate decisions.

Those who care for infants and toddlers also need special qualities, beyond "liking babies." Balaban (1992) includes in her list of important personal qualities the ability to anticipate and plan; provide an interesting environment; elicit language, problem solving, and play; protect, listen, and watch; smooth "jangled feelings"; comfort; cope; facilitate social interactions; facilitate parent-child separation; and care for the whole family.

Teachers' Developmental Stages

Teachers evolve through several stages that are related to their level of experience.

Although the idea of developmental stages is commonly understood and used by teachers of young children, the notion of sequenced steps of development among teachers is not as readily considered. Yet Katz (1977) concludes that teachers also undergo a series of stages, each with unique developmental tasks and training needs. It is helpful to realize that others begin their teaching experiences with similar feelings of inadequacy or anxiety and that these evolve into more advanced stages as competence develops.

- **Stage 1: Survival—**The beginning teachers' main concern through the first year or so of teaching is usually focused on whether they will survive. The realization of the great responsibility they have for the group of children, as well as the discrepancy between the success they expect and the reality of the classroom, result in anxiety and feelings of inadequacy. In general, they are acquiring information about what children are like and what can be expected of them. At this stage, the teacher's main need is for support, encouragement, and guidance, provided onsite, as needed.
- **Stage 2: Consolidation—**Having recognized that they can indeed survive, teachers begin to focus on specific tasks. As they consolidate the information gained from their first year or two, they move their attention more specifically to problem children or to situations that deviate from the general norm. Their needs at this time are for continued on-site training that supports exploration of alternatives to deal with the problem situations.
- **Stage 3: Renewal—**By now, teachers in their third or fourth year begin to seek some new approaches and ideas as they tire of

the way they have been doing things for the past several years. The search for renewal can be met through meetings with colleagues, professional organizations and conferences, professional books and journals, and visits to other programs.

- **Stage 4: Maturity—**This final stage is reached by different teachers at different points and represents a coming to terms with themselves and their profession. Now they ask deeper and more abstract questions, looking at the broader implications of their work in the context of the larger society. Their experience makes these questions more meaningful. Mature teachers need opportunities to read widely, interact with others, and participate in seminars and other forums where such questions are addressed by others searching for similar insights.

STAFFING IN EARLY CHILDHOOD PROGRAMS

The size and complexity of a program will affect the size and complexity of the staffing pattern.

The early childhood teacher, of course, works within a system along with others who share the tasks of the program. Staff members, from the director to the custodian, contribute toward making the program successful. There can be a variety of staffing patterns depending on the type, size, and philosophy of the program as well as on its funding source. A half-day preschool attended by 15 children may, for instance, be staffed by one owner/teacher and one part-time assistant. On the other hand, a not-for-profit child care program in which 160 children are enrolled might involve a board of directors, a director, a curriculum coordinator, a parent coordinator, 12 head teachers, 28 full- and part-time assistants, a variable number of volunteers, a secretary, a cook, a custodian, a list of substitute staff, and various community professionals who serve as resource persons. Figure 4-1 schematically illustrates the staffing patterns of these two hypothetical programs.

Early childhood programs can have various staffing structures and lines of staff authority and responsibility.

The distribution and allocation of responsibility also varies in different programs. Some exhibit a hierarchical structure, fashioned as a pyramid, where power trickles down from the top and each layer in the structure defers to those above. Thus, in some classrooms that follow this model, one teacher is designated as the head or lead teacher and other staff work under her or him, following that teacher's direction and guidance.

Career lattice—Recognizes that the early childhood profession is made up of individuals with varied backgrounds; a lattice allows for both horizontal and vertical movement among positions, with accompanying levels of education, experience, responsibility, and pay.

Yet, in the early childhood field there is often an alternative to this pyramid structure because of the strong interdependence and interconnectedness among staff members, who frequently make decisions by consensus. This can be depicted as a web that allows for more flexible and dynamic relationships than the hierarchical model in which the power structure tends to be static and individuals' responsibilities depend on their position in the structure (Dresden & Myers, 1989). More recently, the term **career lattice** has been suggested as an appropriate symbol for the uniqueness and diversity seen in the early childhood profession. A lattice allows for both horizontal and vertical movement among positions, with accompanying levels of education, experience, responsibility, and pay (Bredekamp & Willer, 1992).

FIGURE 4-1 Organizational Chart Showing Staffing Patterns

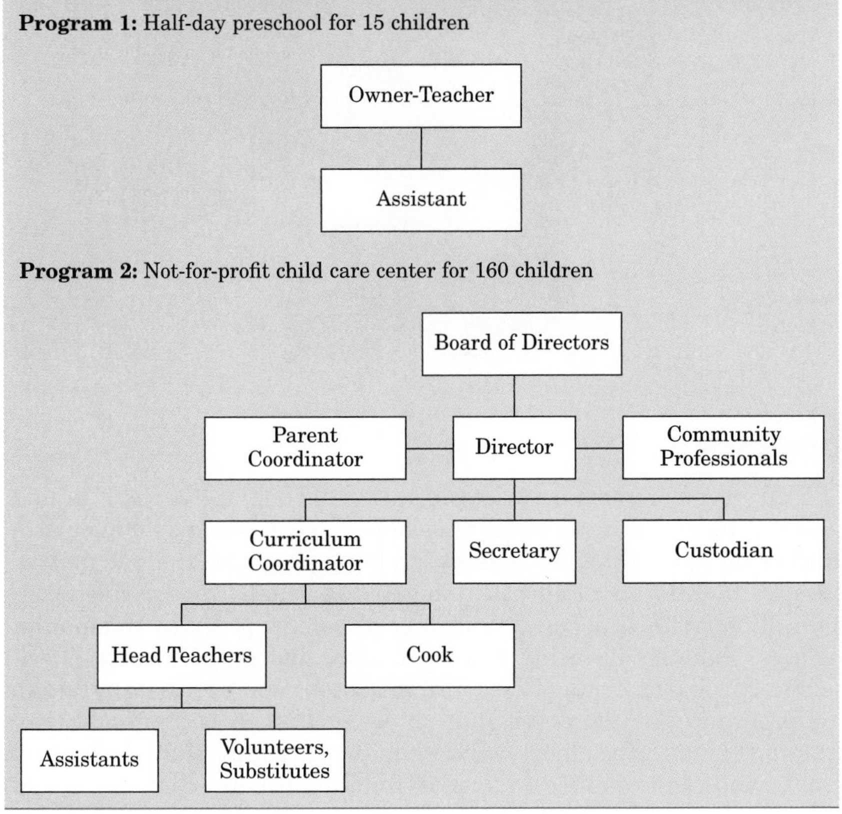

In other programs, classes are cotaught by team teachers who share responsibilities. **Team teaching** is based on a relationship of trust and communication between the two teachers, something that takes time to build. A good team finds many bonuses in this relationship through added flexibility, creativity, problem-solving capabilities, and focus on what each member of the team enjoys most or does best. In addition, the collaboration between the two provides the children with a model for cooperative behavior (Thornton, 1990).

Team teaching—An approach that involves coteaching in which status and responsibility are equal rather than having a pyramid structure of authority, with one person in charge and others subordinate.

Whatever the structure, it is sensible to find out ahead of time what the lines of responsibility are in terms of providing direction, feedback, evaluation, and resources. By learning the lines of authority and communication, you, as a teacher in a program, will know who to seek out for guidance and information, with whom to discuss problems, and where ultimate responsibility for various decisions lies. Whatever the organizational structure of the program, smooth functioning depends in part on a clear understanding of responsibilities and lines of communication and on cooperation among the staff (Click, 1995; Sciarra & Dorsey, 1995). We will now briefly examine some of the positions and their responsibilities held by staff members in early childhood programs.

In many programs, teachers share responsibility equally for the functioning of the classroom through a team-teaching approach.

Director

The role of the director will depend on the size and nature of the program.

The director performs a variety of tasks, depending on the size and scope of the program. In small programs, the director may double as a teacher for part of the day, whereas in large programs the role may be purely administrative. This staff member is usually responsible for financial, personnel, policy, and facility decisions; provides community linkages; handles licensing and regulation; and is the ultimate decision maker in the chain of responsibility in all matters that pertain to the program. The job description often also involves staff selection, training, monitoring, and evaluation. In programs that depend on grants and other outside sources of funding, the director may spend much time writing proposals and meeting with influential decision makers. But a director is often also a plumber, a carpenter, and a counselor because he or she holds the ultimate responsibility for whatever needs to be taken care of!

Teaching Staff

KEY QUESTION #1

Review the four levels of early childhood educators suggested by NAEYC. What are the advantages of such a hierarchy? What are the disadvantages? Since these levels are not extensively used at this time, what needs to happen for wider adoption of such a system?

Although a four-level hierarchy of teacher positions has been suggested, most programs do not include such an elaborate classification system.

Those who work directly with children may hold a variety of titles. In its position statement on nomenclature for early childhood educators, the National Association for the Education of Young Children (NAEYC) suggests four levels (NAEYC, 1984). Although these represent a logical hierarchy for the field, they have not been widely accepted by those who work with young children (Spodek & Saracho, 1988).

- **Level 1: The early childhood teacher assistant** is in a preprofessional position and works under direct supervision of the professional staff. This person holds a high school diploma and must show a genuine liking for children, dependability, and an interest in improving skills.
- **Level 2: The early childhood associate teacher** can implement program activities independently and be responsible for the care and education of a group of children. This person has demonstrated competency in the job, for instance, through an associate degree in early childhood education or a Child Development

Associate (CDA) credential (to be discussed under the topic "Training and Regulation" later in this chapter).

- **Level 3: The early childhood teacher** may perform functions similar to those of the associate teacher, but has a higher level of education and greater theoretical knowledge of child development and early childhood education.
- **Level 4: The early childhood specialist** is involved in supervision, training, administration, or curriculum design. The person at this level has a baccalaureate or advanced degree in child development or early childhood education; specific course work in supervision, administration, and curriculum design; and appropriate teaching experience.

Although these levels are suggested as a way of clarifying roles and expectations, most early childhood programs do not have such an elaborate staff classification system. We will look at two common teaching positions in more depth.

The Head Teacher. It is the responsibility of the **head teacher,** lead teacher, or master teacher to plan and implement the daily program. This involves knowing each child and family well and individualizing the program to meet each one's specific needs. The head teacher usually also takes responsibility for the physical environment of the classroom, setting up equipment, rotating materials, and ensuring a good match between what is available and the children's skill level. The head teacher generally maintains records for the children in the class; is usually involved in parent interactions, both informally at the start and end of each day and formally through conferences or meetings; and takes charge of other staff members who work in the class by providing direction, guidance, and feedback.

Head teacher—The person in charge of a class who is ultimately responsible for all aspects of class functioning.

In many programs, head teachers and assistant teachers with distinct responsibilities are identified for each classroom.

The Assistant Teacher. Also called aide, helper, auxiliary teacher, associate teacher, or small-group leader, the **assistant teacher** works with the head teacher to provide a high-quality program for the children in the class and their families. Depending on the assistant's skill level and experience, this teacher may share many of the head

Assistant teacher—Also called aide, helper, auxiliary teacher, associate teacher, or small-group leader; works under the guidance of the head teacher in providing a high-quality program for the children in the class and their families.

EXPERIENCES

chapter 4

ALEX, Kindergarten Teacher

"The Wicked Stepmother"

We had been talking about various fairy tales, and "Cinderella" was the topic of discussion. The children recounted the story and examined its various aspects. As the conversation touched on Cinderella's stepmother, five-year-old Connie said, "That's just like a stepmother. They're so mean!"

"Yeah," said another child, "Stepmothers are really bad."

Other children chimed in, confirming that, indeed, stepmothers are terrible people. This bothered me because I knew that some of the children in the class were part of blended families, and stepparents were an integral part of their lives. How could we neutralize this fairy tale stereotype that had new meaning in today's society?

I said nothing at that time, but gave it some thought over the next couple of hours. Later in the day, we had another group time and by then I decided on my approach.

"Remember, earlier we were talking about Cinderella and her stepmother? Some of you thought that all stepmothers, like Cinderella's, were mean people."

The children again agreed with this statement.

"But you know, I don't think *all* stepmothers are mean. I want to tell you about my stepmother. After my mother died, my dad remarried another woman, who is now my stepmother. And you know what? She is really nice. She is kind and special and does lots of nice things for me. She loves me and I love her. She's a stepmother . . . my stepmother . . . and she's a wonderful person. So, I can't agree with you that all stepmothers are mean."

The children gave this some thought and discussed the implications of what I had said. Gradually, they verbalized that labels should not be applied uniformly to a group of people. People differ. We talked about the word "stereotype." We considered that not all stepmothers or, for that matter, all stepsisters, were selfish and cruel like the characters in "Cinderella."

Some time into the conversation, one of the children whose parents were both divorced and remarried, joined the discussion. He told the group that he had two moms and two dads, one of each being a stepparent, and that they were really nice people. The other children listened thoughtfully.

Teachers sometimes have to divulge some of their own personal experiences as a way of helping children gain a more balanced perspective. In this case, a sensitive teacher's sharing of his own family background helped the children move beyond what could have developed into a destructive stereotype.

teacher's responsibilities, for instance, participating in curriculum planning, leading large and small group activities, being involved in parent interactions, and arranging the environment. Because of the assistant teacher's close working relationship with the teacher, open and honest communication and mutual respect are vital between the two. In some schools, an assistant teacher may serve as a "floater," moving among classrooms to help with special activities or during specific times of the day.

Support Staff

Most early childhood programs, depending on their size and scope, have some support staff who help with the maintenance and functioning of the program.

Depending on the size and scope of the center, usually some persons serve in a support capacity. These might include (although they certainly are not limited to) persons involved in food preparation, maintenance, and office management.

Large programs often have a cook who is in charge of meal preparation, shopping, and sanitation and maintenance of the kitchen. The cook may also plan meals, if that person has an appropriate background in nutrition, or may participate in classroom cooking projects. A dietitian may serve as a consultant to the program to ensure that children's nutritional needs are appropriately met through the program's meals. In smaller programs, particularly those not serving lunch or dinner, the teaching staff or director may take responsibility for snack planning and preparation.

One of the most important yet difficult tasks of any center serving busy and active young children is maintenance. Daily cleaning, sweeping, vacuuming, sanitizing, and garbage disposal are vital though usually unpopular functions. Large programs may have a custodian as part of the staff, whereas others hold contracts with a janitorial service. Often the expense of a maintenance crew or custodian has to be weighed against other important needs, and the teaching staff finds that its responsibilities include many maintenance chores. Most centers compromise by having the staff maintain a modicum of cleanliness and order while a cleaning service is responsible for intermittent deep cleaning of the facility.

The support staff in an early childhood setting is extremely important in ensuring that the program runs smoothly.

Other support staff take care of office needs. Large programs often have a secretary who maintains records, answers phone calls, manages typing needs, and may handle some accounting tasks. In smaller programs, such tasks may fall to the director. Some programs may employ a part-time accountant or have a receptionist in addition to the secretary. Programs that are part of or housed with other agencies may share custodial and secretarial staff.

Volunteers

Some programs utilize volunteers, have a board of directors who are involved in the decision-making process, and call on community professionals to expand the services of the program.

Some centers avail themselves of volunteers to help with various aspects of the early childhood program. Volunteers can include parents, student teachers or interns, members of such organizations as the Junior League, foster grandparents, and other interested community members. To use volunteers most effectively, however, there has to be a well-planned orientation, training, and monitoring component that helps the volunteer understand the program, its philosophy, and its operation. Although volunteers can provide a wonderful additional resource to a program, the reality is that volunteers are not as plentiful as the potential need for them.

Board of Directors

Board of directors—Policy-making or governing board that holds ultimate responsibility, particularly for a not-for-profit program.

Particularly in not-for-profit centers, some type of policy-making, governing board holds the ultimate responsibility for the program. This board of trustees or **board of directors** may be a very powerful force, making all pertinent decisions that the director then carries out, or it may only be a nominal group, and almost all decisions are left up to the director. Ideally, a board of directors' role falls somewhere between these extremes (Sciarra & Dorsey, 1995).

Boards of directors are usually made up of community persons who come from a variety of spheres of expertise and influence, most of which are not likely to be related to early childhood education. It is wise, however, to include one child development expert on the board. The director serves as a liaison, helping the board understand the rationale for decisions made based on child development knowledge, while utilizing their expertise in areas in which the director is not as well versed. Boards can be very effective in areas such as fiscal management, fund raising, construction and expansion projects, or lobbying for children's rights.

Community Professionals

The resources of a center can be expanded through other professionals in the larger community; for instance, health and mental health professionals, social workers, and therapists. In some instances, families are referred to the early childhood program by a community agency; thus, the program and referring agency can work together to maximize the help provided to the child and family. In other cases, the early childhood program may help connect families with community agencies and professionals to provide needed services. It is important for teachers to recognize the "boundaries of their own professional expertise and know when other professionals need to be consulted" (Sciarra & Dorsey, 1990, p. 369).

TRAINING AND REGULATION IN EARLY CHILDHOOD EDUCATION

As we have discussed, many individuals contribute toward providing a good early childhood program through their levels and types of expertise. Such expertise stems from different types of training. In addition, a variety of regulations and quality controls apply to early childhood programs and the personnel who staff them. We will look at training through academic programs and at one alternative training avenue and then review regulations, licensing, and accreditation of programs.

In addition to college and university training programs, early childhood professionals can receive training and certification through the national Child Development Associate program.

Academic Teacher Training Programs

Because you are reading this text, you are most likely involved in an academic early childhood program whose aim is to prepare qualified teachers and directors of programs for young children through a combination of coursework and practicum experiences. Such programs exist at 2-year associate degree, 4-year baccalaureate degree, and post-graduate degree levels. In more advanced degree programs, greater depth and more theoretical and research knowledge become increasingly important variables. In fact, guidelines for early childhood professional preparation are outlined in position statements from the National Association for the Education of Young Children (NAEYC, 1995). (We will be discussing this association in more detail later in this chapter when we consider professionalism.) In addition, NAEYC has developed a position statement about early childhood professional development (NAEYC, 1994) that delineates six professional categories based on educational attainment, ranging from a person with a doctoral degree to someone currently in training. It is interesting to note that those who teach young children are relatively well educated; about two-thirds of teachers and more than one-half of assistant teachers have taken at least some early childhood or child development course work (Whitebook, Howes, & Phillips, 1989).

Child Development Associate Program

In the 1970s, an alternative model for the training of early childhood teachers was initiated through the **Child Development Associate (CDA)** program. Just as successful completion of an academic program leads to a degree, so does successful completion of the CDA program lead to a professional credential as a Child Development Associate. The CDA credential is available for professionals who work with different age groups and in various settings: preschools, infant/toddler programs, bilingual programs, programs including handicapped children, and family child care. About 60,000 individuals have received a CDA credential, approximately 80 percent coming from Head Start programs. The most recent National Survey of CDAs (Henry, 1995) found that over 95 percent remained committed to early childhood education after receiving their credentials, providing an anchor of

Child Development Associate (CDA)—An early childhood teacher who has been assessed and successfully proven competent through the national CDA credentialing program.

KEY QUESTION #2

Obtain the requirements for the CDA credentialing process (from your instructor or from the Council for Early Childhood Professional Recognition, 1718 Connecticut Ave. NW, Washington, DC 20077). Compare these to the ones required by the program in which you are enrolled. What are the points of similarity and the differences?

stability in a field that suffers from a high turnover rate (Whitebook et al., 1993).

A CDA is defined as an early childhood professional who successfully meets the following six goals (Phillips, 1990):

1. Establish and maintain a safe, healthy learning environment.
2. Advance physical and intellectual competence.
3. Support social and emotional development and provide guidance.
4. Establish positive and productive relationships with families.
5. Ensure a well-run, purposeful program responsive to participant needs.
6. Maintain a commitment to professionalism.

The CDA has been described as an alternative avenue toward professionalism for people who have traditionally been excluded from higher education, specifically those from low-income backgrounds (Peters, 1988). Attaining this credential often encourages a CDA to pursue further education.

Regulation and Licensing

Minimum standards for early childhood teachers are generally described in local or state licensing regulations. Some states require little or no training for those who work with and care for young children; others designate more stringent criteria that specify minimum levels of training in early childhood education and child development and appropriate experiences. Keep in mind that minimum standards are just that—minimums. Professional early childhood educators usually far exceed the minimum, and the children in their care, their families, the overall early childhood program, and the teachers themselves are the beneficiaries of this professionalism and expertise.

Of course, licensing criteria provide guidelines for far more than teacher qualifications. They can cover a wide range of topics related to health, sanitation, safety, child-adult ratio, group size, acceptable guidance and curriculum practices, meal and sleeping arrangements, and so forth. Minimum standards for various aspects of programs for young children are spelled out by all states, although there is considerable variation in what is deemed acceptable. "Such variation reflects differences in the degree of public understanding of children's needs" (NAEYC, 1987, p. 64). Programs that receive federal funding may need to adhere to specified federal regulations as well. Some programs, particularly those that are part of the public school system, may be regulated by a separate agency with different guidelines and regulations to follow.

Accreditation

All programs must adhere to the minimum standards set by state and local licensing regulations, but some programs strive for a higher level of excellence by undergoing accreditation through the National Academy of Early Childhood Programs.

To indicate that they strive for a high level of excellence rather than minimum criteria, many early childhood programs have undergone the voluntary accreditation process of the National Academy of Early Childhood Programs, the accreditation division of the NAEYC, started in 1985. By the tenth anniversary of the accreditation process, more than 4,300 programs had been accredited and an additional 12,000 had begun the first stage toward accreditation (Bredekamp & Glowacki, 1996).

Programs seeking accreditation engage in a self-evaluation, which is reviewed by a validator, who spends time on-site, and a three-person team of early childhood professionals. Specific components of 10 criteria are assessed as acceptable or unacceptable. These 10 criteria include interactions among staff and children, curriculum, staff-parent interactions, staff qualifications and development, administration, staffing, physical environment, health and safety, nutrition and food service, and evaluation. The quality of child-staff interactions and the developmental appropriateness of the curriculum are judged as the most important determinants in the final decision (Bredekamp & Apple, 1986). A recent self-report study of accredited programs confirmed the positive impact of accreditation and also indicated that the process facilitated improvements, which, in turn, led to even higher quality (Herr, Johnson, & Zimmerman, 1993).

PROFESSIONALISM

This book stresses the importance of the early childhood years, early education, and your role as an early childhood educator. To fully realize that importance, however, you must see yourself as a member of a profession. A profession is different from a job by virtue of some specific characteristics, for instance, a defined code of ethics, a specialized knowledge base involving theoretical principles, specialized training founded on that knowledge base, and universal standards of practice that stem from that knowledge base (Katz, 1988; Vander Ven, 1986).

Those who have written at great length about early childhood professionalism, recognizing that there are many inconsistencies and problems to be faced, do not always agree on the degree to which the field meets the criteria of a profession. Increasing dialogue through conferences and written works has helped to focus more sharply on relevant issues—for instance, low pay and shortage of qualified early childhood teachers—as well as on strategies for combatting these (we will discuss some of these later in this chapter). Nonetheless, the expanding concern about professionalism, evident at both national and local levels, should propel early childhood education toward its goals, which include a better definition and greater focus.

Although in many ways the early childhood field has moved toward professionalization, there is concern that professional status is not universally acknowledged by those who work in the field and by the public at large (Dresden & Myers, 1989; Radomski, 1986; Silin, 1985). Those who work with young children need to develop a clearer concept of who they are, what they do, and the importance of their role. At the same time, there is a need for public recognition of the value and status of early childhood educators. As a student embarking on a career in early childhood education, you are in a unique position to develop from the start a sense of professionalism that is furthered by every course you take, every day you spend with children, and every conference you attend. Your competence and recognition of the importance of your role will enhance not only your work with children and families, but also your contributions to the early childhood profession.

Ethics

Code of ethics—Agreed-upon professional standards that guide behavior and facilitate decision making in working situations.

The field of early childhood education has a defined code of ethics, adopted by the National Association for the Education of Young Children.

One of the hallmarks of a profession is its recognition of and adherence to a **code of ethics.** Such a code embodies guidelines for behavior, facilitates decision making, and provides the backing of like-minded professionals when the practitioner takes a "risky but courageous stand in the face of an ethical dilemma" (Katz, 1988, p. 77). Under the leadership of Stephanie Feeney, the NAEYC has adopted a Code of Ethical Conduct that delineates ethical responsibilities to children, families, colleagues, and the community and society (Feeney & Kipnis, 1989).

This code recognizes that many of the day-to-day decisions made by those who work with young children are of a moral and ethical nature. Early childhood teachers, for instance, may find themselves in situations with conflicting values in which it is not clear whether the rights of the child, the parents, the school, other children in the program, or the teachers are most important (Feeney, 1988). A code of

Code of Ethics

It does not take long for new teachers to find out that many of the decisions they face do not have clear-cut answers and often require judgment of a moral or ethical nature. The needs of the four groups with which early childhood professionals interact—children, families, colleagues, and the community and society—must be considered carefully in many decisions. It is to guide such decisions that NAEYC has developed a core set of standards in its *Code of Ethical Conduct and Statement of Commitment,* which outlines ideals and principles in relation to each of these groups.

The foremost guiding principle, which supersedes all others, specifies that "above all, we shall not harm children. We shall not participate in practices that are disrespectful, degrading, dangerous, exploitative, intimidating, psychologically damaging, or physically harmful to children" (Feeney & Kipnis, 1992). This underscores the responsibility of those who work with young children to act on any concerns, including ones related to child abuse and neglect. In addition, the code reflects how important it is for teachers to have a sound knowledge of the fields of early childhood education and child development and to use that knowledge in appreciating, respecting, and supporting each child.

The code also addresses the importance of developing a trusting relationship with the families of the children. This includes recognizing and respecting each family's strengths, values, and decisions. It also involves the importance of helping families better understand their children and the significance of a developmentally appropriate program. In addition, an ethical relationship with families includes open access to the child's classroom, information about the program's philosophy and policies, and participation in decisions that directly affect the child. The code also specifies the need to protect the rights of families and respect their privacy with confidentiality.

Ethical responsibilities to coworkers, employers, and employees are also outlined by the code to support a caring, cooperative work place. The last set of responsibilities involves the community and society. Early childhood professionals are encouraged to work cooperatively with other community agencies and professionals and to use their expertise to be a voice on behalf of children and families. The ideals and principles set forth in the *Code of Ethical Conduct and Statement of Commitment* provide a framework for practice that promotes commitment to high standards, thoughtful decision making, and, as a result, high-quality programming for children and families.

ethics provides common principles for dealing with such dilemmas, principles based on the value of childhood as a unique stage of life, on knowledge of child development, on appreciation of the importance of family and cultural ties, on respect for the dignity and value of children and adults, and on helping individuals reach their potential through trusting, positive relationships.

Because children are particularly vulnerable, those who work with them have an important responsibility that is supported and defined by a code of ethics (Feeney & Kipnis, 1985). As you enter the early childhood profession, it is important to read and utilize NAEYC's Code of Ethical Conduct, which is available in a brochure from the organization or in the journal *Young Children* (Feeney & Kipnis, 1989).

There are numerous professional organizations that early childhood students and professionals can join.

Professional Organizations

KEY QUESTION #3

What are the advantages of belonging to a professional early childhood organization? Review several issues of professional journals such as *Young Children* or *Childhood Education* to gain a sense of what organizations such as NAEYC or ACEI have to offer.

One sign of a profession is the existence of organizations to which members belong and of professional journals that members read. Such organizations and their literature provide its members with support and a sense of common interest and purpose. Early childhood education has several pertinent organizations and journals. We will briefly discuss the two major groups in the field.

National Association for the Education of Young Children (NAEYC)—Largest American early childhood professional organization, which deals with issues of children from birth to age eight and those who work with young children.

1. **The National Association for the Education of Young Children (NAEYC),** the largest early childhood organization, is a powerful voice for children, families, and teachers. Its goals are (a) to improve professional practice and working conditions, and (b) to increase public understanding of and support for high quality in early childhood education (Smith, 1990). The association has a growing membership (reaching 100,000 in 1997) that represents a diverse group of individuals. One of the ways in which NAEYC works toward its goals is through its publications—the bimonthly journal *Young Children,* and more than 80 books and other resources. In addition, NAEYC holds an annual conference that is attended by more than 22,000 early childhood professionals yearly.

Association for Childhood Education International (ACEI)—Professional organization that focuses on issues of children from infancy to early adolescence, particularly those involving international and intercultural concerns.

2. **Association for Childhood Education International (ACEI)** is a professional organization that covers a wider spectrum of educational issues by covering ages ranging from infancy through early adolescence. It also focuses on international and intercultural issues. The ACEI publishes the journal *Childhood Education* five times a year and sponsors an annual study conference.

In addition, numerous organizations focus on more specialized groups, for instance, those involved in for-profit child care, Montessori, Head Start, church-sponsored programs, home care (the National Association of Family Day Care), early childhood special education (for instance the Early Childhood Division of the Council for Exceptional Children), and others. There are regional, stage, and local organizations, such as the Southern Early Childhood Association (SECA); branches of the organizations described previously; and some nonaffiliated, local organizations that meet the needs of a group of people in the community.

As a student entering the early childhood profession, you might consider becoming a member of a professional organization. Some colleges or universities have student member sections of NAEYC or ACEI. By becoming a member, you can keep abreast of new developments, have the opportunity to meet and participate in a support network with others in the same field, and attend workshops and conferences at the local, state, or national level. Information about organizations is readily available through your instructor or those who work in the field.

SOME CURRENT ISSUES AND DILEMMAS

Early childhood education is, in many ways, a field of contradictions and extremes. Those who try to define it often find themselves in a dilemma, not clear on what to include and what to exclude. Where does a program fit that barely meets minimum standards, and what about the program that genuinely strives for excellence in meeting the needs of its children and families? Are the kindergarten teacher, the infant care provider, the Head Start teacher, the preschool master teacher, and the home care provider included? Are the preschool teacher who holds a masters degree in early childhood education and the high school graduate who works in a child care center equals in the same field? Can the child care provider who earns minimum wage for the eight hours a day spent caring for children be lumped together with the kindergarten teacher who earns a public school salary for nine months of teaching?

How can the teacher job description that calls for someone who "likes children" be compared with the one that requires "a degree in early childhood education or child development"? How can the lack of licensing requirements for teachers of young children in many states be rectified with educators' insistence that those who work with young children need specific training? In fact, is there a good reason to justify why you are enrolled in an academic program while others with no academic training may equally qualify for a position?

These questions and others are at the heart of the dilemma facing the early childhood profession. We will review some specific issues and look at some possible ways of addressing these. Although we will divide some of these issues into categories such as teacher shortage and low pay, these are not separable concerns that exist independent of each other.

KEY QUESTION #4

Talk to several teachers of young children. What do they view as the most rewarding parts of their job? What most frustrates them? Compare their answers with your own goals and expectations.

A Historical Perspective

It might be helpful to look at the road travelled by the field of early childhood education to gain a perspective on its current status. Early childhood education today is inextricably linked to the role and status of women in the United States.

Between the mid-eighteenth and mid-nineteenth centuries, "womanhood was redefined, its image re-created and reimagined, its social function reviewed, its links to child rearing and socialization forged, and its authority over the moral and cultural development of the

The history of women over the past two centuries is closely linked with the development of the field of early childhood education.

nation rationalized" (Finkelstein, 1988, p. 12). When, in the latter half of the 19th century, the kindergarten became firmly established as an American institution, women had found their niche in an environment that was not quite domestic, yet not quite public either.

The early twentieth century pioneers of the early childhood movement, while building a scientific basis for child study, continued to see women as the guardians of the young with a specialized role in upholding moral and cultural standards, a noble role above concerns for economic and material comforts. Unfortunately, this legacy of "unselfishness" has followed early childhood educators to the end of this century, endowing them with a realization of the importance of their work, yet placing them in a low-paying profession that has low status in our social structure (Finkelstein, 1988).

Teacher Shortage

The high demand for quality programs for children of working parents, plus the low pay and status of those who work in these programs, have resulted in a serious shortage of early childhood professionals.

Over the past several years, increasing attention has been focused on the shortage of qualified early childhood teachers. This shortage is partly caused by the high demand for child care as increasing numbers of mothers of young children enter the work force. In fact, during the 1990s the demand for preschool teachers increased and is expected to continue to grow as more low income parents enter the work force as a result of welfare reform measures. Yet, particularly in areas where there is low unemployment and a high cost of living, child care workers are scarce.

There also is a shortage of elementary school teachers, compounding the demand for early childhood staff. In addition, fewer college students are opting to pursue education careers, seeking instead more lucrative job opportunities (Whitebook, 1986). Finally, our society is experiencing a decreasing number of people entering the work force as the "baby bust" generation, those born during the years when the national birth rate declined, reaches maturity (Galinsky, 1989).

The contribution of these societal factors to the early childhood teacher shortage tells only half the story, however. What is more serious is the high rate of turnover among teachers of young children. According to the recent National Child Care Staffing Study (Whitebook, et al., 1989), staff turnover nearly tripled between 1977 and 1988, jumping from 15 to 41 percent. The 1988 turnover rate, however, varied according to type of center, ranging from a 74-percent annual staff change in chain, for-profit centers to a 30-percent rate in nonprofit programs.

This high turnover rate appears directly related to low pay, illustrated by the inverse relationship between rate of pay and percentage of turnover. Those at the lower end of the pay scale changed jobs at twice the rate as those at the higher end. At the same time, however, there is less turnover among teachers with early childhood training. A 1995 follow-up survey of CDAs who had earned their credentials during the preceding five years indicated that more than 95 percent of the respondents continued to teach (Henry, 1995). Although this does not provide direct evidence that these teachers were still at the same work site, they continued in the profession. On the other hand, in the early childhood teaching population at large, more than one-third of those who work with young children change occupations each year (Galinsky, 1989).

High staff turnover takes its toll in several ways. The National Child Care Staffing Study (Whitebook et al., 1989) found that in centers with a high turnover rate, children spent less time in social activities with peers and tended more to wander aimlessly. In addition, separation from parents becomes more critical when caregivers change frequently (Galinsky, 1989). Very young children are particularly vulnerable to teacher turnover. Toddlers who lose their primary teacher were found to be more withdrawn and more aggressive two years later (Howes & Hamilton, 1993). Teachers also suffer when their coworkers change frequently because they have to assume the additional burden of orienting and training new staff (Whitebook, 1986).

Resolutions to the issue of high staff turnover, and the related issues of low pay and teacher burnout, are being pursued by professionals and professional organizations. Some of their recommendations will be discussed later in this section.

Low Pay

Low pay and poor benefits for early childhood teachers are directly tied to affordability of child care for parents.

Staffing shortage would undoubtedly be much less of a problem if early childhood teachers were paid adequate salaries and if they received appropriate recognition and status. For most teachers of young children, however, monetary rewards are not equal to their professional training and value. Although there is a wide variation in pay, early childhood teachers are generally paid poorly.

Low pay feeds into a vicious cycle: poor pay causes qualified teachers to seek work elsewhere; as a result, jobs are often filled by unqualified staff; they, in turn, reinforce the low status in which early childhood education is held and negate the need for higher pay (Katz, 1984a). In a recent call for an "all-out" effort to improve compensation and status," Marcy Whitebook (1986), director of the Child Care Employee Project under which the National Child Care Staffing Study was carried out, warned that child care could

> become a less and less attractive career choice despite the many inherently gratifying aspects of working with young children. The most likely and scariest prospect is that the pressure will build at a faster pace to lower standards for child care personnel—some of which are already frighteningly inadequate in many states—in order to fill teaching vacancies. (p. 11)

A follow-up to the original National Child Care Staffing Study found there was little change four years later (Whitebook et al., 1993). The new study, however, confirmed that the rate of teacher turnover is affected by quality, salaries, and program sponsorship. The lowest rate of turnover was found in programs accredited by NAEYC. On the other hand, turnover rates near 80 percent were found for programs that paid low staff wages, for-profit chain centers, for-profit independent centers, and nonprofit church-sponsored centers.

Another issue tied to low pay is the lack of benefits offered to employees of child care programs. The National Child Care Staffing Study found considerable variation in the types of benefits offered. For instance, health benefits were offered by more than 60 percent of nonprofit centers, whereas the percentage dropped to 16, 21, and 24, respectively, for independent for-profit, chain for-profit, and church-sponsored nonprofit child care programs (Whitebook et al., 1989). Generally, early childhood programs sponsored by larger institutions such as hospitals, public school districts, or universities, benefit from the policies of their sponsoring agencies (Galinsky, 1989). In a similar way, employer-sponsored child care programs often also receive their company's benefits package.

The reason for the low remuneration earned by early childhood teachers is directly tied to the issue of affordability of child care. Because staff wages and benefits constitute the largest expenditure in early childhood programs, the cost to parents is most affected by how much is allocated to that portion of the budget; the higher the teacher salaries, the greater the cost. Also part of this balance is the issue of child-adult ratio: the more children per adult, the lower the cost because fewer adults have to be hired. On the other hand, high child-adult ratios are associated with higher levels of teacher stress and decreased responsiveness to children (Phillips & Howes, 1987; Whitebook, Howes, Darrah, & Friedman, 1982).

Yet, the answer is not simply a matter of raising the cost of child care charged to parents. Although some families can afford to pay higher rates to ensure high-quality care offered by well-trained and well-paid professionals, many others cannot. Two-thirds of employed women are either the sole support of their families or are married to men who earn extremely low wages. Families pay as much as one-fourth of their income on child care (Galinsky, 1989). Experts contend that the cost parents pay for child care includes a hidden subsidy—the low wages teachers receive (Willer, 1990).

Many professionals advocate aggressive lobbying for public support for child care. One director proposes that only when child care employees collectively insist on higher wages and benefits—costs that will have to be assumed by parents—will there be sufficient economic impetus to force a solution to the problem, because parents will be sharing it. Parents will not become involved in the political process as long as they can meet their child care costs. According to Morin (1989),

> **Common practice is to shield parents from the true cost of child care by having employees work at compensation levels that subsidize the cost to parents. Our advocacy efforts have been directed primarily toward increasing the supply of affordable care for parents, not to increasing compensation for employees. (p. 19)**

Burnout

Some early childhood teachers experience burnout.

Burnout syndrome—Condition experienced by professionals as a result of undue job stress, characterized by loss of energy, irritability, and a feeling of being exploited.

Intricately tied to staff shortage, staff turnover, and poor salaries is teacher burnout. Burnout is complex, resulting from multiple causes. It is characterized by job dissatisfaction, stress, loss of energy, irritability, and a feeling of being exploited. The **burnout syndrome** has been described as a feeling of exhaustion that results from too many demands on one's energy and resources (Mattingly, 1977).

Low salaries and minimum benefits contribute to burnout, but so do other factors. Some of these, cited in research findings (Whitebook et al., 1982), include long working hours, unpaid overtime, time spent outside working hours in curriculum planning or parent functions, expectations for maintenance duties, lack of breaks, the constant intensity of working closely with children, high child-adult ratios, and lack of power in the decision-making process. Sometimes a change in working conditions, a seminar, or a support group can help a teacher regain a feeling of commitment and renewal.

Although burnout is a final outcome for some of those who work in early childhood programs, many others find great job satisfaction, which balances some of these negative aspects. The opportunity to contribute to and observe the development of their young charges provides a great source of pleasure to early childhood teachers. In addition, they find other aspects of the job gratifying. These include opportunities for reflection and self-development, satisfying staff relations, job flexibility, a level of autonomy, and staff interdependence (Whitebook et al., 1982; Whitebook et al., 1989).

Men in Early Childhood Education

More than 95 percent of early childhood teachers are women, and male teachers leave the field at an even greater rate than female teachers do.

A somewhat different issue concerns the predominance of females in early childhood education, representing between 95 and 97 percent of practitioners (Seifert, 1988; Whitebook et al., 1989). There have been and continue to be male teachers of young children who have a high commitment to the education and well-being of young children. For some children who grow up in single-parent homes without a father figure, a male teacher can fill a particularly special role.

Yet, men leave the field of early childhood education at an even greater rate than women do. Some male teachers who changed careers reported that they were subject to subtle prejudicial attitudes from parents, female coworkers, and administrators. They were considered not as good as women because they had never been mothers. Suspicion that was initially based on vague stereotypes was intensified during the 1980s by several highly publicized cases of sexual abuse in child care settings (Robinson, 1988).

It is more likely that economic reasons preclude more men from entering the field of early childhood education, or cause them to more readily leave the field if they do spend some time as preschool teachers. Robinson (1988) found that 85 percent of his sample of male early

The needs of teachers of young children must be an important priority in early childhood programs. Scheduled time and a pleasant place to relax can contribute to teacher satisfaction. What other factors can improve working conditions for teachers of young children?

childhood teachers were married with at least one child and were the major wage earner of their families. Low pay compelled them to look elsewhere for work. In part, men leave the field or do not enter it because they have more and better paying career choices than women, not because of the nature of the job (Seifert, 1988). The absence of a substantial number of men in the field is undoubtedly a contributing factor to low salaries. Thus, it has been argued that "recruiting more men would enhance the professional self-image of early childhood education" (Seifert, 1988, p. 114).

Empowerment and Activism

The issues and dilemmas facing early childhood education and its teachers are being addressed through vigorous advocacy and lobbying to help bring about change through political action and empowerment of teachers.

KEY QUESTION #5

Professional organizations such as NAEYC have been active in advocating improved working conditions and status for those who work with young children. Review the "Public Policy Report" and "Washington Update" in several issues of *Young Children* to see what kinds of issues are being discussed.

We have raised several urgent issues that face those in the early childhood profession. It is heartening that increasingly more professional and political effort is being devoted to solutions to these issues. Articulate public statements, relevant publications, thoughtful research, and energetic political advocacy and lobbying are making an impact. There is no question that the needs of young children and families, the importance of high quality in child care, and the needs of early childhood teachers are becoming highly visible public matters. From the halls of the capital in Washington, DC, to legislative buildings across all of the states, early childhood education and child care have become high priorities. This is, in many ways, an exciting time to be entering the field!

Changes in the current realities of early childhood education can be brought about through joint political action and the empowerment of teachers (Dresden & Myers, 1989). Training for advocacy is being incorporated into higher education programs at all levels, as students learn how policies are made, how the political system operates, and how they can affect it (Lombardi, 1986). You may well be taking a public policy course as part of your program of study, something that probably would not have been part of the curriculum 15 or 20 years ago. Parents are also often enlisted to support public policy endeavors.

What is clear is the resolve of professionals and professional organizations to push for change. Interest in and support for quality child care comes from many sectors both within and outside of the field of early childhood education, including parents, teachers, administrators, resource and referral agencies, related service providers, professional organizations, teacher trainers and educators, researchers, civic and religious groups, business and labor organizations, volunteer service organizations, philanthropic organizations and foundations, and civic leaders. A coalition including members of such constituency groups can be a powerful force in beginning to address issues (Lombardi, 1990). The National Child Care Staffing Study (Whitebook et al., 1989), which we have been citing throughout this chapter, ends with five major recommendations for change and suggestions for achieving these.

1. **Increase salaries**—To reach this goal, some of the recommendations are to establish salary levels that are competitive with jobs requiring comparable training and education; earmark state and federal money for salary enhancement; raise the minimum wage; and invest more public and private funds in child care to help low-

and middle-income families. The initiation of the Worthy Wage Campaign and the Full Cost of Quality Campaign as well as a variety of federal and state initiatives that specifically enhance salaries of child care workers are hopeful signs (Child Care Employee Project, 1992).

2. **Promote education and training**—This goal can be reached by broader acceptance of a career ladder, inclusion of early childhood teachers in federal and state college loan deferments, and establishment of national stipend programs to cover early childhood training costs.
3. **Adopt standards that will lead to higher quality programs**—Such standards should establish state and federal criteria for child-adult ratios, staff training, education, and compensation; they should be drawn from NAEYC's accreditation guidelines; and they should be required of states seeking federal child care money.
4. **Develop industry-wide standards**—To increase the quality of early childhood programs, recommendations include a minimum allocation of 60 percent of a center's budget for teaching staff expenditures; a benefits package for all teaching staff; inclusion of time for curriculum preparation and staff meetings; and encouragement of staff to join a professional organization.
5. **Promote public education**—To educate the public about the importance of well-trained and adequately paid teachers, it is recommended that administrators, educators, professional organizations, and referral agencies participate in a concerted effort to promote this issue and its importance.

PARENT SUPPORT FOR THE EARLY CHILDHOOD PROFESSION

Parents can be a good source of support for early childhood teachers.

In the last chapter, we discussed the role and responsibility of early childhood teachers toward parents. As indicated, the teacher-parent relationship is a reciprocal process. While teachers provide many services for parents, parents can also be extremely effective advocates for the early childhood education profession. One of the most effective lobbying efforts to promote increased funding allocation for early childhood programs in one state was the appearance of a large group of parents who spoke from their perspective about the importance of that funding. The legislators found the 200 taxpayers who came to promote this bill quite convincing!

Parental support, however, does not begin in the political arena. First and most important, parents must have a sound appreciation of early childhood educators and a clear understanding of the issues they face. Such understanding is promoted in a high-quality program in which teachers act professionally and are articulate about their field. When parents recognize that the quality of education and care their children receive is inextricably tied to improving the status and working conditions of their children's teachers and caregivers, they will be better able to help bring about changes.

SUMMARY

1. Early childhood teachers can be described by some identifiable personal qualities. Consider some predictable stages in their development.
2. The staffs of early childhood programs can include a number of individuals in a variety of roles, including the director, teaching staff, volunteers, support staff, board of directors, and community professionals.
3. A variety of training possibilities and regulating entities are associated with early childhood programs.
   A. Early childhood teachers might receive training through academic channels or through the Child Development Associate program.
   B. Early childhood programs are licensed through local or state regulations, which set minimum standards.
   C. Many programs undergo voluntary accreditation through the National Academy of Early Childhood Programs.
4. Professionalism in early childhood education is noted by such criteria as a code of ethics and the existence of professional organizations.
5. Although early childhood education presents you with exciting challenges, as a student entering this career, it also presents some issues and dilemmas:
   A. Some of the problems faced by early childhood educators are rooted in the historic antecedents of the field.
   B. Early childhood education faces some serious concerns, including teacher shortage, low pay, burnout, and scarcity of men in the field.
   C. Through advocacy and empowerment of early childhood professionals, these issues are beginning to be addressed.

KEY TERMS LIST

assistant teacher
Association for Childhood Education International (ACEI)
board of directors
burnout syndrome
caregiver
career lattice
child care worker
Child Development Associate (CDA)
code of ethics
early childhood educator
early childhood teacher
head teacher
National Association for the Education of Young Children (NAEYC)
team teaching

part III

The Why of Early Childhood Education

Early childhood education meets a number of social needs, as we discussed in earlier chapters. But the importance of this field is also supported by a solid foundation of theory and research, which provides direction to teachers. To address the *why* of early education, we will consider "Rationale Supporting Early Childhood Education" and "Goals, Objectives, and Evaluation."

chapter 5

Rationale Supporting Early Childhood Education

How we approach the education and care of young children depends, to a great extent, on what we believe children are like. Programs for preschoolers are often structured around some underlying assumptions about the nature of children. For instance, a belief that children learn actively by exploring their environment would result in a different type of early education program than one based on the idea that children learn passively by being taught specific information and skills.

Similarly, a belief that children are basically unruly and need strict control so they will learn appropriate behavior would result in a different guidance approach than the notion that children generally strive toward social acceptance from others by conforming to reasonable expectations. In this chapter we will examine the foundations and rationale on which early childhood education has been built.

A LOOK BACK—CHILDREN THROUGH TIME

Interest in the care and education of young children goes back thousands of years. Our Western tradition is traced to ancient Greece, where the writings of philosophers such as Plato and Aristotle reflect a keen sensitivity to the needs of children and the importance of appropriate education in shaping their character. The Greeks saw human development as a transformation from the imperfect state of childhood to the ideal of adulthood (Sameroff, 1983). The Greek tradition, including education for girls as well as for boys, was carried on for several hundred years into the height of Roman times.

Many of the early, enlightened ideas about children were lost, however, during the Middle Ages, when even the concept of childhood seemed to have been misplaced. Children became little more than property and were put to work, for instance, in the fields or tending animals,

Early childhood programs have an extensive and rich history, both in the United States and in other parts of the world.

The concept of childhood and the treatment of children through history have always been tied to economic, religious, and social factors.

just as soon as they were big enough. "The typical man or woman emerged straight out of his babyhood into a sort of junior adult status" (Braun & Edwards, 1972, p. 6). Schools and formal education as a way of passing on cultural traditions had virtually disappeared in Europe except in a few places, particularly in Islamic Spain, where learning was highly valued.

Various religious, political, and economic forces provided impetus for the move out of these Dark Ages, often improving the treatment of children, but at other times exploiting them. Martin Luther, for example, advocated public education for all children in sixteenth-century Germany as a way of promoting religious salvation. In other parts of Europe, some social and political reformers, angered by the injustices that provided an opulent life-style for the nobility at the expense of the starving peasants, developed ideas that focused on children and their education as one way of overcoming such inequities.

By the eighteenth century, as the industrial revolution swept both Europe and America, the economic search for cheap labor led to the abuse of many children in factories. They were kept at spindles or levers up to as many as 16 hours a day, while being fed and housed minimally. Such blatant exploitation also led to reforms, eventually including universal public education and laws prohibiting child labor (Aries, 1962; Borstellman, 1983; Braun & Edwards, 1972; Elkind, 1987a; Ulich, 1947).

During the twentieth century, the view of early childhood as an important part of human development has been particularly promoted.

The twentieth century, while a relatively short period in history, represents an active time in the formation of early childhood education. For one thing, education for all children came to be increasingly accepted, reinforcing the idea that childhood is a separate and important period. Education in the United States, in the eyes of such progressive educators as John Dewey, was a training ground for democracy, a way of equalizing social inequities by imbuing children from a young age with democratic ideals. Philosophers and scientists, who proclaimed the early years as specially relevant, also contributed to the field. Among these, Sigmund Freud focused unprecedented attention on earliest experiences as the foundation of personality.

Child study movement–Occurred earlier in the 20th century in the United States when many university preschools were established to develop scientific methods for studying children.

A third strand was the development of scientific methods of observation that led to the **child study movement,** out of which grew many university preschool laboratory programs designed to facilitate the careful study of young children. Still another contribution to today's field is the notion of early childhood education as a means to social reform. Important programs were developed throughout this century with the idea of rescuing the poor from poverty. A common purpose motivated those who helped move young children out of factories into schools at the turn of the century, and those who developed the Head Start philosophy of the 1960s.

Finally, another change that has profoundly affected early childhood education today is the rising need for child care arrangements, which we discussed in Chapter 1. Although recent changes in the economy and family life have brought the proliferation of child care programs available today, such programs are not new. During World War II, many women were required to work and needed arrangements for care of their young children, which were often publicly subsidized (Braun & Edwards, 1972; Carter, 1987; Greenberg, 1987; Siegel & White, 1982; Weber, 1984).

History and the context of each period have generally determined how children are viewed. Because children are vulnerable and dependent, their image and treatment have been shaped by the needs of the times and by influential thinkers and writers. Today we view children much more benignly than during many periods of the past. We acknowledge that the childhood years are unique and important, we provide children with special environments, and we promote education as a social and personal necessity. Today's view of children is based to a greater extent on theory and research rather than on the religious or political ideas that, in part, dictated the image of children in the past. Let us now turn to some of the important figures in the historical account of early childhood education. The section that follows will then review influential theorists whose conceptualizations have further refined our ideas of young children.

KEY QUESTION #1

Historic events have a great impact on our view of children and how we treat them. What social and political events have taken place during your life that have had an impact on young children and their education? Also ask this question of a relative or friend who was born in an earlier era.

INFLUENTIAL PEOPLE IN THE HISTORY OF EARLY CHILDHOOD EDUCATION

Many, many individuals have contributed to our current view of young children and their care and education. We will touch on the works of only a few of them in this text. Some developed their ideas because of their direct work with children, often the poor and underprivileged; others' theories emerged out of political and philosophical concerns about the problems of society and how reforms could be brought about. Let us now meet some of the people who have contributed to our views, particularly as these relate to the early years.

Jean-Jacques Rousseau (1712-1778)

Rousseau was not an early childhood educator, but his ideas have certainly influenced the field. As a philosopher writing in the context of the corrupt French society of his time, Rousseau developed the idea that society actually hindered human beings from developing according to their nature. Society, with its hierarchy of the few who were rich and powerful, only imposed misery on the masses, a state that is not natural. Rousseau, in fact, considered anything natural and primitive to be good. Thus, he argued, if children could develop without the

Rousseau advanced the notions that children are innately noble and good, that their way of learning is different from that of adults, and that they should be removed from the corrupting influences of society.

Who's Who in ECE? People in the field of early childhood education are, clockwise from top, Jean-Jacques Rousseau, Johann Pestalozzi, Fredrich Froebel, Maria Montessori, Lev Vygotsky, Erik Erikson, Jean Piaget, and B. F. Skinner.

artificial trappings of civilization, they would be able to achieve their true potential of being moral and good.

According to Rousseau, young children are innately pure and noble, but they need to be protected from the evil influences of society to maintain this goodness. It is through close contact with nature that they can develop their senses and form their personalities. In a protected rural environment, they learn from what is concrete, not from the abstract, through trial and error and experimentation. Such learning is natural and satisfying, leading to happiness, because children will know nothing of the artificial needs that society creates. Rousseau recognized that children's mode of thinking and learning is different from that of adults and considered good education to be based on the stage of development of the child, not on adult-imposed criteria. A child-centered, uncorrupted education will, eventually, result in adults who are moral and interested in this common good of society.

Rousseau never worked with children—in fact, he actually abandoned all of his own children to foundling homes—but he wrote extensively about his philosophy in his novels and essays. Today we agree with Rousseau that children have a unique nature that needs to be nurtured and protected. We also recognize the need to provide an appropriate environment for young children, in which their development can be maximized. Although his highly idealistic view of childhood and human nature was never fully adopted by those who followed Rousseau, he nonetheless had a great influence on later early childhood educators, as we shall soon see (Braun & Edwards, 1972; Carter, 1987; Grimsley, 1967; Weber, 1984).

Johann Pestalozzi (1746-1827)

Pestalozzi believed that young children learned actively, from concrete experiences, a philosophy he implemented in the schools he established.

Pestalozzi was deeply influenced by Rousseau's educational ideas. He felt that all people, even the poorest, had the right to an education as a way of helping them develop their moral and intellectual potential. He believed in education according to nature and considered that learning for young children is intricately tied to concrete experiences and observation. Unlike Rousseau, however, he stressed the important role of the mother in children's earliest years.

Also unlike Rousseau, Pestalozzi actually worked with children, developing educational methods that are still used today. For instance, he stressed the importance of recognizing individual differences among children and the relevance of children's self-activity rather than rote as the basis of learning.

What made Pestalozzi successful as an educator of young children, however, was his powerful personality and his selfless and passionate dedication and commitment.

> **His life was devoted to human relationships, a life of the mind, but more a life of feeling and service. . . . His educational doctrine . . . must be followed with devotion, self-forgetfulness, deep and loving concern for children and for the essence of childhood. (Braun & Edwards, 1972, p. 60)**

One of the schools he established became world famous, drawing visitors and students from all over Europe. He is considered to be the first to actually teach young children of preschool age, marking the beginning of the kindergarten movement (Braun & Edwards, 1972; Ulich, 1967; Weber, 1984).

Friedrich Froebel (1782-1852)

Froebel, who is credited with beginning the kindergarten, placed great emphasis on the importance of play.

Froebel was one of the visitors at Pestalozzi's school, observing it with some mixed feelings. He greatly admired Pestalozzi's skills but was concerned over his inability to articulate his methods. Froebel, however, was better able to put into words his educational principles. Like his predecessors Rousseau and Pestalozzi, Froebel believed in the interrelatedness of nature and the child's developing mind. He also advocated that education should harmonize with the child's inner development, recognizing that children are in different stages at various ages. He saw childhood as a separate stage that was not just a transition to adulthood but a stage with great intrinsic value in its own right.

Froebel also strongly stressed the important role of play in young children's development, not merely as a preparation for adult work. He saw play as a pure and natural mode of learning through which children achieve harmony. Froebel developed a carefully programmed curriculum and specific materials. He is, in fact, credited with developing blocks, now a standard early childhood material. His program was centered on play and sensory awareness. Art activities, games, finger plays, songs, blocks, stories, crafts, and other similar endeavors were part of Froebel's kindergartens. His classes were not held in a traditional classroom but in a "garden for children," hence the German word **kindergarten** (Braun & Edwards, 1972; Carter, 1987; Ulich, 1947; Ulich, 1967; Weber, 1984).

Kindergarten—German word, literally meaning "garden for children," coined by Friedrich Froebel for his program for young children.

Maria Montessori (1870-1952)

Montessori, working with slum children in Rome, developed a successful method of early education that is still widely followed today.

A true feminist of her time, Maria Montessori was the first woman to become a medical doctor in Italy. Her psychiatric interest led her to work with retarded children. She felt that their problems were often educational more than medical, and she proved her point when a number of these institutionalized children easily passed regular school exams after she had worked with them. In 1907, the city of Rome asked Montessori to take charge of a children's day nursery that was attached to a housing tenement for the poor. The housing authorities basically wanted someone who would keep the children off the stairs and prevent them from dirtying the newly painted walls. But Montessori found in this "casa dei bambini" (children's house) the opportunity to explore her teaching methods with normal children.

Montessori's methods were based on the principle that young children learn in a way that is fundamentally different from how adults learn. She was particularly impressed with the great capacity of children to learn so much during the first few years of life. She called this capacity the **absorbent mind,** analogous to a sponge soaking up liquid. She felt that all children have a fundamental, inborn intellectual structure that unfolds gradually as they develop, although individual differences are due to different environmental experiences.

Absorbent mind—Maria Montessori's term to describe the capacity of young children to learn a great deal during the early years.

If children's absorbent minds are exposed to appropriate learning experiences in the developmental stages, their minds will grow. This is especially true during **sensitive periods,** times when children are most receptive to absorbing specific learning. For instance, during one sensitive period, children are especially receptive to developing sensory perception; during another, they are concerned with a sense of order in their environment; in yet another, their energies focus on coordination and control of movement.

Sensitive periods—Maria Montessori's term describing the times when children are most receptive to absorbing specific learning.

Montessori developed a curriculum that takes advantage of these sensitive periods by making appropriate experiences available to children at times when they are most ready to learn from them. She used the term **prepared environment** to describe this match of the right materials to children's stages of development. Her school included many learning activities that she herself developed to help children acquire skills. Some of these related to **sensory discrimination,** matching and sorting by size, shape, sound, color, smell, or other dimension; others helped children learn practical skills such as polishing shoes or setting a table. More advanced materials were aimed at teaching reading, writing, and math skills through hands-on manipulation.

Prepared environment—Maria Montessori's term to describe the careful match between appropriate materials and what the child is most ready to learn at any given time.

Sensory discrimination—Involvement in an activity in which one of the senses is used to distinguish a specific feature or dimension of similar materials; it might include matching or sorting by size, color, shape, sound, smell, or taste.

Much of Montessori's philosophy and approach, particularly her self-correcting materials and strong sense of respect for children, have had an enduring impact on early childhood education. Whether by design in contemporary Montessori schools or by common acceptance in other programs, Montessori's influence is still strongly felt today. (Braun & Edwards, 1972; Carter, 1987; Chattin-McNichols, 1992; Elkind, 1983; Gettman, 1987; Simons & Simons, 1986).

INFLUENTIAL THEORISTS OF CHILD DEVELOPMENT

Although many of the predecessors of early childhood education developed a theoretical or philosophical viewpoint about how children develop, it was not until our century that such ideas were founded on a more empirical base through systematic observations and supporting research. Today, the major way in which we view these different concepts is through theories that are based more on empirical information.

A **human development theory** is a way of describing what happens as individuals move from infancy through adulthood, identifying significant events commonly experienced by all people and explaining why changes occur as they do. It is useful to have a grasp of different theories as you develop your own professional identity and beliefs. This not only gives you a way of assessing your personal values but offers some alternative views about how children develop and should be treated (Thomas, 1990b). We will now look at just a few of the most influential developmental theorists whose ideas have contributed, directly or indirectly, to the field of early childhood education today.

Human development theory—A way to describe what happens as individuals move from infancy through adulthood, identifying significant events that are commonly experienced by all people, and explaining why changes occur as they do.

Erik Erikson (1902-1994)

Erikson's psychosocial theory, which spans childhood and adulthood, focuses on specific social tasks that need to emerge for healthy development in each of eight stages.

Erik Erikson, beginning his career in the early decades of this century in central Europe, was a follower of Sigmund Freud. Erikson refined aspects of Freud's theory into his **psychosocial theory.** According to Erikson, each stage of development is defined by a conflict, which leads to opportunities for personal growth. These conflicts, in addition to centering on the person alone, also revolve around relationships with others. Erikson's was the first theory that spanned both childhood and adulthood through, what he considered, eight universal stages. The first four are particularly important because they describe significant tasks that occur in the life of the infant and young child. We will focus on those four in more detail.

Psychosocial theory—The branch of psychology founded by Erik Erikson, in which development is described in terms of eight stages that span childhood and adulthood, each offering opportunities for personality growth and development.

Trust vs. Mistrust—The first stage of development described by Erik Erikson, occurring during infancy, in which the child's needs should be met consistently and predictably.

1. **Trust vs. Mistrust** (birth through approximately 18 months). The basic theme of infancy is the development of trust. This comes about when children's needs for food, warmth, sleep, and nurturing are met consistently and predictably. This stage revolves around the importance of feeding, although Erikson incorporates all aspects of the baby's existence, including sleep and elimination, in this foundation. The helpless infant must rely on the caregiver to provide satisfaction of needs. When children are not cared for adequately, they develop a sense of mistrust in others and in themselves, and they move to future stages by seeing the world as threatening, unpredictable, and hostile.

Autonomy vs. Shame and Doubt—The second stage of development described by Erik Erikson, occurring during the second year of life, in which toddlers assert their growing motor, language, and cognitive abilities by trying to become more independent.

2. **Autonomy vs. Shame and Doubt** (approximately 18 months through 3 years). Toddlers begin to assert their growing motor, language, and cognitive abilities by trying to become more independent. At the same time, they are still very dependent and must reach a balance between reliance on caregivers and the desire to try new things. One potential conflict revolves around toilet training. Success in this stage means that children have increasing self-control, feel good about their own abilities, and also begin to learn the boundaries of the social world. If children are made to feel ashamed of their efforts, they will develop a sense of self-doubt. In early childhood programs, children need to be allowed to exercise their growing independence within the safety of a loving and supportive environment that does not withdraw bodily cuddles and comforts just because the toddler is mobile and naysaying!

Initiative vs. Guilt—The third stage of development described by Erik Erikson, occurring during the preschool years, in which the child's curiosity and enthusiasm lead to a need to explore and learn about the world, and in which rules and expectations begin to be established.

3. **Initiative vs. Guilt** (approximately 3 to 5 years). Preschoolers' social and physical world expands dramatically and they are full of curiosity and desire to try new activities, alone as well as cooperatively with peers. At this age, children enjoy imitating adults, a way of learning about and incorporating adult roles and expectations. Children also acquire an understanding of male and female roles through the subtle expectations of the parent of the opposite sex. If children receive no guidelines or if they are not allowed to explore, satisfy their curiosity, and try new ventures, they will develop a sense of guilt and failure. Thus, in the early childhood setting, it is important to allow children to initiate and try out a variety of experiences and activities and to provide appropriate guidelines within which children can learn the rules and expectations of society.

Industry vs. Inferiority—The fourth stage of development described by Erik Erikson, starting at the end of the preschool years and lasting until puberty, in which the child focuses on development of competence.

4. **Industry vs. Inferiority** (approximately age 6 to puberty). By the end of the preschool years, children begin to focus on the development of competence. They like to plan, carry out, and complete projects, unlike younger preschoolers who are more concerned with the exploratory process of their activities. This period is particularly important in the development of habits of workmanship, persistence, greater understanding of social rules, and citizenship. Children who do not develop an adequate sense of industry will settle for mediocrity and do less than they are able, with a resulting sense of inferiority. Older preschoolers and school-aged children should be allowed time, space, materials, and support to engage in the kinds of activities that build a sense of industry.

Erikson describes four other stages that build on the foundations of the ones we have described. Although all stages occur at critical times in development, they never completely disappear. Thus, trust is still important beyond infancy, children continue to struggle with the balance between autonomy and dependency, and initiative and industry are relevant even beyond the early years, though in a more mature form. Erikson emphasizes the importance of play in meeting the tasks of autonomy and initiative during the early years. Erikson's stages highlight some of the important issues for young children and the balance we must provide to help them achieve healthy development (Erikson, 1963; Maier, 1965; Maier, 1990; Tribe, 1982; Weber, 1984). Gratz and Boulton (1996) suggest that Erikson's stages also provide a suitable framework for teachers of young children to examine and evaluate their own professional development.

KEY QUESTION #2

Observe an early childhood program. What evidence do you see of the influence of one or more theorists, for instance, Piaget, Erikson, or the behaviorists? Ask one of the teachers if he or she draws on any particular human development theories and compare to your observation.

Jean Piaget (1896-1980)

Piaget's cognitive developmental theory, one of the most influential on early childhood education, describes how children's thinking is unique in each of four stages.

One of the most influential forces in early childhood education today is the theory of Jean Piaget. Piaget's **cognitive developmental theory** presents a complex picture of how children's intelligence and thinking abilities emerge. Piaget did not suggest specific educational applications of his work, but educators have transformed his theory into actual models more than any other.

Piaget based his theory of cognitive development on his background and training as a biologist. He conceptualized cognitive development as similar to how all organisms function physiologically, adapting to and organizing the environment around them. A common example illustrates our own biological adaptation to the physical environment: If the temperature becomes too warm or too cold, we sweat or shiver to adapt. In a way similar to this physiological adaptation, we also adapt mentally to changes in the environment. At the same time we adapt, we mentally organize what we perceive in our environment so that it makes sense to us.

In a cognitive sense, **adaptation** is involved any time new information or a new experience occurs. A person must adapt to incorporate any new information or experience into the psychological structure. When something new presents itself, however, the existing mental structure is "upset"—put into **disequilibrium** because this new information or experience does not exactly fit into the old structures.

To return to balance or **equilibrium,** adaptation takes place through the complementary processes of assimilation and accommodation. **Assimilation** occurs when the person tries to make the new information or experience fit into an existing concept or schema. **Accommodation** takes place when the schema is modified or a new concept is formed to incorporate the new information or experience. "Accommodation accounts for development (a qualitative change) and assimilation accounts for growth (a quantitative change); together they account for intellectual adaptation and the development of intellectual structures" (Wadsworth, 1984, p. 16). An example of assimilation and accommodation can be imagined through a visit by a group of young children to a zoo. Raymond, seeing a panther for the first time, says, "Look, there's a black leopard." He has fit the new animal into an

Cognitive developmental theory—The theory formulated by Jean Piaget that focuses on how children's intelligence and thinking abilities emerge through distinct stages.

Adaptation—Jean Piaget's term for the process that occurs any time new information or a new experience occurs.

Disequilibrium—According to Jean Piaget, the lack of balance experienced when existing mental structures and new experience do not fit exactly.

Equilibrium—According to Jean Piaget, the state of balance each person seeks between existing mental structures and new experiences.

Assimilation—According to Jean Piaget, one form of adaptation, which takes place when a person tries to make new information or a new experience fit into an existing concept.

Accommodation—According to Jean Piaget, one form of adaptation, which takes place when an existing concept is modified or a new concept is formed to incorporate new information or a new experience.

existing mental structure because he is already familiar with leopards and just assumes that the panther is a leopard of a different color. He is using assimilation, making the new information fit into what he already knows. Monique, on the other hand, has never visited a zoo and has seen some wild animals only on television or in books. Seeing unfamiliar llamas, she considers what these might be. They resemble horses, but Monique immediately dismisses this category because she knows that horses have smooth hair and shorter necks. She also dismisses camels because she knows they have humps on their backs. She decides finally that this must be an animal she does not know and asks the teacher what it is. Monique is using accommodation, creating a new concept into which this new information can be fitted.

Organization—According to Jean Piaget, the mental process by which a person organizes experiences and information in relation to each other.

Organization is a process that is complementary to adaptation. While adaptation allows for new information and experience to be incorporated into existing mental structures, organization defines how such information and experiences are related to each other. Piaget considers that organization is a basic tendency of all human beings. We all strive to organize our experiences to make them understandable, connected, coherent, and integrated. Intelligence is not just a collection of facts but a way of incorporating these into a framework and context that makes sense.

Consider a pedal. By itself it is a small, flat, rectangular item made of red plastic. However, in proper context, fitted on a tricycle, the pedal takes on an entirely different meaning as it allows the child to turn the wheels that, in turn, make the tricycle move. Organization allows us to expand the visual cues about the pedal to include information about its function as part of a whole.

Schemata—(schema is the singular form)—According to Jean Piaget, cognitive structures into which cognitive concepts or mental representations are organized.

Piaget called the cognitive structures into which we adapt and organize our environment **schemata** (schema is the singular form). Schemata are concepts or mental representations of experiences. We constantly create, refine, change, modify, organize, and reorganize our schemata. One popular analogy of schemata is an index card file. Babies are born with only a few "index cards," but, as they receive new information through their senses, they have to create new cards to incorporate these experiences. Increasingly, their store of information becomes more complex and they create "dividers" in their files into which information can be categorized and organized through some common features.

Stage theorist—Any theory that delineates specific stages in which development is marked by qualitatively different characteristics and accomplishments and where each stage builds on the previous one.

Although the formation, adaptation, and organization of new schemata are ongoing processes in cognitive development, that development is typified by distinct abilities at different ages. As a **stage theorist,** Piaget (like Erikson) conceived of qualitatively different characteristics and accomplishments in cognitive ability during various stages of development. Each stage is built on and incorporates the accomplishments of the previous one. Maturation sets limits on when children are capable of achieving specific cognitive abilities.

Representation—According to Jean Piaget, the ability to depict an object, person, action, or experience mentally, even if it is not present in the immediate environment.

Thus, the infant, dependent on movement and the senses, learns about the environment through those avenues. By age two, however, a distinctly new ability emerges, the ability for mental **representation** of objects, even though they are not present in the immediate environment. This new ability allows the preschooler to move beyond the limits of the immediate physical environment and include past experiences, imaginary ideas, and symbols. While the preschooler's dramatic acquisition of language skills opens up a world of new possibilities, this age group is still limited by the observable characteristics of objects. Reasoning is not yet logical, although by about seven years children begin to apply **logical thinking** to concrete problems. Finally, by adolescence, the young person may be able to apply logic and **abstract thinking** to a wide range of problems.

These changes in thinking ability are the basis for the four periods of cognitive development described by Piaget (Figure 5-1). Although Piaget's stages focus on evolving cognitive abilities, their principles are applied much more widely, to social and moral as well as to physical and mathematical learning.

Early childhood teachers need to be aware of the implications of these stages as they work with young children. Understanding of the characteristics and growing abilities of infants in the sensorimotor period is important for infants and toddlers but also has relevance for those who work with preschoolers. For instance, some young preschoolers may not yet have completely grasped **object permanence,** the recognition that an object continues to exist even if it is out of sight. Thus, the toddler who peels off the collage material to re-find the paste underneath is not naughty but is testing a principle that most children grasp during the earlier sensorimotor stage. Similarly, the preschool teacher needs to understand the concrete operations period for the precocious three-year-old who reads and uses deductive reasoning in exhibiting skills usually not seen in children this young. Teachers of school-aged children need also to be aware not only of the accomplishments of the concrete operations period but of the sensorimotor and formal operations periods as well. An understanding of how children learn as well as their characteristics, abilities, and limits is vital to

Logical thinking—According to Jean Piaget, the ability that begins to emerge around age seven in which children use mental processes to solve problems rather than relying solely on perceived information.

Abstract thinking—According to Jean Piaget, the ability to solve a variety of problems abstractly, without a need to manipulate concrete objects.

Object permanence—Part of Jean Piaget's theory, the recognition that objects exist, even when they are out of view; a concept that children begin to develop toward the end of their first year of life.

FIGURE 5-1 Piaget's periods of cognitive development

Stage 1: Sensorimotor Period (0 to 2 years)

The first period is characterized by motor behavior through which schemata are formed. The child does not yet represent events mentally but relies on coordination of senses and movement, on object permanence development, on learning to differentiate means from ends, and on beginning to understand the relationship of objects in space in order to learn about the environment.

Stage 2: Preoperational Period (2 to 7 years)

Language and other forms of representation develop during this period, although thinking is not yet logical. Children's internal mental representations, which allow them to think of objects even if these are not physically present, is the major accomplishment of this period. Children have an egocentric view of the world, in terms of their own perspective. Early classification, seriation, and role play begin.

Stage 3: Concrete Operations Period (7 to 11 years)

The child has internalized some physical tasks or operations and no longer depends only on what is visible, but can apply logic to solving problems. The child now is able to reverse operations (for instance, $5 - 3 = 2$ is the same as $3 + 2 = 5$). The child can also practice conservation—recognize that an object does not change in amount even if its physical appearance changes (stretching a ball of clay into a snake).

Stage 4: Formal Operations Period (11 to 15 years)

The final period, rare even in adults, is characterized by sophisticated, abstract thinking and logical reasoning abilities applied to physical as well as social and moral problems.

Sensorimotor Period—Piaget's period covering infancy.

Preoperational Period—Piaget's period covering the preschool years.

Concrete Operations Period—Piaget's period covering the elementary school year.

Formal Operations Period—Piaget's period covering adolescence.

Behaviorism—The theoretical viewpoint, espoused by theorists such as B. F. Skinner, that behavior is shaped by environmental forces, specifically in response to reward and punishment.

Behavior modification—The systematic application of principles of reinforcement to modify behavior.

Operant conditioning—The principle of behavioral theory whereby a person deliberately attempts to increase or decrease behavior by controlling consequences.

Reinforcement—In behavioral theory, any response that follows a behavior that encourages repetition of that behavior.

Positive reinforcement—Application of a behavioral principle, which includes any immediate feedback (either through tangible or nontangible means) to children that their behavior is valued.

Social reinforcer—In behavioral theory, a reward that conveys approval through such responses as a smile, hug, or attention.

Shaping—In behavioral theory, a method used to teach a child a new behavior by breaking it down into small steps and reinforcing the attainment of each step systematically.

Extinction—In behavioral theory, a method of eliminating a previously reinforced behavior by taking away all reinforcement, for instance, by totally ignoring the behavior.

Punishment—An aversive consequence that follows a behavior for the purpose of decreasing or eliminating the behavior; not recommended as an effective means of changing behavior.

appropriate teaching (Ginsburg & Opper, 1969; Lavatelli, 1970; Piaget, 1983; Saunders & Bingham-Newman, 1984; Thomas, 1990; Tribe, 1982; Wadsworth, 1984).

B. F. Skinner (1904-1990)

Up to this point, we have considered people whose views are based on a belief that there is an inborn plan according to which children develop. Rousseau, Pestalozzi, Froebel, and Montessori all felt that, given an appropriate environment and understanding adults, children will develop according to nature's plan into healthy, responsible, intelligent adults. Erikson and Piaget likewise believed that development is predetermined and will follow the same stages in each person.

But this view of an innately determined plan is not the only way of viewing human development. An alternative view is that children are not shaped by internal forces but rather by external ones, specifically those emanating from the environment. **Behaviorism** is based on this viewpoint.

B. F. Skinner was one of the behaviorists whose ideas have had widespread influence on all aspects of education, including those encompassing the early childhood years. The application of his theoretical and experimental work can be seen in **behavior modification,** which operates on the underlying principle that behavior can be changed or modified by manipulating the environment, which includes both physical and social components.

Skinner emphasized that almost all behavior is learned through experience. Specific behaviors, according to Skinner, can be increased or decreased as a function of what follows it. In other words, if something pleasant or enjoyable consistently happens after the child engages in a specific behavior (the teacher smiles when Jeremy helps to put away the blocks), he is likely to repeat that behavior. Conversely, if something unpleasant or painful follows a behavior (Lars burns his finger when he touches the stove), he is likely not to repeat it. Deliberately attempting to increase or decrease behavior by controlling consequences, is called **operant conditioning.**

Skinner used the term **reinforcement** to describe the immediate consequence of behavior that is likely to strengthen it. Whether consciously using the behavioral approach or not, early childhood educators frequently use **positive reinforcement** because of its powerful effect on children's behavior. Teachers of young children are most likely to use **social reinforcers**—for instance, a smile, a hug, attention, or involvement—when they see a child engaging in a behavior they consider desirable.

In addition, systematic attention to behavior and its consequences can be used to encourage new behaviors or eliminate undesirable ones. **Shaping** is the method used to help a child learn a new behavior by teaching it in small steps and systematically reinforcing the attainment of each step. **Extinction** is used to eliminate a behavior that had previously been reinforced by taking away all reinforcement, for example, by totally ignoring the behavior. Extinction, however, is not synonymous with **punishment,** which is defined as an aversive consequence that follows the behavior. According to Skinner (and almost all early childhood professionals), punishment is not an effective way of controlling behavior. To summarize, in all of these methods—reinforcement, shaping, and extinction—it is the manipulation of what immediately follows a behavior that affects it.

To return to what we originally said about the distinguishing feature of behaviorism, behavior is considered to be externally controlled, not driven by internal factors. Because behaviorism has attempted to function as a precise science, behavior is defined only by what is **observable**—for instance, actions and words—rather than by nonobservable factors such as motivation or feelings. Behavior is carefully defined, observed, and graphed by representing the rate or magnitude of a given child response in measurable units. Examples of such measures might be the number of times a child hits another child or the number of minutes a child plays appropriately with peers.

Elements of behavioral theory are used in many ways in early childhood programs. Particularly in programs for young children with disabilities and some compensatory programs, behaviorist methods have been widely and systematically applied in attempts to teach children specific skills. When the teacher determines exactly what children should learn, those skills can be organized and presented in the form of **programmed instruction.** More pervasive in early childhood education, however, is the use of a number of behavioral techniques such as reinforcement, extinction, or step-by-step shaping. Teachers in many programs, although they do not strictly adhere to all of the theoretical and applied aspects of behaviorism, nonetheless frequently use a number of its techniques (Braun & Edwards, 1972; Bushell, 1982; Peters, Neisworth, & Yawkey, 1985; Sameroff, 1983; Skinner, 1969; Skinner, 1974; Weber, 1984).

B. F. Skinner, one of the important proponents of behavioral theory, emphasized that almost all behavior is learned and can be increased by positive consequences and decreased by negative consequences.

Observable behavior—Actions that can be seen rather than those that are inferred.

Programmed instruction—(also called direct instruction)—A method of teaching in which the teacher determines exactly what the children should learn, devises a sequence of learning activities to teach specific information, and teaches it directly by controlling the information according to children's responses.

Lev Semanovich Vygotsky (1896-1934)

All of the previously discussed theorists have focused primarily on the child in explaining how development occurs, although the importance of others, especially the family, is certainly not ignored. Other theorists have given much greater prominence to the importance of the cultural and historical context within which a child is socialized. The Russian psychologist Lev Vygotsky, originator of the **sociohistoric theory,** highly stressed the importance of the social environment to development. Vygotsky's ideas have gained greater prominence in recent years, several decades after his death, and have spurred considerable interest in cross-cultural studies of child development and child-rearing practices. Vygotsky proposed that social interaction, especially dialog, between children and adults is the mechanism through which specific cultural values, customs, and beliefs are transmitted from generation to generation.

Vygotsky was particularly intrigued by the question of how young children develop complex thinking. He concluded that the same mechanism through which culture is transmitted—social interaction—is the way in which increasingly more complex thinking develops, as part of learning about culture. Children gain knowledge and skills through "shared experiences" between themselves and adults or older peers. Furthermore, the dialogs that accompany these experiences gradually

Vygotsky's sociohistoric theory stresses the importance of the social context of development; children's learning is often promoted through assistance from adults or older peers who help the child learn new skills within the zone of proximal development.

Sociohistoric theory—Originated by Lev Vygotsky, this theory gives prominence to the social, cultural, and historic context of child development.

EXPERIENCES

chapter 5

ROSALIA, Master Teacher, Mixed-age Class

The Flood

The heavy snows followed by persistent rains caused a flood that devastated parts of the city. Although the children were only three to five years old, they were aware of the flood. When they returned to school, after several days of closure because of impassable roads, we talked about the flood during group time.

"What happened in our area? Does anyone have something to share?"

Several children raised their hands or called out, "It flooded."

"Can you tell me what happened? What do you know about the flood?"

Children had various stories to share. None lived in the low areas near the river where it had flooded, but many had seen the area shown repeatedly on television. Some had gone with their parents to the river to see the devastation. Several had, with their families, helped fill sand bags needed to stave off further potential damage.

"We got to help! It was neat," shared one girl.

Some children elaborated on the flood scenario. Four-year-old Caleb told the following story:

"I was all alone at home when it started to flood. The water kept going up and up, and I knew I had to rescue my dog, Eddie. So, I had to take out the boat to save Eddie. I paddled round the house, went in my bedroom window upstairs, and found Eddie. He was happy to see me because he was getting wet. He got in the boat with me and we left. It was real exciting!" Caleb, who lived down the street from one of the teachers and nowhere near the flooded areas, had seen images on television of people paddling down flooded streets in boats. He used his usual bent for story telling to explain what happened.

Some of the children wanted to know how high the water was. From the newspaper, we found out the height of the flood at its crest, and measured string to that length. This was laid out on the floor to show how deep the water was. We then asked children to lay down along the string, the feet of one against the head of another, to measure "how many children high" the water was. It was twelve children high! Daily, we checked the receding waters' height and adjusted the string accordingly.

We also recreated a flood in the play yard. We dug a gully in the sand to make a river. Along the banks of the river, we placed various toys, such as small cars. Then we filled the "river" with water to its normal height. A flood was created by overfilling the "river." The children were able to see how the force of the water moved the sand and the objects along the banks. They also watched as the water gradually receded, just as our city's river had done.

For weeks discussion of the flood continued. The topic gradually shifted, to one about erosion, for instance. But a significant and memorable event provided great opportunity for activities that truly engaged the children's interest.

become a part of children's thinking. Thus, Vygotsky conceived of cognitive development as dependent on, not independent of, social mediation. This view is in contrast to Piaget's, which conceives of the child as gradually becoming more social and less self-focused; in Vygotsky's view, the child is socially dependent at the beginning of cognitive life, and only becomes increasingly independent in his or her thinking through many experiences in which adults or older peers help.

The child acquires new skills and information within what Vygotsky termed the **zone of proximal development (ZPD).** This is the level at which a child finds a task too difficult to complete alone but which, with the assistance and support of an adult or older peer, the child can accomplish. Infants are frequently guided by adults in tasks they have not yet mastered. Many games adults play with infants encourage the baby to increasingly greater participation; many infant motor skills are preceded by periods in which the baby sits, stands, or walks with adult assistance. Similarly, toddlers accomplish many tasks with the guided assistance of adults. Toddlers' one- or two-word sentences, for example, are often extended by adults into a more complete format, which models as well as provides the structure for more elaborate dialog. Preschoolers also learn many tasks through guided assistance, which, as at earlier and later ages, is adjusted to the child's skill level and gradually withdrawn as the child masters the task. The teacher who tells a child who is struggling to fit a puzzle piece into the frame, "see what happens if you turn the piece around," is working within the zone of proximal development.

Zone of proximal development (ZPD)—In Vygotsky's theory, this zone represents tasks a child cannot yet do by herself but which she can accomplish with the support of an older child or adult.

Vygotsky's ideas have acquired new relevance in early childhood education. The focus on finding the appropriate zone of proximal development for each child has validated the long-held concern with individualization in early childhood programs. Vygotsky's theory also suggests that, in addition to providing a stimulating environment in which young children are active explorers and participants, early educators need to promote discovery by modeling, explaining, and providing suggestions to suit each child's zone of proximal development (Berk, 1994; Gallimore & Tharp, 1990; Seifert, 1993; Wertsch, 1985).

APPLICATION OF THEORIES IN EARLY CHILDHOOD EDUCATION

The work of human development theorists is important to early childhood education if their concepts are translated into practice and methods. In our field, this has happened over the years as a number of **early childhood education models,** founded on a particular theoretical view, were developed. Such models represent a coherent approach to working with young children, including a philosophical and theoretical base, goals, curriculum design, methods, and evaluation procedures. There was a great proliferation of early childhood models in the 1960s and 1970s when educators and researchers were encouraged to develop alternative approaches for Head Start programs. Most models were designed to examine different ways of helping children at risk for later academic failure improve school performance. But models have implications for all children as well (Evans, 1982).

Early childhood education models—Approaches to early childhood education, based on specific theoretical foundations, for instance, the behavioral, Piagetian, or Montessori view.

A number of human development theories have been applied to early childhood education through specific models.

We should not, however, assume that all early childhood programs pursue a carefully prescribed theoretical view. In fact, the majority of programs and teachers of young children probably do not follow a stated philosophical foundation and preference, or they may adhere only to a vaguely recognized theory. An open mind and a practical approach to teaching borne out of sensitive observation and interaction with children are, undoubtedly, equally important.

> Often our theories of growth and development, learning and instruction, or optimal teaching application are hidden and not consciously recognized as theories in the usual sense. Good teachers, like all effective professionals, have sets of guiding principles and outcome expectations that may certainly be considered as theories, at least in a general sense. (Hooper, 1987, p. 303)

It is helpful, however, to examine how some specific models have taken the views of a particular theorist (or theorists) and transformed these into program application. We will examine only five models here, although many alternative approaches exist. These five were selected to illustrate how particular views of child development can be implemented in practice. Included will be a brief overview of Montessori programs as they exist today; the Bank Street approach, which is in part based on the psychosocial view of Erikson; the High/Scope cognitively oriented curriculum, based on Piaget's principles; the Reggio Emilia approach, grounded in part of the theories of Piaget and Vygotsky; and the Bereiter-Engelmann model, founded on behavioral theory.

KEY QUESTION #3

What was your earliest school experience? How does it compare to the type of programs you see for young children today?

Montessori Programs

Today there is great variation among Montessori programs. The traditional Montessori environment and materials include some unique features; the roles of the teacher and the children's activities differ from those in other types of early childhood programs.

Maria Montessori's ideas and methods gradually found a receptive audience in the United States, where Montessori programs have flourished. Although Montessori is not considered a human development theorist, her program, nonetheless, was based on some carefully considered ideas about how young children grow. Today, a wide range of Montessori programs can be found. Some adhere quite rigidly to the original techniques, whereas others follow an approach that has been adapted to better fit the current social context (Chattin-McNichols, 1992). It is interesting to note that although Montessori devised her program to meet the needs of impoverished children and to help them learn important life skills, Montessori programs today are, for the most part, attended by children from more affluent homes.

The Environment. If you visit a traditional Montessori classroom, you will soon observe some of the prominent features of such a program, some similar to other types of early childhood settings, some unique to Montessori. You will quickly notice the sense of order inherent in the room. Child-sized equipment and materials are clearly organized on shelves that are easily accessible to the children. There are distinct areas, each containing materials unique to promoting the tasks to be mastered in that area. The environment is also set up to be aesthetically pleasing, with plants, flowers, and attractive furnishings and materials. The logic, order, and beauty are all integral to the Montessori philosophy.

The Children. You will also note children of different ages involved in individual activities, because the essence of a Montessori program is its individualized nature. Children initiate activities and are free to engage in whichever projects they choose, defining a work space for their selected activity on a mat on the floor or a tabletop. Children are self-directed, working independently or, at times, by twos. Younger children may be learning how to participate in specific activities by observing and imitating their older classmates. The Montessori program is designed as a three-year sequence for children ages three to six.

KEY QUESTION #4

If one is available, observe a Montessori school in your community. How does it differ from other early childhood programs you have seen? How is it similar? What elements of Maria Montessori's original program do you see?

The Teachers. There is little overt adult control. The teacher's involvement is unobtrusive and quiet. She may be observing from a distance or demonstrating to a child how to use a new material. The teacher does not reinforce or praise children for their work since the activities are intended to be self-rewarding, thus, intrinsically motivating. Montessori teachers learn about the methods and curriculum through an intensive course of study at the graduate level.

The Materials. As you look more closely at the materials, you will see that they have some special characteristics. Montessori materials are **didactic,** each designed to teach a specific lesson. In addition, they are **self-correcting** so the child gets immediate feedback from the material after correctly (or incorrectly) completing a task. Materials are graduated from the simple to the more complex; therefore, children are challenged by progressively more difficult concepts. The materials are carefully and attractively constructed, usually made of natural materials such as varnished wood.

Didactic—A term often applied to teaching materials, indicating a built-in intent to provide specific instruction.

Self-correcting—Learning materials such as puzzles that give the child immediate feedback on success when the task is completed.

Daily living—Montessori classroom area that focuses on practical tasks involved in self- and environment-care.

The Curriculum. Different materials fit into each of the three distinct areas of the curriculum. When children first enter a Montessori program, they are introduced to the **daily living** component, in which practical activities are emphasized. Such activities focus on self-help

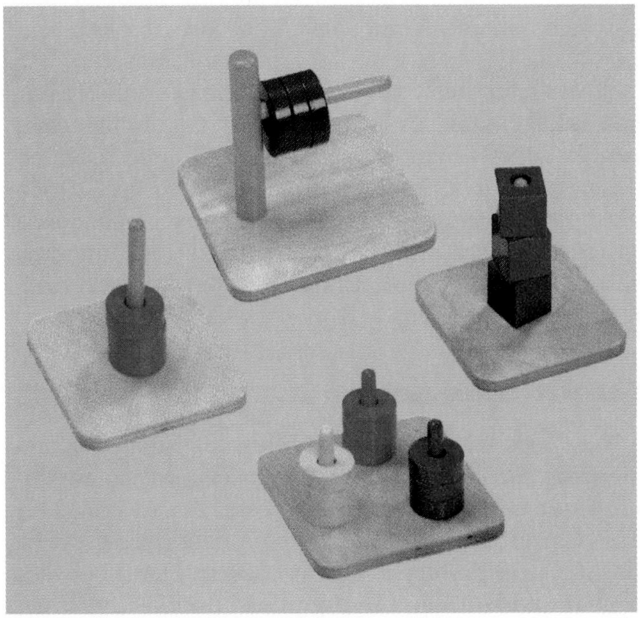

Montessori programs use special equipment and arrange the classroom into centers that are somewhat different from conventional early childhood areas. How does this equipment for toddler infilare exercises differ from that of a more traditional early childhood program?

and environmental care skills such as buttoning, brushing hair, watering plants, washing windows, and sweeping.

Sensorial—Montessori classroom area in which materials help children develop, organize, broaden, and refine sensory perceptions of sight, sound, touch, smell, and taste.

The second set of activities and materials are **sensorial,** helping children develop, organize, broaden, and refine sensory perceptions of sight, sound, touch, smell, and taste. To foster visual discrimination, for instance, children use the Pink Tower, 10 cubes increasing in regular increments of 1 centimeter, stacked from largest to smallest. A more complex visual discrimination task is involved with the set of Color Tablets, which require the child to arrange hues of one color from the darkest to the lightest; an even more advanced task might require the child to find the second darkest hue of each of the seven graded colors when all of the tablets are placed out at random.

Conceptual—Montessori classroom area that focuses on academic materials related to math, reading, and writing.

The third aspect of the program involves **conceptual** or academic materials. The practical and sensorial skills learned in the first two areas have laid the groundwork on which writing, reading, and mathematics are built. Conceptual learning activities are concrete and actively involve the child in multisensory ways. Thus, children use their fingers to trace letters cut out of sandpaper, trace letters in cornmeal, or use the Movable Alphabet to manipulate letters to form words. Many of the math materials are based on a decimal system, for instance, the Golden Beads, which come singly or in units of 10, 100, and 1,000. Other activities promote cultural understanding, including maps and animal and plant pictures to identify and classify.

You may notice that some traditional early childhood activities are absent in the Montessori school. Because Montessori programs are reality based rather than promoting fantasy, you are not likely to find a dramatic play area, a creative art corner, or other activities that invite children to freely use their imagination. You may also note a restriction on how children may use materials. As David Elkind (1983) points out, once children have mastered the use of a particular material in the established manner, they should be free to act on the material and use it freely, in a more experimental way; however, the Montessori method allows materials to be used only in the prescribed procedure. You may also note less emphasis on encouraging language learning.

Montessori schools today vary considerably. Many, in fact, are a blend of the Montessori method and elements of traditional early childhood programs. Relatively little research has evaluated the effectiveness of Montessori programs. Some findings indicate that Montessori children may show greater task persistence and independence, but they appear to score lower on tests of creativity and language development (Chatin-McNichols, 1981; Elkind, 1983; Gettman, 1987; Lillard, 1973; Lindauer, 1993; Simons & Simons, 1986).

The Bank Street Approach

Developmental interactionist model—Foundation of the Bank Street approach, concerned with the interaction among various aspects of each child's development as well as between child and environment.

Since the 1920s, New York's Bank Street College of Education has been one of the leading forces in early childhood education in this country. Its **developmental interactionist model** denotes not only that this program is concerned with all aspects of children's development, but also that it places emphasis on interactions, both between child and environment and between the cognitive and affective areas of the child's development. In other words, children's development in the cognitive and affective domain is not seen as a separate or parallel function but rather as truly an interactive one.

The developmental interactionist approach of Bank Street College is an example of open education, with a strong emphasis on all aspects of children's development.

From such a perspective, this model builds on the works of a variety of theorists, including cognitive theorists such as Piaget, and those who are concerned with the development of **ego strength,** the ability to deal effectively with the environment, such as Erikson. Thus, underlying the program's philosophy is a strong commitment to fostering both intellectual and social-emotional development. Equally important to the acquisition of cognitive skills is the development of self-esteem, identity, competence, impulse control, autonomy, and relationships with other people.

Ego strength—Ability to deal effectively with the environment.

> The school . . . promotes the integration of functions rather than, as is more often the case, the compartmentalization of functions. . . . [It] supports the integration of thought and feeling, thought and action, the subjective and the objective, self-feeling and empathy with others, original and conventional forms of communication, spontaneous and ritualized forms of response. It is part of the basic goal and value system of the school to stimulate individuality and vigorous, creative response. (Shapiro & Biber, 1972, pp. 61-62)

If you were to observe a classroom in which the teachers adhere to the Bank Street philosophy, you would see a program that appears, in most respects, quite similar to a variety of high-quality early childhood programs. The Bank Street approach is considered synonymous with **open education,** a term encompassing programs that operate on the premise that children, provided a well-conceived environment, are capable of selecting and learning from appropriate activities. The program does not aim to teach children a lot of new concepts, but rather to help them understand what they already know in more depth. Children's own experiences are thus the base of the Bank Street program. Because children come to school with a variety of previous experiences, however, the curriculum must remain open and flexible so each child can build on and expand according to her or his own unique conceptual level.

Open education—A program that operates on the assumption that children, provided a well-conceived environment, are capable of selecting and learning from appropriate activities.

The Environment. The classroom is arranged into conventional interest areas such as music, art, reading, science, and dramatic play. The purpose of each area is clearly defined by the materials it contains. Many of those materials are handmade, both by teachers and children. Teacher materials are encouraged because they are designed to meet unique and specific needs of the children in the class. Child-made materials may include books that the children have made as part of the reading center or children's collections that are used as tools for counting in the math center.

The Curriculum. Because this approach is centered on the idea that the child's development must be viewed as integrated, it also specifies that the curriculum and functioning of the classroom be integrated. To promote learning, curriculum is based on a unifying theme, which serves to help children focus on specific concepts and provides a sense of integration. Children's earliest experiences in the Bank Street classroom are designed to help them understand and master their school environment by participating in activities and chores that contribute to its

The environment in the Bank Street programs is organized into conventional interest areas. Children learn by interacting within this environment, broadening their previous experiences.

functioning. Later, learning is extended beyond the classroom to the community to expand the children's understanding of meaningful elements that affect their lives.

The Teachers. The Bank Street approach relies heavily on the abilities of competent teachers. They must have a keen understanding of children's development, of each child's individuality, and of how best to structure an environment that will encourage each child to fulfill his or her potential. Teachers' role both in teaching and guidance is to recognize nuances in the children through their sensitivity and to make changes as appropriate. They recognize the importance of helping the children develop a strong sense of self, to exercise their growing autonomy, to make an impact on and experience mastery over the environment, to make choices, to develop a joy in learning, and to feel enough confidence to take risks and handle contradictions.

In creating a classroom atmosphere that draws on teachers' understanding of the children, teachers match the types and variety of materials and experiences they provide to children's changing needs. They also understand young children's immature control over their impulses and provide rules that protect and build on positive motivation rather than on arbitrary, authoritarian control. Because each child will bring to school his or her personal experience of interactions with adults, the teachers must build on that experience to develop a meaningful relationship with each youngster (Biber, 1984; Shapiro & Biber, 1972; Zimiles, 1993).

The cognitively oriented curriculum, based on the theory of Piaget, revolves around activities that help children learn specific cognitive concepts.

The Cognitively Oriented Curriculum

A number of programs based on the theoretical precepts of Jean Piaget have evolved over the last several decades. One of those, the cognitively oriented curriculum, was developed by the High/Scope Foundation of Ypsilanti, Michigan, under the leadership of David Weikart. This approach was initially designed in the early 1960s as a program for children from impoverished backgrounds, but has since been adopted more widely, partly through the publication of its carefully outlined curriculum manual, *Young Children in Action* (Hohmann, Banet, & Weikart, 1995). In line with Piagetian theory, the cognitively oriented model is based on the premise that children are active learners who construct their own knowledge from meaningful experiences. If you were to visit a cognitively oriented class, you would observe this philosophy in the environment, schedule, activities, and the children's and teacher's behavior.

The Environment. The environment is designed to be stimulating but orderly, where children can independently choose from a wide variety of interesting materials. The classroom is divided into clearly defined work areas, each with a specific set of materials appropriate to that area. A cognitively oriented classroom contains at least a housekeeping, block, art, quiet, and large-group area, although there might also be construction, music and movement, sand and water, and animal and plant work areas as well. Accessible, uncluttered storage spaces in each work area are clearly labeled with silhouettes or pictures, facilitating clean-up and promoting a sense of order.

The Schedule. The daily schedule is integral to the philosophy of the cognitively oriented program. Consistency helps children gain gradual understanding of time. The day is begun with a **planning time,** when children decide what activities they would like to participate in during the ensuing work time. A teacher helps each child individually think through what he or she plans to do, and then records the child's plans. A large block of time is then set aside for **work time,** during which children engage in self-selected activities, supported and assisted by the teachers.

After work time comes **recall time,** usually carried out in small groups, where children review their work-time activities. This **plan-do-review cycle** is the heart of the cognitively oriented curriculum, helping children make deliberate, systematic choices with the help of the teacher. Additional daily periods include clean-up, considered a learning opportunity; a small-group time, which typically includes a teacher-planned activity that reinforces a cognitive concept; large-group time for stories, music, games, and other whole-group activities; outside time; and meals and nap, as appropriate to the length of the program day.

The Curriculum. Throughout the day, teachers focus on extending the cognitively oriented curriculum's **key experiences,** a set of eight concepts based on the characteristics and learning capabilities of preoperational children, as discussed by Piaget. (We will consider some of these concepts in more detail in Chapter 11, when we discuss cognitive development and the early childhood curriculum.) The key experiences give the teachers a framework within which to observe each child's individual performance as well as support and extend children's

Planning time—In the cognitively oriented curriculum, the time set aside during which children decide what activities they would like to participate in during the ensuing work time.

Work time—In the cognitively oriented curriculum, the large block of time during which children engage in self-selected activities.

Recall time—In the cognitively oriented curriculum, the time when children review their work-time activities.

Plan-do-review cycle—The heart of the cognitively oriented curriculum through which children are encouraged to make deliberate, systematic choices with the help of teachers by planning ahead of time, carrying out, then recalling each day's activities.

Key experiences—In the cognitively oriented curriculum, the eight cognitive concepts on which activities are built.

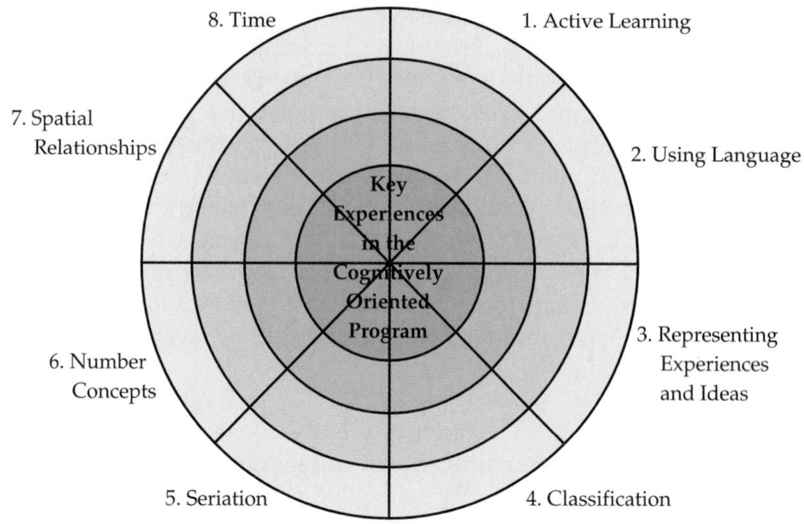

self-initiated activities. Following is a brief description of these eight concepts.

1. Active learning takes place when activities are initiated and carried out by children themselves. It involves learning through all the senses, manipulating and combining materials as a way of discovering their relationships, self-selecting activities and materials, and learning to use equipment and tools.
2. Using language is strongly stressed and encouraged through talking with others about meaningful experiences, describing, expressing feelings, having language written down by a teacher, and playing with language.
3. Representing experiences and ideas—according to Piaget, the hallmark of the preoperational period—allows children to represent the world in nonverbal ways. Key experiences include such activities as recognizing objects through the senses, imitating actions and sounds, role playing, and drawing or painting.
4. **Classification** begins during the preoperational period as children note similarities and differences among objects. Children are encouraged to investigate and describe the attributes of things, sort and match objects, use objects in different ways, talk about characteristics that some things do *not* have, and distinguish between "some" and "all."
5. **Seriation,** the ability to arrange objects along some dimension, is promoted by having children make comparisons, arranging objects in order, and matching.
6. **Number concepts** are the basis for mathematical understanding and are built on many concrete experiences. To promote this concept, experiences are planned to encourage children to compare, count, and engage in one-to-one correspondence.
7. **Spatial relationships** are encouraged through assembling and taking things apart, rearranging and reshaping objects, observing and describing things from different perspectives, working with

Classification—The ability to sort and group objects by some common attribute or property; for instance, color or size.

Seriation—A relationship among objects in which they are placed in a logical order, such as from longest to shortest.

Number concepts—One of the cognitive concepts young children begin to acquire, involving an understanding of quantity.

Spatial relationship—The relative positions to each other of objects and people in space.

shapes, experiencing and representing the child's own body, locating objects in the environment, and experiencing and describing relative positions and distances.

8. Time is a gradually acquired concept involving both understanding of time units and sequencing of events in time. Experiences that help children learn such concepts include signals for stopping and starting actions, experiencing and describing different rates of speed and time intervals, observing seasonal changes, discussing future events, planning, representing past events, and describing the order of events (Hofmann et al., 1995).

The cognitively oriented curriculum provides one illustration of how Piaget's theory has been put into practice. Central is the idea that children are active learners who develop appropriate concepts through interaction with the environment. Through a carefully prepared environment and the guidance of knowledgeable teachers, children attain a deeper understanding of the rules that govern the physical and social world. (Hohmann et al., 1995; Weikart & Schweinhart, 1993).

The Reggio Emilia Approach

Over the past few years, increasing attention has been paid by early childhood educators from around the world to the programs established in Reggio Emilia, in northern Italy. The publicly supported early childhood programs of this region, under the guidance and vision of Loris Malaguzzi, have developed an extraordinary curriculum, based on many theoretical foundations, Piaget's and Vygotsky's included.

The programs of Reggio Emilia in Italy are carefully designed to foster interactions, exploration, and problem solving; much of the curriculum revolves around projects in which children and teachers thoroughly explore a particular concept or topic in myriad ways, over an extended period of time.

The Environment. The physical space in Reggio Emilia is used to promote an inviting, aesthetically pleasing, comfortable environment in which both human relationships and learning are central. The use of space is designed to encourage communication and nurture relationships. Arrangements allow for places in which a child can work with a few children, a larger group of children, a teacher, or alone. Equipment, materials, and activities are arranged to encourage exploration, discovery, and problem solving as well as to offer many choices.

A distinctive feature of each Reggio Emilia school is an atelier, a special studio or workshop in which children and teachers have access to a wide variety of resource materials to depict their experiences. The atelier is used to document the children's work; transcripts of their discussions, photographs of their activities, and representations of their projects are carefully arranged to document the process of learning in relation to various projects. These displays provide deeper insights to children, as they view and review their work and the work of peers, and to teachers and parents, as they consider the process of learning of the children through these projects.

The Curriculum. Projects, in fact, are the central concept around which Reggio Emilia's curriculum revolves. The project approach allows children, usually in small groups, to explore a concept or topic in depth. Projects can be short- or long-term, often lasting well over a month. Because there is no set schedule in Reggio Emilia's schools,

WHO'S WHO IN ECE?

Who?	**Jean-Jacques Rousseau**
When?	Born: June 28, 1712
	Died: July 2, 1778
Where?	Born: Geneva, Switzerland
	Died: near Paris, France
What?	Highlighted the importance of childhood. Saw the child as a "noble savage", pure, in tune with nature. This philosophy was introduced in his novel, *Emile.*
	His ideas strongly influenced Pestalozzi, Froebel, Piaget, Skinner, Montessori, and others
What was he like?	Described as a brilliant yet self-centered, undisciplined, neurotic.
	Profoundly affected by the death of his mother soon after his birth. Raised until age 10 by his father (a watchmaker and a dance teacher), then apprenticed at age 13 to an engraver. In adulthood, abandoned his own 5 children to orphanages.
Where can I read more?	Read more information on pages 105–107.

"Give your pupil no kind of verbal instruction; he should receive none but from experience."

Who?	**Johann Pestalozzi**
When?	Born: January 12, 1746
	Died: February 17, 1827
Where?	Born: Zurich, Switzerland
	Died: Brugg, Switzerland
What?	Set the model for what a teacher of young children should be. Much admired for his teaching methods and his concern for poor children. Espoused the need for active learning and education for the whole child. Influenced many contemporaries, especially Froebel, and later educators, even to today.
What was he like?	Considered to be kind, caring, highly sensitive, charismatic, arousing devotion from others.
	A sickly and awkward child, others made fun of him. He did not get along with his peers or his teachers. From an early age, he believed that teaching should be more kind and humane, a belief that was affirmed when he read Rousseau's *Emile.*
Where can I read more?	Read more information on page 107.

"The first development of thought in the child is very much disturbed by a wordy system of teaching."

Who? **Friedrich Froebel**

When? Born: April 21, 1782

Died: June 21, 1852

Where? Born: Oberweissbach, Germany

Died: near Marienthal, Germany

What? Created kindergarten, literally "garden for children," where play was promoted as the way children learn. Developed early childhood materials, including blocks; materials and activities called "gifts for play".

Twice visited Pestalozzi's schools; had great influence on the early American Kindergarten movement.

"Play is the highest phase of child development."

What was he like? Described as a dreamy and restless child; an idealist as a man, hard working, dedicated, deeply religious.

An unhappy childhood, caused by a distant father and uncaring step-mother, led to his resolve to devote his life to making children happy. A bright spot was working in the garden with his father, reflected as a central feature of the kindergarten.

Where can I read more? Read more information on pages 107–108.

Who? **Maria Montessori**

When? Born: August 31, 1870

Died: May 6, 1952

Where? Born: Chiaravalle, Italy

Died: Noordwijk-on-Sea, Holland

What? Developed the Casa dei Bambini, Children's House, for slum children in Rome; developed comprehensive program, including theoretical formulation, materials, curriculum, and child-sized furnishings.

Influenced by Rousseau, Pestalozzi, Froebel; has had lasting impact through world-wide Montessori schools

"The greatest crime that society is committing is . . . wasting money it should spend for its children."

What was she like? Strong-willed, persistent, ambitious; first woman doctor in Italy; had a mesmerizing personality.

Even as a child, she had a strong sense of the dignity of every person. A teacher commented disparagingly about the expression in her eyes; from that day on she never looked this teacher in the eyes. One of her most important lessons is that every human being, even the smallest child, must be treated with respect.

Where can I read more? Read more information on pages 108–109 and 118–120.

continued

WHO'S WHO IN ECE?—continued

Who? **Erik H. Erikson**

When? Born: June 15, 1902

Died: May 12, 1994

Where? Born: Frankfurt, Germany

Died: Harwich, Massachusetts

What? **PSYCHOSOCIAL THEORY**

Identifies needs of children at different age/stages, beginning with a need for trust for infants, autonomy for toddlers, initiative for preschoolers, and industry for school-aged children; highlights the importance of social interactions in development.

Application: Bank Street Model.

"It is human to have a long childhood; it is civilized to have an even longer childhood."

What was he like? Described as thoughtful, energetic, magnetic; a scholarly thinker and prolific writer.

At 18 wandered through Europe as an artist; stumbled on a job as a teacher in a progressive school in Vienna run by Anna Freud. This proved to be the turning point, his introduction to Freud's work and his life-long involvement with psychoanalytic theory. Later his writings were likened to "works of art," paintings of word pictures with intricate detail and attention.

Where can I read more? Read more information on pages 109–111.

Who? **Jean Piaget**

When? Born: August 9, 1896

Died: September 17, 1980

Where? Born: Neuchatel, Switzerland

Died: Geneva, Switzerland

What? **COGNITIVE DEVELOPMENTAL THEORY**

Intelligence is adaptation to the environment. Thinking is qualitatively different at each stage: infants and toddlers learn through movement and the senses; preschoolers use symbols to organize ideas; school-agers acquire logical structures of thought.

Application: High/Scope, Reggio Emilia, Bank Street.

"We should not allow children a completely free rein on the one hand, nor channel them too narrowly on the other hand."

What was he like? Precocious, with his first publication at 10, and Ph.D. by 22; constantly searching for answers; always ingenious and inventive in his approach.

Perhaps because his mother was in poor mental health, he developed an interest in psychoanalysis. This soon turned into his lifelong fascination with normal development, especially in the thinking of children. Much of his theory was developed by careful observation of his own three children.

Where can I read more? Read more information on pages 111–114.

"Teaching is the expediting of learning: A person who is taught learns more quickly than one who is not."

Who? **B(urrhus) F(rederick) Skinner**

When? Born: March 20, 1904
Died: August 18, 1990

Where? Born: Susquehanna, Pennsylvania
Died: Cambridge, Massachusetts

What? **BEHAVIORISM**

Environment is important in shaping all aspects of behavior. Consistent positive consequences (positive reinforcement) ensure that behavior will be repeated; behavior modification is application of behaviorism.

Application: Bereiter-Engelmann program

What was he like? Ambitious, goal-driven, persistent; seen as the "Darth Vader" of psychology by some, as a brilliant innovator by others.

"Fred" Skinner experienced a calm and nurturing childhood. Perhaps his later theory was shaped by childhood experiences, since his Grandmother Burrhus reinforced good behavior with pie, candy, and letting him win at dominoes.

Where can I read more? Read more information on pages 114–115.

"The maturation of a child's higher mental functions occurs . . . through the adult's assistance and participation."

Who? **Lev Vygotsky**

When? Born: November 5, 1896
Died: June 11, 1934

Where? Born: Orsha, Russia
Died: Moscow, Russia

What? **SOCIOHISTORIC THEORY**

Believed social and historic forces shape intellectual ability: we are the product of our times. Thus, his cognitive theory reflects the Marxist-Leninist philosophy of Russia during his lifetime. Language is a primary tool for conveying society's values.

Application: Reggio Emilia

What was he like? An intense yet very social person with the capacity to inspire others; deeply interested in a variety of fields and topics, many of which he mastered.

His childhood friends called him "little professor" because of his academic pursuits; at age 15 he organized stimulating intellectual discussions for his peers. His ability to structure the environment so others could learn contributed to formulation of his ideas about the zone of proximal development.

Where can I read more? Read more information on pages 115–117.

"Who's Who in ECE?" was compiled with the assistance of Melissa Burnham.

children can work at a leisurely pace because they are under no time constraints in carrying out their projects. Often the representations of learning in projects are expressed in artwork; but, as Forman (1993) points out, children move from learning to draw, to drawing to learn. Art is a vehicle through which children explore the properties of the concept or topic under study.

The subject or theme of projects can emerge from questions asked by children, ideas proposed by children or teachers, or everyday experiences. Thus, there is no preplanned curriculum beyond the general goals set by the teachers. Projects can revolve around most any topic, ranging from shadows, reflections, caves, and the city when it rains, to designing and building an amusement park for small birds.

Forman cites an example of a project, in which children studied a pervasive feature of their community environment during spring—poppy fields. Children begin by drawing the subject, to start thinking about what poppies are like. Teachers and children communicate: they ask questions, examine each others' work, and consider the various aspects of life in a poppy field. After several days of discussing, drawing, and considering questions, such activity is followed by a trip to a poppy field. They have been immersed in poppies for several days now, and are ready to observe, compare, and ponder some of the questions they have asked. The earlier activity has prepared the children to learn about poppies in greater depth now. When they return to the classrooms and again draw poppies, their creations are much more accurate and dynamic. They are, after all, based on careful redefinition of the subject, or assimilation of new information. Immersion in a topic and a time frame for each project set by the interests of the children, not by the adults, allows for much greater depth of learning.

The Teachers. Education, according to Malaguzzi (1993), must be centered on its three important participants—children, teachers, and families. All three must have a sense of well-being if the educational program is to be effective. Teachers in Reggio Emilia schools work in pairs, as co-teachers, which stay with a group of children for three years, from infancy to age three or from three to six. The teachers' role is to be a resource for and, in effect, learning partners with the children. Teachers have the support of a team of pedagogical coordinators and a visual arts teacher. Considerable communication and coordination facilitate the cooperative atmosphere of Reggio Emilia programs. The programs include time for weekly staff meetings and provide ongoing staff development, both of which lead to strong commitment, skill, and a sense of professionalism (Bredekamp, 1993; Forman, 1993; Gandini, 1993; Malaguzzi, 1993).

The Bereiter-Engelmann Model

The Bereiter-Engelmann model, which is based on behavioral theory, uses a direct instruction approach in which the teacher presents carefully planned lessons in three academic areas.

During the height of Head Start program development, several models based on behavioral theory evolved. One was developed by Carl Bereiter and Siegfried Engelmann in the 1960s. Like many of the models developed during that era, it was designed primarily to help children from poverty backgrounds gain some successful experiences that would diminish the likelihood of failure once they started elementary

A Closer Look

Emergent Curriculum

One of the main features of the Reggio Emilia program of Italy is its emergent curriculum. The notion of emergent curriculum is not new, having been promoted for many decades in the United States and elsewhere. In the context of Reggio Emilia, however, the curricular projects that emerge from the children's interests and activities have provided a new emphasis to this approach to curriculum development.

The themes of the emergent curriculum differ from the more traditional thematic approach in which teachers decide what topics should serve as the focus of a given time period, for instance, a week. Emergent curriculum themes literally *emerge* out of the interests of the children in a fluid and flexible way; thus, they are determined by children and teachers rather than by teachers alone. They have no predetermined time frame; some themes may last a few days while others may last several weeks. The complexity of the topic, the children's interest, and the new ideas and questions developed as the theme emerges determine how long children will spend exploring it.

Themes are used to organize curriculum in a way that will interest and engage children in meaningful activity. They build on what is familiar to children—the people and objects of their environment—and expand to assimilate new concepts and information (Diffily, 1996; Katz & Chard, 1989). Furthermore, they provide the chance to integrate curriculum content areas in a natural way (Sheerer, Dettore, & Cypher, 1996). A project should include a broad range of concepts, such as math, science, art, writing, and social studies (Diffily, 1996).

It is important that the emergence of the curriculum is done in a way that actively engages the children in the process of planning, integration, and adaptation (Sheerer et al., 1996). Discussion or shared reading often provides a starting point for a new theme by sparking interest in a topic; this is followed by generation of many questions, a possible field trip, research, planning, and implementation. Often a celebration or exhibit of the process and final project put closure to the theme (Diffily, 1996).

A wide range of ideas, springing from the interest of the children, have provided the content for themes in emergent curricula. Many of these have been documented in articles, books, and films. One intriguing topic from one of the Reggio Emilia schools was titled "An Amusement Park for the Birds," as documented in a film by that name. This four-month project sprang from a conversation in which some of the children thought the birds would enjoy an amusement park in the outdoor area of the school. Topics such as building a town (Bayman, 1995), collecting and classifying rocks (Diffily, 1996), bicycles, building construction, newspaper, and even the all-too-familiar neighborhood McDonald's (Helm, 1996) provide the basis for themes that engage and fascinate children and that provide the foundation for a wide range of learning experiences.

school. The Bereiter-Engelmann model is noticeably different from the other programs we have described because it is based on some very different premises, both about how children learn and about how to best meet their needs.

The program was founded on the assumption that because disadvantaged children were already behind their middle-class peers, they needed not just enrichment activities but a program that would accelerate their rate of learning. Such a program could not be designed to meet all of the needs of preschool-aged children. "A short-term preschool program cannot be expected to produce above normal gains in all areas of development at once; a 'well-rounded' program is therefore incompatible with the goals of catching up: selectivity is necessary" (Bereiter & Engelmann, 1966, p. 19). (It is important to note that when Head Start was initiated, it began as a summer program for children about to enter kindergarten.) Thus, the Bereiter-Engelmann program was designed to meet very specific, teacher-determined learning goals rather than to meet the needs of the "whole child."

Direct instruction (also called programmed instruction)—A method of teaching in which the teacher determines exactly what the children should learn, devises a sequence of learning activities to teach specific information, and teaches it directly by controlling the information according to children's responses.

The Curriculum. The center of this highly structured preschool curriculum is daily lessons conveyed through a **direct instruction** approach. The teacher presents carefully planned lessons, drills, and exercises designed to meet very specific goals. In the Bereiter-Engelmann program, these lessons are offered in three academic areas—language, math, and reading. Precise teacher questions, which require specific verbal answers from the children, are presented in a carefully sequenced order.

The teacher's enthusiasm is important in implementing this approach. Each lesson is designed to help the children master specific skills related to program goals, for example, language goals related to the use of plurals, complete sentences, if-then statements, affirmative as well as negative statements, and polar opposites (big/little, up/down). Other goals relate to color recognition and naming, counting to 20, recognition of letters, ability to rhyme, and development of a sight-reading vocabulary. Constant reinforcement, both in the form of praise and food, is used to motivate and encourage the children.

The Environment. In addition, the environment of the Bereiter-Engelmann model is quite different from that of other early childhood programs. The facility is arranged into small classrooms, where direct teaching activities are carried out, and a large room for less structured, large-group activities. A model floor plan suggested by Bereiter and Engelmann (1966) includes three small classrooms—named the Arithmetic Room, the Reading Room, and the Language Room—each furnished with five small chairs facing a chalkboard (and, presumably, the teacher). The most important feature of these small study rooms should be their acoustic properties, ensuring that they filter out any noise that would distract from lessons. These rooms should also be plain, to minimize distraction from the task at hand. A larger "homeroom," furnished with tables, a piano, and a chalkboard, provides a place for snack and music times.

Bereiter and Engelmann (1966) also suggest that there be very few materials available to the children, mainly ones that will reinforce

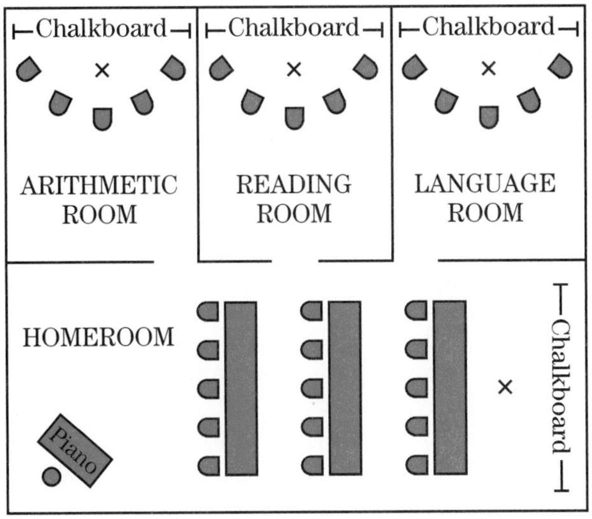

Physical layout of the Bereiter-Engelmann model

concepts taught in the lessons. These might include puzzles, books, tracing materials, paper, and crayons, but not creative materials, because creative development is not a goal of the program. It is assumed that the richness and variety of peer play and games, for example, will be readily available in the child's normal environment.

The Schedule. The daily schedule revolves around three intensive 20-minute lessons in language, math, and reading, each involving five children and one teacher. These small-group periods are interspersed with functional times for eating and toileting and a 15- to 20-minute music period. Music is also a direct instruction activity because it is used to reinforce language. Three teachers work with the children, each teaching one of the three subjects to each of the three groups of children.

The Teachers. Bereiter and Engelmann (1966) suggest that elementary school teachers are more suited to teach in this model than are teachers trained to work with young children. The training of early childhood educators

> has provided them with a deeply ingrained bias against 'forcing' the child in any way; the intensive preschool is premised on 'forcing' the child. Their conception of child development and the emergence of skills is usually diametrically opposed to the viewpoint on which the intensive preschool rests. (p. 69)

Evaluations. Because the Bereiter-Engelmann program operates quite differently from the other programs we have discussed, a few words about how this program fares in research evaluations might be helpful in considering its merits. The Bereiter-Engelmann program was included in a number of comparative studies that sought to examine the impact of this approach. Initial evaluation showed that children had significantly improved IQ and achievement test scores, more so than the other groups studied; however, those gains declined quickly over the next few years, as they did for the children who had been involved in other programs as well.

The levels of curiosity and inventiveness of the children in the Bereiter-Engelmann model seemed lower than those of youngsters who participated in other types of compensatory programs (Miller & Dyer, 1975; Miller & Bizzell, 1983). In part, this may be because the high level of reinforcement, according to research, tends to decrease the intrinsic interest children may have in learning (Lepper, Greene, & Nisbett, 1973). In other words, once the external motivators for learning were removed, the process of learning may have ceased to hold the children's interests.

More recent evaluation of adolescents who had participated in the Bereiter-Engelmann program as preschoolers showed some unexpected outcomes. The youths who had been in a direct instruction program appeared to have higher rates of juvenile delinquency than youths involved in programs where the major teaching method involved self-selection (Schweinhart, Weikart, & Larner, 1986a). The authors of this study speculated in a subsequent publication (Schweinhart, Weikart, & Larner, 1986b) that when young children have control over the activities they participate in, they may well develop a greater sense of responsibility and initiative. They point out that development of such traits is crucial in early childhood, as described by such theorists as Erik Erikson (see page 147). Proponents of the direct instructional approach, however, have questioned these conclusions and expressed concern over the research procedures used in these studies (Bereiter, 1986; Gersten, 1986). Thus, the theoretical approach that is used to help children acquire cognitive skills may have some far-reaching effects, but their measurement is not an easy task.

We have explored some different theoretical ideas about how young children develop and learn, and we have examined several models based on these theories. You have undoubtedly recognized by this time that early childhood education is not a single, unified field based on an agreed-upon philosophy. Let us now briefly examine what research tells us about the effects of early childhood education and, where applicable, what role some of these theoretical precepts play in shaping that effect.

RESEARCH SUPPORT FOR EARLY CHILDHOOD EDUCATION

KEY QUESTION #5

Visit a Head Start program in your community. Which family services and education experiences provided by this program might contribute to the types of long-range positive effects found by the research?

A question that must be asked is whether early childhood education makes a difference. As we have already indicated in several contexts, much of the research about the effectiveness of early childhood education has come from the evaluation of programs designed for children from impoverished backgrounds. The result of such research is important in gauging the value of compensatory education, but it also provides us with more general information about early childhood education. In addition, it is important to understand the effect of early childhood education on all youngsters, particularly with the large number of young children enrolled in child care programs. We will look at these two topics separately.

Research on early intervention programs such as Head Start has shown that they result in long-term, positive effects and cost benefits.

The Effects of Early Intervention

The 1960s can be portrayed as a period of great optimism on the part of the educators and psychologists who had a hand in the development of Head Start. As expressed by Edward Zigler, one of the leaders in the Head Start movement:

> **Intervention was supposed to impart immediate benefits so that class differences would be eliminated by the time of school entry. Furthermore, many expected that the brief preschool experience would be so potent a counteraction to the deficits in poor children's lives that it could prevent further attenuation in age-appropriate performance and a recurrence of the gap between social classes in later grades (Zigler & Berman, 1973, pp. 895-896).**

Head Start, as we now know, did not live up to that idealistic expectation. Many of the early intervention programs showed some short-term results in improved IQ and achievement scores for the first two years of elementary school (Lee, Brooks-Gunn, Schnur, & Liaw, 1990; Royce, Darlington, & Murray, 1983; Schweinhart & Weikart, 1985). But the relatively brief time that children spend in Head Start just cannot make up for the wide variety of social ills that beset the children of poverty. Broader assessments of compensatory programs, however, have demonstrated that early intervention can have important and lasting effects. In a recent survey of outcome evaluations from a number of early childhood programs for children from low-income families, numerous clear long-term benefits were found (Campbell & Taylor, 1996). These include not only IQ gains but higher test scores and better progress throughout the school years. Children of these programs also were better adjusted, had more positive attitudes, and had a higher sense of self. Parents of these children often improved their educational and vocational status and showed reduced incidents of child abuse and neglect. "Early childhood programs clearly do help overcome the barriers of impoverishment" (Campbell & Taylor, 1996, p. 78).

A most interesting set of results comes from the cognitively oriented curriculum, which has been one of the most thoroughly researched early childhood programs for children from low-income families. Follow-up data through adolescence were collected on youngsters who had been enrolled in the program, giving information on their subsequent experiences and functioning within the larger society. When contrasted with a comparable group that had not attended preschool, the cognitively oriented graduates were significantly more likely to have completed high school, experienced job success and satisfaction, and been self-supporting rather than dependent on welfare. They were also less likely to have been arrested, required special education services, or experienced a teen pregnancy.

Further follow-up at age 27 of those who had participated in the program as preschoolers showed continued positive results (Schweinhart, Barnes, & Weikart, 1993). Results indicate that, compared to the control group, these adults had higher earnings, were more likely to own a home, demonstrated a greater commitment to marriage, were less dependent on social services, and had considerably fewer arrests.

Such long-range results indicate that high-quality early childhood programs can and do make a difference, not just to the individual children involved but to society at large. These researchers have estimated that early childhood intervention is a good tax investment that can save up to seven times the amount spent during the early years by offsetting later welfare, special education, and crime costs (Schweinhart et al., 1993).

Longitudinal research has shown that Head Start has some positive, long-range benefits for children, their families, and society.

Similar, positive long-term results were also found for adolescents who had participated in the Syracuse University Family Development Research Program (FDRP) during their infant and preschool years. Most impressive was the highly significant difference in involvement in the juvenile justice system between these teenagers and a comparable (control) group that had not participated in an early intervention program. Not only had far fewer of the FDRP youngsters been involved in juvenile delinquency, but the severity of the offenses, the number of incidents, and the cost of processing were far lower.

Another finding from this study showed that, particularly for girls, early intervention resulted in better school performance and lower absenteeism during adolescence than was found for the control group. The teachers also rated the FDRP girls, compared to the control-group girls, as higher in self-esteem and self-control (Lally, Mangione, & Honig, 1988). Follow-up studies such as these provide evidence that high-quality early childhood intervention programs can and do make a difference.

The Effects of Early Childhood Programs on Low-Risk Children

Research is showing that high quality child care has an effect on all aspects of children's development.

Over the past several decades, much of the research in early childhood education has focused on children at risk because of poverty, as we just discussed. More recently, however, researchers have begun to examine the effects of early childhood programs, especially child care, on all children. Since such a large proportion of American children spend much of their time in child care settings, it is important to have a clear picture of how child care impacts their development. The findings of many studies have made a clear link between the quality of child care and children's social, emotional, cognitive, and language development. Some longitudinal studies have also shown that the quality of an early childhood program affects children's later functioning in school. Such findings are particularly alarming because, as "A Closer Look" in Chapter 3 discussed, the *Cost, Quality, and Child Outcomes Study* (Helburn et al., 1995) found that the majority of young American children are in mediocre or inferior early childhood settings.

A number of studies have found that the quality of child care, especially when measured in terms of positive interactions between teachers and children, impacts children's social development. Several studies conducted during the 1980s found that children's emerging socialization is clearly affected by quality of child care (Phillips, McCartney, & Scarr, 1987; Clarke-Stewart, 1987). Holloway and Reichhart-Erickson (1988) found that positive teaching style results in children who are more prosocial. In two longitudinal studies, Andersson (1989, 1992), followed children who had been in high quality infant and child care to ages 8 and 13. At both later ages, children were more socially competent.

Children's emotional and behavioral development also are affected by child care quality. Children's overall behavior is more appropriate in classrooms where teachers use positive teaching techniques (Peisner-Feinberg & Burchinal, 1997). Another study found that preschoolers' emotional expression is much more positive (more smiling and laughing) when caregivers are more engaged and supportive in their interactions with the children than in centers where teachers ignore or minimally interact with the youngsters (Hestenes, Kontos, & Bryan, 1993). As you will recall from Chapter 1, the caliber of child-adult interactions is an important indicator of quality in early childhood programs. Yet another aspect of emotional development, anxiety, has been linked to child care quality as well. Children in inappropriate classrooms show more stress behaviors than those in developmentally appropriate settings (Burts et al., 1992; Hyson, Hirsh-Pasek, & Rescorla, 1990).

A number of studies have also linked quality in child care to cognitive and language development. Several studies have found that children enrolled in higher quality centers are clearly better communicators (McCartney, 1984; Peisner-Feinberg & Burchinal, 1997). Another study found that children engage in cognitively more complex play in higher quality programs (Howes, Smith, & Galinsky, 1995). Howes (1988) discovered that children who had been in high quality child care earned higher school skill ratings from their teachers, while Field (1991) found a significant relationship between children's enrollment in a high quality infant program and their later inclusion in a gifted program in elementary school. Conversely, Howes (1990) found that children in poor quality child care from an early age were the least task-oriented and most distractible in kindergarten.

A number of factors contribute to child care quality. Among these is the strictness of a state's child care licensing standards. Vandell & Corasaniti (1990) evaluated a sample of middle-class eight-year-olds in a state with minimal child care standards. They found that children who had been in full-time child care since infancy were rated lower on a variety of measures by both teachers and parents than children who had experienced part-time or no child care. They had poorer peer relations, work habits, emotional health, and academic performance, and were more difficult to discipline. A more recent study followed changes in child care standards in the state of Florida, which in 1992 passed more stringent child care regulations related to child-adult ratio and teacher training (Howes et al., 1995). Careful measures before changes were implemented and then later follow-up found that these changes made considerable difference to the children. Their cognitive development, language, behavior, and social competence all improved after the state's child care standards became more stringent.

It is clear to many early childhood professionals that child care quality has an impact, not only in relation to children's behavior and functioning at the time they are in child care, but potentially for many years later. This is why many professionals urge changes that would improve overall quality of child care. But bringing about such changes will take considerable commitment from many sectors, including parents, child care professionals, employers, and government. It is important that we contribute as positively as possible to the future success of young children. Our research right now tells us that many children are not in high quality child care settings, and that this compromises not only their current development, but also their chances for a successful future.

SUMMARY

1. Early childhood education, although relatively new as a formal system, has antecedents that reach far back in history as ideas about children and how they should be treated were shaped.
2. The writings and work of many individuals through history have contributed to our contemporary ideas about young children and early childhood education.
3. Particularly in this century, a number of theorists have proposed models that help us understand the nature of young children and how best to meet their needs.
   A. Some theorists believe that children's development follows an inborn plan.
   B. Others consider that children's development is affected primarily by external factors.
4. Many theories have been applied to early childhood education through the development of specific program models.
5. Research has proven the effectiveness of early education.

KEY TERMS LIST

absorbent mind
abstract thinking
accommodation
adaptation
assimilation
Autonomy vs. Shame and Doubt
behaviorism
behavior modification
child study movement
classification
cognitive development theory
conceptual
concrete operations period
daily living
developmental interactionist model
didactic

direct (programmed) instruction
disequilibrium
early childhood education models
ego strength
equilibrium
extinction
formal operations period
human development theory
Industry vs. Inferiority
Initiative vs. Guilt
key experiences
kindergarten
logical thinking
number concepts
object permanence
observable behavior
open education
operant conditioning
organization
plan-do-review cycle
planning time
positive reinforcement
preoperational period
prepared environment
programmed instruction
psychosocial theory
punishment
recall time
reinforcement
representation
schemata
self-correcting
sensitive periods
sensorial
sensorimotor period
sensory discrimination
seriation
shaping
social reinforcer
sociohistoric theory
spatial relationship
stage theorist
Trust vs. Mistrust
work time
zone of proximal development (ZPD)

chapter

6

Goals, Objectives, and Evaluation

Working with young children and planning a program for them requires a sense of direction and purpose, expressed in a set of broad goals and more specific objectives. Goals and objectives provide the "road map" for the early childhood program "journey." But not just any map will provide the specific information needed for your program. Goals and objectives should reflect the individual character and uniqueness of your class. One way of identifying that individuality is through systematic evaluation. This chapter, therefore, will cover these two discrete but closely related topics—goals and objectives, and evaluation.

GOALS

A **goal** provides an overall, general overview of what you expect the children to gain from the program. Goals should be based on a sound understanding of children's development and needs, reflecting age-appropriate expectations and practices. Goals are often based on facilitating and encouraging healthy development in the social, emotional, cognitive, and motor domains and acquisition of related skills. Goals also reflect the theoretical rationale on which the program is based, such as those discussed in the previous chapter.

Keep in mind that there is no one way of wording goals and objectives. Figure 6-1 lists a few examples of goals that might be included for a group of young children, and some more specific objectives related to these goals.

OBJECTIVES

An **objective** is a more specific interpretation of a general goal, and it provides a more practical and direct tool for day-to-day program planning.

Goal—An overall, general overview of what children are expected to gain from the program.

Goals should be based on an understanding of children and should reflect the program's underlying theoretical base.

FIGURE 6-1 Sample goals and objectives

Sample Goal 1: The children will increase their fine motor skills, gaining better control in tasks requiring use of the hands.

Sample Objectives in Support of Goal 1:

- The children will thread 1-inch beads on shoelaces.
- The children will use scissors to cut pictures of their choice from magazines.

Sample Goal 2: The children will improve their language skills, acquiring larger vocabularies, longer sentence lengths, and more complex sentence structures.

Sample Objectives in Support of Goal 2:

- The children will use three new words in discussions and dramatic play related to bread baking after the visit to the bakery (for instance, *yeast, rising, kneading*).
- The children will retell the story with the flannel board pieces, reflecting the sequence of the story read earlier by the teacher.

Sample Goal 3: The children will gain greater social skills, forming friendships, engaging in more cooperative play, and developing empathy and concern for the feelings of others.

Sample Objectives in Support of Goal 3:

- The children will participate in the cooperative game version of "musical chairs."
- The children will discuss the emotions displayed in the "feeling pictures."

Sample Goal 4: The children will increase their understanding of themselves, their families, and the community within which they live.

Sample Objectives in Support of Goal 4:

- The children will name two functions of the heart, after examining the model of the heart and hearing Dr. Herbert discuss the heart.
- The children will explain the role of the emergency operator and will demonstrate how to dial 911 in case of an emergency.

Objective—An aim; a specific interpretation of general goals, providing a practical and directive tool for day-to-day program planning.

Objectives should facilitate short-term planning and should be part of written lesson plans.

Goals can be identified at the beginning of the program year to provide direction; objectives are useful for short-term planning and should be an integral part of unit and lesson planning, identified for planned activities (discussed in more detail in the next chapter). Objectives will differ, depending on whether they are developed for the group as a whole or for an individual child. We will examine three types of objectives commonly used in early childhood education.

Developmental Objectives

Developmental objective—Purpose or rationale for an activity that specifies that the activity is intended to promote an aspect of physical, social, emotional, or cognitive development.

Developmental objectives specify which developmental domain will be enhanced by an activity.

The purpose of activities is often to promote specific aspects of physical, cognitive, social, or emotional development, each identified as a **developmental objective.** By specifying which developmental domain will be particularly enhanced by each activity, you can ensure that your program provides a good balance of activities that encompasses all areas.

Experienced teachers often develop a sense of this type of balance in program planning. For a beginning teacher, however, it can be very helpful to identify which area(s) of development will be promoted by each activity. This might be done through abbreviations, for instance, letters that identify the area of development (FM = fine motor; L = language). On completing a lesson plan, the teacher, with a quick review of developmental objectives, can ensure that all areas are adequately covered.

Appropriate objectives for early childhood activities support young children's development. Three-year-olds, for instance, are interested in the everyday activities of their world and in what the important people in their lives do. What do you think this three-year-old might learn from serving herself? What objective might the teacher have had in mind in planning this?

Content Objectives

Content objectives relate to the subject matter to be conveyed by the activity.

Objectives are also identified for the content or subject matter of the curriculum (Essa & Rogers, 1992; Lawton, 1988; Peters, Neisworth, & Yawkey, 1985). A **content objective** relates to what an individual activity is conveying, which, in turn, is tied to a unit's topic or theme. Appropriate topics can be drawn from meaningful aspects of the children's environment to expand their understanding of the world.

Content objective—Purpose or rationale for an activity that specifies that the activity is intended to promote specific subject matter.

Content objectives can be met through a variety of activities, although how they are met will depend on the developmental objectives that have been identified (Essa & Rogers, 1992). For instance, a content objective that "children will identify three body parts" can be met through a variety of activities. These might include a language activity (reading a story on the topic), a motor activity (playing a game of "Hokey-Pokey"), or a perceptual activity (gluing cut-out body-part shapes). Generally, you will plan a variety of activities, with different developmental objectives, to help reinforce a specific content objective.

KEY QUESTION #1

Review a lesson plan that contains specific objectives. Do you see a relationship between the objectives and the planned activities? How do the objectives give direction to the teachers who carry out the activities?

A content objective also gives direction to the teacher carrying out an activity. Assume the lesson plan indicates that you will help the children make fruit salad (Essa & Rogers, 1992). What direction does this activity description give you? What will you discuss with the children? The content objective can provide that direction. Different content objectives specify the focus of the activity. For instance, what might be your focus for the following objectives?

- The children will identify fruits that are red, green, and yellow.
- The children will classify fruits as sweet and sour.
- The children will be able to name five different fruits.
- The children will identify that different people, such as chefs, mothers, fathers, and children can make fruit salad.
- The children will follow safety and hygiene rules when making fruit salad.
- The children will be able to measure equal parts of different fruits to put into the fruit salad.

The objectives will determine the focus and purpose of the activity and will help guide your teaching style and handling of the activity.

Behavioral Objectives

Behavioral objective—Aim or goal, usually set for an individual child, that describes in very specific and observable terms what the child is expected to master.

Behavioral objectives are written in very specific, observable terms and usually apply to an individual child.

Although developmental and content objectives usually apply to planning for the total group, a **behavioral objective** is generally used in planning for an individual child. Behavioral objectives are very specific, based on what is observable. As an example, a behavioral objective for a four-year-old might state, "When shown a row containing four blocks—one red, one blue, one yellow, and one green—Simon will point to the red block, when asked, in three out of four trials." The objective does not tell you how to teach red, only how to measure the objective's acquisition (Hendricks, 1986); therefore, it will be tested after a period of time in which Simon will use red play dough, paint, blocks, and Legos, and the teacher will frequently verbalize and encourage Simon to verbalize the color.

Behavioral objectives, because of their precise nature, are often used in working with children who have special needs. This provides a way of pinpointing an area of deficit (Simon cannot identify colors yet); breaking down behaviors into small and manageable steps (we'll start with the color red); documenting progress (it will be clear when Simon points to the red block three times out of four); and providing accountability (Simon has learned the color red!). When federal or state funding provides services for young children with disabilities or children enrolled in a Head Start program, accountability becomes particularly important, and behavioral objectives can contribute.

Notice that the behavioral objective for Simon uses a verb that describes action. When Simon *points* to the red block, there is no guesswork involved on your part; his pointing is observable. Words such as *label, name, identify, match, sort, classify, or order from largest to smallest* relate to a child's actions that you can observe. On the other hand, words such as *think, enjoy, consider, appreciate,* or *be aware of* describe an internalized process. If, for instance, the objective had stated that Simon will *understand* the color red, you would have no way to measure this because you cannot "see" Simon understanding the concept of redness (Deiner, 1993).

A behavioral objective specifies exactly what is expected of the child; for instance, that he will pick out the blue square correctly in three out of four trials.

Behavioral objectives are useful, particularly in planning for an individual child in an area needing attention. Such objectives have also been criticized, however. Because they specify how a child will behave, they eliminate spontaneity, creativity, and playfulness; they preclude a child's internal motivation to master a topic or skill by spelling out and directing the content of activities; they demand a great deal of work from the teacher because each identified behavior will require developing a list of objectives; and, because they are broken into such small components, it is sometimes difficult to keep in touch with the larger goals for the child (Lawton, 1988).

EVALUATION

Evaluation is closely tied to goals and objectives as a beginning, an ending, and an ongoing process. To set appropriate goals and objectives, we need to know something about our group of children, and **preassessment** can help us learn about them; to find out whether the children have met the goals and objectives, we provide **summative evaluation** at the ends of units; and to know whether planned activities, methods, and topics are accomplishing what we want them to, we engage in ongoing **formative evaluation.**

Evaluation can be carried out in many ways. We will discuss both informal and formal types of assessment and the applicability of different approaches; specifically, we will examine observational techniques, teacher-developed rating scales and checklists, and standardized tests. We will also address the potential for misusing evaluation instruments, including the need for sensitivity and care in using them, and the selection of appropriate measures.

Preassessment—A form of evaluation given before teaching a specific concept or topic to assess how much children know about it and to compare later how much they have learned.

Summative evaluation—An assessment that follows a specific lesson or unit to evaluate whether the children have met the objectives.

Formative evaluation—Ongoing assessment to ensure that planned activities and methods accomplish what the teacher intended.

Observation

One of the most effective informal methods of evaluation is through focused observation. Early childhood teachers use observation as a primary method of gaining insight into the various facets of children's development, at different times and in different contexts (Wortham, 1990). Observation can provide us with detailed information about behavior, can help us understand it, and can provide the basis for predicting behavior (Richarz, 1980). One of the most appealing features of observation is that it is unobtrusive and natural. It does not interfere with the child's ongoing activity and behavior, in contrast with more formal tests that require that the child perform specified tasks in an isolated setting.

Observation is an unobtrusive way of gaining information about children.

KEY QUESTION #2

With a fellow student, spend about 15 minutes observing the same child. Each of you write an anecdotal observation involving this child for the exact same period of time. Now compare your two observations. Do they describe the same behaviors, activities, and interactions? Do they convey the same "picture" of this child? If the two observations differ in a significant way, why is this? Are there some subjective elements in either observation that might contribute to this difference?

Types of Observation. Observation can take a variety of forms. One of the most often used is the **anecdotal record,** a brief description or "word picture" of an event or behavior (Cartwright & Cartwright, 1974). A collection of well-written and accurate anecdotes can provide a very descriptive characterization of a child. Anecdotal records come only from direct observation, are written down promptly and accurately, describe the context of the behavior, are factual rather than interpretive, and can focus either on a typical or unusual aspect of the child's behavior (Bentzen, 1993; Wortham, 1990).

Anecdotal record—A method of observation involving a written "word picture" of an event or behavior.

An anecdotal record provides a "word picture" of an event or behavior.

One of the most effective ways of gaining information about the children in your class is through focused observation.

Running record—A type of observation that provides an account of all of the child's behavior over a period of time.

A running record provides a detailed account of everything that occurred during an extended period of time.

A **running record** is a more detailed account of a child's behavior over a period of time (Wortham, 1990). Whereas the anecdote focuses on a single event, the running record keeps track of everything that happens in a specified time period, whether it is a half hour or several months.

Such a record can be very useful when you are trying to pinpoint the source of a problem. It was most helpful in getting a handle on the disruptions in one class, where three-year-old Erin seemed to always be at the center of aggressive outbursts. A careful running record, kept over a period of three days, helped the teachers see that Erin was responding to rather subtle taunts from two other children.

ABC analysis—An observational technique in which the observer records observations in three columns, identifying *a*ntecedent, *b*ehavior, and *c*onsequence.

One helpful device in keeping a running record is the **ABC analysis,** in which three columns identify the *a*ntecedent, *b*ehavior, and *c*onsequence of incidents (Bijou, Peterson, & Ault, 1968). This helps you focus not only on the child's behavior, but also on what precipitates and what follows it as well.

Time sampling—A quantitative measure or count of how often a specific behavior occurs within a given amount of time.

In the time-sampling method, a given behavior is recorded only at specified intervals of time, such as every half hour.

Time sampling provides a way of measuring the frequency of a behavior over a period of time (Wortham, 1990). Time sampling is a quantitative method of observation, in that you count how often the behavior occurs at uniform time intervals (Genishi, 1982). You may, for instance, want to know just how often the adults in the classroom attend to Tracy, because you suspect he is often overlooked and neglected. Since you don't have time to observe Tracy all day long, you might determine that every half hour you will spend 5 minutes watching Tracy, noting every time a teacher attends to or interacts with him. Over a period of a week, you should have a representative sampling of the attention Tracy receives from adults. You might also decide, for purposes of comparison, to observe Sharon at the same time because Sharon appears to get frequent adult attention.

Event sampling—A method of observation in which the observer records a specific behavior only when it occurs.

Event sampling is used to observe and record only when a specified behavior occurs.

When you want to observe a less frequent behavior, **event sampling** can be used (Genishi, 1982; Wortham, 1990). In this case, you wait until a given behavior occurs and then write a descriptive record of the event. Event sampling can be useful if you have noted that Kareem has periodic crying spells, and you have trouble pinpointing the cause. Thus, each time Kareem engages in this behavior, one of the teachers stands back and records carefully what is happening. The

EXPERIENCES

chapter 6

SHERRY, Child Care Director

Teacher Portfolios

We spend a lot of time discussing evaluation of children, how best to carry these out, what methods to use, how to use the results, and what would be the most meaningful approach. We don't spend as much time considering how to evaluate teachers, however.

Over the past several years, we have been developing a portfolio approach in keeping records on our children. Some children begin at our center as infants and stay until they enter first grade. There is much meaningful information that we need to note and use so that we can provide the best possible experience for these little ones. Because each is a unique individual, their portfolios reflect that uniqueness and individuality. Recently, we have taken a similar approach to assessment of teachers.

Each of our teachers is a unique individual, and each is at a different stage in both professional and personal development. Each has different needs, both personally and professionally. Thus, the teacher portfolios reflect that individuality. They are structured around individual goals that help both the teacher as a professional and the program.

Formally, as the director, I meet with each teacher twice a year. At these meetings we discuss performance evaluations and, as part of that, set goals for the following year. Informally we meet individually every six to eight weeks to discuss how they are progressing toward meeting their goals. My question to them is always. "What do you need from me to help you reach your goals?" Content and decisions of these meetings become part of each teacher's portfolio.

Goals of the staff have varied greatly. One year, one teacher's goal was to learn more about infants' emotional development. Another has been learning about inclusion of infants and toddlers with disabilities in the program. Yet another has made it his goal to learn more about effective strategies for collecting data for the children's portfolios. A variety of methods, from attending workshops, to reading books and articles, to taking classes, are facilitated to help the staff reach their goals.

What else goes into the portfolios besides goals and plans for reaching them? That varies from teacher to teacher. My observations of the teacher's performance and peer observations are also included. Documentation of what is working well—for example, successful curriculum plans, assessments, and class projects—can become a part of the portfolio. We also include some appropriate assessment forms, to examine flexibility and willingness to change, learning style, and personality. Some of our assessments, for instance, come from Jorde-Bloom, Sheerer, and Britz's *Blueprint for Action: Achieving Center-Based Change Through Staff Development* (1991, Gryphon House).

Our aim is to provide the best possible program for the children in our center. To achieve this, we have to have the best possible teachers. Nurturing and helping the teachers reach their potential is a collaborative effort, with individualized portfolios as the vehicle.

experiences

ABC method can be very useful in recording such an event because you are trying to get a sense of its causes and consequences (Wortham, 1990).

Good observations need to be objective but at the same time be adequately descriptive. A collection of observations can then be combined and interpreted to better understand the child.

Characteristics of Good Observations. One of the requirements of good observation is that it be objective. Your role as observer is to be as impartial as possible, to stand back and record what you see rather than what you think the child is feeling or experiencing. Compare the two records in Figure 6-2. What distinguishes the two? The first observation tells you how the observer is interpreting the incident; the second describes what is happening. Can the first observer really know that Letitia does not like Erica? that the teacher is angry? that Letitia made a conscious decision to pick on Erica?

Another characteristic of good observation is that it is adequately descriptive. Language is a powerful tool that allows us to conjure up a picture of an event. Cohen and Stern (1978) provide some helpful suggestions to beginning observers in the use of descriptive vocabulary. The verb run, for instance, has many synonyms that can invoke a clearer image of what is being described. Examples include stampede, whirl, dart, gallop, speed, shoot across, bolt, fly, hippety-hop, or dash. Adding descriptive adverbs, adjectives, and phrases will also enliven an anecdote. Although synonyms can add authenticity and life to your observational anecdote, be sure to use the dictionary frequently to ensure that the word you choose actually means what you intend. Can you find some descriptive words in the second example in Figure 6-2 that make the incident come alive?

Good observations also describe nonverbal cues, some of the nuances of body language as well as voice inflection that can give deeper meaning to an anecdote. Children, like adults, share subtle movements

FIGURE 6-2 Sample observations

Observation #1

Letitia comes into the classroom and immediately decides to pick on Erica, whom she doesn't like. She approaches Erica and, in her usual aggressive way, grabs the doll that Erica is playing with. Letitia doesn't really want the doll, she just wants what Erica has. When the teacher sees what has happened, she gets upset with Letitia and makes her give the doll back to Erica. Because of this, Letitia gets really angry and has one of her nasty tantrums, which makes everyone in the class mad.

Observation #2

Letitia marches into her classroom. She looks around for a few seconds, then ambles to the dramatic play area, where Erica is putting a doll into the cradle. Letitia stops 2 feet in front of the cradle, standing with her legs apart and hands on hips. She watches Erica put a blanket on the doll, then steps right up to it, grabs the doll by an arm, and pulls it roughly out of the cradle. She runs with the doll into the block area and turns around to look back at Erica. As Letitia is running off, Erica yells, "No! I was playing with the doll." Erica looks at Mrs. Wendell, whose eyes move toward the dramatic play area. Erica's shoulders drop and she says in a softer whimper, "Letitia took the doll I was playing with," then starts to cry. As Mrs. Wendell walks toward Letitia, Letitia drops the doll and darts to the art area. Mrs. Wendell catches up with Letitia, holds her by the arm, and urges her back to the block area. She picks up the doll. "Letitia, we need to give this doll back to Erica. She was playing with it." Letitia, her lips pressed together over clenched jaws, pulls away from Mrs. Wendell and throws herself on the floor, kicking her feet and screaming.

When a behavior such as a tantrum or crying spell occurs infrequently, event sampling is a good observational method to utilize. Thus, the teacher observes and carefully notes the behavior only when the tantrum or crying event happens.

of face and body and shadings of voice that describe common feelings and reactions. Izard (1982), for instance, uses common facial nuances in infants and children to measure emotion. Body language is not easy to read, requiring experience and practice to interpret accurately. As you begin developing observational skills, you might double-check with a more experienced teacher to verify your reading of such nonverbal cues. Again, looking at Figure 6-2, do you see some descriptions of such nonverbal signs?

Interpreting Observations. As we have indicated, observational information must be gathered objectively, without inserting personal bias. But there comes the point, once you have gathered a collection of anecdotes, when you can look for patterns (Cohen & Stern, 1978). Interpretations, however, should always be kept clearly separate from observations (Cartwright & Cartwright, 1974). In reviewing observations that span a period of time, you should be able to find clues to children's unique ways of behaving and responding. When a set of observations shows repeatedly that a child reacts aggressively to conflict, or becomes pleasurably involved in messy media, or talks to adults far more than to other children, you can see a characteristic pattern for that child.

When recording observations, it is important to note nonverbal cues such as voice inflection or facial expression. These can be revealing. What does this child's body language and expression tell you?

As you interpret observations, keep a clear focus on norms of development for young children. An understanding of the age range within which specific traits and behaviors generally occur (see Chapter 2) will help you interpret observations. Your familiarity with child development, combined with sensitive observation, provide a powerful tool to understanding the children in your care to help you maximize their development.

But interpretation should be undertaken cautiously. Human behavior is complex, not easily pigeonholed, and there is the danger of overzealous interpretation when a pattern is more in the mind of the observer than representative of the child.

Some Observational Techniques. Finding time to observe can be challenging for the busy teacher. Cartwright and Cartwright (1974) recommend developing a pattern and time frame for carrying out observations. Hymes (1981) further suggests setting a goal, a fixed number of anecdotes to record each day. It is helpful to carry a pencil and pad in your pocket while working with children to facilitate jotting down some quick notes and then to set aside a few minutes at the end of the day to write up the records.

Dated anecdotes can be put on file cards to be kept in a file box with a divider for each child in the class. Another handy storage device is to keep a running record in a loose-leaf notebook with separate pages for each child (Bundy, 1989). A file box or notebook can be kept in a spot that is accessible but ensures confidentiality. Keeping such records can also pinpoint children who are being overlooked when, over a period of time, you find very few or no records on some youngsters (Hymes, 1981).

Early childhood student teachers and, in some programs, teachers may be asked specifically to record observations rather than participate in the class for a period of time. If you are assigned a role as an outside observer rather than as a member of the classroom, the observation will require a somewhat different approach. First, you will have more time to engage in a thorough observation, perhaps to keep a running record. If you are observing in the classroom (rather than from behind a one-way mirror), you must be as unobtrusive as possible so that children's behavior is minimally affected by your presence.

A file box with dividers or a notebook helps organize observations and other information about a child.

Seat yourself where you are less likely to be noticed, avoid eye contact with children, and dress simply (Wortham, 1990). If children come to you to ask what you are doing, as invariably they will, give a simple answer that does not invite further conversation, for instance, "I am writing."

Teacher-Designed Instruments

Other frequently used, informal methods of evaluation include **checklists** and **rating scales** designed by the teacher. Both types of instruments are based on specific learning objectives or developmental indicators (Wortham, 1990). Checklists and rating scales are prepared in conjunction with observing the children, but results are recorded with a simple check mark or numerical evaluation rather than a lengthy verbal description.

Checklist—A method of evaluating children that consists of a list of behaviors, skills, concepts, or attributes that the observer checks off as a child is observed to have mastered the item.

Rating scale—An assessment of specific skills or concepts that are rated on some qualitative dimension of excellence or accomplishment.

The primary difference between these two is that checklists simply note the presence or absence of a skill or concept, whereas rating scales evaluate the level of attainment (Wortham, 1990). The advantage of such instruments is that they are quick and easy to use, flexible, and very specific to the needs of your situation. On the other hand, teacher-designed instruments can be time-consuming to prepare and have to be devised with care and thought to be valid and appropriate.

Checklists. A checklist lists behaviors, skills, concepts, or attributes and is followed by a space for noting their presence or absence. They can be devised for individual children (Figure 6-3) or for the entire class (Figure 6-4). Some checklists include space for recording

Checklists and rating scales are ways of checking whether a child or group of children engage in specific behaviors or skills.

FIGURE 6-3 Checklist of selected gross motor tasks (to be completed four times during the year)

Child: ______________________

Instructions: Mark with an "X" when task has been mastered.

	Date of Observation			
Behavior	**1)** ______	**2)** ______	**3)** ______	**4)** ______
Hops on one foot				
Balances on one foot for 5 seconds				
Walks 2-inch balance beam				
Jumps across 12 inches and lands with both feet				
Throws 10-inch ball 6 feet				
Catches 10-inch ball with both arms				
Pumps on swing				
Pedals tricycle				

KEY QUESTION #3

Design a checklist of 10 items to assess social development of a group of preschoolers. How did you decide on which items to include? What resources did you use to put this checklist together? If possible, observe a group of preschoolers and apply this checklist to several of the children.

FIGURE 6-4 Checklist of selected gross motor tasks for the entire class

Date: ____________

Instructions: Mark with an "X" when task has been mastered.

Name	Hops	Balance 5 sec	2-inch Beam	12-inch Broad Jump	Throw Ball 6 feet	Catch Ball	Pedal Trike	Pump on Swing

multiple observations that can be repeated over a period such as a year (Figure 6-3); others are taken at one point in time (Figure 6-4). If you utilize a list that includes all the children in the class to get a sense of which children have and which have not mastered specific tasks, do not post such a record in the classroom where parents will see it and make comparisons.

Rating Scales. Rating scales provide more qualitative information than checklists because they indicate to what extent the child engages in or has mastered a behavior. As a student, you are judged on a rating scale that usually takes the form of letter grades ranging from A (excellent) to F (unsatisfactory), and your cumulative grade point average (GPA) gives a numerical value to all of the ratings (grades) you have received.

The dimensions of ratings applied to children will depend on what you want to measure. You may, for instance, want to determine the frequency of each child's participation in various types of activities (Figure 6-5). In that case you might graph the children on a continuum that goes from "always" to "never" (Wortham, 1990):

Always — Frequently — Occasionally — Seldom — Never

or (Cartwright & Cartwright, 1974):

Always — Usually — Never

FIGURE 6-5 Rating scale of frequency of participation of the children in various classroom activity areas

Dramatic Play

Instructions: Rate each child's frequency of participation in the dramatic play area.

Name	Frequency of Interaction				
	Always	Frequently	Occasionally	Seldom	Never

Rating scales can also be used to show where a child is in the process of mastering certain tasks. You could, for instance, take the checklist of gross motor skills used in Figure 6-2 and turn it into a rating scale by rating each behavior as follows:

1. Performs task all the time
2. Performs task sometimes
3. Performs task rarely
4. Never performs task

It may be appropriate to add a "not observed" category to differentiate between a child who cannot perform a task and one who chooses not to engage in the specific behavior while the teacher is observing.

Standardized or formal tests are more stringently developed and used, and they must follow specific testing criteria.

Standardized Tests

Whereas observations and teacher-devised instruments are informal methods of gathering information about children, standardized tests are considered formal assessments. Such instruments are developed by professionals and are distributed commercially. Standardized tests are developed, tested, and refined so they have validity and reliability. **Validity** means that tests measure what they purport to measure. **Reliability** means they are stable and consistent; you know that when a child's score changes, it is because the child has changed, not the test (NAEYC, 1988). When standardized tests are administered, specific

Validity—A characteristic of a test that indicates that the test actually measures what it purports to measure.

Reliability—A measure of a test indicating that the test is stable and consistent, to ensure that changes in score are due to the child, not the test.

standards for testing conditions are delineated to provide uniformity. Over the past few years, the use of standardized tests with young children has increased; thus, we will examine the general categories of such tests and a sampling of specific instruments.

Screening tests are a quick way of identifying children who might be at risk, but such tests must be followed up with more thorough assessments.

Screening Tests. Screening tests provide a quick method of identifying children who may be at risk for a specified condition, for instance, developmental delay. Screening is not an end in itself but is meant to be followed by more thorough diagnostic testing if the screening instrument shows a possible problem. Most screening tests take about 15 to 30 minutes to administer. They are used by a wide variety of professionals in addition to early childhood educators, including medical and social work personnel. A number of screening instruments have been developed in recent years as a result of the Education for All Handicapped Children Act (Public Law 94-142), which seeks to identify and provide early intervention to young children with disabilities or those at risk for later learning problems (Wortham, 1990).

Screening test—A quick method of identifying children who might exhibit developmental delays; only an indicator that must be followed up by more thorough and comprehensive testing.

Diagnostic testing—Another term for screening, which might indicate that more thorough testing should be carried out.

Denver II—A quick test for possible developmental delays in children from infancy to age six.

Norm-referenced—A test in which scores are determined by using a large group of same-age children as the basis for comparison, rather than using a predetermined criterion or standard of performance.

Developmental Indicators for the Assessment of Learning-Revised (DIAL-R)—A developmental screening test for children ages two to six, assessing motor, concept, and language development.

One widely used screening instrument is the Denver II (Frankenburg & Dodd, 1990), for use with infants and children up to age six. Use of the Denver II can be learned relatively quickly. This test, often used by medical as well as early childhood professionals, examines the child's functioning in self-help, social, language, fine motor, and gross motor areas.

Items on the Denver II are scored in relation to a norm. Such norm-referenced tests provide a large comparison group for each age against which the score can be compared (Goodwin & Goodwin, 1982). For each tested item, the Denver II indicates whether the score of a child is at the 25th, 50th, or 90th percentile or well below or above the functioning of other children who are the same age. If the child fails to accomplish tasks for his or her age group in two or more of the four areas, then more in-depth testing is recommended.

Another widely used screening test is the Developmental Indicators for the Assessment of Learning-Revised (DIAL-R) (Mardell-Czudnowski & Goldenberg, 1990), which screens in the motor, concepts, and language areas. This test, normed for children between the ages of two and six, has separate norms for white and non-

"Can you catch the ball?" Screening tests are based on several simple tasks that the child is asked to carry out.

white children. Like the DDST, this test is easily used with some practice and does not take long to administer.

Developmental tests are thorough assessments of children's development in all or several domains.

Developmental Tests. Frequently, a screening test will indicate the necessity for more complete assessment and is then followed by a more thorough and time-intensive **developmental test.** Such tests measure the child's functioning in most or all areas of development, although some instruments are specific to one or two areas. Various in-depth commercial assessments are available, complete with kits containing necessary testing materials.

Developmental assessments are usually **criterion-referenced** rather than norm-referenced. Thus, children are measured against a predetermined level of mastery rather than against the scores of a group of children of the same age. The criteria in these tests are based on the test developers' educated understanding of what children, at various ages, can be expected to achieve.

One widely used developmental test is the **Brigance Diagnostic Inventory of Early Development-Revised** (Brigance, 1991). With some training, early childhood teachers can use this test. It contains subtests for fine motor, gross motor, language, cognitive, and self-help areas; it does not measure social development. Test materials are designed so that a child's progress can be followed in one booklet over the testing years, from birth to age seven. Testing of many of the items can be incorporated into the curriculum; therefore, a child does not need to be pulled from the class for the Brigance to be administered.

Developmental test—Measures the child's functioning in most or all areas of development, although some such tests are specific to one or two areas.

Criterion-referenced—A characteristic of tests in which children are measured against a predetermined level of mastery rather than against an average score of children of the same age.

Brigance Diagnostic Inventory of Early Development-Revised—A developmental assessment tool for children from birth to age seven.

Intelligence tests measure intellectual functioning and are usually highly structured as to how they can be administered and interpreted.

Intelligence Tests. One of the oldest types of standardized assessments is the intelligence test. Such tests have stirred considerable controversy, much of it loaded with emotion because it raises the question of whether intelligence is a fixed biological trait or whether it is malleable and can be raised through an enriched environment (Jensen, 1985; Woodrich, 1984). Another volatile controversy about such tests has been the concern over culture bias (Goodwin & Goodwin, 1982)—that tests are slanted to white, middle-class norms and experiences.

One of the major applications of intelligence tests with young children has been to identify those who fall well below or above the normal range. Classifications of mental retardation or giftedness, for instance, are generally set by IQ score ranges. One of the concerns with using IQ scores for young children is that these scores are not particularly predictive of later IQ. Most children's scores change between early childhood and adolescence, and some change considerably (Woodrich, 1984).

Such tests are highly structured and must be administered by a psychologist specifically trained in their use. The **Stanford-Binet Intelligence Scale** (Thorndike, Hagen, & Sattler, 1986) is a single test with varying tasks for different ages ranging from two through adulthood. The test yields an IQ score; 100 is the average. The Stanford-Binet yields a single, global IQ score, not breaking down results as do some other tests.

One such test is the **McCarthy Scales of Children's Abilities,** designed for children ages $2^1/_2$ to 8 (McCarthy, 1972). The McCarthy yields a General Cognitive Index, which is similar to the global IQ

KEY QUESTION #4

Have you been tested with a standardized instrument? Recall how you felt about the testing situation and the questions asked. What emotional impact did the test have on you? How might young children feel about being tested? What can a tester do to help children perform to their best ability?

Stanford-Binet Intelligence Scale—A widely used test that yields an intelligence quotient (IQ).

McCarthy Scales of Children's Abilities—An intelligence test, particularly used with children who are mildly retarded or who have learning disabilities.

Children's ability to answer items on readiness tests depends to a large extent on their prior experiences. What kinds of common early childhood experiences will help these five-year-olds answer the types of questions asked on the Metropolitan Readiness Test?

score of the Stanford-Binet, but it also provides subscores on the Verbal Index, Perceptual/Performance Index (nonverbal problem solving), and Quantitative Index. In addition, the McCarthy reports a Memory Index and Motor Index, which are based on separate assessments. The Stanford-Binet is more accurate for children with significant retardation, whereas the McCarthy is considered more appropriate for children who are mildly retarded or may have learning disabilities or processing difficulties (Woodrich, 1984).

In recent years, readiness tests have been increasingly used to determine whether children are prepared to enter a specific program such as kindergarten or first grade.

Readiness Tests. The specific purpose of readiness tests—to determine whether a child is prepared to enter a program such as kindergarten or first grade—differentiates them from other types of assessments. Such tests should not be used to predict school success because they merely measure a child's level of achievement of specified academic tasks at the time of testing (Meisels, 1986). A recent study, in fact, found that the predictive validity of one widely used readiness test when compared to first-grade teacher judgment and report cards was very modest, raising questions about the usefulness of the test and about the potential harm to the many children misidentified as not ready for school (Graue & Shepard, 1989).

Metropolitan Readiness Test—A test to determine whether a child is prepared to enter a program such as kindergarten.

One such instrument used extensively by school districts across the country is the **Metropolitan Readiness Test** (Nurss & McGauvran, 1986). It has been criticized, however, because correct answers rely heavily on exposure to specific concepts rather than on innate ability. Unfortunately, the test does not distinguish between a child who has had limited exposure and the child who has actual learning difficulties. The use of these tests has driven many prekindergarten programs to incorporate activities designed to prepare children for readiness testing, often at the expense of other appropriate activities, particularly exploratory, hands-on experiences (Schickedanz, Hansen, & Forsyth, 1990).

Early childhood professionals have raised some major concerns about the use and misuse of standardized tests, particularly when these lead to developmentally inappropriate practices.

Concerns About Use of Evaluation Instruments

All informal and formal evaluation methods can give us useful insights into the children in our care. But although using a variety of methods to better understand children has always been an important part of early childhood education, there is a growing concern about potential misuses, particularly of standardized evaluations. The 1980s brought an increased emphasis on testing, particularly as a way of proving that educational goals are being met (Wortham, 1990).

One major concern involves the misuse of readiness tests. With increasing frequency, such tests are being used to decide children's placement, for instance, if they will be allowed to move on to first grade, placed in a transitional class, or retained in kindergarten, or if they will be admitted to a particular preschool program (Wortham, 1990). Thus, children are often labeled as failures when, in fact, they are expected to conform to inappropriate expectations (NAEYC, 1988). How devastating such practices are on children's self-concepts! Read the eloquent discussion of these concerns in NAEYC's 1988 "Position Statement on Standardized Testing of Young Children 3 Through 8 Years of Age."

A corollary to this trend is the fact that many early childhood programs have adopted curricula whose main aim is to prepare children for readiness tests (Bredekamp & Shepard, 1989). Thus, preschool and kindergarten programs promote developmentally inappropriate methods to meet such goals, intensifying the problem of "failures" and children who are "unready" (NAEYC, 1988).

It has long been acknowledged that standardized tests have a variety of limitations. For instance, a test cannot ask every possible question to evaluate what a child knows on a topic; but the fewer the questions, the more the chance that the test just happened to include the ones the child does *not* know. On the other hand, the more items there are on the test, the greater the chance that the child will become restless and disinterested and not give a representative picture of her or his ability.

Another criticism of standardized tests has been that they can be culture biased, yet test designers have found it impossible to devise tests that are completely culture free (Wortham, 1990). In addition, it is very difficult to establish reliable and valid instruments for young children, given the rapid changes that occur in development as well as the normal individual variations among children (NAEYC, 1988). This also calls into question the use of norm groups against which individuals are compared.

In addition to the potential problems with a test itself, there are difficulties in evaluating young children that can affect the accuracy of test results. A number of factors can affect how accurately the test reflects the child's ability. These might include the child's attention and interest, the familiarity (or unfamiliarity) with the surroundings, the trust the child has in the adult tester (or whether the child has even seen this person before), the time of day, the fact that the child slept poorly the night before, or the fact that the mother forgot to kiss the child good-bye. In too many instances, tests are given to young children in large groups, a practice that further decreases reliability (NAEYC, 1988).

If so many problems are inherent in standardized tests, what is the answer to the dilemma of their increasing use with young children? NAEYC (1988) recommends that the relevance of tests be

KEY QUESTION #5

Given the information from this chapter about the values and potential misuses of evaluation procedures, develop a set of criteria that might guide you, as an early childhood professional, in using assessments in the most effective way. What do you consider to be the three most important benefits of such testing? What should you avoid?

carefully evaluated by administrators: Will results from the test contribute to improving the program for the children? Will the children benefit from the test? If the benefits are meager in relation to the cost (expense and time), perhaps the test should not be used. Furthermore, it is recommended that

- tests be carefully reviewed for reliability and validity;
- they match the program's philosophy and goals;
- only knowledgeable and qualified persons administer and interpret results;
- testers be sensitive to individual and cultural diversity;
- tests be used for only the purpose for which they were intended; and
- no major decision related to enrollment, retention, or placement in a remedial program be made based on only one test, but that multiple sources of information be used for this purpose.

Some recent alternatives to traditional standardized tests offer a more comprehensive, less intrusive approach to gathering information about young children.

Work sampling system—Samuel Meisel's alternative method of gathering reliable information about young children, using a combination of observations, checklists, portfolios, and summary reports.

High/Scope Child Observational Record (COR)—An alternative method of gathering reliable information about young children; COR utilizes teachers' notes of observations by classifying them into specific categories.

Confidentiality—Requirement that results of evaluations and assessments be shared with only the parents and appropriate school personnel.

To address some of the concerns about inappropriate testing of young children, researchers have been developing some alternative, more comprehensive approaches. Meisels (1993), for example, proposes the **work sampling system,** which combines several types of data over an extended period of time to assess children ages 3 to 8. Teachers' ongoing observations are recorded on developmental checklists, which are categorized into seven domains and include many common, developmentally appropriate activities and expectations. In addition, portfolios of select pieces of the children's work are also compiled, and teachers prepare narrative summary reports at three points during the year. Another alternative testing process is the **High/Scope Child Observational Record (COR),** for children ages $2^1/_2$ to 6 (Schweinhart, 1993). Teachers write brief notes about children's behavior in six categories; initiative, creative representations, social relations, music and movement, language and literacy, and logic and mathematics. These anecdotes are then used to rate children on 30 items, each of which has five levels. Alternatives to traditional, often developmentally inappropriate testing methods, such as the work sampling system and COR, offer promise for those who work with young children.

One final note: It is important to keep in mind that any information gathered about children and their families—whether from test results, observations, or something a parent shared—needs to be treated with **confidentiality** and respect.

Selecting and Using Evaluation Methods

Evaluation methods can provide valuable information about children, give direction for program planning, and contribute feedback to share with parents.

We have looked at a number of formal and informal methods of evaluation, information that can be mind-boggling considering that we have reviewed only a very small number of the many available commercial instruments. Selecting an appropriate method will depend on how the results are to be used. We will briefly examine some suggested methods in terms of three purposes of evaluation: gaining information (1) about children, (2) for program planning purposes, and (3) for parent feedback.

A Closer Look

Portfolio Assessment

Criticism of the more formal methods of evaluating young children has led to the development of alternative methods of assessing their progress. One of these alternatives is portfolio assessment, a collection of meaningful examples of student work that "exemplifies interests, attitudes, ranges of skills, and development over a period of time" (Gelfer & Perkins, 1996, p. 5). What, however, is a portfolio? What does it look like? How is it developed and used?

Gelfer and Perkins (1996) discuss some of the specifics that go into the portfolio assessment process. A portfolio, they say, typically is housed in an expandable file folder. In the folder is a careful selection of the child's work that exemplifies performance and improvement. This could include artwork, writing samples, audio or videotapes, photographs of experiments or projects, teacher or parent observations, anecdotal observations, checklists, self-evaluations, interests inventories, progress notes, log books, reports of parent-teacher communications, and other pertinent examples. Items for the portfolio are carefully selected by the child, teacher, and parents to illustrate the child's changing abilities and development. It is helpful if the teacher meets with each child for a few minutes every few weeks to review the portfolio and select new additions. Gullo (1996) also specifies different types of portfolios, ones that contain works in progress, ones that focus on the current year, and ones that are permanent.

Portfolios can be organized in any way that is meaningful to the child and teacher. It can be arranged by subject area, developmental area, skills, themes, or chronologically. One suggested organizational scheme might be subsections for problem-solving, literacy and language, creativity, personal and social growth, and teacher and family support and involvement.

How do evaluations such as portfolios measure up with more traditional, formal assessments? Meisels and his colleagues have examined the reliability and validity of alternative assessment methods that sample children's work rather than rely on a standardized test. They found that work sampling methods provide a reliable and valid measure of children's achievement when comparing the two approaches (Meisels, Liaw, Dorfman, & Nelson, 1995).

A concern about portfolio assessments has, however, been voiced by those who find implementation of portfolios to be very time consuming (Roe & Vukelich, 1994). They conclude that for portfolios to live up to their promise, support from the wider environment—for instance, school districts—must be given; otherwise, teachers can be caught in a bind of having to use two systems of record keeping—portfolios and more traditional methods.

One way to assess the ability of all children in a class on a task such as scissor use is through systematic observation or use of a checklist.

Information About Children. Effective teaching depends on knowing as much as possible about the children in the class; a variety of data gathering methods can be used as follows:

- Ongoing observation can provide valuable insight into all children, their functioning as part of the class, their growth in all developmental areas, what they particularly enjoy, where they run into difficulties, how they get along with peers and teachers, how they communicate, and so forth.
- A screening test, used with all of the children early in the school year, can help identify those who need further diagnostic testing and those who might benefit from specific intervention programs.
- A developmental assessment can be given to children whose performance on the screening test indicated a need for further evaluation. Such an assessment should be combined with observation, parent interviews, possible professional testing (for instance, by a speech pathologist, audiologist, physical therapist, or doctor), and other sources of information to provide as full a picture of the child as possible. Based on a thorough evaluation, it is possible to make better educational and therapeutic decisions about the child's future. Periodic retesting on the developmental assessment can show whether the child is making progress and can pinpoint areas needing further attention.

Information for Program Planning. One of the main purposes of assessment is to help direct program development. Once you have an idea of strengths and areas that need attention, both for individual children and for the group as a whole, you can plan a prescriptive curriculum (Hendrick's, 1986). Some useful data-gathering methods include the following:

- Information from observations can provide excellent programming direction. You may notice, for example, that the parallel play that predominated earlier in the year is beginning to give way to more and more interactive play (remember our discussion of play in Chapter 2). You might plan activities that require a greater measure of cooperation and set up the class environment to facilitate more social interaction.

- Checklists and rating scales allow you to evaluate the functioning of the group of children on tasks that you identify as important. You may, for instance, discover that the majority of your three-year-olds are not able to hold scissors effectively, let alone cut with them. This information tells you that more activities using scissors should be planned to help children acquire this fine-motor skill. Similarly, these evaluation devices (as well as observations) will help you determine whether children have successfully met the objectives that you set for specific curriculum units.

- Some programs administer either a formal or informal developmental assessment at specific points of the year to evaluate whether children are meeting the overall goals of the program.

Information for Parent Feedback. All forms of evaluation provide information to share with parents. It is important to examine the child's strengths, not just areas that may be problematic, and it is vital that all information be as accurate, realistic, and unbiased as possible. Data carefully collected over a period of time and thoughtfully evaluated provide the basis for good parent-feedback conferences.

There are a number of points to keep in mind when sharing evaluation results with parents. In all instances, tests or other evaluation information should never be given in isolation, out of the context of the child's overall nature. Thus, to tell parents that their child is performing below (or, for that matter, above) the norm in fine-motor skills is only part of the picture. It is equally important to tell them that their child has excellent social skills, shows leadership qualities, has a delightful sense of humor, seems to particularly enjoy sensory activities, and so forth. Such information does not rely solely on the results of a developmental assessment, which yielded the fine motor score, but is reinforced by observations, anecdotes, and the teachers' reflection about the child.

Another point to remember when sharing evaluation results with parents is that you should be able to explain the measures that were applied. Some standardized tests are rather complicated to use, score, and interpret. Be sure that you understand what the test results mean and that you can explain them. It does not help a parent who asks, "What do you mean she scored below the norm?" to be told, "Well, I'm not exactly sure what 'norm' means." If your school uses any kind of standardized test, read its manual carefully, know how the test was constructed, understand how results should be interpreted and used, and be familiar with the terminology.

At the same time, it is also important to keep in mind and convey to parents that tests have their limitations. Consider the preceding discussion about the shortcomings of and concerns about tests and let parents know that these represent only part of the input used in evaluation. Also remind parents, as well as yourself, that children are amazingly flexible and often will experience a quick change or growth spurt in their development that could suddenly modify the test findings. Never present any evaluation results as *the* definitive information about the child's abilities and functioning. Similarly, let parents know that a wide variety of profiles fall within a "normal" range.

Finally, when sharing evaluation results with parents, also be prepared to defend the measures you used. A parent may well ask you, "Why did you give this test to my child?" Be able to answer such a question, because it is certainly logical and valid. You need to feel that the test provides valuable information and you should be able to specify how information will be used. For instance, such measures should help plan relevant learning experiences for the child (Wortham, 1990).

SUMMARY

1. Goals provide an overall, general overview of what is expected of the children.
2. Objectives are a more specific interpretation of goals. There are different types of objectives.
3. Evaluation is an important element in early childhood education and helps assess whether goals and objectives are being met.
   - A. One of the most widely used methods of evaluation is observation.
   - B. Teacher-designed instruments such as checklists and rating scales are another type of evaluation.
   - C. Many commercially produced standardized tests are used for different purposes.
   - D. Although evaluation instruments are widely used, there is also considerable concern about their use.
   - E. Information from evaluations and assessments can be used in different ways.

KEY TERMS LIST

ABC analysis
anecdotal records
behavioral objective
Brigance Diagnostic Inventory of Early Development-Revised
checklist
confidentiality
content objective
criterion-referenced
Denver II
Developmental Indicators for the Assessment of Learning-Revised (DIAL-R)
developmental objective
developmental test
diagnostic testing
event sampling
formative evaluation
goal
High/Scope Child Observational Record (COR)
McCarthy Scales of Children's Abilities
Metropolitan Readiness Test
norm-referenced
objective
preassessment
rating scale
reliability
running record
screening test
Stanford-Binet Intelligence Scale
summative evaluation
time sampling
validity
work sampling system

part IV four

The Where of Early Childhood Education

The environment of the early childhood program is an important factor. Just *where* is it that children and their teachers play and work? What elements do we have to keep in mind as we consider the appropriate environment for programs for young children?

chapter

7

The Physical Environment

Today, many young children spend the bulk of their waking hours in an early childhood program, often in one room for 9 or 10 hours every weekday. They spend some time in the outside play area and occasionally go on excursions into the community, but, by and large, most time for many young children is spent in a relatively confined space.

From research we know that the physical environment affects the behavior of children (Thomson & Ashton-Lilo, 1983). In fact, some theorists propose that **place identity** should be considered part of self-identity, because it contributes to a definition of who the person is. Place identity is integral to self-identity because it is within the environmental context that children's needs are met, that they develop mastery and competence, and that they gain control over the physical world (Proshansky & Fabian, 1987). It is, therefore, extremely important to consider physical environment, its arrangement, and its contents.

EFFECTS OF THE PHYSICAL ENVIRONMENT

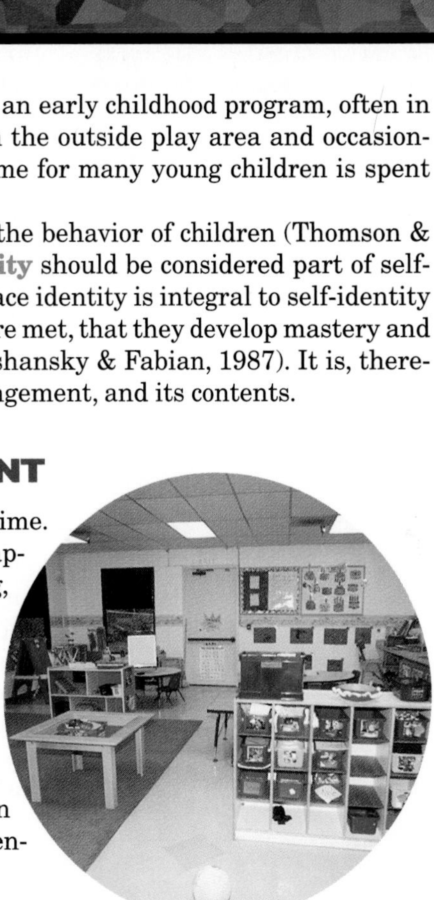

Take a moment to think about a place where you enjoy spending time. What is it about this place that makes it enjoyable? What are its appealing features? Is it because this place is relaxing and soothing, stimulating and exciting, thought-provoking and challenging, orderly and methodical, comfortable and homey, colorful and bright? Now think about a place that you do not particularly like, and consider why it is aversive to you. It may be that this place is boring, messy, stark, disorganized, dark, or uninviting. Think about spending all day in each of these places. What feelings and attitudes does this idea invoke in you? How do you think you would act and react in each place? Can you draw some conclusions about how and why the environment affects you?

Place identity—Considered part of self-identity because it relates to the environmental context within which a child's needs are met, competence is developed, and control over the physical world is gained.

Behavior setting—According to Kounin and Sherman, different environments elicit behaviors that are fitted to the setting; thus, children act "schoolish" at school.

Because children's engagement in activities depends on the environment, teachers need to provide the most appropriate setting possible for learning.

According to researchers (Kounin & Sherman, 1979), when children are in a particular **behavior setting** they behave in a manner appropriate to that locale, following what might be viewed as unspoken rules.

> It is apparent that preschoolers behave "schoolish" when in a preschool. They are diligent creatures who spend 95% of their time actively occupied with the facilities provided and they deal with the facilities appropriately. . . . [T]hey do all of these things in a sort of unwritten private contract between themselves and the setting they enter: teachers and peers infrequently exert any pressure to either enter or leave these settings. (p. 146)

Such research underscores the importance of providing an environment that supports development and learning. If children's engagement in activities is to a large measure prompted by the environment, then it is incumbent upon teachers to provide the most appropriate setting possible.

The quality of the environment has an impact on the behavior of children as well as adults who spend their time in that space (Kritchevsky, Prescott, & Walling, 1977). "Arrangement, organization, size, density, noise level, even the color of the classroom directly and indirectly invite a range of behaviors from children and teachers" (Thomson & Ashton-Lilo, 1983, p. 94).

Effect of the Environment on Children

The environment can help promote or discourage positive peer interaction, independence, and self-esteem in children.

KEY QUESTION #1

Talk to two or three children who are four or five years old. Ask them what they like about their classroom and playground. Are the features they mention ones that you consider particularly interesting and noteworthy? What do their answers tell you about these children's interests, attitudes, and needs in relation to the environment?

The early childhood environment should support the development of children. It has a direct effect on how children behave toward each other. Positive peer interaction is promoted when children are not crowded, when an ample number and variety of items are available, and when socially oriented materials are provided. Classroom arrangement and careful selection of materials also foster cognitive development by providing opportunities for children to classify, find relationships, measure, compare, match, sort, and label (Weinstein, 1987). The environment also enhances both fine and gross motor development through a range of appropriately challenging equipment and materials.

Children's growing sense of independence is supported when they can confidently and competently use equipment and when space and materials are arranged so they can see what is available and make autonomous choices. At the same time, children develop a sense of responsibility when the environment makes it clear how and where materials are to be returned when they finish using them. Children are more productively involved in activities when the purpose of classroom spaces is clearly defined and when materials are developmentally appropriate (Phyfe-Perkins, 1980; Thomson & Ashton-Lilo, 1983). Children are also more likely to follow classroom rules when the environment reinforces these, for instance, if it is important for reasons of safety that children not run inside, classroom furnishings should be arranged in a way that makes walking, rather than running, natural.

The environment also enhances children's self-esteem when it is designed with their needs and development in mind, when it provides space for personal belongings, and when it promotes competence by al-

A pleasant, well-organized environment that provides children with a variety of age-appropriate activity options supports children's development in all domains and enhances learning.

lowing children to function independently (Weinstein, 1987). In addition, the environment should convey a sense of security and comfort through a friendly, warm, and inviting atmosphere; and through "soft" elements such as beanbag chairs, carpeting, or sling swings (Jones & Prescott, 1978; Weinstein, 1987).

Effect of the Environment on Teachers

An appropriate environment must also take the needs of teachers into account.

When the environment is set up to maximize children's development, prevent problem behaviors, and promote appropriate behaviors, teachers' well-being will be indirectly supported. More directly, teachers' jobs are made more pleasant if they work in aesthetically pleasing surroundings, if they have a designated space where they can relax and plan, and if their needs are generally taken into consideration (Thomson & Ashton-Lilo, 1983). Both personal comfort and professional needs should be supported (Harms & Clifford, 1980). Environmental factors such as pleasant temperature, light, color, sound absorption, ventilation, and spatial arrangement can facilitate or hinder staff in carrying out their jobs (Jorde-Bloom, 1988b). Thus, a carefully arranged environment can help prevent teacher burnout by supporting teachers' goals for the children and by making the work site a pleasant place to be.

KEY QUESTION #2

Spend some time in an early childhood classroom and attune yourself to the environment. What do you like? What do you dislike? How would it feel to work all day in this setting? What changes could make this a more pleasant or accommodating environment for adults?

ARRANGING THE INDOOR ENVIRONMENT

As we consider the indoor environment, we must take into account both its fixed features—for instance, size and shape of the room, placement of windows and doors, built-in features such as shelves and storage spaces—and movable or semifixed features, such as arrangement of furnishings and materials, color, and texture (Phyfe-Perkins, 1980).

Fixed features of a room—such as its size and shape, placement of doors and windows, built-in storage, and water access—must be considered when arranging the indoor space.

Fixed Features

Room size will, to a large extent, dictate how many children and how much material can be housed in the space. The maximum number of children allowed in an area is prescribed by licensing regulations. In most states, 35 square feet per child is required, although 50 square feet is often suggested as more desirable (Thomson & Ashton-Lilo, 1983). Some experts recommend as much as 100 square feet per child. (Spodek, 1985). Although the research on the effects of crowding is not clear-cut (Phyfe-Perkins, 1980; Smith & Connolly, 1980), Phyfe-Perkins concludes that "crowding of children which provides less than 25 square feet per child for an extended period of time should be avoided. It may increase aggressive behavior and inhibit social interaction and involvement" (p. 103).

The shape of the room has an impact on arrangement and supervision. A rectangular room seems more adaptable than a square one, and an L-shaped room poses more problems for supervision (Mayesky, 1995).

To some extent, room arrangement will be affected by the amount of natural light available through windows. For instance, color used during art activities is enhanced by clear, bright light; thus, it is desirable to locate the art area near windows. Areas in which children need to attend to close detail, such as the book or language center, should also be located in a well-lighted place. All areas of a room should be well lit, and places not reached by natural light should be provided with adequate electric lighting.

Building materials have an effect on acoustics. Some rooms are constructed with sound-absorbing ceiling, floor, or wall materials, whereas others seem to reverberate with noise. If the room's noise level hinders rather than enhances the children's participation in activities and the communication process, added features such as drapes, carpets, and corkboards can help eliminate much of the noise.

Because many young children's activities are messy, it is important to have water accessible, preferably in the room. Sensory activities, the art center, and cooking projects should be placed near the water source. If there is no running water in or adjacent to the room, an

When arranging the classroom, it is best to take advantage of natural features, for instance, by putting the art area near a window. What other environmental features will have an impact on how the early childhood classroom is arranged?

alternate arrangement, for instance, a bucket with soapy water and paper towels, should be close at hand.

If the room contains built-in storage units, the room should be arranged to best utilize these units. Shelves that are placed at child level should hold materials the children use every day, for instance, blocks, manipulatives, or art implements. Besides built-in storage, easily reachable portable units should be added as needed. If built-in storage space is above the children's reach, such shelves can be used for teacher materials or items not used every day.

Movable Features

An early childhood classroom is made more flexible and can meet the needs of young children by thoughtful arrangement of its movable features such as furniture and equipment.

More than a room's fixed features, it is the movable elements that allow you to arrange a well-planned, developmentally appropriate environment for children. Placement and grouping of equipment and furnishings communicate many messages. They convey the purpose of spaces, set limits on behavior, indicate how many children can comfortably use an area, establish boundaries, invite possible combinations of play through juxtaposition of areas, and encourage quiet or active involvement. Research has provided some guidelines for maximizing the effective use of space. Phyfe-Perkins (1980), in a review of studies that examine the effect of physical arrangements on children's behavior, proposes some helpful principles.

- Children in full-day care need privacy; thus, places where children can be alone should be provided in the environment.
- Soft areas such as beanbag chairs, pillows, or rugs allow children to snuggle and find comfort if "adult laps are in short supply" (p. 103).
- Small, enclosed areas promote quiet activities as well as interaction among small groups of children.
- Physical boundaries around areas can reduce distraction, which, in turn, increases attention to activities.
- Large spaces allow for active, large-group activities that are more boisterous and noisy.
- Clearly organized play space and clear paths can result in fewer disruptions and more goal-directed behavior.

Elizabeth Prescott (1987), one of the leading researchers on effective environments for young children, suggests that recurring guidance or curriculum problems can quite often be resolved by rearranging the classroom. She advises teachers to examine classroom pathways from a child's eye level to ensure that they are clearly defined, that all areas have a path leading to them, and that they are not obstructed.

The walls of a classroom offer an excellent opportunity to convey the philosophy and activities of a classroom. Bulletin boards and other wall space should display the children's creations and should reflect the children's planning and thinking rather than the adults' (Jones & Villarino, 1994).

EXPERIENCES chapter 7

HESTER: Head Teacher, Preschool Class

The New Room

A decision was made by the staff that we would switch the classrooms used by two groups at the end of the year. My class of three- and four-year-olds would move into the space previously used by the kindergarteners, and they would take our room. We had occupied the larger, upstairs area while the kindergarteners had been in the more intimate downstairs room. If you had seen the two rooms before and after the move, you would have seen great differences!

The challenge was to arrange our new downstairs area to fit the needs and interests of my class. I know the characteristics of my kids and what works and what doesn't. The younger ones need more supervision, are more easily distracted, and can be messy. The older ones want plenty of room to carry out activities and projects. All of them love the housekeeping area.

I began by looking for the best large corner for placing housekeeping, separating it like a small room within the classroom. I placed the area for manipulatives next to housekeeping since the children often like to take props from this area to use in their dramatic play. Legos can serve as money, small animals can stimulate the creation of a pet store, and Bristle Blocks double as food items.

The art and sensory areas I placed as close to the bathroom as possible. The shorter the distance between a messy activity and the source of water, the fewer little fingerprints need to be cleaned up later. Luckily, the floor area near the bathroom was linoleum covered. For the blocks, however, I looked for a level carpeted area that would muffle sounds. Some of the younger children in particular love to build towers then knock them down, so carpeting is ideal.

Some activities needed to be placed where there would be minimum distraction, and these I put in the corner nook, where there is little traffic, under the loft. This is where I put the computers and the books, quiet activities that need concentration.

Overall, I was concerned about safety and ease of supervision. We arranged the room so that the teachers could see all areas easily. No high dividers obstruct the view. We have one blind spot in this room, however, a corridor that leads to the exit to the outside; this corridor can't be observed by the teachers. We solved this by talking to the children about the need to stay "on this side of the metal strip" at the edge of the carpet. The children monitor themselves and each other. If someone strays over the line, invariably another child will say, "You're not being safe. You're over the line."

A couple of weeks after we moved into our new room, Clayton said to me, "I like it here. I like that the ceiling isn't so far up and that the walls are close by." For younger children, the room seems to feel secure. I must say, I like the new room, too!

When arranging a classroom environment, the characteristics of the children need to be taken into consideration. The same space should look quite different if it is intended for younger preschoolers than it would for an older group of children.

Learning Centers

Indoor space is often organized into **learning centers** (also called interest or activity areas), which combine materials and equipment around common activities. Learning centers can include art, manipulatives, dramatic play, sensory experiences, blocks, music, science, math, computers, books, language arts, woodworking, cooking, and a variety of other areas that fit the unique interests, needs, and characteristics of a group of children and teachers (Essa & Rogers, 1992). Available space and materials, ages of the children, and licensing regulations also contribute to decisions about numbers and types of learning centers included in a classroom.

Learning centers (also called activity or interest areas)– Where materials and equipment are combined around common activities, for instance, art, science, or language arts.

One effective way of arranging the indoor environment is through organized learning centers that combine materials and equipment around common activities.

Learning centers allow children to make choices from a range of available, developmentally appropriate activities. A curriculum based on learning centers can be considered responsive to the children because it is designed to meet and respond to their specific needs and experiences (Myers & Maurer, 1987). Yet, although learning centers and their activities are planned, structured, set up, and facilitated by teachers, the children determine how to engage in and carry out the activity (Spodek, 1985).

One useful tool in arranging a room into learning centers is to draw a scale model of the classroom, with fixed features such as doors, windows, and built-in furnishings marked. You can then pencil in furniture until you find a workable arrangement. A method that is initially more time consuming but allows more extensive spatial experimentation is to draw and cut out scale models of the furniture and manipulate these on your classroom drawing. Commercial classroom planning guides are also available, which include room layouts and a wide variety of scaled equipment cutouts (one such guide is available from Environments, Inc., P.O. Box 1348, Beaufort, SC 29901). Figure 7-1 offers some suggested guidelines to keep in mind when arranging a classroom for preschool or primary school children.

FIGURE 7-1 Guidelines for organizing classroom space

1. The room arrangement should reflect the program's philosophy. If the program's aim is to foster independent decision making, self-help skills, positive self-concept, social interaction, and more child-initiated than teacher-initiated activities, this should be promoted through room arrangement.
2. Keep in mind the children's ages and developmental levels. As children get older, provide more choices, a more complex environment, and greater opportunity for social play. For young preschoolers, it is best to offer a simple, uncluttered, clearly defined classroom with space for large motor activity. School-aged children need more varied materials and flexible space in which they can plan and carry out complex projects.
3. Any environment in which children as well as adults spend blocks of time should be attractive and aesthetically pleasing. Thought and care should be given to such factors as the arrangement of furnishing, use of colors and textures, and display of artwork. Plants and flowers added to the classroom can enhance its attractiveness.
4. If children are encouraged to make independent choices, then materials should be stored at a level where children can easily see, reach, and return them.
5. If children are to develop self-help skills, toileting facilities and cubbies for coats and boots should be accessible to them. Access to learning materials also contributes to development of self-help skills.

continued

FIGURE 7-1 Guidelines for organizing classroom space—cont'd

6. If the program supports a positive self-concept in children, then there should be individual places for children's belongings, for their projects or art to be saved, and for their work to be displayed.
7. If development of social skills and friendships is encouraged, then the environment should be set up to allow children to participate in activities with small groups of other children without undue interference or disruption.
8. If children are to have many opportunities to select and direct their own activities, then the environment should be set up to offer a variety of activity choices.
9. There should be places for children to be alone if they so wish. Quiet, private spaces can be planned as part of the environment, for instance, a corner with large pillows, a cozy spot in the library area, or a designated rocking chair with cushions.
10. There should be "soft" places in the environment where children can snuggle and find comfort.
11. An environment set up into learning centers should have clearly marked boundaries that indicate the space designated for each given area. Storage shelves and other furnishings can be used to define the edges.
12. Paths to each area should be clear and unobstructed. Children are less likely to use areas that are hard to reach.
13. A pathway to one area should never go through another activity center. This only interferes with ongoing play and can cause anger and frustration.
14. Doorways and other exits should be unobstructed.
15. Quiet activities should be grouped near each other, and noisy ones should be placed at some distance from these. The block area should not be next to the book area, for example.
16. Group those activities that have common elements near each other to extend children's play possibilities. Blocks and dramatic play are often placed next to each other to encourage exchange of props and ideas.
17. Provide areas for individual, small group, and large group activities by setting up different-sized centers.
18. Some areas require more space than others. Block play, for instance, is enhanced by ample room to build and expand block structures.
19. The sizes of various learning centers will, to some extent, convey how many children can play in each area and how active that play should be. Small, cozy areas set natural limits on the number of children and the activity level, whereas large areas send the opposite message.
20. Decrease noise level by using carpeting or area rugs in noisy centers such as the block area.
21. Place messy activities near a water source.
22. Place activities that are enhanced by natural light near windows. Ensure that all areas are well lit, however.
23. Place tables and chairs in or near centers where tabletop activities are carried out. For instance, tables should be placed in the art and manipulative areas but are not needed in the large block center. Tables scattered through the room can take on an added use during snack time.
24. Consider multipurpose uses for space, especially where room size is restricted. When your room allows for a limited number of areas to be set at any one time, some of these might be used for more than one activity. For instance, the area designated for large group activities might also be the block area, music center, or place set aside for large motor activity.
25. Some learning centers may not be part of the classroom on a daily basis. Such centers as woodworking, music, or cooking may be brought into the classroom on a less frequent schedule or may be rotated with other areas for specified periods of time.
26. Be flexible in use of space and open to rearranging it. As children mature and their interests change, so should the center. Also, if repeated problems arise, try solving these by rearranging the environment.
27. Safety should be an overriding, primary concern in setting up an environment for young children.

Periodic assessment of the classroom and, if appropriate, rearrangement of learning centers can capitalize on children's changing interests.

Safety

Safety should be of primary concern as teachers arrange and equip the classroom.

It is also important to be aware of safety considerations when arranging and equipping an early childhood classroom (Click, 1995). Some guidelines will be spelled out in building codes, fire regulations, and child care licensing. But beyond these, additional measures can protect children from foreseeable accidents. Each classroom should have at least two exits to be used in case of emergency. Clearly marked emergency exit routes should be posted and familiar to teachers and children alike, and a well-functioning fire extinguisher and smoke detectors should be installed in each room. Carpeting, drapes, and other furnishings should be treated with fire retardants.

Walls and other surfaces should be painted with lead-free paint. Any potentially hazardous substance, such as those used for cleaning or medical purposes, should be stored out of the classroom or in a locked cupboard. Electrical outlets should be covered. Sharp edges should be eliminated from all furniture and built-in storage units. Any lightweight equipment should be backed against a wall or another sturdy surface so it cannot be knocked or pulled over during vigorous play. In addition, when the classroom is carefully arranged with clearly defined learning areas and paths, the number of accidents will be minimized.

Environments for Infants and Toddlers

An environment for infants and toddlers needs to be designed with many of the same guidelines suggested for preschool and primary environments; it must be developmentally appropriate, safe, secure, comfortable, aesthetically pleasing, and appropriately stimulating. The environment must encourage movement and exploration while meticulously ensuring safety and hygiene. Further, it must be adapted to the needs of very young children by including discrete areas for playing, eating, diapering, and sleeping. Developmental changes are rapid during the first two years of life. The environment must take such changes into account by providing differing levels of stimulation and challenge for different ages (Bredekamp, 1987; Gonzalez-Mena & Eyer, 1989; Harms, Cryer, & Clifford, 1990; Lally & Stewart, 1990).

A Closer Look

Hygiene Practice in Child Care

Parents often note that when they enroll their children in a group child care setting where they are in contact with other children, their rate of illness invariably rises. Children are exposed to more viruses and, as a result, experience more infectious diseases. Respiratory infections, which are the most common illness among young children, are particularly prevalent. Is this rise in illness inevitable, however?

Studies have shown that the incidence of infectious illnesses among child care youngsters can be significantly decreased when the staff pay meticulous attention to hygiene and cleanliness. Several studies, for instance, found a decrease in diarrhea when staff consistently and carefully washed hands when diapering infants and toddlers (e.g., Bartlett et al., 1985).

A more recent study carefully monitored the number of illnesses experienced by infants, toddlers, and preschoolers in one center, both before and after a staff education program to promote infection control was instituted (Krilov et al., 1996). The education program included lectures, written policies, colorful posters about hygiene and disease transmission placed around the classrooms, and involvement of the parents in infection control measures.

The results of these preventive steps paid off. A comparison of number and type of illnesses for the year before and the year after the infection control program showed significant decreases in a number of illnesses. The overall number of illnesses, particularly respiratory infections, was considerably lower after the program was instituted. There was also a somewhat less dramatic decrease in diarrhea, ear infections, and sinus infections. In addition, children had fewer visits to the doctor, took fewer antibiotics, and were absent less from school.

Several measures help to decrease the incidence of illness among children in group care. One of the most important is careful handwashing by staff whenever they change diapers or help children with toileting routines. Cleaning and disinfecting areas where children's diapers are changed, where children eat, and where children play are also very important. Furthermore, toys need to be routinely disinfected, especially for infants and toddlers who frequently mouth toys.

Many playgrounds contain conventional metal structures such as the galvanized pipe geodome climber along with metal swings, slides, and climbers. As you read this chapter, you will see that such playgrounds are being replaced by newer "playscapes."

Arranging the Outdoor Environment

The traditional metal swings and slides of many playgrounds are being replaced by more contemporary playscapes.

Just as the indoor space is arranged with care and thought, considering the children's needs and developmental levels, so should the outdoor environment be carefully designed. The outdoor area should be more than a place where children can let off steam and exercise large muscles. It should also provide opportunities that enhance socialization, cognitive and language development, sensory exploration, creative expression, and an appreciation of nature.

Unfortunately, too often outdoor areas are literally set in concrete, leaving little room for versatility and rearrangement. Most early childhood playgrounds come equipped with either traditional structures such as metal swings, slides, and climbers or with more contemporary **playscapes,** which combine a variety of materials and allow for a range of activities. Such equipment must meet standards of safety and developmental appropriateness. Beyond the immovable components of the outdoor space, however, various elements can enhance and expand children's play, as we will discuss.

Playscapes—Contemporary, often innovative playground structures that combine a variety of materials.

Fixed Outdoor Play Structures

In the early decades of this century, when the playground movement took root in this country, outdoor play areas were generally equipped with swings, slides, seesaws, and sandboxes, not so different from many playgrounds today (Eriksen, 1985). But design of play structures has also come a long way from such traditional, single-purpose pieces of equipment. Through the efforts of child development specialists, professional playground architects, and commercial equipment developers, far more creative and versatile play structures are now available.

Many of today's **creative playgrounds** contain equipment constructed of such materials as tires, cargo nets, railroad ties, telephone poles, large cable spools, barrels, and drainage pipes. A European variation is the **adventure playground** in which children use a wide range of available "junk" materials to create their own environments (Frost, 1992). In fact, research has shown that children engage in a wider variety of social interactions, greater language usage, and more originality on innovative rather than on traditional playgrounds

Creative playgrounds—Outdoor play areas that use innovative materials such as tires, telephone poles, nets, and cable spools.

Adventure playground—A European innovation, a type of outdoor play area in which children use a wide range of available "junk" materials to create their own environment.

Contemporary playgrounds are more versatile in design and construction. They are made of various materials such as wood and plastic and encourage a variety of activities.

(Hayward, Rothenburg, & Beasley, 1974). Where traditional structures were primarily constructed of metal, which could become dangerously hot or very cold during weather extremes, new equipment materials include a variety of treated wood surfaces and "space-age plastics" (Frost & Wortham, 1988).

Guidelines help the early childhood teacher evaluate the safety and developmental appropriateness of outdoor equipment.

Just because equipment is contemporary, however, does not necessarily make it developmentally appropriate or safe (Frost & Klein, 1979). Some guidelines can help ensure that outdoor equipment provides suitable play space for young children.

- Because large structures are relatively fixed in the function they serve, they should be complex in design. For example, while including opportunity for a wide range of motor sills, they can also provide some open spaces underneath, which children can use for dramatic play (Frost & Wortham, 1988).
- Play equipment should provide graduated challenges, offering activities that allow for safe risk taking for children of different ages and developmental levels (Moore, Goltsman, & Iacofano, 1987). An outdoor play area used by a range of children could, for instance, include one gently sloped and one taller, more steeply angled slide; balance beams of different widths; or steps as well as ladders leading to raised platforms.
- Play structures should promote social interaction rather than competition among children. Wide slides, for example, encourage two or three children to slide down together; tire swings invite several children to cooperatively pump; and added props encourage dramatic play. At the same time, there should also be provision for privacy if children want to be alone.
- A final, important factor is the safety of outdoor play equipment. Equipment should be securely anchored to the ground and in good repair with no sharp edges, broken or splintered elements, or loose nuts and bolts. There should be no openings that could trap a child's head, fingers, hands, or feet. Swing seats should be made of a lightweight material. Safety is also fostered when equipment is of appropriate size; climbing heights should not ex-

ceed the reaching height of the children (Frost, 1992; Frost & Wortham, 1988). The surfacing material under swings and climbing structures must also be considered to ensure that children are somewhat cushioned if they fall. In some parts of the country, spiders and other insects like to nest in dark parts of play equipment, for instance, inside tires; thus, frequent safety checks should be carried out and appropriate measures taken in such cases. If there is frequent rain, tires can also trap water, which then stagnates and attracts mosquitos; drilling drainage holes into the bottoms of tires can avoid this problem ("Tire hazards," 1986).

An outdoor play area for infants and toddlers in the sensorimotor stage of development (recall the discussion of Piaget's stages of development in Chapter 5) must encourage basic motor skills and sensory experiences. It must allow for a wide range of movement; stimulate the senses; offer novelty, variety, and challenge; and be safe and comfortable (Frost, 1992).

Flexible Outdoor Play Components

Although not many adjustments can be made with the large equipment, there are other ways in which the outdoor environment can be arranged to enhance and support children's development. By adding equipment and materials, capitalizing on the natural features of the play space, and creating interest areas, the outdoor play space can be made more exciting and flexible.

A variety of movable large equipment components can be added to the outdoor area. When large crates, sawhorses, ladders, ramps, balance beams, tires, pulleys, hollow blocks, or cardboard boxes are provided, children will find a variety of creative ways to incorporate these into their play. Such movable components give children the opportunity to structure and arrange their own environment.

An outdoor play area should also take advantage of all available natural features. The play yard's physical contours, plants, and surfaces provide potential for enhancing the playground. A small hill can

The outdoor environment can be made more flexible by adding movable equipment, by including indoor curriculum activities such as painting or woodworking, and by taking advantage of natural features such as slopes and shady trees.

KEY QUESTIONS #3

Observe a group of children in an outdoor environment. What kinds of activities are the children involved in? Which developmental needs are being met? If you see little involvement in activities that promote one, or several, areas of development (for instance, social, language, cognitive), what changes or additions could be made to bring these about?

Many activities commonly considered indoor activities can be carried out on the playground. Sensory tables and art activities, for example, can be accommodated outdoors as well as inside. What other activities, usually restricted to the indoor environment, could also be set up outside?

let children experience gathering momentum as they run or roll down, or it can be used as the site for a tunnel. A large, grassy area is ideal for large-group movement, ball toss, or parachute activities.

Trees provide shade; shrubs and flowers add to the aesthetic and sensory pleasures of the yard. A flower, vegetable, or herb garden that the children help tend can provide a meaningful science experience. Multiple surfaces such as fine sand for digging, cement on which to ride tricycles, pea gravel or wood shavings under large equipment, grass to sit on, dirt to make mud with, textured paving stones to touch with hands or bare feet—all add to making the outdoor area a good learning environment.

The playground should also accommodate all indoor curriculum areas, for instance, art, music, science, or story time. "The good contemporary playground contains nooks and crannies, amphitheater areas, tables, benches, and so on for full exploration of these subjects (Frost & Wortham, 1988, p. 26). Woodworking, sand, water, and other sensory activities are also portable and very suitable additions to the outdoor environment. An outdoor area can also be enhanced by creating defined learning centers that are more permanent, similar to those used indoors.

ADAPTING THE ENVIRONMENT

The environment can be adapted in a variety of ways so children with special needs can enjoy its use.

Increasingly, early childhood programs are integrating children with disabilities into their facilities. It is important when children with different levels of ability are included to provide a suitable environment in which all of the children can experience appropriate challenges and successes. "Handicapped children have the same need to play as do nonhandicapped children, but, because of personal, social, and physical barriers, it is more difficult for these needs to be fulfilled" (Frost & Klein, 1979, p. 220). Following are suggested adaptations for children with physical and visual disabilities.

Children with severe physical limitations need specialized equipment, such as special chairs or bolsters, to help them participate as much as possible in activities. Children who rely on wheelchairs or walkers for mobility, as well as those with other physical limitations, need wide enough paths and entries to learning centers to maneuver in an unobstructed way throughout the room. Activity opportunities and shelves from which children select materials should be accessible so these children can be as independent as possible. Similarly, outdoor activities and equipment must be accessible through such modifications as wide, gently sloped ramps with handrails; raised sand areas; or sling swings that provide secure body support.

Children with visual impairments require a consistent, uncluttered, and clearly arranged environment that they can recognize through touch. Landmarks such as specific equipment or furniture, and a sensory-rich environment with varying textures, can help blind children orient themselves inside or outside (Frost, 1992).

The environment should always be responsive to children, suited to their unique needs and characteristics. Recognizing that each child is uniquely individual, the play environment should be versatile enough to provide a rich variety of sensory stimuli, opportunities to make and carry out independent choices, and a range of experiences to promote all areas of development in children of varying levels of competence. A sensitive staff can help make the early childhood experience of children with special needs as beneficial as possible through some appropriate environmental modifications.

DEVELOPMENTALLY APPROPRIATE EQUIPMENT

Early childhood **equipment** refers to furniture and other large items that represent the more expensive, long-term investments in an early childhood facility; **materials** refers to the smaller, often expendable items that are replaced and replenished more frequently. Because it is expensive, equipment needs to be acquired carefully. Figure 7-2 lists basic equipment that should be included in classrooms for young children.

Equipment—Large items such as furniture that represent a more expensive, long-term investment in an early childhood facility.

Materials—The smaller, often expendable items used in early childhood programs that are replaced and replenished frequently.

FIGURE 7-2 Basic Equipment and Materials for a Preschool Classroom

A classroom for 16 to 20 young children or a smaller group of infants or toddlers should include, but not be restricted to, the following pieces of equipment:

Equipment		Materials
Basic Furniture		
3-4	Tables that seat 6-8 each (round, rectangular, or both) for meals and activities, as needed	Beanbag chairs, pillows Bulletin boards
24-28	Chairs	
1	Rocking chair	
16-20	Cubbies, one for each child, to store personal belongings	
Dramatic Play Center		
1	Small table	Dress-up clothes, both men's and women's
2-4	Chairs	
4	Appliances	Empty food containers
1	Large mirror	Set of dishes, pots/pans
1	Ironing board	Telephones
4-6	Dolls, different ethnic groups, both sexes	Doll clothes, blankets Dramatic play kits with props for selected themes
1	Doll bed or crib	
Art Center		
2	Easels, two-sided	Variety of paper, paints, crayons, scissors, glue, collage materials, clay
1	Storage shelf for materials	
Block Center		
1	Set unit blocks, 250-300 pieces, 12 shapes	Various props, including people, animals, vehicles, furniture
1	Set hollow blocks	
1	Set cardboard blocks	
3-6	Large wooden vehicles	
Manipulative Center		
1	Storage shelf with individual storage bins	Wide variety of puzzles, pegboards, construction toys, parquetry, beads, lotto and other games
Sensory Center		
1	Sand and water table or deep plastic bins	Variety of props such as funnels, hoses, measuring cups, waterwheels, scoops, containers, shovels

continued

FIGURE 7-2 Basic Equipment and Materials for a Preschool Classroom—cont'd

Equipment		Materials
Language Center		
1	Bookshelf	Wide variety of books
1	Large flannel board	File of flannel board stories
1	Tape recorder	Writing materials
1	Puppet theater	Variety of puppets
Science and Math Center	Animal homes, such as aquarium or cages	Wide variety of natural materials found in nearby environment Variety of scientific instruments, such as microscopes, magnifiers, magnets, thermometers Variety of math materials such as attribute blocks, Cuisinaire rods, items to sort or classify, seriate calendars, timers Variety of old mechanical objects to take apart, such as clocks, watches, cameras, or locks
Music Center		
1	Cassette player	Variety of records
1	Set rhythm instruments	Props for movement activities, such as scarves or streamers
1	Autoharp	
3-4	Tonal instruments such as xylophones, or bells	
1	Storage unit for instruments	
Woodworking Center		
1	Woodworking bench with vises	Soft wood scraps
1	Set tools	Thick Styrofoam sheets
1	Tool storage unit	Variety of nails, screws
Outdoor Equipment		
	Gross motor equipment that allows children to slide, climb, swing, crawl, hang, balance	Sensory materials such as fine-grained sand and access to water (in appropriate weather)
8-10	Wheeled vehicles such as tricycles, wagons, scooters. A play house or other space for quiet or dramatic play	Movable equipment such as tires, crates, planks, cardboard boxes Balls, ropes, parachute
Infant/Toddler Environment		
	Cribs or cots	Soft toys
	Changing table	Mobiles
	Storage near changing table	Colorful displays
	Storage for belongings, toys	Teething toys
	Toddler-sized chairs and tables	Sturdy books
	Mats, carpets	Dramatic play props
	Cassette player	Small blocks
	Strollers, buggies	Nesting toys
		Pull toys
		Mirrors

Note: This suggested equipment and materials list is by no means exhaustive. Many other items could and should be added, selected to suit the program, children, and staff. Discussion of activities in Chapters 9 through 13 can be consulted for additional suggested materials.

Criteria for Selecting Equipment

Equipment must be carefully evaluated to ensure its appropriateness for young children.

Some important questions to ask when selecting equipment include the following:

- **Does this piece of equipment support the program's philosophy?** Equipment should promote children's self-esteem and

Classroom equipment has to be sized appropriately for the children. The chairs and tables in this class of toddlers are smaller than the furnishings in the classrooms of their older peers.

independence, encourage positive social interaction, and support children's development.

- **Is the equipment appropriately sized for the children?** Some pieces of equipment are available in various sizes. For a class of two-year-olds, chairs should be smaller and tables lower than for an older group of preschoolers.
- **Is the equipment safe?** When purchasing equipment, it is important to ensure that safety standards are met and that the equipment will withstand long-term usage. It must continue to be safe for the expected lifetime of the equipment. Manufacturers of outdoor play structures often provide a safety warranty for such equipment.
- **Is the equipment durable?** Early childhood equipment should be well built to withstand hard use by large numbers of children over a period of years. Varnished or plastic surfaces will protect tabletops and shelves. Outside equipment should be finished to resist weathering, rusting, and chipping. It is usually more expensive in the long run to purchase less expensive equipment that is not intended for group use and will have to be replaced sooner.
- **Is there room for this equipment?** The size of the classroom or outside play area will dictate how much equipment (and of what size) can be accommodated. A large outside structure that takes up most of the space in a relatively small play yard may be impractical if it leaves little room for other activities. Storage room should be available if a piece of equipment—for example, a water table or woodworking bench—will not be used all the time.
- **Can the equipment be constructed rather than purchased?** Sometimes teachers, parents, or community volunteers with carpentry skills can make a piece of equipment at a considerably lower cost than would be required to purchase a commercial equivalent. Ensure that a volunteer carpenter understands your standards for safety and performance. Many exciting play yards have been constructed by parent and staff groups; however,

KEY QUESTION #4

Browse through one of the many catalogs in which early childhood materials and equipment are advertised. Evaluate several of the items in the catalog according to the criteria outlined in this chapter for selecting equipment and materials. What conclusions can you draw about selecting developmentally appropriate items for young children?

if you are considering construction of outdoor equipment, get expert advice to assure its safety. One preschool center, with the help of volunteers, had constructed a very interesting, contemporary playground that the children very much enjoyed. About 5 years after the construction of a tire swing, which was suspended from three telephone poles by heavy chains, one of the poles snapped from unsuspected dry rot. One child's nose was broken by falling wood and chain. This preschool decided that homemade equipment, although it offered unique choices, could not be used because of the safety risk to the children and because the liability was too high. Within a year all of the volunteer-made equipment was replaced by commercial units with warranties.

- **Is the equipment aesthetically pleasing?** Consider whether a new piece of equipment will fit harmoniously with existing furnishings. When you purchase a new sofa for your living room, for example, you look for something to match the existing decor; in the same way, consider new equipment in the context of the entire classroom. Many early childhood items are available in attractive natural wood, whereas others come in brightly colored plastics.
- **Is the equipment easy to clean and maintain?** Classroom items should be relatively easy to sanitize and keep clean. Replacement parts such as bolts or gears should be readily available from the manufacturer.

Computers

Computer literacy—Familiarity with and knowledge about computers.

Computers have become a prevalent feature in many early childhood classrooms; in addition, a considerable amount of software has been developed for the use of young children. Software must be carefully evaluated for appropriateness.

Over the past decade, early childhood programs have increasingly invested in the purchase of computers and software for the children's use. A growing number of people today have **computer literacy;** in other words, they are knowledgeable about and capable of using a computer. It is often argued that young children are entering a world in which familiarity with computers will be a requisite for effective functioning; therefore, exposure to computers and development of some basic computer skills should be part of early childhood programs.

Various concerns have been raised about the use of computers with young children. Their development appropriateness for children who have not yet reached the stage of concrete operations (Piaget's stages of development are discussed in Chapters 5 and 11) has been questioned (Barnes & Hill, 1983), although research shows that young children are quite competent in using the symbols of computers appropriately (Clements, 1987).

When computer use first became widespread in early childhood education, an often-heard concern was that children would use the computer in isolation at the expense of peer interaction. This fear has been dispelled by a number of studies and reports that document the positive effects of a computer on socialization and cooperation (Essa, 1987; Swigger & Swigger, 1984; Ziajka, 1983). Another concern has been that the computer could decrease participation in other activities, although research has shown that it augments rather than replaces other centers (Essa, 1987).

The computer should be viewed as neither good nor bad but rather as a tool, similar to the many other educational resources used by children. The selection of computers and computer software for an early childhood program must follow the same principles as the selection of any developmentally appropriate materials. The *"NAEYC Position Statement: Technology and Young Children—Ages Three through Eight"* (NAEYC, 1996) can guide teachers in what may seem to be a complex and difficult task in evaluation of available resources. The statement affirms the important role of the teacher as the one whose professional judgment ultimately deems developmental appropriateness of technological learning materials.

KEY QUESTION #5

If you have access to a computer and early childhood software, try out one early childhood activity on the computer. After you have mastered the activity, evaluate the software according to the criteria presented in this chapter. What do you think young children will learn from the activity? What feature(s) do you think might be appealing, unappealing, or frustrating to preschoolers?

Acquiring a computer for the children's use must also be accompanied by purchasing **software,** the set of "instructions" that direct the computer to perform an activity (Davidson, 1989). Software, which is usually stored on a disk that is inserted into the computer, is available through a variety of commercial sources. This software can then be installed on the hard drive. There is a huge selection of software available for young children, but only about one-fourth of what is on the market is developmentally appropriate; inappropriate "drill and practice" programs, in which there is one right answer, represent the majority of software packages on the market today (Shade, 1996). Haugland and Shade, (1990) propose 10 criteria for judging developmental appropriateness.

Software—The "instructions" that direct a computer to perform an activity, usually stored on a disk or directly in the computer; many such programs are available for young children.

1. **Age appropriateness**—The concepts taught and methods presented show realistic expectations of young children.
2. **Child control**—The children, as active participants, not the computer, decide the flow and direction of the activity.
3. **Clear instructions**—Verbal or graphic directions are simple and precise. Written instructions are not appropriate.
4. **Expanding complexity**—Software begins with a child's current skills, then builds on these in a realistic learning sequence that continues to challenge.
5. **Independence**—Children are able to use the computer and software with a minimum amount of adult supervision.

Many early childhood programs today include computers for children's use. Many of the early concerns about computers for young children, for instance, that computers would discourage peer interaction, have been dispelled. What are some advantages and potential problems in using computers in early childhood programs?

6. **Process orientation**—The intrinsic joys of exploring and discovering are what engage children on the computer. Printouts of completed work can be fun, but they are not the primary objective. Extrinsic rewards such as smiling faces or other reinforcers are not necessary.
7. **Real-world model**—Objects used in software are reliable models of aspects of the world, in appropriate proportion to each other, and in meaningful settings.
8. **Technical features—**Children's attention is better held by high-quality software, with colorful, uncluttered, animated, and realistic graphics, and realistic sound effects. Software also loads and runs quickly, minimizing waiting times.
9. **Trial and error**—Children have unlimited opportunity for creative problem solving, exploring alternatives, and correcting their own errors.
10. **Transformations**—Children are able to change objects and situations and see the effects of their actions.

DEVELOPMENTALLY APPROPRIATE MATERIALS

A wide variety of developmentally appropriate learning materials are available commercially; in addition, many programs also include teacher- or parent-made materials.

In addition to the more expensive furnishings and equipment, an early childhood classroom requires a rich variety of play and learning materials. These include commercially purchased items such as puzzles, crayons, or Legos; teacher- or parent-made games and manipulatives; commercial or teacher-assembled kits that put together combinations of items for specific dramatic play themes or flannel board stories; and donated scrap materials for art or construction activities. Review the recommended basics for an early childhood program listed in Figure 7-2.

Montessori equipment—Early childhood learning materials derived from and part of the Montessori approach.

One special category of learning resources, **Montessori equipment,** stands out because of its specific attributes and prescribed use. These materials are available through special catalogs for use in Montessori programs. Montessori items are of high quality and design, and their cost is also relatively high. The Montessori philosophy does not recommend that these materials be used by non-Montessori schools, although many eclectic programs stock some of these materials. You may want to review the discussion of Maria Montessori's program and its contemporary counter-parts in Chapter 5.

Criteria for Selecting Materials

More than ever before, a great selection of early childhood materials is commercially available. Toy and variety stores, as well as catalogs, display variously priced toys and games that often promise to fully educate or entertain young children. In selecting learning and play materials, some specific criteria must be met to assure their suitability for young children.

Materials need to be carefully selected to ensure that they are developmentally appropriate.

- **Developmentally appropriate**—Materials should match the stage of development of the children. Toddlers just mastering language and locomotion will benefit from play items that encourage vocabulary building, promote a sense of balance, exercise fingers,

Blocks are among the most versatile, open-ended materials because they lend themselves to an infinite variety of uses.

and feed their burgeoning sense of independence. Older preschoolers and primary children, on the other hand, need materials that utilize their more refined skills in all areas of development. All early childhood materials, however, should actively involve children, be interesting, and be safe.

- **Active**—Young children need materials that they can act on. They quickly get bored with items that require no action on their part or that don't stretch the imagination. All early childhood materials should promote active involvement and exploration.
- **Open-ended**—Among the most popular and most frequently used materials are open-ended toys, ones that can be used flexibly and do not dictate how they are to be used. Not all materials in the early childhood program will be open-ended (puzzles, for instance, have only one outcome), but the majority should be.
- **Give feedback**—As children interact with materials, they should receive feedback on the success of their actions. A completed puzzle tells the child that the pieces have been fitted together correctly; when the "bridge" stays up, the child knows that the blocks were stacked successfully; when there is a place setting for each of the four children at the table in the housekeeping area, they know that they have matched children and dishes appropriately.
- **Multipurpose**—Materials or combinations of materials should suggest many possibilities for play. Children's problem-solving skills and imaginations will be enhanced by multipurpose materials. Children of different skill levels should be able to use materials successfully.
- **Safe and durable**—Items purchased for children's use should be sturdy and well constructed. Materials should be of high quality, for instance, hardwood or nonbreakable plastics. Young children should not be given toys that require electricity. All materials should be checked regularly for loose parts, sharp edges, splinters, or chipping paint.
- **Attractive**—Materials' appearance should be appealing and inviting.

Toddlers who have not yet mastered the social skills involved in sharing should have access to more than one of their favorite play materials.

- **Nonsexist, nonracial**—Materials should convey a sense of equality and tolerance rather than reinforce sexist, racial, or cultural stereotypes.
- **Variety**—A wide variety of materials that cater to different interests and that meet all developmental needs is necessary. There should be ample materials to develop fine and gross motor skills, to exercise cognitive processes, to promote language use, to encourage socialization, to provide outlets for emotional needs, and to invite creativity.
- **Duplicate**—Although variety gives children divergent ways through which they can develop skills, there should also be more than one of some items. Toddlers, who have not yet mastered the art of sharing, especially need the assurance of multiples of popular items.

Teacher-Made Materials and Resources

Teachers may develop classroom resource materials, for instance, dramatic play kits, a flannel board story file, or a song and fingerplay file.

Some of the best early childhood materials are not purchased commercially but are ones that an energetic teacher or parent constructs. Homemade toys often are tailored to fit the specific interests or needs of the children. Many resource books offer excellent suggestions and instructions for games and materials that enhance cognitive concepts, fine or gross motor skills, and language development (Baratta-Lorton, 1979; Debelack, Herr, & Jacobson, 1981; Linderman, 1979).

Teachers also can develop and organize classroom resource materials to facilitate planning and programming. One helpful resource is dramatic play kits, which contain a collection of props for common dramatic play themes. Contained in individual labeled boxes, dramatic play kits can include some of the following items:

- **Health theme**—bandages, empty syringes, hospital gowns, stethoscope, empty medicine vials, and similar items donated by local doctors, hospitals, other health care providers
- **Bakery theme**—rolling pins, cookie cutters, baking pans, muffin liners, aprons

Many wonderful early childhood materials have been made by teachers or parents.

- **Self-care theme**—small mirrors, combs, toothbrushes, hair rollers, empty shampoo bottles, other cosmetic containers
- **Grocery store theme**—empty food containers, cash register, register tapes, bags, play money

Another helpful resource is a flannel board story file. The flannel board pieces, a copy of the story, and suggestions for variations can be collected into separate manila envelopes, then labeled and stored in an accessible place. Similar to pulling a book off the bookshelf, flannel board stories will then be readily available to both teachers and children who wish to use them.

A similar collection of favorites can be put into a song and fingerplay file. One way to do this is to type the most frequently used songs and fingerplays on 5″ × 8″ cards, laminate them, punch holes in the upper left corners, alphabetize the cards, and connect them with a key ring. This file can be used by new or substitute teachers and can help refresh the memory of teachers who may have forgotten all the words. Newly acquired songs or fingerplays can be added at any time.

Community resources can provide a variety of interesting materials for early childhood programs.

Numerous community resources can be tapped for useful materials. Often, their scraps can be an early childhood teacher's treasures. Home decorating businesses may be able to contribute color chips and wallpaper or drapery samples. Printing companies may be able to provide trimmings from paper of different colors, sizes, textures, and weights. Carpet sales rooms may make available carpet squares or the heavy inner rolls from carpeting. Businesses that receive copious computer printouts may be able to provide computer printout paper for art and writing projects. Lumber companies are usually willing to share scraps of soft wood or wood shavings. Travel agents may have old travel posters and brochures to contribute. It is a good idea to canvas your community for possible resources.

PARENTS' ROLE IN THE EARLY CHILDHOOD ENVIRONMENT

Parents can be an important resource to the early childhood program in relation to the environment.

Parents can be active participants in matters related to the early childhood environment. They can contribute in a variety of ways to selecting, modifying, or maintaining various aspects of the environment. Some programs have advisory or policy-making parent councils that may be involved in decisions about major purchases or construction. Parents also often have a strong commitment to their children's program and are willing to spend a few weekend hours helping to paint, clean, varnish, or construct. Many parents contribute to their child's center by making learning materials or contributing throwaways that children can use for creative activities. As in all areas of the early childhood center's functioning, parents can be a tremendous resource in matters related to the environment.

SUMMARY

1. The physical environment affects both children and adults.
2. Consider the importance of the indoor environment, focusing on how to use it most effectively to support the development of young children.
3. Consider the outdoor environment and how to maximize its potential.
4. Occasionally the environment must be adapted to meet the requirements of children with special needs.
5. Select developmentally appropriate equipment, with particular emphasis on the role of computers in early childhood programs.
6. Consider criteria for selecting appropriate materials for use in early childhood programs.

KEY TERMS LIST

adventure playground
behavior setting
computer literacy
creative playgrounds
equipment
learning centers
materials
Montessori equipment
place identity
playscapes
software

part V

The How of Early Childhood Education—Curriculum

We will now turn our attention to the *how* of early childhood education, just what it is that involves teachers and children. In Part V, we will examine those aspects of the early childhood program that deal with curriculum.

chapter 8

Scheduling and Curriculum Planning

The schedule is the overall structure into which you must fit the curriculum and activities. The schedule provides a sequence for the events of the day as well as the length of time various components will last. It also allows for many types of interactions: between child and child, between adult and child, and among small and large groups. In addition, the schedule provides time to do activities in a variety of environments (Hohmann, Banet, & Weikart, 1979). But more than that, the schedule reflects your program's philosophy, takes into account the needs and interests of the children, and provides the security of a predictable routine for children and teachers (Essa & Rogers, 1992).

Curriculum is fitted within the structure of the schedule. Planning curriculum is at the heart of your program, an opportunity for thoughtfully building on what the children already know, introducing relevant new topics, and creating a positive attitude toward learning. In this chapter we will examine, in detail, guidelines for good scheduling and for effective curriculum planning.

COMPONENTS OF THE EARLY CHILDHOOD SCHEDULE

Most early childhood programs contain some fairly standard elements. How these components are arranged and how much time is allocated to them reflects the school's as well as the teachers' philosophy and goals. Consider, for instance, a program in which the children spend the bulk of the time in self-selected activities and a program where the teacher directs and controls most of the day's activities. In the first, the philosophy and goals reflect a respect for the child's growing independence, increasing decision-making skills, and ability to draw what is valuable from the day's experiences. In the second example, the teacher feels a need to supervise the children's experiences closely to ensure that they gain specific skills and information. Both approaches are used, although most early childhood professionals prefer the former, where faith is placed in children's ability to learn and flourish in a well-planned environment. Let us now examine standard components of the early childhood program, keeping in mind that these can be arranged in a great variety of ways.

Activity Time

Activity time—Largest block(s) of time in the early childhood program day during which children can self-select from a variety of activities.

One of the largest time blocks in the early childhood schedule is activity time, during which children select from a variety of developmentally appropriate activities.

The largest block(s) of time each day should be reserved for planned activities from which the children can select. **Activity time,** in many programs, is also called self-selected learning activities, free play, play time, learning center time, or other similar names that connote that the children make choices about the activities in which they engage. This is the part of the schedule in which you insert many of the activities we will discuss in the next few chapters. A wide variety of well-planned activities should reinforce and support the objectives and theme of the curriculum. Each day's activities should also provide multiple opportunities for development of fine and gross motor, cognitive, creative, social, and language skills.

In a part-day program, there will usually be only one lengthy activity time block; an all-day child care program will typically have at least one such block in the morning and one in the afternoon. Such time blocks should include at least 45 minutes, and can be as long as 2 hours, to allow children ample time to survey the options, select an activity, get involved in it, and bring it to a satisfactory conclusion. Many children will, of course, participate in more than one activity, but others will spend all of their time with one activity.

Increasingly larger time blocks will be required as children mature and as their attention span increases. Thus, in an after-school program, you may plan up to 2 hours for activity time, assuming, of course, stimulating, age-appropriate activities are available.

A recent study confirms the importance of an adequate-length time block for self-selected play. Christie, Johnsen, & Peckover (1988) compared four- and five-year-olds' social and cognitive levels of involvement in play during a 15-minute and a 30-minute free play period. They found that when the play period was longer, children engaged in more mature play. More specifically, in the longer play period, children engaged in considerably more group play than parallel or solitary play; in the shorter period, there was more onlooker and unoccupied behavior. Similarly, there was significantly more constructive play, in which objects are used to make something, during the longer play period.

Activity time blocks also allow the teachers to interact with children individually or in small groups. Social guidance, informal conversations, well-timed questions, and careful listening give teachers the chance to learn more about the children in the class, develop relationships, introduce or reinforce concepts, evaluate the children's understanding of concepts, or assess developmental status.

When planning the activity time block, consider safety and adequate supervision. Some activities require close attention by an adult, whereas others can be carried out relatively independently by the children. Such activities as cooking and woodworking require constant teacher attention, for example. Water and sand play, other sensory activities, messy media, and blocks also need close supervision.

For each activity time block, it is important to consider the balance between activities that should be closely supervised and those that are more self-directed, particularly in relation to the number of adults available in the class. It can be easy to lose sight of safety needs in an effort to provide a wide variety of interesting and stimulating activities.

Large Group Activities

Most programs include one or more times when all of the children and teachers gather together. **Large group time**—variously called circle, story time, group, or other similar names—can be used for many purposes. Some teachers tend to use it in the same way day after day, and others use such times to meet various objectives. Some programs have several group times, each serving a different purpose, for example, morning business (roll call, calendar), story, or music/movement.

Large group time (also called circle, story, or group time)—Time block(s) during the day when all of the children and teachers join together in a common activity.

Large group times, when teachers and children gather together, can serve a variety of purposes and include many types of activities.

Group times offer the possibility of meeting a wide variety of objectives. For instance, they provide an excellent opportunity to introduce a new curriculum topic or to probe the children's comprehension of concepts and information (Essa & Rogers, 1992). They can also be used for discussions, stories and books, songs, finger plays, movement, socialization, poetry, games, dramatizations, sharing, relaxation exercises, planning and review, calendar or weather, and a host of other activities best carried out with the whole group (McAfee, 1985).

From interviews with and observations of early childhood teachers, McAfee (1985) found that the most popular and frequently observed circle activity was reading of books or stories. In verbal interviews, teachers indicated that music activities were carried out almost as often as book and story activities, but in actual classroom observations McAfee found music used only about one-third as often as reading activities. "Show and Tell" was observed quite regularly, whereas other types of activities were seen relatively infrequently or not at all.

Group times are almost always teacher-initiated and led, although teachers often seek children's input. In fact, older preschoolers and primary children enjoy and are very competent in leading group activities, for instance, "reading" a familiar book, leading songs, and moving the group into transitions. Such opportunities to take over group leadership should, of course, never be imposed and should be conducted as the child chooses.

When guiding large group (as well as small group) activities, it is important to remember how children learn and what constitutes developmentally appropriate group activities. Children, as active learners, will gain more from activities that allow for their input, include active involvement, and encourage flexible problem solving. Asking children to provide answers for which there is a "right" or "wrong," "correct" or "incorrect" response does not support their developmental needs and their growing self-esteem.

In small group activities, the teacher focuses on a specific concept that is presented to five or six children at a similar developmental level.

Small Group Activities

During small group activities, a teacher usually presents a concept to a few children, ensuring that the activity matches their abilities and interests.

Some programs include a small group activity time during which five or six children work with one teacher for a short period, generally 10 to 15 minutes. This can be handled by staggering small groups throughout the program day or by having each teacher take a small group during a designated small group time block. Usually such times focus on teaching specific concepts and are geared to the abilities and interests of the children in the group (Hohmann et al., 1979). Children are often grouped by developmental level for small group activities, although Hohmann and colleagues recommend that small groups represent a cross-section of the classroom population to promote cross-learning. In a small group setting, the teacher has an opportunity to pay close attention to each individual child. As you might expect, careful planning is crucial for successful small group activity times.

Outdoor Activity

Large time blocks should be set aside for outdoor activities.

A large time block for outdoor play should be part of the daily schedule. Some adults think of outdoor play merely as a time for children to expend excess energy and for teachers to take a rest. But outdoor time contains far too many valuable opportunities for learning and development to be dismissed in this way. When you think of outdoor play as an integral part of the early childhood experience, it becomes natural to allocate at least 45 minutes to this time block. Keep in mind that outdoor time requires planning in the same way that indoor activity does, and that it involves the same kinds of teacher-child interactions.

Just as during activity times, the teacher's role when outside includes setting up a stimulating environment, providing for each child's individual needs, guiding children's behavior, providing a variety of experiences, taking opportunities to teach concepts, and encouraging exploration and problem solving. In addition, some unique safety concerns require special attention in an outdoor play area. An important skill that you, as the teacher, should develop is the ability to scan, to keep an eye on the entire outdoor play area. It is particularly important to pay attention to the fronts and backs of swings, slides, climbing

So much learning goes on in the outdoor environment! Large blocks of time for vigorous outdoor play must be an important part of the early childhood schedule.

equipment, tricycles, and other wheeled toys, and the area in and around the sandbox.

Time for outdoor play may be affected by the weather, although the weather should never be used as an excuse for not going outside. Children thoroughly enjoy the snow, for instance, if they are properly clothed. Children do not catch cold from playing outside in the winter.

If inclement weather does prevent the children from enjoying outside time, alternative activities should be made available inside so children can expend energy and engage in large motor activity. Many schools have a selection of large motor equipment, such as tumbling mats or an indoor climbing apparatus, to use on rainy days. If this equipment is in a relatively restricted space, then small groups of children should be allowed to use it throughout the day rather than having the entire group involved at one time.

Cleanup

It is wise to schedule 10 to 15 minutes, particularly after activity times, for children and teachers to participate in putting the classroom back into order. When cleanup time is included in the daily schedule, it conveys that this is an important component of the program.

Other important components that must be considered in scheduling include cleanup, meals, nap, and transitions.

Meals

Sharing food provides a unique opportunity for socialization and learning; thus, almost every program includes at least one snack, if not several meals. A 3-hour program usually includes a snack time around the halfway point of the day. The timing of meals, however, should be dictated by the children's needs, not by a rigid schedule, especially for infants. If it appears that some children get to school having had breakfast several hours before or not having eaten breakfast at all, then an early morning meal should be provided. An alternative, particularly if children's arrival at school is staggered over several hours, is to have snack available for a period of time and allow children to eat as they feel the need to refuel.

KEY QUESTION #1

Visit an early childhood program and look at its daily schedule. What elements are included? Does the schedule seem developmentally appropriate by taking into account the needs of the children? Does it provide the kind of balance discussed in this chapter? Would you change anything in this schedule? Why or why not?

Timing of lunch will depend on the ages of the children, the length of time they are at the center, and when morning snack was served. Younger preschoolers may need lunch at 11:30 a.m. and be ready for a nap by noon. How much time is allocated for each of these meals will depend on the children in the group and the type of meal; generally, however, 15 to 20 minutes for snacks and 20 to 30 minutes for lunch is adequate. Most children can comfortably finish a meal in this period of time.

Nap or Rest

In full-day programs, children should have time for sleep or rest during the middle of the day, usually sometime after, though not immediately following, lunch. Allocating 1 to 2 hours for this time is usually enough (see Chapter 18 for a more detailed discussion). Also be aware of your local regulations for rest time, because some states include specific requirements.

Transitions

Those times between activities are as important as the activities themselves. Failing to plan how children will get from one area to another—from group to the bathroom to snack, or from cleanup time to putting on coats to going outside—can result in chaos. We will discuss transitional techniques in more detail in Chapter 14 in the context of group guidance.

Scheduling for Infants and Toddlers

In an infant and toddler program, the schedule is initially set by the needs of the children and, gradually, shifts toward a more uniform schedule as the children get older. An infant program has to revolve around the eating, waking/sleeping, and elimination patterns of each child. The daily program for each child is uniquely tailored around her or his physiological patterns. As they get older, children begin to eat at times more consistent with adult meals; sleep primarily at night with two time spans, then one time span, for sleep; and regulate their elimination schedule. Thus, by the end of the toddler years, children are ready to enter into a more uniform schedule that applies to the entire group. One of the best ways to meet the needs of infants and toddlers and to help them make the gradual transition from an individual to a group schedule is to provide a consistent caregiver who remains with them throughout this period. See EXPERIENCES for an example of such an arrangement.

GUIDELINES FOR PROGRAM SCHEDULING

In planning a schedule, it is important to balance times when children are active and when they are quiet.

These components of the early childhood day—activity time, large group activities, small group activities, outdoor activity, cleanup, meals, nap or rest, and transitions—can be arranged in the daily schedule in a wide variety of ways. Let's examine some guidelines that will help in setting an effective schedule.

EXPERIENCES

chapter 8

GERRI, Head Teacher, Infant/Toddler Class

Attachment and Continuity

In our center, the three infant/toddler head teachers stay with a group of children for three years. Teachers and children move to new rooms as the children's development indicates new skills and needs. So, over a three-year period, a strong bond is formed between teachers and each of the children in their group. Above everything else, the children gain a good foundation of self-esteem; this, in turn, leads to a strong sense of independence. All other skills develop naturally because the children have gained a strong sense of trust and a strong attachment to their teacher.

At one time, each of the teachers had a group of infants, or one-year-olds, or two-year-olds, for one year. Then the children moved on to a new room and a new teacher; but things are very different now. I've reflected on how this new, three-year rotation has affected all of us, children and teachers. I think that my whole approach is different. When the children were with me for one year, I tended to focus on those that had the greatest needs; not that the others were ignored, but they did not get my wholehearted commitment. Now I find that the three-year period I spend with children gives me a chance to get to know each one intimately and in depth. Somehow, I don't feel the pressure of having to "accomplish" certain goals; these seem to get accomplished anyway, but much more flexibly.

I know the children very well. I know their moods, the nuances of their communication, their body language, their strengths, their needs. And they know me. They know my body language, for instance, what a certain look from across the room means. I use a lot of expressive facial expressions. We can "read" each other. The children are comfortable with me because we have such a long-standing relationship based on trust. I've known them virtually all their lives. The continuity of being with me, an adult to whom they have a strong attachment, for three years provides an anchor for them.

Perhaps the most important aspect of our relationship is that I don't get into power struggles with the children. I try not to limit them and I give them as much independence as possible. In many ways I recognize that there is no need for me to impose an all-or-nothing situation on children. They can make choices about play, about eating, about sleeping, about toileting. I have found that when a child resists I need to step back and reassess the situation. More often than not, I am imposing a decision that the child could have made on her own. So, I always try to examine the child's needs and to give the child a choice whenever possible. When children are allowed to make their own decisions, they are less likely to resist when there is no choice possible.

Increasing research about the needs for consistency and continuity of very young children has given many infant/toddler programs the impetus to change the staffing pattern. By having the same teacher stay with a group of children over an extended period of time, these children are able to develop the self-esteem and independence so important as a foundation to all aspects of development.

experiences

Alternating Active and Quiet Times

Children need time both to expend energy and to rest. A useful rule in scheduling is to look at the total time in terms of cycles of activity and rest, boisterousness and quiet, energy and relaxation. Categorize the descriptions of time blocks listed in your daily schedule in terms of active (for example, activity time, outdoor play, large group activities that involve movement) and less active times (for example, story, small group activities, nap, snack).

In applying this guideline, think about providing the opportunity to be physically active after quiet times and to slow down after active involvement. Also consider the total consecutive time that children are expected to sit quietly. Thus, reconsider a schedule in which children sit at a large group activity from 10:00 to 10:20, then move into a small group activity from 10:20 to 10:35, followed by snack until 11:00. Such a schedule ought to include an active break within that hour, in which children shift from one relatively inactive period to another. Similarly, when children have been engaged in active exploration, a quieter time should follow. One caution: Do not expect children to move immediately from very active involvement, such as outdoor play, to being very quiet, such as nap time. For such times, plan a more gentle transition that helps children settle down gradually.

Balancing Child-Initiated and Teacher-Initiated Activities

KEY QUESTION #2

Consider the issue of child-initiated vs. teacher-initiated activity. Do you agree with the author that there should be ample time for children to make decisions and exercise independence or do you think more teacher control is important? Note that not everyone agrees on this question. Discuss this question with others in your class and consider both sides of the issue.

There should be a balance between child-initiated and teacher-initiated activities to allow children enough time to make decisions and exercise their growing autonomy.

Most early childhood programs provide large time blocks in which children can make decisions about the activities in which they will participate and how they will carry them out. Most programs also include times when teachers direct activities. Typically, activity time and outdoor time accommodate child initiation, whereas small and large group times involve teacher initiation. Some functional activities, such as snack, nap, and cleanup, require children to follow the direction of adults and thus do not entail children's initiative.

A balance between child and teacher control must be considered carefully. When young children are allowed to decide how they will spend their time, they develop qualities such as autonomy, judgment, independent decision making, social give-and-take, initiative, exploration, and creativity. In addition, children are also expected to develop a reasonable amount of compliance, understand the rules of group behavior, and accept the authority and wisdom of adults. Generally, when adults convey respect for and trust in the ability of children to make appropriate decisions, children will reciprocate with enthusiastic participation in adult-initiated activities. Of course, teacher-initiated activities must be developmentally appropriate and engage the interest of the children. Most of the day's activities should, however, be child selected and allow children to move from activity to activity at their own pace (Miller, 1984).

Activity Level of the Children

The activity level of the children is an important consideration in making scheduling decisions.

By nature, young children are active and must have many opportunities for expending energy. Some children, however, are more active than others. Occasionally, you will find that you have a group in which

It is important to consider the children's overall activity level. Sometimes a particularly active group of children needs additional time outdoors. Alternatively, you may want to plan more activities that let children expend excess energy indoors.

a large portion of the children is particularly active. If this occurs, a schedule that has worked for you in the past may not serve as well because the needs of the children are different. In such a case, adjusting the schedule as well as the classroom arrangement and the types of activities planned will help the class run more smoothly. You might, for instance, carry out some activities, which are traditionally indoor ones, outside and plan either a longer or an added outdoor time block.

Developmental Level of the Children

The ages of the children will have an impact on the schedule because older children have longer attention spans and younger children may require more time for some routines.

As children get older, their attention span noticeably increases; thus, your daily schedule should reflect the group's ages and developmental levels (Miller, 1984). For older children, plan longer time blocks for small group, large group, and activity times. On the other hand, younger children require added time for meals, nap, and cleanup. With a group of very young children, you may also want to schedule regular times for toileting, for instance, before going outdoors and before nap.

The length of large group time can be particularly problematic. The time allocated to such activities will depend on the ages and attention spans of the children. Children can, of course, sit for a longer period of time if the activity captivates their interest; but, generally, a well-paced, shorter group time is more rewarding for all. As the program year progresses, reassess the length of group time and adjust it according to the children's interest.

Group Size

Creative scheduling can provide an effective way of working with large groups of children.

Group size may also influence the schedule. Particularly with a large group of children, creative scheduling can be used to allow for more individualized attention to children. One example is a church-supported child care center in which the one large room, in which more than 50 children of varying ages spend the day together, dictates scheduling considerations. Although the children and teachers share the same indoor and outdoor space, the director has created five subgroups of children and teachers who alternate use of the outdoor area, the indoor large-motor area, and the large variety of other learning centers. Thus, while one group is involved in a music activity, another will be outside, while the other groups are engaged in self-selected activities. The children know that they will also have a chance to participate in the other activities because space, teachers, and time blocks are rotated for different groups of children.

Arrival of Children

The schedule also needs to take into account whether children all arrive at school at the same time or whether, as in most child care facilities, their arrival is staggered over a period of time.

How children arrive and leave the center—whether over staggered periods of time or at about the same time—has to be taken into account in scheduling. In most child care centers, the early morning period, until most or all of the children are at school, and the late afternoon period, when children start leaving for home, require some special considerations. The arrival or departure of children makes carrying out teacher-initiated activities difficult because the teacher and other children are interrupted frequently and because the arriving or departing children will not get the full benefit of the teacher-led activity. Thus, self-selected activities, in which children can control engagement and disengagement, should be available during such times. In programs where all the children arrive at the same time, on the other hand, the first activity might be a teacher-initiated group time to introduce the plan for the day.

Seasonal Considerations

In a location where the weather gets very cold or very hot in winter or summer, the schedule may need to be adjusted to include less outdoor time.

In geographic locations where the weather varies considerably from season to season, you may want to adjust the schedule according to the time of year. For instance, during winter in a New England child care program, it would be difficult to keep to a schedule that contains three outdoor time blocks when each involves helping children get into their snowsuits, boots, mittens, and hats and then getting them out of such clothing at the end of the outdoor time. At the same time, a lengthy outdoor time is inappropriate when the temperature is below freezing or, for that matter, when it reaches 100 degrees. Yet once spring arrives and the temperature is balmy, the schedule should allow for longer outdoor time. The weather can certainly affect your schedule, so a flexible approach and attitude are important when working with young children.

TYPES OF SCHEDULES

KEY QUESTION #3

You probably know children like Rita who spend most of their day in a child care center. How are the needs of these children met? How do they differ from a child like David? In what ways can the schedule take the children's needs into consideration?

Schedules for various programs, for instance, infant care, preschool, child care, before- and after-school care, will vary because they meet different needs for the children; the needs of teachers also must be considered in the schedule.

Obviously, the schedules of an infant program, a $2\frac{1}{2}$-hour preschool, a child care center, and a before- and after-school program will differ and must be designed to meet the unique needs of the children and teachers. Take the example of two children to illustrate how the program must meet children's needs. David attends a 3-hour morning preschool program because his parents want him to have an enriching social and learning experience. He gets up around 7:00, eats breakfast with his parents before his father leaves for work, and plays for an hour or so before his mother takes him to school at the nearby recreation center. At lunch his mother picks him up and he has lunch with her and his younger sister Tina, after which he reads or plays with his mother while Tina takes a nap. After dinner, Dad reads the children a story, and they go to bed by 8:00. Rita, who lives with her single mother and two older sisters, has been in child care since she was six weeks old.

She gets up at 6:30 and they are out of the house by 7:15, with or without time for breakfast. She spends the day at the child care center, from about 7:45 to 5:30 in the evening. After picking up her sisters, the family stops at the grocery store or sometimes McDonald's, gets home by about 6:30, followed by dinner, some TV, and bed time. Clearly the two children have very different needs that their respective early childhood programs have to meet.

Although the main scheduling consideration for full-day programs is the needs of the children, the schedule must also take into account the requirements of the staff. Early childhood teachers spend long and difficult hours working with their young charges, a job that can be tiring, energizing, frustrating as well as rewarding. Complementary to the schedule provided for the children has to be a schedule that provides rest, rejuvenation, and planning time for the adults. When the needs of the adults are considered, the children's needs will be better met, and teacher burnout is less likely to occur.

Examples of Schedules

After examining standard components of the early childhood program, guidelines for scheduling, and differences between preschool and child care, you probably have concluded correctly that a daily schedule can be arranged in numerous ways. Figures 8-1, 8-2, 8-3, and 8-4 show four

Schedules for infants and toddlers need to be completely flexible, set by the individual schedules of the children.

FIGURE 8-1 Full-day program for a group of four- and five-year-olds

7:30–9:00	**Staggered Arrival:** Teachers greet children and talk to parents; self-selected activities such as books, manipulatives, play dough, and blocks.
7:30–8:30	Breakfast available.
9:00–9:20	**Group Time:** Introduction of day's activities; story or discussion related to day's topic.
9:20–10:30	**Activity Time:** Self-selected activities from learning centers, or teacher-planned projects.
10:30–10:40	**Cleanup Time.**
10:40–11:00	**Snack.**
11:00–11:15	**Small Group Activity:** Teacher-initiated, small group activity to reinforce specific concepts.
11:15–12:00	**Outdoor Time:** Self-selected activities.
12:00–12:20	**Group Time:** Recap of morning; story; music.
12:20–12:30	**Wash for Lunch.**
12:30–1:00	**Lunch.**
1:00–3:00	**Nap:** Transition to nap and sleep for those requiring a nap.
1:00–1:30	**Rest:** Quiet individual activity for nonsleepers.
1:30–3:00	**Activity Time:** Self-selected activities, both inside and outside; as sleeping children wake, they gradually join others.
3:00–3:20	**Snack.**
3:20–4:00	**Activity Time:** Continued self-selected activities both inside and outside.
4:00–4:10	**Cleanup.**
4:10–4:30	**Group Time:** Closing of day; story; movement activity.
4:30–5:30	**Staggered Departure:** Self-selected activities until all children leave.

FIGURE 8-2 Full-day program for a group of two- to three-year-olds

7:30–9:00	**Staggered Arrival:** Teachers greet children and talk to parents; self-selected activities such as books, manipulatives, play dough, and blocks.
7:30–8:30	Breakfast available.
9:00–9:15	**Group Time:** Introduce day's activities; story.
9:15–10:00	**Activity Time:** Self-selected activities from learning centers, or teacher-planned projects.
10:00–10:15	**Cleanup Time.**
10:15–10:20	**Snack.**
10:20–10:30	**Toileting.**
10:30–11:15	**Outdoor Time:** Self-selected activities.
11:15–11:30	**Group Time:** Story, music, finger plays.
11:30–11:45	**Wash for Lunch.**
11:45–12:15	**Lunch.**
12:15–2:15	**Nap:** Transition to nap and sleep.
2:15–2:45	**Toileting followed by Snack.**
2:45–3:30	**Outdoor Time.**
3:30–4:15	**Activity Time:** Self-selected activities.
4:15–4:30	**Cleanup.**
4:30–4:45	**Group Time:** Story, puppets, movement.
4:45–5:30	**Staggered Departure:** Self-selected activities until all children leave.

FIGURE 8-3 Half-day program for three- and four-year-olds

8:50–9:00	**Arrival.**
9:00–9:20	**Group Time:** Introduce day's activities; story, music.
9:20–9:40	**Snack.**
9:40–10:30	**Activity Time:** Self-selected activities.
10:30–10:40	**Cleanup.**
10:40–11:00	**Small Group Activity.**
11:00–11:40	**Outdoor Time.**
11:40–11:55	**Group Time:** Closing and recap of day.
11:55–12:00	**Departure:** Gather belongings; teachers talk to parents briefly.

FIGURE 8-4 Before- and after-school program

6:00–8:30	**Arrival:** Breakfast available, self-selected activities; outdoor play, weather permitting.
8:30	**Board Bus for School.**
3:00–4:15	**Arrival:** Snack available until 4:15; outdoor play, with organized games available.
4:15–4:30	**Group meeting, discussion.**
4:30–6:00	**Self-selected indoor activities:** Projects, clubs, activity centers, homework, etc.

examples of schedules that consider many variables. Of course, any schedule you devise must meet the unique characteristics of your group and children, your philosophy, and your program.

FLEXIBILITY OF THE SCHEDULE

The schedule provides the framework within which your program functions. You might think of the schedule as the skeleton and the curriculum and activities as the flesh that fills out and defines the character of the inner structure. A sound skeleton is vital to a healthy body, just as a well-put-together schedule is integral to a well-run program.

The daily schedule also provides security, because it gives the day a predictable order. A good schedule provides the predictability that children need, and they soon learn the sequence of activities. Thus, you can say to a child, "I know you are anxious for your mother to come. After we finish cleaning up, we will go outside. Later, when we come back inside, we will read a story, and then your mother will be here." The child can relate to this temporal time frame because he or she is familiar with the schedule.

The schedule should also allow for flexibility, rather than being followed rigidly. There are many occasions when the set time frame should be altered. For instance, if you find that the children are particularly engrossed in activity time, extend that time and shorten a later time block; the clock should not arbitrarily cut off involved play. If it has been raining relentlessly for two weeks and today is a beautiful, sunny day, plan to spend a large portion of the day outside so everyone can enjoy the nice weather. Similarly, if, despite your best efforts, the children are restless and uninterested in your group activity, shorten the time rather than allowing a negative situation to develop. In other words, use cues from the children—and your judgment—to adapt the schedule if it will improve the flow of the day and better meet the needs of the children. You might also ask the children what changes in the schedule they would suggest. Their insights will surprise you!

Young children need the security of a predictable schedule, but the schedule should never be rigid. For instance, activities can be prolonged if the children are engrossed or shortened if they are inattentive.

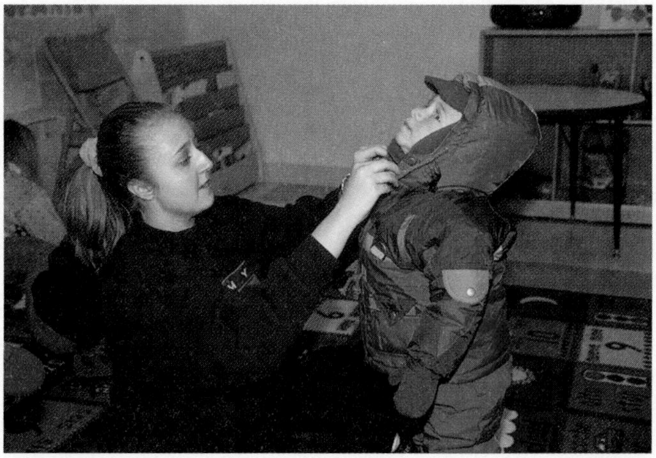

The schedule may need to be rearranged according to the weather. If winters are severe, it would be difficult to help the entire group get in and out of full snow gear several times a day. Think about your own part of the country. What climatic conditions might affect the schedule during different seasons?

Although the daily schedule should be predictable, it also needs to remain flexible. If, for instance, the children seem unusually inattentive and restless at group time, shorten it.

Some large early childhood centers, because they have multiple classes that share some common facilities, establish a centerwide schedule. Such a schedule makes flexibility of certain aspects of the day more difficult, but still allows for some latitude. It may not be possible to alter the time allocated for outside play when classes rotate the use of the playground, or of meals if they share a common dining room; however, self-contained parts of the schedule, such as activity or group time, should be adapted as required.

In infant programs, there are multiple daily schedules. Each child has an individual schedule, set by her own needs and rhythms of being awake and sleeping, eating, and elimination. Furthermore, as children get older, their schedules change and they spend more time alert, playing, exploring their environment, and interacting with peers and nurturing adults. Teachers need to be very flexible, adjusting their own time use to the needs of the children. Toddlers, on the other hand, begin to establish a more predictable routine that resembles that of the other children in the group. Nonetheless, flexibility is still very important because there will be many individual variations in schedule. Especially important parts of the daily schedule for infants and toddlers are arrival and departure times, those transitions between home and school that should promote security and calm for the children as well as facilitate communication among adults (Wortham, 1994).

WHAT IS CURRICULUM?

Curriculum—Overall master plan of the early childhood program, reflecting its philosophy, into which specific activities are fit.

Early childhood professionals view curriculum as dealing with the "whole child," not focused on only one facet such as intellectual development.

Now that we have discussed the daily schedule, let's turn to an examination of the **curriculum**, the content and substance of that schedule. The term curriculum has a somewhat different connotation in early childhood than in elementary, secondary, or higher education. In these settings, curriculum often refers to a course of study on a specific topic, such as a curriculum in history, social studies, physics, reading, or any other subject. Thus, students typically are in the midst of several curricula, which are not necessarily connected to each other. In early childhood, curriculum tends to be viewed more holistically, and all aspects of the program are integrated and related. In fact, in early

A Closer Look

Developmentally Appropriate Practice

You have seen the term *developmentally appropriate practice* (DAP) used on a number of occasions in this text, and you might have asked yourself, What exactly is DAP? NAEYC has published its newly revised edition of the DAP statement (Bredekamp & Copple, 1997), in which there is an expanded discussion and considerable clarification of the ideals and concepts included in this statement. "*Developmentally appropriate practices* result from the process of professionals making decisions about the well-being and education of children" (Bredekamp & Copple, 1997, p. 8).

These decisions are based on an interplay of three sources of information that serve as a foundation for professionals working with young children—general child development; specifics about the strengths, needs, and interests of individual children; and the sociocultural contexts of the children's family lives. None of these can be left out in decisions about programs for young children. In other words, you, as a teacher, continually need to keep in mind information about age norms, each individual child's fit to these, and the family's culture and values as you make decisions about the program.

The newly revised DAP address decisions relevant to curriculum at great length. To be appropriate, curriculum must be challenging, relevant, and interesting to children. The authors consider that too many young children today are subject to developmentally inappropriate curriculum, either because it demands too little or too much (of the wrong things) of them. If curriculum is based on learning a set of narrow, basic skills that address, for instance, items on a standardized test, countless opportunities for more complex learning are lost and children are left bored and unmotivated. In other instances, curriculum is based on the next year's expectations, and children are expected to learn inappropriate content through inappropriate methods, for instance, large group instruction where children must sit still and listen to the teacher.

Curriculum, to be developmentally appropriate, must incorporate all areas of development; include a broad range of content that is relevant and meaningful to the children; build on what children already know by adding depth and complexity; cross traditional subject matter to help children make connections and facilitate concept development; promote development of knowledge, skills, and a positive disposition toward learning; allow children to use scientific principles of inquiry and experimentation appropriate to their age; incorporate their home culture and language as well as the culture of the community; and set goals for children that are attainable and realistic. The DAP statement also expands on the all-important role of the teacher to respect and know each child well and to facilitate learning, peer collaboration, and a sense of responsibility.

What DAP provides is "some reasonably reliable principles for guiding decisions about what's appropriate for any given group in a specific context" (Bredekamp and Copple, 1997, p. 39). As an aspiring teacher of young children, it would be well worth the investment of your time in carefully reading and thinking about Bredekamp and Copple's *Developmentally Appropriate Practice in Early Childhood Programs Serving Children from Birth Through Age 8.*

childhood, even the word *curriculum* is not used uniformly; for instance, some writers replace it with the word program (Almy, 1975).

Most early childhood professionals today view curriculum as integrally tied to a concern for dealing comprehensively with "the whole child," the child's physical, social, cognitive, and emotional development (Williams, 1987). The foundation for sound program development is based on research and theoretical knowledge that helps us understand how children learn, what makes for a good learning environment, and what curriculum material is suitable for young children.

A recent development in early childhood programming that concerns many professionals is the proliferation of curricula and teaching materials aimed at accelerating young children's development (Elkind, 1987b; Gallagher & Coche, 1987; Minuchin, 1987). Advertisements for preschool programs as well as books, kits, and other teaching materials promise parents brighter children, toddlers who read and do math, or future Harvard graduates.

Many accelerated preschool curricula are based primarily on a downward escalation of curriculum, presenting elementary school tasks and methods to younger children (Bredekamp as quoted in Shell, 1989). Elkind (1987b) warns that programs that teach reading, math, ballet, or gymnastics to very young children should be considered "miseducation" because they put children at risk for short- and long-term stress and other problems. There is no research-based support for such practices; on the contrary, research tells us that they tend to be damaging.

So, as you begin to think about an appropriate curriculum for young children, where do you turn? It might be helpful to remember that young children are eager, absorbent learners, curious and interested in learning as much about their world as possible. Children are equipped with a drive to explore and discover, an urge to see and feel and hear firsthand, a thirst for new experiences in both physical and social realms. This suggests that we do not have to force-feed children what we think they should learn. Rather, we can plan a curriculum based on the faith that children's innate interest in their world will lead them to appropriate learning, given a suitable learning environment and knowledgeable adult guidance.

Elements of the Curriculum

Curriculum involves consideration of the program philosophy, goals and objectives, and evaluation.

The early childhood curriculum is the result of both long-range and short-term planning. Many programs start with a master plan that covers a sizable period, a year for instance, and is then filled in with details for shorter segments of time. In other programs, the curriculum is derived from the interests of the children; planning is generally more spontaneous and flexible in such programs. In either case, curriculum has to be integrally related to several important factors—program philosophy, goals, objectives, and evaluation—as we will discuss (Langenbach & Neskora, 1977). These elements form a cyclical pattern: program philosophy guides goals and objectives; these, in turn, lead to development of content and activities; content and activities are evaluated on an ongoing basis; and, returning to the starting point, goals and objectives are reassessed and adjusted as needed, starting the cycle anew (Lawton, 1988).

Appropriate planning is based on developmentally sound goals and objectives. The objectives of a unit on fruits and vegetables are reinforced through a lotto game in which children match and group items.

Program Philosophy and Curriculum. Curriculum takes its direction from the overall philosophy of your program. For instance, underlying beliefs and values about how children learn will have an impact. The contents of the curriculum will be different if you view children as passive receivers of information rather than as active, explorative learners (Langenbach & Neskora, 1977). Another factor shaping the curriculum will be reliance on a particular theorist's works. For instance, programs derived from the theory of Jean Piaget will focus on developmentally appropriate cognitive tasks, whereas programs based on behaviorist theory may rely more on a direct instructional approach.

Finally, your assumptions about how best to meet specific requirements, for instance, of children from low-income families or those with disabilities, will also affect the curriculum. Thus, your program will differ if you think that a special population of children primarily needs positive socialization experiences, or mostly requires improvement in self-concept, or has the greatest deficit in the cognitive area.

Goals and Objectives and the Curriculum. Out of the program's philosophy comes a set of broad goals, which are then translated into more specific objectives. These provide the basis for the curriculum, elevating activities above a utilitarian rationale, such as "but we have to keep the kids busy!" As we discussed in Chapter 6, goals and objectives are designed both to promote and facilitate growth in developmental areas and to convey specific content related to the curriculum. Objectives, in turn, help set direction to the activities that are planned to implement the daily curriculum.

Evaluation and the Curriculum. Curriculum is only as effective as its match to the children in the program. For this reason, evaluation is an important element in curriculum development. It is important, on an ongoing basis, to evaluate whether the topics and activities of the curriculum are appropriate and meaningful for the children. This can be done informally, by observing the children's engagement in activities and reviewing their comprehension of concepts. If your assessment leads you to question aspects of the program, then modify or change the objectives and the curriculum as needed. (Chapter 6 discusses evaluation in more detail.)

Children's Development and Curriculum

KEY QUESTION #4

What are your memories of your earliest school experiences? What kinds of activities were involved? Can you glean from your recollections what type of curriculum your preschool or day care or kindergarten or first grade teacher might have been following?

Particularly important is the match between the children's development levels, abilities, needs, and interests and the curriculum. This involves understanding child development principles and knowing the characteristics of each individual child in the group.

What you include in the curriculum must be directly related to the children in your program. Curriculum that does not fit the comprehension level, abilities, needs, and interests of the children is meaningless. To plan an appropriate program requires knowledge about the age group of your class, about family characteristics and backgrounds, and about the individual variations among the children in the class.

First of all, a sound understanding of child development is essential to curriculum planning. A general comprehension of what four-years-olds are like is basic to planning for a class of fours. Not only does such knowledge tell you what to expect of this age group in terms of physical, cognitive, and social ability, but it also helps you understand what interests four-year-olds often share.

Furthermore, the more you know about the backgrounds of the children, the more specifically you can plan curriculum to meet the characteristics of the group. Any ethnic, cultural, religious, or regional factors unique to the group can be incorporated to enhance the curriculum and to help children feel good about their uniqueness.

In addition, your ability to observe children and glean information from your observations will help you in developing an appropriate curriculum for the individuals in the class. Topics and activities must be matched carefully to the general abilities of the children as a group, but variations within the group and individual needs of children must be recognized. If children with handicaps are integrated into your class, it is particularly important to ensure that your classroom provides an appropriate program for them.

One of the most valuable guides in developing curriculum is NAEYC's *Developmentally Appropriate Practice in Early Childhood Programs Serving Children From Birth Through Age 8* (Bredekamp, 1987). This resource provides a philosophical rationale as well as specific and pragmatic information on appropriate and inappropriate practices when working with young children.

Curriculum Content

Relevant content for an early childhood curriculum should be derived from the children's life experiences and can revolve around the children themselves, their families, and the community.

What, then, is appropriate in an early childhood curriculum? What interests preschoolers? What is relevant to them? What is developmentally relevant, assuming that during the early years children are developing a predictable set of capacities.

Perhaps the best way to define what is appropriate in a curriculum for preschoolers is to say that it should be derived from the children's life experiences, based on what is concrete, and tied to their emerging skills. Consider that young children have been part of their physical and social world for only a very short time. They have so much to learn about the people, places, objects, and experiences in their environment. When you give careful consideration to making the elements of the environment meaningful and understandable to children, you need not seek esoteric and unusual topics. Children's lives offer a

Having a sound understanding of child development gives you the background to plan developmentally appropriate activities.

rich set of topics on which to build a curriculum, including learning about themselves, their families, and the larger community in which they live (Essa & Rogers, 1992).

Children as the Focus of Curriculum. The most crucial skills with which young children can be armed to face the future are feelings of self-worth and competence. Children are well equipped for success if they are secure about their identities, feel good about themselves, and meet day-to-day tasks and challenges with a conviction that they can tackle almost anything. The curriculum can foster such attributes by contributing to children's self-understanding and providing repeated reinforcement and affirmation of their capabilities, individual uniqueness, and importance.

Self-understanding comes from learning more about oneself—one's identity, uniqueness, body, feelings, physical and emotional needs, likes and dislikes, skills and abilities, and self-care. Children enjoy learning about themselves, so a focus on children as part of the curriculum can and should take up a significant portion of time. It is important, however, to ensure that planned activities are age appropriate so they contribute to both self-understanding and positive self-esteem. Two-year-olds, for instance, are still absorbed in learning to label body parts; thus, activities that contribute to sharpening this language skill are appropriate. Older preschoolers and school-aged children, on the other hand, are more interested in finer details. For example, they enjoy examining hair follicles under a microscope or observing how the joints of a skeleton move in comparison to their own bodies.

The Family as the Focus of Curriculum. The family is vitally relevant to children and provides another rich basis for curriculum topics. We can help children build an understanding and appreciation of the roles of the family, similarities among families, the uniqueness of each family, different family forms, the tasks of families, and relationships among family members. Similarly, an examination of the children's family homes, means of transportation, food preferences, celebrations, parental occupations, and patterns of communication

Follow-up activities help reinforce and clarify concepts learned on the field trip. After a visit to the bakery, the children are now kneading bread dough that will be baked in the school kitchen. How does such an activity reinforce what was learned at the bakery?

also provide appropriate curriculum topics. You might invite family members to come into the classroom and share special knowledge and talents. Or, children as well as teachers might bring photographs of their families to share.

A curriculum focus on the family contributes to children's feelings of self-esteem and pride. They can share information about something central to their lives, while at the same time expand their understanding of the family life of the other children. While such learning strengthens children's emerging socialization, it also contributes to cognitive development. Teachers help children make comparisons, note similarities and differences, organize information, and classify various aspects of family structure.

KEY QUESTION #5

What are some of the unique features of your community? Which of these would be of interest to young children? Think of several ways in which your community can be the basis for relevant learning for preschoolers.

The Community as the Focus of Curriculum. Children's awareness of their world can particularly be expanded through the community. Young children have had experience with numerous aspects of their community, especially shopping, medical, and recreational elements. The community and those who live and work in it can certainly extend the walls of your program and offer a wealth of learning opportunities and curriculum material.

From the community and the people who work in it, children can learn about local forms of transportation; food growing, processing, and distribution; health services, including the role of doctors, nurses, dentists, dental hygienists, health clinics, and hospitals; safety provisions such as fire and police departments; communications facilities, including radio and television stations, newspapers, telephone services, and libraries; and local recreational facilities, such as parks, zoos, and museums. Children can visit an endless variety of appropriate places through field trips. (In Chapter 14, we will discuss field trips in more detail.) In addition, community professionals can be invited to visit your class and share information and tools of their professions with the children.

You can help children begin to build an understanding of the community as a social system by focusing on the interrelatedness of the people who live and work in your area. For instance, people are both providers and consumers of goods and services; the dentist buys bread

Cooperative formulating of lesson plans ensures that all teachers are familiar with the objectives and the activities planned to meet these objectives.

that the baker produces, and the baker visits the dentist when he has a cavity.

In addition, the larger physical environment of the area in which you live provides a setting worth exploring with the children in your class. Your approach will differ, depending on whether your community is nestled in the mountains, by the ocean, or in the midst of rolling plains. Most young children living in Kansas, for instance, will not have experienced the ocean. It is difficult to convey what the ocean is like to someone who has never seen it, and this is particularly true for children who rely on concrete, firsthand experience. Therefore, it makes little sense to plan a unit on "the ocean" when it is more than a thousand miles away. Instead, focus on what is nearby and real in the environment, on what children have some familiarity with and can actually experience.

DEVELOPING WRITTEN PLANS

As we discussed earlier, curriculum can be viewed as a comprehensive master plan. Once this larger curriculum is in place, units that cover shorter periods of time, daily lesson plans, and individual activities can be developed to fit into the curriculum. We will examine each of these four elements and briefly discuss staff involvement in planning.

Planning the Overall Curriculum

A written overall curriculum or master plan for a relatively long period of time, such as a year, will facilitate further planning.

The preceding discussions—that curriculum is based on enhancing the total development of children, that it is founded on a good understanding of children, and that it derives its content from children's life experiences—provide direction for curriculum planning. Many programs develop a master plan that spans a typical cycle of time—in most instances, this is a year—and defines some broad topics you wish to cover. Putting together a curriculum master plan requires thoughtful consideration. It should provide a flexible guide, which gives general direction for the year but also allows for input from the children and personalization to reflect the character of the class and its individual children and teachers as the year progresses.

FIGURE 8-5 The Self-Concept Curriculum model

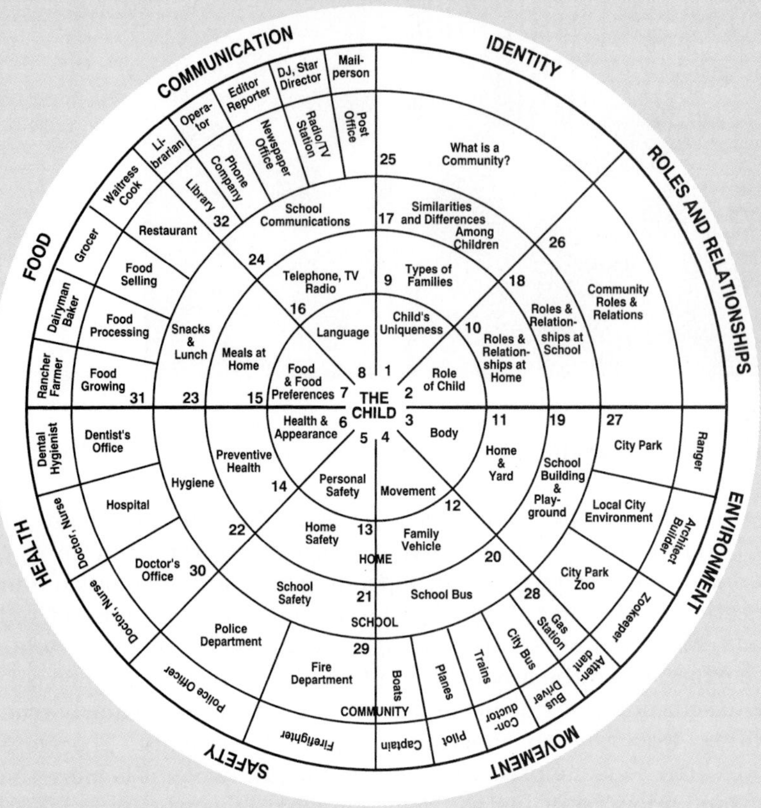

From Essa, E.L., & Rogers, P.R. (1992). *An Early Childhood Curriculum: From Developmental Model to Application.* Albany, NY: Delmar Publishers, Inc.

One example of how to organize a master plan is the Self-Concept Curriculum (Essa & Rogers, 1992), which covers four general areas, beginning with the child, then moving on to home and family, school and friends, and community and community helpers. In this curriculum, each of these four areas is further broken down into eight topics—identity, roles and relationships, environment, transportation, safety, health, nutrition, and communication. Together, these four general areas and their eight subsections result in thirty-two curriculum units (see Figure 8-5). The Self-Concept Curriculum provides a logical progression of topics, which moves from what is closest to the children, to increasingly wider circles of their expanding environment.

Units

Units that revolve around specific themes bring the larger curriculum down to a manageable size for planning and should follow a progression based on how children learn.

Units bring the broad curriculum outline down to a manageable size and provide unifying themes around which activities are planned. A unit can last any length of time, from a day or two to a month or more. It may seem practical to make all units fit into a 1-week framework, but keep in mind that it should be the complexity, interest-value, and relevance of the topic to the children that dictate how much time is spent on a unit. Furthermore, the length of units should be flexible so you can spend more time if the topic intrigues the children or cut it short if the children seem ready to move on. A brief outline of steps in the development of a unit can be found in Figure 8-6.

Planning a unit should begin by carefully considering objectives. What is it that you want the children to learn about the topic? What concept, skills, and information can this unit convey? Most important, are these relevant, age-appropriate, and of interest to the children, and will the children enjoy them? Children have to be the starting point for planning. For instance, if you are planning a unit on bread, you might want the children to learn that

- bread is baked at the bakery,
- the baker is the person who bakes bread,
- many loaves of bread are baked at the bakery (mass production),
- bread is made up of many ingredients, and
- bread is taken by trucks to grocery stores, where it is sold to people such as those in the children's families.

A unit should begin with an introduction through which the theme is initially presented. The length of time spent on the introductory component will depend on the length of the unit and on how new the topic is to the children. Often, the introduction takes place during a large group discussion time.

Introductory components will generally focus on a review of the children's familiarity with the subject or closely related areas and will allow for evaluation of what the children already know about the topic. Thus, if you plan a unit on the topic bread, you can discuss, for instance, types of bread with which the children are familiar, the food group in which bread belongs (assuming you have already spent time discussing nutrition and the basic food groups), the process of baking (for those children who have helped their parents make bread), and the different ways in which bread is used in meals.

Once the topic is introduced, new ideas or information can be presented logically and sequentially. New material should always be presented first in a concrete manner. This often takes the form of a field

FIGURE 8-6 Steps in planning a unit

1. Identification of appropriate objectives
2. Introduction of the new theme through review of familiar aspects of the topic
3. Introduction of new information:
   - First concretely, such as through a field trip
   - Activities that recall the new experience, such as drawing pictures, dictating stories
   - Creative representations of the new experience, such as through art, dramatic play, blocks
4. Summary and evaluation

trip, but concrete experiences can be brought into the classroom through objects or guests. In the case of the bakery unit, you may want to plan a field trip to the local bakery at the beginning of the unit so the children can see how bread is made; on the other hand, some in-class experiences with bread baking can be a wonderful preparation for a trip to the bakery. In either case, it cannot be emphasized enough that any new concept should begin with the concrete, with firsthand experience.

Once children have had a chance to observe and learn through firsthand experience, they can begin to assimilate this information through subsequent activities. After the field trip, children should have opportunities to factually represent what they observed by talking about and dictating accounts of the visit to the bakery, drawing pictures of what they saw on the field trip, kneading bread dough, and otherwise recalling and replicating their visit. This factual recounting allows children to fix the experience in their minds.

Children can begin to use new information in creative ways once it has been integrated into their existing memory and experiential store. They can play with the information through such activities as art, dramatic play, puppets, or blocks. This element of the unit offers a wide variety of possibilities that children can approach in their unique ways.

Finally, a unit is ended through a summarizing component. Children and the teacher review the major features of the unit and what was learned. The teacher can also engage in a final evaluation of how well the children have met the objectives.

Lesson Plans

Lesson plans—The working documents from which the daily program is run, specifying directions for activities.

Daily lesson plans, by specifying activities and objectives, provide the working documents from which the program is run.

Daily **lesson plans** provide the working documents from which a program is run. A lesson plan is fitted into the structure set by the schedule, as discussed earlier. At a minimum, the lesson plan describes each activity planned for that day, objectives for activities, and the time frame within which they are carried out. In addition, it can give information about which teacher will be in charge of the activity, in what part of the classroom each activity is to be carried out, and what materials are needed. Lesson plans can take many forms, but they should be complete enough so that any teacher can pick one up and know for any given day what activities are planned and why they are planned. Figure 8-7 shows a sample lesson plan.

Each lesson plan is part of and fits into the unit and the overall curriculum and, as such, contributes to larger goals and objectives. But each lesson plan should also be a whole in itself by providing a balanced day for the children. Within each lesson plan there should be provision for activities that meet needs in *all* developmental domains—gross and fine motor, cognitive, social, emotional. There should be activities that promote creative expression. Communication should be woven throughout activities, so children exercise receptive and expressive language, as well as a variety of nonverbal means of communication. And there should be opportunity for exploring new topics in a variety of ways through multiple activities, in a leisurely, unrushed manner.

Activities

The smallest element of curriculum planning is the activity, the actual play in which the children will be involved. It is important to be aware of the objectives of a given activity as well as to think through how the activity will be carried out so that the children will gain the knowledge and skills you would like them to acquire. The lesson plan in Figure 8-7

FIGURE 8-7 A sample lesson plan

Class Name: Three-Year-Olds: Half-Day Program **Date:** **Day:** 1
Unit: Senses: Focus on touch
Unit Objectives: The children will develop an awareness that objects feel differently and that there are different textures.

Time Block	Activity	Content Objectives	Devel. Objective	TCHR	Area	Material
9:00–9:15 Circle	Discussion: "How does it feel?" Pass around objects for children to feel and discuss their texture.	Explore and name textures: hard, soft, smooth, rough	L, P, S, C			Apple, sandpaper, velvet, wood block, etc.
9:15–10:10 Activity Time	1. Finger Painting: with corn syrup	Explore and label sticky, smooth	P, Cr, FM			Paper, syrup food colors
	2. Texture Matching	Explore and match textures	P, FM, C, L			Texture samples
	Sensory Bin: popcorn		P, FM, S			Popcorn
	3. Cooking: applesauce	Note difference: hard apples/soft applesauce	P, FM, L, S, C			Ingredients
	Dramatic Play: focus on how objects feel/textures; blankets, stuffed animals	Experience various textures	S, P, M, L, C			Props
10:10–10:20 Cleanup	Focus: on textures as items are put away		M, P, L, C			
10:20–10:35 Snack	Applesauce, apple slices, apple juice, crackers	Compare different textures	P, L, FM, C, S			
10:35–10:50 Small Group	4. Feely box: objects of different textures	Identify items by feel; name textures	P, C, L, FM, S			Feely box, objects
10:50–11:35 Outside	5. Foot Painting	Experience that feet can feel	P, GM, L			Paper, paint, water, towels
11:35–11:50 Large Group	6. Puppetry: select two puppets and have them talk with children about how different things feel.	Review concepts related to sense of touch and different sensations	L, C, S			Puppets
11:50–12:00	Prepare to go home; talk to parents					

Developmental Objectives Codes:

C = Cognitive **GM** = Gross Motor **P** = Perceptual **Cr** = Creative
L = Language **S** = Social **FM** = Fine Motor

From Essa, E.L., & Rogers, P.R. (1992). *An Early Childhood Curriculum: From Developmental Model to Application.* Albany, NY: Delmar Publishers.

describes that day's activities in some detail. Would you, walking into the classroom for which that lesson plan was developed, be able to assume responsibility for some of the activities?

Staff Planning

It is helpful if the staff members who work with the same group of children can be involved in curriculum development. Group planning will ensure that staff members are familiar with objectives and activities, because they took part in their development. It can also lead to greater commitment to the program because everyone's ideas were incorporated. If all staff members are not able to be involved in all steps of planning, it can be helpful if they at least have input into the overall curriculum direction and if their ideas are included in daily lesson plans. The staff's personal investment in the curriculum can contribute to the overall cohesiveness of the program.

PARENT INVOLVEMENT IN THE CURRICULUM

Families' values should be reflected in the curriculum; parents are also a source of support and resources for the curriculum.

As discussed earlier, the curriculum should reflect the backgrounds, needs, and interests of the children. One excellent resource, as you plan curriculum for your group of children, is their parents. Frequent parent-teacher communication and an open policy that conveys the school's emphasis on the importance of the family can encourage parents to be part of the early childhood program.

Parents' expertise and input can greatly enhance the early childhood program. Parents can provide information about special family, cultural, religious, or ethnic customs, celebrations, foods, or dress. They can visit the classroom to share occupational information or special skills. A parent who makes pottery, weaves baskets, plays an instrument, or knows origami will contribute a fascinating element to the classroom.

Some parents may be particularly interested in the direction and content of the curriculum and may want to offer suggestions or ideas. These should be welcomed and incorporated into the program, as appropriate. If, however, the values of a parent seem to be at odds with the program's philosophy, the teacher or director ought to convey that, although she or he respects the parent's views, the school has its own approach founded on child development principles and research. As a last resort, a parent who disagrees with the program's direction has the option of placing the child in another school if the parent is unhappy with the program.

SUMMARY

1. Look at the common components of the daily schedule in an early childhood program.
2. Examine some guidelines for setting an effective schedule.
3. Whether a program operates full-day or part-day will have an impact on the schedule and what it includes.
4. The schedule should be consistent and predictable, but also flexible when needed.
5. Consideration of curriculum includes both definition and examination of its elements.
   A. Curriculum needs to be directly related to the development of the children in the program.
   B. Curriculum must include relevant content to be appropriate.
6. Consider the development of written plans, including the overall curriculum, units, daily lesson plans, and activities.

KEY TERMS LIST

activity time
curriculum
large group time
lesson plans

chapter 9

Creative Development Through the Curriculum

One of the most rewarding joys of working with young children is watching them approach experiences with that spark of freshness and exuberance that opens the door to creativity. Each of us possesses some measure of creativity—some more, some less. This is especially true of young children. Unfortunately, there is a danger of their creativity being stifled through increasing pressure to conform to adult expectations (Mayesky, 1995). In this chapter, we will examine creativity in some detail.

WHAT IS CREATIVITY?

Creativity has been defined in a number of ways. Most definitions include such concepts as originality, imagination, divergent thinking (seeing things from different viewpoints), and the ability to create something new or to combine things in novel but meaningful ways. Creativity is more likely to occur when the person possesses traits such as curiosity, flexibility, and interest in investigation and exploration.

J. P. Guilford (1962), not satisfied with the limited definition of intelligence imposed by tests that measure it by a series of single, "correct" answers, developed a new way of looking at intelligence that includes some of these traits. In Guilford's structure of the intellect, **divergent thinking** is differentiated from **convergent thinking,** both of which are involved in the creative process. Divergence, by one definition, is "the making in the mind of many from one," for instance, by elaborating on a topic as in brainstorming, whereas convergence is defined as "the making of one from many," through narrowing down many ideas to a single, focused point (Hampden-Turner, 1981, p. 104).

One trait often associated with creative thinking is **fluency,** the ability to generate many relevant ideas on a given topic in a limited time.

A definition of creativity includes concepts such as originality, imagination, divergent thinking, novelty, fluency, flexibility, and sensitivity to stimuli.

Divergent thinking—The act of expanding or elaborating on an idea, such as brainstorming.

Convergent thinking—The act of narrowing many ideas into a single, focused point.

Fluency—A measure of creativity involving the ability to generate many relevant ideas on a given topic in a limited time.

Flexibility—A measure of creativity involving the capability to adapt readily to change in a positive, productive manner.

Sensitivity—Related to creativity, it refers to a receptivity to external and internal stimuli.

Five-year-old Michelle wonderfully displayed fluency when she was confronted with a sheet of paper containing 20 circles and was asked to draw as many different items from these circles as she could in 2 minutes. After using some of the circles to make the more conventional face, balloon, ball, sun, orange, and flower, she then created an ashtray, glass, light bulb, and pencil eraser as they would be seen from the top. She had used all but one row of the circles when the teacher told her that she needed to finish in a few seconds. Michelle, after a moment's thought, drew two parallel lines under the remaining row of circles, connected them with crosshatches, then put boxes on top of the circles, creating a quick but recognizable train.

Another measure of creativity is **flexibility,** the capability of adapting readily to change in a positive, productive manner. Three-year-old Ramon showed flexibility when another child accidentally knocked water on the lines that he had carefully painted in different hues of water colors. After a fleeting look of dismay crossed his face, Ramon surveyed his picture and declared, "Look, the water made new colors!"

A third trait related to creativity is **sensitivity,** a receptivity to external and internal stimuli. Creative people have a heightened awareness of their world, their perceptions, feelings, images. They often experience through their senses what others miss (Lowenfeld, 1962). The creative child will, more likely, be the one who points out that a cloud looks like a speeding motorboat, appreciatively sniffs the aroma of freshly sawed wood at the woodworking activity, or delights in the softness of the soapy water when blowing bubbles.

Creativity and the Split Brain

Creativity is associated with the functioning of the right side of the brain, whereas the left side of the brain deals with analytical and logical functions.

Lateralization—The division of the human brain, marked by a specialization in analytical and logical tasks in the left half and intuitive and creative functions in the right half.

Split brain—The term that describes the brain as having two distinct sides or hemispheres, each with different functions.

The human brain has two distinct hemispheres or sides, interconnected by a complex stem of nerves. It has long been recognized that the two sides of the brain serve different functions, but recent research has provided more information to substantiate this (Hampden-Turner, 1981). This division or **lateralization** is very apparent in studies on adults, and research shows that although the young child's brain is still very malleable, there is an innate predisposition toward different functions in the two sides of the brain (Brooks & Obrzut, 1981). Research for the **split brain,** as we shall see, is relevant to understanding creativity.

The left half of the brain, the analytical side, specializes in language and in logical, deductive thinking, and it is associated with concepts of science and mathematics. The right hemisphere is more concerned with processing spatial thinking and visual-motor skills, and it uses a holistic, intuitive approach associated with creativity (Brooks & Obrzut, 1981; Silver, 1982). As a society, we tend to value the verbal and analytical skills of the left brain more highly. We see this attitude reflected in our educational system. Research has also shown that people have a preferred mode of thinking that favors one hemisphere over the other, and this mode is established early in life (Silver, 1982).

Yet the complex crossover of nerve fibers between the two hemispheres shows their strong interrelationship and tells us that we need both sides of the brain for all areas of functioning (Silver, 1982). In fact,

Creative children are more sensitive to the environment, more tuned into its sensations. One trait common to creative people is heightened sensory awareness. What are some other traits of creative children?

optimum brain functioning seems to be the result of full development of both hemispheres of the brain (Brooks & Obrzut, 1981).

What such research about the brain tells us is that from a neuropsychological standpoint, it is equally as important to incorporate elements that encourage creativity as it is to promote more academic skills in programs for young children. Children need a wide variety of experiences in their environments, experiences that encourage right as well as left brain development (Brooks & Obrzut, 1981). As we shall discuss in the following section, activities and materials that promote divergent thinking, problem solving, spatial-perceptual tasks, and visual thinking contribute to development of the whole child.

AN ENVIRONMENT THAT ENCOURAGES CREATIVITY

In our earlier definition of creativity, we examined some traits characteristic of the creative process. The early childhood setting should provide an environment in which these traits are encouraged and valued. Such an environment, however, goes far beyond providing materials for artistic expression. The creative environment is made up not just of the physical arrangement, but is permeated by an attitude of openness, acceptance, and encouragement. We will examine both these aspects, the attitudes that promote creativity and the physical parameters of such an environment.

KEY QUESTION #1

Which of your friends or acquaintances do you consider to be creative? What creative characteristics do they possess? Do they fit the definition of creativity presented in this chapter? How do they use creativity in ways other than the conventional sense (for instance, art or music expression)?

Attitudes That Encourage Creativity

Creativity, as we have seen, is related to flexibility, divergent thinking, and openness to new ideas. Young children's minds strive toward making sense of their world by organizing information and input. Once they become familiar with and master new concepts, they are free to use these in various ways. If we use what we learn in only one way, we are limited and rigid in our approach. Flexible or creative thinking is a mental set that can be encouraged in an open classroom atmosphere. A creative environment promotes new perceptions of and responses to the world.

An open classroom atmosphere, where flexible and imaginative thinking are valued, will encourage creativity.

Creativity has to be nurtured; it does not happen on its own. The teacher plays an important role in fostering creativity by providing a variety of materials and encouraging imaginative use of them. When children are allowed creative expression, each will produce a different outcome. The teacher's acceptance of all the children's work and unique responses gives them the opportunity to learn that people feel and think differently and that this is alright and valued.

In creative activities, the process as much as the product needs to be valued.

Creativity, however, does not always result in a product, although we traditionally tend to think of the picture, the story, or the dance as the creative product. But it is the process as much as the product that is important for young children. In the process, the child can

- experiment ("What will happen if I put this block across the top of these two?");
- enjoy the sensory experience ("Squishing the play dough between my fingers feels nice!");
- communicate ("I'm a bird!");
- relive experiences ("I'll tell the 'baby' she has to go to bed because that's what big people always tell me."); and
- work out fears ("I'll be the doctor, and my dolly will be the baby who gets the shot!").

As children mature, as their motor and perceptual skills improve, and as they plan ahead more, their creative efforts may well result in purposeful products. But toddlers and young preschoolers are much more involved in the process of creative experiences. For a one-, two-, three-, or four-year-old, any end product is usually secondary to the enjoyment of doing the activity.

The teacher, by encouraging children to solve problems, also fosters creativity. By helping children think through different alternatives and find various solutions, the teacher expands their creative capacity. The teacher is a facilitator rather than the one who comes up with answers or solutions, however. Divergent thinking involves the opportunity to go off in different directions and to explore various strategies. The teacher's acceptance of children's suggestions and will-

Creativity is nurtured when children have access to a wide variety of materials and are encouraged to use them in their own unique way.

EXPERIENCES

chapter 9

TINA, School-Aged Summer Camp Coordinator

Why Do People Live in the Park?

One of the philosophies of our summer camp is to emphasize that we should always leave a place better than the way we found it. At the beach, for instance, the lifeguards always remark how responsible our kids are. The children are aware that they play a role in maintaining the environment. This philosophy of a common responsibility seems to permeate other areas; each summer, the children seem to develop a "cause." Last year that cause was the homeless.

On Fridays the group went to a nearby park, taking their lunches along. Soon they noticed that there were several people who seemed to "live" in the park, including a family with two young children. The needs of these people became evident when, after the summer camp children had finished their lunches and thrown away the inevitable leftovers, the homeless would go through the garbage cans and retrieve those leftovers. The summer camp children were disturbed by this as well as curious.

They were full of questions for their teachers. Who were these people? Could they get food from anywhere else, besides the garbage cans? What happens if there is no food to be found in the garbage cans? Where do they sleep? What happens when it's cold or when it rains? Where do they go to the bathroom? What about baths? Above all, they wanted to know why these people were homeless. How could this happen? For this group of affluent children, exposure to the notion of homelessness was frightening and incomprehensible.

But the children were also very touched by the needs of the homeless they saw. Spontaneously they decided that they had to help the people of the park. They collected clothing, especially for the children of the family they met at the park. These they had a chance to give to this family themselves. Several of them made a collection box, a shoe box into which they cut a slot and on which they wrote a sign: Donations for the Homeless. While parents contributed to the cause, some of the money came from the children themselves. For instance, when they went to the skating rink, they brought along money for snacks; but many of the children decided that they would forgo the snacks because that money would be put to better use if it went into the collection box. At the end of the summer the children had collected about $25, which, with input from the adults, they decided to give to the Salvation Army's homeless program.

Empathy, concern, responsibility, care are all qualities that begin to develop at a young age. Sensitive adults can help to provide the setting in which these emerge.

experiences

KEY QUESTION #2

Observe a group of children. What expressions of creativity do you observe? What factors in the environment or in the teachers' behavior encourage or discourage creativity? Does any child stand out as particularly creative in this group? What characteristics does this child possess? Is your criterion for identifying a creative child different from one used to identify a creative adult?

ingness to try these tells them that they are capable of worthwhile ideas.

Another way of accepting and encouraging children's creative work is through uncritical acknowledgment. Well-intentioned praise ("I like your picture.") can stifle creativity because it imposes a value judgment, or becomes meaningless when it is repeated to every child. Rather than evaluating, comparing, or trying to read meaning into nonrepresentational art, a teacher can remark on the process ("You glued the squares on first, then you glued circles over them."); recognize the work that has gone into the picture ("You've really worked hard on this sculpture!"); or comment on its design qualities ("You're using lots of big circles!") (Schirrmacher, 1986).

It is also important in setting an appropriate climate for creativity to provide enough time for children to get involved in and complete their projects. Children need to have ample time blocks during the day in which they can explore and try out their ideas. When the time set aside for child-selected activity is short, children tend not to get very involved (Christie, Johnsen, & Peckover, 1988), thus missing opportunities to engage in creative activity. Children may continue to pursue a creative project over a period of time.

A Physical Environment That Encourages Creativity

A variety of open-ended materials in the environment will encourage creativity.

Open-ended materials—Early childhood materials that are flexible rather than structured and can be used in a variety of ways rather than in only a single manner.

The physical setting can support creativity through provision of and access to a wide range of **open-ended materials,** ones that lend themselves to various uses. Whenever children are confronted with material that has multiple uses, they have to make choices about how to use the material and have to use imagination because it does not dictate a single outcome. Furthermore, each successive time they use the materials, they can do so in a unique way. In fact, children do not need a different art activity each day. When a different set of limited materials is provided every day, children never get the chance to explore in depth or experiment with common, basic materials (Clemens, 1991).

A well-stocked early childhood program will be full of open-ended materials. Examples include a wide variety of art materials, manipulatives, blocks, sensory materials, puppets, dramatic play props, musical instruments, and versatile outdoor equipment. (This is not to say that single-purpose materials—for instance, puzzles—are not important, but they meet different developmental needs and are not particularly suited for creative development.) One study demonstrated that by offering a large array of art materials from which children can choose rather than providing limited materials specific only to one project, children's artwork is significantly more creative, as judged by a panel of artists (Amabile & Gitomer, 1984).

The physical arrangement of the room can also facilitate creativity. Clearly organized classroom areas let children know where they can engage in various creative activities, for instance, where they can build or where they might experiment with messy media. Classroom areas should be set up so that traffic flow does not interfere or disrupt ongoing activity.

The early childhood environment promotes creativity by allowing children to explore freely and to select from a variety of accessible materials.

At the same time, children should be able to move freely from one activity to another. When materials are organized and visible on accessible shelves, the children know what is available for their independent use. These materials should be attractively displayed and uncluttered so that children can see possible new combinations they might try. Such orderly display also conveys a respect for the materials. Similarly, a safe place to store finished products or an area in which these might be displayed also tells the children that their creative endeavors are valued and respected.

The remainder of this chapter examines two specific classroom areas in which creativity is likely to flourish, art and music. This discussion is somewhat arbitrary, however, in that creativity can and should occur in every aspect of the early childhood program. One of the difficulties in writing a book such as this one is that some organizational decisions have to be made that place activities into categories that are not nearly as clear in reality as they appear to be in the book. Although art and music foster creativity, they also promote cognition, socialization, language, emotional release, sensory stimulation, and muscle development. Similarly, language, outdoor motor, or manipulative activities can be very creative (as we will try to point out in the ensuing chapters, where such activities have been placed). As you read on, then, keep in mind that good early childhood activities serve many purposes, meet many needs, and above all contribute to development of the whole child.

ART

Art, in its broadest sense, encompasses the application of creative imagination to a unique product through a wide variety of modes. Art can result in painting, a sculpture, a collage, a song, a dance, a novel, a poem. In the context of early childhood education, art usually refers to the creative process as applied to two-dimensional graphic arts—painting, drawing, print making—and to three-dimensional modeling arts—using clay or play dough, creating sculptures.

Art has been part of early childhood education since its earliest beginnings. Young children seem to gravitate to art activities, where they can express themselves nonverbally; find satisfying sensory experiences; experiment with a variety of materials; and work in a free, uninhibited way not characteristic of many other aspects of their lives.

Theories of Art Development

In its broadest sense, art involves the application of creativity to a unique product through a variety of modes.

You have probably observed a four-year-old boy, crayon in hand, produce a house with door, windows, and chimney; an adjacent tree with curly, green circles atop a brown stem; and a person next to the house, his stick legs floating slightly above ground level and his head reaching the house's chimney. How did this child come to produce such a picture? What does the picture mean? Where did he learn the skills, since not so long ago his pictures were made up of scribbles? How was he able to translate the image of a house, tree, and person into a recognizable depiction? A number of theories have been proposed to answer such questions and explain how children's art develops.

Psychoanalytic theory holds that art emerges from children's emotions and reflects what they are feeling.

Psychoanalytic Theory. This theory proposes that children's art emerges from emotion and reflects what they feel. Art is an expression of the unconscious and can be interpreted to give insight into a child's personality or emotional state. The use of color, line, size, shape, and space, as well as the complexity of art, convey meaning that a psychoanalyst might read. Although some researchers have found support for a link between art and emotional state, others have found little relationship. A number of common early childhood activities stem from the psychoanalytic theory, particularly the use of finger paints, clay, and free-flowing tempera paint. Such activities allow children to release emotion and express themselves freely (Seefeldt, 1987).

Perceptual theory suggests that children draw what they see.

Perceptual Theory. This suggests that children draw what they see. Vision projects an image of the real object on the retina, while perception restructures and interprets the image based on such factors as prior experience, personality, and neurological structure (Schirrmacher, 1990). Part of the perceptual process involves translating a three-dimensional object into a two-dimensional drawing, a challenge to adults, let alone young children. Perceptual theory suggests that a

As children get older, their drawings become more representational, moving from scribbles to recognizable pictures.

drawing will focus on what the child perceives as the most important features of the object because our eyes see more than we consciously perceive. Practical applications of this theory have led to instructional art programs whose goal is to help children focus on detail and to improve their visual discrimination (Seefeldt, 1987).

Cognitive theory assumes that children draw what they know and that their drawings are reflected in a series of stages.

Cognitive Theories. Such theories assume that children draw what they know. The more developed a child's familiarity with a concept or subject, the more detailed or sophisticated the drawing will be. Older children have had a greater number of experiences and more time in which to develop more sophisticated concepts; therefore, their artwork is recognizable.

Piaget discusses the evolution of children's drawings in terms of the developing concept of space (Cox, 1986). In the **scribbling stage,** between the ages of two and four, the child experiments with marks on a page. As the child recognizes that these marks can represent real things, the child begins to give them meaning. Cox tells how her daughter drew a shape, then, in surprise, exclaimed that it was a bird, noting that it needed an eye and adding a dot. In fact, recent research indicates that even very young children's seemingly random scribbles are gestural (as opposed to pictorial) representations. Winner (1986) relates how a $1\frac{1}{2}$-year-old used a marker to hop around the page, leaving marks, and describing how the bunny goes hop-hop.

Scribbling stage—The stage in the development of art in which children experiment with marks on a page.

In the later **preschematic stage,** from approximately age four to age seven, the child does have a subject in mind when beginning a picture, but the actual product will be an inaccurate, crude representation of the real thing. It isn't until a later age, in the **schematic stage,** that the child's representations become more realistic and accurate. Children's art is also related to Piaget's concept of object permanence (Seefeldt, 1987), a recognition that objects continue to exist even when they are out of view. The child, in other words, can evoke a mental image of that object, something necessary to represent the object in a drawing.

Preschematic stage—The stage in the development of art in which children have a subject in mind when they begin a picture, but in which the actual product will be an inaccurate, crude representation of the real thing.

Schematic stage—Older children's drawings, which are more realistic and accurate than younger children's in what they depict.

Developmental theories advocate that children's art develops naturally, through universal stages seen in children from all parts of the world.

Developmental Theories. These advocate that children's art ability develops naturally, through a series of universal stages, and that adult intervention or direct teaching can, in fact, adversely affect this development. The teacher's role is to create a secure environment, make a wide range of materials available, and provide appropriate guidance to facilitate art, a view widely accepted by early childhood educators (Seefeldt, 1987). Gardner (1989) noted an interesting contrast to this approach that he observed during his stay in China, where art techniques are carefully taught to children. The Chinese view would suggest that before people can be creative, they have to achieve competence in using the techniques of the art, techniques that have been developed through long-established traditions that do not need to be reinvented or bypassed.

Interestingly, the traditional view of allowing children's art to develop naturally, without intervention, is being reconsidered by some early childhood educators. Observers of the Reggio Emilia schools (review the discussion in Chapter 5) note the maturity and complexity of the art produced by the children. They also note that Reggio teachers

KEY QUESTION #3

Look at children's artwork. Do you see an age progression from scribbles to shapes to representational pictures?

Basic scribbles—According to Rhoda Kellogg, the 20 fundamental markings found in all art.

Placement patterns—According to Rhoda Kellogg, a way of analyzing children's art by examining the 17 ways in which the total picture or design is framed or placed on the paper.

Diagrams—According to Rhoda Kellogg, the stage in children's art when they begin to use the six recognizable shapes—the rectangle, oval, triangle, X, cross, and the deliberate odd shape.

Combines—According to Rhoda Kellogg, a step in the development of art in which children combine two simple diagrams.

Aggregates—Rhoda Kellogg's term for the step in the development of art in which children combine three or more simple diagrams.

Pictorialism—According to Rhoda Kellogg, the stage in the development of art in which children draw recognizable objects.

Kellogg proposes age-related stages in children's art development, each marked by the emergence of unique elements in their art products.

take art very seriously and do not consider it a frivolous child's activity; they consider it a strong form of symbolic communication, of ideas, feelings, and emotions. Furthermore, children use the same materials and media over and over, taking the time to develop the necessary skills to use them. What changes is the ideas they are encouraged to express with these media (Seefeldt, 1995).

Researchers have proposed developmental stages of art. Congruent with Piaget's and Vygotsky's theories, children's drawings can be described as evolving in three stages, which are influenced by cognitive development and culture (Davis & Gardner, 1993). From ages 1 to 5, the dominance of universal patterns, and ages 5 to 7, the flowering of drawing, children move from universal scribbles into unique expressions of artwork. These stages are followed by the height of cultural influence, from ages 7 to 12, when artistic recreations become much more accurate and realistic and reflect an internalization of the culture.

Rhoda Kellogg (1969), based on her collection of more than 1 million pictures drawn by two- to eight-year-olds from around the world, formulated a series of age-related stages that describe children's artistic development. In addition, she elaborated on the elements of children's art in each of these stages. Two-year-olds use the **basic scribbles,** 20 kinds of markings that form "the building blocks of art" (p. 15), the elements found in any artistic work. These include various straight and curved line patterns. In addition to examining basic scribbles, pictures can be analyzed in terms of **placement patterns,** 17 ways in which the total picture is framed or placed on the paper. By the age of three, children begin to make six recognizable **diagrams** or shapes, specifically the rectangle, oval, triangle, cross, X, and odd-shaped (but deliberate) line. Kellogg considers that "developmentally, the diagrams indicate an increasing ability to make a controlled use of lines and to employ memory" (p. 45).

In children's art, diagrams are seldom found alone, but in **combines,** two diagrams put together, and **aggregates,** combinations of three or more diagrams. Soon diagrams, combines, and aggregates suggest objects, often a face, and thus the transition to **pictorialism** begins between the ages of four and five. Kellogg characterizes early pictorial efforts as humans, animals, buildings, vegetation, and transportation. Because of her extensive cross-cultural study of young children's art, Kellogg concludes that these stages are universal, occurring naturally in all children. She advises teachers and parents not to attempt to judge children's art, nor to provide instruction in how to draw specific objects. Figure 9-1 shows the drawings of children of different ages, illustrating Kellogg's progression in the development of children's art.

Two-Dimensional Graphic Arts

Children's move from scribbling to representational art can be seen in their use of two-dimensional graphic art, which uses a wide range of media.

Young children, as they move from scribbles to gradually more representational depictions, most commonly create these pictures through graphic art media. We will examine graphic arts in terms of drawing, painting, and printmaking.

Drawing. Crayons, nontoxic marking pens, pencils, and chalk are the usual media for drawing. Each produces a different effect and pro-

FIGURE 9-1 The How of Early Childhood Education—Curriculum

The development of young children's art can be seen in these pictures. Typical of two-year-olds' art, Zena's and Ryan's work contain many of the basic scribbles, while Jessie's and Tommy's depictions contain combinations that suggest a face. Jessica's work shows the emergence of shapes and combines. As he was scribbling, three-year-old Bret saw a suggestion of Snoopy emerge; he added some details to enhance the image and named the picture "Snoopy." The older children's work is much more deliberate and recognizable, moving from the crude dinosaurs, sun, and flowers of the four- and five-year-olds to the greater sophistication and humor shown by the school-aged children.

vides satisfaction and enjoyment. Graphic arts are relatively neat—certainly less messy than painting—and may encourage a child, uncomfortable with messy media or reluctant to participate in more uninhibited art activities, to engage in art.

It is important that the drawing tools be appropriate for children. In an art center where children have free access to materials, crayons are often a favorite, partly because most children are already familiar with them. Chunky crayons, especially in small pieces, are easier for toddlers and younger preschoolers to hold because their fine motor coordination is not well developed yet. Crayons lend themselves to experimentation as children become more adept in using them: colors can be mixed, peeled crayons can be used sideways, and pressure in drawing can produce different color effects. Because crayons can be easily controlled (the colors don't run as they do in painting), they facilitate the emergence of shapes, combines, aggregates, and pictorial representations as children move beyond scribbles.

Children also enjoy marking pens because of their vibrant colors and because they are easy to use. It is not necessary to press hard to get a result. Markers come with fine and large tips, allowing children to experiment with different effects. It is important to provide only markers with nontoxic, washable ink because marking pens tend to mark more than the paper; children's tongues, fingers, and clothing are often colored.

Pencils and chalk provide good graphic art alternatives for older preschoolers. The thicker primary pencils with soft lead are best. Chalk offers a novel experience because the colors are soft, smearing and blending easily. Light-colored chalk shows up well on dark paper. Children enjoy drawing with chalk on paper spread with various liquids such as water, buttermilk, or liquid starch; the effect intensifies and seals the colors. A squirt of hair spray can "fix" the picture more permanently. Chalk can also be used on sidewalks to draw easily removable pictures.

Children most often draw on paper, but a variety of other surfaces make for interesting variations. Cardboard, corrugated cardboard, sandpaper, wallpaper samples, wood, and fabric are some of the alternatives to butcher paper, newsprint, manila paper, or construction paper. Even varying the shape and size of the paper can encourage children to try different approaches in their artwork.

Most early childhood educators advise against providing children with dittoes or coloring books because they inhibit creative expression, are not developmentally appropriate because "coloring within the lines" requires fine motor control beyond the abilities of many young children, and serve as poor aesthetic models because the pictures are usually inferior artistic renditions (Mayesky, 1995).

Painting. Painting, with its fluid outpouring of bright colors, is an activity that delights young children, even one-year-olds. Because it is rather messy, painting is something most children do primarily at school. We will survey tempera, watercolor, and finger painting as three common applications of this art form.

Good-quality tempera paints should be a staple in an early childhood program. Such paints come in premixed liquid, in dried blocks that are used like watercolors, or in less expensive powder form. Adding a small amount of liquid detergent to tempera paints makes cleanup of brushes and accidental spills much easier. A pinch of salt keeps the paint from spoiling and growing mold. Because tempera

Painting with good-quality tempera paints is a satisfying activity for young children. This child is painting at the easel, a favorite spot for such an activity. In what other ways could the teacher set up a painting activity?

KEY QUESTION #4

Make a finger painting or collage with materials typically found in an early childhood program. How does this activity make you feel? What benefits can children gain from such activities? Do the same with a music activity, for instance, using rhythm instruments or dancing freely to music, and answer the same questions.

paints are fairly thick, they are best suited to painting on large surfaces with large brushes or other tools. Children can paint on the slanted surface of an easel as well as on a flat surface, such as the floor or a table, and an upright surface, for instance, against an outdoor fence. Painting with tempera paints involves use of large muscles (especially shoulders, arms, and back) as well as the small muscles of the hands.

For younger preschoolers, provide two or three colors at a time, preferably primary colors that the children can then mix to create additional shades. As children get older, variations and new shades of color can revitalize their interest in painting. Although paint is provided in separate containers, each with its own brush, children will invariably mix colors. Keeping small amounts of clean, premixed paints and paper easily accessible promotes independence and allows children to paint when their interest is aroused. It is always a good idea to have a supply of aprons or smocks near paint areas to protect children's clothing. Plastic aprons that slip easily over the head will also encourage independence.

Watercolors are often given to older children who have had some experience with painting, because they require finer control. It is again important to provide good-quality materials; inexpensive watercolors are often weak and yield unsatisfactory results. Children who have begun making representational pictures enjoy using this medium because they can manipulate the materials fairly easily to create people, trees, houses, and other objects.

Watercolors usually come in a tray containing 10 or more individual cakes of color. An accompanying small container of water into which the brush is dipped is needed to wet the colors. When children first use watercolors, they tend to use too much water, swamping and diluting the colors. You might demonstrate to children how to dip the brush in the water and then roll it on the paint, as they begin to use this medium. Give each child a paper towel to wipe the previous color off the brush after it has been rinsed. When children have finished using the watercolors, wipe off excess water and mixed colors.

Finger painting is a multisensory activity that encourages uninhibited use of materials and emotional release. It can be done on large sheets of paper or directly on a clean table surface. Tabletop finger paint creations can be saved by lifting the print on a piece of superimposed paper. Thickly mixed tempera paints are a good finger painting medium, but a wide variety of other media lend themselves to this activity. Liquid starch and wallpaper paste mixed with tempera provide two differing consistencies. Whipped soap flakes (see soap flake recipe in Figure 9-2) makes another excellent finger paint base to which color can be added. Although many teachers and programs object to the use of food as an art medium for ethical reasons (Schirrmacher, 1998) such items as pudding are also widely used. Another food-based finger painting activity is corn syrup and food coloring, which results in an acrylic-like picture (Essa & Rogers, 1992).

Quality is important when purchasing paint brushes because inferior products quickly frustrate and discourage young artists. Good bristles, when carefully cleaned and allowed to air dry after each use, will retain their shape and won't begin to fall out. Provide a variety of brush sizes. Fine-point brushes are good for water colors. Half-inch to 2-inch widths for tempera painting will allow children to experiment with different-sized brush strokes. Even wider sizes can be used, for instance, if children "paint" the outside of the school building with water. Foam brushes provide a different experience. Alternative utensils such as toothbrushes, empty deodorant containers, cotton swabs, sponges, kitchen utensils, feather dusters, or string are often used.

Printmaking. A final graphic art form we will discuss is printmaking, in which children dip into thick paint an object that will leave an imprint when pressed on a piece of paper. Printmaking is different from painting in that the utensil is not moved over the paper but leaves a single imprint with each application. Of course, many children mix painting with printmaking, moving the printing utensil over the paper like a brush or, alternately, leaving single imprints of the brush on the paper. A variety of printmaking objects can be used, such as sponges cut into shapes, cookie cutters, corks, different kitchen utensils, and even body parts.

Three-Dimensional Modeling Arts

Stages in the development of children's art can also be seen in three-dimensional graphic art, which uses a wide range of media, such as clay, collage, and woodworking.

When children use three-dimensional media, they produce artwork that has depth, height, and solidity in addition to color and shape. Just like graphic arts, three-dimensional projects can be abstract or representational. Play dough and clay, collage, and woodworking are three examples of modeling art that we will examine more closely.

Play Dough and Clay. Teacher-made (and child-made) play dough that contains, in a common recipe, flour, salt, water, and a few drops of oil, is a favorite of children and teachers (see Figure 9-2 for some suggested recipes). Well-made and airtight-stored play dough is soft and can be easily manipulated by small hands to provide a satisfying manual and sensory experience or to create shapes and sculptures. Children can punch, squeeze, roll, pull, stretch, and otherwise manipulate play dough; they can roll balls, pull out long snakes, twist snakes into coiled bird nests, and make human or animal figures.

FIGURE 9-2 Art Recipes

1. **Noncooked Play Dough**

   Mix together:

   3 cups flour

   1½ cups salt

   Stir in:

   1 cup water

   ¼ cup cooking oil

   food coloring or dry tempera paint

   Knead ingredients together until well mixed. Add more water if too dry or more flour if too sticky. Store in an airtight container or plastic bag.

2. **Cooked Play Dough**

   Mix together in an aluminum pot:

   2 cups flour

   1 cup salt

   2 cups water

   ¼ cup oil

   1 tablespoon cream of tartar

   food coloring

   Cook these ingredients over medium heat, stirring constantly, until they thicken. Place on a plate to cool enough to handle comfortably. Knead, and then store mixture in an airtight container.

3. **Cornstarch Dough**

   In a pot, bring to a boil:

   3 cups salt

   1 cup water

   In a separate bowl, mix:

   1½ cups cornstarch

   1 cup water

   Add the cornstarch mixture to the boiling saltwater mixture and cook over low heat for several more minutes, until thick. Place on a plate and let the dough cool enough to handle comfortably. Knead well, then store airtight in the refrigerator.

4. **Peanut Butter Clay**

   Combine and knead:

   1½ cups peanut butter

   1 cup powdered milk

5. **Soap Flake Finger Paints**

   2 cups soap *flakes* (not soap powder)

   water

   food coloring

   In a bowl, gradually add water to soap flakes while beating with a rotary or electric mixer. The soap should be the consistency of beaten egg whites, holding soft peaks. Add food color to make desired shade.

6. **Liquid Starch Finger Paints**

   Pour 1 tablespoon of starch on heavy paper; add liquid color.

After children have had ample experience in using play dough with their fingers, tools such as rolling pins, cookie cutters, plastic knives, and other implements that shape or leave interesting imprints can be added. Play dough can be used directly on a table surface or on

Play dough and a variety of tools allow children to manipulate and experiment with shapes, texture, combination, and transformation of a very versatile medium.

an oilcloth table covering, but individual, smooth-surfaced boards make cleanup much easier.

Potter's clay, which is purchased commercially, should be used in addition to, rather than instead of play dough, because it offers a different experience. Adults use this natural clay to create sculptures and utensils, which are fired, glazed, or painted. Children's creations can also be preserved, but the cool clay should be used primarily for the sensory enjoyment it offers. As with play dough, it is very important to store clay in airtight containers. It will be necessary to add water periodically to keep the clay pliable. Sculpting can also be done with sand and water or with mud from a nearby river or lake bank.

Shirrmacher (1998) proposes four stages, not unlike the stages that typify the development of drawing, that children pass through in their experiences with clay and dough. Two-year-olds, in the "What is clay?" stage, explore the properties of clay in a multisensory way. They quickly move into the "What can I do with clay?" stage, where three-year-olds start processing the material manually, rolling, pulling, and patting it. In the "Look what I made!" third stage, four-year-olds creatively combine their clay forms into crude representations, though these happen accidentally as often as they do purposefully. Finally, five-year-olds move into the "Know what I'm going to make out of my clay?" stage, in which they begin with a finished product in mind.

Collage. Collages are a creative combination of materials, kept together by glue or some other binding material. Because they contain varied materials, collages can reinforce shape, texture, and color awareness. An almost infinite variety of materials and techniques can be used in making collages. Some, especially those in which paper is glued to paper, may be almost two-dimensional, whereas others combine components into a three-dimensional sculpture.

Collages need a base, collage materials, and some kind of binding to hold these together. The base can range from various types of paper used to make lightweight collages to cardboard, mat board, Styrofoam sheets, or wood for heavier concoctions. It can be made of paper or plastic plates, meat or TV dinner trays, various commercial plastic packaging containers, milk cartons, or almost any other suitable material.

Collage materials can include torn scraps of foil, tissue, construction, crepe, news-, wall-, or other types of paper; various fabric scraps and fabric trims such as rickrack and bias tape; yarn, string, and heavy thread; buttons, beads, and toothpicks; hardware items such as nuts, bolts, screws, or washers; leaves, twigs, shells, rocks, and other natural collectibles; and almost any nontoxic, small item that lends itself to the art activity. The binding materials used to keep the collage together is usually white glue, but cellophane or masking tape, staples, pipe cleaners, string, toothpicks, straws, or any other material that ties or tacks items to the base and to each other might be suitable for some collages.

Various techniques can also be used for collages. The selection of materials can be provided by the teacher, who may have a specific theme-related product in mind, or by the children from available collage materials stored in the art area. If you encourage children to create collages freely, then it is important to provide a good variety of appealing and neatly organized materials. Boxes with dividers can help keep materials separated. The number of materials can be increased as children become more proficient at using materials, and items should be rotated or changed to stimulate new ideas and interest.

Children can change the shape of collage materials by tearing or cutting paper or fabric. Most young children learn to use scissors through exposure and repeated practice. Appropriate preschool scissors that are both safe but not blunt provide excellent fine motor experience. Children usually begin scissor use by snipping sturdy paper, move on to cutting straight lines, and progress to cutting along curved and angular lines. Cutting out drawn shapes is an advanced skill that does not emerge until children have had many, many experiences manipulating and controlling scissors.

Lefty scissors should be available for left-handed children. In addition, for children who have particular difficulty with fine motor control, double-handled scissors are available, which allow teachers to place their fingers in a second set of holes to guide the child's hand in cutting.

Woodworking. One of the most satisfying experiences for young children three years and older is to successfully saw a piece of wood in two, pound a nail into a tree stump, or combine two pieces of wood with a nail and hammer. Once children have experimented with and achieved some mastery in the use of tools, they use woodworking as the basis for three-dimensional creations as well. How often we hear a child, who has just combined two crossed pieces of wood with a nail, enthusiastically declare, "See my airplane!" School-aged children, who have more highly developed fine motor control and greater skill in planning and implementing more complex projects, find woodworking opportunities particularly gratifying.

Successful and safe woodworking requires high-quality tools, appropriate instruction in using the tools, reasonable rules, and careful supervision. Woodworking tools for children, which can be obtained through various early childhood equipment companies, are not toys. Basic tools should include well-balanced, small claw hammers weighing 8 to 12 ounces; cross-cut saws, up to about 18 inches long; and well-made vises into which the wood can be securely clamped while children saw. Additional tools, once children have had plenty of practice with hammers and saws, can include braces and bits for drilling holes and rasps and planes for shaving the wood. Screwdrivers are generally too difficult for young children to master, and they end up being more frustrating than satisfying. Figure 9-3 shows some of the basic woodworking tools commonly included in early childhood programs.

In addition to the tools, it is important to provide a selection of soft wood, such as pine, which can usually be obtained from the scrap pile of a local lumber wholesaler or carpenter. Nails with fairly large heads in a variety of lengths should also be made available. The teacher can guide children through the problem-solving process of selecting an appropriate nail length for the size of wood being nailed together.

It is very important to help children learn how to use tools appropriately, both for reasons of safety and to minimize frustration. To provide good leverage, hammers are best held with a firm grip toward the end of the handle rather than near the head; in this position, however, the swing of the hammer needs to be more accurate, because it takes greater eye-hand coordination to aim at the nail head from the further distance of the end of the handle. Before a piece of wood is sawed, it should be firmly clamped into the vise to allow the child to use both hands to manage the saw. For inexperienced sawyers, the teacher might want to begin the process by making a small notch as a starting point for sawing. For very young children, wood can be replaced by thick Styrofoam packing material, which is much softer and easier to saw.

FIGURE 9-3 Basic Woodworking Tools for Early Childhood

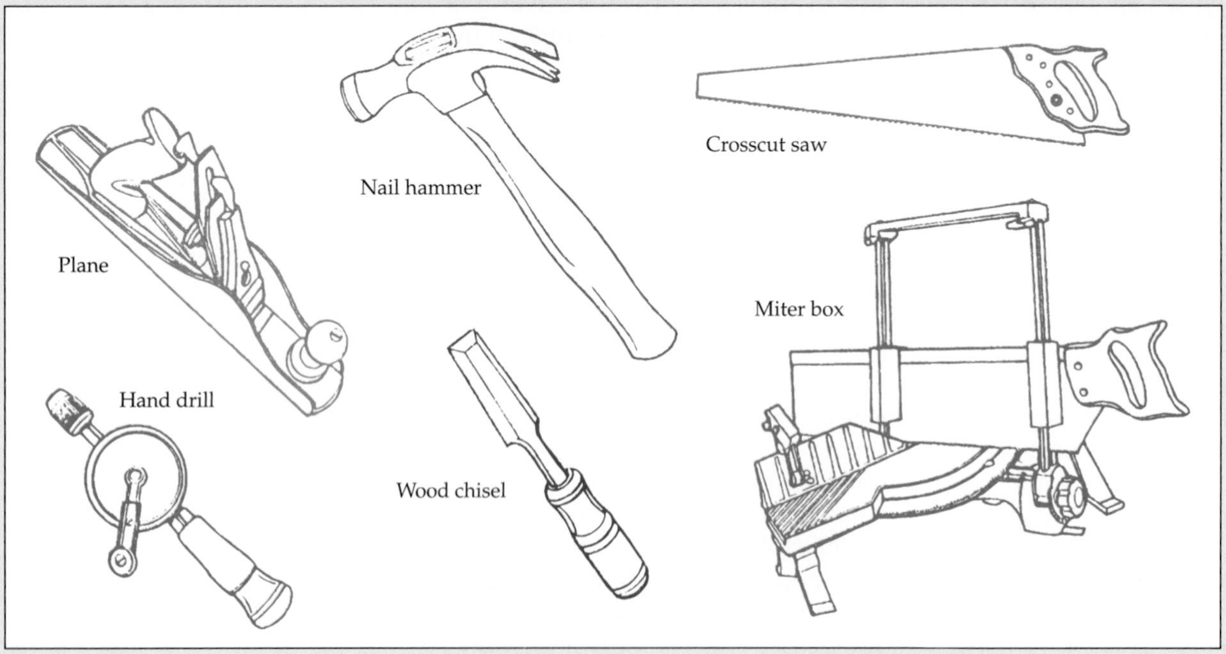

Logical rules should be established and reinforced for woodworking activities to ensure safety and success. Such rules might include an understanding that the tools remain in the woodworking area, that only three or four children are allowed in the area at a time, or that the area can be used only if an adult is in attendance. Similarly, it is important that teachers provide attentive and appropriate guidance. This includes helping children learn how to use the tools, providing appropriate physical guidance as needed, reminding children of the rules, verbalizing the process, and encouraging problem solving.

Older preschoolers and primary children, who have gained proficiency in using the tools and purposefully made objects from wood, will be interested in added props. These should include round objects that suggest wheels, such as wooden spools, slices of large dowels, bottle caps, the metal ends from 6-ounce frozen juice containers, film canister lids, and a variety of other items. Additionally, dowel lengths, knobs, handles, glue and collage materials, and paint and brushes can extend the woodworking activity in many ways.

Aesthetic Appreciation

Aesthetics—Enjoyment and appreciation of beauty, particularly related to all forms of art.

An important aspect of early childhood education is aesthetics, fostering an appreciation of beauty in art and the environment.

Aesthetics, an enjoyment and appreciation of beauty, is related to art in all its forms. Evans (1984) considers the inclusion of aesthetics in education as contributing to a "quality of life that is uniquely human" by exposing children to "sublime experiences" (p. 74), that sense of wonder and enjoyment when we are touched by beauty. Aesthetics includes sensitivity and appreciation for both natural beauty and human creations (Feeney & Moravcik, 1987). A teacher who is sensitive to beauty can help children find it in their surroundings.

One way that aesthetics can be included in the early childhood program is by introducing children to works of art, to "expose not impose" (Schirrmacher, 1998, p. 112). Feeney and Moravcik (1987) suggest age-appropriate ways of exposing children to fine art, for instance, displaying reproductions of artwork in the classroom and taking children on trips to local museums and galleries. From experience with her own children, later extended to her early childhood classroom, Wolf (1990) suggests that art postcards make an excellent vehicle for art appreciation because children can handle them easily. In addition, postcards provide the basis for other related activities such as matching, classification, and, later, learning about the artists.

As co-developers of the nationally recognized early childhood art appreciation program of the Toledo Museum of Art, Cole and Schaefer (1990) have detailed strategies for discussing works of fine art with young children. These involve the following four steps:

1. The first step, description, involves interactive dialogue between teacher and children to describe what the picture portrays. The teacher's questions encourage the children to look closely at the picture, examine details, and relate what they see.
2. In the analysis step, children relate the elements and qualities of the picture. The teacher might ask, "How do the colors get along? Are they quiet or noisy? Fighting or friendly?" or, "Find a line and follow it with your eyes. . . . If it were on a playground, how would you play on it? Slide, swing, climb?" (p. 36).

Some museums have programs for young children that focus on aesthetic appreciation of fine art. Preschoolers enjoy seeing works of art and, through an age-appropriate program, can be helped to describe, analyze, interpret, and judge art as well.

3. The interpretation step invites children to stretch their imaginations by asking, for instance, "What kind of person do you think this man is? What might he say to you?" (p. 36).
4. Finally, in the judgment phase, children are helped to find personal meaning in the artwork by relating it to their own worlds. Questions encourage children to decide whether they would choose this piece for their homes or what elements of the work they like best.

Cole and Schaefer feel that this process has merit not just in the development of aesthetic appreciation, but in the fact that it also fosters cognitive, social, and emotional growth. It involves logical and creative thinking, encourages appreciation and tolerance of others' viewpoints, and helps children put personal feelings into words.

MUSIC

Music is a powerful means of communication. It can be boisterous and joyful, wistful and sad, exuberant and exciting, or soothing and relaxing. Music can match as well as affect our moods. Children have a spontaneous affinity to music, which makes this a natural element to incorporate into the early childhood curriculum, appropriate for infants as well as older children. We will look at the development of music during children's early years, then turn to a more careful examination of appropriate activities related to four components of music in the early childhood curriculum: listening to music, singing, playing instruments, and moving to music.

Music and Child Development

Children develop an awareness of and response to music from a very early age, and the early childhood program should include many music activities to promote musical appreciation and enjoyment.

From earliest infancy, children are aware of and respond to music in their environment. Honig (1995) encourages caregivers to sing, croon, and hum formal as well as spontaneous, made-up songs to babies as early as possible. "From birth, the human baby is biologically primed to respond with pleasure to the human voice" (p. 73). Music is an important vehicle for cognitive, social, and physical development in very young children.

By the time children enter an early childhood program, they have already had numerous musical and rhythmic experiences. Two-year-olds begin to gain some control over their singing voices and enjoy simple songs and finger plays, moving to music, and experimenting with simple rhythm instruments; songs with simple physical actions are favorites of this age group. By age three, because of increasing motor control, attention span, memory, conceptual abilities, and independence, children develop a larger repertoire of songs, begin to note comparisons in sounds, and associate special music for special movement.

Four-year-olds appreciate slightly more complex melodies, enjoy creating words and songs, and experiment with musical instruments. By ages five and six, with continual refinement of abilities in all developmental areas, children begin to appreciate songs and dances that have rules, can follow specific rhythmic patterns, and may pick out simple familiar tunes on musical instruments. Seven- and eight-year-olds may be taking lessons, often are able to read the words of songs, particularly enjoy music with rules, begin to compare sounds and pitches, and like more complex group activities that incorporate music (Jalongo & Collins, 1985; Mayesky, 1995). Whereas the two-year-old can sing an average of 5 different notes, by age five the child has expanded that ability to 10 musical notes (Jalongo & Collins, 1985).

We are all aware that people have varying musical abilities. Mozart was writing musical scores and playing instruments brilliantly at a very early age; on the other hand, we also find individuals who seem to be totally tone deaf. Some children may have a special musical gift while others have talents in other areas. However, inclusion of music in the early childhood curriculum is not a matter of identifying and training special musical talent. Rather, it should promote appreciation and enjoyment of music in all its forms.

In fact, historically, music has been part of early childhood education, suggesting a long standing recognition of its importance. Alper (1987), advocating music education as part of the early childhood curriculum, suggests that music teaches us about ourselves, helps us toward self-actualization, provides a historical link to the past, and facilitates learning. Music, as a process- rather than a product-oriented activity, also allows for creative expression, develops children's aesthetic sense, and provides an enjoyable way of introducing concepts and skills (Bayless & Ramsey, 1982).

Listening

Music activities help sharpen children's listening skills.

Listening is a prerequisite to understanding and using music. Children would not be able to identify environmental sounds, learn new songs, or move to the rhythm of music if they did not first listen. Children can be helped to develop attentiveness and sensitivity to all kinds of sounds, including music. Listening can be promoted in informal ways and through more formal listening activities.

The environment is full of sounds, which can be brought to children's attention. Periodically direct children's attention to the sounds that surround them—the bird song, car horn, airplane drone, slamming door, or flushing toilet. This practice can be begun in infancy. By pointing out sounds, you are focusing children's attention on what often becomes mindless background noise.

In the midst of an activity, for instance, during circle time, you might occasionally suggest that the children close their eyes, listen carefully, and share what they hear. It is amazing how much sound there is in the silence! Listening should not be relegated to a once-a-year topic, when you discuss hearing as one of the senses; it should be a frequent focus of activities. You can also provide good music as an integral part of every day by playing a record or tape during activity time or outdoor time.

In planned, formal listening activities, the primary objectives will be to encourage and sharpen children's skills in listening to music. To help children understand the beat of the music, you can have them clap with the music. You might play very slow music and ask the chil-

Children enjoy all aspects of music, listening to it, singing, playing instruments, and moving to it. Such activities can be both planned and spontaneous.

dren to listen to the tempo or speed, then move their bodies in the same tempo; repeat with a musical selection that has a fast tempo, then one that changes speeds, and discuss the difference with the children. Using a selection whose pitch ranges from high to low notes, you can ask the children to stand on tiptoe when the pitch is high and crouch close to the floor when the pitch is low.

You can also discuss the mood of music by asking children to describe how different selections make them feel. The same music can have different tone color, depending on which instrument plays the piece; let children hear the same melody played by a piano, a xylophone, and a guitar, for instance, and discuss the differences. Children should be introduced to music from a wide variety of **genres,** including classical, popular, jazz, folk, country, and spiritual. Musical selections should certainly include those from the children's cultures.

Genres—Categories or types of music, such as classical, jazz, or country.

Singing

Children enjoy learning new songs and singing spontaneously in a relaxed and accepting atmosphere.

Children usually join readily in song. Many young children are not yet able to carry a tune, although a sense of pitch seems to come more easily to some youngsters (Alper, 1987). However, the main purpose of singing with young children should not be musical accuracy but enjoying and building a foundation for music appreciation. The early childhood program should encourage spontaneous singing and teach a repertoire of new songs.

When children feel relaxed and comfortable in an accepting climate, they will engage readily in spontaneous singing. A child may, for instance, sing a lullaby as he puts a doll in a cradle, expanding his play with a familiar element from his home life. Or a child may verbalize what she is doing, as four-year-old Katrina did, chanting a made-up song identifying the items on the lotto cards she was laying out on the table. Some teachers, who do not feel self-conscious about their voices, model spontaneous singing throughout the day. In one unusual program the author observed, she had a sense of witnessing a fun-filled opera as teachers and children sang rather than talked almost every communication! Singing should certainly be part of infant and toddler programs, as adults frequently use songs to soothe, create interest in sounds, and interact with babies. Music as a daily part of infant care can help babies learn to listen (McDonald & Ramsey, 1982).

Teaching new songs to children is probably the most common music activity in early childhood programs. Children enjoy learning new songs and developing a growing repertoire of music. Early childhood songs have some common characteristics: they have distinctive rhythms, contain understandable lyrics, are often repetitive, stress enjoyment, and use a limited range of notes (Jalongo & Collins, 1985). When selecting a new song, be sure the lyrics are appropriate for young children, because many songs have words that rely on themes or humor suited more for adults than for preschoolers. A child's voice range expands with age, controlled primarily by maturation; thus, songs that have too broad a range should be avoided. McDonald and Ramsey (1982) recommend a range that falls between the B below and the A above middle C on the piano keyboard. Maturity and experience gradually expand the range as children get older.

Some appropriate guidelines can make group singing enjoyable for adults and children (Mayesky, 1995).

- If you are going to teach a new song to children, know the song well first. Listen to and practice a new song until you are comfortable with the melody and lyrics.
- Do not teach the words and music of a new song separately.
- Short, simple songs with repetitive themes can be taught by presenting the entire song at once. Longer, more complex songs can be taught in shorter segments. Let children enjoy listening and join in when they can.
- Musical accompaniment on a piano, autoharp, or guitar or with a record or tape can help reinforce words and melody when a new song is being taught. It is difficult, however, to sing, play an instrument, and observe the reactions of the children simultaneously.
- When you teach a song on a specific topic because it relates to a curriculum theme, do not abandon that song once you have finished the topic. The song has become part of the class repertoire and it should continue to be sung.
- Some children are reluctant to join in singing. Encourage but never force a child to participate.
- Singing should be an enjoyable experience. If the children seem disinterested, bored, or distracted with singing activities, carefully examine what is happening. You may need to teach some new songs, use varying techniques, add action elements to some of the songs, add props suggested by the words, or use rhythm instruments as an accompaniment.

Playing Musical Instruments

Rhythm and melodic instruments provide another means of promoting music appreciation and enjoyment, and they should be part of any early childhood program.

From their earliest pot-banging days, young children enjoy opportunities to make music. Children often use body parts, especially hands and feet, to keep rhythm. Instruments appropriate for the early childhood program fall into three categories: rhythm instruments, which have no pitch and are used for striking or scraping; melodic instruments, which present specific pitches; and accompanying instruments, which produce several tones together, particularly chords that accompany a melody (Alper, 1987). Opportunities to use good instruments, as well as to make rhythm instruments, should be available.

Rhythm instruments are the most common musical tools to which young children are exposed. Commercial sets of rhythm instruments may include several types of drums, rhythm sticks, pairs of wooden blocks, sand blocks that are rubbed against each other, tambourines, triangles, variously mounted bells, castanets, maracas, and cymbals. Each produces a distinctive sound, but, when played together with no ground rules, they can result in a rather deafening din.

It is important, therefore, to introduce rhythm activities properly. Rhythm instruments need to be handled with respect and care. One

Rhythm instruments, particularly when they have cultural relevance, provide an enjoyable music activity for young children.

way of familiarizing children with instruments is by introducing them, one at a time, and demonstrating how they should be used in a small group activity. Each instrument can be played so children are able to hear its distinctive sound and then passed around so all the children have the chance to handle it, examine it, and make sounds with it. It is often best to start small groups of children playing rhythm instruments to an appropriate record or song (one with a strong beat), calling their attention to the rhythm of the music and the unique sound that each instrument makes. Children should have the opportunity to select the instrument they prefer, trade instruments among the players, and try all of them.

Children can also make a variety of rhythm instruments, using assorted materials. Coffee cans and oatmeal cartons, for instance, can be transformed into drums. Film canisters and egg-shaped plastic hosiery containers can be filled with beans, rice, or small pebbles and taped shut to make shakers or maracas. Such craft activities can help children become more familiar with what makes the sound in instruments, but they should not be considered "art" activities, which allow much more latitude and give much less instruction in how to use the materials.

Some simple melodic instruments, such as xylophones and bells, can be included in the early childhood program. These allow children to experiment with different tones, discover ascending and descending notes, and begin to pick out simple tunes. Some schools have a piano in the classroom as well, a good addition if one of the teachers is skilled in playing this instrument. Children can make similar discoveries from a piano, but specific rules should be established to ensure that the piano is handled with care and respect. Color-coded bells or piano keys and simple songs with color-coded notes encourage children to play songs.

Accompanying instruments include the autoharp, guitar, and ukelele. Teachers usually play these instruments during music activities, and then they may be stored in an out-of-the-way place until needed. If children are encouraged to try strumming, they should be familiar with the appropriate rules for the instruments' use.

Movement and Music

Creative movement activities, with or without the accompaniment of music, provide a way to reinforce many concepts.

Small children seem to be in constant motion. Movement activities are a good way of combining this natural inclination with activities that stretch their imaginations, exercise muscles, contribute to formation of spatial and temporal concepts, and build respect for the uniqueness and ideas of others. As with all other aspects of music in the early childhood curriculum, movement activities occur spontaneously as well as in more planned ways.

Because young children still learn very much in a sensorimotor mode, they often use body movement that imitates and is representative of elements of their environment to reinforce what they experience. For instance, children at the edge of a lake will unconsciously squat down in imitation of the birds on the water, seemingly assimilating through active movement what they are observing. Similarly, a child's head might turn round and round as she or he intently watches a spinning top.

Movement reinforces musical beat. Rhythmic movement in time to music begins to emerge around age three, when children are better able to synchronize (McDonald & Ramsey, 1982). Children learn to keep time to music with ample practice. Clapping to music, marching in time to its beat, and taking small steps with short beats and long ones with long beats all reinforce children's emerging synchrony with music.

Creative Movement Activities. Children can also move with the mood of the music. Many lyric pieces invoke feelings of joy or sadness or reflectiveness or whimsy; they invite swaying, bending, rolling, swinging, twirling, or stretching. Asking children to move as the music makes them feel can result in a variety of creative dances. After children have had many opportunities to move their bodies to music, you can add various props to extend this experience. Such props can include scarves, ribbons, balloons, hoops, and streamers.

Another way that children can move creatively is by representing aspects of their environment that they have had an opportunity to observe. Nature provides many fascinating examples: sway like the trees in our play yard, fly like the butterfly we watched outside, walk like the pigs we saw at the farm, grow and open like the tulips on the windowsill that we planted and watered. Children can also be the popcorn they watched pop before snack, the fire engine they saw extend its ladder on the field trip, or the washing machine in which their parents do the laundry. They can make themselves into a ball or a long, long string. Wall mirrors can help children see what they are visualizing. What makes such activities creative is that all children have the opportunity to express themselves in their own unique fashion, not in a way modeled by a teacher. No one rendition of a "tree" or "popcorn" is better than another; each represents a child's own feelings and concepts.

PARENTAL VALUES FOR CREATIVITY

Parents can be helped to value children's creative development in its broadest sense of the term.

Some parents consider their children's creative development an important goal; others focus more on concerns about their children's preacademic success. It is, therefore, important to share with parents the school's philosophy about creativity, particularly in its broad sense of encouraging flexible, open thinking and problem-solving skills. Such information should be part of a philosophy statement that is given to parents when they enroll their children in the program. On an ongoing basis, you can let parents know which activities are planned and what you expect the children to gain from them. Similarly, a focus on creativity can continue to be reinforced individually, as you share with parents information about their child's interests and accomplishments.

Parents also enjoy seeing tangible evidence that their children are involved and productive at school. It is most often art products, which children bring home in great stacks, that provide them with such confirmation. As the teacher, you can help parents appreciate their children's art in relation to the age-appropriateness of the work. It may be easy to dismiss children's scribbles as non-art and value only representation art products. Information on the development of children's art and the importance and sequence of all the stages can provide parents with insight into their children's work. Appropriate handouts, an article in the school's newsletter, an explanatory bulletin-board display, or books on children's art in the parent library can all be good vehicles for conveying such information.

FACTORS THAT DECREASE CREATIVITY

A discussion about creative development should include a few words about the all-too-present factors in our society that often blunt children's creative impulses. As we have discussed, creativity depends on flexible, open, divergent thinking, which is encouraged in children through a flexible and open environment.

Creativity can be stifled when stereotypes are imposed, when children are given few choices, and when they are always shown what to do.

In the same way, however, creativity can also be diminished by socializing factors that narrow, stereotype, or limit ideas. An atmosphere that promotes racial, cultural, or sex stereotypes, for instance, imposes a narrow view of people, which restricts potential. An environment in which the adult is always right and children are expected to do what they are told without asking questions is not conducive to creativity. In addition, when children are given coloring books or dittoes so that each child has an identical end product, they will not develop creativity. When children are always shown how to do tasks, they will not have the opportunity to engage in problem solving and creative thinking. When adults laugh at a child's unique or unusual response, that child is discouraged from expressing other creative ideas.

Television and Creativity

Television viewing can decrease creativity. Both the content of television programs and the amount of time children spend watching television can have a negative impact.

One pervasive factor in children's lives that can affect creativity is television. On the average, children spend more time watching television than in any other activity except sleep (Huston, Watkins, & Kunkel, 1989). What children see—program content—as well as how much time they spend in front of the set can decrease creative thinking.

KEY QUESTION #5

Watch a children's television program, for instance, a cartoon. What messages does this program convey to children? Does it promote stereotypes? If a child watches programs such as this one frequently, how might such viewing affect creativity?

Programs on this medium tend to convey a very stereotyped view of people, one in which recognition and respect are accorded primarily to those who are white, male, young, and beautiful (Liebert & Sprafkin, 1988). Television also generally promotes the view that an

A Closer Look

Television and Children

The effect of the media, particularly television, on young children is a concern that deeply disturbs the many professionals who are in a position to see some of its effects. Since the early 1980s, when children's television was deregulated, the increasingly violent content of programs has heightened concern for the well-being of children because they are continually exposed to inappropriate models and methods of conflict resolution.

The first year's results of the three-year "National Television Violence Study" (1996), which focused on the content of programs, paints a disturbing picture. Researchers analyzed about 2500 hours of programming, from a 20-week period, covering all times of the day. Violence was found in the majority of programs, from a high of 85 percent on premium cable channels to a low of 18 percent on public broadcast channels. On network channels, violent content occurred in 44 percent of programs. Movies had the highest violence ratings and were the most explicit types of programs. Children's programs are not exempt from negative messages either; 95 percent failed to portray any long-term consequences of violence, and 67 percent of programs made light of the violence by showing it in a humorous context.

Even more disturbing was the message sent through these episodes of violence. In 73 percent of all violent scenes, the perpetrator was not punished. In addition, the consequences of the violence were not shown; 47 percent of episodes showed no harm come to the victim, 58 percent showed no pain, and 84 percent portrayed no long-term consequences. In addition, handguns were used in a full 25 percent of violent scenes. Of all these programs with violent content, only 4 percent focused on an anti-violence theme and offered alternatives to violent behavior.

The implications of such information are frightening and demonstrate an uncaring insensitivity to the needs of America's children. Research has clearly shown that television, particularly violent portrayals, affects children and has the potential for great harm. Children respond in different ways, but many become more aggressive, others become insensitive to the suffering of others, and many become fearful. "Exposure to media violence leads children to see violence as a normal response to stress and as an acceptable means for resolving conflict" (NAEYC, 1990).

The "National Television Violence Study" (1996) and NAEYC, in its position statement on media violence in children's lives (1990), outline strong suggestions for the media and policy makers. Both also offer suggestions for those who live and work with children. Teachers are encouraged to be familiar with programs children watch, help children develop nonviolent alternatives to resolve conflicts, discuss their observations of imitation of TV content with parents, and become advocates for more responsible children's programming. In addition, teachers can encourage parents to

- watch television with their children,
- encourage critical viewing by discussing content with their children,
- keep children's developmental level in mind when making viewing decisions, and
- become informed of the potential risks of television violence.

effective way of solving problems is through violence, another narrow attitude that often does not model a variety of constructive problem-solving strategies.

Even more disturbing are the results from a number of studies that have shown that frequent and consistent viewing of violent television programming is strongly related to aggressive behavior (for example, Huesmann, Lagerspetz, & Eron, 1984; Joy, Kimball, & Zabrack, 1986; Singer, Singer, & Rapaczynski, 1984). As one author of a number of important studies concluded, "Aggressive habits seem to be learned early in life, and once established, are resistant to change and predictive of serious adult antisocial behavior" (Huesmann, 1986, p. 129).

The amount of viewing time can also affect creativity. Creative learning is an active process, dependent on ample time spent exploring, investigating, manipulating, and reflecting. The more a child sits in front of the TV, the less time is available for active, self-directed play. Furthermore, research has shown that when children watch violent programs, they tend simply to imitate the aggression of these programs and their play becomes more stereotyped and less imaginative (NIMH, 1982). If, in addition to home television viewing, children spend more hours in front of a TV or VCR at school, cumulative time in passive viewing can be considerable. (See **A Closer Look** for more discussion on this topic.)

There are, certainly, worthwhile children's programs on television, ones that model and teach children positive, **prosocial behaviors,** especially children's programs on public channels, for instance, "Mr. Rogers' Neighborhood" and "Sesame Street." These programs provide high-quality, age-appropriate, sensitive fare for young children. Other programs, some of which are appropriate for preschoolers, are designed to promote appreciation of nature, aesthetics, and culture.

Prosocial behaviors—Positive, commonly valued social behaviors such as sharing, empathy, or understanding.

SUMMARY

1. Consider the definition and discussion of some of the characteristics of creativity. Research on the different functions of the two sides of the brain is relevant to this discussion.
2. Both the teacher's attitude and the physical environment are important in encouraging creativity in young children.
3. One of the early childhood curriculum areas in which creativity can especially flourish is art.
   A. There are several theoretical views of the process of art.
   B. Many types of art activities and materials are appropriate in the early childhood classroom.
   C. Aesthetic appreciation is another element of art that can be nurtured in the early years.
4. A second broad curriculum area that fosters creativity is music. Consider listening to music, singing, playing musical instruments, and creative movement as they relate to children.
5. Some factors discourage and decrease creativity, including television.

KEY TERMS LIST

aesthetics
aggregates
basic scribbles
combines
convergent thinking
diagrams
divergent thinking
flexibility
fluency
genres
lateralization
open-ended materials
pictorialism
placement patterns
preschematic stage
prosocial behaviors
schematic stage
scribbling stage
sensitivity
split brain

chapter 10

Physical Development Through the Curriculum

One of the major tasks of the early years is physical growth and development. At no other time in life is there such a rapid rate of change in size, weight, and body proportions as well as in increased control and refinement in the use of body parts (Allen & Marotz, 1994). Physical changes, which are readily observable, profoundly affect and are affected by all areas of development. As we have emphasized before, a child is a whole, not divisible into components such as physical, social, or cognitive areas, although to be able to manage the information, we do discuss development in such categories. This chapter will examine aspects of physical development and the activities that enhance it.

A DEVELOPMENTAL FRAMEWORK FOR MOTOR DEVELOPMENT

Before we begin discussing theories, we should clarify some terms commonly used in considering physical development. These include **gross motor development**—what is involved in control of the large muscles of the legs, arms, back, and shoulders needed for large body movements such as crawling, running, jumping, and climbing; **fine motor development**—the skills involved in use of the small muscles of the fingers and hands necessary for such tasks as picking up objects, writing, drawing, or buttoning; and **sensory-perceptual development**—which is involved in conveying information that comes through the senses and the meaning that it is given. This chapter will include all three aspects of physical development.

Traditionally, physical development has been considered from a **maturational theory** perspective. This viewpoint is based on information about when children reach development milestones in such functions as sitting, standing, and walking, tasks that are largely determined by the maturation of the nervous system (Wade & Davis, 1982).

Gross motor development—Development of skills involving the large muscles of the legs, arms, back, and shoulders, necessary for such tasks as running, jumping, and climbing.

Fine motor development—Development of skills involving the small muscles of the fingers and hands necessary for such tasks as writing, drawing, or buttoning.

Sensory-perceptual development—Giving meaning to information that comes through the senses.

Maturational theory—Explanation of human development dependent on information about when children achieve specific skills.

Perceptual motor model—A theoretical view of physical development that holds that motor behaviors are a prerequisite for and lead to cognitive abilities.

Physical development involves gross motor, fine motor, and sensory-perceptual development.

The maturational perspective is concerned with when children reach developmental milestones.

The perceptual motor model considers that mastery of physical tasks is a prerequisite for cognitive development.

One of the earliest researchers to carefully observe and record the sequence of motor skill development was Arnold Gesell (Seefeldt & Haubenstricker, 1982), whose pioneering work through the Gesell Institute is still used extensively. Most early research on motor development was descriptive, using observations and films to establish the average age at which children achieve various motor skills. Such information, however, does not explain the underlying process of motor development (Rarick, 1982).

In more recent years, Piaget's theory (as discussed in Chapter 5) has led to the **perceptual motor model** of physical development, a more integrative view proposing that motor behaviors are a prerequisite for and lead to cognitive abilities (Cratty, 1982). As you will remember from the discussion of Piaget's theory, the first level of development is the sensorimotor stage, in which the infant moves through a series of accomplishments, going from primitive reflexes to purposeful manipulation of the environment. In this early stage, covering approximately the first two years of life, the child learns through sensory input and body movement.

Repetition of certain motor patterns leads the child to form schemas, representations of experiences. In early infancy, children use their own body movement to create different schemas. At approximately six months, they begin to explore the effect of their actions on the environment. During the second year, they become active explorers, engaging in rudimentary problem solving to reach their goals (Mussen, Conger, Kagan, & Huston, 1990). As they enter the third year of life, children move into Piaget's second level of development, the preoperational stage. They can now mentally represent or think about objects and events that are not present in the immediate environment. This emerging ability for symbolic representations is based on a foundation of the sensory and motor learning of the first two years.

Because young children learn through physical movement and interaction with the environment, they must be provided with numerous movement opportunities and experiences. Furthermore, this viewpoint also assumes that a child's academic performance can be improved by increasing the amount of motor activity, because cognition is predicated on motor experience (Cratty, 1982). The evidence for this second assumption is still being debated, as we will see later in this chapter.

Reflexive movement phase—According to David Gallahue, the earliest stage of gross motor development during the first year; at first greatly controlled by reflexes then gradually coming under greater voluntary control.

Rudimentary movement phase—According to David Gallahue, the second stage of gross motor development during the second year when body control is gradually developing.

COMPONENTS OF MOTOR DEVELOPMENT

The movement of newborns is primarily reflexive but rapidly becomes more purposeful and controlled as babies learn to grasp objects, move around, and eventually walk. Toddlers and young preschoolers still have rudimentary movement ability and control; but by the time they reach the primary grades, their motions have become much more refined and competent. Gallahue (1993) identifies four phases of motor development: the **reflexive movement phase** of the first year, the **rudimentary movement phase** of the second year, the **fundamental movement phase** of the next four or five years, and the **specialized movement phase,** which begins to appear around age seven. A number of movement components are part of the overall change in motor development.

Body Control

The foundation of the skills that result in increasingly greater control of the body is laid from the very beginning of life. Earliest movements are jerky and large, often controlled by reflexes rather than voluntary, but they become smoother and more purposeful with age. In the very earliest months of life, upper body parts, such as the arms, are more active. By two months, the baby raises herself by the arms, gradually learns to change position from front to back and, by the middle of the first year, begins crawling motions. Many 8-month-olds are able to pull themselves up on furniture and, by 11 months, may be able to stand alone. The first solo step, unsteady as it is, generally appears around the first birthday, although there is great variation in the age of this achievement (Allen & Marotz, 1994; Gonzales-Mena & Eyers, 1989; Wilson, 1995).

Six important elements of body control—walking, running, jumping, hopping, throwing, and balancing—develop during the next few years (Keogh & Sugden, 1985). Walking is the basic means of **locomotion**, self-movement from place to place; running, jumping, hopping, and throwing are fundamental play skills; and balancing provides one way of assessing postural control. All of these important skills become more accurate, controlled, and efficient during the early years.

Subtle changes in walking transform the toddler, whose concern is balance rather than efficiency, to the much more graceful preschooler. As the child gets older, legs and arms alternate, toeing-out decreases, stride becomes more consistent, heels and toes rather than the flat foot are used for landing and takeoff of each step, and feet are placed so they are more parallel. Mastery of stair climbing involves increasing skill in several factors such as moving from supported walking to walking alone, walking up before coming down, and stepping with both feet on each step to alternate stepping (Gallahue, 1993; Keogh & Sugden, 1985). By the time children are four years old, most are able to walk up and down stairs independently using alternating feet (Allen & Marotz, 1990).

Not just a faster version of walking, running makes the child airborne at moments, with both feet off the ground. The earliest form of running is the hurried walk of the 18-month-old, but by age two, most children run, and by ages four to six they are quite skilled, increasing speed and control. Some of the changes involve a longer stride, a shift in the center of gravity as the angle of the legs increases, increased flexion of the knees, and better synchrony between arms and legs (Gallahue, 1993; Keogh & Sugden, 1985). By age four, many preschoolers can start, stop, and move around objects with ease while running (Allen & Marotz, 1994).

Jumping during which both feet leave the ground simultaneously, seems to follow a consistent pattern in its development. The earliest form of jumping occurs when a toddler steps off a step to be briefly airborne. It isn't until the third year that the child leaves a step with both feet, executing a more accurate jump. Another way to view jumping is to observe children jump vertically off the ground, an achievement that usually occurs by their second birthday. The broad jump evolves around age three, with length of jump increasing with age (Gallahue,

Fundamental movement phase—According to David Gallahue, the third stage of gross motor development, from ages 2 to 7, when children refine rudimentary skills so they acquire mature characteristics.

Specialized movement phase—According to David Gallahue, the fourth and final stage of gross motor development, appearing around age 7 and up, when motor skills are applied to special uses, such as specific sports.

Locomotion—Self-movement from place to place, such as in walking.

In development of body control, young children gain mastery in walking, running, jumping, hopping, throwing, and balancing. Each requires complex skills.

KEY QUESTION #1

Observe preschoolers of various ages at play. What differences in physical development do you see as a function of age? What do these abilities tell you about appropriate activities and expectations?

During the early years, children quickly master a variety of gross motor skills. This two-year-old is more secure with a hand to hold as he walks up and down the stairs. Within a couple of years he will negotiate stairs with little problem.

Hopping on one foot becomes easy as children move toward the end of the preschool years.

1993; Keogh & Sugden, 1985). By three children jump in place with both feet, by four most can jump over objects 5 to 6 inches high, and by five they can jump forward on both feet 10 times in a row (Allen & Marotz, 1994).

Achievement of one-legged jumping or hopping generally emerges between ages three and four, beginning with one hop, then increasing the number of hops. Early attempts at hopping usually end with both feet coming back to the ground for support, because children tend to propel their bodies too high by pushing too hard off the ground. Children are better able to hop forward than in place because the forward momentum helps them maintain their balance. Hopping becomes part of other movements such as galloping and skipping, tasks that appear between the ages of four and five and reach mature skill level by six. Skipping appears to be mastered much more easily by girls than by boys (Gallahue, 1993; Keogh & Sugden, 1985).

The objective of throwing is to propel an object forward with accuracy and enough force so that it reaches the target. Before age two, many toddlers execute an overhand throw, but with poor control and speed. By age three, children become more accurate in throwing in a specific direction, and they can usually propel an object 5 to 10 feet. As they get older, children also become more efficient by rotating the body, stepping forward on one foot, and swinging the throwing arm to improve their throwing skills. Boys are generally more skilled at throwing; some children may, with appropriate encouragement and practice, achieve a mature throwing pattern by age six or seven (Gallahue, 1993; Keogh & Sugden, 1985).

Development of balance is essential for children to acquire smooth coordination, which, in turn, leads to self-assurance and success in a variety of activities (Munro, 1986). By age two, children can stand briefly on one foot, but not until after their third birthday can they maintain this posture for at least 5 seconds. Two-year-old children can walk, with steps astride, on a line on the floor; a few months later, they can walk backward in the same way. It isn't until about age four or five that they can walk heel-to-toe forward, then backward. These same steps on a balance beam are more demanding and are mastered at later ages (Keogh & Sugden, 1985).

A final indicator of increased movement control is moving slowly. Although preschoolers improve in their ability to speed up movement—walking, running, throwing, or riding a bicycle faster—executing these movements slowly is more difficult. Between ages four and nine, children show marked improvement in this form of body control (Keogh & Sugden, 1985).

Manual and hand control are evident from early infancy; through the early childhood years, increasing competence can be seen in self-help skills, construction ability, holding grips, and bimanual control.

Manual Control

The infant develops basic grasping and manipulation skills, which are refined during the ensuing years. Very early, the infant reflexively grasps and holds onto objects placed in his palm but cannot let go at will. During the first three months, hand and arm movement become more voluntary and, by three to four months, he can generally reach for and grasp a nearby object, using the entire hand to do so. By about nine months, the infant has perfected the **pincer grasp**, using thumb

Pincer grasp—The use of thumb and forefinger to pick up small objects; this skill develops around nine months of age.

and forefinger adeptly. Toward the end of the first year, fine motor skills have developed enough for the baby to begin taking off clothes, placing objects inside each other, moving a spoon to his mouth, and scribbling spontaneously with a crayon held in his hand. These early skills are gradually refined so that, during the next several years, children become quite adept in self-help, construction, and holding grips (Keogh & Sugden, 1985).

Self-help skills such as feeding, dressing, and grooming involve a variety of manual movements that are mastered during the early years. Between ages two and four, children gain dressing skills of increasing difficulty, pulling on simple garments at the earlier age and learning most of the necessary skills by the later age. Most four-year-olds can bathe, wash hands and face, and brush teeth quite competently, although some supervision is helpful (Keogh & Sugden, 1985). Two-year-olds have some basic self-feeding skills, threes use utensils with increasing competence, fours can use spoon and fork with dexterity, and fives are mastering the use of the knife to spread or cut soft foods. By age eight, the child uses all utensils with skill and ease (Allen & Marotz, 1994).

Self-help skills—Tasks involving caring for oneself, such as dressing, feeding, toileting, and grooming.

Many early childhood manipulative materials are designed to encourage emerging construction skills. One-year-olds begin to stack two to four objects, and by age two children can build a tower of four to six small blocks, place pegs in a pegboard, and turn doorknobs. The three-year-old can make a bridge with blocks, discriminate between and correctly place round and square pegs in a pegboard, and build a tower of 9 to 10 blocks (Allen & Marotz, 1994). As children reach ages four and five, their constructions become more intricate and require more delicate manual dexterity and spatial relations. In the primary grades, children continue to refine their construction skills and often begin assembling models that need detailed attention and control.

The most common tool use requiring a **holding grip** is writing or drawing. By age one and a half, children know how to hold a pencil or crayon, and by four they have a large repertoire of holding grips. Early grips include a **palmar grasp,** in which the pencil lies across the palm of the hand with the fingers curled around it and the arm, rather than the wrist, moves the pencil. Later developments involve variations of

Holding grip—Placement of the hands in using a tool for drawing or writing.

Palmar grasp—A way of holding tools in which the pencil or crayon lies across the palm of the hand with the fingers curled around it, and the arm rather than the wrist moves the tool.

Another accomplishment during the early years is the gradual acquisition of self-help skills. Younger children may still require help with zipping or buttoning, but by the end of the preschool period, most children are quite independent at such tasks.

Young preschoolers may still use a palmer grasp with pencils or crayons.

Tripod grasp—A way of holding tools in which the pencil or crayon is held by the fingers, and the wrist rather than the whole arm moves the tool.

the **tripod grasp,** in which the fingers hold and the wrist and fingers move the pencil. Children will spend varying amounts of time in each of these stages.

Although we consider the development of holding grips to be age related, it also seems to be affected by culture. In one study (Saida & Miyashita, 1979), researchers found that Japanese children achieve the most sophisticated grasp several months before British children do, a result partly attributed to the early mastery of chopstick use in eating. In addition, these researchers found that girls' grasp development is about six months ahead of that of boys.

Bimanual control—Ability to use both hands in tasks for which each hand assumes a different function.

Keogh and Sugden (1985) discuss one other emerging aspect of fine motor development, **bimanual control.** For many tasks we primarily use the dominant hand, but many manipulations require the use of both hands, each one assuming a different function. This is the case when tying shoelaces, holding an orange and separating it into segments, using a manual eggbeater, or manipulating a piece of paper with one hand so the other can cut out a shape. By age four or five, children establish some stability in hand use requiring bimanual control, though little research has been conducted to study this function. Early

As they mature, children develop the tripod grip, which is a more efficient way to hold writing tools.

childhood activities that promote bimanual control should be included in the program.

Sensory-Perceptual Development

Closely intertwined with motor development are sensory and perceptual functioning. Sensory input involves the collection of information through the senses of sight, hearing, taste, smell, and touch and the kinesthetic sense; perceptual input involves attention to, recognition, and interpretation of that information to give it personal meaning. Thus, perception is a cognitive process.

Children's earliest learning about the world is through the senses by seeing, hearing, tasting, touching, smelling, feeling, and the kinesthetic sense; this learning continues to be important throughout the early years.

The Senses. Much of what infants learn about their environment is conveyed through the senses. Because children first learn about their world through the senses, it is important to include activities in the early childhood curriculum that involve all sensory modalities. Traditionally, education tends to encourage visual and auditory learning, often to the exclusion of the other senses, but the world, about which children are continually learning, is made up of more than sights and sounds. It has smells, tastes, and textures as well.

The integration of information from the eyes with movement of the hands is referred to as eye-hand coordination.

Early in life, children begin to discriminate with their visual sense, learning to recognize the familiar, forming preferences for increasingly more complex stimuli, and anticipating events from visual cues. Young children continue to delight in exploring with their eyes. A rich and aesthetic early childhood environment should provide a wealth of opportunities that not only develop visual acuity but also encourage concept formation through exploration. An important integrative development is **eye-hand coordination,** the increasingly accurate use of the hands as guided by information from the eyes. Many early childhood materials, particularly manipulatives such as puzzles or Legos, encourage, exercise, and refine eye-hand coordination.

Eye-hand coordination—Integrative ability to use the hands as guided by information from the eyes.

The sense of hearing is one of the earliest functioning systems, present even before birth. By the time children reach the preschool years, they have achieved a highly sophisticated auditory skill in understanding language and using that understanding to communicate. Of course, the development of language is not only a function of hearing but also involves the perceptual ability to discriminate between

"Can you find a letter that looks just like this one, Erin?" To respond correctly to such a question, Erin must not only hear but also understand what is being asked. Hearing as well as comprehension are involved in use of the highly sophisticated auditory system.

discrete sounds and to focus on the relevant sounds to the exclusion of irrelevant ones. The infant, toddler, and early childhood environment provides a variety of auditory stimuli, but it should also provide many opportunities to focus on, discriminate among, and identify various sounds.

The taste sense is most identified with eating. To a great extent, it reflects learned preferences and socialization, although newborns appear to discriminate among and prefer certain tastes, such as sweet ones, to others, for instance, those that are bitter (Lamb & Bornstein, 1987). But taste is also instrumental in exploration, especially during the first year of life when children put objects in their mouths. Some young preschoolers continue to mouth some things, especially thumbs or other personally comforting objects, although not as indiscriminately as they do during infancy.

A variety of opportunities to explore new tastes through food experiences should be provided in the early childhood setting. In addition, a safe environment will ensure that anything that goes into children's mouths will not be harmful. At the same time, children will learn to discriminate between what is appropriate and what is inappropriate for putting in the mouth.

Smell, a sense in many ways tied to taste, is also present very early in life; newborns, in fact, have been shown to react favorably to the smell of bananas and with disgust to the smell of rotten eggs (Lamb & Bornstein, 1987). Children continue to show olfactory preferences, and they may reject a new food simply because of its smell or dislike a person because "he smells funny." Smell is an important sensory modality in learning to identify and discriminate among various common and uncommon odors, something the early childhood program can encourage and facilitate. Children enjoy matching familiar smells.

Whereas vision involves the eyes, hearing the ears, taste the mouth, and smell the nose, the sense of touch entails our largest organ, the skin. Touch can be soothing or irritating, pleasant or unpleasant, or calming or exciting, and it can project a message of safety or danger. Sensitivity to tactile stimulation develops rapidly during infancy (Lamb & Bornstein, 1987), and, by early childhood, children gain a wealth of information through this sense. Children enjoy stroking different fabrics, mounding wet sand with their hands, or feeling tree bark. A variety of tactile experiences, along with opportunities to verbally discriminate among different textures, should be part of the early childhood program.

Kinesthetic sense—Information from the body's system that provides knowledge about the body, its parts, and its movement; involves the "feel" of movement without reference to visual or verbal cues.

The kinesthetic sense provides knowledge about the movement of the body.

The Kinesthetic Sense. The body's **kinesthetic sense** provides knowledge about the body, its parts, and its movements. It also involves the "feel" of movement without reference to vision or verbal cues (Keogh & Sugden, 1985). All movement experiences add to children's growing understanding of what their bodies can do, their increasing control over their bodies, and their sense of self-confidence in their physical abilities. A child working with hammer and nail in the woodworking center has to make kinesthetic judgments that go beyond visual perception of the location of and distance between nail and hammer; for instance, the child has to know how best to hold the hammer for an effective swing, how to position the body, how hard to swing the hammer, and how to hit the nail head rather than the fingers.

Perceptual Development. As children gain information about the world through the senses of sight, hearing, taste, smell, and touch and the kinesthetic sense, they become increasingly skilled in using this information. Perception involves selecting the important features of a complex environment, focusing on the salient aspects of those features, identifying those features, and discriminating them from others. All of these processes entail cognition, again pointing out the interrelatedness of all aspects of development.

Perception involves being able to select and pay attention to sensory information that is important and relevant.

Most often, perceptual information does not come from just one sensory mode but involves **multimodality** (Allen & Marotz, 1994). If, for instance, you bring a lamb onto the playground, the children will learn about it by seeing it and watching it move, listening to it say "baaaa," smelling its distinctive odor, and feeling its curly fur. Even very young infants demonstrate multimodal abilities. All of this information, coming from the various sensory modalities, contributes to the children's concept of a lamb. From many sensory-perceptual experiences comes **sensory integration,** translation of sensory information into intelligent behavior. Allen and Marotz (1994) provide an excellent example, that of a five-year-old who sees and hears a car coming and waits on the curb for it to pass.

Multimodality—Referring to information that depends on input from several of the senses.

Sensory integration—The ability to translate sensory information into intelligent behavior.

Perceptual Motor Skills. Over the years, a number of theorists and researchers have explored the relationship between motor skills, perception, and academic success. During the 1960s and 1970s, a number of programs focused on helping children with learning disabilities by improving the link between perception and movement. The developers of such programs feel that sensorimotor development (learning through movement and the senses) precedes and is the basis of perceptual and intellectual ability.

In one approach, that of Doman and Delacato (Delacato, 1964; Delacato, 1966; Doman, Spitz, Zucman, & Delacato, 1960), specific exercises are intended to recapture the sequence of sensorimotor development and repeat motor patterns that may have been skipped (for instance, crawling). Generally, perceptual motor programs are intended to enhance academic skills rather than improve motor skills. Considerable research examining the effectiveness of such programs, however, has not supported their claims that such activities improve academic learning (Wade & Davis, 1982). It has been recommended, therefore, that perceptual motor activities be encouraged for their own sake rather than because they might affect other areas of development (Cook, Tessier, & Armbruster, 1987).

Although a number of programs promote perceptual-motor activities to improve academic skills, research has not supported their effectiveness.

We have briefly examined some developmental and theoretical issues related to gross motor, fine motor, and sensory-perceptual functions in young children. The rest of this chapter will look at some early childhood activities that enhance skill development in these areas. Again, keep in mind that this selection is somewhat forced because almost all preschool activities involve motor and sensory-perceptual elements. Similarly, the activities we will review also promote creativity, cognition, language, and social-emotional development.

GROSS MOTOR ACTIVITIES

This section examines gross motor activities, those that involve the large muscles of the body, in three areas. We will examine these activities in relation to physical fitness, consider gross motor activities in outdoor play, and look at them in block usage.

Physical Fitness

Research is finding that most young children do not engage in adequate physical activity; therefore, it is recommended that physical fitness activities regularly be included in the early childhood program.

Gross motor exercise occurs in many early childhood activities. It should be emphasized that vigorous, active play is important not only to muscle development but also to the establishment of lifelong health habits (Seefeldt, 1984). Yet, today's American preschool children are not engaged in adequate physical activity, according to an extensive survey (Poest, Williams, Witt, & Atwood, 1990). In addition, this study found that boys are more physically active than girls, children in preschools engage in more physical activity than those in child care centers, and children whose parents are involved in exercise are more likely to do so as well. Other studies have confirmed that young children have overall low activity levels and simply do not get enough exercise (Werner, Timms, & Almond, 1996). Physical fitness is concerned with overall health, specifically with the development and maintenance of "an adequate level of cardiovascular endurance, muscular strength, muscular endurance, flexibility, and body leanness" (Poest, Williams, Witt, & Atwood, 1990, p. 5). The sizable number of overweight American preschool-aged children further attests to a need for physical fitness (see A Closer Look).

Javernick (1988) feels that teachers of young children often neglect gross motor development, giving it only lip service, and instead emphasize fine motor, cognitive, and social areas in the curriculum. A number of physical educators further express the concern that free play, which often includes various motor experiences, does not adequately meet the motor development needs of young children (Seefeldt, 1984; Skinner, 1979). They advocate that structured physical fitness programs (*not* organized sports) be part of the early childhood curriculum. It is important to note, however, that no national norm exists for what physical fitness in early childhood programs should involve (Poest et al., 1990).

Young children need vigorous exercise each day for fitness. In addition to providing blocks of time for outside play, how can you, as the early childhood teacher, promote physical fitness for children?

The term *physical fitness* often conjures up our own childhood experiences involving games and sports. Play, games, and sports have characteristics that are tied to developmental readiness and appropriateness (Coleman & Skeen, 1985). Play is free from time, space, and rule constraints, and reward is inherent in the play rather than dependent on winning. Play involves such activities as running, crawling, climbing, and throwing. Games are more structured than play, although time limitations and rules can be altered to meet the needs of the players involved. Examples of games include chase, tag, rope jumping, and hopscotch.

Sports, for instance, football, track, or gymnastics, are much more structured and are based on external rewards. Preschoolers do not have the physical, social, emotional, and cognitive skills to participate in sports and in many organized games. Instead, young children need

The Rise in Obesity in Children

Since the early 1960s, the government has been collecting information about the nutritional status of America's children. The National Health and Nutrition Examination Surveys (NHANES) thus provide a unique opportunity to examine trends and changes in children's weight. Thousands of children participate in this research to provide a representative group of the country's youth. The picture that has emerged shows a steady increase in the percentage of overweight children, a trend that was particularly dramatic in the latest cycle of the study (Troiano, Flegal, Kuczmarski, Campbell, & Johnson, 1995).

The study showed that during the past decade, the number of overweight children more than doubled, from 5 to 11 percent. Thus, there are an approximate 5 million obese children in the United States. This figure comes from a more conservative estimate of overweight; if one were to use the study's less conservative measure (one used in other nutritional studies), the figure would jump to 22 percent, closer to 10 million children. Obese children more often than not grow up to become obese adults. This is particularly disturbing because of the clear links between obesity and a multitude of health problems, particularly in adulthood. Obese children also suffer from the social isolation of being different from their peers.

What are some of the reasons for this alarming trend? Body weight represents a balance between food intake and energy output. The increase in the number of overweight children is a factor of both of these elements—an increase in food intake and a decrease in activity level. Dietary patterns have changed over the past decade, and fast foods and snacks, replete with high-calorie fats and sugars, have become a more regular part of children's daily fare. At the same time, children engage in more sedentary activities, watching more TV and playing more video games than ever. Parents may also fear for the safety of their children and thus not send them outside to play as much as in past times.

Experts agree that prevention rather than intervention is the preferred approach to dealing with the problems of overweight. What can you, as an early childhood teacher do to help prevent obesity in children? While your influence extends only over part of the children's day, your contribution to their health and well-being can be significant. The foods you serve for snacks and meals, the example you set in your own eating habits, the exercises and activities you plan and encourage, your reinforcement of healthy eating and physical activity, all contribute to the children's developing acceptance of a healthy lifestyle.

KEY QUESTION #2

If you were asked to plan a physical fitness program for a group of preschoolers, what would you include? Would you plan different activities for three-year-olds than for five-year-olds?

to develop physical capabilities through many play experiences in which they can explore their outside world (Coleman & Skeen, 1985). Children in the primary grades begin to develop the developmental maturity needed for participation in more organized activities. Keep in mind, however, that competitive activities have no place in early childhood programs. Because usually one child wins at the expense of the other participants, the self-concepts of those who do not win are affected negatively, and hostility and ill-will are created.

The challenge to early childhood educators is to develop appropriate gross motor and physical fitness activities. Limited research has shown that specific, guided instruction of preschool children's motor skills can improve performance. Young children do not yet have the endurance to sustain lengthy physical exertion. It is suggested that three to five minutes of vigorous activity, interspersed with time off for recovery, is appropriate for young children (Werner et al., 1996).

Motor skills that emerge during the early years, as discussed previously in this chapter, should be the focus of such activities. Practice helps develop proficiency in motor skills beyond the rudimentary stage (Seefeldt, 1984). Javernick (1988) suggests some gross motor activity guidelines for teachers of young children.

- Motor tasks should be presented in ways that will interest children.
- Physical activities such as calisthenics, "adventurecises," or obstacle courses should be planned for each day.
- Music and movement activities should also be part of every day; many excellent children's records are available to enhance exercise and movement activities.
- Children should be allowed to make choices, for example, "Would you like to be a hopping bunny or an airplane?"
- The teacher must be an active participant in physical activity. Children are much more attracted to activities in which a teacher is enthusiastically involved.
- Outside time should not be treated as free play time during which teachers are merely passive supervisors.

"Simon Says, Everybody sit down! Now Simon Says, Everybody put both arms up!" A variety of group games can be structured to incorporate an exercise component.

The research implies that early childhood teachers need to be more concerned with providing physical fitness as part of the daily program. Vigorous daily activities that are fun and enjoyable contribute to establishing a foundation for lifelong health habits and attitudes.

Outdoor Play

Uninhibited gross motor activity is most likely to occur during outdoor play. Children are not expected to control their voice and activity level and space is not constrained, as it often is indoors. As a result, children feel freer to run, jump, crawl, climb, hang, swing, shout. A variety of interesting and versatile equipment should be available in the outdoor play yard, as we discussed in Chapter 7, "The Physical Environment."

Outdoor play provides one of the best opportunities for physical development, both through self-selected play and specific activities provided by the teacher.

The Benefits of Outdoor Play. The outdoor area and the time children spend outdoors should be integral parts of the early childhood program because of their many inherent values. Outdoor play is not just a time for children to expend excess energy while teachers take a break. Lovell and Harms (1985) summarize some of the educational and development objectives that well-planned outdoor activities in a well-designed, safe playground can meet, as follows:

- Age-appropriate equipment should facilitate a wide range of gross motor activities at different levels of challenge, including balancing, throwing, lifting, climbing, pushing, pulling, crawling, skipping, swinging, and riding.
- Social skills such as sharing, cooperating, and planning together can be encouraged by such equipment as tire swings on which several children swing together, wide slides, or movable equipment with which children can build new structures.
- Activities and equipment should also enhance development of concepts, for instance, understanding spatial relations (up and down, in and out, under and over, low and high) and temporal relationships (fast and slow; first, second, and next).
- Problem solving involving both physical and social skills should be encouraged as children figure out how to move a heavy object or how to share a popular item.
- Children can learn about their natural world by observing and helping care for plants and animals and noting seasonal and weather changes.
- A variety of activities carried on outdoors, such as art, woodworking, or music, can enhance creative development.
- Children can try out and experience various adult roles through dramatic play, for instance, re-creating the fire house, gas station, or airport.
- In addition to stationary equipment, movable components such as planks, climbing boxes, and ladders allow children to create new and different possibilities to enhance their motor, social, language, cognitive, and creative development.

- Exploration and increasing competence help children develop positive self-image and independence.

Outdoor Activities. Although children enjoy the freedom of self-selected ventures while outside, the teacher should also provide and be actively involved in planned activities that enhance motor development. As children get older, they enjoy some noncompetitive games such as "Statues," "Red Light–Green Light," or "Mother May I," which involve both movement and control. Keep in mind, however, that races pitting children against each other, or girls against boys, are inappropriate. Setting up an outdoor obstacle course, which takes advantage of existing places to climb over, crawl through, or jump across, can be enjoyable and provide exercise. A parachute, with children grasping the edges, can be used to reinforce concepts such as up and down and over and under as well as to encourage cooperative effort. The teacher's and the children's creativity are the only limits to how the outdoor play area is used to enhance children's learning and development.

Outdoor play in a separated area should be available for infants and toddlers. Such an area should provide activities and equipment that add opportunities for different movement and sensory experiences. Gentle swings and slides, safe places to crawl and feel new surfaces, places to push, pull, and roll small toys, and opportunity for messy activities should be available outside for this age group.

Blocks

Block play provides excellent opportunities for physical development, through both self-selected play and specific activities provided by the teacher.

Blocks are one of the most versatile and enjoyable materials found in early childhood classrooms. Blocks come in many shapes and sizes, are made of various materials, can be used alone or in combination with other items, and lend themselves to an almost infinite variety of play possibilities.

Benefits of Block Play. Blocks provide many opportunities for motor development. Children use both their large and small muscles during block play as they lift, bend, stretch, reach, turn, and manipulate and balance various types of blocks. In addition, blocks promote concept learning (big and little, tall and short, over and under); are a natural vehicle for learning about matching, similarities and differences, and classification; entail math and science concepts related to quantity, addition and subtraction, weight, and balance; develop vocabulary and visual memory related to shapes, sizes, and patterns; elicit creativity, problem solving, and role playing; encourage cooperative play; and are satisfying, giving a sense of accomplishment and self-worth. Blocks are certainly a versatile medium that meets many needs and provides many opportunities for development!

Children's block play evolves through specific, age-related stages.

Stages of Block Play. As you observe young children using blocks, you will note differences in the type and complexity of such play among children. Children go through stages in their development of block play, stages related to age and experience, but certainly showing considerable individual variation. Toddlers often spend considerable time carrying blocks around, perhaps banging them together, and exploring their feel and weight. In the next stage, children's earliest constructions are either vertically stacked or horizontally laid-out blocks. The flat structure suggests a road, and often the earliest dramatic play with blocks involves small cars driving over such a road.

By three to four years, children begin putting blocks together into more deliberate constructions, for instance, enclosures, bridges, or decorative patterns. Enclosures can lead to dramatic play with animal, people, or furniture accessories as children make houses, farms, or zoos. Bridges often become a challenge for cars driving through, as children gauge and compare size, width, height, distance, and balance. Use of decorative patterns shows children's interest in symmetry, repetition of configurations, and exploration of various designs.

In the final stage, reached between four and six years, children engage in more representational constructions, naming their structures, building to create props for dramatic play, and making quite complex and elaborate edifices (*Blocks,* 1979; Reifel, 1984).

Each of these stages reflects children's increasing understanding of spatial concepts. Well before the age of four, children have mastered basic spatial relationships such as *on, by,* and *in.* In the later stages of block building, they demonstrate more advanced spatial concepts as they manipulate space in symbolic representations of such structures as houses, farms, and other enclosures (Reifel, 1984).

Types of Blocks. The most common type are **unit blocks,** made of hard wood in standardized sizes and shapes. The basic unit is $5\frac{1}{2}$ inches long, $2\frac{3}{4}$ inches wide, and $1\frac{3}{8}$ inches high (*Blocks,* 1979). Variations include the square or half unit, double unit, and quadruple unit, and there are a variety of triangular, cylindrical, arched, and curved units. (See Figure 10-1 for some examples of common unit block shapes.) Unit blocks should be made with precision to ensure mathematically exact relationships among the various units.

Unit blocks—Most common type of blocks, precision made of hard wood in standardized sizes and shapes.

Large, hollow blocks, 11 inches square by $5\frac{1}{2}$ inches high, have one open side and a slit for carrying. Other size variations include a half square and a double square. Hollow blocks are often accompanied by other equipment such as boards, ramps, sawhorses, ladders, and packing crates. Because of their size, hollow blocks encourage a different kind of dramatic play, one in which children can climb into the structures they build to drive the "car," pilot the "boat," or live in the "house." A variety of accessories can extend their play as well. Hollow blocks are used as easily inside as they are outside. They are particularly good for large muscle development because of their bulk and weight (*Blocks,* 1979; Cartwright, 1990).

Cardboard blocks, made of heavy corrugated cardboard resembling large, red bricks, are very useful with toddlers and young preschoolers. These sturdy blocks are lightweight and manageable for very young children, whose motor skills and balance are not yet well developed. They are easily carried around by children in the first stage of block building, are readily stacked by children entering the second stage, and are generally not harmful if knocked over. These blocks are

FIGURE 10-1 Examples of Common Unit Blocks

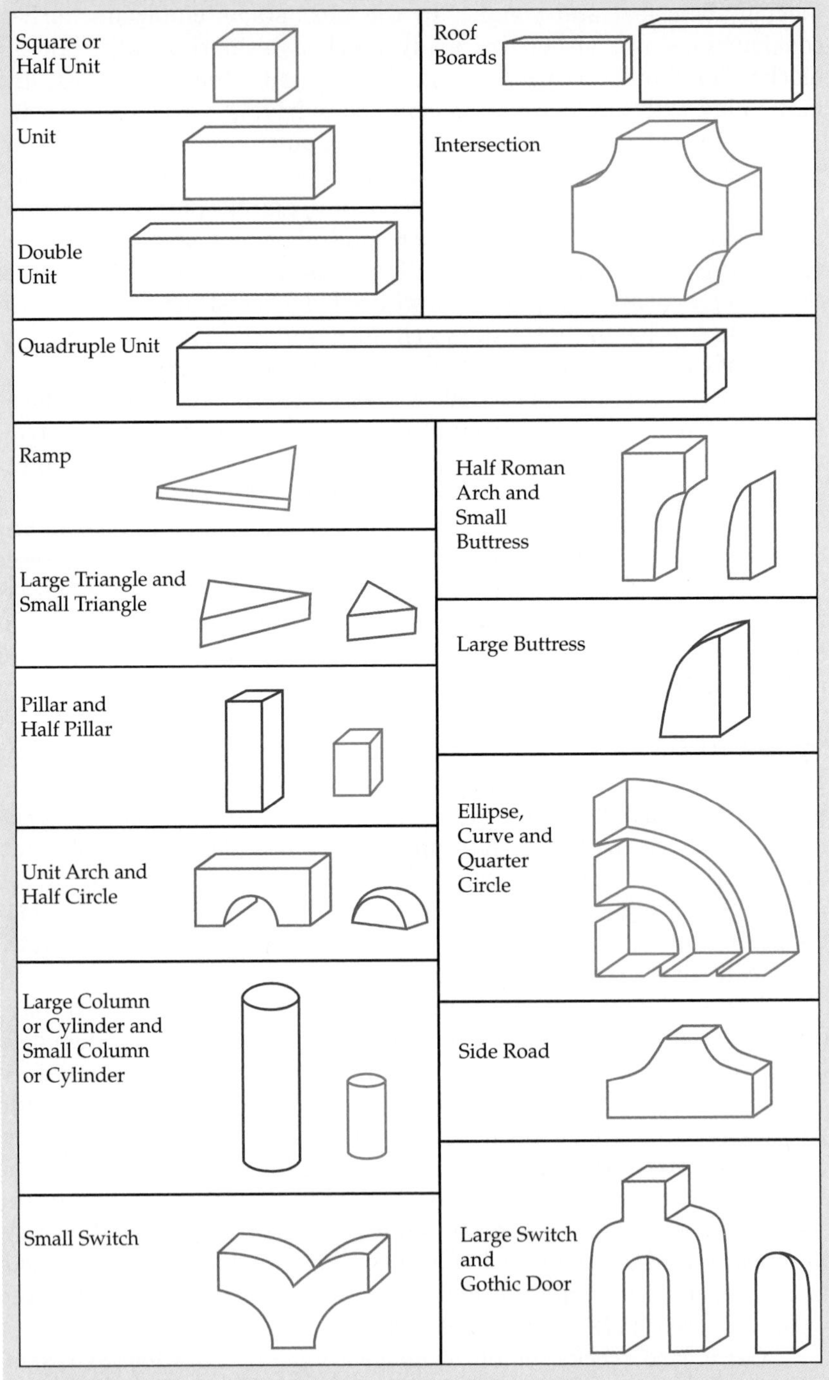

not particularly versatile for more complex block structures, however, because all the blocks are the same size and shape.

A variety of homemade blocks can also be added to your selection of construction materials. Relatively sturdy blocks, for instance, can be made of cylindrical oatmeal boxes and milk cartons. Wooden blocks can

E X P E R I E N C E S

chapter 10

TOSHIKO, Master Teacher, Mixed-Age Class

The Airport

Blocks are one of the most popular materials in our center. Because we are located in a converted house, we decided to dedicate an entire room to blocks. Several classes share all of the rooms, including this one. By having a room just for the blocks, children can keep their block structures up for days or even weeks if they want. This opportunity has led to some very elaborate, creative, and thoughtful block constructions.

It's interesting to see children of various ages playing together with the blocks. From my experience, younger children in a group of age-mates will make relatively simple structures, often towers of stacked blocks or roads of blocks laid end-to-end. When children of various ages are together, however, the younger children seem to be stimulated to develop more elaborate structures, both observing the older ones and being helped by them.

The most frequently used types of blocks are the unit blocks, because they fit together so neatly and because their shapes are so versatile. Most of the time, children will build with these exclusively. Sometimes, however, they will combine many different blocks into very interesting constructions. I have seen them use the large hollow blocks, large cardboard bricks, unit blocks, small alphabet blocks, and, at times, even blocks from manipulative sets for a most interesting effect. We encourage the children to let their imaginations guide what and how they build. Other than safety rules, we try to impose few restrictions on how the children use the blocks.

One of the most exciting uses of the blocks happened after a field trip to the airport. For three weeks after this trip, the children built, rebuilt, and elaborated on a reconstruction of what they had seen. As they worked with the blocks, they discussed in great detail such questions as the configuration of the lines to the ticket counters, the location of the ticket counters, how the luggage got from the ticket counters to the airplanes, how hand luggage went through the X-ray machines, how people went from the waiting areas onto the airplanes, and how the luggage carousels worked. They also included snack bars, bathrooms, and gift shops in their re-creation of the airport. They combined personal memories with recollections from the field trip. They augmented the blocks with items they had constructed in the woodworking area, clothes from the dramatic play area and from home for uniforms, tickets made in the art area, and dolls and action figures to populate the airport. This project was one of the most collaborative efforts I have seen children engage in. The ever-changing airport was an impressive sight!

Since we dedicated an entire room for blocks and are not requiring that the blocks be cleaned up after each use, we have seen a delightful increase in creative block play. Blocks have become a much more important and integral part of our classroom.

experiences

Teachers can help children expand their block play through their interaction and suggestions.

also be constructed by someone who enjoys carpentry, uses high-grade hard wood, is exact in cutting shapes, and sands and varnishes carefully.

Teachers' Role in Block Play. Teachers have to gauge their involvement in block play according to cues from the children. Observation may tell teachers that some children avoid the block area, while others frequently use blocks readily and creatively. Thus, teachers may need to encourage reluctant children to try block play and help the ones who often use blocks to extend their play. In some classes, blocks tend to be a boys' activity, and girls may be unwilling to engage in block play for this reason. In such cases, teachers need to support and encourage girls to try blocks, convey that girls can be as effective as boys in constructions, value all the children's structures, and promote individuality rather than stereotyped views of people (*Blocks,* 1979).

In talking with children about their block constructions, it is better to use descriptive rather than evaluative comments. As we discussed in our last chapter in relation to children's art, judgmental statements tend to discourage and stifle children's creative efforts, because you convey an expectation about what the artwork should be like. Examples of what might be discussed include the names of the blocks used, where they are placed, how many are included, and how the blocks are balanced and connected. In doing this, you convey to the child that you have carefully looked at the construction, you may be promoting language development by using new vocabulary, and you will be encouraging the child to look closely at the work (*Blocks,* 1979).

Teachers can also encourage children's extension of block play into dramatic play. Blocks can help children re-create or act out experiences and take on the role of familiar people in their environment. A variety of props can encourage dramatic play. Wooden or plastic vehicles, animals, and figures of people are traditional block props, but other accessories can include items usually found in the dramatic play, woodworking, manipulative, sensory, or art areas. One alternative to extending block play is to combine the block area with the dramatic play area. Research on just what can happen when the divider between these two areas is removed showed that play with children of the opposite sex increased, as did appropriate use of block and housekeeping materials (Kinsman & Berk, 1982).

One aspect of block play is its relative impermanence. At cleanup time the blocks, which are "nonexpendable materials," usually have to be put back on the shelf. Yet, ownership and permanence are very important aspects of activities in which children engage. Kushner (1989) provides some suggestions to help children achieve these. Photographs can be taken of block constructions and posted, sent home, or mounted in classroom albums. Similarly, slides or videotapes of children's work can be shared at parent events. Sending home enthusiastically written notes about children's play can also give importance to a block activity. Children can also dictate stories about their block structures to verbally preserve what they created. Kushner also encourages teachers to rethink attitudes about cleanup, considering the appropriateness of preserving some block structures beyond the limited play time during which they were constructed.

FINE MOTOR ACTIVITIES—MANIPULATIVES

Fine motor development involves primarily the muscles of the hands and wrists, those needed in precise and small movements. Toys, which require some kind of manipulation with fingers and hands, can be categorized as **manipulatives.** We will consider manipulative materials such as table toys, puzzles, beads, pegboards, and small blocks as they contribute to fine motor as well as other areas of development.

Manipulatives—Toys and materials that require the use of the fingers and hands, for instance, puzzles, beads, and pegboards.

Benefits of Manipulatives

Manipulative toys are important for children of all ages, ranging from safe, interesting small objects for infants to handle and manipulate to the multi-part, interlocking construction toys that older children enjoy. Manipulative toys enhance fine motor development because they require controlled use of hand and finger muscles. But they contribute much more. Manipulatives are sensory materials, involving visual and tactile discrimination; they require skill in coordinating the eyes with what the hands do. Manipulatives can reinforce a variety of concepts such as color, shape, number, and size, as well as encourage one-to-one correspondence, matching, patterning, sequencing, and grouping.

Fine motor development is enhanced by manipulative materials such as puzzles, pegs, and small construction toys; in addition, such materials further other aspects of children's development.

KEY QUESTION #3

Select two different manipulative materials. What do you think children can potentially learn from each of them? Now spend 10 minutes using each manipulative. Would you add any items to your lists of what children can learn?

Some manipulative toys such as puzzles are self-correcting, fitting together in only one specific way. Such toys allow children to work independently and know when they have achieved success. This helps build their sense of self-confidence. Because some manipulative materials have a definite closure point when the child completes the task, they also can contribute to children's growing attention span and the satisfaction of staying at a task until it is completed (*Table Toys,* 1979). One notable feature of Montessori materials (see Chapter 5) is their self-correcting nature, because many are designed with built-in feedback (Gettman, 1987).

Other manipulatives such as Legos and Lincoln logs are more open ended, allowing children to work creatively. In a way similar to the development of art, children use open-ended manipulatives in stages, starting by fitting together and pulling apart pieces to explore their properties, moving on to more purposeful pattern and shape constructions, and finally creating specific, representational objects or structures.

Types of Manipulatives

Many materials and games could be classified as manipulatives, including commercial and homemade items. It is not easy to group manipulatives because different combinations of such toys share some properties, but they also have various differences.

Puzzles. These are among the most popular manipulative materials. Wooden or rubber puzzles are the most durable, but sturdy cardboard puzzles can extend the puzzle selection relatively inexpensively. Children find that puzzles appropriate for their developmental level are very satisfying. First puzzles for toddlers and very young preschoolers should have only three to six pieces, either with each piece as a discrete inset or making a simple fit-together picture. When young children still have difficulty with manual control, pieces with knobs can help them avoid frustration.

Puzzles with an increasing number of pieces and complexity should be available as children's skill level improves. Many five- to eight-year-olds have the dexterity and enjoy interlocking puzzles with 25 to 50 pieces. These lend themselves well to cooperative work. Puzzles pieces are easy to lose or intermingle, however, and some schools have found it helpful to write an identifying name on the back of each individual piece.

Games. A variety of games require manipulative skills and reinforce various concepts. Lotto, bingo, and picture dominoes, for instance, can encourage matching, sorting, and classifying by specific topics. Some board games such as Candyland and Hi-Ho Cherry-O are appropriate for older preschoolers and primary children, if the rules are simple and flexible and the game is played in a cooperative rather than competitive atmosphere.

Construction Toys. The selection and variety of commercial construction toys have increased considerably so that a wide assortment of choices is now available. Duplos, Bristle Blocks, magnetic blocks, and snap blocks are good beginning manipulatives for young children, allowing for easy grip and assembly. Many more complex materials with smaller pieces are available to provide a range of construction possibilities. Some come with different accessories such as small people, wheels, or vehicle bases, which can enhance play. It is best to avoid manipulative sets, such as a helicopter or car, that result in a single outcome. Children quickly lose interest after assembling the pieces a few times, whereas more open-ended materials can be used over and over in an endless variety of ways. Simple toys, such as snap beads and large-sized Legos are available for toddlers. Teachers of very young children who still enjoy mouthing items should be alert, however, to toys that have pieces small enough to be swallowed; these should not be given to toddlers.

Older children often enjoy board games, such as this cooperative game. Not only do board games require manipulative skills, they reinforce other concepts.

Small Blocks. It is possible to find a continuum of open-ended to structured small blocks. Wooden table blocks come in a variety of shapes, similar to the larger unit blocks, and lend themselves to many creative uses. Somewhat more structured are the variety of small block sets that are made up of houses, buildings, and accessories and with which children can build towns, farms, or cities. Playmats and carpets are available that provide the background settings on which such blocks can be used. Because of their angled shapes, **parquetry blocks** are more challenging to assemble into the form board, but they provide a unique perspective and some different pattern possibilities not achievable with the right angles of rectangles or cubes.

Parquetry blocks—Variously shaped flat blocks, including diamonds and parallelograms, that can be assembled into different patterns on a form board.

Miscellaneous Manipulatives. Many other kinds of manipulatives have value for young children. Children can string beads of different sizes and shapes, assembling them in an arbitrary order or following a preset pattern to reinforce matching and sequencing skills. Pegboards with various colored pegs can be used to create designs or follow patterns. Pegboards can be made or purchased in a variety of sizes, with large holes and pegs for toddlers and very young preschoolers and smaller sizes for older children who have refined eye-hand coordination and manual dexterity. Lacing cards help children master a host of motor, perceptual, and cognitive skills.

SENSORY ACTIVITIES

Any activity involves a sensory component because we use sight or hearing or touch almost all of the time. But some activities are specifically geared to enhance sensory awareness. Most young children seem thoroughly to enjoy and get immersed in such activities. We will briefly examine activities that are primarily for tactile enjoyment—specifically, water and sand play—and activities that sharpen sensory acuity.

Water and Sand Play

Water acts like a magnet to young children, who are drawn to this soothing and enjoyable medium. Water play should be considered a requisite activity not only because it is so appealing to children but also because of its many other values. It is as appropriate for infants as it is for school-aged children. Water play can take place indoors, at a water table or plastic bins placed on a table, or outdoors during warm weather. Water can be used with squeeze bottles, funnels, flexible tubes, and pouring containers; to wash dolls, doll clothes, or dishes; or to create bubbles with added liquid soap, straws to blow through, and various-sized bubble-making forms. Children enjoy the sensory stimulation of water but also learn about properties of water such as volume, buoyancy, and evaporation. They also learn to appreciate its importance as they provide water for plants and animals and are exposed to mathematical concepts through pouring activities.

Water and sand play, which promote tactile enjoyment, provide sensory stimulation and can promote learning of a variety of concepts.

Sand play is another multipurpose sensory activity that fascinates and entices children. Many schools provide an outdoor sand play area, but sand can also be provided indoors in a sand table. When available by itself, fine-grained sand lends itself to being manipulated,

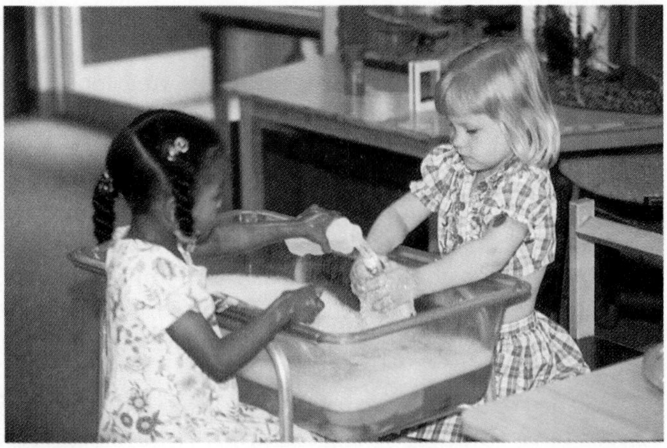

Water play is a soothing sensory experience that provides many learning opportunities. What do you think these two children might be learning from this water play activity?

molded, and smoothed. Added props such as containers, shovels, spoons, sifters, cars, and trucks expand the creative potential of sand play. Some simple rules about both water and sand play let the children know that these materials need to stay in specified areas to protect the children, the classroom, and classroom materials.

Sensory Concepts

Activities aimed at identifying an object by using a singe sense, for instance, touch or smell, help children develop the use of all their senses.

KEY QUESTION #4

Adults generally use their senses of sight and hearing far more than their other senses. Think about how and when you use information from the various senses. Does this suggest activities for young children that could enhance their sensory learning?

Sensory experiences are the foundation of infant learning. The infant and toddler program needs to provide a variety of pleasurable sensory experiences for young children, including colorful, interesting objects to look at and play with; pleasant sounds, including music; a variety of textures to enjoy and contrast and tactile experiences, such as finger painting; and varied taste and smell experiences as part of feeding and special activities.

For older children, sensory experiences can also be pleasurable for their own sake, but they also provide many opportunities for concept development. Each sense is assailed by a range of stimuli, which children gradually learn to identify and discriminate among. Specific sensory activities can provide experiences and reinforcement for these tasks.

We tend to be most adept at identifying objects in our environment through visual cues, because we gather a majority of information through the eyes. But it is also important to be able to use the other senses. Consider the following examples of activities that help children in the task of object identification using a single sensory modality.

- **Touch identification**—Children use only the sense of touch when they put a hand into a feely bag or box and identify an object.
- **Hearing identification**—Children listen to a tape or record of common environmental or animal sounds and identify them using only the sense of hearing. Similarly, during a walk children can be encouraged to listen for and identify the sounds they hear.
- **Smell identification**—Children identify common objects or foods, for instance, a flower or a cotton ball saturated with mint

extract, using only the sense of smell. When an actual object is used, the child should not be able to see it so that smell is the only identifying criterion.

- **Taste identification—**While blindfolded, children are given a spoonful of common foods, which they identify using only the sense of taste.

In addition to using the various senses to identify objects, children also use sensory information to discriminate as they match, seriate, or classify sensory stimuli. Following are some examples of activities that encourage refinement of sensory concepts.

Sensory discrimination involves making distinctions among stimuli, for instance, distinguishing among sounds, or matching a food smell with the picture of the food.

- **Matching—**Children can match like objects using information from primarily one sense. Visual matching can involve color, shape, or size, as well as pairs of objects or pictures that children match based on appearance. A collection of fabrics and sandpaper can provide opportunities for tactile matching. Pairs of sound cans (for instance, film canisters with a variety of objects such as rice, beans, or pebbles) can be matched using the sense of hearing, whereas small jars containing various distinctive smells can encourage smell discrimination.
- **Seriation—**A variety of objects can be seriated (placed in order along a dimension such as height, width, or color) using cues from one sensory modality such as vision or hearing. Children can organize a collection of sticks from longest to shortest, seashells from smallest to largest, or color paint chips from lightest to darkest. Similarly, sound cans can be placed in order from loudest to softest.
- **Classification—**Children can classify sensory stimuli in a variety of ways. They can group foods into such categories as sweet, sour, and salty; organize sounds as soft or loud, high or low, or into those made by household pets or farm animals; and classify objects by such visual cues as color, hue, shape, size, sex, or any of a wide variety of dimensions.

The use and integration of more than one sense can also be promoted in a **cross-modal intersensory activity.** For instance, children can look at an object and then be asked to feel inside a box and pull out the object that matches the one viewed.

Cross-modal intersensory activity—Use and integration of more than one sensory modality, for instance, matching an object that is seen visually to an identical object selected through touch only.

CARING FOR THE BODY

The early childhood program should help lay the foundation for good health habits. In addition to establishing routines and activities that emphasize the importance of physical exercise, children can learn about appropriate nutrition, health, and safety concepts. Keep in mind, however, that the adults in young children's lives ultimately are responsible for their health, safety, and well-being. We can begin to educate children on these topics, but we should never assume that such education is enough. Children need our continued guidance because they do not have the maturity necessary for the enormous responsibility of self-care.

Nutrition Education and Cooking

Young children can learn specific concepts about their need for nutritious foods and the development of good eating habits.

Because food is a basic human need and so often provides great pleasure, nutrition education and cooking experiences should be an integral part of the curriculum. Nutrition concepts can be presented to children in an understandable manner, and they can be reinforced by hands-on cooking activities. The topic of nutrition could have been included in several places in this book; nutrition education, although it contributes toward understanding of a basic physical need, equally involves cognitive, language, creative, and social areas of development as well.

Nutrition Education. The 1969 White House Conference on Food, Nutrition, and Health (1970) identified seven basic nutrition concepts related to nutrition education, attitudes toward food, and food behaviors. This framework has been adapted so that it is more appropriate for young children, resulting in the following list of 10 suggested concepts (Herr & Morse, 1982, p. 154).

1. There is a wide variety of food.
2. Plants and animals are sources of food.
3. Foods vary in color, flavor, texture, smell, size, shape, and sound.
4. A food may be prepared and eaten in many different ways—raw, cooked, dried, frozen, or canned.
5. Good foods are important to health, growth, and energy.
6. Nutrition is how our bodies use the foods we eat for health, growth, and energy.
7. Foods may be classified according to the following categories:
   - Milk
   - Meat and fish
   - Dried peas, beans
   - Eggs
   - Fruits
   - Vegetables
   - Breads
   - Pastas
   - Cereals, grains, seeds
   - Nuts
8. A good diet includes a wide variety of foods from each of the food categories.
9. Many factors influence eating, such as:
   - Attractiveness of food
   - Method of preparation
   - Cleanliness, manners

- Environment, atmosphere
- Celebrations

10. We choose the foods we eat for many reasons, such as:
    - Availability and cost
    - Family and individual habits
    - Taste
    - Aesthetics
    - Social and cultural customs
    - Mass media influence

These concepts, as well as possible additional ones, can be presented to young children through appropriate activities to help them understand the importance of good nutrition. They begin to take into account the complexity of this topic while providing realistically appropriate concepts. You might have noticed that the seventh concept does not recommend the standard classification of foods into the Basic Four Food Groups. Herr and Morse (1982) explain that these groups require too many generalizations based on an abstract grouping of nutrients, which young children often are not able to understand. You will need to tailor nutrition concepts to the ages and ability levels of the children, your own knowledge about nutrition, and the depth with which you plan to approach the subject.

Nutrition is often covered in the early childhood curriculum through a 1-week theme or as a by-product of snack conversation or cooking experiences. Herr and Morse (1982) recommend that nutrition be an integral part of the curriculum, covered on an ongoing basis. One example of a curriculum intended for a 10-week period and covering a variety of appropriate topics related to nutrition is *SHINE!: School-Home Involvement in Nutrition Education* (Haney-Clark, Essa, & Read, 1983). Other nutrition curricula are available, for instance, the National Dairy Council's excellent *Food . . . Early Choices,* featuring Chef Combo (National Dairy Council, 1980).

Cooking Experiences. Among the most enjoyable activities for young children are those that involve food preparation. Such activities are multisensory; involve children in a process they have observed but in which they may not have participated; teach and reinforce a variety of concepts related to nutrition, mathematics, science, and language; and are very satisfying because they result in a tangible (and delicious) end product (Cosgrove, 1991).

Cooking activities can reinforce learning about nutrition as well as promote many other skills and concepts.

KEY QUESTION #5

Plan a cooking activity for preschoolers. How can this activity reinforce nutrition education concepts?

Some cooking activities are more appropriate than others and should be carefully selected to meet specific criteria and objectives. The following are guidelines to keep in mind when planning food activities.

- **The activity should be matched to the children.** For very young preschoolers, select recipes that do not involve heat or sharp utensils and do not require precise fine motor control. Examples include tearing lettuce for a salad, plucking grapes from the stem for fruit salad, mixing yogurt and fruit in individual cups, or spreading tuna salad on crackers with a spoon. Older preschoolers and primary children have more refined muscle control and can follow more complex instructions. More involved recipes that might require use of knives or electrical appliances can be planned.

- **Safety is of utmost importance.** Many cooking tools are potentially dangerous, and careful adult supervision is required. Some steps in cooking require that only one child at a time be involved with a teacher, for instance, flipping pancakes in an electric skillet or griddle. Other cooking activities may well require that the number of children be limited, for instance, to five or six at a time, so that the adult can supervise and observe all of the children adequately. The process can then be repeated with additional groups of children so everyone who is interested has the opportunity to participate. Limitations in the number of children who can be involved at one time have to be thought out before the activity is presented to the children, however.
- **The recipe should involve enough steps so that all of the children in the group make a significant contribution.** Some recipes can be prepared individually by each child in single-serving sizes. Other recipes will require group cooperation. An appealing activity such as cooking should have enough ingredients and steps, for instance, five or six, so that each child in a group is an involved participant. If children are making muffins, for instance, one child can break and stir the eggs while others add and stir in the butter, flour, milk, honey, nuts and raisins, and flavorings and leavening; then they can take turns stirring the dough.
- **Children can be helped to understand the entire process.** It is helpful to prepare a pictorial recipe chart (or use one that is commercially made) that shows ingredients and amounts, allowing children to experience measuring as well as mixing (see Figure 10-2 for an example). School-aged children who have learned how to read may be able to follow recipes with simple words.

Well-planned cooking activities can be a wonderful learning experience that provides opportunities for physical, cognitive, language, and social development.

FIGURE 10-2 Pictorial Recipe Chart for Banana Bread

From Essa, E.L., & Rogers P.R. (1992). *An Early Childhood Curriculum: From Developmental Model to Application.* Albany, NY: Delmar Publishers.

Point out the changes in ingredients as they are mixed with others, for instance, that the flour loses its dry powderiness as it joins the liquids. Discuss and point out the effect of heat, which solidifies the semiliquid dough into firm muffins, for instance.

Young children begin to learn many concepts about health, caring for their bodies, and safety, topics that should be integrated into the early childhood curriculum.

- **The activity should focus on wholesome, nutritious foods.** It is important to set a good example in the planned cooking activities to reinforce nutritional concepts. A wide selection of available cookbooks focus on healthy recipes, some of which are listed in Figure 10-3.
- **The importance of hygiene and cleanliness must be stressed.** Require that children as well as adults wash their hands before participating in cooking experiences. Make sure that cooking surfaces and tools are clean. It contributes to multisensory learning if you allow children to taste at various points during the cooking process; however, instead of letting children use their fingers for tasting, provide individual spoons.

Health

Young children get many messages about health needs and practices from what is expected of them, what they are told, and what adults model. School routines (discussed in Chapter 14) will set many expectations and structure the schedule to encourage and facilitate increasing self-care in toileting, cleanliness, and eating. But health information should also be conveyed as part of the curriculum. Discussions and activities can heighten children's awareness of such topics as the relationship between health and growth, the body's need for both

FIGURE 10-3 Selected Cookbooks that Focus on Nutritious Recipes

Croft, K. B. (1971). *The good for me cookbook.* San Francisco, CA: R and E Research Associates.

Gooch, S. (1983). *If you love me don't feed me junk!* Reston, VA: Reston Publishing Co.

Goodwin, M. T., & Pollen, G. (1980). *Creative food experiences for young children.* Washington, DC: Center for Science in the Public Interest.

Haney-Clark, R., Essa, E., & Read, M. (1983). *SHINE!: School-home involvement in nutrition education.* Reno, NV: Child and Family Center, University of Nevada, Reno.

Harms, T., & Veitch, B. (1980). *Cook and learn.* Menlo Park, CA: Addison-Wesley.

Johnson, B., & Plemons, B. (1984). *Individual child portion cooking: Picture recipes.* Mount Rainier, MD: Gryphon House Press.

Katzen, M. (1977). *Moosewood cookbook.* Berkeley, CA: Ten Speed Press.

Wanamaker, N., Hearn, K., & Richarz, S. (1979). *More than graham crackers: Nutrition education and food preparation with young children.* Washington, DC: National Association for the Education of Young Children.

activity and rest, temperature regulation through appropriate clothing, hygiene practices as part of disease prevention, the importance of medical and dental care, and health professionals and facilities that care for children in the community. In addition, if a child in the class has a specific allergy or a chronic illness, all of the children can be helped to better understand this condition by sensitively including the topic in the curriculum.

It was helpful in one preschool program, for instance, when the teacher discussed why Dorothea could not eat certain foods. The children became more sensitive to Dorothea's diabetes and the restrictions it caused, and they saw that her special snacks were not a privilege but a necessity.

Through repeated experiences, children gradually learn community safety rules, for instance, those related to crossing the street or parking lot safely.

Safety

Young children begin to acquire safety information and precautions, although it is important to remember that adults must be responsible for ensuring children's safety by providing a safe environment and preventing accidents. Because very young children may not process safety information accurately, it should be conveyed with a great deal of caution. Some two-year-olds, or young three-year-olds, may fail to understand the negative message in "don't do . . ." or may get "ideas" from well-intentioned cautions (Essa & Rogers, 1992). Through curriculum topics, older children can gradually acquire information and learn some preventive precautions related to fire, electricity, tools, traffic, potential poisons, and strangers, as well as learn about community safety personnel and resources, and what to do in case of an accident.

Communication between home and school will help in mutual understanding about values related to physical development and self-care.

PARENTAL VALUES RELATED TO PHYSICAL DEVELOPMENT AND CARE

Early childhood teachers and parents share responsibility for the development and care of young children in many areas that once were in the domain of the home. Today, children acquire many personal life skills and habits related to exercise, nutrition, health, hygiene, and safety through their early childhood program. Yet, these areas are also very personal to parents, representing their own lifelong habits and practices. It is important, therefore, to share with parents the school's philosophy about helping children develop healthy patterns that include daily exercise, good nutrition, appropriate care for the body, and safety precautions. It is equally important to be open to the parents' ideas and values on these topics.

One difference between home and school expectations that teachers of young children cite is the desire of some parents to have children sit quietly, learn academic skills, listen to the teacher, and do worksheets. In such an instance, it is particularly important that you, as an early childhood professional, provide appropriate developmental information and make readings available that clearly demonstrate that young children learn through an active not a passive process. You may need to help parents share your concern and recognition that all aspects of children's development need to be furthered. Physical development is an integral part of the whole child, thus, all activities that promote fine motor, gross motor, and perceptual skills deserve prominence in the early childhood program.

SUMMARY

1. Consider the theories that explain physical development.
2. Physical development is complex, involving a number of interrelated components.
   - A. Body control involves mastering a number of skills important for movement and balance.
   - B. Young children gain increasing manual control, the ability to use the hands effectively.
   - C. Sensory-perceptual development involves children's increasing accuracy in interpreting information they gain through their senses.
3. Several early childhood activities encourage and promote use of the large muscles of the body.
   - A. Physical fitness activities and outdoor play provide excellent opportunities for large muscle development.
   - B. Consider the value of blocks and block play for young children.
4. Many manipulative materials and activities promote use and development of the small muscles of hands and fingers.
5. Because of the importance of learning through the senses for young children, consider activities that promote sensory exploration and discrimination.
6. A major aspect of physical development includes learning to care for the body, in relation to nutrition, health, and safety.

KEY TERMS LIST

bimanual control
cross-modal intersensory activity
eye-hand coordination
fine motor development
fundamental movement phase
gross motor development
holding grip
kinesthetic sense
locomotion
manipulatives
maturational theory
multimodality
palmar grasp
parquetry blocks
perceptual motor model
pincer grasp
reflexive movement phase
rudimentary movement phase
self-help skills
sensory integration
sensory-perceptual development
specialized movement phase
tripod grasp
unit blocks

chapter 11

Cognitive Development Through the Curriculum

Young children's thinking ability is quite amazing. Within just a few years of their birth, they have acquired an immense repertoire of information and cognitive skills. A child, who two or three or four years before was a helpless baby responding to the environment mainly through reflexes, is now a competent, thinking, communicating, reasoning, problem-solving, exploratory person. In studying children's **cognition,** we are more concerned with the process of knowing than with the content of what specifically children know (*how* rather than *what*). In particular, we are interested in how children acquire, organize, and apply knowledge (Copple, DeLisi, & Sigel, 1982).

As in each of these chapters that focus on a specific area of development, we will consider some activities that are, by necessity, chosen somewhat arbitrarily. Although we will be highlighting science and math, keep in mind that virtually every activity involves cognition. Children actively learn, use problem-solving strategies, and construct new knowledge from all activities, be they science and math or art, music, movement, manipulatives, story telling, or dramatic play. In no way does this choice imply that such development does not occur in other activities as well.

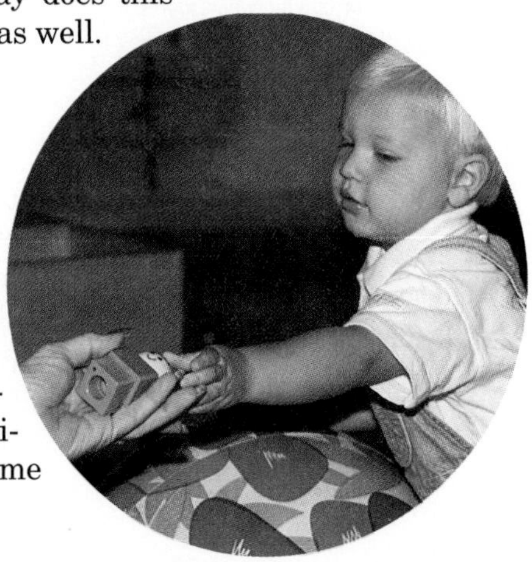

THEORETICAL FOUNDATIONS OF COGNITIVE DEVELOPMENT

Particularly in this century, a number of theories have attempted to explain the development of the intellect. One theory of how children learn that has greatly influenced American education throughout a sizable portion of this century is behaviorism. A far more influential theory on early childhood education, however, is the cognitive developmental theory of Jean Piaget. Another noteworthy, recent, theoretical framework is **information processing,** which is modeled to some extent on the functioning and operation of computers.

Cognition—The process of mental development, concerned more with how children learn than with the content of what they know.

The study of children's cognition is more concerned with how children learn than with what they know.

Information processing—A model of cognitive development, somewhat analogous to how a computer functions, concerned primarily with how human beings take in and store information.

Behavior management—Behavioral approach to guidance holding that the child's behavior is under the control of the environment, which includes space, objects, and people.

The influence of behaviorism on early childhood education has been particularly strong in direct instruction programs, in which the teacher controls most aspects of learning.

Behaviorism

In our Chapter 5 examination of the influence of B. F. Skinner, we noted the foundation of behaviorism as the belief that learning is controlled by the consequences of behavior. When those consequences are pleasant, a child is likely to repeat the behavior, whereas a disagreeable consequence is more apt to result in the child discontinuing the behavior. By careful control of the learning environment through appropriate reinforcement to selected behaviors or responses, behaviorists believe that they can affect children's learning. "Teaching is the art of changing the behavior of students. Thus, one focus of . . . teaching is the systematic management of the consequences of student behaviors" (Bushell, 1982, p. 161).

Behavioral theory is used in early childhood education in both social and learning contexts. In the social context, behavior modification or **behavior management** is used to change a child's behavior by systematically managing consequences. Thus, when a child is aggressive, disruptive, or withdrawn, or acts inappropriately in some other way, a behavior management technique might be used to change the behavior. Chapter 16 will examine some behavior management techniques in more detail, when we consider how to deal with problem behaviors.

Behavioral theory is also applied to teaching children through programmed or direct instruction. In a direct instruction program, the teacher predetermines exactly what children need to know, sets goals accordingly, devises a sequence of learning activities that teach specific information to meet each goal, and directly teaches the children by controlling the information according to their responses. When children respond correctly, they are reinforced; if their responses are incorrect, reinforcement is withheld. In this way, children acquire the specific information prescribed in the goals that the teacher considers to be appropriate for them (Mounts & Roopnarine, 1987). Recall that in Chapter 5 we examined the direct instructional program of Bereiter and Engelmann (1966), which illustrates the application of behavioral theory.

Piaget's Theory of Cognitive Development

Piaget's theory of cognitive development, which holds that children construct their own knowledge out of direct experiences, has been the most influential theory in early childhood education.

Piaget offers a very different view of cognitive development, one based on allowing children to build concepts actively rather than on providing those concepts through direct teaching. He has given us a way to understand how children think, pointing out that their minds work in a way that is different from those of adults, and describing how their thinking develops. Taking Piaget's extensive research and writings, others have developed specific applications of his theory, particularly to educational settings. Over the past several decades, many early childhood educators have incorporated Piagetian principles in their programs to the point where today many of these are often considered common practice. We shall examine these later in this chapter when we review cognitive tasks.

Chapter 5 stated that one function of the mind is to categorize information into schemata. This is an active process by which the child continually finds relationships among objects (Furth, 1969). By physically manipulating and changing objects, the child constructs knowledge about the objects and their relationships. This is an important point: Knowledge is not something that is "poured" into the child by some external source, such as the teacher, but something that the child has to construct for herself or himself.

This is why Piaget's theory is also called a **constructivist theory.** For example, a child trying to place a square block on the top point of a triangular one will, after some trials, construct an understanding of the relationship of these two blocks and which block will or will not support the other one. By transforming the blocks into a new position, the child acquires knowledge (Forman & Kuschner, 1977). Because of this need to manipulate and transform materials in the environment, learning has to be an active, not a passive, process.

Constructivist theory—A theory, such as that of Jean Piaget, based on the belief that children construct knowledge for themselves rather than having it conveyed to them by some external source.

This process is evident at all stages of development. We will now examine in somewhat more depth three of Piaget's stages of cognitive development.

The Sensorimotor Period. Piaget labeled the period covering the first two years of life, the sensorimotor period; as the term implies, learning in infancy is dependent on the senses and on movement. The sensorimotor period is further divided into six stages, which chart the rapid development of the young child.

The infant in the sensorimotor period, which is divided into six substages, learns through the senses and movement.

In the first stage, during the first month of life, babies use the reflexes with which they were born to suck, cry, grasp, hear, and see.

By the second stage, between one and four months, learning begins to replace reflexes; repeated experiences are teaching infants that there are some predictable occurrences. They become more active participants in the social world, engaging in communication with the people around them, and in the physical world, as they look and listen more attentively to stimuli in the environment.

From four to eight months, in the third stage, babies come to recognize that they can cause things to happen. They gleefully repeat actions such as hitting objects to again get that interesting sound, kicking at a mobile to make it turn some more, and throwing a rattle off the high chair because someone will again retrieve it. In other words, they learn that they can affect their environment.

In the next stage, from eight to twelve months, children use "tools" to achieve goals. They might use a stick to retrieve an object out of reach, showing rudimentary problem-solving ability. Object permanence appears, as babies know that something out of sight continues to exist; but this milestone also means that they realize when mom is leaving and may cry as she puts on her coat.

Twelve- to eighteen-month-olds, in the fifth stage, whom Piaget termed "little scientists," are characterized by experimentation. They try to find new ways of using familiar objects. Whereas a couple of months ago they may have been content to bang the pot with a fist, now they experiment with banging it with a spoon, a stick, a cup, and other objects to see what effect these might have.

The final stage, from eighteen to twenty-four months, marks the shift from dependence on actual objects to mental representations of these. Toddlers begin to develop mental pictures of familiar objects, people, and actions; they can now start working out problems and pursuing ideas in their head. This landmark achievement parallels the growth of language, which is a major form of representation. Children in this stage also begin to use this skill to pretend to substitute objects in play. A block pushed along the floor, accompanied by chugging sounds, now may represent a train (Ginsburg & Opper, 1969; Honig & Lally, 1981).

The preschooler, in the preoperational period, employs symbolic representation, the ability to use mental images to stand for something else.

Symbolic representation—The ability acquired by young children to use mental images to stand for something else.

The Preoperational Period. This newly acquired mental ability of **symbolic representation** marks the beginning of the second period, which lasts from about age two to age seven. Symbolic representation is evident when children use symbols such as words and in make-believe play, imitation, and drawing or sculpting to represent something they have experienced or seen. Play is particularly important as children learn about the world, because it gives them the opportunity to assimilate experiences without actually having to adapt to the reality of the world. Recall from Chapter 5 that assimilation is a process through which an experience is made to fit a child's schemata, rather than the child changing to accommodate to reality (Tribe, 1982).

Children who use preoperational thinking are egocentric and rely on perception rather than on logic.

Preoperational children have a limited view of reality, one that comes from their own perceptions, which they rely on to understand what they see. As we all know, our eyes can fool us. As adults, however, we recognize the illusion of appearance—for instance, knowing through logic that although the ball of clay has been stretched out into a long sausage before our eyes, it contains no more or no less clay than it did before. But young children do not yet have that logical ability and rely on their perception, which tells them that it *looks* as if there is more (or less) clay now. This reliance on their own viewpoints contributes to children's egocentricity, the assumption that everyone experiences and sees the world as they do. Young children assume that other people can understand them and what they think because they believe these people's viewpoint must match theirs; there is no other point of view as far as they are concerned.

Reflective abstraction—According to Jean Piaget, part of a child's self-directed activity that allows the child to think about and reflect on what he or she is doing, leading to the development of new mental abilities.

For preschool-aged children to begin to see experiences from a less egocentric point of view, they must have many opportunities to examine, manipulate, modify, transform, experiment, and reflect on objects. Piaget stressed the importance of **reflective abstraction** for children, the opportunity to think about and reflect on what they are doing, which is part of spontaneous, self-directed activity. Through reflective abstraction, new mental abilities can grow because children are actively engaged in the construction of their knowledge. With active control over materials, children gradually learn to differentiate between what they perceive and reality.

School-aged children are in the concrete operations period, which is marked by increasingly logical thought and the acquisition of conservation.

The Concrete Operations Period. From about 7 to 11 years of age, young children continue to build thinking skills, becoming much more reliant on logic than on external appearances. While their thinking abilities are considerably more logical than they had been during the preoperational period, they still rely very much on the concrete presence of objects for understanding. It isn't until the final, formal operational, period that adolescents and adults can think abstractly and hypothetically. Through many of the first-hand experi-

Preschoolers learn from concrete, hands-on experiences. Their environment should be full of objects they can manipulate and explore.

ences in which children acted on objects during the preoperational period, concrete operational children move toward a more logical mode of thinking. They refine the ability to classify and seriate objects (processes we will discuss later in this chapter), which allows them to organize information in increasingly logical ways.

In addition, they integrate the various properties of objects and don't focus only on the most obvious one. This skill helps them achieve **conservation,** recognizing that objects remain the same in amount or number despite perceptual changes. So, while it may look as if there is more liquid when the glass of juice is poured from a short, wide glass into a tall, thin one, concrete operational children know that logically the amount is the same because nothing was added or taken away.

Conservation—Ability to recognize that objects remain the same in amount despite perceptual changes, usually acquired during the period of concrete operations.

During this middle childhood period, children also become much more capable of taking the viewpoint of another person. The egocentricity of early childhood becomes replaced by an increasing ability to see things from the other perspectives (Ginsburg & Opper, 1969).

Thus, from Piaget's theory we gain insight into the growing abilities of young children to think logically. Through this insight come methods of working with young children that suggest that a well-structured environment, ample activities and materials from which children can actively learn, and understanding adults who encourage without interfering will facilitate cognitive growth. Much of this approach is incorporated into many early childhood programs and accepted as developmentally appropriate practice today (Bredekamp, 1987).

Understanding children's thinking processes and limitations helps early childhood educators provide an appropriate environment for cognitive development.

Information Processing

The term *information processing* literally defines itself because it is concerned primarily with how human beings process information. Although information processing provides an alternative view to how children's thinking abilities develop, it shares a number of features with Piaget's cognitive developmental theory. Both approaches try to identify children's cognitive abilities and limitations at different points in their development. Both also acknowledge that later cognitive abilities build on and grow out of earlier, more primitive ones. In addition,

Information processing attempts to identify the processes children use to take in information and relate it to other information already stored in their memories.

both theories consider that existing concepts have a great impact on the acquisition of new knowledge (Siegler, 1986).

But, as is true with behavioral theory, information processing does not focus on stages of cognitive development. Instead, it identifies the exact processes children use to transform information and relate it to other information stored in their memories. As a computer does, the mind relies not only on the information (input) fed into it, but also on its capacity and the strategies (programs) it uses to process the information. (The computer analogy has its limits, of course, because the human mind is so much more complex than any computer!)

Sensory register—In information processing theory, that part of the model describing how information initially comes to our awareness when perceived by the senses.

Short-term (or working) memory—In information processing theory, limited capacity for temporarily remembering information such as a telephone number.

Long-term (or permanent) memory—In information processing theory, the vast store of information and knowledge that is held for a long time.

Central processor—That aspect of the information processing model that governs and coordinates other functions such as sensory input and memory.

An Information Processing Model. Information processing is often depicted as a flow chart or model with several interconnected features (see Figure 11-1). In the process of cognition, information first comes to us through a **sensory register,** being perceived by one of the senses. The second typical part of this model is memory, where the incoming information moves next.

Memory is divided into short-term and long-term components. **Short-term (or working) memory** provides limited capacity for remembering information temporarily, for instance, a telephone number. **Long-term (or permanent) memory** refers to the vast store of information and knowledge that we hold for a long time. This stored information is organized so it can be readily retrieved and linked to new information. A final aspect of the information processing model is the **central processor** that governs and coordinates the other components, for instance, deciding what information should be acknowledged by the sensory register, whether it should remain briefly in short-term memory, or whether it should be stored in long-term memory (Daehler & Bukatko, 1985).

Young children's memories are not as efficient as those of older children and adults.

Memory strategies—Various approaches used especially by older children and adults to help them remember information.

Memory. Children's ability to remember improves over the first years of life, but preschool children do not yet use memory as efficiently as do older children and adults. A number of **memory strategies** are used to remember information, for instance, rehearsal (mentally repeating information over and over), organization (placing items to be remembered into logical categories), and elaboration (making up imaginary connections when there is no logical link among items).

FIGURE 11-1 A simplified information processing model

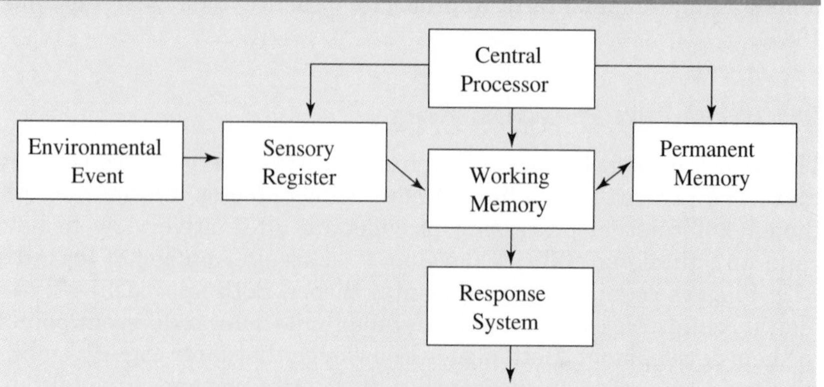

Although preschoolers can learn to use such strategies, they are not very adept at this skill, partly because they have fewer schemata to call up in attempts to organize or elaborate on information. Another reason is that familiarity improves memory, and young children have not had as much opportunity as older children to develop it. It also takes preschoolers longer than older children or adults to retrieve information from both short-term and long-term memory stores. In addition, young children hold considerably fewer pieces of information in their working memories at one time than do older children (Price, 1989; Seifert, 1993; Siegler, 1983; Siegler, 1986).

One aspect of memory that distinguishes older from younger children's thinking is **metamemory,** the ability to think about one's own memory. Older children, for instance, are more realistic in answering the question, "Do you forget?"; younger children often deny that they do forget. Young children are also not very good at estimating how many items they think they will be able to remember, unrealistically predicting that they can remember all of a large number of items. Also, the instruction to "remember what I tell you" does not improve preschoolers' memory when they are later asked to recall, whereas the word "remember" gives older children the cue to use some memory strategies (Daehler & Bukatko, 1985; Siegler, 1983; Siegler, 1986).

Metamemory—The ability to think about one's own memory.

Information processing theory provides some concepts useful in learning how children's cognitive development progresses. Specific consideration of how information is taken in, memory strategies, and metamemory helps us recognize young children's abilities and limitations. The activities planned for young children should be congruent with what we know about their abilities.

ENHANCING INFANTS' COGNITIVE DEVELOPMENT

Infants' cognitive development is best promoted when they are in a safe, loving environment where their basic needs are met. Furthermore, this environment must be rich in appropriate stimuli and sensory experiences that help them explore and learn about their world. Experiences should also be congruent with their particular stages of cognitive development; thus, for babies in Piaget's first and second stages of the sensorimotor period, the awakening awareness of their surroundings should be promoted by frequent interaction with the primary caregiver, loving conversation, gentle sounds, interesting colors and patterns, and the opportunity to view the world from different vantage points.

Infants' cognitive development is best enhanced in a safe, loving environment with experiences that match their stage of sensorimotor development.

In the third stage, babies begin to make the connection between their actions and resulting movement, sounds, and sights. This should be promoted by appropriate toys that allow trial and error and give them feedback. When babies begin to acquire object permanence in stage four, they relish games in which caregivers hide objects while they watch, encouraging the babies to actively search for these. Babies begin to anticipate reactions, and toys and games that provide an expected outcome help them begin to learn about cause and effect.

Toddlers, with the added ability to move about, need many appropriate experiences to help promote cognitive development. They need a variety of materials that can be explored, combined in different ways, put together and taken apart, and in many other ways allow for experimentation. Since object permanence continues to develop, games in which objects are hidden and found are still very appropriate. In addition, games and toys that help children recognize what causes things to happen and that identify them as the causal agent should also be provided. Simple dramatic play props will encourage toddlers' burgeoning ability to pretend (Gestwicki, 1995; Gonzalez-Mena & Eyer, 1989; Honig & Lally, 1981; Wilson, 1995).

COGNITIVE TASKS

In addition to helping us understand how children think, theories of cognition also provide some insights into what cognitive skills children acquire or begin to acquire during the early years. Most of these tasks have been derived from Piaget's theory, particularly what he tells us about thinking and learning abilities in the preoperational and concrete operational periods. This provides a basis for curriculum planning to enhance cognitive development. In this section, we will review classification; seriation; number, temporal, and spatial concepts; and acquisition of information.

Classification

Young children begin to learn classification, the ability to sort and group objects by some similar characteristic.

Classification is the ability to sort and group objects by some common attribute or property. To classify, a child has to note similarities and differences among objects. Classification involves two simultaneous processes, sorting (separating) objects and grouping (joining) objects (Charlesworth & Lind, 1995). For instance, in classifying beads, Liam groups the red beads at the same time that he sorts out the blue and yellow ones; Shanda groups the largest beads and sorts out all other sizes.

If we did not have the ability to classify, every object and experience would represent a separate, isolated piece of information in our minds. Classification allows us to deal "economically with the environment" so that we do not have to go through the process of adaptation each time a new object or experience is encountered (Lavatelli, 1970, p. 81). Although preoperational children use perceptual judgment to classify, for instance, grouping items that *look* the same, true classification is a mental operation that goes beyond such sensory cues. True classification appears later in the concrete operations period, but innumerable early childhood classification experiences contribute to its emergence.

Children classify spontaneously and usually have no problems in finding categories. They frequently use themselves as a basis for social classification, grouping the boys from the girls, the older children from the "babies," or those who get to play with the blocks from those who don't. One teacher, responding to one child's dismay at being excluded from a group of four-year-olds, found that the children's basis for group inclusion was whether their shoes were fastened with Velcro! This child's shoes were tied with more conventional laces.

Of course, children can classify a group of objects in many ways. Features such as color, shape, size, material, pattern, and texture pro-

A variety of early childhood materials lend themselves to grouping and sorting materials in different ways. In what ways are these children classifying with manipulatives? What other common classroom materials contribute to an understanding of classification?

vide concrete attributes by which to group. As children get older, they begin to classify by more abstract commonalities such as the function of items (objects that are used in cooking, things that make music); a common feature among an odd assortment of items (things that have four legs, things that have doors); or association (money, paper bags, and milk are associated with the supermarket; galoshes and rain go together) (Charlesworth & Lind, 1990).

KEY QUESTION #1

Consider the people in the class for which you are reading this book. In how many different ways can you classify these individuals? Think of as many categories as possible. What does this exercise tell you about cognitive skill development in young children?

Because young children sort and group items naturally, the early childhood environment should provide a rich variety of objects and experiences that can be used for such activities.

- Many early childhood materials such as manipulatives, blocks, and science materials lend themselves to being classified.
- Less obvious items in the art, book, dramatic play, and sensory areas also have inherent properties that children will group and sort.
- In addition, teacher feedback should reinforce the value of children's spontaneous classification activities. ("You put all of the green chairs around the round table and the blue chairs at the rectangular table!")
- Structured classification activities should also be part of the early childhood program. In large and small groups, and individually, children can be encouraged to find commonalities among people, objects, and experiences.
- Similarly, children can explore objects and describe their attributes, and articulate similarities and differences.
- Older preschoolers and primary children can be encouraged to group items by two attributes. ("Put together the things that are round *and* hard.")
- Children can also be helped to compare subclasses by distinguishing between "all" and "some" (*all* of these are flowers, but *some* of these are daisies).

"My garage is bigger than your garage!" Children find many ways to compare items in their activities. Such comparative observations contribute to an understanding of seriation.

Seriation

Seriation helps children focus on the relationship among objects, as they place them in a logical order or sequence.

Seriation concerns the relationship among objects and the ability to place them in logical sequence or order. Simple seriation involves concrete objects, for instance, arranging objects from longest to shortest or widest to narrowest. Sensory seriation can include ordering sounds from loudest to softest, tastes from sweetest to sourest, or colors from darkest to lightest. Seriation can also relate to time sequences, for example, what happened first, second, third, and so forth. As children engage in seriation activities, they use and are helped to acquire a vocabulary of comparative words ("this is the longest," "he is older," "I have more pudding," "your hair is lighter than mine," "my blocks are taller").

KEY QUESTION #2

Observe a young child for about 20 minutes. How does this child use cognitive skills? Note the many ways in which this child uses her or his thinking abilities, including evidence of problem solving, symbolic representation, memory, classification, seriation, time and space concepts, and number concepts.

The early childhood environment should include many materials and experiences to encourage seriation.

- Unit blocks and a number of manipulatives such as nesting toys offer many opportunities for children to seriate because they are made in graduated sizes.
- Other materials—for instance, dolls, dishes, props for sand and water play, books, woodworking equipment, and nature collections—should be provided in a variety of sizes to prompt spontaneous ordering and comparison.
- Teachers can also encourage children to note and verbalize comparisons, among each other, among objects, and among sets of objects.
- Instructions in group activities such as "Simon Says" and "Red Rover" can be worded to encourage comparisons.

Number Concepts

An understanding of quantity or number concepts involves more than rote counting; it concerns rational counting as well, the ability to correctly attach a numeral name to each item in a group of objects.

Number is an understanding of quantity, an awareness that entails increasingly more complex concepts. In its earliest form, number understanding involves gross comparison of quantity, identifying *more* and *less*. The young preschooler then begins to make more exact comparisons through **one-to-one correspondence,** pairing socks with shoes or plates with napkins. Preschoolers also acquire a large store of words to label their quantitative understanding, words such as big, small, more, less, tall, short, lots, few. By age four, children understand that adding or taking away objects from a group changes the number. Not until the primary grades, however, are children able to distinguish the absolute number from arrangement, realizing that despite perceptual changes, the number is still the same even if a group of objects is rearranged (Resnick, 1989; Saunders & Bingham-Newman, 1984).

One-to-one correspondence—A way in which young preschoolers begin to acquire an understanding of number concepts by matching items to each other, for instance, one napkin beside each plate.

One aspect of acquiring number concepts is counting. Young preschoolers often learn **rote counting,** reciting numbers as they have been memorized. Rote counting should be distinguished from **rational counting,** which is present when the child attaches a numeral name to a series of objects in a group (Charlesworth & Lind, 1990). Be aware, however, that children do not necessarily have to apply the conventional number names to actually count rationally. Children seem to understand the principle of counting and that number names are attached to each object in a group, even if they count "one, two, three, five, eleven, nine" (Gelman & Gallistel, 1978).

Rote counting—Reciting numbers from memory without attaching meaning to them in the context of objects in a series.

Rational counting—Distinguished from rote counting, in which the child accurately attaches a numeral name to a series of objects being counted.

The good early childhood environment contains many opportunities to encourage use of number concepts.

- Materials such as Unifix cubes, Cuisenaire rods, dominoes, number bingo, and other specific counting and math games can help children acquire number concepts.
- Children will also compare, count, match, add, subtract, and otherwise deal with quantities spontaneously with a wide variety of objects and experiences when they are able to manipulate items actively.
- Being able to move objects around is essential to acquiring an understanding of numbers. This requirement for hands-on involvement is one reason that workbooks are an inappropriate way for children to gain number concepts (Charlesworth & Lind, 1990).

Although children must acquire number concepts through their own efforts, the teacher's role in facilitating this learning is very

Many early childhood materials help children gradually understand number concepts.

important. Constance Kamii, one of the leading interpreters of Piaget's theory, suggests that teachers can encourage children to quantify objects logically through a careful choice of words, for instance, asking a child to "bring just enough cups for everybody" rather than to "bring six cups" (Kamii, 1982, p. 31). She encourages teachers to use everyday experiences, such as distribution of snack food, fair division of game pieces, cleanup time, or collection of permission slips for a field trip, as a basis for using number concepts (Kamii, 1982). She also recommends group games as a way of encouraging numerical concepts, as children count people or objects, use game board counters, and learn about logical rules (Kamii & DeVries, 1980).

Temporal Concepts

Temporal concepts—Cognitive ability concerned with the child's gradual awareness of time as a continuum.

Young children begin to acquire temporal concepts, the sense of time as a continuum that includes the past, present, and future.

Temporal concepts are concerned with the child's gradual awareness of time as a continuum. Infants in the sensorimotor period, not yet able to mentally represent events and experiences, live only in the *now* time frame, in which *before* now and *after* now do not exist. During the preschool years, children become increasingly more aware of temporal relations, such as the order of events and the time relationship between cause and effect ("I hurt my knee because I fell off the climber," rather than "I fell off the climber because I hurt my knee"). Not until early adolescence, however, do children have a true idea of temporal relations (Hohmann, Banet, & Weikart, 1979; Saunders & Bingham-Newman, 1984).

Preschoolers' sense of time is still quite arbitrary and linked to concrete experiences. It would be meaningless to use conventional time measures (clock or calendar) to answer Mark's concern about how long until lunch or Serafina's question about when the field trip to the museum will be. Thus, saying "we will have lunch in a half hour" or "the field trip is tomorrow" conveys very abstract information to young children. It makes much more sense to answer such questions in relation to concrete events, for instance, "we will have lunch after reading this story and washing hands, Mark" or "after school you will go home, Serafina, have dinner, and go to sleep; when you wake up tomorrow and come back to school, we will go on the field trip."

Older preschoolers and young school-aged children begin to recognize that clocks and calendars help us mark time, although this understanding is still very imperfect. Nonetheless, adults should use conventional time measures in their conversations with children to begin exposing them to time-related vocabulary. In addition, concrete experiences with clocks and calendars should be provided. An actual clock alongside a pictorial clock on which key daily events are shown can help children make the connection between the hands on the clock and when snack, outside play time, group time, and other key activities occur. Similarly, a calendar on which the days of the week are accompanied by pictures representing home and school, interspersed with pictures of a child sleeping in bed can help make the passage of day and night or weekdays and weekends understandable. By age seven or eight, many children begin to understand the more abstract representations of time and can learn to use clocks and calendars as adults do.

In everyday experiences and conversations, temporal concepts can be strengthened.

- The daily routine reinforces a consistent time sequence (first comes group time, then activity time, next snack, and so forth) as well as intervals of varying lengths (group time is shorter than activity time).
- Children also need to be exposed to and frequently use temporal words such as before, after, start, stop, first, second, last, next, earlier, later.
- Discussing past occurrences and anticipating future ones gives children the opportunity to use **temporal sequencing,** placing a series of events into their order of occurrence. As an example, children might discuss the steps involved in coming to school in the morning (Essa & Rogers, 1992).

Temporal sequencing—The ability to place a series of events in the order of their occurrence.

Spatial Concepts

Spatial concepts relate to objects and people as they occupy, move in, and use space. Spatial concepts also concern the spatial relationship among people and objects, for instance, standing *behind* the chair, running *toward* the teacher, or putting the triangular block *on top of* the rectangular one. Actually, children are constantly experiencing spatial concepts through their own body movement, their activities, and their physical proximity to others. Their earliest learning, during infancy, was based to a great extent on their motor activity, and this mode of learning continues through the preschool and primary years.

Spatial concepts—A cognitive ability involving an understanding of how objects and people occupy, move in, and use space.

Spatial concepts are concerned with how objects and people occupy or relate to each other in space.

A wide variety of experiences and equipment strengthen children's growing awareness of spatial concepts and relationships.

- Equipment that invites children to explore spatial possibilities is essential in an early childhood setting. Children need to position their bodies in many possible ways in relation to equipment; for example, they should be able to go over, under, around, through, into, out of, and across.
- Such experiences can also be structured through obstacle courses and group games such as "Simon Says" or "Mother May I."
- Active manipulation of objects, such as fitting things together or disassembling them, also strengthens children's spatial understanding. For one thing, children can explore manipulative items from all angles, seeing them from different points of view—from the front, back, side, bottom, or top.
- Puzzles, shape boxes, nuts and bolts. Tinkertoys, nesting blocks, pegboards with pegs, pots and pans with lids, dress-up clothes, woodworking, and collage materials are examples of common early childhood materials and activities that reinforce spatial concepts (Charlesworth & Lind, 1990; Hohmann, et al., 1979; Saunders & Bingham-Newman, 1984).

As is the case with their concept of time, young children's concept of space is viewed from a very subjective perspective. They rely on their perceptions of where, in what position, how close, how far away, or near what an object might be. Space is purely visual to young children, and conventional measures such as inches, yards, or miles are meaningless. Space has to be something concrete, within children's experience. To say that it is 3 miles to the dairy means nothing; instead, saying, "we will be able to sing four or five songs in the bus, and then we'll be at the dairy" is much more concrete (Essa & Rogers, 1992). Be aware also that space and time are often closely related, particularly as children move through space at different speeds. Young children see the distance between the building and the fence as closer if they run than if they walk, because they get to the fence more quickly.

Although young children do not yet understand conventional measuring devices and units of measurement, they nonetheless measure space frequently. They gauge the relative sizes of blocks as they build structures, estimate how much more sand is needed to fill the bucket, or judge whether their bodies will fit through the tunnel in the obstacle course.

- Teachers can help children verbalize measurement concepts by using words such as more, less, short(er), long(er), full, empty, double, or half.
- Activities such as making play dough, woodworking, and cooking can help children recognize the importance of accurate measurement and relative proportions.
- Older preschoolers and primary children also enjoy **mapping**, representing space through such media as marking pens or blocks. For instance, ask children to draw a picture of the route they took to get to school, to make a map with unit blocks of their walk around the neighborhood, or to fill in special features on an outline map you have drawn of the classroom.

KEY QUESTION #3

In this chapter we have considered only math and science as activities in which children use cognitive processes. How is cognition a part of other areas in the early childhood curriculum?

Mapping—A mapmaking activity involving spatial relations in which space is represented creatively through such media as marking pens or blocks.

Acquisition of Information

The early childhood program can help children acquire relevant information through an appropriate curriculum.

While young children learn about the properties of objects, compare objects to discover what makes them similar and different, begin to understand quantity and number concepts, and start to develop a sense of time and space, they also learn a wide variety of facts and information. Some of this information emerges from repeated daily experiences; other items seem to peak children's interest and stick in their memories.

The day after she found an old innersole on a walk with her parents, four-year-old Julie, for instance, told her teacher that she has a "pet paramecium." She made the connection between seeing a picture of a paramecium, an elongated one-celled organism, and the shape of the innersole. Five-year-old Ron is able to recognize pictures of and name more than a dozen kinds of dinosaurs. Elise, aged three, tells the teacher, "I need an ice bucket to keep my milk cold at lunch." She had watched a movie on television the night before and was impressed by the ice bucket into which a bottle of wine was placed! Young children generally do not discriminate between esoteric and practical facts, collecting and storing much information. The early childhood curriculum allows us to select and convey selected information to children.

As we discussed in Chapter 8, appropriate topics for curriculum development can revolve around children, families, and the community. These familiar subjects, which offer innumerable learning possibilities, can then be expanded and built on to help children gain additional information that has relevance in the context of their lives and experiences. It may be charming to hear a young child bring up the subjects of paramecia or ice buckets; however, it makes more sense to help children acquire information that they can connect to existing schemata and that can help them form an increasingly more thorough concept of the world.

Acquisition of information, as well as of the concepts related to classification, seriation, numbers, time, and space, occurs in many ways in the early childhood program. Just about any activity in which young children engage involves one or several of these concepts. Although acquisition of information and concepts is often associated with specific curriculum areas, especially math and science, it is not that easy to place them into discrete categories. Children's thinking is ongoing and involves a constant taking in, sifting, connecting, and storing of experiences, concepts, and information.

The following sections will examine math and science as separate curriculum areas. This is done to reinforce the importance of these subjects as vital parts of the early childhood curriculum, not to imply in any way that these are the major ways in which cognitive development is fostered. Remember also that math and science are as much a part of other activities (for example, blocks, cooking, woodworking, manipulatives, dramatic play, art) as they are separate activities. It is also important to note that the cognitive tasks we discussed earlier are an inherent part of both math and science. It is easy to see that the acquisition of number concepts is central to math. Classification, seriation, and temporal and spatial concepts are equally integral to both math and science. In addition, these concepts supply some of the tools required to carry out math and science endeavors, for instance, measuring, grouping, and comparing.

MATH

Adults often think of mathematics as an abstract discipline involving complex algebraic formulas and geometric calculations. Yet, the foundations of math are grounded in concrete experience such as the exploration of objects and gradual understanding of their properties and relationships. The cognitive concepts we have just discussed—classification, seriation, numbers, time, and space—are all an integral part of the development of mathematical knowledge. Young children are continually involved in mathematical learning, which the early childhood environment and teachers must encourage. The suggested activities listed in the discussion of classification, seriation, numbers, time, and space all contribute to the gradual acquisition of math concepts.

The foundation of more abstract math concepts is formed in early childhood, as children explore concrete objects and understand their properties and relationships.

Much of the previous discussion on cognitive tasks reflects what should be part of a math focus in the early childhood curriculum. Math for young children is not abstract. It is, rather, the provision of many materials that invite the child to handle, explore, compare, measure, combine, take apart, reconstruct, and transform in an infinite variety

Activities such as exploring, comparing, combining, scooping, and measuring at the sensory table reinforce math concepts.

Children in elementary school acquire an essential concept, conservation—the recognition that objects remain the same even if they look different. Grasping the concept of conservation is based on numerous early childhood experiences in manipulating concrete objects.

of ways. By acting on materials, children actively construct knowledge and gradually come to understand mathematical principles.

Central to this gradual understanding is the ability to conserve, recognize that objects remain the same in amount or number despite perceptual changes. As we have discussed before, preschoolers rely very much on their perceptions and think that because materials are rearranged or changed in form, their amount is also changed. Thus, Lisa may think there are more blocks when they are arranged on the floor in a "road" than there were when they are stacked on the shelf; Sylvester will tell you that now that the play dough ball has been made into three snakes, there is more play dough.

This reliance on the observable rather than on an internal understanding that materials do not change unless something is added or taken away is a characteristic of children in the preoperational period. It is through many experiences in arranging and transforming materials that children gradually move to the concrete operational period, in which they are able to conserve. Thus, preschool-aged children usually are not conservers, but they need many concrete experiences on which to build the foundation to acquire this ability to their elementary school years.

The early childhood classroom should contain many materials that lend themselves to acquiring math concepts. These include blocks, sand and water implements, dramatic play props such as dishes and cooking utensils, a variety of manipulatives, art and woodworking materials, and a variety of other items that can be compared, grouped, counted, matched, or placed in a logical order. The class may also contain a specific math learning center, in which materials designed to encourage and enhance math concepts are collected.

SCIENCE

Science is a natural endeavor for young children who are constantly exploring, asking questions, wondering why or why not, observing, touching, tasting. It involves a growing awareness of self, other living things, and the environment through the senses and through exploration

(McIntyre, 1984). Science is not so much a body of specific knowledge as it is a way of thinking and acting, an approach to solving problems (Charlesworth & Lind, 1995). For young children, science is "a reflective attitude toward an object of interest, even during play," a search for answers to interesting questions (Forman & Kaden, 1987, p. 141).

In viewing science as part of the early childhood curriculum, it is important to keep in mind our earlier discussions about the cognitive abilities and limitations of young children. Science concepts need to be concrete and observable. A concept that is abstract and not within the realm of children's experience is not appropriate. Thus, such topics as electricity, water evaporation, the revolution of planets, and matter and energy are inappropriate (Smith, 1982) because they are abstract and nonobservable.

Science activities must be based on concrete, observable elements; children's environments provide many opportunities for such learning.

Science can be classified into two categories, biological science, which deals with living things; and physical science, which concerns nonliving materials.

Biological Sciences

People, animals, and plant life provide fascinating subjects to discover and explore. Children have a natural interest in their own bodies and bodily functions; they also enjoy learning about and caring for animals and plants. In addition, there is the important interrelation between plant and animal life involved in food. Each of these subjects provides a selection of appropriate topics to include in the early childhood curriculum.

The biological sciences provide many fascinating topics for young children related to the study of the people, animals, and plants in their environment.

The Human Body. Toddlers and young preschoolers are still learning the labels of various parts of their bodies, discovering the body's capabilities, and mastering skills in movement and dexterity. Older preschoolers and primary children, on the other hand, have a burgeoning awareness of the less visible parts of the body and want to know why a knee bleeds when someone falls down, where the food goes after it is eaten, or why the heart thumps after a person runs fast.

Children also become increasingly aware of their own growth, relishing the idea of being bigger than they were when they were babies. They are cognizant of each other's characteristics and note that children differ from each other in height, hair length, eye color, and other ways. Following are some topics that can be incorporated into the curriculum to help children increase awareness of their bodies.

- Parts of the body and what they can and cannot do make an intriguing topic for movement activities. "Can you touch your knee with your fingers . . . your ear with your elbow? Can you balance on your bottom . . . on your little fingers?"
- The senses deserve exploration. Every action and activity involves the senses, although we are not always consciously aware of it. Specific activities that encourage children to attend to sensory messages, discriminate between various sensory stimuli, or enjoy sensory stimulation for its own sake should be planned. (See Chapter 9 for more discussion on this topic.)

"Can you touch your ear with your elbow?" Such activities may bring on giggles, but they help children learn what their bodies can and cannot do.

- The concepts of growth and change captivate children. Baby pictures, growth charts, and visits from children's younger siblings can help strengthen these concepts.
- Comparison among children reinforces that each person is unique and that there are many differences among people.
- Care for the body through everyday self-help skills, as well as through activities that focus on the relationship of cleanliness and grooming to health, can be incorporated.
- Older preschoolers and primary children enjoy learning about the inner workings of their respiratory, heart, or digestive systems as long as such information is presented concretely. For instance, a "visit" from a skeleton can help teach the difference between bones and joints. Children can move as the skeleton "moves."

Animals. Any environment contains a variety of animals, for instance, domestic dogs and cats, the classroom gerbil, the sparrows and pigeons that hop in the trees or nest in the eaves of buildings, the horses and cows on nearby farms, the tigers and walruses in the city zoo, the starfish and sea cucumbers in the tide pools, the ants on the playground, the butterflies that flit outside the windows, or the snails that come out after the rain. Children can observe and learn about a wide range of animals in the immediate environment.

The animals that are part of your ecological system provide a rich variety of topics that can be included in the curriculum. If you live in Nevada, why discuss whales when you have not taken time to observe the animals in your desert surroundings? Following are some ideas of ways in which animals can be included in the curriculum.

KEY QUESTION #4

Think of a science class you have taken. What topics from this class might be appropriate concepts for young children? How do you modify information that you, as an adult have learned, to be appropriate for young children?

- Classroom pets provide a natural way for children to learn about, observe, and care for animals. Small animals such as guinea pigs, hamsters, rabbits, gerbils, mice, aquarium fish, parakeets, earthworms, or hermit crabs are often part of early childhood classrooms. It is important to ensure that the animals are in a suitable enclosure, with appropriate food, water, places for rest and privacy, and protection. Be familiar with the needs, characteristics, and care requirements of animals before they become members of your classroom. Although children can participate in caring for the animals, the teachers are ultimately responsible for classroom pets. Also, be aware of any restrictions or limitations spelled out in your local licensing regulations.

- Take time to observe the animals around the school and neighborhood. On the playground or on walks, encourage the children to look or listen for birds, insects, butterflies, squirrels, ducks, and other creatures.
- Animals can be temporary guests in the classroom. Such animals might include a calf or pony on the playground, a child's cat and her new kittens, or caterpillars.
- Plan field trips to nearby animal habitats such as a zoo, farm, aquarium, fish hatchery, or nature preserve. Visit more than one time because there will be much more to see than can be observed on one trip.
- Children's observations about animals should be discussed, both spontaneously and in planned activities.
- Keep records of the children's interactions with animals through photographs, children's pictures, and their stories.
- Through your modeling and through discussion and reminders, help children develop a respect for all animal life.
- Children's exposure to animals through classroom pets, animals that visit the class, neighborhood walks, or field trips should always precede representational activities. Once the children have had ample opportunity to become acquainted with an animal firsthand, they can imitate, discuss, or represent that animal. Thus, the following activities should come only after concrete experiences with animals.
- Through movement activities, children can imitate the walk or characteristic stance of some animals. They can also imitate the animals' sounds.
- The teacher can make various matching games using pictures of animals, or they can be purchased through commercial sources. Once they have observed and learned about specific animals, children might match animals to their habitats (bird to nest, squirrel to tree hole), with their babies, or with their food.
- Children can classify animals by those that fly, live in water, or live on land. Animals can also be classified by other characteristics such as color, size, or number of feet.
- Children can draw pictures, make sculptures, and dictate or write stories of their experiences with animals.

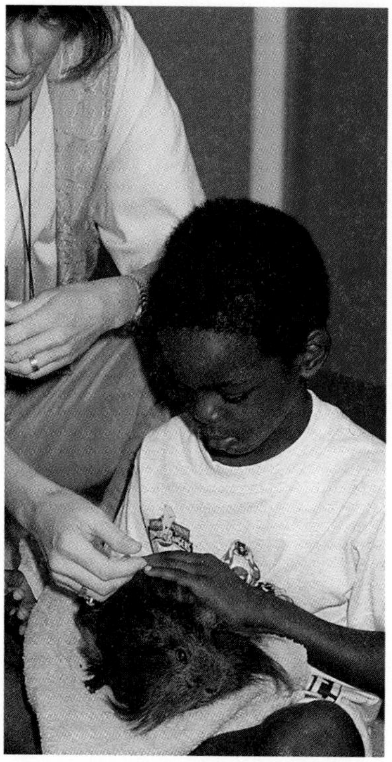

Classroom pets are one way that children can learn about the characteristics and needs of animals firsthand.

Plants. Plant life surrounds us, whether through the vase of flowers in the classroom, the salad at lunch, or the tree in the play yard. Children can expand their understanding of the world by learning

KEY QUESTION #5

What do children learn from the study of animals and plants?

Children learn about living things by helping care for plants and animals in their environment. These young boys have the opportunity to observe and learn about some of the needs of fish in their classroom aquarium.

about plants, their function, needs, aesthetic value, and variety. As is the case in helping children learn about animals, children's increasing understanding about plants should focus on the plants in your environment. The following activities can help children increase their awareness of plants.

- Call attention to and encourage children to describe plants in the environment—the classroom fern, the maple outside the window, the pyracantha across the street. Your enjoyment of plants can help children develop an appreciation for the beauty and variety of plant life.
- Observe and take photographs to record seasonal changes. Compare the photos and discuss the seasons in the context of the children's concrete observations and recollections.
- Help the children understand that plants need water, light, and soil. Note that the leaves droop if a plant does not get enough water, and celebrate as it perks up after an adequate watering. Compare the growth of similar plants on the windowsill and in a shady corner.
- Involve children in observing the growth of plants. Plant seeds in window boxes, pots, an outdoor garden plot, or individual containers that children can take home. (Grass and bean seeds grow very quickly.) Keep a daily record of changes through photographs, measurements, or written records of the children's observations.
- If possible, observe a plant through a growth cycle from seed to blossom to vegetable, fruit, or flower. Plant tomato or zucchini seeds in the spring, care for the plants throughout the summer, and harvest and eat the vegetables in the fall.
- Consider the plants we eat. Visit commercial farms and orchards or a neighborhood garden to see how plants produce the foods we eat.
- Include frequent cooking activities in the curriculum to introduce children to new foods and to learn more about familiar ones.

- Through concrete activities, convey the idea that food helps meet nutritional needs. (See Chapter 9 for a more detailed discussion of cooking and nutrition as part of the curriculum.)

Physical Sciences

Children are in constant contact with and take in information about the inanimate, physical elements of their world, and they acquire many scientific concepts. Patti finds the right length of block to create a bridge, applying an elementary law of physics, for example. Chip mixes water with soil and, through basic chemistry, creates a new substance, mud. Kumalo notices that the black rock he found on the field trip is the same color as the dark band along the face of the mountain. Through such experiences, children begin to construct knowledge about the world and the laws that govern it. We will consider how young children acquire knowledge of physics, chemistry, and meteorology, three examples of physical sciences.

There are many concrete possibilities for learning about the physical sciences, including physics, chemistry, and meteorology.

Physics. Children encounter elements of physics—the relationship of matter and energy—through numerous materials and activities. Blocks, outdoor equipment, water and sand, and manipulatives often present phenomena to be noted and problems to be solved. Children learn about force (throwing the ball hard makes it go further), gravity (cars roll faster down a steep incline), or inertia (a heavy object resists being moved but will move more readily when placed on rollers).

It is not particularly important that children label the laws of physics involved in their actions, although they do delight in acquiring a scientific vocabulary (the swing is a "pendulum" or the slide is an "inclined plane") (Ziemer, 1987). What is important is that children have many experiences in which their actions on objects create movement, for instance, rolling on rollers, jumping, tilting, dropping, blowing, sucking, pulling, and swinging. Children thus experience how their actions affect objects, how they can vary their actions to vary the effect, and how different objects react to their actions (Kamii & Lee-Katz, 1982).

For instance, Sharmila notes that when she kicks a ball, it travels farther away than when she kicks a block; that the lightweight

The laws of gravity can be experienced in everyday activities. If you were this child's teacher, how might you expand the learning potential of this spontaneous activity?

Goals 2000

As the nation approaches the end of the century, it has set some challenging goals of higher standards and achievement for its young people and the institutions that educate them. In 1994 the Goals 2000: Educate America Act was passed, bringing with it a set of expectations and support for improving the educational systems of the country. Many states have joined the campaign by developing their own initiatives toward fulfilling the national agenda.

The eight national educational goals for the year 2000 are that

- all children in America will start school ready to learn;
- all students in America will be competent in the core academic subjects;
- the high school graduation rate will increase to 90 percent;
- American students will be first in the world in math and science;
- every adult American will be literate and possess the skills necessary to compete in the economy of the twenty-first century;
- all teachers will have the opportunity to acquire the knowledge and skills needed to prepare American students for the next century;
- every school in America will be safe, disciplined, and drug-free;
- every school will promote parental involvement in their children's education.

Of particular relevance to early childhood educators is the first of the eight national goals that, by the year 2000, all children will come to school ready to learn. This goal validates what professionals in the field have always recognized, the vital importance of the early years as a foundation for future success. The further recognition given by these goals to the importance of parental involvement in children's education also supports a longstanding value of early childhood educators.

In carrying out plans to meet the eight national goals, a variety of evaluation methods will be utilized. The importance of developmentally appropriate assessment of young children, for instance, as educators gauge their readiness for school, will become even more critical in the future as these are used to help children achieve better school success. Involvement of early childhood educators across the county in implementing Goals 2000 will help to ensure that children are both educated and evaluated in appropriate ways, utilizing the developmentally appropriate practices that have evolved from a considerable body of research and many years of experience in working with young children.

As we get closer and closer to the turn of the century, we may recognize that not all of these goals will be met by the year 2000. They can, however, be continuing goals to help us strive to provide the best for America's children.

beach ball does not travel as far as the heavier rubber ball; and that she can kick with varying degrees of force to move objects different distances. Through repeated experiences, Sharmila begins to develop some generalizations about force and momentum, aided by appropriate questions posed at the right moment by a teacher.

Chemistry. Chemistry deals with the properties, composition, and changes in substances, phenomena that children observe in everyday life. Sensory experiences help children learn about the properties of things around them. Children make intuitive comparisons that tell them that wood is different from metal, which is different from glass, which is different from plastic. They also learn that soap and water result in bubbles, water added to sand makes the sand moldable, and chocolate mixed into milk makes chocolate milk.

Cooking activities are filled with examples of chemistry. Through many cooking experiences, children begin to generalize about how different foods react and are transformed through cutting, mixing, blending, heating, and cooling. For instance, when grapes, banana slices, and orange segments are mixed, they still look like grapes, bananas, and oranges; but when eggs, milk, and flour are mixed, they take on a totally new appearance as batter. When batter is baked, it becomes solid; when potatoes are boiled, they become soft; when eggs are boiled, they become hard. Water can be transformed from a liquid to solid ice after freezing and to elusive steam after boiling. Sugar or salt becomes invisible when stirred into water.

Meteorology. Children are certainly aware of and interested in the weather, an appropriate topic for discussion with young children. Mr. Jenkins encouraged the children in his class to listen to the morning weather forecast and discuss it during the first group time. Throughout the day, then, the children validated what they heard through their own activities and observations. For instance, the children discovered that the wind can blow from different directions. The west wind predicted on the radio made their hair fly in their eyes when they faced the building, whereas an east wind blew their hair out behind them. Kites and streamers further reinforced the idea that the wind can blow from different directions. Storm predictions could be verified by noticing the clouds; they usually meant that the children would plan some alternate, indoor, large motor activities. The children decided what kind of outer clothing they needed. They checked the large outdoor thermometer and compared the level of the temperature line with the adjacent picture of a thermometer on which pictures of a shirt, sweater, jacket, and hat with mittens were pasted at appropriate temperature intervals. Experiments, stories, and poems related to various weather phenomena such as rain, rainbows, the sun, the wind, snow, ice, clouds, and storms can be readily incorporated into the curriculum (Huffman, 1996).

PARENTAL VALUES FOR COGNITIVE DEVELOPMENT

As with all areas of the early childhood curriculum, it is very important to share with parents a clear statement of the school's philosophy about how to support and further children's cognitive development.

The school's philosophy about how young children learn has to be shared with parents.

EXPERIENCES chapter 11

MARK, Bilingual Preschool Teacher

"Twinkle, Twinkle Little Star"

One of the children's favorite songs is "Twinkle, Twinkle Little Star," which we sing quite often. Out of the blue, one of the children asked one day, "Teacher Mark, what is a star?"

I knew that was a difficult question to answer, calling for information beyond my understanding and, I thought, beyond the children's. As a starting point, I asked the children what they thought a star is.

"It's gold," said Maryanne.

"It's a tooth," said another girl, continuing that she thinks that the tooth fairy lives on a star.

"I think it's a planet," contributed John.

"You can see lots of stars," said one of the twins. "Yeah, when you look up at night," said the other.

So the conversation went. Finally, I asked the children to ask their moms and dads that night what a star is and told them I would also see what I could find out. "And, if you have a chance, go outside with your parents when it's dark and look up at the sky. You'll see lots and lots of stars. We'll talk some more about this tomorrow."

The next day, during group time, we returned to the topic of stars. The previous evening I had done some reading to find out more about stars. I told the children, "I learned some more about stars yesterday evening by reading some books. What I found out is that a star is a sun, only much farther away from us."

This information clearly puzzled the children. A sun? But the sun is so bright and so big. How can a star be the same thing?

To try to illustrate the point, one of the other teachers and I decided to help the children see the principles of perspective and distance. I held a large book in my hand and teacher Kathy held a small book. Teacher Kathy stood near the group of children while I went to the farthest corner of the room, away from the children. We held up our respective books.

"Look at these two books that teacher Kathy and I are holding. Which one is bigger?"

The children immediately said that the book teacher Kathy was holding, the smaller one, was bigger. My book, they agreed, was smaller.

"Are you sure?"

They all agreed that, of course, teacher Kathy's book was bigger.

So, I walked toward the children with my larger book held up, and the children noticed that, as I got closer, the book looked larger. Both teacher Kathy and I walked back and forth with the two books and then some of the children took turns holding the two books at different distances.

"You see what happens? When something is close to us it looks bigger, but when it's far, it looks smaller. That's the case with stars. They are as big or even bigger than the sun we see in the sky. But they are so much farther away, that they look much smaller."

It's not always easy to answer seemingly simple questions posed by children. In this case, the teachers' ingenuity helped explain a complex phenomenon. Using concrete examples can help children begin to grasp some rather complex science concepts.

Parents should be aware, for instance, that the program is built on the conviction that children learn best through concrete, hands-on activity; that children are able to select meaningful activities on their own; and that play and learning go together. Conversely, such a philosophy means that the program does not engage in abstract and developmentally inappropriate teaching practices that require the child to sit quietly and inactively.

Today's parents are bombarded by pressures to succeed, which includes having successful children as well. Thus, many well-intentioned parents feel a need to see evidence that their children are indeed learning in their early childhood program. For instance, parents may say to you, "But Marcia does nothing but play all day; when will she learn something?" or "Ron starts kindergarten next year; shouldn't he be learning to read?" or "I want Singh to learn to sit quietly and work on his numbers" or "I'm thinking of enrolling Betsy in the school where my neighbor's son goes; he comes home with dittoes every day and Betsy only brings home paintings." How do you respond in a way that respects the parents' concerns but maintains the integrity of your program?

Conveying to parents your philosophy of how children best learn involves frequent explanation and supportive information. First, it requires that you, as the teacher, are secure in your understanding of how young children learn and acquire concepts so you can answer parents' questions and concerns. It is also important to make information from experts, which supports your approach, available to parents. This might be done through a parent library, well-written articles to be distributed to parents, short quotes by experts placed on the parent bulletin board, speakers at parent meetings, or parent discussion groups with a knowledgeable facilitator. Let parents know that your profession has a position statement, *Developmentally Appropriate Practice in Early Childhood Programs Serving Children from Birth Through Age 8* (Bredekamp & Copple, 1997), that supports your approach. In other words, let parents know that your work with children is founded on and backed by research and theory.

SUMMARY

1. There are three influential theoretical views of cognitive development: behaviorism, cognitive developmental theory, and information processing.
2. Cognition begins to develop in earliest infancy, through movement and sensory experiences.
3. During the preschool years, children begin to acquire some specific cognitive skills.
   A. Consider five cognitive tasks—classification, seriation, number concepts, temporal concepts, and spatial concepts—and activities that can help children master them.
   B. Children also acquire a considerable amount of information during their early years.
4. Two important early childhood curriculum areas to consider are math and science.

KEY TERMS LIST

behavior management
central processor
cognition
conservation
constructivist theory
information processing
long-term (or permanent) memory
mapping
memory strategies
metamemory
one-to-one correspondence
rational counting
reflective abstraction
rote counting
sensory register
short-term (or working) memory
spatial concepts
symbolic representation
temporal concepts
temporal sequencing

chapter 12

Language Development Through the Curriculum

The odyssey of children's early development is particularly astounding when we consider the acquisition of language. The average preschooler has acquired an enormous vocabulary, has a fundamental grasp of the rules of grammar, and understands the subtle nuances involved in the social aspects of communication. In addition, young children begin to develop the skills needed for the complex process of reading and writing, which they master during the primary years. These are truly amazing accomplishments, which children acquire with almost no formal instruction from adults. We know much about this language acquisition process, although language researchers certainly do not understand completely how children learn to communicate with such speed and accuracy (Gineshi, 1987).

As with each of the chapters dealing with how the curriculum supports children's development, the curricular aspects we discuss represent only some of the ways in which language development is fostered. Keep in mind that children's language is used and expanded in almost every early childhood activity in which they participate. In this chapter, we will look more closely at what we know about how language develops and how the early childhood curriculum can encourage and strengthen language development.

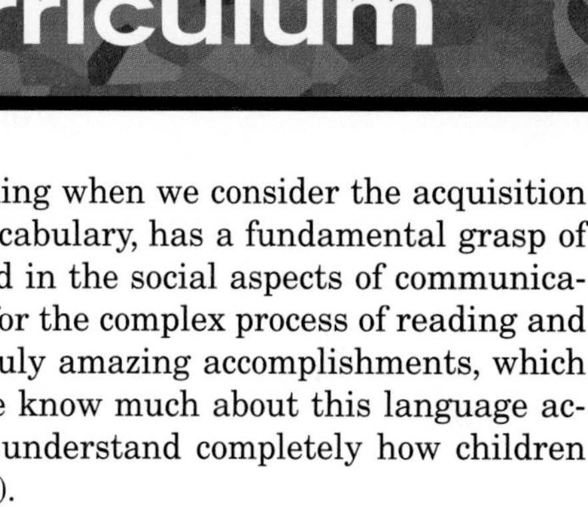

THEORETICAL VIEWS OF LANGUAGE DEVELOPMENT

Theorists and researchers have applied a range of explanations to how the complex process of language acquisition develops in children, often coming to rather conflicting conclusions. The behaviorist view sees language as primarily influenced by external factors such as the modeling and reinforcement of parents; the second, the **innatist view of language development,** considers inborn factors to be the most important component; a third position, the **interactionist view**

Innatist view of language development—The view that inborn factors are the most important component of language development.

Interactionist view of language development—The view that language develops through a combination of inborn factors and environmental influences.

The behaviorist view of language development is that children's language learning is shaped primarily by the responses of parents.

of language development, sees the interaction of innate predispositions to language and environmental influences as most important (Bohannon & Warren-Leubecker, 1985; Lindfors, 1987; Owens, 1984).

Behaviorist View of Language Development

Earlier in this century, the prevalent view of how children learn language was that it is shaped by the environment. B. F. Skinner's classic text, *Verbal Behavior* (1957), describes language acquisition as a learned behavior, subject to the same rules of conditioning (see Chapter 5) as any other behavior being learned.

According to this view, parents reinforce an infant's language development when they respond by smiling, cuddling the baby, and verbalizing. When specific syllables appear in the baby's babbling repertoire, especially ones that sound like "mama" or "dada," the delighted parents redouble their positive feedback to the baby. This behavior serves as further reinforcement, encouraging the baby to repeat the sounds that brought such a response. Gradually, reinforcement becomes more specific, contingent on increasing ability to produce adult-like language. Language becomes more complex because increasingly more complex language is reinforced (Lindfors, 1987). At first, sounds are shaped into words ("mamamamama" becomes "mama"); later word combinations are reinforced for increasing grammatical accuracy. In addition, children learn that language helps them achieve their goals, and this further reinforces and strengthens language acquisition.

Innatist View of Language Development

The innatist view, voiced by theorists such as Chomsky, holds that children are born with a linguistic structure.

At the opposite end of the spectrum of language theories is the innatist view, which considers the capacity for language as inborn. Noam Chomsky (1972), one of the leading proponents of this view, hypothesizes that children are born with a linguistic structure that makes it possible for them to acquire language as quickly as they do during the preschool years.

Deep structure—According to Noam Chomsky, inborn understanding or underlying rules of grammar and meaning that are universal across all languages.

Surface structure—According to Noam Chomsky, specific aspects of language that vary from one language to another.

He believes that every person starts life with an innate **deep structure,** the underlying rules of grammar and meaning that are universal across all languages. Thus, children are "wired" to know without being taught that communication has meaning or that it can affirm, negate, question, and command. Beyond this deep structure, then, children have to learn the specific vocabulary and grammar of their language, what Chomsky calls the **surface structure.** The deep structure includes the common features of all languages, whereas the surface structure involves the specifics that vary from language to language.

Because language is innate, it is linked to biological maturation and follows an internal clock, needing to emerge during the "critical age" for language acquisition (Lennenberg, 1967). Children who do not learn language in early childhood have a much more difficult time later, just as learning a second language later in life is not nearly as easy as acquiring it in the early years (Bohannon & Warren-Leubecker, 1985). Language, however, does not emerge automatically; rather, it is triggered by exposure to verbal communication in the environment.

Language, according to the interactionist view, develops from a combination of inborn and environmental factors. Internal readiness and reinforcement from positive interactions with adults are needed.

Interactionist View of Language Development

A compromise between the behaviorist view, in which external environment is all important, and the innatist view, in which inborn factors are the key, is the interactionist view, which takes important elements from the other two theoretical extremes. Thus, children are seen as neither passive recipients of language training from their parents nor the active language processors whose internal structures are the primary determinants of language acquisition. Interactionists see many factors such as the social environment, maturation, biology, and cognition at play in the development of language. These elements interact with and modify each other (Bohannon & Warren-Leubecker, 1985).

The interactionist view suggests that there is an interplay between inborn and environmental factors in children's language learning.

There are two major approaches to this view—the **cognitive interactionist view of language development** and the **social interactionist view of language development.** As proponents of the former view, Piaget (1926) and other cognitive theorists considered that children's understanding of language is rooted in their cognitive development, requiring, for instance, the ability to represent objects mentally. Language is one way of expressing representational or symbolic thought.

Cognitive interactionist view of language development—The view that children's language is rooted in cognitive development, requiring, for instance, ability to represent objects mentally.

Social interactionist view of language development—Theoretical view that considers language closely tied to and dependent on social processes.

Social interactionist theorists deem that language is intimately tied to social processes. Children's language development is guided by internal factors, but the critical fact is that it must emerge within the social environment provided by the parents. Furthermore, the social interaction that triggers language is a two-way operation, in which children cue their parents and parents, in turn, supply appropriate language experiences (Bohannon & Warren-Leubecker, 1985). Vygotsky (1962), one of the leading proponents of the social interactionist view, considers that the young child's primary social tool is language. (See Chapter 5.)

COMPONENTS OF LANGUAGE

Language is a complex system involving a variety of components. Included are learning as well as understanding words, knowing the rules for using words accurately, learning the rules for putting words together meaningfully, and obtaining a growing grasp of the appropriateness of what is being communicated. As each theory of language development indicates, children's early years are particularly crucial in the evolution of language skills. To better grasp the complexity of this task, we will take a closer look at early language development as well as at some of these components related to meaning and rules of language.

Early Language Development

Babies' language moves from cooing to babbling to the emergence of recognizable words in the first year; toddlers become increasingly adept, acquiring both more words and some rudimentary grammatical rules.

Cooing—The language of babies in the first half of the first year, consisting primarily of strings of throaty vowels sounds.

Babbling—The language of babies in the second half of the first year, consisting of strings of vowels and consonants that are often repeated over and over.

Language does not begin when babies speak their first words around the end of the first year. It has been developing from their earliest days. Newborns prefer the human voice over other sounds and can even distinguish their mother's voice from another woman's at a very early age. Their early communication takes the form of **cooing,** throaty vowel sounds, later combined with laughter, which delights adults as they "converse" with babies. Remember from Chapter 11 that infants discover their own power to make interesting things happen again; the same holds true for language. Babies gradually recognize they can repeat interesting sounds to their own delight and amusement.

In the second half of the first year, cooing is replaced by **babbling,** strings of consonants and vowels that are repeated in a form of play with sounds. Babies also begin to imitate sounds and participate in give-and-take conversation, taking turns talking and listening. Toward the end of the first year, words like "mama, dada," and a few other familiar labels appear. Intonation, tone, and pitch become more varied and expressive.

During the second year, more and more recognizable words become part of and eventually replace babbling. At first, one word may communicate an entire thought; later toddlers put two words together, for instance "more juice" or "truck bye-bye," very effectively conveying what they mean. Children learn the labels for familiar objects, begin to use negatives (no!) and possessives (mine), and learn some action words. By the end of the second year, many toddlers have a vocabulary of 25 to 50 words (Allen & Marotz, 1994; Anisfeld, 1984; Dyson & Genishi, 1993; Honig & Lally, 1981; Wilson, 1995).

Language Meaning

Young children's vocabulary expansion is quite astounding, estimated to average two to four new words every day.

Vocabulary. One way of studying children's language development is to examine the rapid acquisition of vocabulary. For instance, one early study reported that between the ages of two and a half and four and a half, children acquire 2 to 4 new words per day on the average (Pease & Gleason, 1985); a more recent report estimates that young children learn about 10 words every day (Miller & Gildea, 1987). A three-year-old has a vocabulary of 900 to 1,000 words, a four-year-old's vocabulary typically contains 1,500 to 1,600 words, and a five-year-old has acquired a vocabulary of 2,100 to 2,200 words (Owens, 1984). Vocabulary continues to grow rapidly beyond the preschool years. A six-year-old learns as many as 5 to 10 new words a day and has a vocabulary of 10,000 to 14,000 words (Allen & Marotz, 1994). Estimates of vocabulary size vary, but they are impressive when you consider that a young child has picked up such a large amount of information in such a short time.

Although vocabulary counts provide interesting figures, their use in understanding language development is limited. For one thing, it is difficult to determine whether a child really understands the words he uses. When Colin says, "We're going to Disneyland and we're going to stay there a million days," does he really understand the word "million"? While he clearly does not have a grasp of "million" as an absolute amount, he nonetheless knows that it has quantitative meaning (Lindfors, 1987). This is a case in which the study of semantics is relevant.

Semantics. Children learn the meanings of words in the context of their experiences. The study of **semantics** examines the understanding of word meanings. One significant part of semantics is a scrutiny of emotion-laden words; the most common examples are those connected to racism. In addition, name-calling depends on the negative impact of certain words. For instance, an "unloaded" word such as "red" simply refers to a color, whereas labeling a person "a Red" makes this straightforward word derogative. The importance of this aspect of semantics in the handling of children is that they tend to hurt one another through such verbal attacks as name-calling.

Children's growing understanding of word meanings, including those that have an added emotional context, is called semantics.

Semantics—Related to understanding and study of word meaning.

In addition, word meaning is related to the **semantic network,** the interrelationship among words (Pease & Gleason, 1985). Fourteen-month-old Monica calls the family pet by its name, "Lucky," then applies the same word to other dogs and even some other four-legged animals she comes across. This **overextension** is typical of toddlers learning their first words, and it reflects their vocabulary limitations (Clark, 1978b).

Semantic network—The interrelationship among words, particularly related to word meaning.

Overextension—Application of a word to a variety of related objects, especially used by toddlers.

As they get older, however, children narrow the meanings of words until they become closer to adults' meanings. Monica will gradually learn that Lucky is a dog, that dogs are animals, and that other creatures can also be called animals. Thus, the semantic network includes an increasing understanding of classification (see Chapter 11) through this relationship among the various words (Gleason, 1985; Moskowitz, 1982).

Children learn the meaning of words in the context of experience. Modeling of positive social interaction, for instance, using words in socially constructive rather than destructive ways, helps children relate more sensitively to their peers.

The meanings of some words, which adults take for granted, pose some problems for young children. For instance, they only gradually acquire an understanding of prepositions. It isn't until their third year that preschoolers comprehend the word *in,* followed by *on* and *under.*

More complex prepositions, for instance, *between* or *beside,* are not grasped until ages four to five (Clark, 1978a; Johnston & Slobin, 1979). Thus, when a teacher tells a group to "wait beside the sink to wash your hands," and three-year-old Jimmy is under a table, the teacher must recognize that Jimmy may not be "not listening" but rather "not understanding." Young children also have difficulty understanding a sentence in which a sequence is not in its logical order (Goodz, 1982). Therefore, it is harder for preschoolers to understand "before you go outside put on your coat" than "put on your coat before you go outside."

Language Rules

Morphology—The study of word rules, for instance, tense, plurals, and possessives.

Morphology refers to children's learning of rules about words, for instance, how to make a verb into the past tense or how to make the plural form.

Morphology. As children acquire words and understand their meanings, they also learn rules that apply to these words; the study of such word rules is called **morphology.** Some examples of morphological word rules include verb tense, plurals, and the possessive form. Researchers have identified a fairly predictable sequence in which children learn specific morphemes (Brown, 1973; deVilliers & deVilliers, 1973). Among the first such rules children learn are the present progressive form (-ing ending), the words in and on, and the regular plural (-s ending). Irregular verb forms and contractions (isn't, we're) are learned later.

Syntax—Involves the grammatical rules that govern the structure of sentences.

KEY QUESTION #1

Listen to a young child's spontaneous language usage. What components of language do you note? Consider the child's understanding of the meaning of language as well as the child's grasp of language rules.

Syntax. Rules also apply to combinations of words. **Syntax** involves the grammatical rules that govern the structure of sentences. Even very young children show a grasp of such rules in their construction of two-word sentences. A toddler is much more likely to say "my car" than "car my" or "more juice" than "juice more," indicating a sensitivity to conventional word order in sentences.

Whereas very young children often use simple nouns and verbs to convey meaning, older children elaborate on these to create increasingly more complex noun phrases and verb phrases as parts of longer sentences. In addition, somewhere between the ages of two and four, children begin to combine more than one idea in one complex sentence rather than saying two simple sentences (Gineshi, 1987). Children also become progressively more adept at asking questions and stating negatives (deVilliers & deVilliers, 1979). Thus, their language, though limited in vocabulary, can take on infinite variety in its forms of expression. Careful analysis of how children learn grammatical rules indicates that they are not merely imitating what they have heard from adults, but that they are constructing a cohesive language system of their own (Gleason, 1985).

Learning the social rules of conversation is called pragmatics.

Pragmatics—Rules that govern language use in social contexts.

Pragmatics. One additional set of rules governs our system of language. That aspect of communication governed by the social context is called **pragmatics.** Children gradually learn the give-and-take rules of becoming a conversationalist. They learn that during certain times it is appropriate to remain quiet (for instance, when the teacher is reading a story), whereas at other times their verbal input is desired. They also come to understand that different forms of communication are expected in different situations. Depending on the conversational partner, children learn to use different words, apply different levels of formality, and give different types of responses to questions. Accordingly, they modify how they speak when they talk to a younger child, to a friend, to a visitor at school, or to the teacher; or when they assume the role of Superman, a parent, or a fireman in role playing (Shatz & Gelman, 1973). A child may say to a neighbor at snack, "Gimme the milk" while to the teacher, "May I have the milk, please?" (Owens, 1984).

BILINGUALISM

Early childhood programs increasingly include children from other linguistic and cultural backgrounds, children who may speak only a language other than English, children who are in the process of acquiring English as a second language, and children who have grown up acquiring more than one language simultaneously. In some programs, English-speaking children are exposed to a second language, particularly if that language and culture are important parts of the community. **Bilingualism,** although it is often considered primarily a matter of language learning, also needs to be viewed as intricately tied to cultural and social dimensions (Hakuta & Garcia, 1989). Awareness of and sensitivity to family values is particularly important in working with children learning English as a second language (Sholtys, 1989).

Children generally have little difficulty learning more than one language.

Bilingualism—Ability to use two languages.

In general, young children have little difficulty acquiring more than one language and eventually speaking each of them with no interference from the other (Obler, 1985). In learning a second language, children follow a process similar to that used to acquire the first language (Hakuta, 1988). In fact, common principles of learning are seen as the foundation for acquiring both languages (McLaughlin, 1984). Although bilingual children gain the elements of semantics, morphology, syntax, and pragmatics of two languages, they also have to acquire a sense of when it is appropriate to use each language. To function

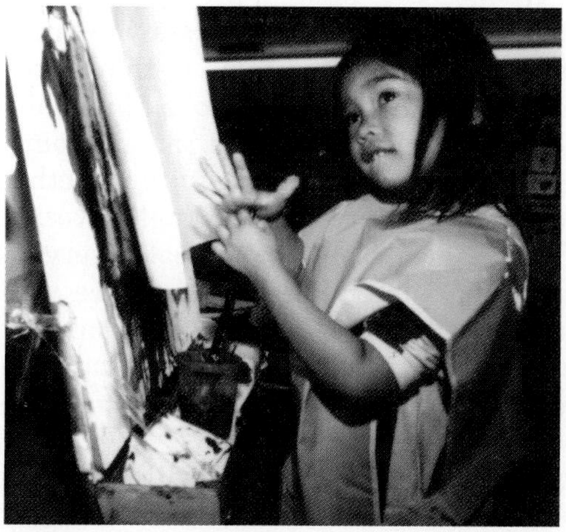

Early childhood programs increasingly enroll children from other cultures whose primary language is not English.

Code switching—Ability to switch appropriately from one language system to another.

Code switching refers to bilingual children's ability to learn in which context it is appropriate to use each language.

Simultaneous language acquisition—A child learning two languages at the same time or before the age of three.

Successive language acquisition—Learning a second language after the age of three.

Immersion programs—An approach to teaching a second language to children by surrounding or immersing them in that language.

Nonimmersion programs—Approach to teaching a new language that involves using both the primary and second languages, with a gradual shift from emphasis on the first to the second.

Different approaches to teaching a second language include immersing children in the new language without using the primary language and using both the new and old languages at the same time.

effectively in their multilanguage environment, bilingual children have to become proficient at **code switching,** shifting from one language system to the other.

A distinction needs to be made between **simultaneous language acquisition** and **successive language acquisition.** A child who learns two languages at one time or a second language by age three, is considered to be acquiring the languages simultaneously; learning a second language after age three is deemed as successive acquisition (McLaughlin, 1984). At first, children who are learning more than one language simultaneously from the beginning are a little slower in acquiring vocabulary because each object or event has two words attached to it, but they soon catch up with children who are learning only one language (deVilliers & deVilliers, 1979). In addition, young simultaneous language learners tend to engage in some language mixing, but this is naturally followed by increasing awareness that the two languages are separate and different (Owens, 1984).

Often, however, young children in an early childhood program are successive language learners, being first exposed to English in the school setting. Different bilingual education approaches have been developed, although such models are most likely to be found where large populations of children speak a language other than English, for instance, Head Start programs in southwestern states.

Immersion programs use only the second language, and the children are treated as if they were native speakers of that language. In **nonimmersion programs,** both the native and second language are used, with a gradual shift from the former to the latter over time (Garcia, 1982). Teachers in nonimmersion programs are most often bilingual, helping children begin to learn English while also furthering the children's native language. Unfortunately, little research has focused on the relative effectiveness of such programs for young children; what seems clear is that measuring bilingual program effectiveness is a complex matter involving many factors.

A single child or a few children from another linguistic and cultural background are often enrolled in an early childhood program, leaving teachers who are not familiar with the child's language to use their ingenuity in helping such youngsters learn English. More often than not, a less systematic approach is followed, taking cues from the child's reactions and apparent needs.

The following examples of Nina and Hoang illustrate why more than language has to be considered. When Nina came to the United States from San Salvador with her family, she was enrolled in a daily preschool program to help her learn English. Nina, an outgoing, friendly four-year-old, found little problem interacting with the other children and the teachers. She quickly acquired a basic English vocabulary and, combined with nonverbal cues, soon communicated very effectively. Hoang, on the other hand, entered the United States as a refugee and experienced considerable hardships as well as a series of unsettling changes, including the recent death of his mother. He seemed to find his kindergarten bewildering and rarely participated in activities, standing at the sidelines in somber silence.

Although the approach to helping Nina acquire English involved encouraging peer interactions, exposure to stimulating activities, and a

A Closer Look

NAEYC Position Statement on Linguistic and Cultural Diversity

The *NAEYC Position Statement: Responding to Linguistic and Cultural Diversity—Recommendations for Effective Early Childhood Education* (NAEYC, 1996) makes a very strong statement about bilingualism. Children who are learning English as a second language must be encouraged to continue development in their primary language. In this important statement, NAEYC urges professionals to value and recognize the importance of a child's primary language and culture and to work with all parents toward the common goal of optimizing each child's potential for development.

"Development of children's home language does not interfere with their ability to learn English . . . because knowing more than one language is a cognitive asset" (p. 5). This statement, supported by considerable research, should encourage early childhood professionals to view a child who knows, or is learning, more than one language as having a decided advantage, not a deficit. The statement, however, must be taken in the context of interaction within the family. The family's primary language and culture have to be valued and respected. This message must be conveyed clearly to children and their parents, through the attitudes and actions of teachers. When use of the primary language is maintained at home, even if a child is learning English at school, the child can maintain that all-important link to the values, cultural heritage, and traditions of the family.

The position statement makes some valuable recommendations for professionals' work with young children. The importance of recognizing that all children are connected in cognitive, language, and emotional ways to their home culture underscores the philosophy of the statement. Furthermore, recognizing that children can demonstrate their abilities in many ways throughout the curriculum, and recognizing the importance of context to learning, are also emphasized. The latter is particularly important because language should never be conveyed in abstract, meaningless ways; in fact, often it is the knowledge acquired in the first language that can make it easier to learn the second language, particularly in learning more complex concepts. Thus, continuing to become proficient in the primary language at home builds depth in the understanding of one language, which serves as a foundation of learning concepts in the new language.

To help children reach their potentials, it is vital that teachers and parents work together. This means two-way communication, even if a translator has to be involved. The position statement clearly asks teachers to "encourage and assist all parents in becoming knowledgeable about the cognitive value for children of knowing more than one language, and provide them with strategies to support, maintain, and preserve home-language learning. If parents, who are themselves limited in their ability in English, speak only English to their children, they are limiting and impoverishing the parent-child communication. Children are less likely to hear complex ideas, which are important to cognitive development. Thus, the natural, day-to-day interactions of parents and children are vital to all aspects of development.

Children will acquire English even if they continue to use their home language, as long as that language is respected and valued. Not only teachers but administrators need to incorporate wholehearted support and encouragement of children's primary language into their program's philosophies.

language-rich environment, Hoang's needs were clearly different. Before language learning could be addressed, his emotional needs had to be considered. After almost 2 months, Hoang began to establish a relationship with one of the teachers and gradually became involved in activities. Throughout this time of silence, Hoang had nonetheless been surrounded by language, and eventually it became clear that he had attended to much of what he heard. Once Hoang felt stability in his home and school life, his mastery of English progressed significantly.

Lily Wong Fillmore (1991) raises some provocative questions about teaching English to young non-English speaking children. She cites studies in which a growing gulf separates parents, especially from immigrant families, who do not speak English and their children who have learned English in school and gradually forget their native language. For these children, the home language often represents barriers to participation in the American culture while English become the language for success. Fillmore proposes that educational practices, which replace rather than augment the child's home language with English, erode families by breaking down communication to the point where parents cannot effectively socialize and teach their children. She suggests that more thought be given to practices that impose English on young children until they have more firmly acquired skill in their own first language.

Second-language Teaching Strategies

Although there are no definitive guidelines for helping children learn a second language, some strategies can be helpful in this process (Saville-Troike, 1982; Sholtys, 1989). As you read this list, notice that many of these suggestions are equally important for all young children, not only those learning a new language.

KEY QUESTION #2

Talk to someone you know who learned English as a second language. What are this person's recollections about this learning process? What was most difficult and what was easiest? What strategies or techniques were most helpful in this learning process? Talk with others in your class and compare the findings of those whose friends learned English at an early age and those who learned it later in life.

- A new experience such as school can be bewildering to any young child, particularly if the child cannot understand the language. A friendly, consistent, supportive atmosphere can help make the child feel welcome and comfortable, which, in turn, will facilitate learning English.

The teacher can encourage the children in the class to talk to and invite their non-English-speaking classmate to join in their activities. What are some ways you might help this child become an integral part of her new class?

- If someone who speaks the child's first language is available, enlist that person to help the child learn the routines and expectations, as well as the new language. If another child in the class speaks the language, interaction between the two should be encouraged, although certainly not forced.
- At the same time, encourage all of the children to talk to and include the child in activities.
- Use the child's name frequently, being sure to pronounce it properly when talking to the child.
- A non-English-speaking child should not be forced to speak, because the natural process of learning a second language usually entails a time of silent assimilation. Even if not yet actively speaking it, the child is still acquiring the language.
- Involve the child in the classroom through nonlanguage activities, for instance, helping to set the table for snack, to help the child become part of the group.
- Language should be presented in a natural, meaningful way, in the context of the child's experiences and interests.
- Concrete objects or demonstration of actions should be paired with new words. Say the word "milk" when helping the child pour it at snack; pair the word "cut" with a demonstration using scissors.
- Repetition of new language learning is important, provided it is done naturally. Meaningless drill does not help. Consistently using the same wording each day, for instance, to signal classroom transitions, will help the child connect words and meaning more easily.
- When a child shares feelings or an idea verbally, such communication should be encouraged through uncritical acceptance. Correcting grammar or pronunciation tends to inhibit rather than foster language.

Dialects

Some children enter the early childhood program speaking a dialect of English. A **dialect** is a regional variation of a language different in some features of vocabulary, grammar, and pronunciation. **Ebonics** is one of this country's most widely used dialects, spoken throughout the South and in many urban areas in other parts of the country. The complex grammatical system of Ebonics has been studied extensively (Labov, 1970). Thus, what may appear to someone unfamiliar with Ebonics to be poor grammar actually represents a different set of grammatical rules (for instance, "we be here" or "I ain't finished"). It should be noted that certainly not all black Americans speak Ebonics, and numerous other dialects exist, often developed as part of the culture of a given area or group.

It is important for teachers of young, Ebonics-speaking children to recognize that they have language competence in the same way that all children do, having already acquired the morphology, semantics,

Some young children speak a dialect, which is a regional variation of the primary language.

Dialect—A regional variation of a language that differs in some features of vocabulary, grammar, and pronunciation.

Ebonics—Term identifying the dialect spoken by some black children, which has a complex grammatical system of its own.

Some black children may use Ebonics, a dialect that has a complex set of grammatical rules of its own.

syntax, and pragmatics of Ebonics. An atmosphere of genuine acceptance and value of black children's language and culture, coupled with an environment in which standard English is spoken, can help them acquire the language that predominates in the larger culture of the country. In addition, children can be encouraged to gain skill in code switching, deciding which form of the language is appropriate in which situations.

LANGUAGE AND THE EARLY CHILDHOOD CURRICULUM

The following sections will examine several important aspects of language. First, we will discuss the informal, ongoing use of language that should be a natural accompaniment to whatever children are doing. We next will look at some specific activities that teachers plan to enhance language development. Finally, we will examine children's emerging literacy, their awareness that language extends to reading and writing, and how this is supported through integrated language experiences.

Spontaneous Language

Because language is so integral to all parts of the early childhood program, much language learning occurs spontaneously.

Because language is so pervasive in almost everything children do, it must be central to the early childhood program. Children are constantly involved in communication—in listening, hearing, talking, interpreting, writing, reading. All forms of language surround them as they interact with each other, with adults, with media, with activities, and with varied materials. Language activities do not need to be structured to *teach* language because by preschool age children have already acquired an elaborate and complex language system. Rather, early childhood language experiences should emerge from natural and meaningful conversations and experiences between adults and children and among children. Such talk is used to inform, tell stories, pretend, plan, argue, discuss, express humor, and so on (Gineshi, 1987). Classrooms for young children, therefore, are not quiet. They are abuzz with language almost all of the time.

EXPERIENCES

chapter 12

TERRI, Head Teacher, Class of Four-Year-Olds

"Pandy"

This year's class was just not interested in literacy activities, as some of the previous classes had been. The writing table and book area were not used as enthusiastically as they had been in past years. We decided to enlist the help of the parents by sending an activity home with the children.

"Pandy," a large stuffed panda bear was put in a shopping bag along with a box of crayons and paper. The children were told Pandy really wanted to get to know each of them and that they would take turns taking Pandy home for a few days. At the end of Pandy's stay they were to tell a story about what they had done while Pandy visited their house, either by writing their story with the help of their parents or drawing a picture. The children were enthusiastic and all wanted Pandy to go home with them first. The order of Pandy's home visits was to be determined by a random drawing of names, however.

When Little Eagle's name was the first drawn, we were concerned. Little Eagle was a very nonverbal child who often resorted to aggression to communicate with others. It had been hard to engage him in activities, conversations, or, in fact, any engagement with the other children or the teachers. He lived with his mother and grandmother after his abusive father was jailed a few months previously. We were worried about what would happen to this activity with Little Eagle setting the tone.

A few days later, Little Eagle brought Pandy back to school. His mother told us, "This has been the most wonderful thing for him!" Little Eagle had taken Pandy's visit very seriously, nurturing and caring for the bear in a way that was very unusual for him. Every night, for instance, he would brush Pandy's teeth, put pajamas on him, and tuck him carefully under the covers of his bed.

With information from the mother, we were able to help Little Eagle during group time to share what he and Pandy had done over the past few days. The other children were fascinated. And, Little Eagle's approach to Pandy set the tone for the activity for the rest of the class.

Somehow, this activity, which was merely intended as a home literacy project, was a pivotal experience for Little Eagle. He gradually showed more empathy toward his classmates, for instance, watching with concern from the sidelines when someone was hurt or cried. He smiled and laughed more often as time passed and even developed some friendships with the other children.

Could a stuffed animal make that kind of difference in the life of a young child? Ask Pandy.

experiences

Language is used and reinforced countless times in the early childhood program, as teachers and children, as well as children and children, interact and converse informally.

Almost every aspect of the early childhood environment and program facilitates language. For instance, the knowledgeable teacher, who values what children have to say and listens to them carefully, promotes language development. Similarly, a daily schedule (as we discussed in Chapter 8) that provides large blocks of time in which children can become immersed in activities and interactions fosters language usage. In addition, language growth is encouraged by a curriculum that introduces interesting and stimulating objects, experiences, and concepts, just as a classroom environment that is set up to invite small groups of children to work together promotes language.

Effective conversations between teachers and children are responsive to the child rather than being controlled by the teacher.

KEY QUESTION #3

Observe a teacher of young children engage in spontaneous conversation with children. What techniques does she or he use? How are the children encouraged to interact with each other as well as with the teacher? Did you hear examples of language play or humor?

Conversations. A natural way of using language is through conversation. This begins in earliest infancy. In good early childhood programs, there is an almost constant, ongoing buzz of conversations between children and teachers and among children. For children, conversation is an art that takes time to develop, since it involves learning a number of elements such as how to initiate and end conversations, maintain coherent dialogue, take turns, and "repair" a conversation that breaks down (McTear, 1985). It is important, therefore, that there be many, many opportunities for children to practice their emerging conversational skills.

Equally an art is teachers' ability to engage in effective conversations with children. Dialogue between adults and small groups or individual children is essential (Lay-Dopyera & Dopyera, 1987). Unfortunately, research has found that there is generally little extended conversation between teachers and young children.

An in-depth study of one skilled teacher's conversational strategies revealed some significant differences between her approach with young children and that of other teachers (Rogers, Perrin, & Waller, 1987). For one thing, Cathy (the teacher) maintained an equalitarian relationship in her conversation; the number of words and length of sentences were relatively equal to those used by the child. Analysis of another teacher-child dialogue showed that the child used far fewer words and shorter sentences. Particularly important was Cathy's genuine interest in what the child was telling her. Although other teachers often asked the child perfunctory questions, Cathy's interactions were based on the child's actions and interests and, more often than not, were in response to the child's initiation.

The most concrete finding of this study was Cathy's avoidance of "know-answer questions," questions to which the teacher already knows the answer (for instance, "what color did you paint the sky?" or "how many cookies are on your plate?"). Such questions, which many teachers use frequently, are followed by a simple, often one-word response from the child and an evaluation of the correctness of the answer by the teacher. Children may, in fact, fear giving a wrong answer and therefore hesitate to engage in any conversation with the teacher. Thus, teacher-child conversations should arise from natural situations and be based on genuine interest in what the child is doing. Cathy, in other words, listened to and took her conversational cues from the children.

Once children have a good grasp of the principles of language, they begin to play with it through humor, nonsense words, rhymes, or "dirty" words.

Playing With Language. Another facet of language that teachers can use to enrich its use in the early childhood setting is children's language play. Infants delight in physical humor such as tickling. Once children have a good grasp of the principles of language and the correctness of a concept, they delight in confirming this by expressing the opposite, usually accompanied by much laughter and giggling (Geller, 1985). Expressions of humor through silliness, nonsense words or rhymes, and "dirty" words particularly enthrall young children. Children enjoy humor, and teachers can use it to capture and maintain children's attention, both in the stories they read or tell and in their conversations with children.

One basis for humor is children's increasing ability to recognize incongruity (Honig, 1988b). For preschoolers, this can involve changing the words of favorite rhymes ("Mary had a little bleep"), an absurd element in a picture (a cat's head on a goldfish's body), or calling a known object by an obviously inappropriate name.

Most riddles and jokes that depend on the double meaning of a word are too sophisticated for preschoolers, who do not yet have the cognitive skills to comprehend this level of linguistic incongruity but are grasped by many primary children. Seven-year-old Caleb asks his family at dinner, "What did the dog say when he saw the top of the house?" His parents and four-year-old sister Nancy laugh when he tells them, "Roof, roof!" Then Nancy decides to relate a riddle as well. "What did the kitty say when he saw the top of the house?" Nancy's answer—"Miaow, miaow!" and her accompanying laughter indicate that she does not yet understand that words sometimes have double meanings, although she does understand that a joke is something funny that people enjoy sharing.

Children usually know when they are using a naughty word, and this is also a source of humor for them. "Bathroom language" is a particular favorite of many four-year-olds, who can dissolve into paroxysms of laughter as they recite a litany such as "poo-poo-poo-poo." Usually, such language is best ignored. If it seems unduly disruptive, you might tell the children involved that bathroom language is restricted to the bathroom. Children also enjoy repeating adult swear words, usually unaware of their meaning but knowing that such words are somehow inappropriate. Let children know that swear words are not acceptable at school. This is particularly important if children use

Young children delight in language play. The teacher can structure activities that tickle the children's funny bones, or, as often is the case, children will find their own ways to play with language. Silly words, nonsense words, bathroom terms, and rhyming words are favorites.

words that are intended to hurt others, for instance, racial or ethnic slurs.

Language Activities

In addition to the ongoing use of language in the early childhood program, specific activities based on language use and elaboration are also incorporated. Such activities are often presented at large or small group times, enhancing not just language but listening skills, group social skills, creative thinking, concept formation, and other areas of development.

Stories, in their various forms, are the most popular vehicle for such activities. Stories can be told or read by teachers, children, or both together; they can be enacted by children or with flannel board pieces, puppets, or play dough; or they can come from the rich store of children's literature or be made up out of the fabric of the children's experiences. We will briefly look at some of the ways in which stories can be used and presented.

Book reading is one of the most popular language activities; good children's books on a variety of topics are available.

Books. The most popular story activity in most early childhood programs is book reading. Very young children enjoy book reading, and teachers should certainly incorporate reading into the routine of infants and toddlers. Because so many excellent books are available for young children, they provide a wealth of ways to contribute to language experience, reinforce concepts, entertain, stimulate thought, and offer emotional support.

Many children have had happy experiences with books all of their lives. They approach book reading activities anticipating enjoyment; they also have developed the concentration and attention required for full involvement. Others may not have had many such opportunities and may need some individual, more intimate story reading time to help them acquire a greater appreciation for books.

Some techniques help engage children in the book reading process. For one thing, teachers play a vital role in how children respond to story reading. In a sense, they endorse the story through their enthusiasm, interest in the story, animation, and the use of their voices

Book reading remains a perennial favorite among language activities for young children. The teacher makes the book come alive through her voice inflection and animation.

as tools in making the characters and action come alive. In addition, book reading—whether with the large group, a small group, or an individual child—should be interactive rather than a one-way endeavor. Children should have opportunities to comment on and discuss the story and illustrations, speculate on what might happen next, and relate the story to their personal experiences. When children listen only passively, learning is less likely to be taking place, and many children may well tune out. It is important to keep in mind that it is not the words themselves, but the relevance of those words to the children's lives that make books meaningful; that relevance is explored through discussion between children and teacher (Teale & Martinez, 1988).

Many wonderful books are available for young children, spanning a wide range of appropriate and relevant topics. Among these are storybooks on familiar topics, fairy tales and fables, informational nonfiction books, wordless books, alphabet books, and therapeutic books (see the discussion on bibliotherapy in Chapter 17) (Machado, 1985). A school should have a good selection of children's books in its own library, rotating them as curriculum topics and the children's interests change. In addition, the local community library can expand the available supply. Figure 12-1 lists guidelines for selecting children's books.

KEY QUESTION #4

Read a book written for preschool-aged children. Does this book appeal to you? Do you think it will appeal to children? Evaluate this book using the criteria outlined in Figure 12-1.

Poetry. In many early childhood programs, poetry is a sadly neglected aspect of literature, perhaps because teachers have not had much exposure to poetry themselves. This is unfortunate, because appropriate poems can broaden children's experiences and add a magical aspect to language activities (Andrews, 1988). The cadence of well-rhymed words, as is true with music, invites attention and involvement. Poetry's strongest appeal is its "singing quality" (Sutherland & Arbuthnot, 1986). Poems, like any literature, must interest children, speaking to a familiar experience or delighting with their nonsense and humor. For instance, children can relate to Robert Louis Stevenson's poem, "Bed in Summer" (1985), a child's complaint about having to go to bed when the sky outside is still blue—just as they enjoy the silly image of the "Mother Goose" cow jumping over the moon or Shel Silverstein's humorous poems.

FIGURE 12-1 Criteria for selecting children's books

The books you select for children should meet the best standards, both for literary and artistic quality. Although more than 2,000 children's books are published every year, the fact that a book is in print does not necessarily assure that it is good (Sword, 1987). There are some published guides to selecting high-quality children's books (for instance, the monthly *Bulletin of the Center for Children's Books,* the bimonthly *Horn Book Magazine,* or the American Library Association's *Notable Children's Books*), and resource persons such as children's librarians can prove extremely helpful. But it is also important to develop a sense of what constitutes a good book (Glazer, 1986). As you review books to read to children, apply the following guidelines (Glazer, 1986; Goodman et al., 1987; Machado, 1985; Sword, 1987).

Overall Impression

- The length of the book should be appropriate to the ages of the children. Although engrossing stories of increasing length should be presented as children get older, 5 to 10 minutes (not including discussion) is generally a good time limit for children over age three. Primary children will listen for longer periods to an engrossing story.
- The amount of text per page should also be considered. Especially young preschoolers will find long text with few pictures difficult.
- The size of the book is important, particularly when you read to a group of children. Very small books should be kept for one-on-one reading sessions. Children do enjoy many of the new oversized books.
- The binding of a book is important if you are planning to buy it for the school library. Sturdy binding will ensure durability. Some schools prefer buying less expensive books such as paperbacks, which won't last as long but the cost is only one-third or one-fourth that of hardbound books. Sturdy cardboard and cloth books are available for infants and toddlers.

Text Elements

- Read the book carefully and consider whether the plot or story line is coherent and interesting. The plot doesn't have to be complex, but it should be plausible and logical. The adventure of Max in Maurice Sendak's *Where the Wild Things Are* is a good example of a well-written plot that appeals to young children.
- The characters of the book should be distinctive and memorable, should not be stereotyped, and should provide children something with which they can identify. Children have no trouble remembering mischievous Curious George or spunky Madeline from their books.
- Characters in many books represent diversity according to racial, gender, age, and ability diversity. Ensure that such portrayals are sensitive and accurate, promote inclusion, and help strengthen children's value of differences.
- Many books revolve around a theme, for instance, friendship, emotional reactions, or exploration (Smith, 1989). If there is a theme, it should not sound like a sermon. A theme should also be relevant to young children's lives and worth sharing with them. Ann Scott's *On Mother's Lap* contains the common theme of jealousy over a new sibling, an experience with which many children can relate.
- As you review a book, pay close attention to the style of writing. Language should be simple but vivid and evoke appropriate mood and images. Because children delight in repetition and humor, look for some books that incorporate these elements. Children love to chime in the refrain of Wanda Gag's *Millions of Cats* as the old couple's acquisition of cats reaches the ludicrous stage with "hundreds of cats, thousands of cats, millions, and billions, and trillions of cats!"

Illustrations

- Above all, pictures should be aesthetic, complementing and enlivening the words of the story. Many skilled artists' talents enrich children's books. Illustrators use numerous, effective ways to convey the story in pictures. As you browse through some children's classics, compare the whimsical characters of Dr. Seuss, the humorous pen-and-ink drawings of Maurice Sendak, or the impressionistic watercolors of Brian Wildsmith.
- Pictures should be placed adjacent to the text so the story and illustrations work in harmony.

Storytelling. Telling rather than reading a story from a book can be a more direct, intimate experience (Machado, 1985) and can stimulate children's imagination as they visualize the story line and characters. The story can be original, pulled from a proficient teacher's imagination, or it can be a paraphrased version of a book or folktale. Of course, the teacher's skill in holding the children's attention through eye contact, voice variation, and dramatic pauses contributes considerably to storytelling.

Stories can also be told by children, either individually or as a group activity. In particular, older children, who have well-developed language fluency and vocabulary, enjoy making up original stories, which can be recorded in writing by an adult or tape recorded if you wish to preserve them. Although storytelling can be prompted by showing children a picture or a wordless book, many children will tell much more elaborate stories without such guides (Hough, Nurss, & Wood, 1987). In fact, research links beginning reading skills and the development of literacy to opportunities for telling as well as listening to stories.

Flannel Board Stories. A version of storytelling with props, flannel board stories easily capture children's attention as they look forward to seeing what will be put on the board next (Machado, 1985). A flannel- or felt-covered board serves as a background, while felt, fabric, or pellon cutouts of characters are used to relay the story. A selection of favorite stories can be available for the teachers' and children's use through a flannel board story file (see the discussion of teacher-made materials in Chapter 7).

Poetry, storytelling, flannel board stories, lap board stories, story enactment, and puppets are variations of language activities that children enjoy.

Flannel board stories can be derived from a variety of sources including favorite books and poems, nursery rhymes, teacher-made stories, and stories based on the children's experiences such as field trips. A new flannel board story can be presented during a group time, then the props left out so the children can retell the story in their own way later. In addition, a selection of familiar flannel board stories can be placed in the language arts area of the classroom for children's everyday use.

Lap Board Stories. Another variation of storytelling, which includes both children and the teacher, is lap board stories (Essa & Rogers, 1992). Two elements are involved: the children, with the teacher's prompting, tell a story while the teacher creates the characters, props, and action of the story with play dough. Manipulating the play dough on a small board in her lap, the teacher "illustrates" the emerging story that the children tell. These depictions of the story, however, are not artistically formed but merely suggest what they represent (for instance, a ball of dough with two "ears" pinched into the top can be a dog). In fact, if the teacher pays too much attention to sculpting perfect forms, this tends to be too time consuming and distracting in lap board stories.

As the story emerges, the pieces can be moved around to show action, they can disappear by merging back into the larger play dough mass, and they can grow by adding more play dough. One group of preschoolers, who had watched two neighborhood squirrels pick up some crackers the children had left outside, decided to retell what they had observed in a lap board story. They were delighted to see the play dough "cookies" disappear as the hungry "squirrel" gobbled them up; in turn, the squirrel grew fatter with each cookie it engulfed. Children who participate in lap board storytelling find the emerging play dough enactment a good stimulus to storytelling.

Story Enactment. Children respond with great enthusiasm to opportunities to enact favorite stories. Story enactment involves both language and social skills as children cooperate and share the roles of a given story. Stories such as "The Three Little Pigs," "Goldilocks and the Three Bears," "Caps for Sale," And "Stone Soup" provide important elements such as repetitive dialogue, strong action lines, and familiarity. These stories can and should be adapted as needed, however, to incorporate the children's interests, increase repetitive elements, elaborate on what is most familiar to the children, simplify the plot if it is too complex, or challenge sex-role stereotypes. For instance, several children can play the role of Goldilocks while the teacher takes on the other roles, Papa Bear can cook the porridge, or a female hunter can save Little Red Riding Hood and Grandma (Ishee & Goldhaber, 1990).

Puppets. Another way to enact stories is to use puppets as the actors. A makeshift stage made from a table set on its side, or a more elaborate one with curtains, can provide the backdrop; alternately, puppets can be used to enact a story without such a setting. A variety of commercial, teacher-made, or child-made puppets can help enact the story. Teachers can use puppets to convey a story during group time because children enjoy watching a lively puppet show. The puppets can be left out for the children to reenact the story or to make up a different one later. Puppets can be an ongoing part of the language arts center, however, inviting children to engage in puppetry at other times. Puppets allow children to project onto another character ideas and feelings that they might hesitate to express as their own. Puppets can also help a shy child by allowing that child to speak through an intermediary.

Emergent Literacy

Emergent literacy acknowledges that reading and writing are ongoing processes that begin early in life.

Emergent literacy—The ongoing, dynamic process of learning to read and write, which starts in the early years.

As we have seen, children learn to understand and express language in a natural way, through a process that begins very early in life. Similarly, children also begin to form an understanding of reading and writing, something that has come to interest researchers and educators only relatively recently. The term **emergent literacy** acknowledges that learning to read and write (in other words, to become literate) is a dynamic, ongoing, emerging process. In fact, all aspects of language—listening, speaking, writing, and reading—are intertwined and develop concurrently, not sequentially (Teale & Sulzby, 1986). A Closer Look illustrates one teacher's strategies to encourage emergent literacy in her class.

Children develop this understanding of reading and writing through a supportive literate environment, starting at home and furthered in the early childhood program. Catherine Snow concludes that when parents read to their young children, these children's language is more complex than it is during other times of play. Furthermore, in the process of early reading, parents help their children acquire some of the basic rules of literacy, learning that books are for reading rather than manipulating or that books represent an autonomous fictional world (Snow & Ninio, 1986). Both home and school experiences with books provide children with further insights, for example, that print should make sense, that print and speech are related, that book language is different from speech, and that books are enjoyable (Schickedanz, 1986). Out of many experiences with the printed form of the language come the foundations for writing and reading.

Learning to Write. The beginnings of writing emerge early in life through a number of antecedent steps. Vygotsky (1978) (recall the discussion of his theory in Chapter 5) traces the roots of writing to earliest infant gestures, described as "writing in the air." During the preschool years, children become aware of the differences between drawing and writing, a distinction that is evident in their own efforts. By age three, many children begin to use **mock writing,** a series of wavy, circular, or vertical lines that deliberately imitate adult writing and are distinctly different from drawing. Within the next couple of years, mock writing increasingly becomes a mixture of real letters and innovative symbols.

By early elementary school, most children who have grown up in a pleasurable, literate environment and who recognize most or all of the letters of the alphabet begin to use **invented spelling** by finding the speech sound that most closely fits what they want to write (Atkins, 1984). Five-year-old Abby wrote, "I M GNG TO DRV MI KAR AT HOM" (I am going to drive my car at home) in one of her stories, accompanied by a picture of Abby atop a blue vehicle. Analysis of the errors seen in invented spelling indicates that children are trying to work out a system of rules, just as they did when, as toddlers, they were acquiring oral language. Because reading and writing are intertwined processes, such early attempts at phonemic spelling are soon replaced with more conventional forms as children repeatedly come across the same words in their reading (Atkins, 1984).

Young children engage in mock writing, which is distinctly different from drawing and scribbling.

Mock writing—Young children's imitation of writing through wavy, circular, or vertical lines, which can be seen as distinct from drawing or scribbling.

KEY QUESTION #5

Examine some samples of children's artwork. Do you see examples of mock writing? Are there letters included? Are there any recognizable words written in invented spelling by the child?

Some older preschoolers may begin to use invented spelling by finding speech sounds that most closely fit what they want to write.

Invented spelling—Used by young children in their early attempts to write by finding the speech sound that most clearly fits what they want to convey.

Mock writing is distinct from children's scribbling or drawing and appears at a relatively early age. A three-year-old, for instance, may tell you he is "writing a letter," using mock writing in a deliberate imitation of adult writing. Look at samples of children's artwork and see if you can find examples of mock writing.

The ability to read also emerges gradually, as children increasingly make sense out of print.

Learning to Read. When children read and write, they are *"making sense out of or through print"* (italics used in original text), although this sense does not require an understanding of a conventional alphabetic code (Goodman, 1986, p. 5). Eventually, children do acquire this understanding as they learn the consistent relationship between the letters of the alphabet and their use in the written form. Early literacy, however, is based on the growing awareness that print means something, for instance, that a stop sign indicates "step on the brake."

Two-year-olds often already display such awareness, for example, pointing to a word in a book and saying, "That's my name" (Walton, 1989). By age three, children clearly have substantial understanding of why and how print is used. Many four-year-olds have developed the ability to recognize a variety of words when these are presented in their appropriate context, for instance, common labels and signs. Experiences in recognizing words in their environmental context help children learn about the process of reading and lead to eventual recognition of these words out of their context (Kontos, 1986).

Children actively seek to make sense of print in their environment by using a variety of strategies that they themselves invent (Willert & Kamii, 1985). Younger preschoolers' strategies focus on such clues as the first letter of a word ("That's my name," says Paul, "because it's got a 'P'."); looking at the shape of the word, such as its length or spacing if there is more than one word in a configuration; and using pictures as clues to help decipher accompanying words. As children get older and more experienced in acquiring reading skills, they use some additional strategies. Included are looking for familiar letters or combinations of letters in words; spontaneously and repeatedly practicing the spelling and copying of words; and inventing a phonological system to sound out words, similar to that used in inventive spelling. Gradually they internalize the conventional rules of reading, as they become proficient readers in the early grades.

Implications. As the preceding discussions suggest, young children have a natural interest in the print environment around them, an interest most of them express through their own inventive attempts at writing and reading. This view of how children learn to read and write is far removed from some of the stereotyped notions of reading and writing as formal subjects best begun in first grade. Thinking of literacy merely as recognizing words or the sounds of letters "is as dangerous as it is erroneous" (Gibson, 1989, p. 30).

Yet, all too often, young children are placed into high-powered, rigid, formalized programs that focus on isolated skills involved in the reading process, rather than on the integration of all aspects of language. In fact, a statement expressing concern over this developmentally inappropriate practice was jointly prepared by a consortium of relevant organizations (International Reading Association, 1986).

Reading and writing emerge from many successful and enjoyable experiences with language, both oral and written. According to research, literacy best develops through meaningful context in an informal, supportive environment (Kontos, 1986). As Judith Schickedanz (1982), one of the leading authorities in children's emergent literacy, writes:

Commonly seen words that appear on labels and signs are among the first that children "read." This four-year-old recognizes the word "milk" on the carton.

> **We need to abandon ideas and practices that assume early literacy development to be simply a matter of teaching children a few basic skills such as alphabet recognition or letter-sound associations. Much more is involved. Limiting children's reading experiences to contacts with bits and pieces of print isolated from meaningful contexts may actually prevent them from developing broader and more complex insights that are the key to understanding what written language is all about. (p. 259)**

Promoting Literacy Development. Literacy, like oral language, emerges in a natural way that does not require formal teaching to prompt interest. What it does need is a language-rich environment to encourage its development. Literacy is best promoted in the context of a **whole language approach,** one in which high-quality oral and print language surrounds children, children can observe others using literacy skills, and they are encouraged to experiment with all forms of language. Such an approach integrates all forms of communication, including speaking, listening, writing, reading, art, music, and math (International Reading Association, 1986). It is also dependent on the support, modeling, and mediation of adults and more experienced peers within the zone of proximal development, as described by Vygotsky (Manson & Sinha, 1993). Recall from Chapter 5 that, according to Vygotsky, children can acquire new skills that are too difficult for them to complete alone but which they can accomplish with some guided help from someone more experienced. While the whole language approach is widely supported, it is also suggested that it be combined with other methods that can help children develop literacy and acquire reading and writing skills. NAEYC's revised *Developmentally Appropriate Practice in Early Childhood Programs Serving Children from Birth Through Age 8* (Bredekamp & Copple, 1997), for instance, recommends a balance between the whole language approach and the more traditional teaching of phonics. The following suggestions for supporting literacy development come from a variety of sources.

A whole language approach surrounds children with high-quality oral and written language and encourages them to use language in all its forms.

Whole language approach—Strategy for promoting literacy by surrounding children with high-quality oral and print language.

- The aim of supporting literacy development in young children should be to enhance their *desire* to read and write by building on their intrinsic motivation to learn these skills (Willer & Kamii, 1985).

- A language-rich environment must contain many materials, opportunities, and experiences for planned and spontaneous interaction with language, both oral and written. This means providing appropriate materials and scheduled time blocks for children to pursue language activities (Machado, 1985; Teale & Martinez, 1988).
- A carefully selected library of high-quality children's books must be available. Good books attract children's interest so they often seek them out to browse through or to ask a teacher to read.
- Stories should not just be read but should be discussed. Children understand stories better when they have opportunities to ask and answer questions about the plot and characters of a story and relate the story to their own lives (Teale & Martinez, 1988; Walton, 1989).
- One important skill for early reading is story awareness. Children need many story-reading experiences to acquire a sense of what a story is and how it is organized. Knowing, for instance, how a story begins and ends and the story's sequence of events is important to literacy development (Jensen, 1985).
- Books should be read more than one time. Children are more likely to reenact a book on their own if they have heard it at least three times (Teale & Martinez, 1988).
- Children should be encouraged to "read" to each other, whether or not they actually know how to read (Teale & Martinez, 1988).
- If some children in the class seem to have had few one-on-one reading experiences at home, time should be set aside for story reading, for instance, during self-selected activity blocks when a teacher can spend time reading to just one or two children (Jensen, 1985).
- Print awareness can be supported through books as well as through other forms of print in the school environment. Charts, lists, labels, and bulletin boards that surround children in the environment contribute to print awareness, as does a teacher who

Children enjoy reading to each other as well as hearing an adult read to them. A favorite story, heard many times, can be "read" to an interested audience.

interprets, calls attention to, and gets the children's input when creating print (Goodman, Smith, Meredith, & Goodman, 1987; Schickedanz, 1986).

- Children gradually learn that there is a relationship between written and spoken words. When children are read certain books frequently, they often become so familiar with the stories that they know which words correspond with which pages. Such experiences contribute to making the connection between speech and print (Schickedanz, 1986).
- Children should be provided with a variety of reading and writing materials to incorporate into their play. For example, paper, pencils, markers, and other implements in the art, language arts, dramatic play, science, and math areas should be included to suggest a link between the activities that go on in those areas and reading/writing.
- Given a supportive atmosphere, children will engage in story writing. Although children may not be using conventional letters and words, their stories as well as the writing process are still full of meaning. The sensitive teacher must carefully attend to what children are conveying to understand that meaning (Harste, Short, & Burke, 1988).
- One way of promoting storytelling and writing is to include a "writing table" as an ongoing activity center in the classroom (Bakst & Essa, 1990). The teacher writes down children's dictated stories but also encourages the children to write their stories.
- Stories should be shared, something that can be done informally as other children come to the writing table or more formally during a large group activity. When their stories are shared, children develop **audience awareness,** an appreciation that their stories are a form of communication that should make sense to others (Bakst & Essa, 1990).
- Some children show little interest in reading and writing, perhaps because they have had little access to materials that promote these activities. One successful strategy to stimulate this interest is to provide a "writing suitcase" that the children can take home overnight or over a weekend. This suitcase can include such materials as various sizes and shapes of paper and notebooks; chalk and chalkboard, pencils, crayons, and markers; magnet, cardboard, or plastic letters and stencils; favorite picture books; scissors; and tape, glue, stapler, hole punch, and ruler (Rich, 1985).

Audience awareness—Children's growing awareness that their stories are a form of communication that should make sense to others.

PARENTAL VALUES FOR LANGUAGE DEVELOPMENT

Parents and teachers share the task of providing the experiences that will best promote language acquisition in young children. Language learning is furthered when teachers and parents share goals, insights, and information through regular communication. By the very fact that

Working closely with parents ensures support for language and emergent literacy development.

parents do not set out to "teach" their young children oral language, they consciously or unconsciously appreciate that language learning is a natural process that they promote through modeling and interaction. It is assumed that children will learn language.

Yet parents often do not have the same intuitive understanding of children's literacy learning, although they may well be providing many high-quality language experiences that will lead to competent, literate children. Some parents assume that learning to read and write begins in elementary school and is best left until the child reaches the appropriate age. Others, anxious that their children will succeed in school, may seek formal reading and writing training in the preschool years to give their children a head start. It is important, therefore, that as an early childhood teacher you convey to parents your philosophy of a whole language approach to language and literacy development.

Share with parents information through articles and books that point out the early beginnings of literacy development. You might, for instance, provide parents with a copy of the International Reading Association's statement, published in *Young Children* in 1996, which addresses appropriate and inappropriate reading practices. Help parents recognize the many ways in which their children engage in reading and writing every day and how they, as parents, facilitate this.

Also reinforce that the many activities they already engage in with their children—book reading, talking, shared time, outings, matching and sorting games, identifying food labels and road signs—contribute immensely to language and literacy development. Following are some suggestions for enhancing this development, which you can share with parents (Mavrogenes, 1990).

- Provide an environment that conveys the value of literacy. Let children see their parents reading and writing. Make books, magazines, and newspapers an important part of the home. A literate environment need not be expensive when the community library or a lending library from the early childhood program is used.
- Make reading time with the child a special daily occasion. Read as well as discuss books.
- Give books as presents for birthdays and holidays.
- Make writing materials available to children. A special writing area with paper, pencils, markers, envelopes, memo pads, and forms from school, restaurants, or the doctor's office will encourage writing as well as incorporation of writing into pretend play.
- Help children write letters to friends and relatives or to the author of a favorite book.
- Write special word or picture notes to children and put these in their lunch boxes.
- Write out grocery lists and recipes with children to illustrate the usefulness of writing.
- Share with parents the titles of favorite school books that their children particularly enjoy.

It is reassuring to parents when teachers frequently reinforce the point that children are enthusiastic and active learners in all areas, including language and literacy. It is particularly important that teachers find ways to communicate this message to parents whose children are learning English as a new language. Usually, in such a case, there is also a language barrier between teachers and parents. Teachers can meet this challenge by finding an interpreter to help in communication, by learning some words and phrases in the family's primary language and using these in combination with nonverbal messages, and by recommending English instruction for the parents, if this is appropriate.

Finally, teachers of infants and toddlers can reinforce the importance of reading to very young children by encouraging parents to use simple picture books with their little ones. When parents see sturdy books included in infant and toddler rooms, or note teachers routinely reading to babies, they may be encouraged to engage in this activity at home as well.

SUMMARY

1. There are several divergent theoretical views of language development.
2. Some components of language can help us understand the complexity of all that children attain during their early years.
3. Because many early childhood programs include children who speak a language other than English, consider bilingualism and effective strategies for teaching children a second language.
4. Many components of the early childhood program support and reinforce language learning:
   A. Conversations and language play offer many spontaneous opportunities for language learning.
   B. Also consider some of the many types of planned activities aimed at enhancing language.
   C. Emergent literacy is children's ongoing process of learning reading and writing.

KEY TERMS LIST

audience awareness
babbling
behaviorist view of language development
bilingualism
code switching
cognitive interactionist view of language development
cooing
deep structure
dialect
Ebonics
emergent literacy
immersion programs
innatist view of language development
interactionist view of language development
invented spelling
mock writing
morphology
nonimmersion programs
overextension
pragmatics
semantic network
semantics
simultaneous language acquisition
social interactionist view of language development
successive language acquisition
surface structure
syntax
whole language approach

chapter 13

Social Development Through the Curriculum

One major function of the early childhood program is to facilitate the process of **socialization,** the means through which children become a functioning part of society and learn society's rules and values. Socialization is a lifelong process that begins from the first day of life; during the early years, the foundation for later attitudes, values, and behaviors is laid.

Unquestionably, socialization begins with the parent-child relationships in infancy, where patterns of response, need fulfillment, and give-and-take have their roots. When children come to the early childhood program they have already had a lifetime of socializing experiences. They may have learned to trust or be wary of others, to meet new experiences enthusiastically or with caution, to care about others' feelings because their needs have always been considered, or to think of others as competitors for affection or resources.

Because socialization is such an important responsibility of the early childhood teacher, we will consider some of its facets in more than one chapter. This chapter will focus primarily on the development of social competence as it is facilitated and supported through the curriculum; the following chapters discuss guidance techniques that facilitate the development of positive social skills. The term *curriculum* as used in this chapter does not refer solely to the planned activities of the day, but also includes all the elements in the environment that lead to conversations and activities that promote socialization.

THEORETICAL VIEWS OF THE SOCIALIZATION PROCESS

Recall that in Chapter 5 we considered the work of Erik Erikson, whose psychosocial theory of young children's stages of development has had

Socialization—The process through which children become a functioning part of society and learn society's rules and values.

KEY QUESTION #1

As we discuss in this chapter, becoming socialized into society is a complex process. Which early childhood activities and teacher behaviors do you think contribute to this goal?

An understanding of Erikson's theory is important for developing an appropriate social environment for young children.

tremendous influence on early education. Although we will not review this theory in detail here, keep in mind Erikson's emphasis on the importance of providing for children a social environment in which people can be trusted, children can safely exercise their growing independence, and many opportunities to explore and experience competence are available. A good early childhood program is built on the premise that children's needs for trust, autonomy, initiative, and industry must be met.

We will consider three theoretical views that are pertinent to our discussion of socialization. One important view of how children become socialized has stemmed from the work of Jean Piaget. This approach centers on the idea that children construct all knowledge, including social knowledge. This contrasts with the behaviorist idea that social knowledge is transmitted through environmental and cultural means (Edwards, 1986). A third view, the sociohistoric theory of Lev Vygotsky, focuses on the role of adults and more experienced peers in the transmission of social values.

The constructivist view of socialization holds that children gain social knowledge through the same process used in gaining other knowledge, by constructing it from their experiences.

Social cognition—Organization of knowledge and information about people and relationships.

The Constructivist View of Socialization

In the Piagetian view of social development, social knowledge is acquired much in the same way as other knowledge (refer to Chapter 11). Children use their evolving **social cognition,** or understanding of other people's problems and how they feel, to organize and structure information about people and relationships in a way similar to the one used in organizing and structuring information about the physical properties of their world (Kohlberg, 1966). For instance, children classify the people they meet in relation to themselves and their own existing schema, which have, of course, been shaped by their culture. As with all other learning, such understanding comes from the child's active involvement, not from passive transmission of information. As part of a complex world, children need to make sense of themselves and others. "Simply by being born into the human family, then, young children are challenged to understand self, others, social and moral relations, and societal institutions" (Edwards, 1986, p. 3).

Social learning theory suggests that children learn social behaviors through observation and imitation.

Social learning theory—Theoretical view derived from but going beyond behaviorism, which considers that children learn not just from reinforcement but from observing and imitating others.

Observational learning—In social learning theory, the process of learning that comes from watching, noting the behavior of, and imitating models.

Modeling—In social learning theory, the process of imitating a model.

Model—In social learning theory, those whom children imitate, particularly because of some desirable feature or attribute.

The Behaviorist View of Socialization

In contrast to Piagetian theory, the traditional behavioral assumption is that children are taught about the social world when their responses are reinforced by the adults who shape their behavior. **Social learning theory,** which is derived from but goes beyond traditional behaviorism, does not consider reinforcement as always necessary for social learning. From the social learning perspective, children also learn social behaviors through **observational learning,** by observing, noting the behavior of, and imitating or **modeling** their behavior on that of a **model.** Adults and peers can be models. Research has shown that particularly nurturant and warm adult models influence children's social behaviors (Yarrow, Scott, & Waxler, 1973). It is possible that children imitate those they like because they want to be like them. In addition, children are more likely to imitate models they observe being rewarded (Bandura, 1977).

The Vygotskyan View of Socialization

In Chapter 5 you were introduced to Lev Vygotsky, whose sociohistoric theory is particularly pertinent to a consideration of social development. Social development is inseparable from cognitive and language development. It is through language that the child's mind is "joined" with the minds of others to gain insight into the world. "A basic premise of Vygotsky's theory is that all uniquely human, higher forms of mental activity are jointly constructed and transferred to children through dialogues with other people" (Berk, 1994, p. 30). Vygotsky dwells on the role of adults and more experienced peers in transmitting information about the culture and about social skills and expectations. The role of teachers is particularly meaningful in the context of this theory, which underscores their contribution to children's socialization into the larger society. Within the zone of proximal development, the range of tasks that a child is not yet able to do alone but can accomplish with help, teachers are available to children as they learn a variety of skills. In Vygotsky's terms, adults provide **scaffolding**, an evocative term when we think about the type of support and guidance teachers offer children to help them learn socially relevant skills.

Vygotsky helps explain how the development of language is intricately tied to socialization as adults and more experienced peers help transmit culturally and socially relevant information to young children.

Scaffolding—In Vygotsky's sociohistoric theory, the support provided by adults and older peers to help children learn the new tasks they are not yet able to accomplish on their own.

DEVELOPMENT OF SOCIAL COMPETENCE

As increasing numbers of young children enter group care, they experience increasingly intimate peer contact (Howes, 1987). By age three or four, most children are part of a social world that is truly egalitarian, a world of peers who are equals (Moore, 1982). In this world, children are expected to share and cooperate, to learn the rules and expectations. As young children go through this process of becoming socialized to the peer society, they gain skill and competence in peer interaction, enter into friendships, develop gender identity, adopt racial and cultural attitudes, form a sense of morals and values, and acquire a host of prosocial behaviors.

The opportunity to develop multicultural, multiracial, and multieconomic acceptance will, to a large extent, depend on the integrative

A good early childhood program is an ideal setting for children to gain skills in positive peer socialization. Sensitive adult guidance and an appropriate environment and program are important in this process.

A Closer Look

What Early Childhood Educators Have Always Known

Very recently, the media, politicians, and the general public have "discovered" the importance of the first three years of life. Yet early childhood educators have always recognized the vital significance of the earliest years of development in a child's life. Two decades of research on the development of the brain caught the public eye and became newsworthy; this information was promoted by national publications such as *Newsweek* (Begley, 1996) and *Time* (Nash, 1997), an ABC television special called "I Am Your Child," and a White House Conference on Early Childhood Development and Learning. In addition, an increasing number of states are funding programs that promote the well-being of young children and families. Babies, and by implication their care and nurture, have become a matter of public attention.

Many early childhood professionals see this heightened awareness as a not-to-be-missed opportunity to build public support for the field of early childhood education. "With plans to make further links between science and education, early childhood professionals and advocates may find increased support for our cause—public understanding and support for child care that guarantees proper nutrition, well-planned physical environments, and developmentally appropriate practices to ensure the most promising future for all young children and families" (Newberger, 1997, p. 9).

The public has been made aware of the miracle of early brain development but has also been cautioned about the possibility of irreversible loss when a baby does not form secure attachments or receive the love, attention, nurture, and consistency needed for optimal development. In a widely circulated publication called *Starting Points: Meeting the Needs of Our Youngest Children,* the Carnegie Corporation (1994) announced its conclusions that our country is facing a "quiet crisis" through its neglect of young children's needs. Indicators include the inadequate prenatal care experienced by nearly one-fourth of pregnant women; the increase in number of single parents and isolation from family support systems; substandard child care; the poverty of one-fourth of the families with children under the age of three; the rising infant mortality rate and declining immunization rate; the increase in child abuse, neglect, and injury; and the insufficient attention many young children receive in terms of intellectual stimulation to prepare them for school.

The Carnegie report also underscores the critical importance of the first three years of life, particularly in the link of brain development and the importance of a secure, loving environment. The social environment within which the baby is raised is all-important in optimizing the potential of the brain. "Brain development is much more vulnerable to environmental influence than we ever suspected. . . . the environment affects not only the number of brain cells and number of connections among them, but also the way these connections are 'wired'" (Carnegie, 1994, p. 4).

Such information has heightened public awareness so that there is an increased base of support for what early childhood educators have intuitively known and supported: "warm, everyday interaction—cuddling infants closely or singing to toddlers—actually helps prepare children for learning through life. More and more we begin to understand the biological reasons behind this" (Newberger, 1997, p. 5).

nature of the early childhood program. Although programs can help children learn about people from diverse backgrounds, early childhood programs tend to be rather homogeneous, joining children from a common racial, cultural, and economic milieu.

Children have many opportunities each day to learn to be helpful and consider the needs of others. Recall the discussion in Chapter 1 of the advantages of mixed-aged grouping. What are some other positive effects on social development in the class that this three-year-old and five-year-old are part of?

Peer Interaction

Peer interaction is an essential ingredient in the process of childhood socialization, in fact, to the total development of the child (Hartup, 1983). Such interactions begin in infancy, when as early as two months of age, babies show an interest in peers. By the middle of the first year, they direct smiles and vocalizations toward other infants. The imitation that becomes a part of babies' repertoire is also integrated into peer play; very young children often develop games based on imitation that they play with each other (Ladd & Coleman, 1993).

The early childhood setting offers an ideal opportunity for young children to develop social skills with peers. As with any skill, it is through practice in real situations that children develop competence in peer interaction. The many naturally occurring opportunities of day-to-day life allow children to be sympathetic and helpful to peers (Honig, 1982). These social skills include the many strategies children learn to help them initiate and continue social interactions, to negotiate, and to settle conflicts (Smith, 1982).

For young children who are just entering peer relationships, adult guidance—not interference—is important; as children get older and less egocentric, the presence of an adult becomes less necessary (Howes, 1987; Oden, 1982). The teacher, in facilitating social development, first must provide children with ample time and space and appropriate materials to facilitate social interaction. A child who has difficulty engaging in social play can be helped through sensitive teacher guidance, for instance, directing that child to a group with similar play interests or pairing the child with a more socially competent peer (Rogers & Ross, 1986).

The early childhood teacher facilitates development of positive peer relationships from infancy on by means of guidance and by setting an appropriate environment.

Older children also provide excellent models for younger peers. In one study, the pretend play of two-year-olds was characterized as much more cooperative and complex when they were paired with five-year-olds than with fellow toddlers (Howes & Farver, 1987). This research supports the idea of providing children in child care with some opportunities for mixed-age interaction.

Friendship

One special type of peer relationship is friendships, that close link between people typified by mutual concern, sharing, and companionship. Recent research points to the importance of early friendship to later emotional well-being (Flaste, 1991). Young children's concept of friendship is limited, primarily revolving around the immediate situation with little thought to the enduring nature of friendship. As children grow older, their friendships typically become more stable (Damon, 1983).

Toddlers begin to develop friendships, although early friendships are more concerned with the immediate situation than with long-term commitments.

KEY QUESTION #2

What is your earliest recollection of a friendship? Can you recall why this friendship developed? How long did it last? What was special about this particular friend? What feelings does your recollection of this friendship evoke right now?

Nonetheless, there is growing research evidence that toddlers form early friendships, showing preference for and affection toward

These friends enjoy a special reunion each morning when they get to their preschool. Many young children begin to form friendships, forging a unique and close bond with a peer.

specific peers. Such early friendships, which sometimes continue on for many years, also have strong affective ties and show characteristics similar to the attachment behavior seen between young children and adults (Ladd & Coleman, 1993).

Preschoolers view friends in terms of their accessibility, physical attributes, and actions rather than their personality traits (Rubin, 1980). In other words, a friend is "someone you play with a lot," "someone who wears a Batman T-shirt," "someone who invites you to her birthday party," or "someone who isn't mean." Another insight into early friendship can be found in the often-heard question, "Are you my friend?" which can be translated to mean, "Will you play with me?" (Edwards, 1986).

Preschoolers expect friendships to maximize enjoyment, entertainment, and satisfaction in play (Parker & Gottman, 1989). Young children are focused on themselves, their own feelings and needs; not until later in childhood do they shift to a greater awareness of the needs and feelings of others (Rubin, 1980). Yet, as many observers have noted, young children are also surprisingly capable of caring about and giving emotional support to each other (Levinger & Levinger, 1986); for instance, observe the concern of onlookers when a child cries because he is hurt or distressed.

By the time children enter elementary school, their peer group has become a much more important source of support. Peers are influential in determining many aspects of primary children's lives, including what to wear, how to behave, and how to speak. Children's self-esteem is more strongly affected by peers than in earlier years. Children also become more selective in their choice of "best friends," almost always of the same sex, the one or few other children to whom they have a strong attachment (Click, 1994).

Trust is the basic foundation on which friendship is built. Children who are trustworthy, who share and cooperate, are more likely to be considered as friends by their peers. Trust in the peer relationship, however, does not simply emerge, but is built on the sense of trust that children established early in life (as described by Erikson), when nurturing adults met their needs consistently. Teachers can help children develop a sense of trust, which can enhance friendships, through their support and guidance. More specifically, they can help children recognize their own needs and goals and those of others, develop more effective social skills (strategies will be discussed in more detail in the next chapter), recognize how their behavior affects others, and become aware of their own social successes so they can be repeated (Buzzelli & File, 1989).

Gender Role Development

Children tend to choose playmates of the same sex, a tendency that increases with age.

Research has shown that one of the most powerful determinants of peer interaction and friendship is the children's sex. If you work with young children, you will have observed that the majority of their playmate choices are of the same sex. This holds true in all cultural settings, not just in America (Maccoby, 1990). Cross-sex friends are not uncommon; however, as they get older, girls increasingly choose to play with other girls and boys seek out other boys as play partners.

EXPERIENCES chapter 13

KELLY, Head Teacher, Infant/Toddler Class

Best Friends . . . At Age One

Our children grow up with each other. For instance, Matt and Jared started in our infant class when they were six weeks and three months old. Now they are two and best of friends. Sometimes it's hard to think of friendship in relation to very young children. But the moment when Matt and Jared's special relationship began can be exactly pinpointed.

Matt was 10 months old and Jared was 8 months old. Both were mobile, loving to crawl around the infant room. One day, by chance, both crawled around the same chair, one from the right, the other from the left. They met in front. They looked at each other, turned around, and crawled back the way they had come. Then they circled the chair again. When they met at the front this time, they smiled at each other. A game was forming. They did this again, then again and again. Soon they were laughing with great glee at their game of hide and seek. They repeated the same game a number of times over the next few weeks.

A friendship had formed. From that time on, they spent a lot of time together. They would follow each other, sometimes Matt crawling in the lead and sometimes Jared. Whoever got to school first would keep a close eye on the door and, when the other arrived, would break into a big smile. When one left before the other at the end of the day, the remaining boy would crawl to the window, pull himself up, and look to see his friend depart. They had also developed their own form of communication, long before oral language had developed. They knew what the other's gestures and expressions meant. Through their second year of life, they increasingly played near each other, usually engaging in parallel play.

Now, at age two, they are best of friends. When the second one arrives in the morning, they hug and kiss each other, showing how happy they are to be together. Their budding verbal skills have increased the scope of their play, but they still know each others' nonverbal cues. From across the room one can sign to the other in an unspoken language to say, "Let's play." At snack and lunch, they sit next to or across from each other. They go down the wide slide together, giggling and laughing all the way. When they play with cars, they invariably bang them into each other, resulting in great outbursts of hilarity. One of their favorite joint activities is to dig in the sand together. Recently, Matt's family went on vacation. Every day, Jared asks, "Where's Matt?" He wants reassurance that Matt will be back.

So, can infants form friendships? Matt and Jared would answer that question with a resounding "yes!" The child care environment places very young children in the unique position of getting to know their peers very well so the magic of friendship can evolve.

experiences

Sex cleavage—Distinct separation based on gender, evident in children at a very young age.

This **sex cleavage,** or distinct separation based on gender, begins to be evident before children reach age three (Howes, 1988). Four-year-olds play with same-sex peers nearly three times as often as with children of the opposite sex; two years later, this preference has increased to elevenfold (Maccoby & Jacklin, 1987). Children choose same-sex friends spontaneously, and attempts to change or influence their choices to encourage more cross-sex interaction have generally not been very successful (Howes, 1988; Katz, 1986; Maccoby, 1990).

KEY QUESTION #3

Observe a group of young children during a time when they can self-select activities. Note with whom they interact. How many of the children interact primarily with peers of the same sex? How many interact with peers of the opposite sex? Estimate the proportion of same-sex and cross-sex interactions.

Much speculation exists about the reasons for this sex cleavage. Eleanor Maccoby (1990), who has been involved in research on gender differences for many years, hypothesizes that girls avoid boys because they find it aversive to interact with unresponsive play partners. She speculates that girls generally dislike boys' competitive, rough-and-tumble play styles and, more importantly, find that they seem to have little influence over boys. The issue of influence becomes increasingly important during early childhood as children learn to integrate and coordinate their activities with those of playmates. In attempts to influence others, girls typically are more polite whereas boys are much more direct; over the span of the preschool years, boys increasingly disregard girls, and girls, in turn, increasingly avoid boys because their efforts to influence them are not successful.

At a very young age, children identify themselves as boys or girls, although they do not realize until between the ages of five and seven that gender is permanent and cannot be changed.

How does this awareness of sex differences develop? Lawrence Kohlberg (1966) discusses a developmental process in the formation of sex-role attitudes. It begins with **gender identity,** when even very young children, often before their second birthdays, accurately identify and label themselves and others as boys or girls based on observable physical cues. Between the ages of five and seven, children acquire **gender stability.** Younger children do not yet realize that they will always remain the same sex; this sense of constancy emerges in middle childhood at about the same time as the development of such cognitive concepts as conservation, for instance, that the amount of clay in a ball does not change even if its shape is changed.

Gender identity—Identification with the same sex.

Gender stability—The recognition by children by age five to seven, but absent in younger children, that sex is constant and cannot be changed.

Another development in this process, evolving during the preschool years and becoming very pronounced by the time the child enters elementary school, is value of the same sex and whatever per-

It is most common for children to seek out same-sex playmates. Boys tend to play typically with male toys; girls usually find typically female toys.

tains to it. Children value the concrete symbols of their gender that confirm their maleness or femaleness, and they construct and adopt a rigid set of rules and stereotypes about what is gender appropriate. This rigidity is consistent with a similar approach to other cognitive concepts. In acquiring same-sex values, children also form an identity with like-sex persons.

When teachers are sensitive to providing a nonsexist, nonstereotyped atmosphere, children will be more likely to develop attitudes based on respect for each person as an individual.

Guidelines for Nonsexist Teaching. This rigidity, children's gravitation toward same-sex peers, and their engagement in gender-stereotyped activities is often troublesome to adults who want children to be broad-minded and tolerant of others. Despite many parents' and teachers' efforts to present nonsexist models to the children in their lives, these same children will often display highly sex-stereotyped behaviors and attitudes. In fact, by the end of the primary years, children often become quite antagonistic toward peers of the opposite sex, engaging in teasing and quarreling (Click, 1994). Some guidelines can help the early childhood teacher lay the foundation for nonbiased attitudes based on respect for each person as an individual.

- **Value each child as an individual.** Focus on the strengths and abilities of each child as a person, and help children recognize and value these characteristics.
- **Help children learn that gender identity is biologically determined.** Before they develop gender constancy, children may feel that it is their preference for boy or girl activities that makes them boys or girls. Reassure them that their bodies, not their activities, determine their sex (Derman-Sparks, 1989).
- **Be aware of possible gender biases in your own behavior.** Studies have shown, for instance, that adults tend to protect girls more, react to boys' misbehaviors more, encourage independence more in boys, and expect girls to be more fearful (Honig, 1983).
- **Listen carefully to all children.** Adults tend to interrupt or speak simultaneously more with girls than with boys, suggesting that what girls have to say is less important (Honig, 1983).
- **Help children find the words to get their nurturance needs met.** Little boys are not as likely to ask for a hug or a lap to sit on as girls are. Teachers can help all children find the right words to communicate their needs for affection (Honig, 1983).
- **Use language carefully, avoiding bias toward male identity.** The English language tends to assume male identity when sex is not clear. We generally say "he" when we don't know whether an animal, person, or storybook character is male or female, and this tricks children into thinking that "hes" are more important and more pervasive than "shes" (Sheldon, 1990).
- **Provide materials that show males and females in a variety of roles.** Puzzles, lotto games, posters, and photographs can portray males and females in nontraditional roles. Dramatic play props can draw children into a variety of roles sometimes stereotyped as male or female.

Boys are less likely to ask for a hug than girls are. It is important, therefore, to help children find the right words to express their needs for nurturance.

- **Select children's books that portray nonsexist models.** Children's literature includes a gamut of characters from the very sex-stereotyped to the very nonsexist. A study of widely read children's books, including award-winning ones, showed that male and female roles are often distorted and stereotyped. Males appear far more often; females, when they are portrayed, tend to be shown as passive and dependent (Flerx, Fidler, & Rogers, 1976).
- **Plan a wide range of activities and encourage all children to participate.** Children will participate in and enjoy a variety of activities—cooking, woodworking, blocks, housekeeping, book browsing, sewing, sand and water, art—if they are well planned and the teacher's words or attitudes do not promote sex stereotyping.
- **Provide gender-neutral toys for infants and toddlers.** Avoid giving the blue rattles and car-shaped teething rings to the boys and the pink, feminine toys to the girls. Similarly, avoid offering gender-specific toys to toddlers; they will quickly pick up the message that dolls are for girls while trucks are for boys!
- **Discuss blatant sex stereotyping with children.** Older preschoolers and primary children, especially if they have been around adults who are sensitive to using nonbiased concepts and vocabulary, can engage in discussions about sex stereotypes in books, favorite television programs, or movies.

Racial and Cultural Awareness and Attitudes

Children develop an awareness of racial differences at an early age.

KEY QUESTION #4

Look around an early childhood classroom to assess how it promotes positive (or negative) attitudes toward other people in relation to sex, race, culture, or disability. What recommendations can you make for setting up a nonbiased classroom?

Similar to their early recognition of gender differences, children also develop an awareness of racial variations at an early age. Although little research has been conducted to document this with children under the age of three, many three-year-olds and most four-year-olds not only recognize racial cues, but also show racial preferences (Katz, 1983). Thus, children at a very young age already have a sense of racial difference. Preschoolers use the most readily visible physical differences as cues; skin color in particular, as well as hair and eye color, provide a basis for comparison and classification.

In a way similar to the process of acquiring gender identity, young children also do not seem to understand fully the permanence of race until they reach the stage of concrete operations in middle childhood. It may be somewhat more difficult for children to develop a sense of racial permanence because many youngsters have limited contact with people of other races, growing up in fairly homogeneous environments. For many children, the primary encounter with people of other races is through television, movies, and books rather than in real life. In addition, children witness contradictory evidence when they see that skin color can be changed by the sun. Some young children, in fact, think that all people start out white but become darker through tanning, dyeing, or painting (Edwards, 1986).

A rather subtle variation in learning about different people arises when children begin to discover cultural differences. Family, neighbor-

hood, school, church, books, and mass media can introduce children to the fact that people meet their daily needs in different ways. All people need to communicate, but they may do so in different languages; all people need to eat, but they don't all eat the same types of foods; all people require clothing, shelter, and transportation, but they meet these needs in unique ways. A focus on the similarities among people should be the basis of multicultural programming for young children.

Although children's cognitive development steers them toward noting differences and classifying accordingly, society applies the comparative values that lead to stereotypes and prejudice. Children are bombarded with subtle and not so subtle messages about the worth of people. Parents, as the primary socializers of their children, seem the obvious transmitters of racial and cultural attitudes; yet, research has shown little relationship between children and their parents in this respect (Katz, 1982). A more plausible source of racial and cultural information may be television, movies, and books that, by their portrayals or by their omissions, imply superiority of some and inferiority of other groups.

In forming their own attitudes, young children continually strive to fit together the multiple and often contradictory sources of information about other people. This was poignantly illustrated to the author a number of years ago by four-year-old Tory, an aggressive child with few friends. Tory stood at the edge of the playground, looking at Muanza, an affable, outgoing child from Kenya. Using a very derogatory term he had heard used about blacks, he said in a sad tone, "The ________ is my only friend." His use of this word stood in sharp contrast to his actual experience with Muanza.

The early childhood curriculum should provide many opportunities for children to learn about themselves and others, to value their own and others' races and cultures, and to develop appreciation and acceptance of diversity.

Guidelines for Teaching About Race and Culture. The early childhood program is an ideal place to help children learn about themselves and others, learn to value and have pride in themselves, and learn to respect others. This involves conveying accurate knowledge about and pride in children's own racial and cultural groups, accurate knowledge about and appreciation of other racial and cultural groups, and an understanding of racism and how to counter it (Derman-Sparks, Higa, & Sparks, 1980). One excellent resource for helping teachers of young children in this task is Louise Derman-Sparks' *Anti-Bias Curriculum: Tools for Empowering Young Children* (1989). This book sensitively and succinctly discusses and suggests strategies for helping children learn about and respect racial, gender, cultural, and physical differences, and to promote antidiscrimination and activism.

The following guidelines are gleaned from various sources (Derman-Sparks, 1989; Dimidjian, 1989; Edwards, 1986; Phenice & Hildebrand, 1988; Ramsey, 1982; Ramsey, 1987; Suggestions for Developing Positive Racial Attitudes, 1980). They can help you provide children with a developmentally appropriate understanding of other races and cultures.

- **When children bring up racial/cultural differences, discuss them honestly.** Help children recognize that there are differences among people, but that these differences do not make them superior or inferior to others. Stress the unique personality of each individual.
- **Help children develop pride through positive racial/cultural identity.** Children's self-concepts are tied to feeling good about all aspects of their beings. Acknowledgment and positive comments about the beauty of different skin, hair, and eye colors is important to developing feelings about self-worth.
- **Help children develop positive attitudes about other races.** Children need accurate information about other races and must be guided to appreciate others. Modeling acceptance and appreciation of all races is an important factor.
- **Help children see skin color variations as a continuum rather than as extremes.** Color charts to which children can match their own skin color can help them recognize that everyone is a shade of brown.
- **Help children learn that dark-skinned people are not dirty.** A common misconception among children is that they think that a dark-skinned child is dirty or unwashed. Doll-washing ac-

Positive relations with peers from different racial, ethnic, and cultural backgrounds are fostered by sensitive and knowledgeable teachers. What guidelines will help you, as a teacher, promote positive relations in a class of children from diverse backgrounds?

tivities, for instance, bathing an obviously dirty Anglo doll and a clean dark-skinned doll, can help begin to dispel this notion.

- **Post photographs of children and their families.** This can help children begin to acquire the concept of racial constancy as teachers point out similarities (as well as differences) among family members. Help dispel misconceptions about racial constancy as these come up spontaneously. Be prepared for questions if a child in your class was adopted by parents of a different race.
- **Ensure that the environment contains materials representing many races and cultures.** Books, dolls, pictures, posters, dramatic play props, manipulatives, puzzles, and other materials should portray people of all colors and cultures in very positive ways. This is particularly important if your class is racially/culturally mixed; it is also important, however, to expose children in homogeneous classes to different racial and cultural groups through the environment. Include such materials in infant and toddler rooms as well.
- **Discuss incidents of racism and racial stereotypes with the children.** Model antiracist behaviors by challenging incidents of racism or racial stereotyping. Help children find alternative words if they use racial slurs in arguments with each other.
- **Focus curriculum material about cultures on similarities among people rather than on differences.** Children can identify with shared experiences engaged in by people of other cultures. All people eat, wear clothes, need shelter, share special occasions, and value family activities. Focusing on "exotic" aspects of a culture only points out how different these are and robs them of the shared human factor. Focusing on differences develops stereotypes, whereas focusing on shared similarities builds understanding.
- **Avoid a "tourist" approach to teaching about cultures.** Do not teach children about other cultures out of context. For instance, avoid using only the holidays celebrated by other cultures or a one-shot "cultures" week to focus on this topic (Monday—Mexico, Tuesday—Japan, Wednesday—Africa, Thursday—Germany, and Friday—France). Also avoid using an ethnic cooking activity and a display of ceremonial clothing as the main components of these occasions. Such an approach is disconnected from everyday life, trivializes cultural diversity, and merely represents multi-culturalism as a token gesture rather than as a genuine reflection of life around the world.
- **Make cultural diversity part of daily classroom activity.** Integrate aspects of the children's cultures into the everyday life of your class to emphasize that culture is pervasive to all groups. Consider that the typical housekeeping corner in many early childhood classrooms conveys a single culture: a white, middle class model. Many ways of life should be reflected throughout the classroom. For instance, you can include dolls of different races,

post pictures showing different ethnic groups, introduce food packages in the housekeeping cupboard that reflect cultural preferences, or include home or cooking implements used by the culture of some of the children.

- **Convey the diversity of cultures through their common themes.** Read about different cultures to find out how various cultural groups meet their physical needs, engage in celebrations, and adapt to their environment. For instance, although Americans carve pumpkins into jack-o'-lanterns at Halloween, other cultures also commonly carve fruits and vegetables on certain occasions.
- **Consider the complexity involved in celebrating holidays when their observance might be counter, even offensive, to some families' beliefs or cultures.** The celebration of Christmas could offend the non-Christian families with children in your program. Thanksgiving as a holiday might be an occasion of loss rather than celebration for Native American families. The celebration of holidays should not be avoided but should be considered carefully, taking into account the attitudes, needs, and feelings of the children, families, and staff. Holiday celebrations should focus on respect and understanding of cultural observances.
- **Do not single out a minority child in a way that would make that child feel "different."** Learning about a child's culture should be done in the context of learning about all of the children's cultures. Help such a child and the others in the class recognize that a particular culture is shared by many other people in the world.
- **Involve children's families.** Families are a prime source of information about cultural diversity. Invite parents to participate in the class and share ideas about how all of the children can learn more about their unique backgrounds. Particularly in child care centers, parents may not have the time to join the class, but they should always feel welcome.

Sensitivity Toward the Disabled

The early childhood curriculum should help children develop sensitivity toward those with disabilities.

Children can also learn to develop understanding, acceptance, and an attitude of helpfulness toward those who have special needs. As we discussed in Chapter 2, many children with disabilities are included in early childhood programs. But integrating disabled and nondisabled children in and of itself does not assure interaction and acceptance.

Children need accurate information about why a peer (or a teacher) looks, moves, sounds, or behaves differently. Children need the chance to express fears or misgivings and to ask questions. It is not unusual for children to be apprehensive about things that are unfamiliar and different or to worry that the disability could happen to them as well. Offering a simple, honest explanation will answer the child's concern and respect the disabled person's disability (Derman-Sparks, 1989).

When a child with cerebral palsy was enrolled at one school, Martin called her "a baby." The teacher explained, "Roberta cannot walk because there is something wrong with the muscles in her legs. She can get around on this scooter board by using her arm muscles. Would you like to ask Roberta if you can try her scooter board so you can see what it feels like?"

In addition to helping children accept and include peers with disabilities, the early childhood program can also incorporate activities in the curriculum that are specifically aimed at dispelling stereotypes and helping to build an accepting atmosphere. One such curriculum, *Including All of Us* (Froschl, Colon, Rubin, & Sprung, 1984), provides many excellent activities to meet these goals.

Moral Development

Moral development—The long-term process of learning and internalizing the rules and standards of right and wrong.

One primary aim of socialization is for children to learn and internalize standards of what is right and wrong, in other words, to develop a conscience. **Moral development** is a long-term process to which many factors contribute. Children are surrounded by a social climate in which the actions of others convey degrees of fairness, consistency, respect, and concern for others. Children's observations of how others behave, how they are treated, and their own cognitive maturation contribute to their emerging sense of morality.

Moral development is concerned with children's development of conscience through internalization of society's rules and standards.

Children adopt a more mature set of standards if they are raised in an atmosphere of clearly set and enforced standards, support and nurturance, open communication in which the child's viewpoint is valued, and other-oriented reasons for expected behavior (Maccoby & Martin, 1983). There is also evidence that the onset of the distinction between right and wrong may be an inborn trait, emerging by children's second birthday (Kagan, 1987).

Certainly, the transition from infancy to the preschool years is an important time for laying the foundation for understanding right and wrong. Such learning occurs most effectively when, as Erik Erikson (see Chapter 5) points out, infants have developed a strong sense of trust through loving, caring relationships with significant adults. On this foundation of trust, toddlers' growing assertion of independence can develop in a healthy way by nurturing, encouraging adults who set appropriate limits on behavior; for instance, toddlers are helped to curb aggressive impulses and learn alternative, socially acceptable behaviors. This was supported by a study (Howes & Hamilton, 1993) that found that when toddlers lost a teacher with whom they had developed a secure and trusting relationship, they became more aggressive, a trait that was seen at age four.

Interpersonal moral rules—Considered as universal, including prohibitions against harm to others, murder, incest, and theft.

Conventional moral rules—Standards, which are generally culture-specific, arrived at by general consensus.

Another factor with which children have to contend, especially in a pluralistic society such as ours, is that moral standards vary in different cultures. Some universal **interpersonal moral rules**—ones prohibiting harm to others, murder, incest, theft, and family responsibility—are found across cultures. Other **conventional moral rules** are arrived at by general consensus and are more culture specific, such as wearing clothes in public or chewing with your mouth closed. In addition, each society specifies some regulations that ensure orderly and safe functioning, for instance, stopping at red lights. Implied in this differentiation is that some rules are more important than others. This is usually reflected in the classroom, where some transgressions, for instance, harm to others, are considered more serious than others (Edwards, 1986).

Piaget's View of Moral Development. Much of today's theoretical writing about moral development derived from Piaget's work on children's developing understanding of rules (Piaget, 1932). From his observations of children at play, Piaget formulated a stage theory of moral development that moves from a higher authority (for instance, God or parents) to the more mature perspective that rules are made by and can be changed through mutual consent of the players. Interestingly, even though young children see rules as inflexible, they also change them to suit their own interests; this is not a contradiction, but rather a reflection of their limited understanding of the nature and purpose of rules as reciprocal. Piaget also described young children as unconcerned with intentions, because they focus on the concrete and observable outcome. Thus, a preschooler will think that a child who breaks one plate while trying to get a forbidden cookie is less at fault than a child who accidentally breaks several plates while helping his mother set the table. During middle childhood, children gradually move toward a more flexible view and take into account intention when judging moral behaviors.

Kohlberg's Stages of Moral Development. Lawrence Kohlberg (1969) took Piaget's stage theory and developed a more elaborate framework for considering moral development based on why people make certain choices rather than on what those choices are (Edwards, 1986). He describes three levels, each divided into two substages, that relate to the person's view of social "conventions," thus, the terms, *preconventional, conventional,* and *postconventional.* Furthermore, these levels coincide with Piaget's cognitive developmental stages (Shweder, Mahapatra, & Miller, 1987), which we discussed in Chapters 5 and 10.

Preconventional level of moral development—According to Lawrence Kohlberg, the stage during which moral decisions are made based on personal preference or avoidance of punishment.

1. The **preconventional level of moral development** occurs approximately during the preoperational stage of cognitive develop-

Four-year-olds generally understand the concept that if they do something nice for someone, that person may well do something nice in exchange.

ment (about ages 2 to 7). Moral decisions are founded on personal preference, based on emotion and on what the child likes. They typify young children's egocentric thinking. External rewards and punishment determine right and wrong. Children will engage in behavior because it is pleasurable or because they might risk punishment if they do not. By age four, many children develop an understanding of reciprocity; doing something for another person can result in that person doing something for the child.

2. The **conventional level of moral development** coincides with the stage of concrete operations (approximately ages 7 to 12) and is more concerned with group approval and consensus. Pleasing others becomes important, and authority is to be respected.
3. The **postconventional level of moral development** dovetails with the stage of formal operations (reached by some adolescents) and is based on a higher moral sense of what is right and principled. Socially agreed-on values are accepted. However, these may be transcended if personal ethics, based on a universal morality, are violated. (Note that not all people reach this stage.)

Conventional level of moral development—According to Lawrence Kohlberg, the stage concerned with pleasing others and respect for authority.

Postconventional level of moral development—According to Lawrence Kohlberg, the stage in which moral decisions are made according to universal considerations of what is right.

William Damon's research (1977, 1983) further delineates young children's thought processes as they move through stages of moral development, especially as they relate to concepts of authority and fairness. His studies are based on interviews with children aged four and older.

- Four-year-olds base decisions on self-interest, not really differentiating their own perspective from that of adults. Justification for a choice is simply, "I should get it because I want it."
- By age five, children recognize the potential conflict between what they want and external rules, and they obey to avoid the consequences. They also begin to view authority as an obstruction to their own desires. Justification for their choices is based on visible external cues such as size or sex, for instance, "We should get more because we're girls."
- Over the next year, children show respect for authority because of the authority figure's social or physical power, which is considered

To a greater extent, young children's moral development is based on personal preference, but gradually evolves to consider the need for rules and the role of authority figures.

almost as omnipotent. They also progress to a view of strict equality, where everyone gets the same amount when resources are distributed.

- Subsequent stages show more complex thinking, as children see authority figures in terms of their special attributes that invest them with leadership qualities. Their view of fair distribution of resources increasingly considers more factors, for instance, looking at competing claims and at compromising.

Guidelines for Promoting Moral Development. As a teacher of young children, you will be primarily concerned with children who are still developing morally. It is important to recognize their abilities and limits in terms of moral reasoning and to guide children on the road to moral understanding. The following guidelines will help in this task (Edwards, 1986; Sunal, 1993).

- **Use other-oriented reasoning with children.** When giving children reasons for doing or not doing something, help them understand this in terms of the impact their action will have on others. Rather than stating, "Our rule is that we don't run inside," use wording that implies potential consequences to others: "We don't run inside because we could hurt other children by bumping into them." When adults use reasoning and encourage children to be concerned about the welfare and feelings of others, they have higher levels of moral development.
- **Use stories to promote thinking and discussion about moral issues.** Favorite children's stories often pose interesting moral dilemmas that, with teacher guidance, can help children articulate their thinking. The teacher's role is not to judge or seek consensus but to encourage discussion by asking appropriate questions.
- **Provide ample time for child-selected play and materials that promote cooperation.** Dramatic play allows children to

Activities that give children opportunities to talk about and identify feelings contribute toward heightening their awareness of emotions and emotional needs.

take the viewpoints of others; equipment that requires more than one child to operate encourages cooperation; and group games promote turn taking and social coordination. Any group activity in which the children work toward a common goal will invite cooperation.

- **Provide activities that help children become more aware of how the face conveys emotions.** Collages, masks, photos, acting out feelings, and "emotion puzzles" can strengthen this awareness.
- **Initiate thinking games that encourage children to seek multiple alternatives for social problems.** Flannel board characters or puppets can enact a common social dilemma, for instance, one dealing with sharing, and children can generate as many alternative solutions to the situation as possible.
- **Plan thinking games that deal with moral intentionality.** Children over the age of four can begin to differentiate between intended naughtiness and an accident that happened while a child was trying to help. Discuss the context of consequences in each instance.
- **Realize that not all cultures share the same values.** Communication with parents can help teachers find which values are important to families and help to reinforce these as appropriate with the children.

Development of Prosocial Behaviors

Peer relations, friendship, gender role acquisition, racial and cultural awareness, and moral development are all part of an intertwined process that involves the emergence of a number of other related traits. Researchers have looked at how such social characteristics as nurturance, empathy, altruism, generosity, sharing, and tolerance evolve in young children. Children's social cognition will affect how they respond to others. With age comes greater comprehension, although a higher level of understanding will not ensure that children's responses will necessarily be appropriate. Other factors contributing to the emergence of prosocial behaviors include the modeling of the significant people in children's lives as well as the kinds of other-oriented values that have been stressed (Schickedanz, Hansen, & Forsyth, 1990).

An early childhood program in which adults model, emphasize, and value prosocial behaviors will facilitate development of such traits in children. Alice Honig (1988a), who considers a prosocial curriculum based on caring and kindness as a crucial goal of early childhood programs, has highlighted the importance of such behaviors.

Prosocial behaviors are best promoted in an early childhood program that stresses caring and kindness.

Previous sections of this chapter presented activities and strategies that can help encourage developmentally appropriate and positive social attitudes and behaviors. In the context of supportive atmosphere, understanding of child development, concern for children's needs, respect for their opinions, encouragement of their autonomy, support for their individuality, and provision of a stimulating program and environment, such activities will help promote positive socialization.

A dramatic play area is a must for an early childhood program. Such play allows children to try on different roles, learn social skills, and work through feelings.

Sociodramatic play takes place when a group of children is jointly involved in symbolic or pretend play; it provides children with valuable opportunities to learn about themselves in peer relationships and to take on someone else's identity.

Sociodramatic play—Children's dramatic or symbolic play that involves more than one child in social interaction.

SOCIODRAMATIC PLAY

Although the development of positive social traits is fostered in a variety of preschool activities and learning centers, it is perhaps most naturally facilitated in dramatic and sociodramatic play. In dramatic play, children use symbols such as words, actions, or other objects to represent the real world; in **sociodramatic play,** they expand this symbolic play to include other children (Fein, 1979; Smilansky, 1968).

Theorists and researchers have postulated a relationship between sociodramatic play and the development of social competencies. For instance, through such play children have many opportunities to learn about social rules by taking on someone else's identity and enacting common situations, as well as by negotiating with peers when conflicts arise (Doyle & Connolly, 1989). Most, though not all, children engage in sociodramatic play. If children have very limited skills, the teacher can facilitate such play by directly participating or helping the child enter into the play of an ongoing group. Vygotsky's theory has relevance to such a teacher role since it suggests that teachers adapt their level of support to the skill level of the child.

In many cases, children assist peers who are not as skilled in entering sociodramatic play. For instance, four-year-old Felix most often engaged in onlooker behavior during child-selected activity times, usually standing on the outskirts of social groups. On one day in November, Yasmine, just five, deftly included Felix, who stood at the edge of the housekeeping corner observing a "family" group prepare dinner. The participants had assumed all the obvious roles, including that of family dog. The "mother," Yasmine, took Felix by the hand, led him to the play oven, and declared, "You can be the turkey." She helped Felix fit himself into the oven and closed its door. A few seconds later she opened the door, checked Felix's doneness by squeezing his thigh, and declared, "Turkey's done!" Everyone gathered around as the turkey was helped out of the oven. Felix's big grin testified to his delight at being assigned such an important role!

An appropriate classroom environment and the teacher's guidance will facilitate children's involvement in sociodramatic play.

Most young children engage in dramatic pretend play naturally; however, such play should also be purposefully encouraged and enhanced in the early childhood setting. Every early childhood classroom, including toddler classes, should have an area set aside and equipped for dramatic play. Most commonly, dramatic play props and children's engagement in dramatic play will center on housekeeping because home-related roles and activities are most familiar to young children. Children recreate and enact what happens at home: meal preparation and consumption, bedtime routines, visitors, child rearing, even arguments. Home-related kitchen, living room, and bedroom items, as well as a selection of dolls, dress-up clothes, and mirrors, stimulate children's creative and social engagement in housekeeping play. (See Chapter 7 for additional suggested dramatic play props.) Materials for toddlers and younger preschoolers should be realistic, whereas they should be more abstract for older preschoolers and primary children, to encourage pretending (Fein, 1982). Children can be further encouraged to broaden their concepts and dramatic play through displays and pictures of people of all ages and different ethnic groups engaged in common household activities.

Dramatic play can also revolve around any other theme familiar to the children—health care, shopping, and recreation are usually particularly relevant to young children because they invariably have visited the doctor, grocery store, or park. Children will also enact favorite book, television, or movie roles and stories. It is important, however, that children be thoroughly familiar with a topic through concrete, firsthand experience before they engage in dramatic play. Following a field trip, for instance, appropriate props in the dramatic play area can help children assimilate and integrate information from the trip.

COOPERATIVE GAMES

Cooperation can be promoted in the early childhood environment through activities and games that join the children in working together toward a common goal; there is no place in the early childhood program for competition.

One prosocial goal that early childhood educators cite for young children is cooperation, the force that unites people into working together toward a common objective. In an effort to promote cooperation, there should be no place in the early childhood program for competitive activities in which all but one child end up as losers, even if they are called "second winners." Races, board games, musical chairs, and similar activities in which one child emerges as the winner only promote feelings of resentment, anger, failure, and lack of confidence. Yet, often such games can be easily adapted to keep the element of fun while eliminating competition. For instance, the game of musical chairs can be changed so that all the children share the decreasing number of chairs, until everyone is piled on (and around) the last chair, usually dissolved in gales of laughter!

Writers such as Terry Orlick (1978a, 1978b, 1982) have expressed concern over the destructive outcome of competitive games and have proposed as an alternative cooperative games in which no one is a loser and everyone is a winner. The rationale for cooperative games is not just the avoidance of situations in which most of the participants lose, but is much broader, extending to a general concern for the quality of life, emphasis on peace and harmony, and decrease in societal aggressiveness. Figure 13-1 contains a selection of cooperative games for young children.

FIGURE 13-1 Cooperative Games

1. "Sticky Popcorn"
   Children begin by jumping or hopping up as they "pop." Because the popcorn is sticky, whenever a piece of popcorn touches another they stick together. Once stuck, they continue to pop together until all the popcorn kernels make one big popcorn ball.
2. "Musical Hugs"
   With energetic music playing, children skip around the room. When the music first stops, children give a big hug to someone nearby. When the music starts again, pairs of huggers can skip together if they want. The next time the music stops at least three children hug together, and so on, until everyone is joined in one massive hug.
3. "Shoe Twister"
   The children each remove one shoe and place the shoes in a pile. While holding hands in a circle around the shoe pile, the children pick up someone else's shoe (the method for doing this is left up to the children's imagination). After locating the owners of the shoes, they exchange the footwear without breaking the circle.
4. "Big Turtle"
   Seven or eight children get on their hands and knees under a "turtle shell"—a tumbling mat, tarp, or blanket. Children have to work together to move without dropping the shell.
5. "Toesies"
   With bare feet, pairs of children lie stretched out on the floor, toes touching. They try to roll across the floor while maintaining their toe touch.
6. "Beach Ball Balance"
   Pairs of children try to hold a large ball between them without using their hands. They try to find as many different ways of doing this as possible (between their stomachs, knees, foreheads, hips, and so on). Next they try to walk without losing the ball.
7. "Lap Ball"
   The children sit close together in a circle and try to pass a large ball from lap to lap without using their hands. A less difficult version of "Lap Ball" and "Beach Ball Bounce" can be arranged by having four children each hold a corner of a towel and keeping a ball bouncing on a towel through cooperative effort.
8. "Elbow-Nose Reverse"
   With the children in a circle, one child starts by pointing to her or his elbow and saying, "This is my nose." The second child passes this message to the next one, and so on. When this has gone around the circle, a new confusing message is sent.

Sources:
Orlick, T. (1978). *The cooperative sports and games book.* New York: Pantheon Books.
Sobel, J. (1983). *Everybody wins: Non-competitive games for young children.* New York: Walker & Co.

Activities involving two or more players can be considered cooperative if one or more of the following is involved: shared goals, joint decision making, shared ideas and materials, negotiation and bargaining, coordination of efforts to meet goals, and evaluation of progress toward goals (Goffin, 1987). Although Orlick recommends organized group games as a vehicle for promoting cooperation, this trait can be encouraged in more indirect and less structured ways as well.

Classroom space can be organized to encourage interactions, and ample time blocks can be allocated for child-selected play. Cooperative endeavors may well require more space and more time than activities in which children act alone. In addition, materials should be selected for their cooperative properties. Open-ended materials such as dramatic play props, blocks, water and sand, and puppets particularly promote cooperation. Teachers can also set up activities so that more than one child is involved. Instead of simply putting out beads and yarn as

Cooperation should be fostered in the early childhood program. Whether children share materials or engage in cooperative games, they learn social skills that enhance their self-concepts.

a fine motor activity, try laying long pieces of yarn across the table, with beads at each end, so that two children can work cooperatively on one yarn piece (Goffin, 1987).

KEY QUESTION #5

Try one of the cooperative games listed in this chapter with a group of young children. What was their reaction?

REFLECTING THE FAMILY'S CULTURE AND VALUES

Communication with families about values as well as about cultural and racial identity are very important.

Communicating with parents is particularly important in clarifying home and school values about socialization and about children's cultural and racial identities. Although the school is responsible for conveying to parents what values it tries to instill in the children through its curriculum and guidance techniques, the school also is responsible for obtaining similar information from parents about what they value for their children.

Teachers need to be sensitive to the many variations among families of different cultures, and they must be particularly aware of their own attitudes and biases. It is easier to convey positive messages to a family whose parenting style and values you are familiar with and agree with than it is to understand and accept an approach different from your own. Furthermore, it is important not to make assumptions about children's home life based on cultural generalizations; such stereotypes can best be avoided through thoughtful and ongoing parent-teacher communication.

Derman-Sparks (1989), in the *Anti-Bias Curriculum,* suggests that in addition to open communication in which values and ideas can be shared by parents and teachers, the school can provide accurate information to parents about the development of children's sexual, racial, and ethnic identities and attitudes. A series of parent group meetings can inform and invite discussion about such topics as gender identity and sexism, the creation of nonsexist environments, the development of racial identity and awareness, the creation of antiracist environments, and evaluation of children's books for sexist and racial stereotypes. Such groups can help parents gain information about the school's philosophy, help teachers attain insight into parents' values and attitudes, and provide parents with strategies for antibiased socialization of children.

SUMMARY

1. Consider the theoretical views of how socialization takes place.
2. Consider the development of social competence.
   A. An important element in the development of social competence is peer interaction and friendships.
   B. Children also develop gender role identity; consider nonsexist teaching strategies that promote positive gender attitudes.
   C. Racial and cultural attitudes, and attitudes toward the disabled, are formed early in life; review guidelines that can help promote accepting attitudes toward others.
   D. The foundations for moral development and positive social skills and behaviors are also formed during the early years.
3. There are two types of activities that can promote positive social interaction, specifically, sociodramatic play and cooperative games.

KEY TERMS LIST

conventional level of moral development
conventional moral rules
gender identity
gender stability
interpersonal moral rules
model
modeling
moral development
observational learning
postconventional level of moral development
preconventional level of moral development
scaffolding
sex cleavage
social cognition
social learning theory
socialization
sociodramatic play

part VI

The How of Early Childhood Education—Guidance

Another important part of the *how* of early childhood education is guidance, the principles that teachers use in directing the social behavior of young children.

chapter 14

Guiding Routines and Group Activities

In a well-managed classroom, children and teachers are involved, busy, happy, organized, and smoothly functioning, working within a flexible schedule and curriculum. Children know what is expected and behave according to those expectations. The classroom atmosphere is one in which the children are continually learning to be responsible for their own and the group's behavior. Such a classroom does not just happen, however. Teachers set the stage through their guidance techniques.

Two guidance aspects of the early childhood program deserve special consideration. The first of these is routines, such as meals or naps, which, by necessity, are a part of all programs. In infant programs, such routines take up the major part of the day and are determined by individual needs; in toddler, preschool, and before- and after-school programs, many of these elements become increasingly more scheduled for the group as a whole. The other guidance aspect of early childhood programs has to do with the times when all of the children participate in the same activity at one time as a group. This chapter will consider some strategies to facilitate both routines and group guidance.

ARRIVAL AND DEPARTURE TIMES

The first order of the day, the transition from home to school, has to be considered carefully, because leaving their parents can be very difficult for children. One factor affecting the ease of arrival at preschool or child care is children's general enjoyment of school. Another consideration is the security of children's **attachment** to their mothers, which is related to the quality of the mother-child relationship; young children most distressed at separation often also show signs of anxious attachment (Fein & Schwartz, 1982). When babies have established a secure attachment to a familiar caregiver, this relationship can help ease and cushion separation from the parent

Attachment—The child's bond with the mother, established during the first year of life.

Separation anxiety—Emotional difficulty experienced by some young children when leaving their mothers.

Some young children experience separation anxiety on leaving their parent. This is especially characteristic of older infants and toddlers.

Stranger anxiety—Displays of fear and withdrawal by many infants beginning around six months of age, when babies are well able to distinguish their mother's face from the faces of other people.

A well-thought-out procedure for arrival, particularly when children don't all arrive at the same time, will help get the day off to a good start.

KEY QUESTION #1

Observe children arriving at school with their parents. What differences in the way they leave their parents do you note?

(Raikes, 1996). Feelings of **separation anxiety** are normal and common in older infants and toddlers and also often are exhibited by preschoolers (Hinde, 1983). Other factors, particularly what happened at home as a child was getting ready that morning, also have an impact.

Arrival procedures need special thought in infant and toddler programs. It is the time when parents share relevant information with caregivers. Generally, young infants do not react adversely when left by the parent, but around six months, babies begin to exhibit **stranger anxiety**. They are now well able to distinguish the familiar face of the parent from other faces. By nine months and often continuing well into the next year, many babies display more active separation anxiety, crying and clinging, whereas before they may have had no trouble going to a familiar caregiver. This behavior is usually as hard on the parent as it is on the child. A gentle, unrushed transition, where the parent can spend a few moments and the teacher focuses on the child, often helps children's adjustment. A security object from home, such as a favorite toy or blanket, can also help (Gonzalez-Mena, 1990; Wilson, 1995).

In classrooms for preschoolers and primary children, it is important also to think through the arrival procedure and individual children's reactions and needs. Especially in a child care setting in which many children will be spending a large portion of their waking hours and where they arrive at different times of the morning, it is best to provide a low-keyed opening for the day. A few quiet activities, some soft music, and available teachers to ease anxiety or welcome enthusiastic children can help the day get off to a good start. This allows Jesse to sit quietly in a teacher's lap with his thumb in his mouth until he feels fully awake; lets Katrina take her father to check on the guinea pig babies she has been talking about since their birth last week; provides time for Thui's mother to spend a few minutes until Thui gets involved in an activity; or gives Larry's mother a chance to tell the teacher that her husband was in an auto accident the previous day and that Larry might be upset.

In any program, whether infant, toddler, preschool or before- and after-school, provision must be made for a teacher to welcome each child and parent individually. It is reassuring to a parent on parting from his or her child to know that someone is aware of and pleased about the child's presence at school. Similarly, children need to know that the teacher is glad to see them and is looking forward to mutual enjoyment during the day. This time also provides a chance for the parent to share pertinent information, which might affect the child's behavior that day, with the teachers. Morning is not, however, a time for the teacher to bring up concerns with the parent.

Morning Health Check

A morning health check conveys an interest in the children's health, sends a subtle but strong message that ill children do not belong at school, and gives the teacher a few moments to greet each child and parent individually.

Many schools use this early morning greeting as an opportunity to give each child a health check, before the parent rushes off to work. This conveys their interest in the children's health as well as their concern that ill children not remain at school. A quick visual inspection of the child can tell you whether the child appears unusually listless, has dull or heavy eyes, is developing a rash, has a runny nose, or looks flushed. A hug or touch can further indicate unusually warm skin.

A Closer Look

The Importance of Consistency in Routines for Infants and Toddlers

The consistency and routine of child care, important for all children, is particularly vital for infants and toddlers. Babies are in the process of developing many concepts about self, others, relationships, and the environment. Much of what very young children learn is dependent on the foundation of a secure social and emotional relationship, something traditionally provided on a one-on-one basis by mothers. But today, 23 percent of children under age one, 33 percent of one-year-olds, and 38 percent of two-year-olds are cared for by someone other than family (Willer, et al., 1991). Another survey reported that over 53 percent of mothers return to work within a year of their baby's birth (Carnegie Corporation, 1994).

Considerable discussion has focused on whether infants in child care are able to form successful attachments to their mothers. Lally (1995) raises the further question of how child care can facilitate identity formation of infants and toddlers, who "are in the process of forming [a] preliminary sense of self" (p. 59). He stresses the importance of the earliest years in young children's formation of identity, and suggests reconsideration of policies and practices to most effectively support this development.

Lally criticizes the trend that considers infant care as not serious and the notion that "anyone" can take care of infants and toddlers with little or no training. He reviews research that underscores the importance of sensitivity to and understanding of the signals sent by babies to caregivers. The caregivers' behavior in responding to very young children is crucial in the formation of many lessons related to the child's sense of self. These include perceptions of how to act in various situations, how people act toward the child and others, and how emotions are expressed. These are all vital in the formation of a sense of self and the child's ability to relate to others.

Lally makes several suggestions for policy and practice related to infant and toddler care. He strongly recommends that children be in the care of one primary caregiver, with one or two backups, who can provide a sense of trust and security. Frequent staff turnover, part-time and volunteer staff, and team approaches interfere with a young child's need for a caring, predictable relationship. In addition, he recommends that, for the first three years of life, children remain with the same caregiver to provide continuity. Babies' sense of self-identity is closely related to the identity of important others in their lives with whom they have formed attachments. When such important people change on a regular basis, children's task of identity formation becomes much more difficult. Lally also feels that small groups are vital to provide an intimate setting for infant and toddler care. In small groups, babies have more personal contact with their caregiver, get more one-on-one attention, can feel safer in their explorations, and develop a sense of belonging. Additionally, he recommends a curriculum that is responsive to babies rather than selected for intellectual stimulation only. Babies need the freedom to make their own choices about what they want to experience in their world. Finally, Lally considers it very important that caregivers provide cultural and language continuity from home to the child care setting. Part of identity formation involves the family culture and history, which is best promoted and reinforced by a caregiver who is sensitive to and knowledgeable about the child's culture. Attention to these issues will, according to Lally, improve infant and toddler care in this country.

If you suspect that a child is ill, discuss this with the parent and help find an alternative child care arrangement, if necessary. Working parents often find it difficult to cope with ill children, but a child who is sick should not be allowed to remain at school, for the well-being of the child as well as the health of the other children. Some communities have sick-child care arrangements, of which parents should be apprised early in the school year. Your school might also have a list of people willing to come into the home of a family with a sick child.

The New Child at School

A number of strategies can help the new child adjust to the early childhood program.

A special example of arrival at school, which often causes great anxiety for children, is the initial entry into an early childhood program. This experience can be traumatic, fraught with the unknown. It is difficult for a child, with a mode of concrete thinking, to conjure up a mental image of what school is, and without such an image the idea of school can be very frightening. Therefore, it is important for the child to have the chance to gradually become familiar with school, with the security of the parents nearby, rather than being thrust into a first day with no introduction or transition.

Ideally, a new child should visit the school with a parent before her or his first day. After this visit, the child can stay for a short period while the parent leaves briefly, which can help the child realize that she or he has not been abandoned. After that, the parent can be encouraged to stay a few minutes at the beginning of the first few days, as the child needs additional reassurance. If such an arrangement cannot be made because of parents' work schedules, urge the parents to allocate a little extra time at the beginning of those first few days.

It is important to help the parent, as well as the child, say good-bye when it is time for Dad or Mom to leave. Parents should be encouraged to establish a routine that maintains trust, for instance, always waving good-bye from the door, rather than one that undermines trust, such as sneaking out when the child is not looking.

One designated teacher should be available to welcome and spend some time with a new child. It is good for the child to have a reliable

When they are dropped off at school, children are not always ready for their parents to leave. Particularly for a child who is new to the school, a gentle and gradual transition is important.

adult to turn to with questions or concerns. This teacher also should be prepared to deal with the child's fears, anger, or tears, if necessary.

Other children, those who are veterans of the program, often help ease the new child into the center. You might facilitate this by introducing the newcomer to another child who can show that child the classroom. As children get older, peers become increasingly more important in supporting separation from mother (Gunnar, Senior, & Hartup, 1984). For some children, a classroom pet can help ease the anxiety of the new school experience.

The first few days at school can be difficult for the new child, the parents, and the teachers. This experience can be even more disconcerting, however, when not just one new child but many or all of the children, starting a new school year, find themselves in unfamiliar surroundings. In such a case, it is best to encourage parents to stay with anxious children. Another approach is to plan a phased-in start to school, with only a few new children beginning at a time.

Departure Time

The end of the school day can bring challenges to early childhood teachers as well as to children and parents. This time may provide opportunity for teachers and parents to exchange information when parents are not as rushed as they may be in the morning. On the other hand, the latter part of the day is also the time when everyone is tired and, perhaps, stressed after a long day. It is, therefore, important for teachers to give some thought to what is the most important positive aspect of the child's day to share with the parents; an accomplishment, an exciting discovery, or a painting could help send the parent and child on their way home with an affirmative message about the day. Such information sharing is especially important for parents of infants and toddlers who cannot verbally share what happened during their day.

Departure time, at the end of the day, can be stressful for children, parents, and teachers, but is a time that provides an opportunity to share something positive with the parents about the child's day.

A young child who shows no interest in the arrival of the parent or even actively resists leaving school may make the parent feel insecure and guilty. The teacher can reassure the parent of the normalcy of such behavior. Preparing the child for the imminent arrival of the parents, for instance, saying, "It is almost time for Mom or Dad to pick you up," can provide the cue needed to get ready for the end-of-day transition.

MEALS AND EATING BEHAVIOR

Meals are an important element of the early childhood program because they fulfill a vital physiological need, as well as social and emotional needs. Care and thought must be given to feeding routines and menu planning, whether children will be eating a single, daily snack in a part-day program or breakfast, lunch, and two snacks in a child care program. Young children take in relatively few calories, yet they need a wide range of nutrients; thus, foods that maximize nutritional value should be selected. Meeting children's nutritional needs is particularly important because many of today's parents do not do so as reliably as did parents of past generations (Rothlein, 1989).

It is challenging but important to provide nutritious, healthy foods for meals and snacks eaten at school because these must be considered part of the child's daily intake of nutrients.

Feeding Infants

Infants subsist on breast milk or formula for the first several months, after which semisolid foods are gradually added. Feeding babies provides an opportunity to establish and affirm a sense of trust.

Infants up to four to six months of age can obtain all of their nutrient needs from milk. Mother's milk is ideally suited to provide for all the nutritional needs of the baby, as well as provide immune protection against some infections. Mothers who wish to breast feed should be encouraged and accommodated by the program. Some mothers who cannot come to the school to feed their babies may express their breast milk and make a day's supply available in bottles. Other infants are fed formula milk, one of many commercially available products that is fortified with nutrients in amounts similar to those found in human milk. When babies are fed by bottle, they should be held by a caregiver who provides full and nurturing attention. Feeding is one of the most important times for babies to establish a sense of trust.

Babies must be allowed to set their own schedule for feeding. How much food they require varies according to the child as well as the sensitivity of adults to the child's cues about hunger and satiety (Pipes, 1993). At two months, babies may take 28 to 32 ounces of milk. When semisolid foods are added, about 4 ounces per day of cereal, fruit, or juice is an appropriate beginning amount (Pipes & Trahms, 1993).

Current recommendations suggest the addition of iron-fortified cereals between four and six months; between six and eight months strained vegetables, fruits, and meats can be added, followed by finger foods and well-cooked, mashed table foods.

Nutritional Needs of Young Children

How much older children of the same age and sex will eat varies widely, with boys generally taking in somewhat more than girls (Pipes, 1989a). Even with this variation, the relative percentages of protein, fat, and carbohydrate consumed remain similar (Hitchcock, Gracey, Gilmour, & Owles, 1986). The U.S. Department of Agriculture has issued The Food Guide Pyramid (Figure 14-1), which emphasizes the relative quantities of foods needed from the major food groups. Figures 14-2 and 14-3 contain some guidelines that will help clarify appropriate expectations and serving amounts for preschool and young primary children.

When children spend the bulk of their day in an early childhood program, it is important that the meals and snacks they eat at school contribute to their overall nutritional intake.

FIGURE 14-1 The Food Guide Pyramid

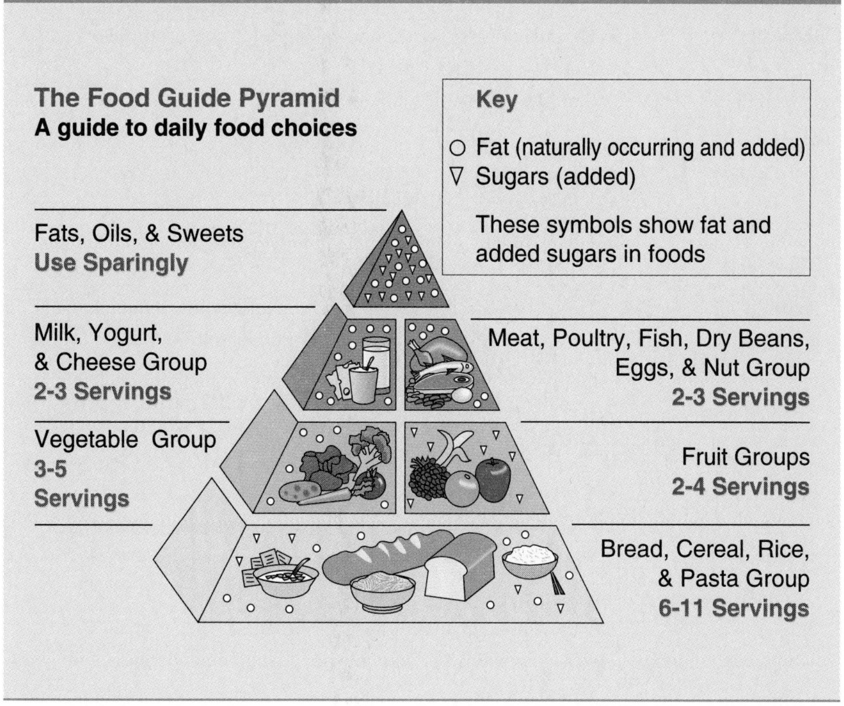

Minimum daily nutritional requirements have been established for the nutrients that children of different ages need for growth, health, and well-being. Nutrients include proteins, fats, specific vitamins, and specific minerals (see Figure 14-2). Using this information, you can provide carefully thought-out meals that meet all of these nutritional needs.

To help in planning meals, these nutrient requirements have been organized into four basic food groups. Nutritionists have identified how many servings a day are appropriate and what the serving size should be, which depends on the age of the children. Figure 14-3 outlines the number and size of servings for younger preschoolers (age three and younger) and older ones (ages four to six). Keep in mind that if children are at your center all day, you may be providing as much as three-fourths of their daily food intake, an important responsibility.

Providing Nutritious Meals That Children Will Eat

It is challenging to meet children's nutritional needs, not only in terms of including the needed nutrients in their diets but also because children often are picky eaters. Let's look at some guidelines that can be helpful in providing nutritious foods that children will eat.

Some specific mealtime guidelines can help encourage children, including finicky eaters or those who are overweight, to form good eating habits.

- **Provide variety.** A long-range menu, for instance, for a month at a time, can help ensure that children are not repeatedly being

FIGURE 14-2 Guide to Nutrients and What They Do

Protein	• Essential for growth and lifelong body maintenance. • Builds resistance to disease.
Sources:	Animal foods and plant foods such as dry peas or beans.
Minerals	
Calcium	• Forms healthy bones and teeth. • Aids in normal blood clotting. • Helps nerves and muscles react normally.
Sources:	Milk and other dairy products.
Iron:	• Helps blood cells carry oxygen from the lungs to body cells. • Protects against some forms of nutritional anemia.
Sources:	Liver, meat, egg yolks, dry beans, dark greens. • Other minerals are important too, such as **zinc, iodine, phosphorus,** and **magnesium.** Eating a wide variety of nutritious foods will provide them.
Fats	• Carry vitamins A, D, E, and K. • Source of energy (calories); best used in limited amounts.
Sources:	Meat group and milk group.
Carbohydrates	• Inexpensive source of energy. • Best when consumed as fruit sugar or starch.
Sources:	Whole-grain bread, cereal, rice, pasta, or potatoes.
Vitamins	
A	• Protects eyes and night vision. • Helps keep skin healthy. • Builds resistance to disease.
Sources:	Deep yellow/orange or very dark green vegetables.
B-complex	• Protects the nervous system. • Keeps appetite and digestion in working order. • Aids body cells in using carbohydrates, fat, and protein for energy. (The more important B-complex vitamins include **thiamin, riboflavin, folic acid, niacin, B_6, B_{12}.)**
Sources:	Whole-grain products, enriched rice, wheat germ, beans, peas, nuts, peanut butter, fish, and leafy green vegetables.
C	• Keeps body cells and tissues strong and healthy. • Aids in healing wounds and broken bones.
Sources:	Citrus fruit, melon, strawberries, broccoli, tomatoes, raw cabbage.
D	• Aids in absorption and use of calcium and phosphorus by body cells. • Helps build strong bones and teeth.
Source:	Vitamin D fortified milk.

Adapted from Rothlein, L. (1989). Nutrition tips revisited: On a daily basis, do we implement what we know? *Young Children, 44*(6), 30–36.

offered the same food items. One useful tool that ensures variety but helps avoid the need for constant meal planning is a cycle menu. Each cycle contains a set of three to four weekly menus for a particular season, and these menus can be repeated for a 3-month period (Endres & Rockwell, 1980).

FIGURE 14-3 Number of Servings and Serving Size of the Basic Four Food Groups Required Each Day for Preschool Children

	Age	
	3 and Under	**4 to 6**
Meat Group: Meat, poultry, fish, organ meats, or substitutes.		
Servings:	2	2
Size:	1 ounce each	1½ ounces each
(Substitutes: 1 egg, 1 ounce cheese, ¼ cup cottage cheese, ¼ cup peanuts, ⅓ cup other nuts, ½ cup cooked dry peas or beans, 2 tablespoons peanut butter)		
Milk Group: Whole, skim, dry, or evaporated milk; buttermilk; yogurt; cottage cheese; and other dairy products.		
Servings:	2 cups	2 cups
(Substitute for the calcium in 1 cup milk: 1 cup yogurt, 1⅓ cups cottage cheese, 1½ cups ice cream, 1¼ ounce [⅓ cup grated] natural cheese, 1¾ ounces processed cheese)		
Fruit/Vegetable Group: One vitamin C source per day and one vitamin A source every other day. In addition to those rich in vitamins A and C (listed in Figure 14-1), others should be added.		
Servings:	4 or more	4 or more
Size:	3 tablespoons each	3 tablespoons each
Bread/Cereal Group: Whole-grain or enriched bread, cereal, rice, and pasta.		
Servings:	3	4
Size:	1 slice or ½ cup	1 slice or ½ cup
Total Calorie Needs: Will vary among children.		
Calories:	1,300	1,800

Adapted from Rothlein, L. (1989). Nutrition tips revisited: On a daily basis, do we implement what we know? *Young Children, 44*(6), 30–36.

- **Take advantage of fresh seasonal fruits and vegetables.** Children enjoy watermelon in the summer or grapes in the fall, when these foods are available and inexpensive. Fruit, as part of a snack or as dessert, will provide some important nutrients in children's diets. Similarly, fresh vegetables can add enjoyment as well as a learning experience. Not all children have had the chance to see that peas do not grow in freezer packages or cans but come in pods!
- **Offer simple foods.** Most young children prefer unmixed foods; thus, noodles, hamburger, and broccoli as three separate dishes are preferable to a beef-noodle-broccoli casserole. Generally, young children are suspicious of foods that are not readily recognizable.
- **Introduce children to new foods carefully.** Children often reject foods they are not familiar with, so plan with care when you present something new. In fact, young children do not readily accept new foods unless they are sweet (Birch, Johnson, & Fisher, 1995). Introduce only one new food at a time, and serve it with familiar foods; talk about the color, texture, shape, and taste of the food; encourage but do not force tasting; introduce the food in a

In planning meals for young children, it is important to include a variety of healthy foods, take advantage of seasonal fruits and vegetables, and keep foods tasty but simple.

cooking activity; and be a good model for good eating habits (Rothlein, 1989).

- **Limit sugar in the foods you provide.** Too much sugar leads to dental caries and provides too many empty calories, quickly satiating children's small appetites without contributing to their nutritional needs. Avoid foods with added refined sugar, such as processed desserts, canned fruits, soft drinks, or punch; read food labels to help you avoid the hidden sugars in many foods (for instance, peanut butter is manufactured both with or without added sugar); use alternative natural sweeteners such as fresh fruits or fruit juices, and reduce the amount of sweetener called for in recipes (Rogers & Morris, 1986).
- **Provide healthy snacks that contribute to the daily nutrient intake.** Cheese, whole-grain crackers or toast, fresh fruit, unsweetened fruit juices, milk, vegetables and dip, yogurt popsicles, and unsweetened peanut butter are a few simple, yet nutritious snack ingredients that children enjoy.
- **Time meals carefully.** Children should not feel hungry between meals, yet they should have enough appetite to eat an adequate amount. Children's capacity is small, so meals should be relatively frequent, with small servings (Alford & Bogle, 1982). Plan snacks so that they are served at least 2 hours before the next meal (McWilliams, 1986).
- **Give special names to dishes sometimes, which adds to the fun of eating** (Lambert-Lagace, 1983). "Ants-on-a-log," celery sticks with peanut butter and raisins, are a favorite at many schools.
- **Vary the location of meals now and then.** Most meals and snacks will be eaten inside the school, but an occasional picnic on blankets on the playground or at a nearby park, a bag lunch or snack taken on field trips, or a meal shared with another class at the school can add to the enjoyment of eating. Even a picnic eaten on a blanket inside the classroom can provide a change from routine. Similarly, a holiday buffet or cafeteria-style meal can add variety (Endres & Rockwell, 1980).
- **Be sensitive to children's cultural food preferences as you plan meals.** Such awareness helps you establish rapport with children and families in your program (Endres & Rockwell, 1980). If the majority of children at your center come from the same cultural or ethnic background, daily meals should incorporate foods from that culture. If one or two children in your class are from a diverse environment, periodically plan to include foods with which they are familiar. Parents and ethnic cookbooks can help provide appropriate recipes.

Encouraging Healthy Eating Habits

In any given class, you will find children who are vigorous eaters, enjoying whatever is served, and others who are picky and selective.

Even individual children will vary considerably in appetite from day to day or meal to meal (Alford & Bogle, 1982). Let's look at some suggestions for encouraging the formation of good eating habits and for dealing with some eating problems.

- **A relaxed, comfortable atmosphere is important to good eating.** Mealtimes should be an important part of the social and learning experiences of the program. The focus should be on enjoying the food and on pleasing mealtime conversations, not on nagging children to "eat up." An aesthetic table setting, with child-sized plates and utensils, will also contribute to pleasant mealtimes.
- **Teachers should sit and eat with the children during all meals.** In doing so, they are partners, not supervisors, of the experience and can model good eating habits.
- **Children should never be forced to eat a food against their will, but they should be encouraged to taste all menu items.** Forcing will generally have the opposite of the desired effect, and children may become all the more adamant in insisting that they hate this food, even if they have never tasted it!
- **Food preferences and aversions are formed at an early age.** Birch (1980b) suggests that early childhood may be a particularly sensitive period in the formation of food likes and dislikes; thus, the preschool and primary years are important in helping children acquire healthy eating patterns. Innate as well as cultural factors affect which foods will appeal to an individual, but learning and exposure to different foods can modify this.
- **Children should be allowed to be as independent as possible at mealtimes.** Provide finger foods and foods that are easy to scoop in a spoon or spear with a fork, especially for toddlers and younger preschoolers whose fine motor control is still developing. Let children serve themselves in a family-style approach to help them develop decision-making skills about how much they can eat.
- **It is important to be aware of foods that put young children, especially those under the age of three, at risk of choking.** Especially problematic are foods that are hard, slippery, or of a size that can plug up the throat, such as raisins, carrots, or grapes (Pipes, 1989a).

Problem-Eating Behaviors

Some children are finicky eaters. Innate as well as learned preferences seem to play a role in developing food habits (Trahms, 1989). In some cases, children are picky eaters because they have learned that such behavior gets them attention (Essa, 1995). By not focusing on children's eating behavior in your conversations, you take away that attention while directing it to something more pleasant. You are, in essence, giving children responsibility for their eating behavior. As you converse with the children, you might talk about how crunchy the orange carrot sticks are, but not focus on the child who refuses to eat those carrots. Peers can also influence children's food choices (Birch, 1980a) as can repeated exposure to a new food (Birch, Marlin, & Rotter, 1984).

Overweight children pose a special concern because of long-range social and health problems associated with obesity (American Academy of Pediatrics, 1985). It is very likely that obese children will become obese adults, so early intervention is crucial (Garn & Clark, 1976; Pipes, 1989b).

A variety of reasons have been suggested as the cause for obesity, but regardless of the underlying cause, obesity results when more calories are taken in than are expended. Thus, overweight children need to both reduce their food and increase their activity level. Not just an obese child, but all children will benefit from a healthy, low-sugar, low-salt menu. You can monitor the food intake of overweight children and help them serve themselves reasonably sized portions. Also encourage children to eat slowly, perhaps put their forks down between bites, because overweight young children have been shown to chew their food less and eat more quickly than other children (Drabman, Cordua, Hammer, Jarvie, & Horton, 1979). Encouragement to increase activity level is also important for overweight children.

Food Assistance Programs

Public assistance programs are available to families with low incomes and to some early childhood programs.

Because the nutritional status of children is of national concern, a number of public assistance programs are available for families and early childhood programs. Your school may already avail itself of one or more of these programs or may be eligible for assistance. Similarly, families with low incomes may be able to get food assistance through local, state, and federal programs. Your familiarity with such programs can help improve the nutritional status of the children in your care.

Availability of such programs depends on local resources and your state's participation in federal programs. Food commodities or cash subsidies are available to child care centers through the Child Care Food Program, the School Breakfast Program, and the Special Milk Program. A Summer Food Service Program for Children provides funding for summer camps in which children from low-income families are enrolled. Families can receive assistance through the Food Stamp Program, the Commodity Supplemental Food Program, and the Special Supplemental Food Program for Women, Infants, and Children (WIC). In addition, other programs address the needs of Native American, Appalachian, and migrant populations (American Academy of Pediatrics, 1985; Marotz, Rush, & Cross, 1993; Pipes, 1993).

These programs are administered through different agencies, depending on where you live. A call to the local education, welfare, health, or social services agencies can provide a starting point for information about such programs if your school is eligible or if you are concerned about the nutritional status of one of your center's families.

DIAPERING AND TOILETING

Diapering of infants and toilet training of toddlers are important parts of the daily routine.

Infants and toddlers are dependent on responsive adults to make them comfortable when their diapers are wet or soiled. Diapering routines are important parts of the day not only because of babies' comfort but because they afford many opportunities for quality interaction and communication. The diapering routine has to be carefully considered to ensure the safety of the children as they are changed, convenience for the caregiver, and hygiene. The area should be sanitized after every use and soiled diapers appropriately disposed of; the caregiver must thoroughly wash hands with warm water and soap before and after the baby is changed (Gonzalez-Mena, 1990; Wilson, 1995). In addition, caregivers can wash toddlers' hands to establish a foundation for handwashing as part of the toileting routine.

Toileting is also important because it helps children become more independent and establishes habits of good hygiene. Toileting takes on particular significance in groups of toddlers, who are in the process of toilet training, and young preschoolers, who are in the process or have recently mastered bowel and bladder control. Even with older preschoolers, it is good to remind ourselves that these children were still in diapers just a couple of years ago!

Teachers in toddler programs are often required to guide their young charges in toilet training. Children between the ages of two and three (and sometimes later) usually signal their readiness to be toilet trained, often by telling the teacher they have wet or soiled their diaper, staying dry for several hours, or watching older children in the bathroom with interest. Early pressures to use the potty are usually futile and result in resistance rather than compliance. Toilet training should be pleasant, never a stressed or punitive experience. Accomplishments should be acknowledged and praised and accidents handled in a matter-of-fact manner. It is particularly important that parents and teachers communicate during toilet training, so they are on the same schedule, use the same methods, and are aware of progress while the child is not with them (Gonzalez-Mena, 1990; Wilson, 1995).

Before toileting becomes a matter-of-fact routine of life, young children may go through a period when they are especially interested in the acts of urinating and defecating as well as everything that surrounds them. Toddlers and young preschoolers may enjoy flushing the toilet repeatedly, watching others sit on the toilet, or talking about their accomplishments. It is best to react in a matter-of-fact way that acknowledges the child's interest but does not convey shame or self-consciousness about these natural bodily functions.

With young children who are just mastering bladder control, you may need to provide reminders or periodically ask children if they need to go to the bathroom. Be particularly aware of signs such as wiggling or holding, which indicate a need to urinate. Some young children are reluctant to go to the bathroom because they fear losing the activity in which they are involved. If this seems to be the case, reassure them that you will ensure their place at the play dough table or protect their block structure until they return.

Many preschools have a common bathroom for all children, not separating boys from girls. This provides a setting in which children can observe and note sex differences without any attending mystery or fuss. School-aged children, however, will require more privacy.

EXPERIENCES
chapter 14

SYLVIA, Master Teacher, Infant/Toddler

Where's The Potty?

Toilet training is a long process that begins long before children go anywhere near a potty. Even when they're little babies and don't understand my words, I begin to talk to them about what's happening. Diapering times are ideal for descriptive language.

"You're all wet . . . Now you have a new diaper and you're dry. It feels nice to be dry."

"Oh, you're bottom is all red and irritated. It must be sore!"

When I "catch" them in the act of having a bowel movement, I tell them, "One day you're going to put that in the toilet. I put it in the toilet. Mommy puts it in the toilet. Daddy puts it in the toilet. And you're going to put it in the toilet too when you're a big boy."

Such language helps children be aware of their bodies. Gradually, as they learn the meaning of words, they connect them with concepts like wet and dry, which they have to understand before they begin to use the potty. They also gradually recognize when they have to go to the bathroom. I tell the children that their bodies talk to them. "Listen to what your body is telling you," helps them tune in to their needs.

This recognition of being wet, of the difference between wet and dry, and of the urge to eliminate are important prerequisites to toilet training. I begin actual potty training only when individual children send cues that they are developmentally ready. This happens at different times for different children. Going to the bathroom is the child's choice, not my choice, and so the start of toilet training depends on each individual child.

When do my kids get toilet trained? My expectation is that by age three most will still need help, may still be wearing diapers, and will have accidents. Most young three-year-olds are still working on mastering toileting. Only a few have gotten there. It's so much easier to allow children's individual development to dictate when they will learn how to care for their own toileting needs. When toileting becomes an issue of power and control between adults and children, no one is the winner. And, as I tell parents, I have never met a college student in diapers! They all master it sooner or later.

Toileting is a major accomplishment of toddlers. An individualized approach that respects the rights of children to set their own pace accomplishes the task without undue stress for adults or children.

Toilet Accidents

Occasional toileting accidents should be expected in a group of young children and should never be considered a cause for punishment or shame.

In a group of young children, toilet accidents are inevitable. Children who have just recently mastered bladder and bowel control may not yet have the timing worked out, perhaps getting caught up in play and not leaving an activity quickly enough to get to the bathroom. Older preschoolers and at times primary children will also have periodic accidents, which should not be a cause for concern or shame. It is critical that teachers handle toilet accidents gently and sensitively.

Children will react differently to toilet accidents. For some, an accident will be embarrassing and upsetting, whereas for others it will be, at most, a minor irritant. In neither instance should a child ever be lectured, shamed, or chastised for a mishap. Accidents should be handled in a matter-of-fact manner that does not call attention to the child and conveys acceptance of the accident as "no big deal."

Any school should have a supply of extra underwear, pants, and socks available in case of accidents. For a group of younger children, parents might be asked to bring a change of clothing for possible mishaps. When children have an accident, the teacher should furnish the needed change of clothes and encourage them to change themselves. Make sure a child has privacy to avoid embarrassment or ridicule by others. Also keep a stock of plastic bags for storing soiled clothes.

One contributing factor to accidents may be the clothing that children wear. For young children to be independent, they have to be able to get their clothes off easily and quickly. Small buttons, overalls, belts, and back fasteners can frustrate a child trying to undress to use the toilet. Simple clothes with elastic waistbands are the easiest for children to handle.

Sometimes children will suddenly have repeated accidents long after they have achieved toileting independence. If this is the case, it would be wise to try to determine the reason for this behavior. Could the child have a bladder infection that is affecting control? Is the child reverting to a younger behavior to regain an earlier status, for instance, after the birth of a new sibling? Is the child using accidents to get attention? Each of these reasons will require a different approach.

Bathroom Facilities

Child-sized toilets and sinks can help decrease toileting accidents and facilitate independence.

It is beneficial to children if toilets and sinks are child-sized and easy to reach. If only adult facilities are available, sturdy, wide steps should be placed in front of toilets and sinks to promote independence. Children should also be able to reach toilet paper, soap, and towels with ease. Having to overreach can cause accidents.

Bathrooms should be adjacent to the classroom and easy to supervise. Children are more likely to have an accident when they have to ask for permission to go to the bathroom than when they can go on their own when they need to. Some schools have one large bathroom that all of the classrooms share, rather than a bathroom for each class. If so, teachers need to think through an arrangement that promotes independence but still lets them know where each child is at all times. Children should not be taken to the bathroom in large groups. Such a procedure, in which children have to wait unnecessarily, only promotes

Child-sized bathroom fixtures facilitate independent self-help skills. Learning about going to the toilet and washing hands is easier for these two-year-olds because the toilets and sinks are just the right size for them.

pushing, shoving, frustration, and even toilet accidents if a child just can't wait.

Toothbrushing

Especially in child care centers, toothbrushing supplies are often located in the bathroom. Wet toothbrushes should not be stored in a closed cabinet, but in an out-of-the-way place where they can air out after each use. Each child should have an individual, clearly marked brush; disposable paper cups can be used for rinsing. The teacher should dispense the toothpaste, preferably from a pump. It is important to the establishment of good hygiene habits that children from an early age be allowed to brush their teeth after meals.

SLEEP AND REST TIMES

A nap or rest is important for children who spend all day in a child care center.

Newborns spend a majority of their time sleeping, but sleep needs decrease as children get older. When older children spend all day at a child care center, a rest or nap time should be an integral part of the day. Not all children need a nap, especially as they get older, but for children who are on the go all day, a time to slow down is important. According to Dr. Richard Ferber (1985), director of the Center for Pediatric Sleep Disorders in Boston, most children by age two sleep 11 to 12 hours at night, with a 1- to 2-hour nap after lunch. Children continue to take naps until at least age three, though some children still nap until they are five.

Infant Sleep Patterns and Needs

Infants set their own sleep patterns, spending much of the earliest months sleeping. Around the end of the first year, they generally take one nap per day.

Infants' sleep must follow each individual child's schedule rather than being imposed for the group. Some babies have a fairly consistent sleep-wake cycle, while others are more unpredictable in their schedules. In the first couple of months of life, babies will sleep most of the time. As they reach the middle of the first year, their sleep needs continue to decrease and sleep patterns become more predictable, including two or three naps during the day. By the age of one, most children take only one nap a day.

Babies signal tiredness by yawning, rubbing their eyes, fussiness, crying, or by falling asleep toward the end of feeding. Some children will fall asleep readily when put in their cribs, while others need to be held and gently rocked to encourage sleep. Sleep space for babies should be away from active areas, and not contain stimulating toys, bright colors, or other distractors. Each baby should have an individual crib (Gonzalez-Mena, 1990; Wilson, 1995).

Children Who Don't Need to Sleep

A variety of arrangements can be made for older children who do not take a nap in the middle of the day. In some programs, children are asked to lie on a cot quietly for a period of relaxation; if this is not handled punitively, children can enjoy a short period of rest and quiet. In other centers, children who do not sleep are allowed to engage in a quiet activity, such as book browsing, while they are on their cots. Nonsleepers are usually placed apart from those who are expected to fall asleep, so they are not disturbed. Some children, when they lie down in a relaxed atmosphere, will eventually fall asleep. Those who don't can get up after about a half hour and move into an activity apart from the sleepers. Another alternative is to have a quiet time, where nonnappers, rather than lying down, participate in a period of individual, restful activity, for instance, book browsing or playing quietly with manipulatives.

Nap Guidelines

Sleep, which is a natural part of the body's daily rhythm, requires that the body and mind be relaxed and at ease. If children are anxious or wound up, they will have a difficult time falling asleep. Thus, the way you prepare for nap time and set up the environment will either facilitate or hinder sleep.

A consistent pre-nap routine and a relaxing atmosphere facilitate sleep.

Children should not be expected to move directly from a high-energy activity, such as outdoor play, into nap; rather, a transition is needed to let children slow down gradually. A predictable prenap routine that is followed every day is as important as the nap itself (Ferber, 1985). For instance, a leisurely 10-minute period is set aside for children to go to the bathroom, get a drink of water, take off shoes and tight clothing, get a favorite stuffed animal and blanket, and settle down on cots. The lights are dimmed, and drapes or shades are drawn. Cots are spaced far enough apart, and friends who enjoy talking are separated, to facilitate sleeping. Once all the children are settled down, a teacher may read a story or play a story record, sing softly, or lead the children in relaxation exercises.

After these preliminaries, the teachers move from child to child, gently rubbing backs, whispering a soothing word, or stroking children's hair. Children who need a midday nap will fall asleep in a conducive atmosphere in which lighting is dim, the temperature is comfortable, the room is relatively quiet, and the teachers convey a gentle, soft mood.

Not all children need a nap, but children who spend all day in an early childhood setting do need time to rest. Quiet book browsing is a good activity for rest time.

If the policy of the center dictates all children will lie down for a nap, special provisions may need to be made for children who do not sleep during this time. At one center, teachers have found "rest packs" to be effective for nonsleepers. Rest packs contain two to four items for quiet play, which children can use while on their cots. Teachers can prepare several rest packs to be distributed generally or can make individual packs for each child. The contents of rest packs, for instance, books, crayons, paper, small puzzles, or manipulatives, should be changed frequently.

Because sleeping children would need extra help to move out of the building in case of an emergency, it is especially important that teachers be aware of exits and alternative escape routes.

Children should not sleep for too long; an average of an hour to two suffices for most children. Some children need time to wake up gradually, so an unstructured transition in which children can join the class at their own pace is helpful. An afternoon snack, to which children can move as they are ready, often helps provide that transition.

Problem Sleepers

KEY QUESTION #2

A three-year-old in your class consistently refuses to go to sleep during nap, but then almost always falls asleep later in the afternoon. What strategies might you use in such a situation?

Occasionally you will encounter children who consistently resist sleep, even though they need the rest. A few children have genuine sleep problems, stemming from such conditions as chronic middle ear infection, the use of certain medications, and some cases of brain damage. For other children, falling asleep represents a letting go, where anxieties and fears can surface, and their sleep reluctance comes from a need to avoid such scary thoughts. Most children's difficulty in falling asleep, however, results from poorly established sleep habits and routines (Ferber, 1985).

Three-year-old Becky had a very hard time going to sleep, both at home and at school, and engaged in a variety of disruptive stalling techniques to avoid nap time. Often, by late afternoon she was grumpy and tired, and she invariably fell asleep in the car on the way home or "crashed" in the classroom around 4:00 p.m. Her teachers eventually decided that it was not worth trying to put Becky down for nap with the other children because she prevented everyone from sleeping when she was in the nap room. Instead, once the other children had fallen asleep, one teacher would sit with Becky in the rocking chair and read a quiet story to her. This seemed to work about 3 days out of the week, when Becky would fall asleep on the teacher's lap and then be put down on her cot.

PARENTAL CONCERNS ABOUT ROUTINES

Regular exchange of information between parents and teachers about routines will help provide consistency in expectations and experiences for children.

As with all aspects of the early childhood program, the school's philosophy about meals, toileting, nap or rest, and group guidance should be shared with parents. An exchange of information between teachers and parents helps provide a consistent set of expectations for children.

To help children achieve a balanced diet, parents and teachers need to cooperate. One way to further this goal is for the school to post a detailed menu of all meals and snacks served. The school may also compile and distribute a "cookbook" of healthy alternatives for snacks and lunches.

Some families have particular restrictions or preferences in their dietary habits, and these need to be honored. Moslems and some Jewish families do not eat pork, for instance, so children from these religious backgrounds should not be served luncheon meats or hot dogs made of pork. Some families are vegetarian because of religious, ethical, or health reasons; the school will need to make special provisions to furnish appropriate meals for vegetarian children or make arrangements with the family to provide alternative foods.

Parents may convey concerns about their children's eating patterns, and the teachers' advice and informed responses can be very reassuring. One frequent parental concern involves lunch box meals, particularly if food items remain uneaten. Teachers can share the school's philosophy about meals, suggest alternative menu items, and discuss appropriate serving sizes for preschoolers, depending on the circumstances.

Toileting, especially if children take home plastic bags with wet or soiled clothing, can be a cause of concern for parents. If toilet mishaps seem to be happening too frequently in relation to the child's age, explore potential causes with the parents. Check with parents about possible stressful events in the child's life and assure them that toilet accidents are not uncommon among young children. Share the school's nonpunitive philosophy toward accidents. Your matter-of-fact perspective can be reassuring.

Parents may also feel concern over naps, particularly if they affect evening bedtime. Some children, if they sleep too long during the day, are not ready for sleep at night until quite late. This puts a burden on parents who want their children in bed at a reasonable time. It may take some coordination to meet the needs of the child, the family, and the school, but effective parent-teacher communication is the important ingredient to reaching such a goal. Parents may also seek your advice in dealing with their children's nighttime sleep problems. Your advice or recommendations for further readings can help establish a consistent and pleasant bedtime routine and recognize factors that can disrupt sleep patterns.

Parents of infants and toddlers especially need consistent and thorough information about their children's routines. A special form, on which information about the child's eating, sleeping, elimination, play, and developmental progress are briefly noted should be available for parents at the end of each day.

FACTORS THAT AFFECT GROUP BEHAVIOR

Each of the previously discussed routine elements of the young child's day is important and needs careful consideration as you decide how best to guide the group of children in your care. We will now turn to another aspect of guidance, those times of the day when all the children participate together in a common activity. Although it is important to consider each child as an individual within that group, some factors can facilitate group guidance.

The Physical Environment

Group guidance can be facilitated by such factors as a well-set-up environment, schedule, activities, materials, and expectations that are appropriate for the developmental level of the children. When expectations are inappropriate, frustration or boredom are likely to result.

For one thing, it is important to examine the physical environment in relation to group behavior. Are several children running in the classroom, for instance, although the rule is "walk inside, run outside"? Perhaps too much open space invites children to run. Critically examine room arrangement in relation to group behaviors. (See Chapter 7 for more detail on this topic.)

Developmentally Appropriate Expectations

Another important factor in setting expectations for the group is the developmental level of the children. Carefully examine activities, the daily schedule, and materials to be sure they are appropriate to the ages of the children. Keep in mind the attention span, social ability, activity level, muscle control, and cognitive skills of your group and plan accordingly (look back at Chapter 2). Realistic expectations are essential to good group guidance and have to be aligned with the children's developmental level so you do not have either under- or over-expectations. Frequently refer to NAEYC's *Developmentally Appropriate Practice in Early Childhood Programs Serving Children From Birth Though Age 8* as a guide (Bredekamp & Copple, 1997).

Children who are expected to behave beyond their capability will become frustrated, and frustration results in misbehavior. Similarly, if the expectations are too simple for the children's abilities, the children will easily get bored; this can also lead to misbehavior.

A relevant incident occurred recently in one child care center's two-year-old class during large group time. About 12 children were grouped on the floor in front of a standing adult, who flashed alphabet cards while reciting the letters "*A, B, C,. . . .*" During this activity, one child was crying, another poked her neighbor, several stared vacantly into space, one untied his shoelaces with the help of a friend, and two were about to get up to look for an alternative activity. There was also a distinctive smell that indicated that at least one child in the group

Active young children should not be expected to wait in lines to go outside, go to the bathrooms, get a drink, go to lunch, or for any other reason. What alternatives to lining up could you suggest to the teacher of these children to get them outside?

had a physical need more immediate than hearing the alphabet recitation. The well-intentioned teacher was pleased that she was furthering the academic development of the children in her class.

A better grasp of child development would have helped her recognize the inappropriateness of the activity and the normalcy of the inattentive children's reactions. Activities have to be age appropriate, and this is an important responsibility of the teacher.

Another example in which the need for understanding of child development provides the teacher with guidance is in the pacing of activities. Avoid occasions in which a group of children must wait for more than a minute or two. For instance, *it is generally unrealistic to make children wait until everyone is seated to start, or until everyone is finished to move on to the next activity. Also, standing in line to wait for a turn to get a drink, go outside, go to the bathroom, go to lunch, or wash hands is difficult for active preschoolers.* By the time children are in the primary grades, they have a better capacity for waiting a few minutes, although waits should not be excessive. There are other methods of moving children from one place to another without chaos, which we will discuss later in this chapter.

Also keep in mind that although developmental guidelines help you identify appropriate expectations for the age of the children, each child is an individual and will conform to some but not to other developmental milestones. You may also have children in your class who have special needs and in some ways do not fit the profile for their age group. Be sensitive to their unique needs and characteristics, make alternate arrangements if they cannot be expected to participate in the same way as the other children in some activities, but help them fit into the group as smoothly as possible.

Conveying Expectations

Young children are exuberant and active, so you may find times when their voices or activity levels get too high. Shouting instructions to "quiet down!" or "settle down!" will only add to the confusion. A more effective way of controlling children's voice levels is to whisper softly. Move from small group to small group and speak in a soft, slow voice. Children will quiet their pitch so they can hear you. You will find the noise level quickly reduced by your modeling.

You might want to let the children know that it will be "shout time when we go outside." Similarly, an elevated activity level, if it seems unproductive, also can be reduced by a quiet voice, dimmed lights, or soft music that induces relaxation rather than agitation.

As individual children quiet or settle down, let them know with a smile or nod that you appreciate how they are speaking or behaving, rather than calling attention to inappropriate behavior; appropriate behavior can be contagious. Teachers will frequently praise the behavior of one compliant child publicly in the hopes that others will behave similarly because they also want to be acknowledged. According to Hitz and Driscoll (1988), however, research shows that praise given in this manner can lead to resentment and anger because it is manipulative rather than sincere. Teachers of young children "may get away with blatant manipulation and fool themselves into thinking that it works. But eventually most children come to resent this type of control" (p. 10).

KEY QUESTION #3

Ask three teachers what rules they set for the young children in their class. Are there commonalities among the rules listed by the different teachers? Are there differences? Which rules seem reasonable and understandable to preschoolers? Do any of the rules seem inappropriate?

Rules

Children are most apt to follow rules if there are few of them and if they understand the reasons for these rules.

Another way of encouraging good behavior from the group is by letting the children know just what is expected. This can be done through a few simple, established rules. Children should know what the limits are and why they are set. Like adults, children are much more likely to follow rules if they understand the reasons behind them. Rules should be discussed with children to emphasize and explain them. Another way of reinforcing rules is by posting them so that children can easily "read" them. One example is a picture poster of dos (smiling face) and don'ts (frowning face) with contrasting photographs or sketches for the two categories (for instance, pounding clay versus hitting another child). For primary children who are beginning readers, rule charts can use simple sentences reinforced by pictures.

Such posters makes it easy to call children's attention to a rule if there is an infraction and to encourage them to verbalize the expected behavior. Rules can also be reinforced through a "rehearsal" procedure, particularly if you need to establish some special rules for a special event (for instance, walk, field trip, visitor). Puppets, a flannel board story, or a role-playing situation can help you anticipate problems and reinforce the rules and the rationale behind them. A rehearsal can give children a sense of security that, in itself, can help them behave appropriately.

Group behavior, as indicated in the previous discussion, can be affected by such factors as room arrangement, developmental level of the children, and clearly spelled out expectations and rules. These factors are, in a sense, constants that do not change from day to day, although they do change over longer periods of time as the children change. They provide a framework for the group guidance techniques that relate to specific parts of the daily schedule and that a teacher uses in the minute-by-minute functioning of the class.

GROUP GUIDANCE AND THE DAILY SCHEDULE

In Chapter 8, we discussed some guidelines for planning the daily schedule. Many have a direct effect on group guidance because the schedule is a very important element in successful control of group behavior and needs to be thought through carefully (Essa & Rogers, 1992). The actual sequence and timing of the daily schedule, as well as the length of activities, will have a bearing on group guidance.

There must be a logical rhythm and flow to the sequence of daily activities that relates to the developmental level of the children. If children are expected to sit quietly for several activities in a row, they will tend to find unacceptable ways to release some of the energy that is pent up during this overly long period; if too many boisterous activities are scheduled one after another, the children may tire or get too keyed up. All elements of the schedule should be carefully timed to avoid boredom because activities last too long or frustration when activities are not long enough.

Let's look at some specific aspects of the daily routine in relation to group guidance techniques. At certain times in the schedule, careful forethought and planning can make the difference between a chaotic and a well-ordered classroom.

Arrival and Departure Times

When children arrive and leave over a staggered period of time, it is a good idea to provide a selection of activities that are self-directed, easy to clean up, and easy to disengage from.

Morning arrival can be a difficult time because much is going on. Children, parents, and staff are starting a new day for which information needs to be shared. If parents bring the children to school individually (rather than children arriving in a group by bus), one teacher needs to be available near the door to exchange greetings and a few words with arriving children and parents. To free this teacher from classroom chores, it would be helpful to have a few, simple activities available for children who arrive early. These activities should be relatively self-directed, easy for the children to disengage from, and easy to clean up. Puzzles and other manipulative materials serve well for this purpose. Also, if there are not enough teachers to supervise all areas of the classroom adequately at the beginning of the day, some areas can be announced as "off limits." You can do this by posting a large, construction-paper stop sign or by stringing a rope across the entrance to specified areas.

If the children arrive in a group, for instance, at 3:00 for the after-school program, you can move into your scheduled first activity immediately. A good starting point might be a large group activity to orient the children to what will happen that day.

Departure at the end of the day should be handled similarly. If all parents come for their children at about the same time or if the children go home by bus, a cleanup period followed by a group activity works well. If children are picked up over a period of time, some selected activities that are easy to clean up and disengage from should be made available. Manipulative materials, book browsing, table games, or outdoor play are examples of appropriate activities. When a parent arrives, the child can finish and put away the activity while a

A good part of the daily schedule will be devoted to time blocks in which children can select from a variety of available activities and materials.

teacher chats for a few moments with the parent. The transition from school to home, as well as from home to school, will be much smoother if you plan carefully.

Activity Time

Problems may arise during activity time if too many children flock to one activity; the number of children who engage in a particular activity at one time can be controlled.

A good part of the day will be scheduled for activities that children select from several planned by the teachers or from the classroom learning centers. Children have the opportunity to engage in a decision-making process at these times (Hohmann, Banet, & Weikart, 1979). Some group guidance principles can help keep activity time blocks running smoothly.

One of the main guidance problems during activity time can arise from the grouping and distribution of children among activities. What if 10 children want to participate in the water play activity, 8 more are in the housekeeping area, and only 1 chooses to do the art project you planned so carefully? Chances are problems will develop at the water table and in dramatic play. How can you avoid such a situation?

One way to establish limits is to post happy faces in a conspicuous place at the entrance to each learning center. The number of happy

It is best to make some activities simple and easy to clean up, such as book browsing, available during the early and late parts of the day, when children are arriving and leaving.

faces corresponds with the number of children who can be in a given area at one time. Thus, four happy faces above the water table means that only four children at one time may be in that area. The teacher can help the child count the number of happy faces and match it to the number of children in the area. In this concrete way, a child can be helped to understand why there is no more room. The child can then be redirected to another area with an assurance that she or he will be informed if a child leaves the desired area and there is room for one more.

The number of children can also be limited by the availability of materials and equipment in an area. Thus, five chairs around the art table indicates how many artists can work at one time; six play dough boards tells how many youngsters can engage in that activity; four hard hats set the limits in the block area, and so forth. Your imagination and ingenuity as a teacher will help you determine how such controls can best be set.

Meals

Pleasant mealtimes result when children help set up, when they are not required to wait, when there is relaxing conversation, and when they know what cleanup is expected after they finish eating.

Breakfast, lunch, dinner, or snack can pose group guidance problems if these times are not carefully planned. What happens before, during, and after a meal will directly affect group control, not to mention digestion.

Before the children sit down to eat, tables should be set and the food ready. Children should be involved in this process. It provides an excellent opportunity for young children to be engaged in a practical activity that builds self-concept, self-confidence, social competence, eye-hand coordination, and cognitive skills. Special helpers can assist in setting the table; putting out a plate, napkin, and silverware for each child; pouring juice or milk; and passing food.

Once the children have washed their hands and are ready to sit down, waiting should be kept to a minimum. Especially young children should not have to wait for everyone to be seated. Older preschoolers and primary children, in whom patience is beginning to develop, can wait a few minutes until all the children at their table are seated. If, for some reason, the children are at the table and have to wait for more

Both children and teachers find mealtimes more enjoyable in a comfortable and relaxed atmosphere. Pleasant conversation is an asset to meals and should be facilitated by the teacher.

than a minute, initiate a song or finger play to keep the youngsters occupied until they can eat. Waiting for any prolonged period, especially quietly with hands folded in their laps, only frustrates children and is an invitation to guidance problems.

During the meal, establishing a few simple rules about eating (as discussed earlier in this chapter) and a pleasant, relaxed atmosphere are important. Conversation with peers and adults should be encouraged; silence is not an asset to a pleasant mealtime. The focus should be on appropriate eating and social behaviors. Children will seek your attention by doing what is expected if you praise and attend to those behaviors.

After the meal, children should again follow a few simple rules about clearing their dishes and cleaning their area at the table. Children should not have to wait until everyone is finished eating. They should be able to engage in a self-directed, quiet activity such as book browsing or move individually to the next activity. The staff should be distributed according to where the children are. As more children finish eating and move to another area, so should more of the staff move. One staff member should stay with the eaters until all are finished and then clear away all food and utensils (unless there is a separate kitchen staff that does this).

Group Times

Effective group activities require careful planning and preparation, as well as forethought to seating arrangement.

One of the most rewarding as well as most difficult parts of the early childhood day occurs when children participate in teacher-initiated group activities. Good guidance is particularly important at group times because the success of such activities may well depend on your ability to keep the group attentive. This is no simple task because you are trying to move children gradually from their egocentric focus toward some specific social behaviors, ones that are particularly important in primary school. The control you maintain over the group will, to a great extent, be a function of the environment and activities you provide for group times.

The physical environment within which group activities are conducted has to be carefully thought out. It should be relatively free from distractions so the children focus on the activity. If, for instance, a shelf of attractive materials competes for the children's attention, a simple covering of butcher paper or fabric can be used during group activities. Also, if children cannot see you or are crowded, they will respond with frustration or lose interest in the activity.

Therefore, arrange the group seating with thought. A carpeted area works best; children should be physically comfortable. Depending on the activity, a circle or semicircle around which children sit works well. If the activity is basically verbal with no visual props, such as group discussion, use a circle. If there is something to look at such as a book or flannel board, a semicircle works better, because in a circle the children next to the teacher will not be able to see the visuals very well. The visual prop should be held at or slightly above the children's eye level; if it is too high, the children will have to tilt their heads back at an uncomfortable angle. Get down on the floor with the children to see what they see or how they see it.

Careful attention to how children are seated during group activities can prevent behavior problems. Young preschoolers have a tendency to creep closer and closer to the teacher. This often results in children not being able to see the book well.

Sometimes, however, as much as you try to delineate an outer edge for the group, the children gradually creep closer and closer until you have a knot of little people sitting in no designated order. This may particularly happen with a group of toddlers and younger preschoolers. Some things can help children stay on the periphery of the group area. You might simply outline the area with masking tape and mark Xs or dots at intervals where children are to sit. Or, you may use carpet samples from a local carpet or interior design business; carpet squares can provide a colorful and appealing outline for your group area. You can set out the squares yourself, or you can have the children select a color and place the square in the circle to sit on.

Another way of keeping the shape of the circle is to set out cues on the floor that the children must then match. You might, for instance, use the youngsters' name tags (whether these are just printed names, photographs, individual symbols, or a combination). You could use some other cue with which the children are not familiar. In this way you can achieve three things: (a) you delineate the outline of the group area, (b) you incorporate an active cognitive task with your group activity, and (c) you can arrange seating and thus control potential problems by separating children who tend to distract each other.

The timing of group activities is also important. Be aware of the developmental abilities of your group to sit quietly and pay attention. Begin the year with relatively short group times and lengthen these as the children are able to sit for increasingly longer times. You may plan several short group times at the beginning of the year and fewer longer ones later in the year. Although ability to sit and listen will vary depending on the children in the group, there are some rough guidelines for length of group time. For groups of one- and two-year-olds, 5 minutes of group time is plenty; toddlers should not, however, be required to sit for group but should be invited to join and free to leave if they wish. Three-year-olds should be able to manage a 10-minute group, whereas four- and five-year-olds can handle 15 to 20 minutes. School-aged children can sit longer for an interesting activity. Keep in mind, however, that children in an after-school program have spent the day in fairly structured activities. They may be more responsive to activities they can self-select.

A stimulating, longer group activity is sometimes fine, but as a rule don't expect children to sit quietly and attend for extended periods. It may also happen that although the group as a whole can pay attention for a certain period of time, one child lacks the maturity of the rest. In such a case, provide that child with a quiet alternative away from the group, rather than punishment for something the child is developmentally not capable of.

What happens during group times is very important to group guidance. Your activities must be age appropriate to hold the children's interest. A wide variety of appropriate activities can be included during group time. Most popular among early childhood teachers are books, stories, and music activities (McAfee, 1985), but there are many other possibilities, as we discussed in Chapter 8.

It is also important to be prepared for whatever you plan to cover during group time; you should have read the stories, have all props prepared and at hand, and know songs and finger plays by heart. If you try to "wing it," you may well lose the all-important sense of pacing. Several group guidance techniques help keep the children's attention while you are reading or telling a story.

If you see a child's attention wavering, you might try saying, "And do *you* know what happened next, Amy?" to gently bring Amy back to the group. To involve children in the story process, plan enough time to stop every so often to ask the children questions or to have them find something in a picture. Another way to heighten interest in a story is to periodically substitute the names of some of the children in the group for those of the characters in the story.

When you are using finger plays and song during group activity, keep in mind that some of these excite and others quiet children. Have a repertoire of songs and finger plays on hand to use as a stimulant or a relaxant, as needed. Children should learn an increasingly larger number of songs and finger plays as the year goes on. Remember, young children enjoy and need repetition, so when you introduce a new song, give the children enough time to learn it thoroughly, then continue to use it periodically thereafter.

Songs and finger plays serve an excellent group guidance function at the beginning and end of group time. At the beginning, they provide a good transition from the previous activity; start a familiar song as soon as a couple of children are seated in the group area, or even before children arrive as a signal that the group is starting.

Don't wait for everyone to be seated before you start. You can also end your group with a familiar song or finger play, particularly if you need a good transitional device to move children to the next activity. (This will be discussed in more detail in the discussion on transitions, which follows.)

Show-and-tell—A common group activity in which children can share something special and personal with their classmates.

One more group activity, a favorite of many teachers, is **show-and-tell** or "sharing time," which is often used to allow children to share something special and personal with their classmates. Such an activity can be tiresome and difficult, or it can provide a rich learning experience for all of the children (Oken-Wright, 1988).

Show-and-tell gives children a chance to be in the limelight as well as to practice talking before a group. But show-and-tell has to be planned and carried out carefully. As with other early childhood activities, you should keep in mind the attention span of the group. It is not necessary for all of the children to participate on the same day. The ages of the children will determine how many youngsters should share on one day.

One alternative to show-and-tell, especially for young preschoolers, is to select a "special child" for each day. Part of what the special child can do on his or her day is to share something from home. One thing to consider is storage for the children's personal treasures. It is not a good idea to allow the entire group to play with a special item, in case it is broken or lost. Instead, arrange a place to store these items, whether in the children's own cubbies or in a specially designated place. When a child shares a treasured item, be sure you are very interested in what the child shows and tells about. A half-hearted comment from you could be crushing.

TRANSITIONS

A very important, though often unplanned for or neglected part of the day's schedule, is not the daily activities but what happens in the gaps or transitions between them (Alger, 1984). Transitions really have to be thought of as part of the routine, a part that provides many opportunities for children to learn. Learning certainly takes place as children have to cooperate and be considerate of each other during toileting before lunch; classify, seriate, match, and organize during cleanup; or bend, lift, stretch, and pull in putting outdoor toys into storage before coming back inside.

A beautifully planned day can fall apart if no thought is given to transitions between activities. Carefully think through what has to happen at the beginning of an activity, at the end of an activity, and between activities. In fact, to help you plan transitions, role play with the rest of the staff what occurs during transition times. Fix in your mind the sequence and steps of various transitions so your guidance and expectations of the children are appropriate.

Children should always be aware of upcoming transitions, and you can do this in a variety of ways. For instance, you might use a cue or signal to let children know a change is coming. A song, chant, record, bell, flick of the lights, or specific clapped or drummed beat can be used regularly as transitional signals. For instance, such cues can announce cleanup time, group time, or outside time.

Children best respond to upcoming transitions, such as cleanup time, if they know what to expect, therefore, a warning a few minutes before the change will help them be prepared for it.

Even before you announce the end of an activity, however, and the transition to the next, give children a warning. Do this to help children finish activities they may still be involved in. For older preschoolers and primary children who are more product oriented with projects or who are concerned with completing a game, a longer warning will be needed. As a rough guide, allow 1 minute of warning for each year of age (2 minutes for two-year-olds, 3 minutes for threes). Tell children, "In a few minutes, I will ask you to put your blocks away so we can get ready for snack." This is the first warning, to be followed within a few minutes by the cue that signals cleanup time.

As you give the warning, and later as you encourage cleanup, do not make a megaphoned announcement to the class as a whole. Rather, move from small group to small group with your message. In

KEY QUESTION #4

Observe a preschool class during transitions between activities. What strategies does the teacher use? Do these strategies reflect a sense of preparedness and forethought? Did the transitions go smoothly or were there some problems? How could these transitions be improved?

supervising cleanup, remember that the children are cleaning up with some help from the teachers, not vice versa. Your role is that of teacher and guide. Be as specific in your verbal instructions as you can. Rather than telling children, "Put everything away," say, "Jimmy, you get to put the shoes on the shelf and the purses and hats on the hat rack; Lesley, please stack the dishes in the cupboard on the top shelf; Tom, you can put all the long blocks on top of the red rectangle on the block shelf."

Cleanup will, of course, be facilitated by an orderly, well-thought-out environment (also see Chapter 7), where every item has a logical place. Sometimes you may have to devise games to encourage cleanup, especially for reluctant helpers, until they accept it as part of the routine. Suggestions to "drive your truck into the garage" or "swim like a fish to the sink and get the sponge to wash this table" can help encourage cleanup participation.

Sometimes a transition needs to be used to limit the flow of children to the next activity. For instance, you may have snack following group activity, with hand washing between the two. Sending 20 children at one time to a bathroom with two sinks is asking for problems. Think through ahead of time how many children can be in the bathroom comfortably at one time, and plan accordingly. A familiar song or finger play is a good device for such controlled flow. For instance, sing "Five Little Monkeys" using five children as participants at one time, and send each "monkey" to the bathroom as it "falls off the bed."

Teachers need to think through how children will move through activities and where the adults should be stationed to provide appropriate assistance when it is needed.

The position of teachers, as in the previous example of moving children from group to bathroom to snack, is an important factor in smooth transitions. The teachers should be positioned in key places (in the bathroom, in the group area, at the snack table). As the bulk of the group moves to the next area, so should the adults.

It is important to consider and plan for transitions as part of the program, because children spend a considerable part of their day involved in transitions. In an analysis of time spent in various activity categories in five different early childhood settings, Berk (1976) found that children spent from 20 to 35 percent of their total time in transitions. Because the teachers involved in this study ranked transitions low in relation to other activities, Beck suggests that teachers need to consider transitions a legitimate part of the curriculum.

THE UNUSUAL SITUATION

A regular schedule and routine are essential to help young children work comfortably in their environment; they need the security and regularity. But sometimes the unusual or unexpected comes along. It is important that children be able to handle deviations from the usual since life is full of the unexpected.

Some guidance techniques will help you give the children in your group the coping skills to deal with unusual situations if and when they come up. It should be noted, by the way, that if children are allowed to make choices frequently, they won't panic when the unexpected happens. Unusual situations can be grouped into two categories—the planned and the unplanned.

Planned Unusual Events

These include such changes from the regular routine as special events, special circumstances that you know about ahead of time, and field trips. Children can be prepared for expected changes, although it is advisable not to prepare them too far in advance to avoid undue anxiety or disappointment if they become ill. Also keep in mind that children's time sense is not the same as adults'; a week can seem like an eternity! When you prepare children, tell them exactly what will happen during the special event. If Santa Claus is coming tomorrow, tell the children that they will sing some songs for Santa and then they will each have a chance to sit on Santa's lap if they would like. A calendar that refers to the special coming event can help older preschoolers and primary children "see" the time span in a concrete way.

If you can anticipate a special circumstance that will involve a change—for instance, if you will be away from school for a few days next week and a substitute teacher will be taking your place—prepare the children. Discuss your upcoming absence and reassure the group that you will still be their teacher, even if you are gone for a few days. If possible, have the substitute teacher visit your class so the children have a concrete idea of who that person is.

Field Trips. This is probably the most common example of a planned unusual event, and some of the principles we just discussed also apply here. Children should be well prepared ahead of time so they know what to expect. Review with them what the schedule for the field trip will be, what the rules are, when they will be returning ("we'll get back just before lunch"), the transportation arrangements, and the transportation rules. It is particularly important to review safety rules with the children. If necessary, role play or present a flannel board story to cover key points that the children need to know before leaving. Before leaving, also put a name tag on each child's outer garment with the child's name and the school's name and phone number.

Careful planning and forethought are important to ensure safety and enjoyment on field trips and walks.

If you are going by car, assign children and adults to a specific car in which they must go and return. This avoids a child being left behind

Field trips are fun, but they require advance planning and particular attention to safety. Children should understand safety rules; for instance, that they must stay seated in the car with the seatbelt buckled.

KEY QUESTION #5

You are going to take a group of children on the first field trip of the year. How will you and the other staff members prepare for this trip? How will you prepare the children?

accidentally because everyone assumes she is in the other car. In the car, be strict about safety rules and expectations. If the children do not comply with the rules (and in the excitement of the trip this could well happen), pull the car to the nearest curb and tell the children that the trip will continue when everyone obeys the safety rules again. Be familiar with the child safety restraint laws of your state and follow these carefully on car trips. Before and frequently during the trip, count noses. It is also advisable to get extra adult supervision for field trips (parents are often willing to go along and help) because any environment outside the school will be less familiar and less controlled, and therefore less safe.

Walks. Similar to field trips but with some different guidelines are walks. When you take the group on a walk, you again need to inform the children of expectations and safety rules. A buddy system works well. Children are paired off, and each partner is responsible for the other by holding hands. It's a good idea to establish an engine and a caboose if the children have to walk in a line (such as along a sidewalk). An adult at the beginning and end of the line are essential on a walk. Any additional adults can walk in between or act as rovers.

An alternate arrangement is to have each adult in charge of a small group of children, but enough adults must be available for this to work. Especially with a group of toddlers and young preschoolers, there may be some strayers in the group. If you know who they are, be sure an adult is holding their hands. If there are too many strayers in the group, it is probably better not to leave the building at all or to use a group stroller which can seat six children. One thing that works with some children who tend to run off is a rope. Take a sturdy, smooth, long rope and have the children hold onto it at intervals; knots tied in the rope can indicate handholds. Often a strayer will hang onto a piece of rope but not a hand.

One way to ensure that no stragglers are lost when taking children on a walk is to use a buddy system—children hold the hand of a partner or the teacher.

Unplanned Unusual Situations

Children cannot be prepared for all unexpected or emergency situations, whether these be fire drills, a broken window, or an injury; but some specific teacher strategies can help them respond calmly.

There are times when the really unexpected occurs. A fire drill or a real fire, a serious accident to a child, or any other emergency can throw the class into an agitated state or even panic. Although you cannot foretell unplanned unusual events, you can prepare the children for these situations with some discussion and practice. As with planned unusual happenings, you can role play, present a flannel board story, use puppets, or otherwise pose hypothetical problem situations so children know what may happen and what they are to do.

Emergency procedures should be thought through so that teachers as well as children know what to do. A written policy for handling emergencies should be visibly posted. Such a policy statement can be written in another language if some of the parents or staff are not native English speakers. One example of a carefully planned emergency procedure is fire drills. These should be part of any early childhood program. It can also be helpful to have an "emergency pack" available by the exit, which might include a class list, phone numbers, a flashlight, and a couple of favorite children's books in case there is a wait.

Another type of emergency situation that is helped by forethought occurs if a child is seriously injured. One teacher should stay with the child while another moves the rest of the group away. It should be agreed on ahead of time who is responsible for which tasks; a teacher who has had first aid training should, of course, stay with the hurt child. If necessary, a responsible child can be sent to get additional help—the director, secretary, cook, janitor—so arrangements for needed medical care can be made. Once the emergency is settled, review with the children what happened so they can express their concerns and feelings and be reassured.

It is a good idea to devise a cue for emergencies that tells children that this is a "red flag" situation. A combined visual and auditory signal can let children know that the teacher's attention needs to be focused on one child. This cue tells the children what they are to do—for instance, move to a self-directed, independent activity. This can be especially useful if one teacher is in charge of a group.

The unexpected does not always have to be a dire emergency. Less serious occurrences such as broken glass, spilled paint, or a minor injury can still be disconcerting to children. If children realize that the teacher's attention must be focused temporarily on the calamity, they can take responsibility for being self-directed if they have been prepared to do so.

The teacher should set the stage by verbalizing what is happening: "Usually we get ready for snack at this time. But because this window was broken, we will have to take care of the broken glass first. So instead of snack right now, we get to do something else. Jenny, get the 'Goldilocks' flannel board pieces and all of you help Jenny tell the story. Bobby, please get the broom and dustpan from the bathroom. Anita and Todd, go to the office and tell Mrs. Arnold we have a broken window." When adults are organized—even in unexpected situations—know what to do, and do not panic, children will respond in a similarly calm manner, particularly if they have been prepared for unexpected events.

SUMMARY

1. Consider four routine times: arrival and departure, meals, toileting, and sleep. All four have strong emotional significance for the child and need sensitive handling by the teachers.
2. Some important factors affect group behavior, particularly the developmental appropriateness of expectations and activities.
3. Forethought and planning can help ensure an orderly classroom during specific time blocks within the daily schedule.
4. Transitions, those times when children move from one activity to the next, deserve special attention.
5. Consider occasions when the out-of-the-ordinary happens, either planned—such as a field trip—or unplanned—for instance, an accident.

KEY TERMS LIST

attachment
separation anxiety
show-and-tell
stranger anxiety

chapter 15

Guiding Social Behaviors

When we discuss guidance of children's behaviors, we are not considering just what we expect of them today, but we are looking at the beginning of a lifelong process. It may sound like a cliche, but today's children *are* tomorrow's adults. In that context, guiding the behavior of young children takes on an important and delicate meaning. Every time you give children direction, ask their help, stop an argument, step in before a fight starts, discipline a misbehavior, or convey your expectations to them, you are affecting not just their immediate behavior. You are shaping future behavior. You are, in essence, contributing another grain to the growing hill of such grains that is becoming the child's character. In this chapter, then, we will discuss the guidance of children's behavior.

WHAT BEHAVIORS DO WE EXPECT OF YOUNG CHILDREN?

Parents and early childhood educators in general hope to help develop children who are friendly, sociable, acquiring a conscience, responsible, helpful, cooperative, and considerate (Moore, 1982). Such a repertoire of behaviors, however, does not emerge without thoughtful and consistent guidance from parents and teachers.

Among the qualities of children that parents and teachers often value is an ability to care about others, to share willingly, to be altruistic and empathetic, and to be understanding of the needs of others. Such prosocial behaviors are most likely to appear in children who live in a nurturing environment, where understanding and caring are modeled, where responsibility is expected, and where **inductive reasoning** is used (Mussen & Eisenberg-Berg, 1977). Induction involves an approach in which adults help children see the consequences of their behavior on other people through logic and reasoning.

Inductive reasoning—A guidance approach in which the adult helps the child see the consequences of a behavior on other people through logic and reasoning.

KEY QUESTION #1

List the behaviors you think are desirable in young children. Then make a list of the characteristics you like to see in adults. Now compare the two lists. Are the qualities on your two lists similar? Do you see a link between your expectations of children's behaviors and the outcomes you find desirable in adults?

Prosocial behaviors have to be nurtured in an atmosphere of acceptance, in which inductive reasoning is used and children are helped to take the rights and feelings of others into consideration.

Thoughtful and respectful guidance practices result in children who are socially competent and responsible.

One correlate of prosocial qualities in children appears to be development of self-control. This, in turn, leads to self-regulation, in which the child's judgment about the situation dictates the response (Kopp, 1982). Internal rather than external control is critical, for it means the child does what is right, not because she or he might be rewarded (or punished), but because she or he knows this action is the morally responsible thing to do. Development of inner control, a long process tied to the gradual evolution of ego strength and moral judgment, is fostered through many opportunities for the child to make decisions and to experience the consequences of those decisions (Kamii, 1984).

A climate in which such opportunities are offered is child-centered and nurturing, based on trust, and respectful of the child's growing autonomy. Adults in the child's world are careful to use inductive reasoning, focusing on explanations that stress the rights and feelings of others rather on punitive admonitions or restrictions (Honig, 1985; Maccoby & Martin, 1983). Thus, the child is told, "It really makes Ingrid feel unhappy and hurt when you tell her nobody likes her," rather than "Don't you say that, you selfish brat!"

In an article titled, "Obedience Is Not Enough," Constance Kamii (1984) differentiates between morality of autonomy—based on an inner sense of integrity—and morality of obedience—based on doing what one is told to do. To achieve morality of autonomy, children need, from an early age, many opportunities to develop a sense of personal values, for instance, recognizing that honesty is important because it is the foundation for trust from another person; "children who can see that adults cannot believe or trust them can be motivated to think about the necessity of telling the truth" (p. 12). Development of values comes from the chance to exchange viewpoints with others and from opportunities to make decisions.

An interaction style between adult and child, in which the child is given a reason for what the adult expects, has also been shown to produce children who are socially competent; have positive interactions with peers; and are self-controlled, assertive, self-reliant, generally happy, and explorative (Baumrind, 1967). The adult engages in verbal give and take with the child, provides opportunities for decision making, and is consistent in setting and enforcing rules and expectations (Baumrind & Black, 1967).

Research supports the fact that the process of child rearing and child care giving is tied to the characteristics that the child displays. A consistent, loving, firm, reasonable, inductive environment helps lead to children who are morally responsible, considerate of others, independent, and assertive. These findings give direction to early childhood settings, which are partners with parents in the process of child rearing.

PHILOSOPHIES OF GUIDANCE

A number of philosophies and approaches deal with children's behaviors. These are, quite often, addressed to parents but have relevance to teachers as well. The common aim of these approaches is to contribute positively to the development of productive and responsible youngsters by giving parents and teachers a consistent method and workable strategies. We will discuss three such programs—those of Rudolf Dreikurs, Thomas Gordon, and behaviorists—each stemming from a very different underlying theory and philosophy and with a different thrust, but also sharing some commonalities.

Dreikurs' Child Guidance Centers

According to Dreikurs, all children's misbehaviors stem from one of four underlying goals: attention, power, revenge, and inadequacy; logical consequences is one of Dreikurs' most widely used techniques.

Psychiatrist Rudolf Dreikurs, through his Child Guidance Centers, promoted a program based on the work of Alfred Adler (an associate of Sigmund Freud in his early career). Adlerian theory that people are goal-seeking organisms led Dreikurs to identify four underlying goals of all misbehavior—attention, power, revenge, and inadequacy (Dreikurs & Soltz, 1964). Thus, in keeping with the psychoanalytic underpinnings of his approach, Dreikurs felt that one cannot effectively change a child's misbehavior without analyzing and understanding which goal motivates the child.

Appropriate reaction to the child's behavior will depend on the child's goal (Dreikurs & Cassel, 1972). For instance, it is best to deal with the child who seeks attention, the usual first step in misbehavior, by ignoring the bid for attention. This is not to say that attention should not be given to the child; on the contrary, attention for positive behavior should be given freely and frequently. But inappropriate bids for attention need to be ignored.

The child who feels that bids for attention are still not getting what is needed will often escalate the behavior pattern and turn to power seeking. To respond to the child whose goal is power, it is best to disengage from any power struggle; a power contest is no contest if you, as the opponent, refuse to participate. Children need to feel important, but the way to establish their importance is not through disobedience, tantrums, and arguments. You can help the child find legitimate and productive ways of asserting that power, but not through power plays.

The next step if the child continues to feel discouraged in attempting to assert those needs is revenge. The aim is to get even for feelings of hurt and rejection by hurting others. It is important to recognize that the child's attempts to hurt you reflect the child's own pain; do not let the child see your feelings of hurt, since this will only reinforce the child's actions. Above all, do not retaliate. Instead, work on making the child feel accepted, enlisting another child if appropriate, and be as encouraging as possible.

Children sometimes engage adults in a power struggle. Power seeking, according to Rudolf Dreikurs, is one goal of misbehavior.

The fourth goal, inadequacy, is perhaps the easiest to identify as stemming from discouragement (which, according to Dreikurs, underlies all four goals of misbehavior). People around the child have often suggested to that child that he or she is inept, or the child misinterprets environmental cues and comes to such a conclusion (Dreikurs, 1972). To help the child shed such helplessness, you cannot accept these expressions of inadequacy. You continually need to convey encouragement, faith in the child's ability, praise, and support.

Dreikurs suggests that instead of reward and punishment, parents and teachers use encouragement and logical consequences. Encouragement focuses on increasing children's confidence by accepting them as they are rather than as they might be (Dreikurs & Cassel,

1972). It builds on children's strengths, thus boosting self-esteem. Encouragement is also differentiated from praise; praise focuses on your perception and approval of the child ("I'm so proud of you for helping clean the class!") whereas encouragement centers on the child's accomplishment and ability ("How nice our classroom looks now!"). Praise rewards the child's action and makes it dependent on your approval; encouragement puts the action in the context of the child's contribution to the total group.

Logical consequences—Rudolf Dreikurs' technique of allowing children to experience the natural outcome of their actions.

One of the most widely used tools suggested by Dreikurs is **logical consequences.** By allowing children to experience the natural outcome of their actions, you provide a real learning experience. If they do not come to the table for snack, they miss snack; if they do not stay with the group on a walk, they cannot go on the next outing; if children consistently put their shoes on the wrong feet, they will feel uncomfortable. As the teacher, you are not inflicting a punishment in any of these instances; the consequence of the behavior is in a child's control to change. Logical consequences also follow positive actions and provide natural reinforcement for a variety of prosocial behaviors.

Gordon's Teacher Effectiveness Training

Gordon's approach focuses on building mutual respect and acceptance between child and adult; the type of technique the adult uses depends on whether the problem is "owned" by the child, the adult, or their relationship.

The second guidance approach was developed by Thomas Gordon, a humanistic psychologist. In humanistic psychology, the basic, underlying tenet is mutual respect and acceptance between adult and child (Gordon, 1974; Gordon, 1976). His books, *P.E.T. (Parent Effectiveness Training in Action)* and *T.E.T. (Teacher Effectiveness Training)* have been used widely. The foundation for mutual respect is laid in early infancy, as adults handle and respond to babies in a way that conveys respect for what they are communicating. According to Gordon, it is important that you, as the adult, identify which behaviors are acceptable and which are not. Then, when a problem arises, you can examine the situation and decide who "owns" the problem; some problems are owned by children, some by adults, and some by the relationship between the two. The method of dealing with the issue will depend on "ownership."

Active listening—Thomas Gordon's term for the technique of reflecting back to children what they have said as a way to help them find their own solutions to problems.

When the child owns the problem, she is sending a cue that something is wrong. In this case, you use **active listening,** a technique in which you reflect on what the child is saying to help the child find her own resolution. You respect the child's right to solve her own problem and do not solve it for her through more standard reactions such as advice giving, moralizing, or distracting. Active listening conveys acceptance and thus encourages the child to reveal the true, underlying cause of her distress.

For example, if Carol reacts with an angry outburst when asked to clean up the blocks she has been playing with, your active listening response might be, "You sound awfully angry" rather than, "Carol, I need you to clean up the blocks *now.*" Carol, seeing that you accept her feelings rather than focusing on your own, can respond more openly by acknowledging her anger or by shifting to another cause of her reaction, for instance, "Nobody likes to play with me any more." Your listening and reflecting her feelings helps Carol acknowledge and find her own solutions to her problems.

Active listening, a technique suggested by Thomas Gordon, is used to help children find solutions to their problems. The adult carefully listens to the child and, as if holding a mirror, reflects back what the child has said. According to Gordon, this method can also be used with very young children.

On the other hand, when you, the adult, own the problem, a different technique is called for. If, for instance, Carol does not want to help pick up the blocks because she is more excited about joining the story another teacher is reading to two of her friends in the library area, the problem of the blocks on the floor is yours. In this case, you respond with an **I-message**, telling Carol how you feel, rather than a **you-message**, which focuses on her character. Thus, you might say, "When I find the blocks all over the floor, I'm afraid someone will trip and get hurt, and that really upsets me," rather than, "You are being very irresponsible."

I-message—Thomas Gordon's term for a response to a child's behavior that focuses on how the adult feels rather than on the child's character.

You-message—Thomas Gordon's term for a response to a child's behavior that focuses on the child's character (usually in negative terms) rather than on how the adult feels.

When the ownership of the problem is a joint one, belonging to both adult and child, Thomas suggests a third strategy. A process of no-lose problem solving, in which those involved discuss and negotiate until they find a mutually satisfactory resolution, is used.

Behavior Management

The behavior management approach is derived from behavioral theory. The underlying philosophy is that the child's behavior is under the control of the environment (which includes space, objects, and people), which can be changed by the adult through some kind of environmental manipulation. It is based on the notion that the consequences of behavior are vital, that children respect behaviors that are reinforced and cease behaviors that are not reinforced. A number of techniques have been developed as part of behavior management; some are used frequently in early childhood settings, and we will concentrate our discussion on these. (Recall our discussion of the principles of behaviorism in Chapter 5.)

Behavior management is based on the notion that children's behavior can be changed by changing the environment; techniques such as positive reinforcement for desirable behaviors and ignoring for undesirable behaviors are used.

Behavior management focuses on observable traits that can be noted and measured, such as crying, hitting, or whining, as opposed to unobservable qualities, such as jealousy, insecurity, or separation anxiety. The observable can be defined and is objective rather than relying on subjective interpretation.

When a misbehavior is to be changed, it is carefully measured (for instance, the number of occurrences are counted or the duration is timed) and quantified, as in a graph (Essa, 1995). If, for instance,

Positive reinforcement, whether it comes in the form of a hug, a smile, or a thank you, is an effective way to encourage children to continue desirable behaviors.

Edward has been hitting other children frequently, it is more accurate to know that after 2 weeks of a behavior management program he has decreased his rate of hitting from an average of five times a day to two times a day than to conclude that the program is not working because Edward is still hitting.

Positive reinforcement is perhaps the most widely used application of behavior management. You use it every time you smile at the children who are playing cooperatively in the dramatic play area, gently touch the head of the child who is engrossed in putting together a puzzle, or say thank you to the children for helping to clean up after snack; such subtle social reinforcers come naturally to most teachers. Your reaction is conveying approval of these behaviors. The principle applied in behavior management is that children will continue to display behaviors for which they get acknowledgment or attention. In behavior management, reinforcers are often used systematically to encourage specified behaviors. If Julio gets positive attention every time he hangs up his coat, he is more likely to repeat the behavior.

Behaviorists may resort to more powerful reinforcers such as food, toys, tokens, or privileges to reward a child, but only if that child does not respond to social reinforcement (Sheppard, 1973). Reinforcement, because it follows the behavior ("Everyone who helps in cleanup will get a special sticker") needs to be distinguished from bribes ("If I give you a special sticker, will you help clean up?").

It is important that reinforcement immediately follow the behavior to be effective, although the frequency of reinforcement will vary. When you first attempt to help a child acquire a new behavior (for instance, Julio hanging up his coat when he comes inside), the reinforcement must be applied every time the behavior appears; however, once the child is on the way to remembering to hang up his coat, the reinforcement schedule can be decreased gradually until eventually Julio is reinforced for this behavior about as frequently as the other children (Patterson & Gullion, 1971).

Ignoring—A principle of behavior management that involves removing all reinforcement for a given behavior to eliminate that behavior.

Just as positive reinforcement strengthens behaviors, withdrawing it, through **ignoring** or extinction, can weaken and eliminate behaviors. We often inadvertently reinforce a negative behavior by our reactions: frowning when a child shouts in the classroom; repeatedly saying, "Stop shouting, you are disturbing everyone!"; or taking the child aside and sitting with her until she promises to stop making noise. Each of these reactions tells children that they have successfully gotten our attention. Ignoring can extinguish the behavior, if it is persistent and complete. But ignoring is not always the best method to use, particularly if aggression is involved (Essa, 1995; Morrison, 1988). Aggressive behavior must be dealt with more firmly and quickly for the safety of all involved.

Time-out—Technique in which the child is removed from the reinforcement and stimulation of the classroom.

One variant of ignoring is **time-out,** when the child is given time away from both the reinforcement and the stimulation of the classroom. Consistent time-out can be effective in eliminating undesirable behaviors, but it should be used sparingly and only for situations in which the removal of the child is the best response, such as following an angry, aggressive outburst. "Time-out must not be used to get rid of the child, but to weaken specific behavior" (Peters, Neisworth, & Yawkey, 1985, p. 126).

Modeling, advocated by social learning theorists, is effective because research has told us that children are likely to imitate those they admire and like. Observational learning occurs frequently in the classroom, and we use it when we model politeness, friendliness, or caring, although modeling is not a simple cause-effect phenomenon. Certain conditions, for instance, children seeing a model being reinforced, will be more likely to result in imitation of the behavior (Bandura, 1977).

Shaping is another behavioral technique, perhaps used more frequently with children who have special needs. A behavior is broken down into smaller steps, and **successive approximations** to the desired behavior are reinforced, until the final behavior is achieved (Peters et al., 1985; Sheppard, 1973). Thus, each time children come closer to the goal or target behavior, they are reinforced. For instance, to increase a child's attention to any given activity when that child remains at one task only for an average of 3 minutes, the time required for reinforcement is increased gradually, moving from 3 minutes to 5 minutes to 8 minutes to 10 minutes to 15 minutes (Peters et al., 1985).

Successive approximations–Breaking a complex behavior into smaller steps and reinforcing a child for each step as the child comes closer to attaining the final behavior.

We will consider a final method advocated by behaviorists—**cuing,** a technique used to help children remember what is expected. Thus, teachers may use a specific cue such as a bell to tell children that it is time to come in from outside play, or a specific song to signal a transition time, as we discussed in Chapter 14. It may suffice for the teacher to catch a child's eye and give a nod of the head to remind the child of what is expected.

Cuing–A technique used to help children remember what is expected by giving them a specific signal.

Factors in Selecting a Guidance Technique

Where do you begin? What approach to guidance should you use? The examples we cited are only three of a number of approaches that professionals advocate. Some guidelines may help you select an approach to working with young children.

First, try to think through your own values and expectations as they relate to the care of young children. Do this in the context in which you were reared, because your own background will affect your views. If you were raised in a family that used firmness and fairness, you will most likely bring your own experiences to the task of guiding young children. If your family was authoritarian—you were expected to follow rules because someone bigger than you said these were the rules—then you will need to examine whether you carry this attitude into your work. Self-understanding is very important in working with young children; if you acknowledge your strengths and identify areas you might want to change, you will emerge with a more solid foundation.

As you examine your own values, keep in mind your aim in working with the children whose parents have entrusted them into your care. As was stated at the beginning of this chapter, guidance is a long-term process, contributing to the evolution of children into adults. If the aim is to develop caring, competent, self-directed adults, this process begins early in life. What matters is that the guidance principles applied are congruent with the desired outcome.

It is also important to be aware of the philosophy of the early childhood program in which you work. Some follow a specific guidance

Teachers' own values and background will affect their philosophy of guidance and the way they interact with children.

KEY QUESTION #2

Consider the three philosophies of guidance discussed in this chapter. Does one appeal to you more than the others? Why? Are there specific features in the approaches that you think would be effective as you work with children?

An eclectic approach to guidance allows teachers to select those features of various approaches that work best for them.

Eclectic Approach–Describing an approach in which various desirable features from different theories or methods are selected; drawing elements from different sources.

KEY QUESTION #3

Observe a teacher at work with young children. What guidance techniques do you see this teacher using? Can you relate these techniques to any particular theory? Is this teacher's approach based on one theory or does it seem to be eclectic?

Guidance–Ongoing process of directing children's behavior based on the types of adults children are expected to become.

Discipline–Generally considered a response to children's misbehavior.

Positive discipline–Synonymous with guidance, an approach that allows the child to develop self-discipline gradually.

philosophy for which training is often provided and which all employees are expected to use. If you are comfortable with the philosophy, there is no problem; if you don't agree with the approach, then you have the choice of discussing your reservations with the director or finding another position. Many programs, however, do not have a firmly stated philosophy and rely on the good judgment of the staff.

As we reviewed Dreikurs', Gordon's, and the behaviorists' approaches to guidance, we discussed the main features of these three divergent philosophies. Good early childhood educators use many of these techniques. When you select the salient features from different programs that you think will work, you are using an **eclectic approach**. Being eclectic, for instance, allows you to utilize logical consequences, positive reinforcement, and active listening, consciously aware that these are features of different philosophical methods; in so doing, you may be developing an approach that works best for you.

Developing a personal style of guidance takes time, and it may well change over the years of your professional involvement and development. What is important is that you are comfortable with the guidance approach you use because it is effective and supports children's development in a positive, nurturing manner.

IMPORTANT DEFINITIONS

We have been using the word *guidance* throughout this chapter. Before continuing, let's briefly examine this word and differentiate it from some other related ones. One definition of **guidance** in *Webster's Dictionary* is "the act of directing . . . to a particular end." This implies, as we discussed earlier, that guidance is an ongoing process and that techniques must be congruent with the kind of people you want children to grow up to be. Guidance is also related to **discipline,** which, for many adults, connotes a reaction to a misbehavior by the child who did not follow the rules (Morrison, 1988). **Positive discipline** helps children achieve self-discipline and can be considered interchangeably with guidance (Gordon & Browne, 1993).

One form of discipline is punishment, which implies inflicting a painful consequence for a misbehavior and which relies on retribution rather than correction (Gartrell, 1987). Early childhood experts discourage punishment because of its long-term ineffectiveness in changing behavior. Physical punishment may, in fact, increase undesirable behaviors such as aggression (Maccoby & Martin, 1983; Patterson, 1982) because it models the very behavior it is intended to discourage.

Although the word *discipline* often has negative connotations, the terms *guidance* and *positive discipline* are more concerned with the ongoing process involved in socializing children.

Punishment emphasizes what the child should not do, without giving any indication of what the desired behavior is; it is a one-time rather than an ongoing occurrence; it focuses on obedience rather than on development of self-control; it undermines self-esteem; and it makes a decision for the child rather than allowing the child to think through a solution (Gordon & Browne, 1993). Children will also learn to dislike and avoid those who punish them (Sheppard, 1973).

Punishment as a technique is discouraged because it is ineffective in the long run.

SOME TECHNIQUES OF GUIDANCE

Keep in mind that your attitude toward your job and toward children, your skill as a teacher, your ability to be consistent as well as flexible—and a good sense of humor—all contribute to setting the tone for the classroom. A respect for all children and a willingness to get to know each child as an individual are basic ingredients in positive guidance. So is a sense of partnership with the children ("me with the children") rather than a "me against them" attitude. There is no doubt: you, the teacher, are central to establishing a productive, lively, happy environment for children and adults.

We have discussed guidance from the viewpoint of what kinds of adults we would like children to grow up to be, within the context of some different philosophical approaches, and as it is related to and distinguished from some other terms. Let us now turn to some specific techniques that can help you better deal with children's behavior.

How Do You Handle Infants?

Babies do not require discipline. It is the responsibility of adults to meet their needs in a way that contributes trust, the underlying prerequisite in the process of socialization. Sometimes infants lose control, reflecting some kind of discomfort or distress rather than a problem behavior. Gonzalez-Mena and Eyer (1989) recommend that babies may need to be held close and tight to help them regain control.

Toddlers, because they are mobile and verbal, require guidance to help them develop control over their impulses. Developing internal control over behavior is a slow, long-term process. It is important to set clear limits for toddlers to ensure their safety and provide a sense of security. Toddlers are notorious for testing the limits adults impose; without stretching these limits, they cannot find out exactly where the boundaries are (Gonzalez-Mena & Eyer, 1989; Wilson, 1995).

Thorough and Creative Planning

Remember, when children are engrossed in meaningful activities that they find rewarding and interesting, they are much less likely to misbehave. Good curriculum is integrally tied to your guidance approach

("Good discipline . . . ," 1987) and will in itself provide a key preventive technique.

Reinforcement

Reinforcement should never be given gratuitously or thoughtlessly. Rather, for praise to be effective it must be personalized to what the child is doing in a way that is encouraging.

We examined positive reinforcement from the viewpoint of behavior management as a way to maintain desired behavior. Reinforcement can be a powerful tool in guiding children by attending to them when they are engaged in positive rather than negative behaviors. Be aware, however, that ineffective praise, for example, general or gratuitous statements such as "Good job!" or "Good boy!", can actually be counterproductive to the intended goal (Hitz & Driscoll, 1988).

Rather than fostering positive self-concept and autonomy, ineffective praise can lower self-confidence and lead to dependency because the teacher has placed herself in the position of telling children what is right or wrong (Kamii, 1984). Ineffective praise can also decrease motivation by making the reward rather than the activity the goal. When praising one child's appropriate behavior is used to encourage the others to follow suit, children may react with anger and resentment because they feel manipulated.

Effective praise—A form of encouragement that focuses on children's activities rather than on teacher evaluation of their work; praise that is meaningful to children rather than general or gratuitous.

Instead, it is recommended that you use **effective praise** or encouragement, which focuses on the activity and process, allows children to evaluate their own work, and discourages competition. Following are some examples of encouragement, as proposed by Hitz and Driscoll (1988, p. 12):

- Denise played with Jimmy at the sand table. They experimented with funnels for more than 20 minutes.

  Encouraging statement: "You and Jimmy played together for a long time at the sand table."

- Sue seldom talks in the group, but today she told a short story about Halloween.

  Encouraging statement: "That was a very scary story you told. When you told that story, I could just picture ghosts in our classroom. It gave me goosebumps."

Effective praise focuses on the child's activity and accomplishment. Thus, the teacher may comment on the combination of colors or shapes, or the techniques used in the art project rather than give a gratuitous statement of praise.

- Daniel just finished a painting. He comes to you, the teacher, and says, "Look at my painting, isn't it beautiful!"

  Encouraging statement: "You look happy about your painting. Look at all the colors you used."

Attention

Reinforcement is a form of attention, but attention is more than reinforcement. All human beings need acknowledgment of their existence, affirmation of their linkage to others, acceptance of their membership in the human race. Sometimes we communicate through nurturance, caring, gentleness, sensitivity, and tenderness; we do this not because we are reacting to a desired behavior, as in reinforcement, but simply because we are responding to a human need.

Whereas positive reinforcement is given as a consequence for a desirable behavior, unconditional attention is not linked to any particular behavior. It conveys to children that they are valued as people in their own right.

Reinforcement is given conditional on the child responding in a specific way, but children also need **unconditional attention.** Such attention makes an enormous difference to a child. Unconditional acceptance and response begin in earliest infancy and lay the foundation for feelings of trust. As a result, many children, receiving such attention in ample supply at home, have strong, trusting relationships in their lives. These children usually come to school full of independence and openness to new experiences. Other children, whose foundation for trust is not as firmly established or has been shaken by a disruptive experience such as divorce, may seem unduly demanding; they may constantly seek your attention, possibly through misbehavior.

Unconditional attention—A way of conveying acceptance to children by letting them know they are valued and liked; attention that is not given in response to a specific behavior.

Most often, a child who engages in a lot of attention-getting behavior is expressing a need for attention. It is not wise to provide attention when a child expresses that need through some form of misbehavior; that only reinforces the child's mistaken notion that the main way to get attention is to do something unacceptable. Such attention is generally negative and will not help the child feel good about herself. Two kinds of attention should be provided instead. One is reinforcement of appropriate behavior, as we have already discussed. The other is unconditional attention.

Unconditional attention tells the child that you value *her,* as a person in her own right, not just because she behaves as you want her to behave. You can give unconditional attention in a number of ways. Many teachers express it as they greet children at the beginning of the day with genuine statements such as, "Good morning, Jenny! I'm so glad to see you!" During the day, teachers also provide such attention when they smile at, hug, cuddle, or soothe a child or when they respond to the child who requests help or attention.

One mechanism for providing unconditional attention to a child who particularly seems to need extra attention is **special time** (Essa, 1995). The teacher sets aside just a few minutes a day, or even two or three times a week, just for the child. This one-on-one time is *not* conditional on the child behaving in a particular way (for instance, "If you ________, then we will spend special time") but is unconditional, not at all tied to the child's behavior. Special time should be allowed just for the child alone with the teacher. The teacher conveys the message, "I want to spend time with just you because you are you." The teacher can ask what the child would like to do for special time and then follow up

Special time—A method for spending a few minutes a day with just one child as a way of providing unconditional attention.

Special time, during which an adult spends a few minutes giving undivided attention to one child, can have great payoffs.

on that suggestion, whether it is going for a short walk, reading a book, or playing a game; the specific activity is less important than the teacher's undivided attention during this time together.

Such a time investment can have great payoffs. Early childhood teachers who have used special time with children who seem to be seeking extra attention have found that these children seem to feel better about themselves and greatly decrease their acting-out behavior. Some schools also recommend this method to parents (Keele, 1966), with the result that children whose parents regularly spend a few minutes using an individual time formula in one-on-one interaction seem much more self-assured and secure.

Ignoring

Particularly for attention-seeking and annoying behavior, ignoring can be an effective technique; however, any time a behavior is ignored, the attention that is withdrawn through the ignoring has to be given at other times in a positive way.

Another behavioral technique that early childhood teachers use frequently is ignoring, although it is always important to replace the removed attention by ignoring in another way (especially for the opposite of the behavior you are trying to remove). The principle of extinguishing a behavior by removing all reinforcement works well in many instances in which the behavior can safely be ignored, when all adults consistently and totally ignore the behavior, and when the child is not getting reinforcement for the behavior from other sources.

You need to think carefully about whether ignoring is the best tactic to use when you are examining a behavior of concern. Ignoring works well for annoying behaviors that are clearly a bid for your attention. Such behaviors, however, should not harm or potentially harm the child or other children. Persistent and repeated instances of whining, pouting, baby talk, crying as a means of getting attention, tantrums (for toddlers and younger preschoolers), and deliberately creating annoying noises are some examples of behaviors that can be changed through ignoring.

In all of these instances, let the child know clearly that you will not respond to the attention-getting behavior, but also tell the child clearly how to get your attention. Of course, you are bound to carry through and provide attention when the child asks you a question without whining or requests your interaction without pouting, particularly at first. It is not always possible to give the child immediate attention, but it is important to provide it when you are trying to show the child that appropriate behavior can be rewarding.

For ignoring to be effective, attention needs to be removed totally. This means that all teachers in the class have to agree to use ignoring. It is counterproductive if you remove attention from the child who throws a tantrum and another teacher goes to the child and attends in the old ways. Before using this technique then, all teachers should discuss the behavior thoroughly, agree on an approach, and help each other stick to implementing it. A caution about ignoring: One problem that makes this technique difficult to use is that the child, who has been used to getting attention for a given behavior, will often redouble his or her efforts and increase the behavior to regain the old response; thus, the behavior gets worse before it gets better (Peters et al., 1985). Ignoring, therefore, should not be tried for a day or two and then deemed a failure.

Ignoring works only if your attention, as the teacher, is the main source of reinforcement for the behavior. If the child is getting reinforcement from other sources, for instance, the other children, ignoring will probably not work. Thus, before using it, check what the child seems to expect as a result of the behavior. Does David look at you or another adult before he throws the blocks across the room? If he does, your attention is what he is most likely expecting for his efforts. If, however, other children laugh every time he engages in the behavior, and this brings out a little smile on his face, ignoring probably won't be very effective.

One well-intentioned teacher decided to try ignoring to stop three-year-old Bunny (who had three teenaged brothers) from swearing. Unfortunately, the result was that several children started using Bunny's choice vocabulary and the problem multiplied. The teacher failed to note Bunny's delighted reaction to the vocabulary expansion of the other children!

Time-Out

Time-out is a technique in which the child is removed for a few minutes from the stimulation and reinforcement of the class. It should be used very sparingly.

Although consistent ignoring should gradually eliminate an undesirable behavior, behaviorists recommend time-out as a method for speeding up the removal of reinforcement that maintains the behavior. Time-out should be used only when a child engages in a behavior consistently, not for one-time occurrences. It is also most effective when used infrequently and for short durations, 2 to 3 minutes (Sheppard, 1973). Time-out has been shown to be most effective when paired with ample attention for appropriate social interactions (Risley & Baer, 1973).

Time-out is usually carried out in an identified location, such as a chair placed in an area of the classroom with the least amount of stimulation and chance for reinforcement. If the child engages in a behavior such as hitting, the teacher matter-of-factly takes the child to the time-out area, calmly explains the reason for being removed, then leaves the child there for a few minutes. The teacher tells the child, "You hit Arthur. Hitting is not allowed in our class, so you will have to sit here until I tell you that you may get up" (Sheppard, 1973). After a

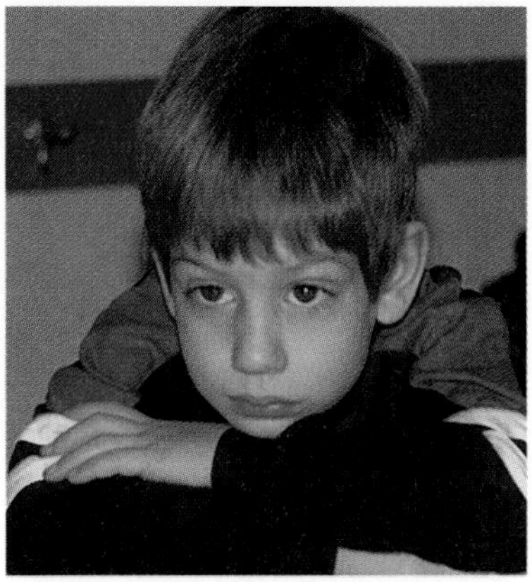

Time-out provides the child with a brief time away from the stimulation and reinforcement of ongoing activities. Because time-out is often overused, what guidelines could you suggest to ensure that this technique is not abused?

Self-selected time-out—A technique in which children are given the responsibility for removing themselves from the classroom if they feel they are about to lose control.

few minutes, the teacher gets the child from the time-out area and helps that child find an activity in which to engage.

It is often recommended that if a child engages in a tantrum or crying while in time-out, the child should remain in time-out as long as this secondary behavior continues (Patterson & Gullion, 1971; Sheppard, 1973). More recent research (Mace, Page, Ivanic, & O'Brien, 1986) has tentatively concluded that in some cases, for instance, with preschool children, such contingent delay of removal from time-out may not change the effectiveness of time-out in relation to the behavior being eliminated.

In some situations, time-out allows the child to get away from the overstimulation of the class for a few minutes rather than be removed from reinforcement. It is used to allow children a few minutes to regain their composure when they lose self-control. It should be reemphasized that time-out should not be overused. It should also never be considered the primary method of disciplining children, although, as one writer notes, time-out seems to be the most prevalent disciplinary method used in a majority of child care centers (Clewett, 1988).

One variation of this is **self-selected time-out** (Essa, 1995), in which children are given the responsibility of removing themselves from the class if they sense that they are about to lose control. In one center, a child who seemed to be overly affected by the stimulation of a busy, active preschool classroom, was given the option to remove himself from the class whenever he felt upset. He was able to go to a nearby office, which was equipped with a small table and some low-key toys. It was made clear to him that coming to this room was not a punishment but an aid to help him regain control. The opportunity to remove himself from the class when he felt the need made all the difference for this three-year-old, whose frequent tantrums and disruptive behaviors decreased dramatically.

Prevention

Prevention is an excellent guidance technique in which the teacher steps in when noting a potential problem situation before the problem actually occurs.

It is much easier on you, as the teacher, as well as on children to prevent problems before they occur. Prevention is an excellent guidance technique because you step in to stop a potential problem before tempers flare. One way to use preventive guidance is to keep an eye on as much of the group as possible; both inside and on the playground, position yourself with your back to a wall or fence where you can watch the majority of the children, even though generally you are with an individual child or a small group. Prevention is particularly important at the beginning of the school year, when you set expectations for the rest of the year. It is an especially effective technique to use with toddlers and young preschoolers, who are just beginning to acquire self-control and learn about social expectations.

Also know what triggers certain children's problem behaviors. If Shane tends to hit others when he gets frustrated, be available when you see him trying a difficult puzzle; if Rhonda cries when she does not get to be "Mommy" in housekeeping play, be available to guide children's role selection if needed; if Susannah has a difficult time sharing, keep a close eye on the block area when you see Andy approaching Susannah to join her construction project. You are not stepping in to solve the children's problems but to be available to guide them if needed in learning problem-solving skills.

Redirection

One way to prevent potential problems is by redirection. For instance, distract Sylvia if she is about to kick over the block tower by steering her to the water table, or provide Yusuf with an alternative toy to replace the one he is about to snatch from Richie. Redirection works particularly well with toddlers and very young preschoolers whose self-control is just emerging and who do not yet have the verbal and social skills required for sharing. Sensitive teachers can help one- and two-year-olds develop these attributes over time and through many positive interactions. Redirection should not be used routinely with older children, however, who need guidance and practice in handling social situations effectively (Essa, 1995).

Toddlers and younger preschoolers can sometimes be distracted from a potential problem situation, although this should not be used at the expense of helping children learn problem-solving techniques.

Distraction through humor is used very effectively by some teachers ("Laughing," 1988). Many potential "me-against-you" situations in which a heavy hand is needed can be avoided by using the light touch—distraction to something interesting and fun, directions in the form of a jingle or song, or a joke, *not* at the child's expense, of course.

Humor helps avoid power struggles because the teacher and children are joint participants in a fun-filled friendship. Telling a child, "Now . . . let . . . me . . . see . . . you . . . walk . . . slow . . . slow . . . like . . . a . . . turtle" will be more effective than saying, "How many times do I have to tell you not to run in the classroom?"

Discussion

Talking about behavior can be effective with some children. A teacher can often enlist the child's help in changing an undesirable behavior by discussing it with the child. Older preschoolers and primary children often respond well to such discussion, particularly if they have adequate verbal skills, the budding ability to look at themselves, and the motivation to change a behavior that makes them unhappy. In essence, the teacher and child form a partnership: The child agrees to try to make some behavioral changes while the teacher promises to support the child and be there to help or remind. (See the example of Victor on p. 421.)

Some older children respond well to talking about their problem behavior, particularly if they feel motivated to change this behavior with help from the teacher.

Problem Solving

Our goal for children is that they eventually learn constructive ways of dealing with and resolving conflicts, whether among themselves or with adults. Teachers can help children develop creative problem-solving skills and strategies. Earlier in this chapter, we reviewed Thomas Gordon's approach to guidance. One of Gordon's strategies involves a no-lose method of conflict resolution in which the outcome ensures that both parties are winners and no one is a loser.

The long-range goal, which is that children learn constructive ways of solving problems, can involve a no-lose method of conflict resolution.

The teacher's role in implementing this method begins with helping children identify and clarify the problem, done best through active listening. Children are then enlisted in brainstorming some possible

Sometimes children are ready to discuss a misbehavior because they are motivated to change it. The child and the teacher, in essence, become partners in their attempt to help the child change the behavior.

ways of dealing with the problem, evaluating these possibilities, selecting the one that best satisfies both parties, and finding ways of implementing and affirming the solution. The key to this approach is to avoid having one person, child or adult, impose his or her position on the other person. This method conveys a sense of mutual respect based on the equality of both rather than on the power of one over the other.

WHAT IS THE DIFFERENCE BETWEEN NORMAL AND PROBLEM BEHAVIOR?

When you view guidance as an ongoing process that contributes to the socialization of the child, it is easier to consider a solution to a problem behavior as a change that has a far-reaching impact, rather than as a stopgap measure to make your class run more smoothly. Although many children go through temporary periods in their early years that can be difficult for the adults around them, children pass through these without too many residual effects. The negative stage of many twos, for instance, often dissolves within a few months into a period of cooperation. But some behaviors persist and become more problematic as children get older. It is such behaviors that we will discuss in this section.

All children misbehave at times; the early childhood educator, using child development knowledge and exploring available information, distinguishes between normal behaviors and those that merit concern and intervention.

Problem behaviors are one of the greatest challenges facing teachers of young children. Remember that all children misbehave at some time; it is normal for them to test the limits. Some children, although they misbehave, can easily be rerouted by the adults around them. Other children have identifiable deficits (for instance, diagnosed attention deficit hyperactivity disorder) that give direction to handling problem behaviors. And then some children totally frustrate all their teachers' attempts to deal with them. Teachers can go through a series of up-and-down feelings about their own competence as they try to cope with such children in the classroom.

But which behaviors are normal, and which should send up a red flag? Some guidelines follow that can help you make that distinction.

- Know the developmental stages of the children in your class, particularly as they relate to social, emotional, and moral development. Many children of a given age go through a phase that will

All young children misbehave at times. It is important, however, to recognize signs that distinguish the normal testing of limits from behavior problems that signal a more serious difficulty. As you have interacted with young children, have you felt that some behaviors go beyond the limits of normal behavior?

most likely pass. Many toddlers go through a stage in which they assert their growing autonomy by throwing spectacular tantrums, which gradually taper off and disappear as children gain better inner control. Similarly, four-year-olds often have the propensity to blur the line between truth and fantasy; but this certainly does not predict a life of dishonesty and pathological lying.

- Realistic expectations for the age group, tempered by a recognition of individual variations among children, are important. However, if a child appears extremely immature in relation to her or his peers—for instance, a four-year-old who acts more like a two- to three-year-old in social behavior—the child may be developmentally delayed, particularly if other areas of development also are delayed.
- Look for signs of possible medical causes for problem behaviors. As we will discuss later in this chapter, a chronic infection, allergy, nutritional deficiency, or sensory deficit can profoundly affect behavior. If, in addition to disruptive social behavior, the child frequently rubs the eyes, winces when urinating, or appears unduly clumsy, consider a possible link between the social behavior and an underlying health problem.
- When the behavior of a child in your class is out of hand so frequently that you feel there is a preponderance of negative experiences between you and the child, it is probably time to bring in professional assistance to help you deal with the situation. This holds particularly true if other teachers, who are generally very effective in dealing with children, share your experience and feel as baffled and frustrated by this child as you do. Griffin (1982) suggests that if a child is so frequently disruptive and not able to get along in the early childhood program without continuous help, that child needs professional, one-to-one help that cannot be given in a group school setting.
- We generally notice acting-out children because they force our attention to their behavior. But also be alert to the extremely withdrawn child who stays away from social interactions, is reluctant to participate in activities, avoids eye contact, or refuses

to talk. Many children are shy and exhibit reluctance in social situations; however, extreme withdrawal might signal a deeper problem for which help should be sought.

- A child whose behavior changes suddenly and drastically may be signalling a problem requiring attention. You should feel concerned about the generally happy, outgoing child who suddenly becomes antisocial, or the active, assertive child who inexplicably becomes withdrawn and passive, particularly if the changed behavior persists for more than a few days and is not a sign of illness. Your first source of information, of course, is the child's parents. But if they too are baffled, a more thorough search for the cause of the change is in order.
- Finally, if you notice unexplainable bruises, abrasions, cuts, or burns on a child, consider the possibility of child abuse. Other forms of abuse do not leave physical scars but are just as damaging. Unfortunately far too many children are subject to physical, verbal, and sexual abuse and neglect. An abused child usually also exhibits behavioral symptoms of the problem. If you have reason to suspect child abuse, speak to your director so the concern can be followed up by notifying the appropriate authority. (We will discuss this issue further in the next chapter.)

When a competent teacher finds that a particular child's behavior is just beyond his capacity to cope, it is time to look beyond his own resources. It is wise to remember that many community professionals, in addition to early childhood teachers, share responsibility for the care and guidance of young children. Medical, mental health, special education, and social work professionals provide an expanded network of resource persons to call on in any community.

FACTORS THAT AFFECT CHILDREN'S BEHAVIOR

Many times the causes of misbehavior are not within the control of the child but come from some source beyond the child's ability to change.

In dealing with a child's misbehavior, it is important to examine all potential factors that might be affecting that behavior. All kinds of subtle influences undoubtedly contribute to behavior, for instance, the weather (Essa, Hilton, & Murray, 1990; Faust, Weidmann, & Wehner, 1974). But misbehaviors can be precipitated by more identifiable causes, some external, others internal. Particularly when you are concerned about a repeated misbehavior, it is wise to give careful thought to what might be triggering the problem. It is easy to blame children for problem behaviors—"he is aggressive" or "she is disruptive"—and look no further for reasons before working to eliminate the problem. But the approach to changing a problem behavior is often in the control of the adult rather than the child. We will now examine some of the factors that can affect children's behavior.

KEY QUESTION #4

Why is it important to consider the underlying cause of a child's misbehavior? Consider the consequences for a child who is continually berated or punished for a behavior that she is not able to control.

Clear-cut Guidelines

Children need to understand what is expected of them; a few clear-cut and logical rules will help children comply with such expectations.

Children generally abide by rules if they are logical, simple, and not too numerous. There is no need to overwhelm children with too many rules. Four to six simple rules, focused on personal safety and respect

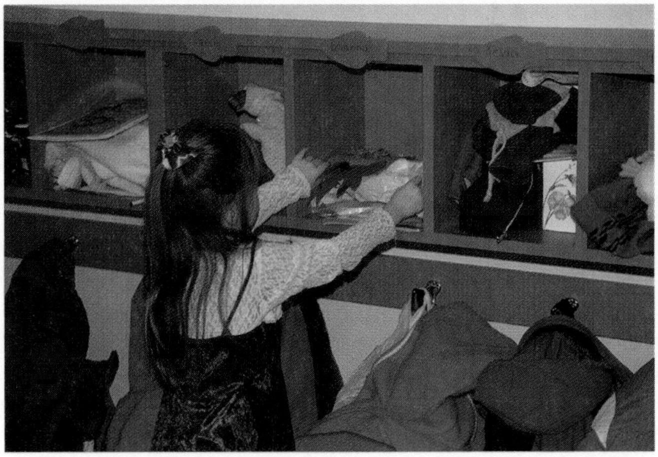

Children need to understand what the expectations are. A few simple classroom rules that make sense to children can avoid problems based on misunderstandings.

for the rights of others, can be set with the help of the children, posted in the classroom, and discussed periodically. Chapter 14 discusses rules in the context of group guidance in more detail.

Sometimes children's behavior is a function of not understanding what is expected. When a child engages in a new misbehavior, do not jump to the conclusion that the child is misbehaving deliberately. The child may simply be acting out of ignorance or misunderstanding of the expectations of the setting. For example, by their second week in school, four-year-old twins Trevor and Teddy seemed constantly to be testing the preschool program limits. One day they climbed over the 6-foot chain-link playground fence. Another time they were each swaying in the tops of two trees on the playground; on yet another day, they were found exploring and sampling the contents of the refrigerator in the school's kitchen.

The teachers were disconcerted by what they perceived as the boys' constant misbehavior. It occurred to one teacher that Trevor and Teddy may not have understood the expectations. Indeed, in talking to their mother, the teacher found that the type of exploration the boys engaged in at school was encouraged at home. The teacher decided to talk to the boys about the school rules, which no one had reviewed with them as relative newcomers to preschool. Once the children discussed these with the teacher, they agreed that the rules made sense. They diverted their abundant energy to other, more acceptable activities with the help of the staff, who made greater efforts to inform the boys of the acceptable parameters of their new preschool.

Health and Related Problems

Children often react in unacceptable ways because their bodies are not functioning well or are sending messages of discomfort or pain. When children do not feel well, they cannot be expected to behave normally. Think how you feel when your stomach is upset, your head hurts, or your nose is stuffy. Most of us become very irritable under such circumstances, and children are no different. In fact, children have fewer resources to control their behavior when they don't feel well (Essa, 1995).

When children are not feeling well, they may respond with unacceptable behaviors; other physiological factors that can affect behavior include allergies, sensory deficits, and poor nutrition.

When infants are unduly fussy or children are misbehaving, consider whether they might not be feeling well. Ill children should not be at school where they can infect others; but many children have debilitating, chronic health problems such as asthma or low-grade infections, and in spite of them, they continue to attend school. It is important to know what health limitations children might have and emergency medical procedures, if these are called for.

Allergies—Physiological reactions to environmental or food substances that can affect or alter behavior.

Many children are also affected by environmental or food **allergies**, which can change their behavior in unpredictable ways. It is not uncommon for children to be allergic to dust, animal hair, milk, or other food products, and if exposed to these, children may respond by being cranky or overactive, or by having a short attention span. Miranda was an extraordinarily bright, verbal, sociable, and creative preschooler, but she had a severe sensitivity to all milk and corn products. The school she attended was very careful to avoid giving her any food with even a small amount of milk or corn, which was difficult because so many commercially prepared products contain some form of these two foods. Inadvertently one day, Miranda ate some crackers that had cornstarch in them. The effect was swift and dramatic; the horrified staff watched as this very competent preschooler was suddenly transformed into a hyperactive, uncontrollable whirlwind bouncing through the class. Certainly Miranda was not able to control her disruptive behavior, but the adults around her had the power to control her diet so such episodes would not occur.

It is only possible to wonder what Miranda would have been like if her allergies had not been identified and controlled; the world most likely would have been deprived of a young woman who today has a great artistic and musical gift. It is also important to consider how many children suffer behavioral alterations because of unidentified allergies.

Sensory deficit—A problem, particularly of sight or hearing.

Some children have an undetected **sensory deficit** that may be affecting their behavior. Could the clumsy child who is unwilling to try anything new have a vision deficit? Might the child who is often distractible and seems to ignore what you tell him have trouble hearing? Three-year-old George proved a great frustration to his teachers; he constantly wandered from activity to activity, was uncooperative when

A child's inattention to what the teachers tell him may be a result of a sensory defect, for instance, inability to hear well or distinguish sounds, not a sign of deliberate misbehavior.

asked to help with cleanup, never sat for more than 2 or 3 minutes at circle time, and was overly loud at other times. His mother was concerned that the school was not meeting his needs because there was no problem with his attention at home, where he would sit for long periods while she read to him and where he was compliant to her requests. At the suggestion of the director, George's mother had his hearing tested. It turned out that he had a severe hearing loss from frequent ear infections, a situation that was remedied when tubes were inserted in his ears. George then became an entirely different child, attending, responding to adults and children, and becoming involved in activities; he could hear and interpret specific sounds rather than experiencing only undifferentiated noise as he had before the tubes were inserted.

Some children's behavior may be related to exposure to any of a variety of substances during their prenatal development. Children exposed prenatally to alcohol, nicotine, some prescription drugs, and many illicit drugs may suffer permanent effects. Restlessness, poor ability to attend to tasks, short attention span, lack of impulse control, and other symptoms may appear to be behavior problems that the child can control but are, in reality, side effects of a circumstance they inherited at birth.

Nutrition, both the quality and the quantity of food, is another factor that can affect children's behavior (Lozoff, 1989). A child who comes to school hungry will be irritable or listless; a basic physiological need must be met before that child can be expected to participate effectively. A child whose diet is imbalanced and lacks certain nutrients may not work to potential or may misbehave. Studies have linked nutrition to behavior and learning (Lucas, 1993; Van Heerden, 1984). In our society, children from all social strata are at risk for malnutrition and undernutrition. Although children from low-income families may not get proper nutrients because of the cost factor, middle-class children often subsist on a diet high in sugar, fats, additives and preservatives, and empty calories, also putting them at risk.

Individual Temperament

To a large degree, children's personalities are molded by their environment, but research has also shown that children are born with a certain temperament, which persists and affects them as they grow up (Thomas & Chess, 1969). Behavior is often a by-product of the child's inborn temperamental disposition, further shaped by how people have reacted to the child.

Children are born with individual temperaments–some basically easy, others difficult–that affect how they respond to the world around them. Difficult children generally have a harder time complying with expectations; in turn, adults find it more challenging to deal with such children.

Thomas, Chess, and Birch (1968), after extensive and in-depth observations and interviews of children beginning in their infancy, classified children into three general categories: easy, slow to warm up, and difficult. They concluded that the largest group in their sample—40 percent—were classified as easy children, whereas 15 percent belonged to the slow-to-warm-up category and 10 percent to the difficult category; 35 percent of the children did not fit neatly into any of these categories.

Easy children, from their earliest days, follow a regular cycle in sleeping, eating, and eliminating; are readily adaptable to change and are open to new experiences; have a reasonable attention span; are

Children are born with different temperaments. Some have an easygoing, even disposition; others have a more difficult temperament with more extreme reactions.

easily distractible; display a moderate level of activity; are not overly sensitive to stimuli in their environment; and have a generally happy disposition. Difficult children, on the other hand, show opposite traits such as irregularity, intensity in reactions, an inability to adapt, and a high activity level, and they are often out of sorts. Slow-to-warm-up children fall in between these two extremes.

It is not easy to deal with difficult children because they often defy all attempts to pacify or engage them. "When children are difficult, less confident adults will doubt themselves, feel guilty, and be anxious about the child's future and their relationship" (Soderman, 1985, p. 16). Thomas and Chess (1969), in discussing their findings, encourage parents to accept a difficult child positively by seeing his or her traits in terms of self-assertion rather than obstreperousness. Soderman advises teachers to deal with difficult children through respect, objectivity, environmental structure, effective limits, positive interaction, patience, and cooperation with colleagues and parents, all characteristics of sensitive, effective teachers. She further warns against inappropriate reactions such as ignoring the difficult behaviors, coercing compliance, shaming or comparing children to peers, labeling children with derogatory words, or punishing children verbally or physically.

As you pursue your early childhood teaching career, you likely will be entrusted with one or more temperamentally difficult children. Many beginning (as well as veteran) teachers have found this to be a real test of their self-confidence. Keep in mind that consistent, positive guidance skills and ingenuity can help channel the child's energy, perhaps into a leadership role, rather than into that of an unhappy outcast. Rely on your teaching strengths, examine and acknowledge your own feelings, and then continue to view each child—whether easy or difficult—as an individual worthy of your respect and support.

Children's misbehavior may be a reaction to stress they are experiencing at home. A variety of family changes, including divorce, a new sibling, or a parent's job loss, can upset children because they sense their parents' distress.

The Child's Family

A child's behavior may be a reaction to stress or change at home. Statistics tell us that a large number of young children will experience their parents' divorce, enter a single-parent family where there will most likely be financial as well as emotional stresses, or experience reconstitution of a family as one of their natural parents remarries (Halpern, 1987). Such major changes, even when parents are very sensitive to and mindful of the needs and feelings of their youngsters, are invariably upsetting to children who cannot fully understand what is happening. Other changes, such as a new baby in the family, a visit from grandparents, a parent away on a business trip, the death of a family member or pet, or moving to a new house, can also trigger behavioral responses. (These topics are discussed further in the next chapter, in which we will examine stress and young children.)

It is important to maintain frequent and open communication with parents to find out what is happening at home. If you know that Eddie's parents are heading toward a divorce, you can better understand his sudden angry outbursts, or you can see why Lisa is suddenly sucking her thumb and clinging to you since her baby brother was born. You cannot put Eddie's family back together or make Lisa's brother disappear, but you can convey to the children that you understand their distress and are there for them. If Eddie hits out at other children, you can let him know that you do not condone his behavior and will take measures to stop it, but that you do acknowledge his pain.

Parenting style can also affect children's behavior; poor parental discipline and monitoring have been shown to result in escalating antisocial behaviors.

Behavior problems have also been linked to parenting style. Patterson, DeBaryshe, and Ramsey (1989) have proposed a developmental model of antisocial behavior. Poor parental discipline and monitoring can lead to child conduct disorders in early childhood; in middle childhood, such parenting practices may result in rejection by peers and academic failure; finally, in later childhood and adolescence, poor parenting can lead to affiliation with a deviant peer group and delinquency. Certain family variables appear to correlate with development of antisocial behavior in children. These include a history of antisocial behavior by other family members, particularly parents and grandparents; family demographics, including education, income, occupation, race, and neighborhood; and family stressors such as unemployment, marital conflict, and divorce.

The authors, in summarizing the literature on intervention efforts, conclude that intervention at adolescence produces short-term results; thus, for the most part, it is ineffective. But intervention at earlier ages has proven to be more effective. This has implications for working with both parents and children when ineffective parenting seems to sustain behavior problems.

DEALING WITH SPECIFIC BEHAVIOR PROBLEMS

The early childhood teacher will encounter many behavior problems in his or her career. We will examine two such concerns in this chapter and look at case study examples of how some teachers have dealt with children who display these behaviors. We will discuss aggression in some detail, with three specific examples, because it is probably the one behavior that most concerns and ignites adults' emotions. Then we will examine two different examples of children who are shy or uninvolved.

Aggressive Children

Aggression—Behavior deliberately intended to hurt others.

Aggressive children deliberately hurt others; aggression should never be acceptable and teachers can use a variety of strategies to change aggressive behavior.

Children who exhibit **aggression** deliberately hurt others. It is their intent to hurt that makes the act aggressive, not just the fact that someone was hurt, although the unobservable "intent" is difficult to assign (Caldwell, 1977). Because of this difficulty, intention is generally just one criterion in the definition of aggression, others include the antecedents of the act, its form and intensity, the extent of injury, and the role of both victim and perpetrator (Parke & Slaby, 1983).

One thing that makes dealing with aggression so difficult is an ethical dilemma, the potentially conflicting needs of the total group for a reasonably safe and peaceful environment and the child's need for appropriate guidance (Feeney, 1988). Countless teachers who cope with aggressive behaviors each day have used many approaches to decrease it; these methods often prove effective, although equally often they do not. Some guidelines for dealing with aggressive behaviors follow.

- **Under no circumstances should aggression be acceptable.** A classroom rule should ensure each child's right not to be hurt, spell out a child's responsibility not to hurt others, and underline the teachers' obligation to make aggression unacceptable. Stating such a rule lets everyone know that even if a child hurts another, the behavior is not condoned and will be dealt with.
- **Aggression should never be ignored.** It is equally important to recognize that simply ignoring aggression will not make it go away. When an adult does not respond to an aggressive act, the child is given the subtle message that the adult approves of the behavior (Caldwell, 1977).
- **Prevention through vigilance is important in handling aggression.** If you know that a child engages in frequent aggression, it makes sense to keep an eye on that child. Be prepared to avert trouble if you see it brewing. You may be able to mediate an argument, or you may have to restrain the child who is raising a fist to hit out.
- **When the child is not being aggressive, it is important to take time to work on acceptable alternative behaviors.** Some children who engage in aggressive behaviors also exhibit good prosocial skills, indicating that they perhaps participate in more social interactions of all kinds (Caldwell, 1977). Such children will need careful guidance to channel them toward using the more positive skills they already have mastered in their interpersonal behavior. Other children, however, have a limited repertoire of social skills and need to be taught more systematically how to play with others, how to share, or how to be gentle. This can be done both through modeling and coaching of appropriate social responses (Parke & Slaby, 1983). Careful observation will tell you whether an aggressive child has adequate social skills or whether that child needs your help to learn them.
- **The aggressive child should be provided with positive attention.** A child who uses excessive aggression often needs to unlearn the idea that the main way to gain teacher attention is to

A Closer Look

Aggression In Young Children

Every teacher of young children has had experiences with aggressive behavior and children who frequently act aggressively. Such behaviors are a major concern to those who work with young children because at least one child gets hurt and another has engaged in a behavior that is deemed unacceptable. Aggression is not a solitary affair, but a behavior inherent in a relationship, involving more than one child. A study by Farver (1996) carefully studied aggression in the context of social groupings rather than individuals and came up with some interesting findings.

The researcher set out to examine whether patterns of aggression can be linked to a clique of children, not just to a specific child who has been identified by the teachers as aggressive. She also examined how aggressive behavior within the context of social groups relates to other traits that have been identified with children who act aggressively. These included gender, because boys have been found to be more aggressive than girls; temperament, because "difficult" children tend to elicit negative reactions from peers and adults; and social competence, because children who act aggressively may be rejected by their peers or, conversely, may find a subgroup of peers who are also aggressive and rejected by the majority of children in the class. The last point is supported by the observation that children gravitate toward those who are like them.

Farver did, in fact, find a link among these variables in the groups of four-year-olds she observed extensively during free play. In social groups made up of children who were more aggressive, had difficult temperament, and had lower social competence there were greater levels of aggressive behavior. The temperamental characteristics of these "difficult" children included such traits as high activity level, above-average distractibility, intense reactions, and negative mood. This study found that children seek out peers to whom they are similar and then they behave similarly, mutually strengthening the attitudes and values of the others in their clique. When the norm of the group is to solve problems by using aggression, then the behavior is encouraged and furthered by the group. "These results may confirm informal observations made by early childhood educators that aggressive behavior among preschoolers is 'contagious' and seems to occur in small groups of highly active and temperamentally 'difficult' children" (Farver, 1996, p. 346).

How can you, as a teacher, use the information from this study to help you in your work with children? The author of this research suggests that teachers might begin to think of intervention in terms of the larger peer group rather than in terms of individual children. The dynamic of the group may be what is continuing and promoting aggressive behavior more than factors within an individual child. Teachers could help children broaden their circle of friendships by grouping children for specific activities and projects with others in the class; this could open the door to new friendships. The author also suggests that the teacher can verbally interpret a conflict rather than simply intervening; this can help children find alternative ways of resolving problems. Thus, in your work as a teacher of young children, consider the social group implications of aggression the next time an aggressive incident occurs. You might find new insights by viewing such incidents in this light.

KEY QUESTION #5

Observe a group of children and note any aggressive behavior. What was the nature of the aggression? How did the aggressive child act? How did the victim of the aggression react? What did the teacher do? Was the teacher's action or reaction effective? Why or why not?

hurt someone else. It is important to reinforce appropriate social behaviors systematically as well as to provide a message of acceptance through unconditional attention, for instance, through special time.

- **Environmental factors that may contribute to aggression should be minimized.** Many children's aggression seems to be heightened when they are in a crowded situation. Think through ahead of time how group size can be controlled (for instance, only four children at a time at the woodworking table) or position an adult next to a child who seems sensitive to the proximity of others during circle time. Research has shown that crowding can be a particular problem if there is not enough play equipment to keep all the children busy (Parke & Slaby, 1983). Thus, adequate amounts of equipment and materials can also help minimize frustration and potential aggression. Finally, another environmental problem that can lead to aggression is an inappropriate schedule, particularly if children are not given enough opportunity to expend physical energy or if they are expected to sit passively for too long.

Toddlers Who Bite

Biting is a common toddler behavior that may stem from a variety of causes; biting should not be allowed.

One especially difficult form of aggression common among toddlers, is biting. Some young children whose teeth are still erupting may bite out of discomfort. A teething ring or other toy on which they can safely bite can provide an appropriate alternative. Toddlers may also bite in the process of exploration, out of curiosity; because they are bidding for attention and know that an adult will quickly attend to them if they sink their teeth into another child; in anger; out of frustration because of their limited verbal ability in conveying their needs or as an expression of power, since their sharp little teeth can be a potent tool with which to inflict damage (Gonzalez-Mena & Eyer, 1989). Toddlers are just beginning to learn the rules of socially acceptable behaviors, so reactions like biting should be expected. Because of their limited language ability, apologies should not be expected. One program involves children

Providing frequent and consistent positive attention to children is one way to discourage aggressive behaviors. Children tend to repeat behaviors that are reinforced.

EXPERIENCES

chapter 15

JEAN, Head Teacher, Infant/Toddler Class

Sharp Little Teeth

One-year-olds are biters. Biting starts when they become mobile and have a few teeth, around 10 months. It seems to peak between 15 and 20 months. I've found over the years that there is at least one biter in each group. But often, there are more. Sometimes, in fact, most of the children in a group bite at one time or another. Some bite back when they are bitten, doubling the problem. Groups of children vary, with some groups having few or (rarely) no biters and others groups having many. In general, two or three bites a day are not unusual.

Biting is serious, so we do many things to prevent biting. It's really important to know each child very well. Often biting is a result of frustration, so knowing what tends to frustrate each child is one way of being preventive. Any child who bites frequently for a period of time is shadowed by a teacher to try to prevent biting incidents. We also find that children respond differently to different approaches. For one child we suggested, "Why don't you give kisses instead of bites?" This really took her fancy, and now she kisses other children instead of biting them. Our lavish reactions, like, "Yeah! You gave him a kiss!" helps her see that we like her behavior. We always verbalize that biting hurts and try to model empathy and caring for the child who was bitten.

We keep a record of every biting occurrence, and this helps us look for patterns. Through this log, we found that a majority of biting occurs during transitions between activities as we move toward new activities, for instance, times for cleanup, snack and lunch, diapering, or going outside. Those are the times we are extra vigilant. We have also restructured transitions to take away some of the uncertainty and stress for the children. One child, for instance, reacted with biting when he was asked to put away his toys because it was time for a new activity. Now we tell children ahead of time, "Soon we will put the toys away," so they have a warning of what is to come. We also have one teacher stay with this child to help him through the transition.

There seems to be a strong relationship between improved language and social skills and decrease in biting. Generally, by the time children are two and a half, biting has decreased and gradually stops. When children are better able to articulate their desires and learn some of the give-and-take involved in playing with peers, they use alternative methods for getting their needs met. Leading up to this point, however, we have to be constantly available to facilitate and model positive interactions with peers.

Biting is a likely occurrence in groups of toddlers. Watchful, gentle, empathic guidance from caregivers can help young children emerge from this period with positive skills for negotiating their social world.

experiences

who bite in providing comfort and first aid for bitten children to "foster their social and emotional development" (Best, 1997, p. 3).

Biting should not be condoned. Toddlers need to hear adults verbalize that biting hurts, thus modeling empathy for the victim's feelings. For very young children, probably the best deterrent to biting is prevention. Careful vigilance, especially of children who have bitten before, is important. Observation of the child can provide clues to what happens just before a child bites, time of day when the child bites, or what activities tend to be associated with biting. A "biting log" will help identify circumstances under which biting is most likely to occur (Best, 1997). Such clues will facilitate prevention.

Let's now look at three examples of aggressive children and how their teachers dealt with aggression. In each example, a different approach proved effective. This underscores the need to examine carefully what factors might be affecting the behavior and to be flexible, creative, and open when dealing with behavior problems. No two children and no two situations are alike.

Brenda

Brenda was ninth in a family of 11 children, used to jockeying for position and attention and to helping herself get what what she wanted. She had good verbal skills, and her Head Start teachers considered her to be outgoing. Brenda often resorted to hitting other children if she did not immediately get what she wanted. She commonly hit out when another child was playing with a toy she wanted, if a snack was not passed to her quickly enough, or if someone got to a tricycle she wanted before she reached it. The head teacher talked with Brenda about the unacceptability of hitting, stressed that it hurt others to be hit, and encouraged her to use words to ask for what she wanted. Teachers tried to prevent hitting incidents whenever they could, and Brenda was willing to verbalize what she wanted when a teacher was with her to guide her behavior. But after 2 months, Brenda was still hitting others when a teacher was not there to discourage the behavior.

The teachers felt that Brenda understood what the expectation was, but chose to ignore it. As one said, "Brenda continues to get what she wants, *and* she is also getting our attention because we spend time talking with her after she has hit someone." They decided to try systematic time-out. They also discussed the importance of ample positive feedback to Brenda when she appropriately asked for a toy, shared, and took turns.

On the day they were going to start, the head teacher took Brenda aside and explained to her in simple terms what would happen from now on if she hit. Within the first hour, Brenda hit Jack because she wanted to use the blue paint he was using. A teacher went to Brenda, took her by the hand to the designated time-out chair, and said, "You hit Jack and I cannot allow you to hurt other people. You need to sit here until I tell you that you can get up again." The teachers were relieved when Brenda sat quietly in the chair.

After 3 minutes, the same teacher took her out of time-out and helped her find another activity. She did not discuss Brenda's hitting with her because it was clear from the previous 2 months' experience that Brenda understood why she should not hit. That same day, Brenda was placed in time-out three more times for hitting. The next day Brenda again spent four times in time-out, but on the third day, she was there only twice. After that, she hit only occasionally over the next 2 weeks, and then ceased hitting all together.

Brenda had learned during her first few years of life that hitting was an effective way of getting something she wanted as well as getting attention. Systematic time-out worked well in Brenda's case because it helped her unlearn this behavior by removing her from the enjoyment of the activity and taking away the teachers' attention. At the same time, Brenda was also helped to learn more appropriate social skills.

Victor

In his after-school program, seven-year-old Victor was notoriously aggressive. He hurt other children frequently and in a variety of ways, especially if he did not get what he wanted, if others would not let him join them in play, or if he had one of his numerous "bad moody days." The teachers had tried to change Victor's behavior through a variety of techniques, but the aggression persisted. One day, as the children were sitting at the snack table a little after 3 o'clock, Victor turned to Margaret, one of the teachers, and said rather sadly, "The other kids just don't like me because I hit them." After a moment of reflection, Margaret used an active listening technique saying, "You are concerned because the other children don't like you when you hit them." "Yeah," answered Victor and then, after a pause, added, "I don't like hitting." Margaret suggested that she and Victor talk about what he might do to stop hurting the other children and that she, as his friend, would help him change the behavior.

Later, during outdoor time, Margaret asked the other teachers to cover for her while she and Victor went for a walk to talk about his desire to stop hurting others. Victor conveyed a fear that he couldn't stop himself. Margaret, in turn, asked him if he could tell when he was getting so mad that he would soon want to hit. Victor thought about this, then indicated that he did feel "funny and tight inside" when he was getting mad. Margaret suggested that Victor be alert for this "funny, tight" feeling and seek out Margaret immediately when he felt that way. She promised to help him work out the problem. She also promised to help him protect his rights, because he was concerned that he might lose a turn in a game by coming to talk to her.

Over the ensuing months, Victor made a definite attempt to curb his aggression, although for some time not always successfully. He learned increasingly to seek out Margaret and tell her when his anger was rising. She, in turn, went with him back to where the problem had occurred and mediated a verbal solution. Other children sensed Victor's attempts and were amazingly supportive of him, joining in congratulating him for successfully solving his problems. Victor had the maturity and motivation to change his behavior, and with the help of a sensitive teacher and the other children he was able to learn the necessary social skills.

Ryan

Ryan, who had recently made the transition from only child to new brother, was two and a half when he started at the preschool. He had also been in a car accident recently and had a cast on his left forearm. He was one of the most aggressive children the staff had ever experienced. "If I blink, Ryan has three children crying," said one frustrated teacher. Because of the teachers' immediate concern, the director observed Ryan one morning during his first week at the school. She joined the staff in their deep concern when she counted 40 acts of hitting, kicking, hair pulling, chopping with the arm cast, and choking within a half-hour period. The whole cohesiveness of the class was disintegrating, the other children felt terrorized, and parents were complaining. Something had to be done immediately.

An emergency staff meeting was called to discuss Ryan. One teacher felt that his parents should be asked to remove him from the program, but others wanted to try working with him first, before this last resort was used. The staff brainstormed on the methods to try, but rejected most of them as too slow. They felt an urgency to do something immediate. What finally emerged was a decision to inundate Ryan with positive reinforcers. Another teacher would be brought into the room so that one of the regular staff members would be free to work just with Ryan.

The next day, Mrs. Prater greeted Ryan when he arrived at school and stuck with him wherever he went. About every 15 seconds she would give Ryan verbal praise, which took quite a bit of ingenuity on her part. In addition, every 2 minutes, he was given a star sticker and told, "Ryan, you are playing really nicely this morning! You get to put a sticker on your chart." Ryan enjoyed the attention and the stickers, but he also simply did not have the time to hurt anyone. The morning passed without any aggressive acts, although Mrs. Prater was worn out with her constant vigilance!

The next day, Mrs. Prater and another teacher took turns following Ryan and giving him constant reinforcement. By the third day, the rate of reinforcement was decreased, although a teacher still stuck with Ryan. Amazingly, no aggressive acts had occurred for 3 days. Over the next few weeks, this one-on-one attention was reduced considerably, although all the teachers continued to keep a watchful eye on Ryan. Ryan still hit other children, but the rate decreased to 2 or 3 aggressive acts per morning rather than the 40 per half hour that he had started with.

Once this frequent aggression was curbed, the teachers were able to work with Ryan on acquiring some positive social skills. At the same time, the director also worked with Ryan's mother on parenting skills. The mother, who spent some time observing in the classroom, noticed the difference in Ryan's behavior and also noted the techniques the teachers were using. She reported trying a more positive approach, spanking less frequently, and spending more time playing with Ryan.

Two years later, Ryan was still at the preschool. He had acquired some effective social skills, was very popular among his peers, and emerged as a leader of a group of boys. His aggression was turned to assertiveness, and he had no problems getting what he wanted through verbal give-and-take. Later, when he reached high school, Ryan was a good student, was elected to a student body office, and played on the football team.

Shy Children

Shy children may need the teacher's assistance to help them become assimilated into the social environment of the early childhood classroom.

Most children experience shyness at some times in their lives, although some children can be characterized as basically shy whereas others are generally outgoing (Honig, 1987). Evidence suggests that shyness is perhaps more influenced by hereditary factors than any other personality trait (Plomin & Daniels, 1986), and physiological differences have been found between children who are shy and outgoing (Garcia Coll, Kagan, & Reznick, 1984).

These findings do not, however, preclude environmental factors, because children of shy parents also tend to be shy, whether or not they were adopted (Plomin & Daniels, 1986). A cultural effect is also indicated, evidenced in one study in which young Chinese children were consistently rated as more inhibited whether they attended full-time child care or were at home with their mothers full time (Kagan & Reznick, 1986). Thus, the reasons for shyness are not easy to pinpoint. It is important, however, to identify shy children and provide assistance in social assimilation if this is called for.

Teachers can use a variety of methods to help shy children acquire some effective social strategies.

Shy children, because they feel inhibited and fearful in social situations, often have less opportunity to learn and practice social skills. Their self-concepts suffer because they are ignored, and this reinforces their feelings of isolation. Honig (1987) proposes many excellent suggestions for helping shy children.

- Observing the shy child trying to join others in play can provide insight into ineffective social strategies. From this, the teacher might identify some social skill words and phrases that she can teach the child as an entree into social situations. The teacher can also role play how to join others in their play with the child.
- Small social groups, rather than large ones, are easier for the shy child to handle, and there is also evidence that shy children may play more effectively with younger playmates. Activities should

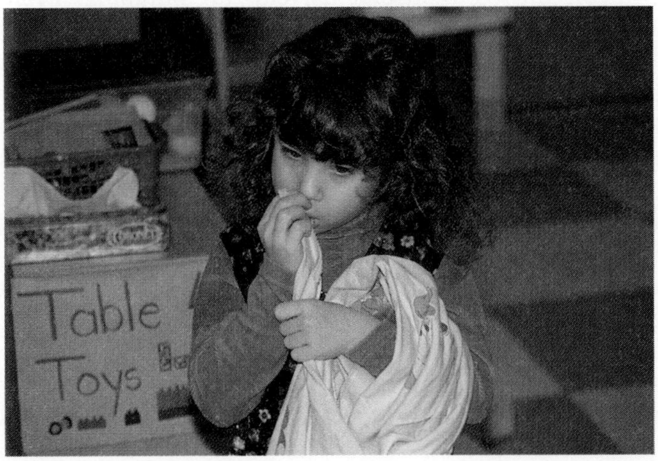

Shy children often engage in solitary activities because they have a more difficult time approaching and interacting with peers. It is important for the teacher to be aware of quiet, withdrawn children and help them become more integrated into the class if this is warranted.

be cooperative, not competitive. The teacher should be a facilitator for situations in which the shy child can experience success.

- The teacher's consistency, nurturance, and acceptance will help the shy child feel more secure. In such an environment, the child can be safe enough to take some social risks.

Bibliotherapy—The use of books that deal with emotionally sensitive topics in a developmentally appropriate way to help children gain accurate information and learn coping strategies.

- **Bibliotherapy** can also help the child, as the teacher selects books that focus on shy children and how they find friends (to be discussed in more detail in the next chapter).

Let's now examine two examples, one of a shy child and the other of a noninvolved child, and how their teachers helped them participate more fully in their programs.

Devon

Devon's mother told the child care staff that he had always been a shy child, reticent around people he did not know, and finding it hard to get involved in anything unfamiliar. He cried during his first days at school, even while his mother stayed with him, because he knew she would soon be leaving to start her new, part-time job. Since then, although he adjusted to being at the center, he still found it difficult to be part of activities and almost never joined other children in play. He observed often from the sidelines, his thumb in his mouth.

The beginning of the day seemed hardest for Devon, and it often took him an hour to get involved in any activity. He related well to Andrea, one of the aides, and she was most successful in inviting him to enter into play. He felt most comfortable with quiet activities such as art, manipulatives, and books, and he rarely participated in dramatic play or played with blocks. He never spoke during group activities.

Over the months, Devon continued his quiet presence. On his fourth birthday, he brought a special toy to share with the class. His dilemma was written on his face; he was torn between wanting to share and having to speak before the group. He finally showed the toy without any accompanying explanation. Later, Andrea encouraged Devon to talk to another child, who came up to him to ask if he could play with the toy. The two boys played quietly together for 10 minutes.

Shy children often observe others at play from the sidelines because they are not sure how to join in. What methods could you use to help this girl learn some of the social skills needed to join in more interactive play?

At times Devon played alongside Alycia, an outgoing, even-tempered, three-year-old. Andrea created opportunities for Devon and Alycia to work together, occasions that became very successful. Alycia announced that "Devon is my special friend," and Devon, in turn, became more relaxed and spontaneous in playing with Alycia. Sometimes on weekends Devon visited Alycia's home or she came to his house.

By the time he was five, Devon was still basically a quiet, shy child, but he was much more involved in the class. He was most comfortable with only a few children and felt secure enough to talk when there were no more than four or five in a group. He still preferred quiet activities, although he did not completely avoid those that were more boisterous. The teachers were careful not to force him into an activity he was not ready to enter; they were successful by being gentle and supportive.

Cheryl

Cheryl started at the university lab school at age three and a half, her first experience away from her mother. For 5 months Cheryl remained totally mute at school, although everyone heard her competent use of language as soon as she was out of the building with her mother at the end of the day. She did not participate in any form of social play and only occasionally entered into a solitary manipulative or art activity. Although she sat with other children at circle time, she never participated in songs, finger plays, or discussions. Cheryl did not smile and avoided eye contact. She was, more than anything, a silent, uninvolved observer at the preschool.

The teachers were concerned and discussed Cheryl at length. Parent conferences disclosed that Cheryl, in her parents' opinion, was a precocious child with both language and social competence. She played with cousins and a neighborhood child at home with no problems. Cheryl's parents were aware of her behavior at school, but advocated patience. "Just wait and see. She'll come around," they advised.

The teachers tried many strategies to get Cheryl to participate. They coaxed, encouraged other children to invite her in their play, planned enticing projects, and spoke to her frequently about the joys of participating. They made every effort to provide a secure and friendly environment. None of this helped. Cheryl continued to ignore all attempts to include her in the school system of the class.

After 5 months, the head teacher decided that it was time to reassess the situation because everyone felt discouraged with Cheryl's nonprogress. Another parent conference was scheduled to discuss Cheryl's home life, life history, and statements about school in more depth. A couple of new, although not startling, facts emerged from this parent conference: Cheryl had been very upset about being enrolled in the preschool and had initially cried about not wanting to go, even though she stopped protesting once she started school; and Cheryl's parents considered one of her major personality characteristics to be stubbornness.

At the same time, an observer was assigned to record Cheryl's school conduct carefully, describing nonverbal behavior, body language, and facial expressions as thoroughly as possible. The observer's notes repeatedly mentioned that Cheryl frowned, had a "grim set" to her mouth, and assumed a stiff posture when she first arrived at school each morning. The observations also noted that she carefully watched what the other children and the teachers were doing, but looked away if she saw anyone looking at or approaching her. "It's almost as if she were angry about being here but also interested," said one teacher, and this conclusion suddenly made sense to other staff as well.

As they talked more about a combination of factors—anger, stubbornness, covert interest, refusal to respond to teachers' overtures—a plan emerged. The staff decided to give Cheryl a little more "space" by ceasing their frequent attempts to involve her. They would treat her matter-of-factly, as they did the other children, but not make any more special attempts to invite her. For a week, Cheryl received considerably less attention than she had been getting during the past few months. One day, Cheryl suddenly approached another child in the class who was putting a doll to bed in the housekeeping area and joined in the play. She then went to the art area and asked if she could make a picture, then later sang with the other children during group time. It was as if she had been socially involved in the class all along. The teachers remained calm and matter-of-fact, but they were totally taken by surprise.

What did they conclude? They decided that Cheryl had been very angry at being sent off to school when she was perfectly happy to be at home; that she was "punishing" her mother and the teachers by refusing to participate, because everyone made it clear that was what they wanted of her; that she became interested in what was happening at school, but felt she could not become involved because she was too invested in her "statement" of noninvolvement; and that when everyone backed off and stopped focusing on her, she felt she could slip into the school routine in an unobtrusive way that did not call attention to her.

WORKING WITH PARENTS TO SOLVE BEHAVIOR PROBLEMS

When parents ask for help in dealing with children's behavior problems, it is important to build on an atmosphere of trust and mutual understanding.

Perhaps the topic most frequently brought up by parents when they talk with teachers is child behavior. Similarly, a child's behavior often prompts a teacher to want to consult with parents. Because parents and early childhood teachers share responsibility in the socialization of young children, it is important that effective communication, based on mutual understanding, take place.

It is critical to recognize that a child cannot be viewed in isolation, solely within the context of the hours spent at school. What happens during the other hours, the people with whom the child interacts, the quality of these interactions, and the overall quality of the lives of these other people all affect the child. Thus, to understand the child well, you must also get to know the other important people in the child's life; the most basic way to do this is through frequent, informal, positive contact (Herrera & Wooden, 1988). When a problem behavior becomes a concern to the parents, the teachers, or both, a trusting relationship that facilitates communication has already been established.

Morgan (1989) recommends that when parents bring up concerns about their child's behavior, it is helpful for you, as the teacher, to keep certain points in minds. For instance, never forget the depth of the emotional investment parents have in their children and acknowledge underlying feelings such as anger, defensiveness, or frustration. One underlying message may be a parent's need for reassurance that he or she is a good parent; whenever appropriate, provide sincere feedback. Also recognize that parents may have different values and beliefs about appropriate guidance, for instance, in relation to spanking. Acknowledge the parent's view nonjudgmentally, while stating your philosophy. If suitable, you may use such an opportunity to help the parent explore an alternative method of guidance. In some instances, clarifying the parent's misconception about child development can be reassuring and can help parents see a child's behavior in better perspective.

While helping parents deal with behavior concerns, it is also important to keep in focus the concept of guidance as an ongoing, positive process and to convey this philosophy to parents. Let parents know that your approach to guiding children is concerned primarily with helping them develop inner control and self-direction rather than merely a matter of dealing with problems. Many adults think of working with children in terms of discipline; however, you can help parents see guidance more broadly by framing your philosophy in terms of laying a foundation for lifelong patterns of creative problem-solving, positive interactions, and concern for the needs of others.

SUMMARY

1. Consider the kinds of behaviors we expect of children.
2. Examine workable philosophies of guidance.
   A. These include the approaches of Rudolf Dreikurs, Thomas Gordon, and the behaviorists.
   B. Look at how to select a personal guidance approach.
3. Consider definitions and distinctions among words related to guidance and discipline.
4. Look at a variety of guidance techniques and when these are used most effectively.
5. Consider where to draw the line between behaviors that fall within the normal range and behaviors for which professional help should be sought.
6. Consider the underlying causes of misbehavior, factors that in both subtle and direct ways affect the way children behave.
7. Two specific behavioral concerns, aggression and shyness, are of particular concern to many teachers.

KEY TERMS LIST

active listening
aggression
allergies
bibliotherapy
cuing
discipline
eclectic approach
effective praise
guidance
ignoring
I-message
inductive reasoning
logical consequences
positive discipline
self-selected time-out
sensory deficit
special time
successive approximations
time-out
unconditional attention
you-message

chapter 16

Helping Children Cope With Stress

Stress is inevitably a part of life. Hane Selye, the "father" of stress research, considered stress to be any demand on our ability to adapt (1980). Stress causes disequilibrium to which we have to make some kind of adjustment (Doyle, Gold, & Moskowitz, 1984). Undoubtedly, you know exactly what the word stress means and can define it in terms of your own experiences. We all experience stress.

A variety of internal and external causes of stress are an inevitable part of life for young children as well. In this chapter, we will examine stress and young children.

DEFINING STRESS AND COPING

Stress has proven a difficult term to define, surrounded by "conceptual cloudiness" (Garmezy, 1984, p. 44) because researchers who study stress use the word in different ways. A broad definition, however, would include an environmental change that triggers the stress and some kind of resulting emotional tension in the individual that interferes with normal functioning (Garmezy, 1984). Yet stress is not in itself a negative force and, in fact, often provides the challenge and motivation to improve, grow, and mature. In her excellent two-part research review of stress and coping in children, Alice Honig (1986a, 1986b) points out that

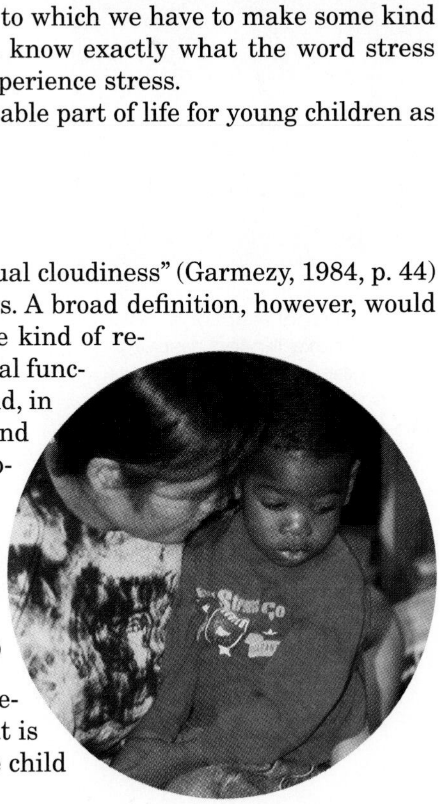

> stress continues to mark the achievement of developmental milestones. How often an infant, on the verge of toddling, stumbles, lurches, falls, crashes, and recommences bravely. Not all stresses are harmful. The struggle to learn to walk is a good example of how some stresses can be perceived as challenges that impel a child to strive toward more mature forms of behavior. (1986a, p. 51)

Other stressful experiences can be more negative, however, requiring the child to deal with an emotional or physical situation that is unsettling, frustrating, painful, or harmful. More often than not, the child

Stress—Internal or external demand on a person's ability to adapt.

Stress has been defined in a variety of ways, but a definition usually includes the concept of an environmental change that brings about a response that interferes with normal functioning.

KEY QUESTION #1

What have been the most stressful events in your life? What were your reactions? How did you cope? What feelings did you experience? Can you think of a stressor in your life that has had a positive effect on you?

Stress is not necessarily negative; if it makes demands on children beyond their ability to cope, it can be harmful.

Coping strategies—Mental or physical reactions, which can be effective or ineffective, to help deal with stress.

Stress involves both physical and emotional reactions. Young children have limited resources to help them deal with their stress and may, in fact, feel a total sense of powerlessness.

Children undergo identifiable stages of stress.

is helpless and unable to cope with this kind of stress (Arent, 1984). This is particularly true of infants, who are totally dependent on adults to relieve the cause of their stress. It appears to many professionals that the number and severity of childhood stresses have greatly increased over the past two decades. To add to this concern about increased stresses, "people who work with children report an uneasy sense that youngsters today have fewer sources of adult support, affirmation, and love than in the recent past" (Brenner, 1984, p. 1).

From our own experience, we are aware that stress causes emotional reactions, for instance, anxiety, fear, guilt, anger, and frustration in some cases, or joy, euphoria, and happiness in other instances. Behind these emotional responses are physiological, neurochemical reactions involving many bodily changes, such as in hormones, heart rate, blood flow, skin, and muscles (Ciaranello, 1983). It is important to recognize that stress is as much a physical as an emotional phenomenon because children often respond to stress in physical ways. The complexity of responses to stress has made its study a challenge to researchers and those who work with young children.

In response to stress, we use different **coping strategies** to ease the tension. Coping always involves mental and/or physical action and can take such forms as denial, regression, withdrawal, impulsive acting out, or suppression, as well as humor (Brenner, 1984) and creative problem solving. Coping reactions vary according to the stressful situation, and they depend on such innate factors as temperament, the age and cognitive functioning of the child, and a variety of learned responses and social factors (Allen, 1988; Brenner, 1984). Children also begin to develop certain patterns of coping with specific stressors through habituation and adaptation (Brenner, 1984). Some coping strategies are more effective and more socially acceptable than others; when a child uses aggression as a coping reaction to rejection by peers, we view such behavior as less acceptable than if the child uses a problem-solving approach. Later in this chapter, we will discuss in more detail how to help children cope with stress.

Stages of Stress

Alice Honig (1986a) has identified four stages of response to stress.

1. The **stage of alarm** involves involuntary physical changes, as discussed previously, for instance, adrenaline being released into the bloodstream or acid being produced by the stomach. If stress persists, such responses can result in psychosomatic illness (not an "imaginary" illness, but a case of the mind and body working together to produce a physical problem).
2. The **stage of appraisal** is concerned with the cognitive process of evaluating and giving personal meaning to the stressful situation. The child's age and psychological makeup will affect this process.
3. The **stage of searching for a coping strategy** can include both adaptive and maladaptive responses. A child may, for instance, cry, throw a tantrum, ignore the situation, find a compromise, or find a substitute.

4. In the **stage of implementing coping responses,** children will react in different ways, depending on their personal experiences and resources. A child responding defensively may distort, deny, or respond with rigid and compulsive behaviors. Responding through externalization means tending to blame others rather than looking at using the child's own resources in coping. On the other hand, a child who uses internalization is more likely to accept responsibility for dealing with the stressor. With either internalization or externalization, it is not blame for cause of the stress but the responsibility for dealing with it that is at issue here.

SOURCES OF STRESS IN CHILDREN'S LIVES

Today's children grow up in a complex world that contains a host of potential and actual stressors. A helpful framework for viewing sources of tension for children is the **ecological model** developed by such researchers as Urie Bronfenbrenner (1979). This approach takes into account the various interconnected ecological contexts within which children exist (this model was discussed in more detail in Chapter 3). Stress sources as well as potential moderating influences within the social system (Doyle, Gold, & Moskowitz, 1984) can come from any of the interacting and overlapping systems. These systems can include the family (the microsystem); its interactions (the mesosystem); the family's social network, friends, school, and extended family (the exosystem); and the larger society, with its values and beliefs (the macrosystem).

Ecological model—A framework for viewing development that takes into account the various interconnected contexts within which individuals exist, for instance, the family, neighborhood, or community.

Because stress is an individual's unique reaction to a specific event or circumstance, there is an infinite variety of possible stressors. Young children's stressors most often have their roots in the microsystem and mesosystem, and to some extent the exosystem; however, the larger macrosystem also affects young children as social forces and policies have an impact on their families. For purposes of discussion, we will focus on some common contemporary sources of stress, many of which have received the attention of researchers and theorists.

Family Stressors

Children's security is anchored in their families. Ideally, this security is created by a caring family that provides a protected, predictable, consistent environment in which challenges and new experiences occur as the child is able to handle them successfully. But families do not have such control over the environment and increasingly are caught up as victims of forces that produce enormous stress. Today's families face innumerable struggles—family violence, hostile divorces, custody battles, poverty, homelessness, unemployment, hunger, slum environments, neighborhood gang wars, AIDS, drug and alcohol abuse—that can shatter their control and sense of security.

Divorce. One of the most pervasive stressors that today's children face is divorce. It is estimated that 40 to 50 percent of the children

Many young children experience the divorce of their parents, one of the major sources of stress for today's youngsters.

Children's behavior often is a reflection of the stress in their lives. It is particularly important to maintain close contact with each child's family so you, as the teacher, have a better understanding of unexpected or uncharacteristic behaviors.

KEY QUESTION #2

Talk to a teacher of young children and ask her what types of family stressors are experienced by the children in her class. How do these stressors affect the children? How does the teacher help the children deal with their stress?

growing up in this decade will experience their parents' divorce, live in a single-parent family for a period of time, and probably experience their parents' remarriage (Hetherington, Stanley-Hagan, & Anderson, 1989). Although divorce is stressful for everyone involved, it is probably most difficult for children, particularly young ones (Medeiros, Porter, & Welch, 1983).

Young children in the midst of a divorce see what is happening from an egocentric viewpoint. They tend to attribute the departure of one parent to their own "bad" behavior, in essence a punishment for something they did wrong (Brenner, 1984). Accompanying this anxiety is the worry that the other parent may also abandon them (Wallerstein, Corbin, & Lewis, 1988), a situation so stirringly depicted in the 1979 film, "Kramer vs. Kramer." Wallerstein (1983) has found that after a divorce young children are likely to regress behaviorally, for instance, experience sleep disturbances and be tearful, irritable, and more aggressive.

Divorce is usually accompanied by a range of other occurrences that can have a profound effect on young children. Before the divorce there is often parental anger, discord, and open fighting, which can be very frightening to children. After the divorce, about 90 percent of children end up living with the custodial mother (Hetherington et al., 1989), not only experiencing a shift from a two-parent to a single-parent arrangement but also undergoing a shift to a lower income bracket, having fewer resources, possibly living in less expensive housing or with a transitional family (for instance, grandparents or mother's new boyfriend), living with a parent who is stressed in new ways, and perhaps entering or spending more hours in child care (Hilton, Essa, & Murray, 1991). All these changes, on top of the loss of one parent, can be very traumatic.

A sizable number of American families live in poverty; this includes a rapidly increasing number of homeless families. Poverty and homelessness are grave sources of stress for young children.

Poverty and Homelessness. Another area of stress on which increasing attention has been focused recently is the plight of children whose families lack adequate resources to meet basic needs. (In 1991, over 20 percent of American children lived in poverty (Annie E. Casey Foundation, 1994). This represents a disproportional number of minority children, including approximately 43 percent of African-American, 38 percent of Spanish-American, and 16 percent of Anglo children

A Closer Look

Welfare Reform and Child Care

In 1996, the president signed the Personal Responsibility and Work Opportunity Reconciliation Act, which fundamentally reformed the welfare system of the United States. Much of the control for distribution of funds now rests with the states, which, by mid-1997, set into motion their own plans for implementing the various aspects of the law. This act is expected to have some profound effects on the child care system of the country because of the implications of many of its provisions.

The centerpiece of this welfare reform is the requirement that people must move from welfare to work within a specified time. This emphasis on work "will create significant stress on the existing system of early childhood services. It has broad ramifications for quality, accessibility, and affordability of services for poor as well as working families" (Gnezda, 1996, p. 55). Millions more people will be entering the work force over the next several years, and many of them will have young children who will require care while their parents are at work. In fact, of the children whose families receive welfare support, more than half are under the age of six (Kisker & Ross, 1997). More child care providers will be needed to meet this new demand. There is concern, however, that this dramatic increase in demand may lead to lowered standards.

Compounding the problem is the change in child care funding. Previous sources of government support for child care are now consolidated into block grants over which the states have more control. Monies previously designated for child care during job training, child care for at-risk children, and transitional child care have been put into one pot of limited funding. Restructuring of child nutrition programs, while encouraging new providers in low-income communities, may discourage providers in other neighborhoods whose reimbursement is reduced. Furthermore, while previous child care reimbursement recognized that age and ability of a child affects the cost of care, the new system does not require that differential rates be specified according to age or special needs of children.

While the law specifies that a minimum amount must be spent to improve child care quality, the word "quality" is loosely defined. As many new families seek child care for their children, it is important to keep in mind that these children should be provided with high-quality, not minimal, care. A related concern raised by welfare reform is that work with young children must be considered a viable occupation for which providers are appropriately compensated. "We must work to protect children by ensuring that good-quality child care is accessible and affordable to poor families and that the expansion of the child care market promotes the professionalization of our field" (Gnezda, 1996, p. 58). To address some of these issues, NAEYC issued a *Position Statement on State Implementation of Welfare Reform* (NAEYC, 1997) which urges setting new policies and maximizing resources to meet the changes brought about by the welfare act. The impact of welfare reform on child care will be felt for a long time. Child care professionals and advocates are being challenged in many new ways by this law.

(Chafel, 1990). Chronic poverty can interfere intrusively with effective parenting and may lead to insecure mother-child attachment (Honig, 1986a).

The number of homeless families with children in the United States is also increasing. It is estimated that as many as 100,000 children have no permanent home. Children under the age of five now make up over half of the number of homeless children (Klein, Bittel, & Molnar, 1993). Such children tend to suffer health and emotional problems, developmental delays, nutritional defects, and irregular school attendance. The capacity for effective parent-child bonding is affected by the lack of privacy experienced by homeless families. Homeless children "are robbed of the most basic and essential element of childhood—reliable, predictable, safe routines" (Boxhill, 1989, p. 1). A small but growing number of public and nonprofit organizations are starting to provide services, including child care, to homeless families and children.

Other Family Stressors. We can easily recognize that experiences such as divorce, poverty, and homelessness can be grave sources of stress for young children. Children may also experience stress from family occurrences that to adults may not appear on the surface to be as stressful. For some children, for instance, the birth of a new sibling triggers regression to earlier behaviors, increased crying, and sleep problems (Honig, 1986a). Other stressors can include any event that causes a change, such as the death of a pet, relatives who are visiting, or a parent's prolonged business trip.

Children from affluent families, whose parents have a fast-paced, hectic lifestyle, can also experience stress.

Fast-Paced Family Life. Some children, who at first glance might appear to be privileged, actually experience a great deal of stress. Some dual-income professional families, in which both parents work 60 or more hours a week to keep up with their medical, law, or executive jobs, may produce a different kind of stress for themselves and their children. Parents are frequently rushed and beset by the constant need to make quick and important decisions. Their children may be in the care of nannies, are enrolled in special schools, and attend ballet or tennis classes for tots.

Leisure time is spent at special resorts that are often more oriented toward adults than children, a fact recently brought home to the author by five-year-old Nina, who was overheard discussing her recent vacation at Club Med. When looking at the child from a high-power family, surrounded by abundant material possessions, keep in mind that this child may be involved in a fast-paced and stressed lifestyle, which can take its toll.

Child Abuse and Neglect

Children who are abused or neglected are beset by multiple sources of stress.

Child abuse and neglect—Any action or inaction that harms a child or puts that child at risk.

Stress is certainly an issue for children who are victims of abuse or neglect, although the more pervasive danger is that serious harm can befall them. Because young children are inexperienced and because they depend on adults to care for their needs, they are particularly vulnerable to abuse. Most often, although certainly not always, **child abuse and neglect** occur within the family. Garbarino (1990) identifies three basic causes of child abuse.

1. Our culture supports domestic violence by permitting a range of behaviors by adults against children.
2. We have strong ideas about family privacy that reduce community responsibility for children, so that problems are viewed as "someone else's" rather than everyone's.
3. Family stresses stemming from social and economic factors often lead to parental feelings of inadequacy and frustration, which can explode in abuse against children.

Ray Helfer, one of the world's leading authorities on the subject, views child abuse and neglect as disruptions in the normal developmental process of children, with long-term repercussions. During childhood, youngsters begin to formulate and practice many skills that are precursors to important adult skills; opportunities for such practice occur naturally, as part of normal development. Parents and other adults who interact with the child have a great impact on this process. When the normal course of development is disrupted through what Helfer terms "the world of abnormal rearing" (W.A.R.), serious developmental deficiencies occur. "Adults who are victims of the W.A.R. truly have 'missed out on childhood,' that is, missed learning many of those basic skills necessary to interact with others" (Helfer, 1987, p. 68).

Meddin and Rosen (1986) define child abuse and/or neglect as "any action or inaction that results in the harm or potential risk of harm to a child" (p. 26), including the following:

KEY QUESTION #3

Check what the procedures are for reporting suspected child abuse and neglect in your local community. Which agency or agencies should be contacted? What procedure will be set in motion by such a report? What is the involvement of the person who makes the report?

- **Physical abuse** is manifest in such signs as cuts, welts, bruises, and burns.
- **Sexual abuse** includes molestation, exploitation, and intercourse.
- **Physical neglect** involves such signs as medical or educational neglect and inadequate food, clothing, shelter, or supervision.
- **Emotional abuse** occurs through any action that may significantly harm the child's intellectual, emotional, or social functioning or development.
- **Emotional neglect** is considered inaction by the adult to meet the child's needs for nurture and support.

Physical marks or unusual behavior may tell you that a child has been or is at risk of being abused or neglected, although it is not always easy to read such signs. Cigarette burns on a child's body are more recognizable as abuse, for instance, than a child's inability to sit for any length of time because of sexual molestation (Meddin & Rosen, 1986). Emotional abuse and neglect are particularly difficult to read because the behavioral symptoms could be the result of any number of causes. Figure 16-1 lists some physical signs of child abuse, whereas Figure 16-2 outlines some behavioral indicators of physical and emotional abuse that can help identify children who are being victimized. It is your skill as a careful observer, combined with your knowledge of child development, that can best provide clues about abnormal or unusual evidence that could indicate abuse or neglect (Meddin & Rosen, 1986).

Early childhood educators need to be able to recognize potential signs of abuse. It is their ethical and legal responsibility to report suspected child abuse or neglect.

FIGURE 16-1 *Physical Signs of Child Abuse and Neglect*

- The child has bruises or wounds in various stages of healing, indicating repeated injuries.
- Multiple injuries are evident on two or more planes of the body, for instance, a head injury and bruises on the ribs, which are not likely to have happened in a single fall.
- Injuries are reported to be caused by falling but do not include the hands, knees, or forehead, the areas most likely to be hurt when a child attempts to break a fall.
- The child has oval burns left by a cigarette, shows doughnut-shaped or stocking-mark signs of being immersed in a hot substance, or has identifiable burn imprints of such items as an electric stove burner.
- A child's discomfort when sitting, which could be caused by sexual abuse.
- A child has sexual knowledge too sophisticated for the child's age, evident in conversations or through inappropriate play, which may indicate a victim of sexual abuse.
- A child dressed inappropriately for the weather, for instance, wears sandals or no coat on a snowy day, which could be reason to suspect neglect.
- A child steals food because he or she does not get enough to eat at home, which may be another sign of neglect.

Adapted from Meddin, B. J., & Rosen, A. L. (1986). Child abuse and neglect: Prevention and reporting. *Young Children, 41*(4), 28.

Another source of information about whether a child has been or is at risk of being abused or neglected is the cues you might pick up from the child's parents. As you interact with parents informally, you might note whether parents convey unrealistic expectations for the child, seem to rely on the child to meet their own social or emotional needs, lack basic knowledge and skills related to child rearing, or show signs of substance abuse (Meddin & Rosen, 1986). Chronic family problems and frustrations stemming from unemployment, illness, and poverty often also result in child abuse and neglect. The majority of parents who abuse or neglect their children can be helped through intervention (Kempe & Kempe, 1978).

It is important to stress that it is your ethical as well as legal responsibility as a professional to report suspected child abuse or neglect to an appropriate child welfare or protection agency. Every state mandates that professionals report suspected cases, and specific laws protect them from any liability for that report (Meddin & Rosen, 1986). It is not easy to make the decision to report a family for suspected child abuse or neglect. You may be aware of stress afflicting the family and be reluctant to add to it through your report; the evidence of abuse may not be clear-cut or the child may tell you that he or she fell rather than he or she was hit. But it is your responsibility as an early childhood educator and caregiver to act on your concern and speak for and protect young children.

Health Stressors

Children who suffer from chronic illness or experience a serious illness or accident are faced with many health-related stressors.

Another source of childhood stress derives from health-related problems. Children suffering from chronic asthma, facing a tonsillectomy, undergoing chemotherapy for cancer, or enduring the aftermath of a serious automobile accident experience stress. This stress is a combination

FIGURE 16-2 Behavior Patterns of Abused Children Younger Than Age Five

Physically Abused Children

Expressiveness and apparent sense of self

- Bland affect, no tears, no laughter
- No curiosity/exploration
- Unable to play; no sense of joy
- Shows no affect when attacking another child
- Afraid of dark, being hurt, being alone
- Reluctant to try messy activities
- Aggressive, hyperactive, or withdrawn

Response to frustration or adversity—withdraws or has tantrums

- Language and learning
- Lack of speech or delayed language development
- Delayed motor development
- Short attention span

Relationships with peers

- Grabs objects from others without trying to retain them
- Inept social skills
- Avoids or is aggressive toward peers
- Can't wait or take turns

Relationships with parents

- Shows no expectations of being comforted; no distress at separation
- Alert for danger
- Solicitous of parent's needs
- Constantly aware of parent's reactions
- May defy parent's commands
- Difficult to toilet train

Relationships with other adults

- Relates indiscriminately to adults in charming and agreeable ways; seeks affection from any adult
- Avoids being touched
- Responds negatively to praise
- Always seems to want/need more objects, attention, and so forth

Emotionally Abused Children

Expressiveness and apparent sense of self

- Comforts self through rocking and sucking
- Does not play
- Has difficulty sleeping
- Is passive and compliant or aggressive and defiant
- Rarely smiles

Language and learning—speech disorders or delayed language development

Relationships with peers—inept social skills

Relationships with parents

- Affectless, detached from parents or solicitous of them
- Fussy, unresponsive, irritable
- Watchful, yet avoids eye contact

Relationships with other adults

- Relates indiscriminately to adults in agreeable ways
- Seeks attention and always seems to want/need more

Adapted from Brenner, A. (1984). *Helping children cope with stress.* Lexington, MA: Lexington Books, pp. 98–99, 101.

Health problems, whether the child is ill or is distressed over a parent's illness, can be a source of great stress.

of factors surrounding the physical problem—pain and discomfort—as well as of related elements such as fear of the unknown, limited understanding of what is happening, a strange environment populated by strangers, an exotic medical vocabulary that can conjure up terrifying images, and, perhaps most frightening, fear of being abandoned by the parents (Medeiros et al., 1983). This last factors causes particular distress for very young children facing hospitalization, because attachment and separation are important issues at this age. In addition, children who are seriously ill or face surgery are also aware of their parents' anxiety, and this adds further to their own stress (Rutter, 1983).

A parent's serious health problem, whether physical or mental, is also a source of stress for children. If a parent is hospitalized, the child's familiar routine is disrupted and the remaining parent or another adult fulfills some of the absent parent's functions. These changes produce stress, particularly if a new caretaker is involved. During the parent's convalescence, the child may also have to adapt to changes in the ill parent's personality, energy level, and preoccupation with health.

Death

Although young children have a limited view of death, they nonetheless experience bereavement after the loss of a significant person in their lives.

Inevitably, as a teacher of young children, you will find a need to discuss and explain death, perhaps because the classroom parakeet was lying stiffly on the floor of the bird cage, when the children arrived in the morning or because one of the children's relatives had died. Most young children encounter death, whether it is the death of a grandparent, a friend, a sibling, a parent, a family or classroom pet, or a dead worm found in the backyard.

Preschoolers' Understanding of Death. Young children's understanding of death is a function of their cognitive development. Children in the preoperation stage of cognitive development do not yet have the mental ability to grasp fully the concepts involved in understanding death; nonetheless, anecdotes as well as research show that even toddlers have some cognitive awareness of death (Essa & Murray, 1994). Young children's limited understanding can lead to misconceptions based on the child's "magical or other pre-logical explanation" (Wass, 1984, p. 12) when they come face to face with death. Some preschoolers' reactions cited by Wass (1984, from Schilder & Wechsler, 1934, and Anthony, 1972) include:

- "My grandfather died by eating too much dinner."
- "If people don't go for a walk, they die."
- "Boys don't die unless they get run over. If they go to a hospital, I think they come out living."

Death is not a single concept, but involves several subcomponents. Finality is an understanding that death cannot be reversed by magic, medicine, or other means, which is something preschoolers often believe can happen. Inevitability involves an understanding that death eventually comes to all living things, though preschoolers consider death to happen only to others. Recognizing that death involves

EXPERIENCES

chapter 16

LORI, Head Teacher, Mixed-age Class

"Wheat"

As soon as we got to school that morning, we realized something was wrong with our guinea pig, Wheat. He was acting sickly, not breathing well, lethargic, having trouble moving.

"What's wrong with Wheat, Teacher Lori?" asked several concerned children.

"Let's call a vet and see what we can find out."

A call to the local veterinary school brought a student vet to the classroom within an hour. She took one look at Wheat and said he probably would not last the day. She took Wheat with her to her lab and said she would call with news later.

That afternoon the vet called to say that Wheat had died. She planned to bring him back to the class so the children could see Wheat one more time and say good-bye to him. At the end of the day, the parents were told that the class pet, Wheat, had died and that the funeral would be tomorrow.

The next day, Wheat was lying on a piece of paper in the middle of the table, where the children gathered around him.

"Wheat is dead. His heart stopped and he stopped breathing. He can't move. But he is also not hurting anymore. You can pet Wheat if you want to."

Some children petted Wheat and others didn't.

"What do you remember about Wheat? What's your favorite memory of him? Let's write these down so we can remember what we enjoyed most about Wheat."

Some of the children with the teachers wrote lists of stories and sentences about Wheat. Others drew pictures.

"I liked the way Wheat ate the carrots I brought in my lunch for him."

"I liked how he squeaked when I came to his cage."

"I liked how his hair hung over his eyes."

"I liked how soft he felt."

Later Wheat was buried on the shores of a nearby lake. The stories and pictures were buried with him. One child brought flowers she had picked for Wheat, and these were placed on his grave.

For a long time children talked and asked questions about Wheat. Some of their older siblings, who had known Wheat when they were in preschool, sent notes or pictures that they had made. The children in the class continued to write stories and draw pictures of Wheat, which became part of a wall display about him. Most of the stories began something like, "I miss Wheat so much because . . ." or "Wheat was a great pet because. . . ."

Death is not an uncommon occurrence to young children. The opportunity to articulate their feelings and ask questions in a supportive and understanding atmosphere will help them deal with the feelings of loss and grief surrounding death.

experiences

the cessation of all bodily functions, including movement, thought, and feeling, is another concept difficult for preschoolers to grasp. Between the ages of five and seven, children generally gain an understanding of these three concepts. In addition, the concept of causality, that death is caused by internal factors such as illness or old age, rather than external factors, seems the most difficult one for children to grasp; most do not gain this understanding until a somewhat later age (Essa & Murray, 1994).

Bereavement—The grief over a loss, such as after the death of a loved one.

Bereavement. Young children's limited understanding of death does not mean that they do not experience genuine grief at the loss of someone who was important in their lives. **Bereavement** is a natural process, an essential reaction to loss, which needs to be worked out and supported (Ketchel, 1986). Children's reactions to death will vary. Although some children will show no overt signs of mourning or may even seem indifferent to the death, others may react with anger, tantrums, and destructive rages. Children, like adults, pass through stages of mourning that include denial, anger, bargaining, depression, and, finally, acceptance (Kubler-Ross, 1969).

It is important that adults, for instance, teachers, provide strong support and help in the mourning process of young children who have experienced the death of someone close. The early childhood teacher can offer such support by being willing to discuss the death, recognize and accept the child's feelings, and answer questions (Furman, 1982). This is particularly crucial for a child who has lost a parent, "the worst bereavement," because no other loss or separation is like it (Furman, 1982, p. 239).

A special example of death occurs when a young child in your class battles cancer unsuccessfully or is killed in an accident. Almost a year after the death of five-year-old Robbie, one of the children in our center, there was still considerable discussion and expressions of grief by peers in his class. During his 10 months of illness, chemotherapy, and hospitalizations, Robbie continued to see his friends and visited his class a few times. When Robbie died, the grief process involved the children, their parents, and the center staff. Frequent discussions, prompted by questions or angry outbursts, continued. Some of the older children expressed anger that they had lost a good friend whom they would never see again, while the younger children sought frequent affirmation of the finality of Robbie's death ("Robbie won't be back because he is dead, right?"). Underlying many of the children's comments was a sense of their own vulnerability, the fear that they too might die. The staff and some of the parents also engaged in discussions, both to deal with their own fears and grief and to consider how best to help the children. Robbie's death was a painful experience, but also one that brought growth and understanding for everyone involved.

Children's Fears

Almost all young children experience some common fears, for instance, the unknown, abandonment, animals, the dark, or monsters.

Lisl's mother had gone to the apartment next door, when the thunderstorm broke. Lisl was five years old, and the remembered boom of that thunderclap, while she was all alone, continued to frighten her for many years. Even long after Lisl learned about the physical workings of storms, thunder had the power to cause stress, to accelerate her heartbeat and make her mouth feel dry.

This early experience is not uncommon, and you can undoubtedly recall some generalized feeling of unease or a precise incident that caused a specific fear for you. Everyone experiences fear at some time because "fear is a normal emotional response to a perceived threat that may be real or imagined" (Sarafino, 1986, p. 15). Fear is an important self-protective response because it alerts us to danger. Children facing an unknown situation for the first time, for example, a visit to the dentist, will experience natural apprehension. In other instances, a fear can turn into a **phobia,** which is intense and irrational and stems directly from a specific event such as the thunderstorm just mentioned. A more generalized, vague feeling of uneasiness that cannot be traced to any specific source is labeled **anxiety,** and it is the most difficult form of fear to deal with (Sarafino, 1986). Overcoming phobias and anxieties often requires professional help, although teachers can support children as they struggle to understand the source of the fears and their feelings.

Phobia—An intense, irrational fear.

Anxiety—A general sense of uneasiness that cannot be traced to a specific cause.

Young children's cognitive characteristics influence the types of fears they experience. For example:

- Young children often confuse reality, dreams, and fantasy.
- They often attribute human or lifelike qualities to inanimate objects.
- Concepts of size and relationship are just developing during the early years.
- The relationship between cause and effect is not well understood yet at this age.
- Young children are often helpless and not in control of what is happening around them.

These characteristics, reflecting incomplete or inaccurate understanding, combine to contribute to children's fears (Myers-Walls & Fry-Miller, 1984).

It is not always easy to recognize fearfulness in young children. Hyson (1986) gives three examples of children who are afraid of dogs: one child runs away from an approaching dog, another stands frozen in panic, a third constantly asks questions about and looks for dogs. The source of these three children's fear is the same, but their different reactions do not make it equally easy to recognize their fear. The third child's response for instance, might be mistaken for interest or fascination rather than fear.

Although all people develop fears based on their unique experiences, some common fears of young children can be identified. Pervasive fears include the unknown and abandonment, apprehensions that commonly emerge when children deal with divorce, hospitalization, and death. Other frequent sources of fears are animals, the dark, doctors, heights, school, monsters, nightmares, storms, and water (Sarafino, 1986). Children have experienced such fears throughout time; in addition, modern society has created the source of some unique fears for children. Today's children worry not just about the dark or the "boogie man"; they also are victims of feelings of powerlessness and helplessness in an age of nuclear war, meltdown, and sophisticated missiles (Allen & Pettit, 1987). Fears are powerful stressors for young children.

Community Violence

Increasing numbers of children grow up in violent communities; early childhood programs can serve as one stable, supportive environment in their lives.

Increasingly, focus has been placed on children who grow up in violence-riddled inner cities, which have been likened to "war zones" (Garbarino, Dubrow, Kostelny, & Pardo, 1992). Every day, young children witness or fall victim to violent acts, assaults, and death in their communities. The United States has the dubious distinction of being labeled as the most violent country, with far larger numbers of murders, assaults, and rapes than any other industrialized nation (Dodd, 1993). Often an early childhood program is the only safe haven in young children's lives; thus, early childhood educators have taken the plight of children from violent neighborhoods seriously.

In 1993, NAEYC, concerned about the escalation of community violence in which increasing numbers of young children live, adopted a Position Statement on Violence in the Lives of Children (1993). This statement articulates two goals. The first goal is to decrease violence in children's lives through advocacy; the second aims to enhance educators' ability to help children and families cope with violence through improved professional practice in early childhood programs.

CHILDREN'S REACTIONS TO STRESS

Responses to stress can take many forms; they can be manifested through emotional reactions, affect thinking processes, be evidenced through aggression or withdrawal, or result in body responses such as loss of bladder control.

Stress can result in a wide variety of reactions. The reaction will depend on the child as well as on the nature of the stressful event. Behavioral reactions have been classified into four categories (Blom, Cheney, & Snoddy, 1986) as follows:

1. **Feeling—**This category includes such reactions as crying, temper tantrums, shyness, fearfulness, loneliness, low self-confidence, sadness, anger, and depression.
2. **Thinking—**Such reactions may involve short attention span, distractibility, and confusion.
3. **Action—**Active reactions could include fighting, stealing, teasing, withdrawal, overdependency, impulsiveness, hiding, and running away.
4. **Body response—**Physical manifestations of stress might entail tics, hyperactivity, headaches, stuttering, loss of bladder or bowel control, clumsiness, nail biting, stomach complaints, and thumb sucking.

As we discussed in the chapter on dealing with children's misbehaviors, it is important to consider what triggers a problem. The previous categorization indicates that children may respond to stressful events in a variety of negative ways. But behind the overt behavior is often a stressor that precipitates the behavior. Getting to the root of problem behaviors requires a thoughtful, observant teacher who gath-

It is important to recognize that children react to stress in different ways. Physical reactions to stress may include nail biting, thumb sucking, or stomach complaints. What other behaviors may signal that the child is under stress?

ers pertinent information and considers many factors when dealing with a child.

Resilient Children

Some children, despite incredible stress, are stable and optimistic; such youngsters are called resilient children.

It is important to be aware of what factors cause stress and that stress can result in a variety of undesirable or harmful behaviors. Yet, such a focus on the negative effects of stress should be balanced by considering that not all children respond adversely to stress. Some researchers have focused their attention on children who appear to be stable, healthy, outgoing, and optimistic in spite of incredibly stressful lives. They have been called **resilient children,** resistant, vulnerable but invincible, and superkids (Werner, 1984). Honig (1986b), however, cautions that although some children are incredibly resilient, "there are no super children who are impervious to all stresses in life" (p. 51).

Resilient children—Children, who despite extremely stressful lives, appear to be stable, outgoing, and optimistic.

Researchers have found some shared characteristics among resilient children. They tend to have an inborn temperamental character that elicits positive responses from adults, being cuddly, affectionate, good natured, and easy to deal with as infants. They have established a close bond with at least one caregiver, enabling them to establish a basic sense of trust. As preschoolers they have been shown to have a marked independence, playing vigorously, seeking out novel experiences, showing fearlessness, and being self-reliant. They are highly sociable and often develop a close bond with a favorite teacher. In fact, they have been described as being adept at actively recruiting surrogate parents. In spite of poverty, abuse, a broken home life, and other chronic distress, reslient children grow up to feel in control of their destinies, loving, and compassionate (Werner, 1984).

Resilient children seem to be able to establish a close bond with a caregiver. Their even-tempered nature seems to elicit positive responses from adults.

An awareness of the "self-righting tendencies" of children under stress can help early childhood teachers focus on development of traits that contribute to such resilience. Werner (1984) suggests that to "tilt the balance from vulnerability to resiliency" (p. 71), teachers need to be accepting of children's individuality and allow them to be challenged but not overwhelmed; convey a sense of responsibility and caring and reward cooperation and helpfulness; encourage special interests as a source of gratification; model a positive outlook despite adversities;

and encourage children to reach out to adults outside their family for support.

TECHNIQUES TO HELP CHILDREN COPE WITH STRESS

As an early childhood educator, you have the power to help children cope with some of the stresses in their lives, although you do not have the ability to change the source of most of their stressors. You cannot reconcile divorcing parents, make the new baby sister go away, change the rushed pace of hectic lives, or disperse the monsters in the closet. But you can help children develop some of the skills that will enable them to handle stress more effectively. As we will discuss, the kind of atmosphere you establish and your skills as a good communicator are part of a stress-reducing approach. We will also examine bibliotherapy, relaxation techniques, and play as they contribute to stress reduction in young children. Figure 16-3 contains Alice Honig's (1986b) valuable list of suggested strategies for teachers to help children cope with stress.

A Consistent, Supportive Atmosphere

When children are stressed, it is particularly important to provide a supportive, stable, predictable, developmentally appropriate environment.

A good early childhood program—one that is child oriented, supports children's development, is consistent and predictable, provides experiences that are not boring or overly demanding, affords appropriately paced challenges, and is staffed by knowledgeable and nurturing teachers—is one important element in reducing children's stress. Establishing such a program allows you to provide direct help to stressed children. One underlying component of stress is that it results from something unknown and potentially scary over which the child has little control. Thus, a safe and predictable school environment, in which children can experience success and their actions are valued, will contribute to reduced stress. In the NAEYC Position Statement on Violence in the Lives of Children (1993), provision of a developmentally appropriate program is, in fact, one of the most important contributors to helping children cope with violence.

The NAEYC publication, *Reducing Stress in Young Children's Lives* (McCracken, 1986), contains a collection of articles drawn from the journal, *Young Children.* Many of the papers deal with helping children cope with stressful events in their lives and with ways of strengthening families. In addition, about half of the articles, under the heading "Making Sure We Don't Contribute to Children's Stress," focus on ensuring that the early childhood setting is developmentally appropriate. Similarly, a child care provider's guide entitled *Day Care, Families, and Stress* (1985), published by the Texas Department of Human Resources, focuses much of its discussion on providing a well-thought-out program for young children. A recent study validated such recommendations by its finding that children in developmentally appropriate kindergarten classes exhibited less stress behavior than children in inappropriate classrooms (Burts et al., 1992).

These publications underscore the importance of the early childhood program's role in providing some elements of stability and

FIGURE 16-3 How Teachers Help Children Cope With Stress

How teachers can help children cope with stress

Considering the large number and variety of stressors that children's lives entail, and considering the fragility of coping skills and the scarcity of buffering supports in some children's lives, what can parents and teachers do to help children cope with stress? Most of the suggestions given here focus on preschoolers and school-aged children rather than infants. Some will be useful for caregivers of children of all ages. Adults who care for children in stressful life situations need to have a *wide* variety of techniques and ideas to help young children adjust better in classrooms, at home, and in stressful situations such as temporary foster care or hospitalization.

1. Fundamental to helping children cope with stress is the development of well-honed adult **noticing skills.** Recognize when a child is stressed. Be alert to changes in behavior (more quarrels with playmates, bedwetting, poor concentration) that signal stress. Parents and teachers who are sensitive to telltale signs of stress can tune in more effectively. Learn the signs of stress.
2. **Demonstrate self-control and coping skills yourself.** Be fair and sensitive to differences and problems. Demonstrate brave behaviors: Keep calm even when classroom problems arise and stresses (such as crying, diarrhea, acting-out) seem to be especially prevalent or aggravating on a particular day. If a teacher's voice is exasperated, whiny, disappointed, aggrieved, or angry fairly often, then young children learn that these are acceptable models of coping with stress.

   As a parent or teacher, **find social supports in your own life** so that you are energized for adaptive coping with problems that arise with young children. Your "feeling of confidence or faith that things will work out as well as can be reasonably expected and that the odds can be surmounted" contributes to children's effective coping (Werner, 1986, p. 192).
3. **Enhance children's self-esteem** wherever and whenever possible through encouragement, caring, focused attention, and warm personal regard. You are the mirror that reflects the personal worth of each child (Briggs, 1970).
4. Encourage each child to develop a special interest or skill that can serve as an **inner source of pride and self-esteem** (Werner, 1986).
5. **Use proactive intervention to avoid unnecessary stress.** Give children plenty of time before a transition. For example, use verbal, musical, or light-dimming signals so children can gradually put away toys and get ready for lunch. Anticipate stressful occasions.

   Preventive actions lessen the possibility and impact of stressful events. Frequent fire drills make children less terrified of loud alarms or sudden commotions. Children who have experienced drills and other such procedures become used to their occurrence and the rules to be followed, so that a fire drill does not become an occasion for panic.
6. Help children understand the consequences and implications of negative, acting-out behaviors on others and on themselves. Shure and Spivack (1978) provide daily activities to help young children improve **skills in consequential thinking.**
7. **Acknowledge children's feelings and encourage verbal mediation.** Help children learn that they are not alone in having uncomfortable feelings. Give them permission to feel scared, lonely, or angry (as when a peer squashes their sandpie). Help them *decenter*—become able to see how others also feel upset if their play or rights are interfered with. Give children *words* to express their negative feelings so that they will not have to be aggressive or disorganized when stressed. "I" statements help a child communicate personal upset and strong wishes rather than accusing, hurting, or threatening others (Gordon, 1970).

   Impulsive behavior often causes peer troubles. Help children think about the situation and their impatient feelings so they can avoid a fuss with friends. Use Gordon's (1970) active listening: "You wish you could have the new trike all morning, but other children want to ride too, so we need to take turns. "You are trying so hard to sit still until the crackers are passed to you. You are wiggling and *waiting.* Good for you."

   The "Think Aloud" lessons (Camp & Bash, 1981) teach children to deal with cognitive and interpersonal problems through verbal mediation. Children learn to talk to themselves in effective and skillful ways to identify their problem, to make plans for coping, and to weigh the merits of different solutions.
8. **Help children distinguish reality from fantasy.** Having strong angry wishes about a brother did not cause that brother to become ill. Papa did not leave home because you were a sloppy eater or were mad at him for not buying you two ice cream cones.
9. **Use gentle humor** when possible to *help children reframe* their negative thoughts and feelings. Then they can perceive mild stressors as possible opportunities or challenges. For example, if Jonathan accidentally knocked down his own block tower, you could comment matter-of-factly with a smile, "Jonathan, your elbow sure was a giant tower-smasher. Now you have a chance to design your next tower even fancier and taller."
10. If the stressor on a child is peer aggression, **focus directly on the stressor.** If a class bully gets others to tease or jeer at a child, *you must stop the bullying.* Talk to the children in your class about attitudes and values that permit bullying or threatening. Speak with the children and their parents separately. Aggression that is not addressed does not go away (Caldwell, 1977). Teachers need to be brave and direct in handling hurting. Children cannot be allowed to hurt others. A child who scapegoats needs to have other ways to feel good about herself or himself.
11. **Help children view their situation more positively.** Some stressors make a child feel ashamed as well as hurt. *Shame eats at a child's self-esteem.* Having a single parent can be such a stressor. As Blom, Cheney, and Snoddy (1986) have noted in their excellent resource for teachers: "A child can be helped to view the single-parenthood status of his mother as acceptable, not uncommon, and preferable to having both parents together and quarreling. [The child's] perception can be altered and the impact of the stress thereby reduced" (p. 82).
12. **Structured classroom activities to enhance cooperation** rather than competition. A cooperative climate in the classroom can help reduce stress. Children will flourish where they can grow and achieve at a pace comfortable

continued

FIGURE 16-3 How Teachers Help Children Cope With Stress—continued

for each. Required helpfulness has been found to increase children's sense of effectiveness and coping. Devise cooperative games to play (Honig, 1985a; Honig 1985b; Honig, Wittmer, & Gibralter, in press, Sobel, 1982).

If a child is unpopular with peers, arrange for *cooperative activities* that require children to work together. When you provide friendly younger peers as companions in mixed-age classes, unpopular children increase their social skills (Roopnarine & Honig, 1985).

13. **Modify classroom situations and rules.** Make choices and expectations easier to understand and to meet. *Rearrange environments to decrease stress.* Quiet reading corners should not be set up adjacent to tricycle riding or block building areas. Define activity areas with clear rules so that fewer tensions will arise in play.
14. **Find individual talk time** with troubled children. Find out how children perceive threats or stresses. A child may feel picked on or that nobody likes her or him. Help children think of a variety of possible solutions for their problems. *Generating alternatives* will increase a child's coping resources.
15. **Mobilize other children to help.** For example, if a handicapped child is entering preschool class, talk with the children about strengths and troubles every child, and particularly the handicapped child, might have in making friends, using materials, or negotiating spaces. Honig and McCarron (1986) have shown that normal preschool children in a mainstreamed classroom can be very helpful, empathic, and prosocial toward handicapped peers. If a child has a seriously ill sibling, *enlist classmates* of the well child to provide peer support and attention.
16. **Use bibliotherapy.** Adults can find many materials to read aloud with children to help them identify with stressed characters and how they cope. Some representative titles from the Human Sciences Press are *My Grandpa Died Today, The Secret Worry, Two Homes to Live In: A Child's Eye View of Divorce,* and *Dusty Was My Friend.* Walker Publishers have books such as *That New Baby* and *About Handicaps.* Sunal and Hatcher (1985), Jalongo (1983), and Fassler (1978) provide guides to the use of such books when children are having troubles in their lives.
17. **Have regular classroom talks, in a safe calm atmosphere,** about different stressors. Ask children who are comfortable about their experiences to share what it was like: to go to the hospital for surgery; to move to a new house or school; when a new baby was born in the family; when a parent had to go away for a long while; when there was a violent storm; when a fierce looking dog barked at them; and when a child thought she or he was lost while shopping with a parent.

    Arent (1984) has written a guide to symptoms, situations, and strategies for dealing with child stress, which can stimulate your ideas for talks. Such talks give courage to a child who may be hiding secret sorrows, thinking she or he is all alone with these troubles, or the only one scared by them.

    In the Bessell and Palomares "Magic Circle" program (1973), children sit in circles and share pleasant and unpleasant feelings, secure that they will not be judged.

    Provide verbal stems for children who may find it difficult to talk in circle time: "One time when I really felt scared, I . . ."; "My friend made me feel really good when . . ."; "One time I was very worried when . . ."

    Such openers help a teacher evaluate the appraisal reactions of young children to stressors and to learn the range and efficacy of coping strategies that children have used.
18. **Use art.** Many young children cannot verbally express fears and anger about the painful stressors in their lives. Paint, clay, and other art tools allow a child to express upsets and act out private feelings. A big, brown, smeary painting can be the way a child feels about the ambulance that came to take Papa away when he suddenly became ill.
19. **Encourage children to act out coping skills** with dolls and other dramatic play. For example, if a particular child is stressed because of a recent or future move, "doll houses, housekeeping equipment, and boxes are good for helping a child act out a moving experience. Toy telephones allow imaginary communication with friends in other places and friends that the child would like to know better" (Long, 1985, p. 8). Early in the school year, doll play can help children deal with separation from home.

    Use puppets to act out positive problem-solving responses to ordinary daily stressors that a child might encounter. Some sample topics might be forgetting to bring lunch or lunch money to school; wanting a turn on the slide and finding a lot of children ahead of you; wanting a teacher to read to you right away when she or he is busy helping another child; feeling another child unfairly got a bigger portion than you.
20. **Involve parents.** Recommended good books about recognizing and managing child stress (Arent, 1984; Brenner, 1984; Kersey, 1985; Wolff, 1969). Remind parents about how important rest and good nutrition are for coping with stressful situations (see Honig and Oski, 1984, for a discussion of iron deficiency symptoms of irritability and solemnity in infants and young children).

    Listen empathetically if parents are able to share some of their life stresses. Together, you and the child's family can be a mutually supportive human system to reduce stress effects and to enhance the security of a child who is troubled.

From Honig, A. S. (1986). Stress and coping in children (Part 2): Interpersonal family relationships. *Young Children, 41*(5), 55-57.

security for young children under stress. The tentative results of a recent study support the basic premises of these publications. The researchers compared a developmentally appropriate and a developmentally inappropriate classroom and found significantly higher

One way in which the early childhood teacher can reduce stress in young children is to provide a supportive, developmentally appropriate classroom environment.

rates of stress in the children involved in the latter (Burts, Hart, Charlesworth, & Kirk, 1990).

Communication

The teacher's communication, through understanding and acknowledgement of the child's feelings, can help a child cope with stress.

One of the most important ways that you, as a teacher of young children, can help mitigate stress is by how and what you communicate. The process (how you communicate) as well as the content (what you say) of communication are important. Thus, it is important that someone share the child's concern, acknowledge how the child feels, and provide reassurance by hugging, holding, or rocking. Allen (1988) suggests that such responses are particularly important for very young children and for older children who are extremely distressed. Listening carefully to what children say and encouraging them to ask questions, express feelings, and discuss their perceptions are important in helping children deal with stress in their lives.

In addition to such responses, it is also important to give accurate and developmentally appropriate explanations and information to children old enough to understand. Vague reassurances such as "don't worry about the doctor" do not help the child develop control and alternative coping skills. On the other hand, information about what the doctor will do and what instruments will be used will help reduce the child's sense of helplessness (Hyson, 1986, p. 5).

Four-year-old Percy, whose parents were in the process of getting a divorce, spent most of his time at the child care center involved in activities and play. But when he was confronted with minor frustrations, he would fly into angry outbursts, using abusive language and exhibiting unmanageable behavior. Such conduct was quite different from Percy's former competent approach to life. His teacher, Ann, had been in close contact with Percy's mother and recognized his behavior as resulting from stress. Ann did several things for Percy. She spent extra time with him, encouraging him to talk about his father, his fears, and his anxieties. She also tried to give Percy accurate information about the divorce, based on what she had learned from his mother. When Percy flew into one of his rages, Ann would quickly pick him up, move with him away from centers of activity in the class, and hold him in her lap and rock him. This calmed him, and within 5 or 10 minutes he was usually ready to return to an activity or sit quietly looking at a book.

Bibliotherapy

Some excellent children's books, that deal with sensitive topics, can help children gain accurate information and learn coping strategies.

KEY QUESTION #4

Review several children's books, such as those listed in Figure 16-4, that deal with sensitive issues. How do these books address such topics as loss, divorce, or fear? Could a young child identify with the characters? Do the books offer alternatives to the child who is experiencing a similar stressor?

The term *bibliotherapy* refers to the use of books that deal with emotionally sensitive topics in a developmentally appropriate way that helps children gain accurate information and learn coping strategies. Jalongo (1986) defines bibliotherapy as "using literature for the purpose of promoting mental health or the use of books in a therapeutic sense" (p. 42). Bibliotherapy provides a relatively comfortable form of dealing with difficult topics because book reading is a familiar activity for both teachers and children (Blom et al., 1986). Jalongo (1986, pp. 42–43) identifies three potential advantages of such books.

1. **Information—**It stimulates the adult-child exchange of ideas on significant topics.
2. **Relevance—**It encourages the child to make meaningful connections between school experiences and daily life.
3. **Acceptance—**It legitimizes the child's emotional responses to crisis situations.

Today, many books are available that deal with such issues as death, divorce, new siblings, separation, sexuality, disabilities, hospitalization, and fears (*Day Care, Families, and Stress . . .*, 1985; Jalongo, 1986). Books can help children replace a frightening mental image with a more realistic one by presenting accurate facts about a topic, for instance, helping children relieve the anxiety of facing the first day of school (Kleckner & Engel, 1988).

But, as Jalongo (1986) cautions, just because a book deals with a sensitive topic does not necessarily make it a good book for young children. In addition to the general guidelines for evaluating good children's literature presented in Chapter 14, crisis-oriented children's books also need to have settings and characters with which children can identify, accurately depict and explain the crisis situation, examine the origins of emotional reactions, consider individual differences, model good coping strategies, and display optimism (Jalongo, 1986). Figure 16-4 lists selected books for bibliotherapeutic use with young children.

Relaxation Techniques

Relaxation techniques and imagery can help children reduce some of the tension associated with stress.

Children can be helped to reduce some of the physical tension associated with stress through guided relaxation exercises. Relaxation routines can easily be incorporated into the early childhood program, for instance, as part of movement activities or during rest or pre-nap time. Some programs schedule a regular relaxation period for specific exercises.

Progressive relaxation—A technique in which various specified muscle groups are tensed then relaxed systematically.

One approach to relaxation is to experience muscle tension followed by muscle relaxation (Humphrey & Humphrey, 1985). For instance, children can be instructed to make themselves stiff as a board, then to become as floppy as a Raggedy Ann or Andy doll. A more systematic approach, called **progressive relaxation,** asks children to

FIGURE 16-4 Suggested Bibliotherapeutic Books

Loss, Death, and Dying

Burningham, J. (1984). *Granpa.* New York: Crown. **Ages 3–8.**

Buscaglia, L. (1982). *The fall of Freddie the Leaf: A story of life for all ages.* Thorofare, NJ: Charles B. Slack, **Ages 4 and up.**

Clifton, L. (1983). *Everett Anderson's goodbye.* New York: Holt, Rinehart and Winston. **Ages 4–8.**

DePaola, T. (1981). *Now one foot, now the other.* New York: Putnam. **Ages 4–8.**

Hickman, M. W. (1984). *Last week my brother Anthony died.* Nashville, TN: Abingdon. **Ages 3–8.**

Sharmat, M. W. (1977). *I don't care.* New York: Macmillan. **Ages 3–5.**

Wilhelm, H. (1985). *I'll always love you.* New York: Crown. **Ages 3–8.**

Family-Related Matters

Alexander, M. (1979). *When the new baby comes, I'm moving out.* New York: Dial Press Books. **Ages 3–7.**

Baum, L. (1986). *One more time.* New York: Morrow. **Ages 4–8.**

Cain, B. S., & Benedek, E. P. (1976). *What would you do? A child's book about divorce.* New York: Saturday Evening Post. **Ages 4–7.**

Caines, J. (1977). *Daddy.* New York: Harper & Row. **Ages 4–8.**

Drescher, J. (1986). *My mother is getting married.* New York: Dial Press Books. **Ages 4–8.**

Galloway, P. (1985). *Jennifer has two daddies.* Toronto: Women's Educational Press. **Ages 3–8.**

Girard, L. W. (1987). *At daddy's on Saturday.* Niles, IL: Albert Whitman. **Ages 3–8.**

Lapsley, S. (1975). *I am adopted.* New York: Bradburg. **Ages 2½–6.**

Lasky, J., & Knight, M. B. (1984). *A baby for Max.* New York: Scribner. **Ages 4–7.**

Perry, P., & Lynch, M. (1978). *Mommy and Daddy are divorced.* New York: Dial Press Books. **Ages 4–8.**

Smith, P. (1981). *Jenny's baby brother.* New York: Viking Press. **Ages 3½–7.**

Stinson, K., & Reynolds, N. L. (1985). *Mom and Dad don't live together anymore.* Toronto: Annick Press. **Ages 3–5.**

Vigna, J. (1982). *Daddy's new baby.* Niles, IL: Albert Whitman. **Ages 4–7.**

Vigna, J. (1988). *I wish daddy didn't drink so much.* Niles, IL: Albert Whitman. **Ages 3–7.**

Fears

Aylesworth, J. (1985). *The bad dream.* New York: Albert Whitman. **Ages 4–8.**

Bunting, E. (1987). *Ghost's hour, spook's hour.* New York: Clarion. **Ages 3–7.**

Dragonwagon, C. (1977). *Will it be OK?* New York: Harper & Row. **Ages 4–8.**

Howe, J. (1986). *There's a monster under my bed.* New York: Atheneum. **Ages 4–8.**

Jonas, A. (1984). *Holes and peeks.* New York: Greenwillow. **Ages 2–5.**

Jones, R. (1982). *The biggest, meanest, ugliest dog in the whole wide world.* New York: Macmillan. **Ages 3–7.**

Mayer, M. (1969). *There's a nightmare in my closet.* New York: Dial Press Books. **Ages 4–7.**

Robinson, D. (1981). *No elephants allowed.* New York: Houghton Mifflin. **Ages 4–7.**

Szilagyi, M. (1985). *Thunderstorm.* New York: Bradbury Press. **Ages 3–6.**

Viorst, J. (1972). *Alexander and the terrible, horrible, no good, very bad day.* New York: Atheneum Press. **Ages 3–6.**

Viorst, J. (1988). *The good-bye book.* New York: Atheneum Press. **Ages 3–7.**

Illness and Hospitalization

Brandenberg, F. (1978). *I wish I was sick, too!* New York: Puffin. **Ages 3–8.**

Hautzig, D. (1985). *A visit to the Sesame Street hospital.* New York: Random/Children's Television Workshop. **Ages 2–7.**

Krementz, J. (1986). *Taryn goes to the dentist.* New York: Crown. **Ages 3–4.**

Rockwell, A., & Rockwell, H. (1982). *Sick in bed.* New York: Macmillan. **Ages 3–6.**

Rockwell, A., & Rockwell, H. (1985). *The emergency room.* New York: Macmillan. **Ages 2–5.**

Rockwell, H. (1973). *My doctor.* New York: Macmillan. **Ages 2–6.**

Rogers, F. (1986). *Going to the doctor.* New York: Putnam. **Ages 3–6.**

Wolde, G. (1976). *Betsy and the chicken pox.* New York: Random House, **Ages 3–6.**

First Day at School

Bram, E. (1977). *I don't want to go to school.* New York: Greenwillow. **Ages 3–6.**

Frandsen, K. (1984). *I started school today.* Chicago: Childrens Press. **Ages 4–7.**

Gross, A. (1982). *The I don't want to go to school book.* Chicago: Childrens Press. **Ages 5–8.**

Hamilton-Merritt, J. (1982). *My first days of school.* New York: Simon and Shuster. **Ages 4–6.**

Howe, J. (1986). *When you go to kindergarten.* New York: Alfred Knopf. **Ages 5–6.**

Oxenbury, H. (1983). *First day of school.* New York: Dial Press Books. **Ages 2½–4.**

Rogers, F. (1985). *Going to day care.* New York: Putnam. **Ages 3–6.**

Wolde, G. (1976). *Betsy's first day at nursery school.* New York: Random House. **Ages 3–6.**

Sources:

Cuddigan, M. & Hanson, M. B. (1988). *Growing pains: Helping children deal with everyday problems through reading.* Chicago: American Library Association.

Day care, families, and stress. (1985). Austin, TX: Child Development Program Division, Texas Department of Human Resources.

Jalongo, M. R. (1986). Using crisis-oriented books with young children. In J. B. McCracken (Ed.), *Reducing stress in young children's lives.* Washington, DC: National Association for the Education of Young Children, p. 46.

The bookfinder: A guide to children's literature about the needs and problems of youth aged 2–15 (vol. 1). (1977). Circle Pines, MN: American Guidance Service.

"Now, make yourselves as floppy as a Raggedy Ann or Andy doll." Relaxation exercises are an enjoyable way to reduce tension.

tense and then relax various specified muscle groups. For instance, squeeze your eyes shut tightly, then relax; make fists with both hands, then relax; push your knees together hard, then relax (Humphrey & Humphrey, 1985). A game such as Simon Says can be used to promote relaxation activities.

Imagery—A relaxation technique in which a mental image such as "float like a feather" or "melt like ice" is invoked.

Imagery, a mental image that helps in the process of relaxation, can also be used effectively with young children. After children are lying in a comfortable position, they can be asked to "float like a feather" or "melt like ice." A poem or story, read very slowly and softly, can help children visualize an image in their own way. Humphrey and Humphrey (1985, p. 150) suggest two poems to help children create a relaxing image:

SNOWFLAKES
Snow!
Snowflakes fall.
They fall down.
Down, down, down.
Around and around.
Could you move like
a snowflake?

MR. SNOWMAN AND MR. SUN
See Mr. Snowman.
See Mr. Sun.
Mr. Snowman sees Mr. Sun.
Mr. Snowman is going.
Going, going, gone.
Mr. Snowman is gone.
Be Mr. Snowman.

Play and Coping with Stress

Play is one important outlet for children as they attempt to assimilate and cope with stressful events.

Play provides a natural outlet for children to cope with and work out stressors in their lives. Play furnishes a safe setting in which children can confront fears and anxieties, express anger, and find solutions to problems. Role playing or sociodramatic play in particular allows children to reenact frightening experiences, feel what it is like to take on the perspective or role of others, and make reality more acceptable (Allen, 1988). Taking on the role of the doctor by using a stethoscope or giving a doll an injection with an empty syringe can help dispel some of the fears associated with an upcoming visit to the doctor's office.

Another effective approach to decreasing fear is to increase understanding about something unknown. For instance, one study reported that children who used the game Hospital Windows, a med-

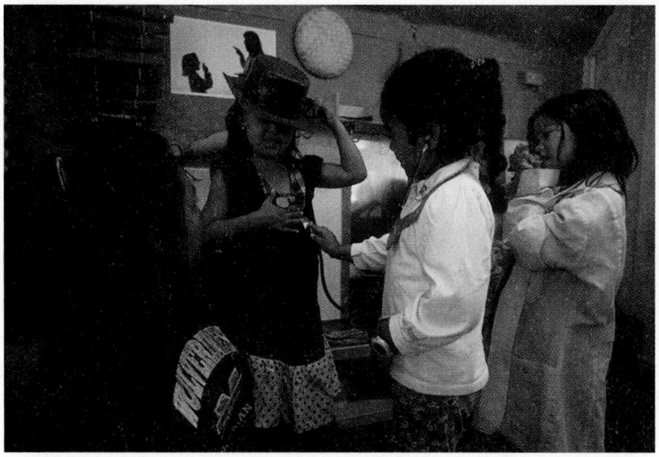

Play is one of the most important ways for children to deal with stress by facing their feelings in a safe setting. Children often gravitate to dramatic play when medical props are available.

ically oriented lotto game that helps children gain accurate information, increased their knowledge of health care concepts significantly, while decreasing their fear of medical equipment and procedures (Henkens-Matze & Abbott, 1990).

Gunsberg (1989) suggests a format for contingent play as a very effective method for working with young abused and neglected children. Such children exhibit primitive and disorganized play behavior, are disruptive, and often are hostile toward or avoid adults. Gunsberg cites the case of a four-year-old abused child whom the teacher engaged in a repeated, simple play episode. By structuring play that responded repeatedly and predictably to the actions of the child, the teacher helped her form a perception of a nurturing and attentive adult. Repeated, positive play experience was used to help the child not only develop more mature and effective play patterns, but also to promote trust, a sense of control and power, and enjoyment.

SELF-PROTECTION PROGRAMS

A number of programs designed to help children protect themselves against abuse have been developed; however, research has found little evidence that such programs actually meet their goals for young children.

With increased social awareness and concern about child sexual abuse has come a proliferation of programs aimed at teaching children some self-protection techniques. Specially designed programs such as Child Assault Prevention, Touch Safety, Body Rights, Drug Free, or "Bubbylonian Encounter" are usually presented to groups of young children by volunteer, law enforcement, or social agencies. They address such topics as the difference between "good" and "bad" touching and the child's right to say "no," and they present some specific protective techniques, including running away from a potential assailant and rudimentary karate moves.

Although such programs are well-intentioned, their effectiveness has been questioned. In fact, a critical review of research evaluating child sexual-abuse prevention programs found little evidence that such programs for preoperational children actually meet their goals (Reppucci, & Haugaard, 1989). These authors raise serious questions about the developmental readiness of young children for meaningful understanding of the concepts these programs teach. It is a fundamentally important point that adults, not children, are responsible for

KEY QUESTION #5

Observe a self-protection program presentation for young children. What concepts are being presented? Are these concepts appropriate for the cognitive and emotional abilities of young children? What do you think young children might learn from this program? Do you see any drawbacks or potential problems from this program?

providing protection against abuse (Furman, 1987; Jordan, 1993). Young children are too inexperienced to be given such a serious responsibility. We need to protect them through our consistent and constant supervision, modeling of appropriate interaction with strangers, and teaching respect and ownership of the body through nurturing care.

HELPING FAMILIES COPE WITH STRESS

Usually a stressed child comes from a stressed family; teachers may be able to help families cope with stress.

A stressed child most likely comes from a stressed family. Although all families experience stress, the circumstances and their available resources for coping with stress will differ. Early childhood programs can function as important family-support systems for parents of young children, although traditionally they have focused more on the child than on the family system (Powell, 1987b). Certainly from an ecological perspective, the child cannot be separated from the family (Weiss, 1987); thus; a good early childhood program includes a family support component.

As an early childhood educator, you can help families cope with life stressors, whether through your support, modeling, education, or referrals. Gestwicki, in her book *Home, School, and Community Relations* . . . (1992), provides some helpful guidelines for teachers interacting and working with stressed parents.

- **Reassure parents—**Through empathy and caring, teachers can encourage parents and reassure them about such things as the amount of time needed to readjust after a divorce or the grief process. Suggested books for both children and adults can also provide reassurance.
- **Know available community resources—**Teachers' expertise is in working with children rather than in professional counseling; thus, their role with highly stressed parents is to provide emotional support, information, and a listening ear. Beyond that, they should refer the parents to appropriate community agencies. It is important that early childhood teachers be aware of what is available in their own areas. Different communities have different services, for instance, family and children's services or United Way agencies. There are also mutual support groups such as Parents Without Partners, organizations for parents who have abused their children, and associations for parents of children with disabilities. The yellow pages of the telephone directory often have appropriate listings under the heading "Social Services."
- **Be aware of legal agreements—**It is important to know both legal and informal agreements between parents, particularly when custody battles are involved. A written statement from every family listing authorized persons who can pick up the child should be on file.
- **Keep requests light—**It is important to be sensitive to the stress level of parents and not to ask an overwhelmed, single parent to bake two dozen cookies for tomorrow's snack.

- **Be aware of your own attitudes and feelings**—It is sometimes easy to lay blame, be judgmental, or get angry at parents, especially when the teacher perceives them as inadequate. Teachers should examine their own attitudes and work especially hard to get to know the parents and their special circumstances so that true empathy can develop.

In addition to these suggestions, teachers can also assist parents through modeling positive guidance techniques, respect for children's ideas, and enforcement of reasonable limits. For some parents, it may be necessary to accompany modeling with verbal explanations and a discussion of alternatives (*Day Care, Families, and Stress . . .*, 1985).

It is also important to differentiate between a family that is coping adequately and continuing to carry out its family functions in the face of stress and a family that is in trouble and may require intervention. Some signs of parents who may be at the breaking point include the following (*Day Care, Families, and Stress . . .*, 1985):

- **Disorganized behavior**—Parents frequently forget vital things, for instance, the child's jacket on subzero days, or the child's lunch.
- **Frustration**—Parents have perpetually worried expressions, are unduly impatient with a slow child, threaten punishment, express lack of confidence in their parenting ability, or appear confused about how to handle the child.
- **Inability to accept help**—Parents get defensive and become verbally aggressive or walk away from a teacher who tries to discuss the child, perhaps in response to their own sense of guilt, failure, or inadequacy.
- **Concern more for themselves than for their child**—Parents seem more focused on their own problems and bring them up any time the teacher tries to talk about the child.

If you suspect that a parent is under so much stress that she or he is temporarily unable to cope, discuss your concerns with other teachers who interact with the parent, as well as with the director. A poorly functioning parent puts the child at risk. Your school's decision may be to contact a social service agency, which, in turn, may recommend that the child be temporarily removed from the home, that parental counseling be required, or that some other form of support be provided for the parent.

SUMMARY

1. Define stress and coping and look at the stages of stress.
2. A variety of possible sources for stress exist in young children's lives.
   A. Family stressors, including divorce, poverty and homelessness, and fast-paced family life, can have a serious effect on children.

   B. Child abuse and neglect, in addition to the potential for severe harm, is a serious source of stress for young children.
   C. Health problems and dealing with death are other stressful occurrences for children.
   D. Children may also be stressed by their fears and the violence in their environment.
3. Children may have a wide variety of adverse effects from stress.
4. The early childhood teacher can use a number of effective techniques to help children cope with the stress in their lives.
5. Some programs are designed to teach young children self-protection from potentially harmful encounters.

KEY TERMS LIST

anxiety
bereavement
child abuse and neglect
coping strategies
ecological model
imagery
phobia
progressive relaxation
resilient children

References

Alexander, N.P. (1986). School-age child care: Concerns and challenges. *Young Children, 42*(1), 3–10.

Alford, B.B., & Bogle, M.L. (1982). *Nutrition during the life cycle*. Englewood Cliffs, NJ: Prentice-Hall.

Alger, H.A. (1984). Transitions: Alternatives to manipulative management techniques. *Young Children, 39*(6), 16–25.

Allen, J. (1988). Children's cognition of stressful events. *Day Care and Early Education, 16*(3), 21–25.

Allen, J., & Pettit, R.B. (1987). Mighty Mouse and MX missiles: Children in a violent society. *Day Care and Early Education, 15*(1), 6–9.

Allen, K.E., & Marotz, L. (1994). *Developmental profiles: Birth to six.* Albany, NY: Delmar Publishers

Almy, M. (1975). *The early childhood educator at work*. NY: McGraw Hill Book Co.

Almy, M., Monighan, P., Scales, B., & Van Hoorn, J. (1984). Recent research on play: The teacher's perspective. In L.G. Katz (Ed.), *Current topics in early childhood education* (Vol. 5, pp. 1–26). Norwood, NJ: Ablex Publishing Corp.

Alper, C.D. (1987). Early childhood music education. In C. Seefeldt (Ed.), *The early childhood curriculum: A review of current research* (pp. 211–236). NY: Teachers College Press, Columbia University.

Amabile, T.M., & Gitomer, J. (1984). Children's artistic creativity: Effects of choice in task materials. *Personality and Social Psychology Bulletin, 10*, 209–215.

American Academy of Pediatrics. (1985). *Pediatric Nutrition Handbook* (2nd ed.). Elk Grove Village, IL: American Academy of Pediatrics.

Ames, L.B., Gillespie, C., Haines, J., & Ilg, F.L. (1980). *The child from one to six: Evaluating the behaviour of the preschool child*. London: Hamish Hamilton.

Anastasiow, N. (1988). Should parenting education be mandatory? *Topics in Early Childhood Special Education, 8*(1), 60–72.

Anderson, B.E. (1992). Effects of day-care on cognitive and socioemotional competence of thirteen-year-old Swedish school children. *Child Development, 63*, 20–36.

Anderson, B.E. (1989). Effects of public day-care: A longitudinal study. *Child Development, 60*, 857–866.

Andrews, J.H. (1988). Poetry: Tool of the classroom magician. *Young Children, 43*(4), 17–25.

Anisfeld, M. (1984). *Language development from birth to three*. Hillsdale, NJ: Lawrence Erlbaum.

Annie E. Casey Foundation (1996). *Kids count data book.* Baltimore, MD: Annie E. Casey Foundation.

Annie E. Casey Foundation (1994). *Kids count data book: States profiles of child well-being*. Greenwich, CT: The Annie E. Casey Foundation.

Anthony, S. (1972). *The discovery of death in childhood and after*. NY: Basic Books.

Arent, R.P. (1984). *Stress and your child: A parents' guide to symptoms, strategies, and benefits*. Englewood Cliffs, NJ: Prentice-Hall.

Aries, P. (1962). *Centuries of childhood: A social history of family life.* (R. Baldick, Trans.). NY: Alfred A. Knopf.

Arnett, J. (1987). Caregivers in day care centers: Does training matter? Paper presented at the biennial meeting of the Society for Research in Child Development, Baltimore, MD.

Atkins, C. (1984). Writing: Doing something constructive. *Young Children, 40*(1), 3–7.

Ayers, W. (1989). *The good preschool teacher: Six teachers reflect on their lives*. NY: Teachers College Press, Columbia University.

Bakst, K., & Essa, E.L. (1990). The writing table: Emergent writers and editors. *Childhood Education, 66*, 145–150.

Balaban, N. (1992). The role of child care professionals in caring for infants, toddlers, and their families. *Young Children, 47*(5), 66–71.

Bandura, A. (1977). *Social learning theory*. Englewood Cliffs, NJ: Prentice-Hall.

Baratta-Lorton, M. (1979). *Workjobs: Activity-centered learning for early childhood education*. Menlo Park, CA: Addison-Wesley Publishing Co.

Barnes, B.J. & Hill, S. (1983). Should young children use microcomputers: LOGO before LEGO? *The Computing Teacher, 10*(9), 11–14.

Bartlett, A.V., Moore, M., Gary, G.W., Starko, K.M., Erben, J.J., & Meredith, B. (1985). Diarrheal illness among infants and toddlers in day care centers. *Journal of Pediatrics, 107,* 495–502.

Baumrind, D. (1967). Child care practices anteceding three patterns of preschool behavior. *Genetic Psychological Monographs, 75,* 43–88.

Baumrind, D., & Black, A.E. (1967). Socialization practices associated with dimensions of competence in preschool boys and girls. *Child Development, 38,* 291–327.

Bayless, K.M., & Ramsey, M.E. (1982). *Music: A way of life for the young child.* St. Louis, MO: The C.V. Mosby Co.

Becher, R.M. (1986). Parent involvement: A review of research and principles of successful practice. In L.G. Katz (Ed.), *Current topics in early childhood education* (Vol. 6, pp. 85–122). Norwood, NJ: Ablex Publishing Corp.

Begley, S. (1996). I am your child. *Newsweek,* February 19, 55–61.

Bentzen, W.R. (1997). *A guide to observing and recording behavior* (3rd ed.). Albany, NY: Delmar Publishers.

Bereiter, C. (1986). Does direct instruction cause delinquency? *Early Childhood Research Quarterly, 1,* 289–292.

Bereiter, C., & Engelmann, S. (1966). *Teaching disadvantaged children in the preschool.* Englewood Cliffs, NJ: Prentice-Hall.

Berk, L.E. (1994). Vygotsky's theory: The importance of make-believe play. *Young Children, 50*(1), 30–39.

Berk, L.E. (1976). How well do classroom practices reflect teacher goals? *Young Children, 32*(1), 64–81.

Berns, R.M. (1994). *Child, family, community: Socialization and support* (3rd ed.). NY: Holt, Rinehart and Winston, Inc.

Berrueta-Clement, J.R., Schweinhart, L.J., Barnett, W.S., Epstein, A.S., & Weikart, D.P. (1984). *Changed lives: The effects of the Perry Preschool program on youths through age 19.* Monographs of the High/Scope Educational Research Foundation, #8. Ypsilanti, MI: High/Scope Press.

Best, M.B. (1997). What we have done about biting. *Young Children, 52*(4), 3.

Biber, B. (1984). *Early education and psychological development.* New Haven, CT: Yale University Press.

Bijou, S.W., Peterson, R.F., & Ault, M.H. (1968). A method to integrate descriptive and experimental field studies at the level of data and empirical concepts. *Journal of Applied Behavior Analysis, 1,* 175–191.

Birch, L.L. (1980a). Effects of peer models' food choices and eating behaviors on preschoolers' food preferences. *Child Development, 51,* 489–496.

Birch, L.L. (1980b). Experiential determinants of children's food preferences. In L.G. Katz (Ed.), *Current topics in early childhood education* (Vol. 3, pp. 29–46). Norwood, NJ: Ablex Publishing Corp.

Birch, L.L., Johnson, S.L., & Fisher, J.A. (1995). Children's eating: The development of food-acceptance patterns. *Young Children, 50*(2), 71–78.

Birch, L.L., Marlin, D.W., & Rotter, J. (1984). Eating as the "means" activity in a contingency: Effects on young children's food preferences. *Child Development, 55,* 431–439.

Bjorklund, G., & Burger, C. (1987). Making conferences work for parents, teachers, and children. *Young Children, 42*(3), 26–31.

Blocks: A creative curriculum for early childhood. (1979). Washington, DC: Creative Associates, Inc.

Blom, G.E., Cheney, B.D., & Snoddy, J.E. (1986). *Stress in childhood: An intervention model for teachers and other professionals.* NY: Teacher's College Press, Columbia, University.

Bohannon, J.N., & Warren-Leubecker, A. (1985). Theoretical approaches to language acquisition. In J.B. Gleason (Ed.), *The development of language* (pp. 173–266). Columbus, OH: Charles E. Merrill Publishing Co.

Borstellman, L.J. (1983). Children before psychology: Ideas about children from antiquity to the late 1800s. In P.H. Mussen (Ed.), *Handbook of child psychology* (4th ed.). *History, theory, and methods* (Vol. 1, pp. 1–40). NY: John Wiley and Sons.

Boxhill, N.A. (1989, December). Quoted in S. Landers, Homeless children lose childhood. *The APA Monitor,* pp. 1, 33.

Brady, J.P. (1994). Risk and reality: Implications of prenatal exposure to alcohol and other drugs. ERIC Document #ED397986.

Braun, S.J., & Edwards, E.P. (1972). *History and theory of early childhood education.* Worthington, OH: Charles A. Jones Publishing Co.

Brazelton, T.B. (1990, September 9). Why is America failing its children? *New York Times Magazine,* pp. 40–43, 50, 90.

Bredekamp, S. (1993). Reflections on Reggio Emilia. *Young Children, 49*(1), 13–17.

Bredekamp, S. Quoted in E.R. Shell (1989, December). Now, which kind of preschool? *Psychology Today,* pp. 52–57.

Bredekamp, S. (Ed.) (1987). *Developmentally appropriate practice in early childhood programs serving children from birth through age 8.* Washington, DC: National Association for the Education of Young Children.

Bredekamp, S., & Apple, P.L. (1986). How early childhood programs get accredited: An analysis of accreditation decisions. *Young Children, 42*(1), 34–37.

Bredekamp, S., & Copple, C.E. (Eds.) (1997). *Developmentally Appropriate Practice in Early Childhood*

Programs Serving Children from Birth Through Age 8 (Rev. ed.). Washington, DC: National Association for the Education of Young Children.

Bredekamp, S., & Glowacki, S. (1996). The first decade of NAEYC accreditation: Growth and impact on the field. *Young Children, 51*(3), 38–44.

Bredekamp, S., & Shepard, L. (1989). How best to protect children from inappropriate school expectations, practices, and policies. *Young Children, 44*(3), 14–24.

Bredekamp, S., & Willer, B. (1992). Of ladders and lattices, cores and cones: Conceptualizing an early childhood professional development system. *Young Children, 47*(3), 47–50.

Brenner, A. (1984). *Helping children cope with stress.* Lexington, MA: Lexington Books.

Brigance, A.H. (1991). *Brigance diagnostic inventory of early development.* North Billerica, MA: Curriculum Associates.

Briggs, B.A., & Walters, C.M. (1985). Single-father families. *Young Children, 40*(3), 23–27.

Bronfenbrenner, U. (1986). Ecology of the family as a context for human development: Research perspectives. *Developmental Psychology, 22*, 723–742.

Bronfenbrenner, U. (1979). *The ecology of human development.* Cambridge, MA: Harvard University Press.

Bronfenbrenner, U. (1971). Who cares for America's children? *Young Children, 26*(3), 157–163.

Bronfenbrenner, U., & Crouter, A.C. (1983). Ecology of the family as a context for human development research perspectives. In P.H. Mussen (Ed.), *Handbook of child psychology, Vol. 1: History, theory and methods.* NY: John Wiley and Sons.

Brooks, R.L., & Obrzut, J.E. (1981). Brain lateralization: Implications for infant stimulation and development. *Young Children, 36*(3), 9–16.

Brown, R. (1973). *A first language.* Cambridge, MA: Harvard University Press.

Bruner, J. (1980). *Under five in Britain.* Ypsilanti, MI: High/Scope Foundation.

Bullock, J. (1986). Teacher-parent conferences: Learning from each other. *Day Care and Early Education, 14*(2), 17–19.

Bundy, B.F. (1991). Fostering communication between parents and preschools. *Young Children, 46*(2), 12–17.

Bundy, B.F. (1989). Effective record keeping. *Day Care and Early Education, 17*(1), 7–9.

Bureau of Labor Statistics. (1996). Occupational Outlook Handbook. Washington, D.C.: U.S. Government Printing Office.

Burts, D.C., Hart, C.H., Charlesworth, R., Fleege, P.O., Mosely, J., & Thomasson, R.H. (1992). Observed activities and stress behaviors of children in developmentally appropriate and inappropriate kindergarten classrooms. *Early Childhood Research Quarterly, 7*, 297–318.

Burts, D.C., Hart, C.H., Charlesworth, R., & Kirk, L., (1990). A comparison of frequencies of stress behaviors observed in kindergarten children in classrooms with developmentally appropriate versus developmentally inappropriate instructional practices. *Early Childhood Research Quarterly, 5*, 407–423.

Bushell, D. (1982). The behavior analysis model for early education. In B. Spodek (Ed.), *Handbook of research in early childhood education* (pp. 156–184). NY: The Free Press.

Buzzelli, C.A., & File, N. (1989). Building trust in friends. *Young Children, 44*(3), 70–75.

Caldwell, B.M. (1977). Aggression and hostility in young children. *Young Children, 32*(2), 4–13.

Campbell, F.A., & Taylor, K. (1996). Early childhood programs that work for children from economically disadvantaged families. *Young Children, 51*(4), 74–80.

Carnegie Corporation (1994). *Starting points: Meeting the needs of our youngest children: The report on the task force on meeting the needs of young children.* New York: Carnegie Corporation.

Carter, D.B. (1987). Early childhood education: A historical perspective. In J.L. Roopnarine & J.E. Johnson (Eds.), *Approaches to early childhood education* (pp. 1–14). Columbus, OH: Merrill Publishing Co.

Cartwright, C.A., & Cartwright, G.P. (1974). *Developing observation skills.* New York: McGraw-Hill Book Co.

Cartwright, S. (1990). Learning with large blocks. *Young Children, 45*(3), 38–41.

Cass, J.E. (1973). *Helping children grow through play.* New York: Schocken Books.

Cataldo, C.Z. (1987). *Parent education for early childhood: Child-rearing concepts and program content for the student and practicing professional.* NY: Teacher's College Press, Columbia University.

Chafel, J.A. (1990). Children in poverty: Policy perspectives on a national crisis. *Young Children, 45*(5), 31–37.

Charlesworth, R., & Lind, K.K. (1995). *Math and science for young children.* Albany, NY: Delmar Publishers.

Chattin-McNichols, J. (1992). *The Montessori controversy.* Albany, NY: Delmar Publishers.

Chattin-McNichols, J.P. (1981). The effects of Montessori school experience. *Young Children, 36*(5), 49–66.

Child Care Employee Project. (1992). On the horizon: New policy initiatives to enhance child care staff compensation. *Young Children, 47*(5), 39–42.

Children's Defense Fund. (1998). *The state of America's children: Yearbook 1998.* Washington, DC: Children's Defense Fund.

Children's Defense Fund. (1991). *The state of America's children 1991.* Washington, DC: Children's Defense Fund.

Children's Defense Fund. (1990). *Children 1990: A report card, briefing book, and action primer*. Washington, DC: National Association for the Education of Young Children.

Chomsky, N. (1972). *Language and mind*. NY: Harcourt Brace Jovanovich, Inc.

Christie, J.F., Johnsen, E.P., & Peckover, R.B. (1988). The effect of play period duration on children's play pattern. *Journal of Research in Childhood Education, 3*, 123–131.

Ciaranello, R.D. (1983). Neurochemical aspects of stress. In N. Garmezy & M. Rutter (Eds.), *Stress, coping and development in children* (pp. 85–105). NY: McGraw-Hill Book Co.

Clark, E.V. (1978a). Non-linguistic strategies and the acquisition of word meaning. In L. Bloom (Ed.), *Readings in language development* (pp. 433–451). NY: John Wiley & Sons.

Clark, E.V. (1978b). Strategies for communicating. *Child Development, 49,* 953–959.

Clarke-Stewart, K.A. (1988). Evolving issues in early childhood education: A personal perspective. *Early Childhood Research Quarterly, 3*, 139–149.

Clarke-Stewart, K.A. (1987a). In search of consistencies in child care research. In D.A. Phillips (Ed.), *Quality in child care: What does research tell us?* (pp. 105–120). Washington, DC: National Association for the Education of Young Children.

Clarke-Stewart, K.A. (1987b). Predicting child development from child care forms and features: The Chicago Study. In D.A. Phillips (Ed.), *Quality in child care: What does research tell us*? (pp. 21–41). Washington, DC: National Association for the Education of Young Children.

Clarke-Stewart, K.A. (1984). Day care: A new context for research and development. In M. Perlmutter (Ed.), *Parent-child interaction and parent-child relations in child development: The Minnesota symposia on child psychology* (Vol. 17, pp. 61–100). Hillsdale, NJ: Lawrence Erlbaum Associates.

Clarke-Stewart, K.A. (1983). Exploring the assumptions of parent education. In R. Haskins & D. Adams (Eds.), *Parent education and public policy* (pp. 257–276). Norwood, NJ: Ablex Publishing Corp.

Clarke-Stewart, K.A., & Gruber, C. (1984). Daycare forms and features. In R.C. Ainslie (Ed.), *Quality variations in daycare* (pp. 35–62). NY: Praeger.

Clemens, S.G. (1991). Art in the classroom: Making every day special. *Young Children, 46*(2), 4–11.

Clements, D.H. (1987). Computers and young children: A review of research. *Young Children, 43*(1), 34–44.

Clewett, A.S. (1988). Guidance and discipline: Teaching young children appropriate behavior. *Young Children, 43*(4), 26–31.

Click, P. (1998). *Caring for school-age children* (2nd ed.). Albany, NY: Delmar Publishers.

Click, P.M. (1996). *Administration of schools for young children* (4th ed.). Albany, NY: Delmar Publishers.

Cochran, M. (1988). Between cause and effect: The ecology of program impacts. In A.R. Pence (Ed.), *Ecological research with children and families: From concepts to methodology* (pp. 143–169). NY: Teachers College Press, Columbia University.

Cohen, D.H., & Stern, V. (1978). *Observing and recording the behavior of young children* (2nd ed.). NY: Teachers College Press, Columbia University.

Cole, E., & Schaefer, C. (1990). Can young children be art critics? *Young Children, 45*(2), 33–38.

Coleman, M., & Skeen, P. (1985). Play, games, and sports: Their use and misuse. *Childhood Education, 61*, 192–198.

Cook, R.E., Tessier, A., & Armbruster, V.B. (1987). *Adapting early childhood curricula for children with special needs*. Columbus, OH: Merrill Publishing Co.

Copple, C.E., DeLisi, R., & Sigel, E. (1982). Cognitive development. In B. Spodek (Ed.), *Handbook of research in early childhood education* (pp. 3–26). NY: The Free Press.

Cosgrove, M.S. (1991). Cooking in the classroom: The doorway to nutrition. *Young Children, 46*(3), 43–45.

Cox, M.V. (1986). *The child's point of view: The development of cognition and language*. NY: St. Martin's Press.

Cratty, B.J. (1982). Motor development in early childhood: Critical issues for researchers in the 1980s. In B. Spodek (Ed.), *Handbook of research in early childhood education* (pp. 27–46). NY: The Free Press.

Daehler, M.W., & Bukatko, D. (1985). *Cognitive development*. NY: Alfred A. Knopf, Inc.

Damon, W. (1983). The nature of social-cognitive change in the developing child. In W.F. Overton (Ed.), *The relationship between social and cognitive development* (pp. 103–141). Hillsdale, NJ: Lawrence Erlbaum Associates, Publishers.

Damon, W. (1977). *The social world of the child*. San Francisco: Jossey-Bass.

Davidson, J.I. (1989). *Children and computers together in the early childhood classroom*. Albany, NY: Delmar Publishers.

Davis, J., & Gardner, H. (1993). The arts and early childhood education: A cognitive developmental portrait of the young child as artist. In B. Spodek (Ed.), *Handbook of research on the education of young children* (pp. 191–206). New York: Macmillan.

Day, B.D. (1988). What's happening in early childhood programs across the United States. In C. Warger (Ed.), *A resource guide to public school early childhood programs* (pp. 3–31). Alexandria, VA: Association for Supervision and Curriculum Development.

Day care, families, and stress: A day care provider's guide. (1985). Austin, TX: Child Development Program Division, Texas Department of Human Resources.

Debelack, M., Herr, J., & Jacobson, M. (1981). *Creating innovative classroom materials for teaching young children*. NY: Harcourt Brace Jovanovich, Inc.

Deiner, P.L. (1993). *Resources for teaching children with diverse abilities* (2nd ed.). New York: Harcourt Brace.

Delacato, C.H. (1966). *Neurological organization in terms of mobility.* Springfield, IL: Charles C. Thomas.

Delacato, C. H. (1964). *The diagnosis and treatment of speech and reading problems.* Springfield, IL: Charles C. Thomas.

Derman-Sparks, L. (1989). *Anti-bias curriculum: Tools for empowering young children*. Washington, DC: National Association for the Education of Young Children.

Derman-Sparks, L., Higa, C.T., & Sparks, B. (1980). Children, race and racism: How race awareness develops. *Interracial books for children bulletin, 11*(3–4), 3–9.

deVilliers, J.G., & deVilliers, P.A. (1973). A cross-sectional study of the acquisition of grammatical morphemes in child speech. *Journal of Psycholinguistic Research, 2*, 267–278.

deVilliers, P.A., & deVilliers, J.G. (1979). *Early language*. Cambridge, MA: Harvard University Press.

Diffily, D. (1996). The project approach: A museum exhibit created by kindergartners. *Young Children, 51*(2), 72–75.

Dimidjian, V.J. (1989). Holidays, holy days, and wholly dazed: Approaches to special days. *Young Children, 44*(6), 70–74.

Dinkmeyer, D., & McKay, G.D. (1976). *Systematic training for effective parenting: Parent's handbook*. Circle Pines, MN: American Guidance Services.

Dodd, C. (1993). Testimony before the Joint Senate-House Hearing on Keeping Every Child Safe: Curbing the Epidemic of Violence. 103rd Congress, 1st session, March 10.

Doman, R.J., Spitz, E.B., Zucman, E., & Delacato, C.H. (1960). Children with severe brain injuries: Neurological organization in terms of mobility. *Journal of the American Medical Association, 174*, 257–262.

Doyle, A.B., & Connolly, J. (1989). Negotiation and enactment in social pretend play: Relations to social acceptance and social cognition. *Early Childhood Research Quarterly, 4*, 289–302.

Doyle, A.B., Gold, D., & Moskowitz, D.S. (Eds.) (1984). *Children and families under stress*. San Francisco, CA: Jossey-Bass Inc., Publishers.

Drabman, R.S., Cordua, G.D., Hammer, D., Jarvie, G. J., & Horton, W. (1979). Developmental trends in eating rates of normal and overweight preschool children. *Child Development, 50*, 211–216.

Dreikurs, R. (1972). *Coping with children's misbehavior: A parent's guide*. NY: Hawthorne Books, Inc.

Dreikurs, R., & Cassel, P. (1972). *Discipline without tears*. NY: Hawthorne Books, Inc.

Dreikurs, R., & Soltz, V. (1964). *Children: The challenge*. NY: Duell, Sloan and Pearce.

Dresden, J., & Myers, B.K. (1989). Early childhood professionals: Toward self-definition. *Young Children, 44*(2), 62–66.

Dunst, C.J., & Trivette, C.M. (1988). Toward experimental evaluation of the family, infant, and preschool program. In H.B. Weiss & F.H. Jacobs (Eds.), *Evaluating family programs* (pp. 315–346). NY: Aldine de Gruyter.

Dyson, A.H., & Genishi, C. (1993). Visions of children as language users: Language and languages education in early childhood. In B. Spodek (Ed.), *Handbook of research on education of young children* (pp. 122–136). New York: Macmillan.

Edwards, C.P. (1986). *Promoting social and moral development in young children*. NY: Teachers College Press, Columbia University.

Elkind, D. (1988). The resistance to developmentally appropriate educational practice with young children: The real issue. In C. Warger (Ed.), *A resource guide to public school early childhood programs* (pp. 53–62). Alexandria, VA: Association for Supervision and Curriculum Development.

Elkind, D. (1987a). The child yesterday, today, and tomorrow. *Young Children, 42*(4), 6–11.

Elkind, D. (1987b). *Miseducation: Preschoolers at risk.* NY: Alfred A. Knopf, Inc.

Elkind, D. (1983). Montessori education: Abiding contributions and contemporary challenges. *Young Children, 38*(2), 3–10.

Endres, J.B., & Rockwell, R.E. (1980). *Food, nutrition, and the young child*. St. Louis, MO: C.V. Mosby Co.

Eriksen, A. (1985). *Playground design: Outdoor environments for learning and development*. NY: Van Nostrand Reinhold Co.

Erikson, E.H. (1963). *Childhood and society* (2nd ed.). NY: Norton.

Essa, E.L. (1999). *Practical guide to solving preschool behavior problems* (4th ed.). Albany, NY: Delmar Publishers.

Essa, E.L. (1987). The effect of a computer on preschool children's activities. *Early Childhood Research Quarterly, 2*, 377–382.

Essa, E.L., Hilton, J.M., & Murray, C.I. (1990). The relationship of weather and preschool children's behavior. *Children's Environments Quarterly*.

Essa, E.L., & Murray, C.I. (1994). Research in review: Young children's understanding and experience with death. *Young Children, 49*(4), 74–81.

Essa, E.L., & Rogers, P.R. (1992). *An early childhood curriculum: From developmental model to application*. Albany, NY: Delmar Publishers.

Ethics Commission. (1987). Ethics case studies: The working mother. *Young Children, 43*(1), 16–19.

Evans, E. D. (1984). Children's aesthetics. In L.G. Katz (Ed.), *Current topics in early childhood education* (Vol. 5, pp. 73–104). Norwood, NJ: Ablex Publishing Corp.

Evans, E.D. (1982). Curriculum models and early childhood education. In B. Spodek (Ed.), *Handbook of research in early childhood education* (pp. 107–134). NY: The Free Press.

Everts, J., Essa, E.L., Cheney, C., & McKee, D. (1993). Higher education as child care provider. *Initiatives, 55*(4), 9–16.

Fallen, N.H., & Umansky, W. (1985). *Young children with special needs* (2nd ed.). Columbus, OH: Charles Merrill Publishing Co.

Farver, J.M. (1996). Aggressive behavior in preschooler's social networks: Do birds of a feather flock together? *Early Childhood Research Quarterly, 11,* 333–350.

Faust, V., Weidmann, M., & Wehner, W. (1974). The influence of meteorological factors on children and youths. *Acta Paedopsychiatrica, 40,* 150–156.

Federman, J. (1997). National Television Violence Study: Executive Summary (vol. 2). Santa Barbara, CA: Center for Communication and Social Policy, University of California at Santa Barbara.

Feeney, S. (1988). Ethics case studies: The aggressive child. *Young Children, 43*(2), 48–51.

Feeney, S. (1988). Ethics case studies: The divorced parents. *Young Children, 43*(3), 48–49.

Feeney, S., & Chun, R. (1985). Effective teachers of young children. *Young Children, 41*(1), 47–52.

Feeney, S., & Kipnis, K. (1989). NAEYC code of ethical conduct and statement of commitment. *Young Children, 45*(1), 24–29.

Feeney, S., & Kipnis, K. (1992). *NAEYC Code of ethical conduct and statement of commitment.* Washington, DC: National Association for the Education of Young Children.

Feeney, S., & Kipnis, K. (1985). Professional ethics in early childhood education. *Young Children, 40*(3), 54–56.

Feeney, S., & Moravcik, E. (1987). A thing of beauty: Aesthetic development in young children. *Young Children, 42*(6), 7–15.

Fein, G.G. (1982). Pretend play: New perspectives. In J.F. Brown (Ed.), *Curriculum planning for young children* (pp. 22–27). Washington, DC: National Association for the Education of Young Children.

Fein, G.G. (1979). Play and the acquisition of symbols. In L.G. Katz (Ed.), *Current topics in early childhood education* (Vol. 2, pp. 195–225). Norwood, NJ: Ablex Publishing Corp.

Fein, G., & Schwartz, P.M. (1982). Developmental theories in early education. In B. Spodek (Ed.), *Handbook of research in early childhood education* (pp. 82–104). NY: The Free Press.

Ferber, R. (1985). *Solve your child's sleep problems.* NY: Simon & Shuster, Inc.

Fernandez, J.P. (1986). *Child care and corporate productivity.* Lexington, MA: Lexington Books.

Field, T. (1991). Quality infant day-care and grade school behavior and performance. *Child Development, 62,* 863–870.

Fillmore, L.W. (1991). Language and cultural issues in the early education of language minority children. In S.L. Kagan (Ed.), *The care and education of America's young children: Obstacles and opportunities* (pp. 30–49). Chicago: University of Chicago Press.

Finkelstein, B. (1988). The revolt against selfishness: Women and the dilemmas of professionalism in early childhood education. In B. Spodek, O.N. Saracho, & D.L. Peters (Eds.), *Professionalism and the early childhood practitioner* (pp. 10–28). NY: Teachers College Press, Columbia University.

Flaste, R. (1991, April 28). Sidelined by loneliness. *New York Times Magazine*, pp. 14–15, 23–24.

Flerx, V.C., Fidler, D.S., & Rogers, R.W. (1976). Sex role stereotypes: Developmental aspects and early intervention. *Child Development, 67,* 998–1007.

Forman, G. (1993). The constructivist perspective to early education. In J.L. Roopnarine & J.E. Johnson (Eds.), *Approaches to early childhood education* (2nd. ed., pp. 137–155). New York: Merrill.

Forman, G., & Kaden, M. (1987). Research on science education for young children. In C. Seefeldt (Ed.), *The early childhood curriculum: A review of current research* (pp. 141–164). NY: Teachers College Press, Columbia University.

Forman, G.E., & Kuschner, D.S. (1977). *The child's construction of knowledge: Piaget for teaching children.* Monterey, CA: Brooks/Cole Publishing Co.

Frankenburg, W.K., & Dodd, J.B. (1990). *Denver II screening manual.* Denver: Denver Developmental Materials.

Fraser, A.S. (1989, Spring). The changing American family. *In Context*, pp. 13–16.

Friedman, D. (1989, August). A more sophisticated employer response to child care. *Child Care Information Exchange*, pp. 29–31.

Froschl, M., Colon, L., Rubin, E., & Sprung, B. (1984). *Including all of us: An early childhood curriculum about disability.* NY: Educational Equity Concepts, Inc.

Frost, J.L. (1992). *Play and playscapes.* Albany, NY: Delmar Publishers.

Frost, J.L., & Klein, B.L. (1979). *Children's play and playgrounds.* Boston: Allyn and Bacon, Inc.

Frost, J.L., & Wortham, S.C. (1988). The evolution of American playgrounds. *Young Children, 43*(5), 19–28.

Fullerton, H.N. (1989). New labor force projections, spanning 1988 to 2000. *Monthly Labor Review, 112*(11), 3–12.

Furman, E. (1987). More protection, fewer directions. *Young Children, 42*(5), 3–7.

Furman, E. (1982). Helping children cope with death. In J.F. Brown (Ed.), *Curriculum planning for young children* (pp. 238–245). Washington, DC: National Association for the Education of Young Children.

Furth, H.G. (1969). *Piaget and knowledge: Theoretical foundations*. Englewood Cliffs, NJ: Prentice-Hall.

Galinsky, E. (1990). Why are some parent/teacher partnerships clouded with difficulties? *Young Children, 45*(5), 2–3, 38–40.

Galinsky, E. (1989). Update on employer-supported childcare. *Young Children, 44*(6), 2, 75–77.

Galinsky, E. (1988). Parents and teacher-caregivers: Sources of tension, sources of support. *Young Children, 43*(3), 4–12.

Galinsky, E. (1981). *Between generations: The six stages of parenthood*. NY: Times Books.

Galinsky, E., Howes, C., Kontos, S., & Shinn, M. (1994). The study of children in family child care and relative—key findings and policy recommendations. *Young Children, 50*(1), 58–61.

Gallagher, J.M., & Coche, J. (1987). Hothousing: The clinical and educational concerns over pressuring young children. *Early Childhood Research Quarterly, 2*, 203–210.

Gallahue, D.L. (1993). Motor development and movement skill acquisition in early childhood education. In B. Spodek (Ed.), *Handbook of research on the education of young children* (pp. 24–41). New York: Macmillan.

Gallimore, R., & Tharp, R. (1990). Teaching mind in society: Teaching, schooling, and literate discourse. In L.C. Moll (Ed.), *Vygotsky and education* (pp. 175–205). New York: Cambridge University Press.

Gandini, L. (1993). Fundamentals of the Reggio Emilia approach to early childhood education. *Young Children, 49*(1), 4–8.

Garbarino, J. (1990, June). Child abuse: Why? *The World and I*, pp. 543–553.

Garbarino, J., Dubrow, N., Kostelny, K., & Pardo, C. (1992). *Children in danger: Coping with the consequences of community violence*. San Francisco: Jossey-Bass.

Garcia, E.E. (1982). Bilingualism in early childhood. In J.F. Brown (Ed.), *Curriculum planning for young children* (pp. 82–101). Washington, DC: National Association for Young Children.

Garcia Coll, C., Kagan, J., & Reznick, J.S. (1984). Behavioral inhibition in young children. *Child Development, 55*, 1005–1019.

Gardner, H. (1989). Learning, Chinese-style. *Psychology Today, 23*(12), 54–56.

Gargiulo, R.M. (1985). *Working with parents of exceptional children*. Boston: Houghton Mifflin.

Garmezy, N. (1984). Stressors of childhood. In N. Garmezy & M. Rutter (Eds.), *Stress, coping and development in children* (pp. 43–84), NY: McGraw-Hill Book Co.

Garn, S.M., & Clark, D.C. (1976). Trends in fatness and the origins of obesity. *Pediatrics, 57*, 443–456.

Gartrell, D. (1987). Punishment or guidance. *Young Children, 42*(3), 55–61.

Gelfer, J.I., & Perkins, P.G. (1996). A model for portfolio assessment in early childhood education programs. *Early Childhood Education Journal, 24*, 5–10.

Geller, L.G. (1985). *Word play and language learning for children*. Urbana, IL: National Council of Teachers of English.

Gelman, R., & Gallistel, C.R. (1978). *The child's understanding of number*. Cambridge, MA: Harvard University Press.

Genishi, C. (1982). Observational research methods for early childhood education. In B. Spodek (Ed.), *Handbook of research in early childhood education* (pp. 564–591). NY: The Free Press.

Gersten, R. (1986). Response to "Consequences of three preschool curriculum models through age 15." *Early Childhood Research Quarterly, 1*, 293–302.

Gestwicki, C. (1995). *Developmentally appropriate practice: Putting theory into practice in early childhood classrooms*. Albany, NY: Delmar Publishers.

Gestwicki, C. (1992). *Home, school, and community relations: A guide to working with parents* (2nd ed.). Albany, NY: Delmar Publishers.

Gettman, D. (1987). *Basic Montessori: Learning activities for under-fives*. NY: St. Martin's Press.

Gibson, L. (1989). *Through children's eyes: Literacy learning in the early years*. NY: Teacher's College Press, Columbia University.

Gineshi, C. (1987). Acquiring oral language and communicative competence. In. C. Seefeldt (Ed.), *The early childhood curriculum: A review of current research* (pp. 75–106). NY: Teacher's College Press, Columbia University.

Ginsburg, H., & Opper, S. (1969). *Piaget's theory of intellectual development: An introduction*. Englewood Cliffs, NJ: Prentice-Hall, Inc.

Glazer, J.I. (1986). *Literature for young children* (2nd ed.). Columbus, OH: Charles Merrill Publishing Co.

Gleason, J.B. (1985). Studying language development. In J.B. Gleason (Ed.), *The development of language* (pp. 1–35). Columbus, OH: Charles E. Merrill Publishing Co.

Gnezda, M.T. (1996). Welfare reform: Personal responsibilities and opportunities for early childhood advocates. *Young Children, 52*(1), 55–58.

Goelman, H. (1988). The relationship between structure and process variables in home and day care settings on children's language development. In A.R. Pence (Ed.), *Ecological research with children and families: From concepts to methodology* (pp. 16–34). NY: Teachers College Press, Columbia University.

Goffin, S.G. (1987). Cooperative behaviors: They need our support. *Young Children, 42*(2), 75–81.

Gonzalez-Mena, J. (1990). *Infant-toddler caregiving: A guide to routines*. Sacramento: California Department of Education.

Gonzalez-Mena, J., & Eyer, D.W. (1989). *Infants, toddlers, and caregivers*. Mountain View, CA: Mayfield.

Good discipline is, in large part, the result of a fantastic curriculum! (1987). *Young Children, 42*(3), 49–51.

Goodman, K.S., Smith, E.B., Meredith, R., & Goodman, Y.M. (1987). *Language and thinking in school: A whole-language curriculum* (3rd ed.). NY: Richard C. Owen Publishers, Inc.

Goodman, Y.M. (1986). Children coming to know literacy. In W.H. Teale & E. Sulzby (Eds.), *Emergent literacy: Writing and reading* (pp. 1–14). Norwood, NJ: Ablex Publishing Corp.

Goodwin, W.L., & Goodwin, L.D. (1982). Measuring young children. In B. Spodek (Ed.), *Handbook of research in early childhood education* (pp. 523–563). NY: The Free Press.

Goodz, N.S. (1982). Is before really easier to understand than after? *Child Development, 53*, 822–825.

Gordon, A.M., & Browne, K.W. (1996). *Beginnings and beyond: Foundations in early childhood education* (4th ed.). Albany, NY: Delmar Publishers.

Gordon, T. (1976). *P.E.T. in action*. NY: Peter H. Wyden Publisher.

Gordon, T. (1974). *T.E.T.: Teacher Effectiveness Training*. NY: Peter H. Wyden Publisher.

Gould, R.L. (1978). *Transformations: Growth and change in adult life*. New York: Simon and Shuster.

Gratz, R.R., & Boulton, P.J. (1996). Erikson and early childhood educators: Looking at ourselves and our profession developmentally. *Young Children, 51*(5), 74–78.

Graue, M.E., & Shepard, L.A. (1989). Predictive validity of the Gessell School Readiness Test. *Early Childhood Research Quarterly, 4*, 303–315.

Greenberg, P. (1987). Lucy Sprague Mitchell: A major missing link between early childhood education in the 1980s and progressive education in the 1890s–1930s. *Young Children, 42*(5), 70–84.

Griffin, E.F. (1982). *Island of childhood: Education in the special world of nursery school*. NY: Teachers College Press, Columbia University.

Grimsley, R. (1976). Jean-Jacques Rousseau. In P. Edwards (Ed.), *The encyclopedia of philosophy* (Vol. 7–8, pp. 218–225). NY: Macmillan Publishing Co., Inc., & The Free Press.

Guilford, J.P. (1962). Creativity: Its measurement and development. In S. Parnes & H. Harding (Eds.), *A sourcebook for creative thinking* (pp. 151–168). NY: Charles Scribner's Sons.

Gullo, D.F. (1966). Evaluating student learning through the analysis of pupil produced products. Presentation at the annual meeting of the National Association for the Education of Young Children, Dallas, TX.

Gunnar, M.R., Senior, K., U. Hartup, W.W. (1984). Peer pressure and the exploratory behavior of eighteen- and thirty-month-old children. *Child Development, 55*, 1103–1109.

Gunsberg, A. (1989). Empowering young abused and neglected children through contingent play. *Childhood Education, 66*, 8–10.

Hakuta, K. (1988). Why bilinguals? In F.S. Kessell (Ed.), *The development of language and language researchers* (pp. 299–318). Hillsdale, NJ: Lawrence Erlbaum Associates, Publishers.

Hakuta, K., & Garcia, E.E. (1989). Bilingualism and education. *American Psychologist, 44*, 374–379.

Halpern, R. (1987). Major social and demographic trends affecting young families: Implications for early childhood care and education. *Young Children, 42*(6) 34–40.

Hampden-Turner, C. (1981). *Maps of the mind: Charts and concepts of the mind and its labyrinths*. NY: Collier Books.

Haney-Clark, R., Essa, E., & Read, M. (1983). *SHINE!: School-home involvement in nutrition education*. Reno, NV: Child and Family Center, University of Nevada, Reno.

Hanson, M.J., & Lynch, E.W. (1989). *Early intervention: Implementing child and family services for infants and toddlers who are at-risk or disabled*. Austin, TX: Pro-Ed.

Harms, T., & Clifford, R.M. (1980). *Day care environment rating scale*. NY: Teachers College Press, Columbia University.

Harms, T., Cryer, D., & Clifford, R.M. (1990). *Infant/toddler environment rating scale*. New York: Teachers College Press, Columbia University.

Harris, J.D., & Larsen, J.M. (1989). Parent education as a mandatory component of preschool: Effects on middle-class, educationally advantaged parents and children. *Early Childhood Research Quarterly, 4*, 275–287.

Harste, J.C., Short, K.G., & Burke, C. (1988). *Creating classrooms for authors: The reading-writing connection*. Portsmouth, NH: Heninemann Educational Books, Inc.

Hartup, W.W. (1983). Peer interaction and the behavioral development of the individual child. In W. Damon (Ed.), *Social and personality development: Essays on the growth of the child* (pp. 220–233). NY: W.W. Norton & Co.

Haskins, R. (1985). Public school aggression among children with varying day care experience. *Child Development, 56*, 698–703.

Haugland, S.W., & Shade, D.D. (1990). *Developmental evaluations of software for young children*. Albany, NY: Delmar Publishers.

Hayward, D., Rothenburg, M., & Beasley, R. (1974). Children's play and urban playground environments: A comparison of traditional, contemporary, and adventure playground types. *Environment and Behavior*, *6*(2), 131–168.

Head Start: A child development program. (1990). Washington, DC: U.S. Government Printing Office, Department of Health and Human Services.

Helburn, S., Culkin, M.L., Howes, C., Bryant, D., Clifford, R., Cryer, D., Peisner-Feinberg, E., Kagan, S.L. (1995). *Cost, quality, and child care outcomes in child care centers*. Denver: University of Colorado at Denver.

Helfer, R.E. (1987). The developmental basis of child abuse and neglect: An epidemiological approach. In R.E. Helfer & R.S. Kempe (Eds.), *The battered child* (4th ed., pp. 60–80). Chicago, IL: The University of Chicago Press.

Helm, J.H. (Ed.) (1996). *The project approach catalog.* Urbana, IL: ERIC Clearing House on Elementary and Early Childhood Education.

Hendricks, J. (1986). *Total learning: Curriculum for the young child* (2nd ed.). Columbus, OH: Merrill Publishing Co.

Henkens-Matzke, A., & Abbott, D.A. (1990). Game playing: A method for reducing young children's fear of medical procedures. *Early Childhood Research Quarterly*, *5*, 19–26.

Henry, M. (1995). The 1994 national survey of CDAs: A research report. ERIC No. ED385394.

Herr, J., Johnson, R.D., & Zimmerman, K. (1993). Benefits of accreditation: A study of directors' perceptions. *Young Children*, *48*(4), 32–35.

Herr, J., & Morse, W. (1982). Food for thought: Nutrition education for young children. In J.F. Brown (Ed.), *Curriculum planning for young children*. Washington, DC: National Association for the Education of Young Children.

Herr, J., & Zimmerman, K. (1989). *Results of the 1989 national campus child care study*. Menomonie, WI: University of Wisconsin-Stout.

Herrera, J.F., & Wooden, S.L. (1988). Some thoughts about effective parents-school communication. *Young Children*, *43*(6), 78–80.

Hestenes, L.L., Kontos, S., & Bryan, Y. (1993). Children emotional expression in child care centers varying in quality. *Early Childhood Research Quarterly*, *8*, 295–307.

Hetherington, E.M., Stanley-Hagan, M., & Anderson, E.R. (1989). Marital transitions: A child's perspective. *American Psychologist*, *44*, 303–312.

Hills, T.W. (1987). Children in the fast lane: Implications for early childhood policy and practice. *Early Childhood Research Quarterly*, *2*, 265–273.

Hilton, J.M., Essa, E.L., & Murray, C.I. (1991). Are families meeting the nonphysical needs of their children? A comparison of single parent, one-earner and two-earner households. *Family Perspectives*, *25*(2), 41–56.

Hinde, R.A. (1983). Ethology and child development. In P.H. Mussen, (Ed.), *Handbook of child psychology* (4th ed.). M.H. Haith & J.J. Campos (Eds.), *Infancy and developmental psychobiology* (Vol. 4, pp. 27–93). NY: John Wiley & Sons.

Hitchcock, N.E., Gracey, M., Gilmour, A.I. & Owles, E.N. (1986). *Nutrition and growth in infants and early childhood: A longitudinal study from birth to 5 years.* New York: Karger.

Hitz, R., & Driscoll, A. (1988). Praise or encouragement? New insights into praise: Implications for early childhood teachers. *Young Children*, *43*(5), 6–13.

Hofferth, S.L. (1989). What is the demand for and supply of child care in the United States? *Young Children*, *44*(5), 28–33.

Hofferth, S.L., & Phillips, D.A. (1987). Child care in the United States, 1970 to 1995. *Journal of Marriage and the Family*, *49*, 559–571.

Hohmann, M., Banet, B., & Weikart, D.P. (1995). *Young children in action: A manual for preschool educators*. (2nd ed.) Ypsilanti, MI: The High/Scope Press.

Holloway, S.D., & Reichhart-Erickson, M. (1988). The relationship of day care quality to children's free-play behavior and social problems-solving skills. *Early Childhood Research Quarterly, 3,* 39–53.

Honig, A.S. (1995). Singing with infants and toddlers. *Young Children, 50*(5), 72–78.

Honig, A.S. (1993). Mental health for babies: What do theory and research tell us? *Young Children*, *48*(3), 69–76.

Honig, A.S. (1988a). Caring and kindness: Curricular goals for early childhood educators. In G.F. Robertson & M.A. Johnson (Eds.), *Leaders in education: Their views on controversial issues* (pp. 58–70). NY: University Press of America.

Honig, A.S. (1988b). Humor development in children. *Young Children*, *43*(4), 60–73.

Honig, A.S. (1987). The shy child. *Young Children*, *42*(4), 54–64.

Honig, A.S. (1986a). Stress and coping in children (Part 1). *Young Children*, *41*(4), 50–63.

Honig, A.S. (1986b). Stress and coping in children (Part 2): Interpersonal family relationships. *Young Children*, *41*(5), 47–59.

Honig, A.S. (1985). Compliance, control, and discipline. *Young Children*, *40*(3), 47–52.

Honig, A.S. (1983). Sex role socialization in early childhood. *Young Children*, *38*(6), 57–70.

Honig, A.S. (1982). Prosocial development in young children. *Young Children*, *37*(5), 51–62.

Honig, A.S. (1979). *Parent involvement in early childhood education*. Washington, DC: National Association for the Education of Young Children.

Honig, A.S., & Lally, J.R. (1981). *Infant caregiving: A design for training*. Syracuse, NY: Syracuse University Press.

Hooper, F.H. (1987). Epilogue: Deja vu in approaches to early childhood education. In J.L. Roopnarine & J.E. Johnson (Eds.), *Approaches to early childhood education* (pp. 301–314). Columbus, OH: Merrill Publishing Co.

Hough, R.A., Nurss, J.R., & Wood, D. (1987). Tell me a story: Making opportunities for elaborated language in early childhood classrooms. *Young Children, 43*(1), 6–12.

Howes, C. (1997). Children's experiences in center-based child care as a function of teacher background and adult–child ratio. *Merrill-Palmer Quarterly, 43,* 404–425.

Howes, C., Smith, E., & Galinsky, E. (1995). *The Florida Child Care Quality Improvement Study: Interim report.* New York: Families and Work Institute.

Howes, C. (1990). Can the age of entry into child care and the quality of child care predict adjustment in kindergarten? *Developmental Psychology, 26,* 292–303.

Howes, C. (1988). Relations between early child care and schooling. *Developmental Psychology, 24,* 53–57.

Howes, C. (1988). Same- and cross-sex friends: Implications for interaction and social skills. *Early Childhood Research Quarterly*, *3*, 21–37.

Howes, C. (1987a). Quality indicators in infant and toddler child care: The Los Angeles Study. In D.A. Phillips (Ed), *Quality in child care: What does research tell us*? (pp. 81–88). Washington, DC: National Association for the Education of Young Children.

Howes, C. (1987b). Social competency with peers: Contributions from child care. *Early Childhood Research Quarterly*, *2*, 155–167.

Howes, C. (1983). Caregiver behavior in center and family day care. *Journal of Applied Developmental Psychology*, *4*, 99–107.

Howes, C., & Farver, J.A. (1987). Social pretend play in 2-year-olds: Effects of age of partner. *Early Childhood Research Quarterly*, *2*, 305–314.

Howes, C., & Hamilton, C.E. (1993). The changing experience of child care: Changes in teachers and in teacher-child relationships and children's social competence with peers. *Early Childhood Research Quarterly*, *8*, 15–32.

Howes, C., & Marx, E. (1992). Raising questions about improving the quality of child care: Child care in the United States and France. *Early Childhood Research Quarterly*, *7*, 347–366.

Huesmann, L.R. (1986). Psychological processes promoting the relation between exposure to media violence and aggressive behavior by the viewer. *Journal of Social Issues*, *42*, 125–139.

Huesmann, L.R., Lagerspetz, K., & Eron, L.D. (1984). Intervening variables in the TV violence-aggression relation: Evidence from two countries. *Developmental Psychology*, *20*, 746–775.

Huffman, A.B. (1996). Beyond the weather chart: Weathering new experiences. *Young Children, 51*(5), 34–37.

Humphrey, J.H., & Humphrey, J.N. (1985). *Controlling stress in children*. Springfield IL: Charles C. Thomas Publisher.

Huston, A.C., Watkins, B.A., & Kunkel, D. (1989). Public policy and children's television. *American Psychologist*, *44*, 424–433.

Hymes, J.L. (1981). *Teaching the child under six* (3rd ed.). Columbus, OH: Merrill Publishing Co.

Hyson, M.C. (1986). Lobster on the sidewalk: Understanding and helping children with fears. In J.B. McCracken (Ed.), *Reducing stress in young children's lives* (pp. 2–5). Washington, DC: National Association for the Education of Young Children.

Hyson, M.C., Hirsh-Pasek, K., & Rescoria, L. (1990). The Classroom Practices Inventory: An observational instrument based on NAEYC's guidelines for developmentally appropriate practices for 4- and 5-year old children. *Early Childhood Research Quarterly, 5,* 475–494.

International Reading Association (1986). Literacy development and pre-first grade: A joint statement of concerns abut present practices in pre-first grade reading instruction and recommendations for improvement. *Young Children*, *41*(4), 10–13.

Ishee, N., & Goldhaber, J. (1990). Story re-enactment: Let the play begin. *Young Children*, *45*(3), 70–75.

Izard, C. (1982). *Measuring emotions in infants and children*. NY: Cambridge University Press.

Jalongo, M.R. (1986). Using crisis-oriented books with young children. In J.B. McCracken (Ed.), *Reducing stress in young children's lives* (pp. 41–46). Washington, DC: National Association for the Education of Young Children.

Jalongo, M.R., & Collins, M. (1985). Singing with young children! Folk singing for nonmusicians. *Young Children*, *40*(2), 17–22.

Javernick, E. (1988). Johnny's not jumping: Can we help obese children? *Young Children*, *43(2),* 18–23.

Jenkins, S. (1987). Ethnicity and family support. In S.L. Kagan, D.R. Powell, B. Weissbourd, & E.F. Zigler (Eds.), *America's family support programs: Perspectives and prospects* (pp. 282–294). New Haven, CT: Yale University Press.

Jensen, A. R. (1985). Compensatory education and the theory of intelligence. *Phi Delta Kappan, 66,* 554–558.

Johnston, J.R., & Slobin, D.I. (1979). The development of locative expressions in English, Italian, Serbo-Croatian, and Turkish. *Journal of Child Language*, *6*, 529–545.

Jones, E., & Prescott, E. (1978). *Dimensions of teaching–Learning environments, II: Focus on day care.* Pasadena, CA: Pacific Oaks College.

Jones, E., & Villarino, G. (1994). What goes up on the classrooms walls—and why? *Young Children, 49*(2), 38–40.

Jordan, N.H. (1993). Sexual abuse prevention programs in early childhood education: A caveat. *Young Children, 48*(6), 76–79.

Jorde-Bloom, P. (1988a). *A great place to work: Improving conditions for staff in young children's programs.* Washington, DC: National Association for the Education of Young Children.

Jorde-Bloom, P. (1988b). Teachers need "TLC" too. *Young Children, 43*(6), 4–8.

Jorde-Bloom, P., Sheerer, M., & Britz, J. (1991). *Blueprint for action: Achieving center-based change through staff development.* Mt. Rainer, MD: Gryphyn House.

Joy, L.A., Kimball, M.M., & Zabrack, M.L. (1986). Television and children's aggressive behavior. In T.M. Williams (Ed.), *The impact of television: A natural experiment in three communities* (pp. 303–360). Orlando, FL: Academic Press, Inc.

Kagan, J. (1987). Introduction. In J. Kagan & S. Lamb (Eds.), *The emergence of morality in young children* (pp. ix–xx). Chicago: The University of Chicago Press.

Kagan, J., & Reznick, J.S. (1986). Shyness and temperament. In W.H. Jones, J.M. Cheek, & S.R. Briggs (Eds.), *Shyness: Perspectives on research and treatment* (pp. 81–90). NY: Plenum Press.

Kagan, S.L. (1990). The changing world of early care and education. Retrofitting practice and policy. *Child and Youth Care Quarterly, 19*(1), 7–20.

Kamii, C. (1984). Obedience is not enough. *Young Children, 39*(4), 11–14.

Kamii, C. (1982). *Numbers in preschool and kindergarten.* Washington, DC: National Association for the Education of Young Children.

Kamii, C., & DeVries, R. (1980). *Group games in early childhood.* Washington, DC: National Association for the Education of Young Children.

Kamii, C., & Lee-Katz, L. (1982). Physics in preschool education: A Piagetian approach. In J.F. Brown (Ed.), *Curriculum planning for young children* (pp. 171–176). Washington, DC: National Association for the Education of Young Children.

Karnes, M.B., & Lee, R.C. (1979). Mainstreaming in the preschool. In L.G. Katz (Ed.). *Current topics in early childhood education* (Vol. 2, pp. 13–42). Norwood, NJ: Ablex Publishing Corp.

Katz, L.G. (1988). Where is early childhood education as a profession? In B. Spodek, O.N. Saracho, & D.L. Peters (Eds.), *Professionalism and the early childhood practitioner* (pp. 75–83). NY: Teachers College Press, Columbia University.

Katz, L.G. (1984a). The education of preprimary teachers. In L.G. Katz (Ed.), *Current topics in early childhood education* (Vol. 5, pp. 209–227). Norwood, NJ: Ablex Publishing Corp.

Katz, L.G. (1984b). The professional early childhood teacher. *Young Children, 39*(5), 3–10.

Katz, L.G. (1980). Mothering and teaching: Some significant distinctions. In L.G. Katz (Ed.), *Current topics in early childhood education* (Vol. 3, pp. 47–63). Norwood, NJ: Ablex Publishing Corp.

Katz, L.G. (1977). *Talks with teachers: Reflections on early childhood education.* Washington, DC: National Association for the Education of Young Children.

Katz, L.G. (1972). Teacher-child relationships in day care centers. ERIC document #046 494.

Katz, L.G., & Chard, S. (1989). *Engaging children's minds: The project approach.* Norwood, NJ: Ablex Publishing Corp.

Katz, L.G., Evangelou, D., & Hartman, J.A. (1990). *The case for mixed-age grouping in early education.* Washington, DC: National Association for the Education of Young Children.

Katz, P.A. (1986). Modification of children's gender-stereotyped behavior: General issues and research considerations. *Sex Roles, 14*, 591–602.

Katz, P.A. (1983). Developmental foundations of gender and racial attitudes. In R.L. Leahy (Ed.), *The child's construction of social inequality* (pp. 41–78). NY: Academic Press.

Katz, P.A. (1982). Children's racial awareness and intergroup attitudes. In L.G. Katz (Ed.), *Current topics in early childhood education* (Vol. 4, pp. 17–54). Norwood, NJ: Ablex Publishing Corp.

Keele, V.S. (1966). Individual-time formula: The golden formula for raising happy secure children. Unpublished paper.

Kelker, K., Hecimovic, M., & LeRoy, C.H. (1994). Designing a classroom and school environment for students with AIDS. *Teaching Exceptional Children, 26*(4), 52–55.

Kellogg, R. (1969). *Analyzing children's art.* Palo Alto, CA: Mayfield Publishing Co.

Kelly, F.J. (1981). Guiding groups of parents of young children. *Young Children, 37*(1), 28–32.

Kempe, R.S., & Kempe, C.H. (1978). *Child abuse.* Cambridge, MA: Harvard University Press.

Keogh, J., & Sugden, D. (1985). *Movement skill development.* NY: Macmillan Publishing Co.

Ketchel, J.A. (1986). Helping the young child cope with death. *Day Care and Early Childhood, 14*(2), 24–27.

Kinsman, C.A., & Berk, L.E. (1982). Joining the block and housekeeping areas. In J.F. Brown (Ed.), *Curriculum planning for young children* (pp. 28–37). Washington, DC: National Association for the Education of Young Children.

Kisker, E.E., & Ross, C.M. (1997). Arranging child care. *The Future of Children, 7*(1), 99–109.

Kleckner, K.A., & Engel, R.E. (1988). A child begins school: Relieving anxiety with books. *Young Children, 43*(5), 14–18.

Klein, T., Bittel, C., & Molnar, J. (1993). No place to call home. Supporting the needs of homeless children in the early childhood classroom. *Young Children, 48*(6), 22–31.

Kohlberg, L. (1969). Stages and sequence: The cognitive-development approach to socialization. In D.A. Goslin (Ed.), *Handbook of socialization theory and research* (pp. 347–480). Chicago: Rand McNally.

Kohlberg, L. (1966). A cognitive-developmental analysis of children's sex-role concepts and attitudes. In E.E. Maccoby (Ed.), *The development of sex differences* (pp. 82–173). Stanford, CA: Stanford University Press.

Kontos, S. (1986). What preschool children know about reading and how they learn it. *Young Children, 42*(1), 58–66.

Kopp, C.B. (1982). Antecedents of self-regulation: A developmental perspective. *Developmental Psychology, 18*, 199–214.

Kounin, J.S., & Sherman, L.W. (1979). School environments as behavior settings. *Theory Into Practice, 18*(3), 145–151.

Krilov, L.R., Barone, S.R., Mandel, F.S., Cusack, T.M., Gaber, D.J., & Rubino, J.R. (1996). Impact of an infection control program in a specialized preschool. *American Journal of Infection Control, 24,* 167–173.

Kritchevsky, S., Prescott, E., & Walling, L. (1977). *Planning environments for young children: Physical space.* Washington, DC: National Association for the Education of Young Children.

Kubler-Ross, E. (1969). *On death and dying.* New York: MacMillan.

Kushner, D. (1989). "Put your name on your painting, but . . . the blocks go back on the shelves." *Young Children, 45*(1), 49–56.

Labov, W. (1970). *The study of nonstandard English.* Urbana, IL: National Council of Teachers of English.

Ladd, G.W., & Coleman, C.C. (1993). Young children's peer relationships: Forms, features, and functions. In B. Spodek (Ed.), *Handbook research on the education of young children* (pp. 57–76). New York: Macmillan.

Lally, J.R. (1995). The impact of child care policies and practices on infant toddler identity formation. *Young Children, 51*(1), 58–67.

Lally, J.R., Mangione, P.L., & Honig, A.S. (1988). The Syracuse University Family Development Research Program: Long-range impact on an early intervention with low-income children and their families. In D.R. Powell (Ed.), *Emerging directions in parent-child intervention* (pp. 79–104). Norwood, NJ: Ablex Publishing Corp.

Lally, J.R., & Stewart, J. (1990). *Infant-toddler caregiving: A guide to setting up environments.* Sacramento: California Department of Education.

Lamb, M.E., & Bornstein, M.H. (1987). *Development in infancy: An introduction.* NY: Random House.

Lambert-Lagace, L. (1983). *Feeding your child: From infancy to six years.* NY: Beaufort Books, Inc.

Landau, S., & McAninch, C. (1993). Young children with attention deficits. *Young Children, 48*(4), 49–58.

Langenbach, M., & Neskora, T.W. (1977). *Day care curriculum considerations.* Columbus, OH: Charles E. Merrill Publishing Co.

Laughing all the way. (1988). *Young Children, 43*(2), 39–41.

Lavatelli, C.S. (1970). *Piaget's theory applied to an early childhood curriculum.* Boston, MA: American Science and Engineering, Inc.

Lawton, J.T. (1988). *Introduction to child care and early childhood education.* Glenview, IL: Scott, Foresman & Co.

Lay-Dopyera, M., & Dopyera, J.E. (1987). Strategies for teaching. In C. Seefeldt (Ed.), *The early childhood curriculum: A review of current research* (pp. 13–33). NY: Teachers College Press, Columbia University.

Lee, V.E., Brooks-Gunn, J., Schnur, E., & Liaw, F.R. (1990). Are Head Start effects sustained? A longitudinal follow-up comparison of disadvantaged children attending Head Start, no preschool, and other preschool programs. *Child Development, 61,* 495–507.

Leister, C. (1993). Working with parents of different cultures. *Dimensions of Early Childhood, 21*(2), 13–14.

Lennenberg, E.H. (1967). *Biological foundations of language.* NY: John Wiley & Sons, Inc.

Lepper, M. R., Greene, D., & Nisbett, R.E. (1973). Undermining children's intrinsic interest with extrinsic reward: A test of the "overjustification" hypothesis. *Journal of Personality and Social Psychology, 28*, 129–137.

Lerner, J.V., & Abrams, L.A. (1994). Developmental correlates of maternal employment influences on children. In C.B. Fisher & R.M. Lerner (Eds.), *Applied developmental psychology.* New York: McGraw-Hill.

Levinger, G., & Levinger, A.C. (1986). The temporal course of close relationships: Some thoughts about the development of children's ties. In W.W. Hartup & Z. Rubin (Eds.), *Relationships and development* (pp. 111–133). Hillsdale, NJ: Lawrence Erlbaum Associates, Publishers.

Levinson, D.J. (1978). *The seasons of a man's life.* NY: Alfred Knopf.

Liebert, R.M., & Sprafkin, J.N. (1988). *The early window: Effects of television on children and youth* (3rd ed.). NY: Pergamon Press.

Lillard, P.P. (1973). *Montessori: A modern approach*. NY: Schocken Books.

Lindauer, S.L.K. (1993). Montessori education for young children. In J.L. Roopnarine & J.E. Johnson (Eds.), *Approaches to early childhood education* (3rd ed., pp. 243–259). Columbus, OH: Merrill Publishing Co.

Linderman, C.E. (1979). *Teachables from trashables: Homemade toys that teach*. St. Paul, MN: Toys'n Things Training and Resource Center, Inc.

Lindfors, J.W. (1987). *Children's language and learning* (2nd ed.). Englewood Cliffs, NJ: Prentice-Hall, Inc.

Lombardi, J. (1990). Developing a coalition to reach the full cost of quality. In B. Willer (Ed.), *Reaching the full cost of quality in early childhood programs* (pp. 87–96). Washington, DC: National Association for the Education of Young Children.

Lombardi, J. (1986). Training for public policy and advocacy: An emerging topic in teacher education. *Young Children, 41*(4), 65–69.

Lovell, P., & Harms, T. (1985). How can playgrounds be improved? A rating scale. *Young Children, 40*(3), 3–8.

Lowenfeld, V. (1962). Creativity: Education's stepchild. In S. Parner & H. Harning (Eds.), *A sourcebook for creative thinking* (pp. 157–158). NY: Charles Scribner's Sons.

Lozoff, B. (1989). Nutrition and behavior. *American Psychologist, 44*, 231–236.

Lucas, B. (1993). Nutrition and the school-age child. In P.L. Pipes & C.M. Trahms (Eds.), *Nutrition in infancy and childhood* (5th ed., pp. 142–164). St. Louis, MO: Mosby.

Maccoby, E.E. (1990). Gender and relationships. *American Psychologist, 45*, 513–520.

Maccoby, E.E., & Jacklin, C.N. (1987). Gender segregation in childhood. In H.W. Reese (Ed.), *Advances in child development and behavior* (Vol. 20, pp. 239–288). NY: Academic Press.

Maccoby, E.E., & Martin, J.A. (1983). Socialization in the context of the family: Parent-child interaction. In P. H. Mussen (Ed.), *Handbook of Child Psychology* (4th ed.), M.H. Haith & J.J. Campos (Eds.), *Infancy and development psychobiology* (Vol. 2, pp. 1–101). NY: John Wiley and Sons.

Mace, F.C., Page, T.J., Ivancic, M.T., & O'Brien, S. (1986). Effectiveness of brief time-out with and without contingent delay: A comparative analysis. *Journal of Applied Behavior Analysis, 19*, 79–86.

Machado, J.M. (1985). *Early childhood experiences in language art* (3rd ed.). Albany, NY: Delmar Publishers.

Maier, H.W. (1990). Erikson's developmental theory. In R.M. Thomas (Ed.), *The encyclopedia of human development and education: Theory, research, and studies* (pp. 88–93). NY: Pergamon Press.

Maier, H.W. (1965). *Three theories of child development*. NY: Harper and Row.

Malaguzzi, L. (1993). For an education based on relationships. *Young Children, 49*(1), 9–12.

Mann, J. (1991). Congress remembers the children—finally. *Young Children, 46*(2), 81.

Manson, J.M., & Sinha, S. (1993). Emerging literacy in the early childhood years: Applying a Vygotskian model of learning and development. In B. Spodek (Ed.), *Handbook of research on the education of young children* (pp. 137–150). New York: Macmillan.

Mardell-Czudnowski, C.D., & Goldenberg, D.S. (1990). *Developmental Indicators for the Assessment of Learning—Revised (DIAL-R)*. Circle Pines, MN: American Guidance Service.

Marotz, L.R., Rush, J.M., & Cross, M.Z. (1997). *Health, safety, and nutrition for the young child* (4th ed.) Albany, NY: Delmar Publishers.

Marshall, H.H. (1989). The development of self-concept. *Young Children, 44*(5), 44–51.

Mattingly, M. (1977). Introduction to symposium: Stress and burnout in child care. *Child Care Quarterly, 6*, 127–137.

Mavrogenes, N.A. (1990). Helping parents help their children become literate. *Young Children, 45*(4), 4–9.

Mayesky, M. (1998). *Creative activities for young children* (6th ed.). Albany, NY: Delmar Publishers.

McAfee, O.D. (1985). Circle time: Getting past "two little pumpkins." *Young Children, 40*(6), 24–29.

McCarthy, D. (1972). *Manual for the McCarthy Scales of Children's Abilities*. New York: Psychological Corp.

McCartney, K. (1984), Effect of quality of day care environment on children's language development. *Development Psychology,* 20, 244–260.

McCracken, J.B. (Ed.) (1986). *Reducing stress in young children*. Washington, DC: National Association for the Education of Young Children.

McDonald, D.T., & Ramsey, J.H. (1982). Awakening the artist: Music for young children. In J.F. Brown (Ed.), *Curriculum planning for young children* (pp. 187–193). Washington, DC: National Association for the Education of Young Children.

McIntyre, M. (1984). *Early childhood and science*. Washington, DC: National Science Teachers Association.

McLaughlin, B. (1984). *Second-language acquisition in childhood: Preschool children* (Vol. 1, 2nd ed.) Hillsdale, NJ: Lawrence Erlbaum Associates, Publishers.

McTear, M. (1985). *Children's conversations*. Oxford England: Basil Blackwell.

McWilliams, M. (1986). *Nutrition for the growing years*. NY: John Wiley & Sons.

Meddin, B.J., & Rosen, A.L. (1986). Child abuse and neglect: Prevention and reporting. *Young Children, 41*(4), 26–30.

Medeiros, D.C., Porter, B.J., & Welch, I.D. (1983). *Children under stress*. Englewood Cliffs, NJ: Prentice-Hall, Inc.

Meisels, S.J. (1993). Remaking classroom assessment with the Work Sampling System. *Young Children, 48*(5), 34–40.

Meisels, S.J. (1986). Testing four- and five-year-olds: Response to Salzer and to Shepard and Smith. *Educational Leadership, 44*(3), 90–92.

Meisels, S.J., Liaw, F., Dorfman, A., & Nelson, R.F. (1995). The work sampling system: Reliability and validity of a performance assessment for young children. *Early Childhood Research Quarterly, 10,* 277–296.

Miller, C.S. (1984). Building self-control: Discipline for young children. *Young Children, 40*(1), 15–19.

Miller, G.A., & Gildea, P.M. (1987, September). How children learn words. *Scientific American*, pp. 94–99.

Miller, L.B., & Bizzell, R.P. (1983). Long-term effects of four preschool programs: Sixth, seventh, and eighth grade. *Child Development, 54*, 727–741.

Miller, L.B., & Dyer, J.L. (1975). Four preschool programs: Their dimensions and effects. *Monographs of the Society for Research on Child Development*, (Serial No. 162), Nos. 5–6.

Minuchin, P. (1987). Schools, families, and the development of young children. *Early Childhood Research Quarterly, 2*, 245–254.

Mitchell, A., & Modigliani, K. (1989). Young children in public schools? The 'only ifs' reconsidered. *Young Children, 44*(6), 56–61.

Moore, R.C., Goltsman, S.M., & Iacofano, D.S. (1987). *Play for all guidelines: Planning, design and management of outdoor play settings for all children*. Berkeley, CA: MIG Communications.

Moore, S.G. (1982). Prosocial behaviors in the early years: Parent and peer influences. In B. Spodek (Ed.) *Handbook of research in early childhood education* (pp. 65–81). NY: The Free Press.

Morado, C. (1986). Prekindergarten programs for 4-year-olds. *Young Children, 41*(5), 61–63.

Morgan, E.L. (1989). Talking with parents when concerns come up. *Young Children, 44*(2), 52–56.

Morin, J. (1989). We can force a solution to the staffing crisis. *Young Children, 44*(6), 18–19.

Morrison, G.S. (1988). *Education and development of infants, toddlers, and preschoolers*. Glenview, IL: Scott, Foresman/Little, Brown College Division.

Moskowitz, B.A. (1982). The acquisition of language. In *Human communication: Language and its psychobiological bases: Readings from Scientific American* (pp. 121–132). San Francisco, CA: W.H. Freeman & Co.

Mounts, N.S., & Roopnarine, J.L. (1987). Application of behavioristic principles to early childhood education. In J.L. Roopnarine & J.E. Johnson (Eds.), *Approaches to early childhood education* (pp. 127–142). Columbus, OH: Merrill Publishing Co.

Munro, J.G. (1986). Movement education: Balance. *Day Care and Early Education, 14*(2), 28–31.

Mussen, P., & Eisenberg-Berg, N. (1977). *Roots of caring, sharing, and helping: The development of prosocial behavior in children*. San Francisco: W.H. Freeman and Co.

Mussen, P.H., Conger, J.J., Kagan, J., & Huston, A.C. (1990). *Child development and personality* (7th ed.). NY: Harper & Row Publishers.

Myers, B.K., & Maurer, K. (1987). Teaching with less talking: Learning centers in the kindergarten. *Young Children, 42*(5), 20–27.

Myers-Walls, J.A., & Fry-Miller, K.M. (1984). Nuclear war: Helping children overcome fears. *Young Children, 39*(4), 27–32.

NAEYC. (1997). NAEYC position statement on state implementation of welfare reform. *Young Children, 52*(2), 42–45.

NAEYC. (1996). NAEYC position statement: Responding to linguistic and cultural diversity—recommendations for effective early childhood education. *Young Children, 51*(2), 4–12.

NAEYC. (1996). NAEYC position statement: Technology and young children—ages three through eight. *Young Children, 51*(6), 11–16.

NAEYC. (1995). *Guidelines for early childhood professional preparation.* Washington, DC: National Association for the Education of Young Children.

NAEYC. (1995). NAEYC position statement on quality, compensation, and affordability. *Young Children, 51*(1), 39–41.

NAEYC. (1994). NAEYC position statement: A conceptual framework for early childhood professional development. *Young Children, 49*(3), 68–77.

NAEYC. (1993). NAEYC position statement on violence in the lives of children. *Young Children, 48*(6), 80–85.

NAEYC. (1990). NAEYC position statement on media violence in children's lives. *Young Children, 45*(5), 18–21.

NAEYC. (1988). Position statement on standardized testing of young children 3 through 8 years of age. *Young Children, 43*(3), 42–47.

NAEYC. (1987). Position statement on licensing and other forms of regulation of early childhood programs in centers and family day care homes. *Young Children, 42*(5), 64–68.

NAEYC. (1984). NAEYC position statement on nomenclature, salaries, benefits, and the status of the early childhood profession. *Young Children, 40*(1), 52–55.

NAEYC. Information Service. (1990). *Employer-assisted child care: An NAEYC resource guide.* Washington

DC: National Association for the Education of Young Children.

Nash, M. Fertile minds. *Time,* February 3, 48–56.

National Dairy Council (1980). *Food . . . Early choices: A nutrition learning system for early childhood.* Rosemont, IL: National Dairy Council.

National television violence study: Key findings and recommendations. (1996). *Young Children, 51*(3), 54–55.

Nauta, M.J., & Hewett, K. (1988). Studying complexity: The case of the child and family resource program. In H.B. Weiss & F.H. Jacobs (Eds.), *Evaluating family programs* (pp. 389–405). NY: Aldine de Gruyter.

Neugebauer, R. (1991, January/February). How's business: Status report #7 on for profit child care. *Child Care Information Exchange*, pp. 46–50.

Newberger, J.J. (1997). New brain development research—a wonderful window of opportunity to build public support for early childhood education! *Young Children, 52*(4), 4–9.

NIMH (National Institute of Mental Health). (1982). *Television and behavior: Ten years of scientific progress for the 80s. Vol. I: Summary report.* Washington, DC: U.S. Government Printing Office.

Nurss, J.R., & McGauvran, M.E. (1986). *Metropolitan Readiness Assessment Program* (5th ed.). Orlando, FL: Harcourt Brace Jovanovich.

Obler, L.K. (1985). Language through the life-span. In J.B. Gleason (Ed.), *The development of language* (pp. 277–305). Columbus, OH: Charles E. Merrill Publishing Co.

Oden, S. (1982). Peer relationship development in childhood. In L.G. Katz (Ed.), *Current topics in early childhood education* (Vol. 4, pp. 87–118). Norwood, NJ: Ablex Publishing Corp.

Oken-Wright, P. (1988). Show-and-tell grows up. *Young Children, 43*(2), 52–58.

Orlick, T. (1982). *The second cooperative sports game books*. NY: Pantheon Books.

Orlick, T. (1978a). *The cooperative sports and games book: Challenge without competition*. NY: Pantheon Books.

Orlick, T. (1978b). *Winning through cooperation*. Washington, DC: Acropolis Books, Ltd.

Owens, R.E. (1984). *Language development: An introduction*. Columbus, OH: Charles E. Merrill Publishing Co.

Parke, R.D., & Slaby, R.G. (1983). The development of aggression. In P.H. Mussen (Ed.), *Handbook of child psychology* (4th ed.), E.M. Hetherington (Ed.), *Socialization, personality, and social development* (Vol 4, pp. 547–641). NY: John Wiley and Sons.

Parker, J.G., & Gottman, J.M. (1989). Social and emotional development in a relational context. In T.J. Berndt & G.W. Ladd (Eds.), *Peer relationships in child development* (pp. 95–131). NY: John Wiley & Sons.

Parten, M.B. (1932). Social participation among preschool children. *Journal of Abnormal and Social Psychology*, *27*, 243–269.

Patterson, G.R. (1982). *Coercive family practices.* Eugene, OR: Castalia Press.

Patterson, G.R., DeBaryshe, B.D., and Ramsey, E. (1989). A developmental perspective on antisocial behavior. *American Psychologist*, *44*, 329–335.

Patterson, G.R., & Gullion, M.E. (1971). *Living with children: New methods for parents and teachers.* Champaign, IL: Research Press.

Pease, D., & Gleason, J.B. (1985). Gaining meanings: Semantic development. In J.B. Gleason (Ed.), *The development of language* (pp. 103–138). Columbus, OH: Charles E. Merrill Publishing Co.

Peisner-Feinberg, E.S., & Burchinal, M.R. (1997). Relations between preschool children's child-care experience and concurrent development: the Cost, Quality, and Outcomes Study. *Merrill-Palmer Quarterly, 43,* 451–477.

Peters, D.L. (1988). The Child Development Associate credential and the educationally disenfranchised. In B. Spodek, O.N. Saracho, & D.L. Peters (Eds.), *Professionalism and the early childhood practitioner* (pp. 93–104). NY: Teachers College Press, Columbia University.

Peters, D.L., Neisworth, J.T., & Yawkey, T.D. (1985). *Early childhood education: From theory to practice.* Monterey, CA: Brooks/Cole Publishing Co.

Phenice, L., & Hildebrand, L. (1988). Multicultural education: A pathway to global harmony. *Day Care and Early Education*, *16*(2), 15–17.

Phillips, C.B. (1990). The Child Development Associate program: Entering a new era. *Young Children*, *45*(3), 24–27.

Phillips, D., McCartney, K., & Scarr, S. (1987). Child-care quality and children's social development. *Social Psychology, 23,* 537–543.

Phillips, D., & Whitebook, M. (1986). Who are child care workers? The search for answers. *Young Children*, *41*(4), 14–20.

Phillips, D.A. (1987). *Quality in child care: What does research tell us*? Washington, DC: National Association for the Education of Young Children.

Phillips, D.A., & Howes, C. (1987). Indicators of quality child care: Review of research. In D.A. Phillips (Ed.), *Quality in child care: What does research tell us?* (pp. 1–20). Washington, DC: National Association for the Education of Young Children.

Phillips, D.A., Scarr, S., & McCartney, K. (1987). Dimensions and effects of child care quality: The Bermuda Study. In D.A. Phillips (Ed.), *Quality in child care: What does research tell us?* (pp. 43–56). Washington, DC: National Association for the Education of Young Children.

Phyfe-Perkins, E. (1980). Children's behavior in preschool settings: A review of research concerning the influence of the physical environment. In. L.G. Katz (Ed.), *Current topics in early childhood education* (Vol. 3, pp. 91–125). Norwood, NJ: Ablex Publishing Corp.

Piaget, J. (1983). Piaget's theory. In P.H. Mussen (Ed.), *Handbook of child psychology* (4th ed.). W. Kessen (Ed.), *History, theory, and methods* (Vol. 1, pp. 103–128). NY: John Wiley and Sons.

Piaget, J. (1932). *The moral judgment of the child.* NY: Harcourt, Brace & World.

Piaget, J. (1926). *The language and thought of the child.* London: Routledge & Kegan Paul.

Pipes, P.L. (1993). Infant feeding and nutrition. In P.L. Pipes & C.M. Trahms (Eds.), *Nutrition in infancy and childhood* (5th ed., pp. 87–120). St. Louis, MO: Mosby.

Pipes, P.L. (1989a). Between infancy and adolescence. In P.L. Pipes (Ed.), *Nutrition in infancy and childhood* (4th ed., pp. 120–142). St. Louis, MO: Mosby.

Pipes, P.L. (1989b). Special concerns of dietary intake during infancy and childhood. In P.L. Pipes (Ed.), *Nutrition in infancy and childhood* (4th ed., pp. 268–300). St. Louis, MO: Mosby.

Pipes, P.L. & Trahms, C.M. (1993). Nutrient needs of infants and children. In P.L. Pipes & C.M. Trahms (Ed.), *Nutrition in infancy and childhood* (4th ed., pp. 30–58). St. Louis, MO: Mosby.

Plomin, R., & Daniels, D. (1986). Genetics and shyness. In W.H. Jones, J.M. Cheek, & S.R. Briggs (Eds.), *Shyness: Perspectives on research and treatment* (pp. 63–80). NY: Plenum Press.

Poest, C.A., Williams, J.R., Witt, D.D., & Atwood, M.E. (1990). Challenge me to move: Large muscle development in young children. *Young Children, 45*(5), 4–10.

Poest, C.A., Williams, J.R., Witt, D.D., & Atwood, M.E. (1989). Physical activity patterns of preschool children. *Early Childhood Research Quarterly, 65*, 367–376.

Powell, D.R. (1989). *Families and early childhood programs.* Washington, DC: National Association for the Education of Young Children.

Powell, D.R. (1987a). After-school care. *Young Children, 42*(3), 62–66.

Powell, D.R. (1987b). Day care as a family support system. In S.L. Kagan, D.R. Powell, B. Weissbourd, and E.F. Zigler (Eds.), *America's family support programs: Perspectives and prospects* (pp. 115–132). New Haven, CT: Yale University Press.

Powell, D.R. (1986). Parent education and support programs. *Young Children, 41*(3), 47–53.

Prescott, E. (1987). The environment as organizer of intent in child-care settings. In C.S. Weinstein & T.G. David (Eds.), *Spaces for children: The built environment and child development* (pp. 73–88). NY: Plenum Press.

Price, G.G. (1989). Mathematics in early childhood. *Young Children, 44*(4), 53–58.

Proshansky, H.M., & Fabian, A.K. (1987). The development of place identity in the child. In C.S. Weinstein & T.G. David (Eds.), *Spaces for children: The built environment and child development* (pp. 21–40). NY: Plenum Press.

Radomski, M.A. (1986). Professionalization of early childhood educators: How far have we progressed? *Young Children, 41*(4), 20–23.

Raikes, H. (1996). A secure base for babies: Applying attachment concepts to the infant care setting. *Young Children, 51*(5), 59–67.

Ramey, D., Dorvall, B., & Baker-Ward, L. (1983). Group day care and socially disadvantaged families: Effects on the child and the family. In S. Kilmer (Ed.), *Advances in early education and day care* (Vol. 3, pp. 69–132). Greenwich, CT: JAI Press.

Ramsey, P.G. (1987). *Teaching and learning in a diverse world: Multicultural education for young children.* NY: Teachers College Press, Columbia University.

Ramsey, P.G. (1982). Multicultural education in early childhood. In J.F. Brown (Ed.), *Curriculum planning for young children* (pp. 131–142). Washington, DC: National Association for the Education of Young Children.

Rarick, G.L. (1982). Descriptive research and process-oriented explanations of the motor development of children. In J.A.S. Kelso & J.E. Clark (Eds.), *The development of movement control and co-ordination* (pp. 275–291). NY: John Wiley & Sons.

Reiber, J.L., & Embry, L.H. (1983). Working and communicating with parents. In E.M. Goetz & K.E. Allen (Eds.), *Early childhood education: Special environmental, policy, and legal considerations* (pp. 152–183). Rockville, MD: Aspen Publications.

Reifel, S. (1984). Block construction: Children's developmental landmarks in representation of space. *Young Children, 40*(1), 61–67.

Reppucci, N.D., & Haugaard, J.J. (1989). Prevention of child sexual abuse: Myth or reality. *American Psychologist, 44*, 1266–1275.

Resnick, L.B. (1989). Developing mathematical knowledge. *American Psychologist, 44*, 162–169.

Rice, K.S. (1992). Behavioral aspects of fetal alcohol syndrome. ERIC document #ED344355.

Rich, S.J. (1985). The writing suitcase. *Young Children, 40*(5), 42–44.

Richarz, A.S. (1980). *Understanding children through observation.* St. Paul, MN: West Publishing Co.

Risley, T.R., & Baer, D.M. (1973). Operant behavior modification: The deliberate development of behavior. In B.M. Caldwell & H.M. Ricciuti (Eds.), *Review of child development research* (Vol. 3, pp. 283–329). Chicago IL: University of Chicago Press.

Robinson, B.E. (1988). Vanishing breed: Men in child care programs. *Young Children, 43*(6), 54–57.

Roe, M., & Vukelich, C. (1994). Portfolio implementation: What about R for realistic? *Journal of Research in Childhood Education, 9,* 5–14.

Roedell, W.C., Jackson, N.E., & Robinson, H.B. (1980). *Gifted young children*. New York: Teachers College Press, Columbia University.

Rogers, C.S., & Morris, S.S. (1986). Reducing sugar in children's diets: Why? How? *Young Children, 41*(5), 11–16.

Rogers, D.L., Perrin, M.S., & Waller, C.B. (1987). Enhancing the development of language and thought through conversations with young children. *Early Childhood Research Quarterly, 2*, 17–29.

Rogers, D.L., & Ross, D.D. (1986). Encouraging positive social interaction among young children. *Young Children, 41*(3), 12–17.

Rogers, F., & Sharapan, H.B. (1991). Helping parents, teachers, and caregivers deal with children's concerns about war. *Young Children, 46*(3), 12–13.

Rothlein, L. (1989). Nutrition tips revisited: On a daily basis, do we implement what we know? *Young Children, 44*(6), 30–36.

Roupp, R., Travers, J., Glantz, F., & Coelen, C. (1979). *Children at the center: Final report of the National Day Care Study*. Cambridge, MA: Abt Associates.

Royce, J.M., Darlington, R.B., & Murray, H.W. (1983). Pooled analyses: Findings across studies. In The Consortium for Longitudian Studies, *As the twig is bent . . . Lasting effects of preschool programs* (pp. 411–459). Hillsdale, NJ: Lawrence Erlbaum Associates.

Rubin, K.H. (1977). Play behaviors of young children. *Young Children, 32*(6), 16–24.

Rubin, Z. (1980). *Children's friendships*. Cambridge, MA: Harvard University Press.

Rutter, M. (1983). Stress, coping, and development: Some issues and some questions. In N. Garmezy & M. Rutter (Eds.), *Stress, coping, and development in children* (pp. 1–41). NY: McGraw-Hill Book Co.

Saida, Y., & Miyashita, M. (1979). Development of fine motor skill in children: Manipulation of a pencil in young children aged two to six years old. *Journal of Human Movement Studies, 5*, 104–113.

Sameroff, A.J. (1983). Developmental systems: Contexts and evolution. In P.H. Mussen (Ed.), *Handbook of child psychology* (4th ed.). *History, theory, and methods* (Vol. 1, pp. 237–294). NY: John Wiley & Sons.

Samuels, S.C. (1977). *Enhancing self-concept in early childhood*. NY: Human Sciences Press.

Sarafino, E.P. (1986). *The fears of childhood: A guide to recognizing and reducing fearful states in children.* NY: Human Sciences Press, Inc.

Saunders, R., & Bingham-Newman, A.M. (1984). *Piagetian perspectives for preschools: A thinking book for teachers*. Englewood Cliffs, NJ: Prentice-Hall, Inc.

Saville-Troike, M. (1982). The development of bilingual and bicultural competence in young children. In L.G. Katz (Ed.), *Current topics in early childhood education* (Vol. 4, pp. 1–16). Norwood, NJ: Ablex Publishing Corp.

Scarr, S., Phillips, D., & McCartney, K. (1990). Facts, fantasies and the future of child care in the United States. *Psychological Science, 1*(1), 26–35.

Schickedanz, J.A. (1986). *More than ABCs: The early stages of reading and writing*. Washington DC: National Association for the Education of Young Children.

Schickedanz, J.A. (1982). The acquisition of written language in young children. In B. Spodek (Ed.), *Handbook of research in early childhood education* (pp. 242–263). NY: Free Press.

Schickedanz, J.A., Hansen, K., & Forsyth, P.D. (1990). *Understanding children*. Mountain View, CA: Mayfield Publishing Co.

Schilder, P., & Wechsler, D. (1934). The attitudes of children toward death. *Journal of Genetic Psychology, 45*, 406–451.

Schirrmacher, R. (1998). Art and creative development for young children (3rd ed.). Albany, NY: Delmar Publishers.

Schirrmacher R. (1993). *Art and creative development for young children* (2nd ed.). Albany, NY: Delmar Publishers.

Schirrmacher, R. (1986). Talking with young children about their art. *Young Children, 41*(5), 3–10.

Schweinhart, L.J. (1993). Observing young children in action: The key to early childhood assessment. *Young Children, 48*(5), 29–3.

Schweinhart, L.J., Barnes, H.V., & Weikart, D.P. (1993). *Significant benefits: The High/Scope Perry Preschool study through age 27*. Ypsilanti, MI: High/Scope Press.

Schweinhart, L.J., & Weikart, D.P. (1985). Evidence that good early childhood programs work. *Phi Delta Kappan, 66*, 545–551.

Schweinhart, L.J., Weikart, D.P., & Larner, M.B. (1986a). Consequences of three preschool models through age 15. *Early Childhood Research Quarterly, 1*, 15–45.

Schweinhart, L.J., Weikart, D.P., & Larner, M.B. (1986b). Child-initiated activities in early childhood programs may help prevent delinquency. *Early Childhood Research Quarterly, 1*, 303–312.

Sciarra, D.J., & Dorsey, A.G. (1995). *Developing and administering a child care center* (3rd ed.). Albany, NY: Delmar Publishers.

Seaver, J.W., & Cartwright, C.A. (1986). *Child care administration*. Belmont, CA: Wadworth Publishing Co.

Seefeldt, C. (1995). Art—a serious work. *Young Children, 50*(3), 39–45.

Seefeldt, C. (1987). The visual arts. In C. Seefeldt (Ed.), *The early childhood curriculum: A review of current research* (pp. 183–211). NY: Teacher's College Press.

Seefeldt, V. (1984). Physical fitness in preschool and elementary school-aged children. *Journal of Physical Education, Recreation, and Dance, 55*(9), 33–40.

Seefeldt, V., & Haubenstricker, J. (1982). Patterns, phases, or stages: An analytical model for the study of developmental movement. In J.A.S. Kelso & J.E. Clark (Eds.), *The development of movement control and co-ordination* (pp. 309–318). NY: John Wiley & Sons.

Seifert, K. (1988). Men in early childhood education. In B. Spodek, O.N. Saracho, & D.L. Peters (Eds.), *Professionalism and the early childhood practitioner* (pp. 105–116). NY: Teachers College Press, Columbia University.

Seifert, K.L. (1993). Cognitive development in early childhood education. In B. Spodek (Ed.), *Handbook of research on the education of young children* (pp. 9–23). New York: Macmillan.

Seitz, V., Rosenbaum, L.K., & Apfel, N.H. (1985). Effects of family support intervention: A ten-year follow-up. *Child Development, 56*, 376–391.

Seligson, M., & Allenson, M. (1993). *School-age child care: An action manual for the 90s and beyond*. Westport, CT: Auburn House.

Selye, H. (Ed.) (1980). *Guide to stress research* (Vol 1). NY: Van Nostrand Reinhold.

Shade, D.D. (1996). Software evaluation. *Young Children, 51*(6), 17–21.

Shapiro, E., & Biber, B. (1972). The education of young children: A developmental-interaction approach. *Teachers College Record, 74*, 55–79.

Shatz, M., & Gelman, R. (1973). The development of communication skills: Modifications in the speech of young children as a function of listener. *Monographs of the Society for Research in Child Development, 38*(5, #152).

Sheehy, G. (1976). *Passages: Predictable crises of adult life*. NY: Dutton.

Sheerer, M.A., Dettore, E., & Cyphers, J. (1996). Off with a theme: Emergent curriculum in action. *Childhood Education Journal, 24*, 99–102.

Sheldon, A. (1990). "Kings are royaler than queens": Language and socialization. *Young Children, 45*(2), 4–9.

Sheldon, J.B. (1983). Protecting the preschooler and the practitioner: Legal issues in early childhood programs. In E.M. Goetz & K.E. Allen (Eds.), *Early childhood education: Special environmental, policy, and legal considerations* (pp. 307–341). Rockville, MD: Aspen Systems Corp.

Sheppard, W.C. (1973). *Teaching social behavior to young children*. Champaign, IL: Research Press.

Sholtys, K.C. (1989). A new language, a new life. *Young Children, 44*(3), 76–77.

Shweder, R.A., Mahapatra, M., & Miller, J.G. (1987). Culture and moral development. In J. Kagan and S. Lamb (Eds.), *The emergence of morality in young children* (pp. 1–83). Chicago: The University of Chicago Press.

Siegel, A.W., & White, S.H. (1982). The child study movement: Early growth and development of the symbolized child. *Advances in Child Development and Behavior, 17*, 233–285.

Siegler, R.S. (1986). *Children's thinking*. Englewood Cliffs, NJ: Prentice-Hall, Inc.

Siegler, R.S. (1983). Information processing approaches to development. In P.H. Mussen (Ed.), *Handbook of child psychology* (4th ed.). W. Kessen (Ed.), *History, theory, and methods* (Vol. 1, pp. 103–128). NY: John Wiley & Sons.

Sigel, I.E. (1987). Does hothousing rob children of their childhood? *Early Childhood Research Quarterly, 2*, 211–225.

Silin, J.G. (1985). Authority as knowledge: A problem of professionalization. *Young Children, 40*(3), 41–46.

Silver, R. A. (1982). Developing cognitive skills through art. In L.G. Katz (Ed.), *Current topics in early childhood education* (Vol. 4, pp. 143–171). Norwood, NJ: Ablex Publishing Corp.

Simons, J.A., & Simons, F.A. (1986). Montessori and regular preschools: A comparison. In L.G. Katz (Ed.), *Current topics in early childhood education* (Vol. 6, pp. 195–223). Norwood, NJ: Ablex Publishing Corp.

Singer, J.L., Singer, D.G., & Rapaczynski, W. (1984, Spring). Family patterns and television viewing as predictors of children's beliefs and aggression. *Journal of Communication*, pp. 73–89.

Skinner, B.F. (1974). *About behaviorism*. NY: Alfred A. Knopf.

Skinner, B.F. (1969). *Contingencies of reinforcement: A theoretical analysis*. NY: Appleton-Century-Crofts.

Skinner, B.F. (1957). *Verbal behavior*. NY: Appleton-Century-Crofts.

Skinner, L. (1979). *Motor development in the preschool years*. Springfield, IL: Thomas Publishers.

Smilansky, S. (1968). *The effects of sociodramatic play on disadvantaged children*. NY: Wiley.

Smith, C.A. (1989). *From wonder to wisdom: Using stories to help children grow*. NY: New American Library.

Smith, C.A. (1982). *Promoting the social development of young children*. Palo Alto, CA: Mayfield Publishing Co.

Smith, M.M. (1990). NAEYC annual report. *Young Children, 46*(1), 41–48.

Smith, P., & Connolly, K. (1981). *The behavioral ecology of the preschool.* Cambridge, England: Cambridge University Press.

Smith, P.K., & Connolly, K.J. (1980). *The ecology of preschool behaviour*. Cambridge, England: Cambridge University Press.

Smith, R.F. (1982). Early childhood science education: A Piagetian perspective. In J.F. Brown (Ed.), *Curriculum planning for young children* (pp. 143–150). Washington, DC: National Association for the Education of Young Children.

Snow, C.E., & Ninio, A. (1986). The contracts of literacy: What children learn from learning to read books. In W.H. Teale & E. Sulzby (Eds.), *Emergent literacy: Writing and reading* (pp. 116–138). Norwood, NJ: Ablex Publishing Corp.

Soderman, A.K. (1985). Dealing with difficult young children. *Young Children, 40*(5), 15–20.

Spodek, B. (1985). *Teaching in the early years* (3rd ed.), Englewood Cliffs, NJ: Prentice-Hall, Inc.

Spodek, B., & Saracho, O.N. (1994). *Dealing with individual differences in the early childhood classroom.* New York: Longman.

Spodek, B., & Saracho, O.N. (1988). Professionalism in early childhood education. In B. Spodek, O.N. Saracho, & D.L. Peters (Eds.), *Professionalism and the early childhood practitioner* (pp. 59–74). New York: Teachers College Press, Columbia University.

Spodek, B., & Saracho, O.N. (1982). The preparation and certification of early childhood personnel. In B. Spodek (Ed.), *Handbook of research in early childhood education.* NY: The Free Press.

Sponseller, D. (1982). Play and early education. In B. Spodek (Ed.), *Handbook of research in early childhood education* (pp. 215–241). NY: The Free Press.

Stevenson, R.L. (1985). *A child's garden of verse.* M. Forman (Illustrator). NY: Delacorte Press.

Suggestions for developing positive racial attitudes (1980). *Interracial books for children bulletin, 11*(3–4), 10–15.

Sunal, C.S. (1993). Social studies in early childhood education. In B. Spodek (Ed.), *Handbook of research on the education of young children* (pp. 176–190). New York: Macmillan.

Sutherland, Z., & Arburthnot, M.H. (1986). *Children and books* (7th ed.). Glenview, IL: Scott, Foresman and Co.

Swick, K.J. (1994). Family involvement: An empowerment perspective. *Dimensions of Early Childhood 22*(2), 10–13.

Swigger, K.M., & Swigger, B.K. (1984). Social patterns and computer use among preschool children. *AEDS Journal, 17*(3), 35–41.

Sword, J. (1987). Help! I'm selecting children's books. *Day Care and Early Education, 15*(2), 26–28.

Table toys: A creative curriculum for early childhood. (1979). Washington, DC: Creative Associates, Inc.

Teale, W.H., & Martinez, M.G. (1988). Getting on the right road to reading: Bringing books and young children together in the classroom. *Young Children, 44*(1), 10–15.

Teale, W.H., & Sulzby, E. (1986). Emergent literacy as a perspective for examining how young children become writers and readers. In W.H. Teale & E. Sulzby (Eds.), *Emergent literacy: Writing and reading* (pp. vii to xxv). Norwood, NJ: Ablex Publishing Corp.

Thomas, A., & Chess, S. (1969). *Temperament and development.* NY: New York University Press.

Thomas, A., Chess, S., & Birch, H.G. (1968). *Temperament and behavior disorders in children.* NY: New York University Press.

Thomas, R.M. (1990a). Basic concepts and applications of Piagetian cognitive development theory. In R.M. Thomas (Ed.), *The encyclopedia of human development and education: Theory, research, and studies* (pp. 53–56). NY: Pergamon Press.

Thomas, R.M. (1990b). *The encyclopedia of human development and education: Theory, research, and studies.* NY: Pergamon Press.

Thomson, C.L., & Ashton-Lilo, J. (1983). A developmental environment for child care programs. In E.M. Goetz & K.E. Allen (Eds.), *Early childhood education: Special environmental, policy, and legal considerations* (pp. 93–125). Rockville, MD: Aspen Systems Corp.

Thorndike, R.L., Hagen, E.P., & Sattler, J.M. (1986). *Stanford-Binet intelligence scale: Fourth edition.* Chicago: Riverside Publishing Co.

Thornton, J.R. (1990). Team teaching: A relationship based on trust and communication. *Young Children, 45*(5), 40–43.

Tire hazards, woodworking, and crib safety. (1986). *Young Children, 41*(5), 17–18.

Tizard, B., Mortimer, J., & Burchell, B. (1981). *Involving parents in nursery and infant schools.* Ypsilanti, MI: The High/Scope Press.

Trahms, C.M. (1989). Factors that shape food patterns in young children. In P.L. Pipes (Ed.), *Nutrition in infancy and childhood* (4th ed., pp. 160–170). St. Louis, MO: Mosby.

Tribe, C. (1982). *Profile of three theories: Erikson, Maslow, Piaget.* Dubuque, IA: Kendall/Hunt Publishing Co.

Troiano, R.P., Flegal, K.M., Kuczmarski, R.J., Campbell, S.M., & Clifford, L.J. (1995). Overweight prevalence and trends for children and adolescents: The National Health and Nutrition Examination Surveys, 1963 to 1991. *Archives of Pediatrics and Adolescent Medicine, 149,* 1085–1092.

Ulich, R. (1967). Johann Heinrich Pestalozzi. In P. Edwards (Ed.), *The encyclopedia of philosophy* (Vol. 5–6, pp. 121–122). NY: Macmillan Publishing Co., Inc. & The Free Press.

Ulich, R. (1947). *Three thousand years of educational wisdom*. Cambridge, MA: Harvard University Press.

Vandell, D.L., & Corasaniti, M.A. (1990). Variations in early child care: Do they predict subsequent social, emotional, and cognitive differences? *Early Childhood Research Quarterly, 5*, 555–572.

Vander Ven, K. (1986). "And you have a ways to go": The current status and emerging issues in training for child care practice. In K. Vander Ven & Tittnich (Eds.), *Competent caregivers—competent children: Training and education for child care practice*. NY: Hawthorne Press.

Van Heerden, J.R. (1984). Early under-nutrition and mental performance. *International Journal of Early Childhood, 16*(1), 10–16.

Vygotsky, L.S. (1978). The prehistory of written language. In M. Cole, V. John-Steiner, S. Scribner, & E. Souberman (Eds.), *Mind and society: The development of higher psychological process* (pp. 105–119). Cambridge, MA: Harvard University Press.

Vygotsky, L.S. (1962). *Thought and language*. NY: John Wiley & Sons, Inc.

Wade, M.G., & Davis, W.E. (1982). Motor skill development in young children: Current views on assessment and programming. In L.G. Katz (Ed.), *Current topics in early childhood education* (Vol. 4, pp. 55–70). Norwood, NY: Ablex Publishing Corp.

Wadsworth, B.J. (1984). *Piaget's theory of cognitive and affective development* (3rd ed.). NY: Longman.

Wadsworth, D.E., & Knight, D. (1996). Meeting the challenge of HIV and AIDS in the classroom. *Early Childhood Education Journal, 23,* 143–147.

Walker, D.K., & Crocker, R.W. (1988). Measuring family systems outcomes. In H.B. Weiss & F.H. Jacobs (Eds.), *Evaluating family programs* (pp. 153–176). NY: Aldine de Gruyter.

Wallerstein, J., Corbin, S.B., & Lewis, J.M. (1988). Children of divorce: A ten-year study. In E.M. Hetherington & J. Arasteh (Eds.), *Impact of divorce, single-parenting and stepparenting on children* (pp. 198–214). Hillsdale, NY: Paul Erlbaum, Associates.

Wallerstein, J.S. (1983). Children of divorce: Stress and developmental tasks. In N. Garmezy & M. Rutter (Eds.), *Stress, coping, and development in children* (pp. 265–302). NY: McGraw-Hill Book Co.

Walton, S. (1989). Katy learns to read and write. *Young Children, 44*(5), 52–57.

Wash, D.P., & Brand, L.E. (1990). Child day care services: An industry at a crossroads. *Monthly Labor Review, 113*(12), 17–24.

Washington, V., & Oyemade, U.J. (1985). Changing family trends. Head Start must respond. *Young Children, 40*(6), 12–18.

Wass, H. (1984). Concepts of death: A developmental perspective. In H. Wass and C.A. Corr (Eds.), *Childhood and death*. NY: Hemisphere Publishing Corp.

Weber, E. (1984). *Ideas influencing early childhood education*. NY: Teachers College Press, Columbia University.

Wechsler, D. (1944). *The measurement of adult intelligence*. Baltimore, MD: Williams and Wilkins.

Weikart, D.P., & Schweinhart, L.J. (1993). The High/Scope curriculum for early childhood care and education. In J.L. Roopnarine & J.E. Johnson (Eds.), *Approaches to early childhood education* (2nd ed., pp. 195–208). New York: Merrill.

Weikart, D.P., & Schweinhart, L.J. (1987). The High/Scope cognitively oriented curriculum of early education. In J.L. Roopnarine & J.E. Johnson (Eds.), *Approaches to early childhood education* (pp. 253–267). Columbus, OH: Merrill Publishing Co.

Weinstein, C.S. (1987). Designing preschool classrooms to support development. In C.S. Weinstein & T.G. David (Eds.), *Spaces for children: The built environment and child development* (pp. 159–185). NY: Plenum Press.

Weiss, G., & Hechtman, L.T. (1986). *Hyperactive children grow up: Empirical findings and theoretical considerations*. NY: The Guilford Press.

Weiss, H. (1987). Family support and education in early childhood programs. In S.L. Kagan, D.R. Powell, B. Weissbourd, & E.F. Zigler (Eds.), *America's family support programs* (pp. 133–160). New Haven, CT: Yale University Press.

Werner, E.E. (1984). Resilient children. *Young Children, 40*(1), 68–72.

Werner, P., Timms, S., & Almond, L. (1996). Health stops: Practical ideas for health-related exercise in preschool and primary classrooms. *Young Children, 51*(6), 48–55.

Wertsch, J.V. (1985). *Vygotsky and the social formation of mind*. Cambridge, MA: Harvard University Press.

White House Conference on Food, Nutrition, and Health: Final report. (1970). Washington, DC: U.S. Government Printing Office.

Whitebook, M. (1986). The teacher shortage: A professional precipice. *Young Children, 41*(3), 10–11.

Whitebook, M., Howes, C., Darrah, R., & Friedman, J. (1982). Caring for the caregiver: Staff burnout in child care. In L.G. Katz (Ed.), *Current topics in early childhood education* (Vol. 4, pp. 211–235). Norwood, NJ: Ablex Publishing Corp.

Whitebook, M., Howes, C., & Phillips, D. (1989). *Who cares? Child care teachers and the quality of care in America: Executive summary, national child care study*. Oakland, CA: Child Care Employee Project.

Whitebook, M., Phillips, D., & Howes, M. (1993). *National Child Care Staffing Study revisited: Four years in the life of center-based child care*. Oakland CA: The Child Care Employee Project.

Wilderstrom, A.H. (1986). Educating young handicapped children: What can early childhood education contribute? *Childhood Education*, *63*(2), 78–83.

Willer, B. (1990). Estimating the full cost of quality. In B. Willer (Ed.), *Reaching the full cost of quality in early childhood programs* (pp. 55–86). Washington, DC: National Association for the Education of Young Children.

Willer, B. (1987). Quality or affordability: Trade-offs for early childhood programs? *Young Children*, *42*(6), 41–43.

Willer, B.S., Hofferth, L., Kisker, E., Divine-Hawkins, P., Farquhar, E., & Glantz, F.B. (1991). *The demand and supply of child care in 1990: Joint findings from the national child care survey 1990 and a profile of child care settings.* Washington, DC: National Association for the Education of Young Children.

Willert, M.K., & Kamii, C. (1985). Reading in kindergarten: Direct vs. indirect teaching. *Young Children*, *40*(4), 3–9.

Williams, L.R. (1987). Determining the curriculum. In C. Seefeldt (Ed.), *The early childhood curriculum: A review of current research* (pp. 1–12). NY: Teachers College Press, Columbia University.

Wilson, L.C. (1995). *Infants and toddlers: Curriculum and teaching* (3rd ed.). Albany, NY: Delmar Publishers.

Winner, E. (1986). Where pelicans kiss seals. *Psychology Today*, *20*, 24–35.

Wolery, M., Holcombe, A., Venn, M.L., Brookfield, J., Huffman, K., Schroeder, C., Martin, C.G., & Fleming, L.A. (1993). Mainstreaming in early childhood programs: Current status and relevant issues. *Young Children*, *49*(1), 78–88.

Wolf, A.D. (1990). Art postcards--Another aspect of your aesthetics program? *Young Children*, *45*(2), 39–43.

Wolfe, J. (1989). The gifted preschooler: Developmentally different, but still 3 or 4 years old. *Young Children*, *44*(3), 41–48.

Woodrich, D.L. (1984). *Children's psychological testing: A guide for nonpsychologists*. Baltimore, MD: Paul H. Brookes Publishing Co.

Wortham, S.C. (1994). *Early childhood curriculum: Developmental bases for learning and teaching*. New York: Merrill.

Wortham, S.C. (1990). *Tests and measurement in early childhood education*. Columbus, OH: Merrill Publishing Co.

Yarrow, M.R., Scott, P.M., & Waxler, C.Z. (1973). Learning concern for others. *Developmental Psychology*, *8*, 240–260.

Ziajka, A. (1983). Microcomputers in early childhood education. *Young Children*, *38*(5), 61–67.

Ziemer, M. (1987). Science and the early childhood curriculum: One thing leads to another. *Young Children*, *42*(6), 44–51.

Zigler, E., & Berman, W. (1973). Discerning the future of early childhood intervention. *American Psychologist*, *38*, 894–906.

Zigler, E.F., & Freedman, J. (1987). Head Start: A pioneer of family support. In S.L. Kagan, D.R. Powell, B. Weissbourd, & E.F. Zigler (Eds.), *America's family support programs* (pp. 57–76). New Haven, CT: Yale University Press.

Zimiles, H. (1993). The Bank Street approach. In J.L. Roopnarine & J.E. Johnson (Eds.) *Approaches to early childhood education* (2nd ed., pp. 261–273). Columbus, OH: Merrill Publishing Co.

Zuckerman, B. (1991). Drug-exposed infants: Understanding the medical risks. In R.E. Behrman (Ed.), *The future of children: Drug-exposed infants*. Los Altos, CA: The David and Lucile Packard Foundation.

Glossary

A

ABC analysis — An observational technique in which the observer records observations in three columns, identifying antecedent, behavior, and consequence.

Absorbent mind — Maria Montessori's term to describe the capacity of young children to learn a great deal during the early years.

Abstract thinking — According to Jean Piaget, the ability to solve a variety of problems abstractly, without a need to manipulate concrete objects.

Accommodation — According to Jean Piaget, one form of adaptation, which takes place when an existing concept is modified or a new concept is formed to incorporate new information or a new experience.

Active listening — Thomas Gordon's term for the technique of reflecting back to children what they have said as a way to help them find their own solutions to problems.

Activity time — Largest block(s) of time in the early childhood program day during which children can self-select from a variety of activities.

Adaptation — Jean Piaget's term for the process that occurs any time new information or a new experience occurs.

Adventure playground — A European innovation, a type of outdoor play area in which children use a wide range of available "junk" materials to create their own environment.

Aesthetics — Enjoyment and appreciation of beauty, particularly related to all forms of art.

Aggregates — Rhoda Kellogg's term for the step in the development of art in which children combine three or more simple diagrams.

Aggression — Behavior deliberately intended to hurt others.

Allergies — Physiological reactions to environmental or food substances that can affect or alter behavior.

Anecdotal record — A method of observation involving a written "word picture" of an event or behavior.

Anxiety — A general sense of uneasiness that cannot be traced to a specific cause.

Assimilation — According to Jean Piaget, one form of adaptation, which takes place when a person tries to make new information or a new experience fit into an existing concept.

Assistant teacher — Also called aide, helper, auxiliary teacher, associate teacher, or small-group leader; works under the guidance of the head teacher in providing a high-quality program for the children and families in the class.

Association for Childhood Education International (ACEI) — Professional organization that focuses on issues of children from infancy to early adolescence, particularly those involving international and intercultural concerns.

At-risk children — Because of adverse environmental—factors, for instance, poverty or low birth weight—children considered at risk for developmental delay.

Attachment — The child's bond with the mother, established during the first year of life.

Attention deficit disorder (ADD) — Difficulty in concentration on an activity or subject for more than a few moments at a time.

Attention deficit hyperactivity disorder (ADHD) — Manifested by short attention span, restlessness, poor impulse control, distractibility, and inability to concentrate.

Audience awareness — Children's growing awareness that their stories are a form of communication that should make sense to others.

Authority stage — Stage of parenting defined by Ellen Galinsky typifying parents of young preschoolers who are defining rules as well as their own parenting role.

Autism — A socioemotional disorder of unknown origin in which the child's social, language, and other behaviors are inappropriate, often bizarre.

Autonomy vs. Shame and Doubt — The second stage of development described by Erik Erikson, occurring during the second year of life, in which toddlers assert their growing motor, language, and cognitive abilities by trying to become more independent.

B

Babbling — The language of babies in the second half of the first year, consisting of strings of vowels and consonants that are often repeated over and over.

Basic scribbles — According to Rhoda Kellogg, the 20 fundamental markings found in all art.

Behavior management — Behavioral approach to guidance holding that the child's behavior is under the control of the environment, which includes space, objects, and people.

Behavior modification — The systematic application of principles of reinforcement to modify behavior.

Behavior setting — According to Kounin and Sherman, different environments elicit behaviors that are fitted to the setting; thus, children act "schoolish" at school.

Behavioral objective — Aim or goal, usually set for an individual child, that describes in very specific and observable terms what the child is expected to master.

Behaviorism — The theoretical viewpoint, espoused by theorists such as B. F. Skinner, that behavior is shaped by environmental forces, specifically in response to reward and punishment.

Bereavement — The grief over a loss, such as after the death of a loved one.

Bibliotherapy — The use of books that deal with emotionally sensitive topics in a developmentally appropriate way to help children gain accurate information and learn coping strategies.

Bilingualism — Ability to use two languages.

Bimanual control — Ability to use both hands in tasks for which each hand assumes a different function.

Board of directors — Policy-making or governing board that holds ultimate responsibility, particularly for a not-for-profit program.

Brigance Diagnostic Inventory of Early Development-Revised — A developmental assessment tool for children from birth to age seven.

Burnout syndrome — Condition experienced by professionals as a result of undue job stress, characterized by loss of energy, irritability, and a feeling of being exploited.

C

Career lattice — Recognizes that the early childhood profession is made up of individuals with varied backgrounds; a lattice allows for both horizontal and vertical movement among positions, with accompanying levels of education, experience, responsibility, and pay.

Caregiver or child care worker — Term traditionally used to describe a person who works in a child care setting.

Center-based programs — A program for young children located in a school setting, usually including larger groups of children than are found in home-based programs.

Central processor — That aspect of the information processing model that governs and coordinates other functions such as sensory input and memory

Checklist — A method of evaluating children that consists of a list of behaviors, skills, concepts, or attributes that the observer checks off as a child is observed to have mastered the item.

Child abuse and neglect — Any action or inaction that harms a child or puts that child at risk.

Child-adult ratio — The number of children for whom an adult is responsible, calculated by dividing the total number of adults into the total number of children.

Child advocacy — Political and legislative activism by professionals to urge change in social policies affecting children.

Child Development Associate (CDA) — An early childhood teacher who has been assessed and successfully proven competent through the national CDA credentialling program.

Child study movement — Occurred earlier in the 20th century in the United States when many university preschools were established to develop scientific methods for studying children.

Classification — The ability to sort and group objects by some common attribute or property for instance, color or size.

Code of ethics — Agreed-upon professional standards that guide behavior and facilitate decision making in working situations.

Code switching — Ability to switch appropriately from one language system to another.

Cognition — The process of mental development, concerned more with how children learn than with the content of what they know.

Cognitive developmental theory — The theory formulated by Jean Piaget that focuses on how children's intelligence and thinking abilities emerge through distinct stages.

Cognitive interactionist view of language development — The view that children's language is rooted in cognitive development, requiring, for instance, ability to represent objects mentally.

Combines — According to Rhoda Kellogg, a step in the development of art in which children combine two simple diagrams.

Computer literacy — Familiarity with and knowledge about computers.

Conceptual — Montessori classroom area that focuses on academic materials related to math, reading, and writing.

Concrete Operations Period — Piaget's period covering the elementary school years.

Confidentiality — Requirement that results of evaluations and assessments be shared with only the parents and appropriate school personnel.

Conservation — Ability to recognize that objects remain the same in amount despite perceptual changes, usually acquired during the period of concrete operations.

Constructivist theory — A theory, such as that of Jean Piaget, based on the belief that children construct knowledge for themselves rather than having it conveyed to them by some external source.

Content objective — Purpose or rationale for an activity that specifies that the activity is intended to promote specific subject matter.

Conventional level of moral development — According to Lawrence Kohlberg, the stage concerned with pleasing others and respect for authority.

Conventional moral rules — Standards, which are generally culture-specific, arrived at by general consensus.

Convergent thinking — The act of narrowing many ideas into a single, focused point.

Cooing — The language of babies in the first half of the first year, consisting primarily of strings of throaty vowels sounds.

Coping strategies — Mental or physical reactions, which can be effective or ineffective, to help deal with stress.

Creative playgrounds — Outdoor play areas that use innovative materials such as tires, telephone poles, nets, and cable spools.

Criterion-referenced — A characteristic of tests in which children are measured against a predetermined level of mastery rather than against an average score of children of the same age.

Cross-modal intersensory activity — Use and integration of more than one sensory modality, for instance, matching an object that is seen visually to an identical object selected through touch only.

Cuing — A technique used to help children remember what is expected by giving them a specific signal.

Curriculum — Overall master plan of the early childhood program, reflecting its philosophy, into which specific activities are fit.

D

Daily living — Montessori classroom area that focuses on practical tasks involved in self- and environment-care.

Deep structure — According to Noam Chomsky, inborn understanding or underlying rules of grammar and meaning that are universal across all languages.

Deficit or impairment — A problem in development, usually organic, resulting in below-normal performance.

Denver II — A quick test for possible developmental delays in children from infancy to age six.

Developmental delay — A child's development in one or more areas occurring at an age significantly later than that of peers.

Developmental Indicators for the Assessment of Learning-Revised (DIAL-R) — A developmental screening test for children ages two to six, assessing motor, concept, and language development.

Developmental interactionist model — Foundation of the Bank Street approach, concerned with the interaction among various aspects of each child's development as well as between child and environment.

Developmental objective — Purpose or rationale for an activity that specifies that the activity is intended to promote an aspect of physical, social, emotional, or cognitive development.

Developmental test — Measures the child's functioning in most or all areas of development, although some such tests are specific to one or two areas.

Diagnostic testing — Another term for screening, which might indicate that more thorough testing should be carried out.

Diagrams — According to Rhoda Kellogg, the stage in children's art when they begin to use the six recognizable shapes—the rectangle, oval, triangle, X, cross, and the deliberate odd shape.

Dialect — A regional variation of a language that differs in some features of vocabulary, grammar, and pronunciation.

Didactic — A term often applied to teaching materials, indicating a built-in intent to provide specific instruction.

Direct instruction (also called programmed instruction) — A method of teaching in which the teacher determines exactly what the children should learn, devises a sequence of learning activities to teach specific information, and teaches it directly by controlling the information according to children's responses.

Discipline — Generally considered a response to children's misbehavior.

Disequilibrium — According to Jean Piaget, the lack of balance experienced when existing mental structures and new experience do not fit exactly.

Divergent thinking — The act of expanding or elaborating on an idea, such as brainstorming.

E

Early childhood education models — Approaches to early childhood education, based on specific theoretical foundations; for instance, the behavioral, Piagetian, or Montessori view.

Early childhood teacher or educator — A specifically trained professional who works with children from infancy to age eight.

Ebonics — Term identifying the dialect spoken by some black children, which has a complex grammatical system of its own.

Eclectic — Describing an approach in which various desirable features from different theories or methods are selected: drawing elements from different sources.

Ecological model — A framework for viewing development that takes into account the various interconnected contexts within which individuals exist, for instance, the family, neighborhood, or community.

Educable mentally retarded — A child who has noticeable delays in most areas of development, including cognitive, but can function quite well in a regular early childhood program.

Effective praise — A form of encouragement that focuses on children's activities rather than on teacher evaluation of their work; praise that is meaningful to children rather than general or gratuitous.

Ego strength — Ability to deal effectively with the environment.

Emergent literacy — The ongoing, dynamic process of learning to read and write, which starts in the early years.

Empowerment — Helping parents gain a sense of control over events in their lives.

Equilibrium — According to Jean Piaget, the state of balance each person seeks between existing mental structures and new experiences.

Equipment — Large items such as furniture that represent a more expensive, long-term investment in an early childhood facility.

Event sampling — A method of observation in which the observer records a specific behavior only when it occurs.

Exosystem — According to family systems theory, that part of the environment that includes the broader components of the community that affect the functioning of the family, such as governmental agencies or mass media.

Extended family — Family members beyond the immediate nuclear family; for instance, aunts and uncles, grandparents, or cousins.

Extinction — In behavioral theory, a method of eliminating a previously reinforced behavior by taking away all reinforcement; for instance, by totally ignoring the behavior.

Eye-hand coordination — Integrative ability to use the hands as guided by information from the eyes.

F

Family child care homes — Care for a relatively small number of children in a family home that has been licensed or registered for that purpose.

Family involvement — The commitment of parents to the early childhood program through a wide variety of options.

Family systems theory — A view of the family as an ever-developing and changing social unit in which members constantly accommodate and adapt to each other's demands as well as to outside demands.

Fetal alcohol syndrome (FAS) — Irreversible birth abnormalities resulting from mother's heavy alcohol consumption during pregnancy. Children are usually retarded and hyperactive, and may have small head size, small overall size, and various limb or face abnormalities.

Fetal alcohol effect (FAE) — Not as serious or noticeable as fetal alcohol syndrome, FAE, nonetheless, can leave children at a disadvantage in ability to learn and reach optimal development.

Fine motor development — Development of skills involving the small muscles of the fingers and hands necessary for such tasks as writing, drawing, or buttoning.

Flexibility — A measure of creativity involving the capability to adapt readily to change in a positive, productive manner.

Fluency — A measure of creativity involving the ability to generate many relevant ideas on a given topic in a limited time.

Formal Operations Period — Piaget's period covering adolescence.

Formative evaluation — Ongoing assessment to ensure that planned activities and methods accomplish what the teacher intended.

Fundamental movement phase — According to David Gallahue, the third stage of gross motor development, from ages 2 to 7, when children refine rudimentary skills so they acquire mature characteristics.

G

Gender identity — Identification with the same sex.

Gender stability — The recognition by children by age five to seven, but absent in younger children, that sex is constant and cannot be changed.

Generativity — According to Erik Erikson, the stage of human development in which the mature adult focuses on the care and nurture of the young.

Genres — Categories or types of music, such as classical, jazz, or country.

Gifted children — Children who perform significantly above average in intellectual and creative areas.

Goal — An overall, general overview of what children are expected to gain from the program.

Gross motor development — Development of skills involving the large muscles of the legs, arms, back, and shoulders, necessary for such tasks as running, jumping, and climbing.

Guidance — Ongoing process of directing children's behavior based on the types of adults children are expected to become.

H

Head teacher — The person in charge of a class who is ultimately responsible for all aspects of class functioning.

High/Scope Child Observational Record (COR) — An alternative method of gathering reliable information about young children; COR utilizes teachers' notes of observations by classifying them into specific categories.

Holding grip — Placement of the hands in using a tool for drawing or writing.

Home visit — A one-on-one interaction between the teacher and the parent(s) of the child that takes place in the child's home.

Hothousing — Term taken from horticulture in which plant growth is speeded up by forced fertilization, heat, and light; refers to accelerated learning programs for young children.

Human development theory — A way to describe what happens as individuals move from infancy through adulthood, identifying significant events that are commonly experienced by all people, and explaining why changes occur as they do.

I

I-message — Thomas Gordon's term for a response to a child's behavior that focuses on how the adult feels rather than on the child's character.

Imagery — A relaxation technique in which a mental image such as "float like a feather" or "melt like ice" is invoked.

Ignoring — A principle of behavior management that involves removing all reinforcement for a given behavior to eliminate that behavior.

Immersion programs — An approach to teaching a second language to children by surrounding or immersing them in that language.

Individualized Education Plan (IEP) — Mandated by Public Law 94-142, such a plan must be designed for each child with disabilities and must involve parents as well as teachers and other appropriate professionals.

Individualized Family Service Plan (IFSP) — Required by the 1986 Education of the Handicapped Act Amendments for handicapped children under the age of three and their families; the IFSP, often developed by a transdisciplinary team that includes the parents, determines goals and objectives that build on the strengths of the child and family.

Inductive reasoning — A guidance approach in which the adult helps the child see the consequences of a behavior on other people through logic and reasoning.

Industry vs. Inferiority — The fourth stage of development described by Erik Erikson, starting at the end of the preschool years and lasting until puberty, in which the child focuses on development of competence.

Information processing — A model of cognitive development, somewhat analogous to how a computer functions, concerned primarily with how human beings take in and store information.

Initiative vs. Guilt — The third stage of development described by Erik Erikson, occurring during the preschool years, in which the child's curiosity and enthusiasm lead to a need to explore and learn about the world, and in which rules and expectations begin to be established.

Innatist view of language development — The view that inborn factors are the most important component of language development.

Integrated curriculum — A program that focuses on all aspects of children's development, not just cognitive development.

Interactionist view of language development — The view that language develops through a combination of inborn factors and environmental influences.

Interpersonal moral rules — Considered as universal, including prohibitions against harm to others, murder, incest, and theft.

Interpretive stage — Stage of parenting defined by Ellen Galinsky typifying the parent of an older preschooler or school-aged child who faces the task of explaining and clarifying the world to the child.

Invented spelling — Used by young children in their early attempts to write by finding the speech sound that most clearly fits what they want to convey.

K

Key experiences — In the cognitively oriented curriculum, the eight cognitive concepts on which activities are built.

Kindergarten — German word, literally meaning "garden for children," coined by Friedrich Froebel for his program for young children.

Kinesthetic sense — Information from the body's system that provides knowledge about the body, its parts, and its movement; involves the "feel" of movement without reference to visual or verbal cues.

L

Large group time (also called circle, story, or group time) — Time block(s) during the day when all of the children and teachers join together in a common activity.

Latch-key or Self-care children — School-aged children who, after school, return to an empty home because their parents are at work.

Lateralization — The division of the human brain, marked by a specialization in analytical and logical tasks in the left half and intuitive and creative functions in the right half.

Learning centers (also called activity or interest areas) — Where materials and equipment are combined around common activities, for instance, art, science, or language arts.

Least restrictive environment — A provision of Public Law 94-142 that handicapped children be placed in a program as close as possible to a setting designed for children without disabilities, while being able to meet each child's special needs.

Lesson plans — The working documents from which the daily program is run, specifying directions for activities.

Locomotion — Self-movement from place to place, such as in walking.

Logical consequences — Rudolf Dreikurs' technique of allowing children to experience the natural outcome of their actions.

Logical thinking — According to Jean Piaget, the ability that begins to emerge around age seven in which children use mental processes to solve problems rather than relying solely on perceived information.

Long-term (or permanent) memory — In information processing theory, the vast store of information and knowledge that is held for a long time.

M

Macrosystem — According to family systems theory, the broadest part of the environment, which includes the cultural, political, and economic forces that affect families.

Manipulatives — Toys and materials that require the use of the fingers and hands, for instance, puzzles, beads, and pegboards.

Mapping — A mapmaking activity involving spatial relations in which space is represented creatively through such media as marking pens or blocks.

Materials — The smaller, often expendable items used in early childhood programs that are replaced and replenished frequently.

Maturational theory — Explanation of human development dependent on information about when children achieve specific skills.

McCarthy Scales of Children's Abilities — An intelligence test, particularly used with children who are mildly retarded or who have learning disabilities.

Memory strategies — Various approaches used especially by older children and adults to help them remember information.

Mesosystem — According to family systems theory, the linkages between the family and the immediate neighborhood and community.

Metamemory — The ability to think about one's own memory.

Metropolitan Readiness Test — A test to determine whether a child is prepared to enter a program such as kindergarten.

Microsystem — According to family systems theory, that part of the environment that most immediately affects a person, such as the family, school, or workplace.

Mixed-age grouping — Programs in which children of different ages—for instance, three- to six-year-olds—are together in one class.

Mock writing — Young children's imitation of writing through wavy, circular, or vertical lines, which can be seen as distinct from drawing or scribbling.

Model — In social learning theory, those whom children imitate, particularly because of some desirable feature or attribute.

Modeling — In social learning theory, the process of imitating a model.

Montessori equipment — Early childhood learning materials derived from and part of the Montessori approach.

Moral development — The long-term process of learning and internalizing the rules and standards of right and wrong.

Morphology — The study of word rules, for instance, tense, plurals, and possessives.

Multimodality — Referring to information that depends on input from several of the senses.

N

National Association for the Education of Young Children (NAEYC) — Largest American early childhood professional organization, which deals with issues of children from birth to age eight and those who work with young children.

Nonimmersion programs — Approach to teaching a new language that involves using both the primary and second languages, with a gradual shift from emphasis on the first to the second.

Norm-referenced — A test in which scores are determined by using a large group of same-age children as the basis for comparison, rather than using a predetermined criterion or standard of performance.

Nuclear family — The smallest family unit made up of a couple or one or two parents with child(ren).

Number concepts — One of the cognitive concepts young children begin to acquire, involving an understanding of quantity.

Nurturing stage — Stage of parenting defined by Ellen Galinsky into which the parents of an infant fit, as they form an attachment with and integrate the new baby into the family.

O

Object permanence — Part of Jean Piaget's theory, the recognition that objects exist, even when they are out of view; a concept that children begin to develop toward the end of their first year of life.

Objective — An aim; a specific interpretation of general goals, providing a practical and directive tool for day-to-day program planning.

Observable behavior — Actions that can be seen rather than those that are inferred.

Observational learning — In social learning theory, the process of learning that comes from watching, noting the behavior of, and imitating models.

One-to-one correspondence — A way in which young preschoolers begin to acquire an understanding of number concepts by matching items to each other, for instance, one napkin beside each plate.

Open education — A program that operates on the assumption that children, provided a well-conceived environment, are capable of selecting and learning from appropriate activities.

Open-ended materials — Early childhood materials that are flexible rather than structured and can be used in a variety of ways rather than in only a single manner.

Operant conditioning — The principle of behavioral theory whereby a person deliberately attempts to increase or decrease behavior by controlling consequences.

Organization — According to Jean Piaget, the mental process by which a person organizes experiences and information in relation to each other.

Overextension — Application of a word to a variety of related objects, especially used by toddlers.

P

Palmar grasp — A way of holding tools in which the pencil or crayon lies across the palm of the hand with the fingers curled around it, and the arm rather than the wrist moves the tool.

Parent-cooperative — A program staffed by one professional teacher and a rotating staff of parents.

Parent education — Programs aimed at enhancing parent-child relations and improving parenting competence.

Parent-teacher conference — A one-on-one interaction between the teacher and the child's parent(s).

Parquetry blocks — Variously shaped flat blocks, including diamonds and parallelograms, that can be assembled into different patterns on a form board.

Perceived competence — Children's belief in their ability to succeed in a given task.

Perceptual motor model — A theoretical view of physical development that holds that motor behaviors are a prerequisite for and lead to cognitive abilities.

Personal control — The feeling that a person has the power to make things happen.

Phobia — An intense, irrational fear.

Pictorialism — According to Rhoda Kellogg, the stage in the development of art in which children draw recognizable objects.

Pincer grasp — The use of thumb and forefinger to pick up small objects; this skill develops around nine months of age.

Place identity — Considered part of self-identity because it relates to the environmental context within which a child's needs are met, competence is developed, and control over the physical world is gained.

Placement patterns — According to Rhoda Kellogg, a way of analyzing children's art by examining the 17 ways in which the total picture or design is framed or placed on the paper.

Plan-do-review cycle — The heart of the cognitively oriented curriculum through which children are encouraged to make deliberate, systematic choices with the help of teachers by planning ahead of time, carrying out, then recalling each day's activities.

Planning time — In the cognitively oriented curriculum, the time set aside during which children decide what activities they would like to participate in during the ensuing work time.

Playscapes — Contemporary, often innovative playground structures that combine a variety of materials.

Positive discipline — Synonymous with guidance, an approach that allows the child to develop self-discipline gradually.

Positive reinforcement — Application of a behavioral principle, which includes any immediate feedback (either through tangible or nontangible means) to children that their behavior is valued.

Postconventional level of moral development — According to Lawrence Kohlberg, the stage in which moral decisions are made according to universal considerations of what is right.

Pragmatics — Rules that govern language use in social contexts.

Preassessment — A form of evaluation given before teaching a specific concept or topic to assess how much children know about it and to compare later how much they have learned.

Preconventional level of moral development — According to Lawrence Kohlberg, the stage during which moral decisions are made based on personal preference or avoidance of punishment.

Preoperational Period — Piaget's period covering the preschool years.

Prepared environment — Maria Montessori's term to describe the careful match between appropriate materials and what the child is most ready to learn at any given time.

Preschematic stage — The stage in the development of art in which children have a subject in mind when they begin a picture, but in which the actual product will be an inaccurate, crude representation of the real thing.

Programmed instruction (also called direct instruction) — A method of teaching in which the teacher determines exactly what the children should learn, devises a sequence of learning activities to teach specific information, and teaches it directly by controlling the information according to children's responses.

Progressive relaxation — A technique in which various specified muscle groups are tensed then relaxed systematically.

Prosocial behaviors — Positive, commonly valued social behaviors such as sharing, empathy, or understanding.

Psychosocial theory — The branch of psychology founded by Erik Erikson, in which development is described in terms of eight stages that span childhood and adulthood, each offering opportunities for personality growth and development.

Punishment — An aversive consequence that follows a behavior for the purpose of decreasing or eliminating the behavior; not recommended as an effective means of changing behavior.

R

Rating scale — An assessment of specific skills or concepts that are rated on some qualitative dimension of excellence or accomplishment.

Rational counting — Distinguished from rote counting, in which the child accurately attaches a numeral name to a series of objects being counted.

Recall time — In the cognitively oriented curriculum, the time when children review their work-time activities.

Reflective abstraction — According to Jean Piaget, part of a child's self-directed activity that allows the child to think about and reflect on what he or she is doing, leading to the development of new mental abilities.

Reflexive movement phase — According to David Gallahue, the earliest stage of gross motor development during the first year; at first greatly controlled by reflexes then gradually coming under greater voluntary control.

Reinforcement — In behavioral theory, any response that follows a behavior that encourages repetition of that behavior.

Reliability — A measure of a test indicating that the test is stable and consistent, to ensure that changes in score are due to the child, not the test.

Representation — According to Jean Piaget, the ability to depict an object, person, action, or experience mentally, even if it is not present in the immediate environment.

Resilient children — Children, who despite extremely stressful lives, appear to be stable, outgoing, and optimistic.

Rote counting — Reciting numbers from memory without attaching meaning to them in the context of objects in a series.

Rudimentary movement phase — According to David Gallahue, the second stage of gross motor development during the second year when body control is gradually developing.

Running record — A type of observation that provides an account of all of the child's behavior over a period of time.

S

Scaffolding — In Vygotsky's sociohistoric theory, the support provided by adults and older peers to help children learn the new tasks they are not yet able to accomplish on their own.

Schemata (schema is the singular form) — According to Jean Piaget, cognitive structures into which cognitive concepts or mental representations are organized.

Schematic stage — Older children's drawings, which are more realistic and accurate than younger children's in what they depict.

Screening test — A quick method of identifying children who might exhibit developmental delay; only an indicator that must be followed up by more thorough and comprehensive testing.

Scribbling stage — The stage in the development of art in which children experiment with marks on a page.

Self-concept — Perceptions and feelings children may have about themselves, gathered largely from how the important people in their world respond to them.

Self-correcting — Learning materials such as puzzles that give the child immediate feedback on success when the task is completed.

Self-esteem — Children's evaluation of their worth in positive or negative terms.

Self-help skills — Tasks involving caring for oneself, such as dressing, feeding, toileting, and grooming.

Self-selected time-out — A technique in which children are given the responsibility for removing themselves from the classroom if they feel they are about to lose control.

Semantics — Related to understanding and study of word meaning.

Semantic network — The interrelationship among words, particularly related to word meaning.

Sensitive periods — Maria Montessori's term describing the times when children are most receptive to absorbing specific learning.

Sensitivity — Related to creativity, it refers to a receptivity to external and internal stimuli.

Sensorial — Montessori classroom area in which materials help children develop, organize, broaden, and refine sensory perceptions of sight, sound, touch smell, and taste.

Sensorimotor Period — Piaget's period covering infancy.

Sensory deficit — A problem, particularly of sight or hearing.

Sensory discrimination — Involvment in an activity in which one of the senses is used to distinguish a specific feature or dimension of similar materials; it might include matching or sorting by size, color, shape, sound, smell, or taste.

Sensory integration — The ability to translate sensory information into intelligent behavior.

Sensory-perceptual development — Giving meaning to information that comes through the senses.

Sensory register — In information processing theory, that part of the model describing how information initially comes to our awareness when perceived by the senses.

Separation anxiety — Emotional difficulty experienced by some young children when leaving their mothers.

Seriation — A relationship among objects in which they are placed in a logical order, such as from longest to shortest.

Sex cleavage — Distinct separation based on gender, evident in children at a very young age.

Shaping — In behavioral theory, a method used to teach a child a new behavior by breaking it down into small steps and reinforcing the attainment of each step systematically.

Short-term (or working) memory — In information processing theory, limited capacity for temporarily remembering information such as a telephone number.

Show-and-tell — A common group activity in which children can share something special and personal with their classmates.

Simultaneous language acquisition — A child learning two languages at the same time or before the age of three.

Slow learner — A child with mild cognitive delay and general immaturity.

Social cognition — Organization of knowledge and information about people and relationships.

Social interactionist view of language development — Theoretical view that considers language closely tied to and dependent on social processes.

Social learning theory — Theoretical view derived from but going beyond behaviorism, which considers that children learn not just from reinforcement but from observing and imitating others.

Social reinforcer — In behavioral theory, a reward that conveys approval through such responses as a smile, hug, or attention.

Socialization — The process through which children become a functioning part of society and learn society's rules and values.

Sociodramatic play — Children's dramatic or symbolic play that involves more than one child in social interaction.

Sociohistoric theory — Originated by Lev Vygotsky, this theory gives prominence to the social, cultural, and historic context of child development.

Software — The "instructions" that direct a computer to perform an activity, usually stored on a disk or directly in the computer; many such programs are available for young children.

Spatial concepts — A cognitive ability involving an understanding of how objects and people occupy, move in, and use space.

Spatial relationship — The relative positions to each other of objects and people in space.

Special time — A method for spending a few minutes a day with just one child as a way of providing unconditional attention.

Specialized movement phase — According to David Gallahue, the fourth and final stage of gross motor development, appearing around age 7 and up, when motor skills are applied to special uses, such as specific sports.

Split brain — The term that describes the brain as having two distinct sides or hemispheres, each with different functions.

Stage theorist — Any theory that delineates specific stages in which development is marked by qualitatively different characteristics and accomplishments and where each stage builds on the previous ones.

Stanford-Binet Intelligence Scale — A widely used test that yields an intelligence quotient (IQ).

Stranger anxiety — Displays of fear and withdrawal by many infants beginning around six months of age, when babies are well able to distinguish their mother's face from the faces of other people.

Stress — Internal or external demand on a person's ability to adapt.

Successive approximations — Breaking a complex behavior into smaller steps and reinforcing a child for each step as the child comes closer to attaining the final behavior.

Successive language acquisition — Learning a second language after the age of three.

Summative evaluation — An assessment that follows a specific lesson or unit to evaluate whether the children have met the objectives.

Surface structure — According to Noam Chomsky, specific aspects of language that vary from one language to another.

Symbolic representation — The ability acquired by young children to use mental images to stand for something else.

Syntax — Involves the grammatical rules that govern the structure of sentences.

T

Team teaching — An approach that involves coteaching in which status and responsibility are equal rather than having a pyramid structure of authority, with one person in charge and others subordinate.

Temperament — Children's inborn characteristics such as regularity, adaptability, and disposition that affect behavior.

Temporal concepts — Cognitive ability concerned with the child's gradual awareness of time as a continuum.
Temporal sequencing — The ability to place a series of events in the order of their occurrence.
Time-out — Technique in which the child is removed from the reinforcement and stimulation of the classroom.
Time sampling — A quantitative measure or count of how often a specific behavior occurs within a given amount of time.
Total communication approach — Used with hearing impaired children, utilizing a combination of methods such as sign language, speech reading, and hearing aids.
Tripod grasp — A way of holding tools in which the pencil or crayon is held by the fingers, and the wrist rather than the whole arm moves the tool.
Trust vs. Mistrust — The first stage of development described by Erik Erikson, occurring during infancy, in which the child's needs should be met consistently and predictably.

U

Unconditional attention — A way of conveying acceptance to children by letting them know they are valued and liked; attention that is not given in response to a specific behavior.
Unit blocks — Most common type of blocks, precision made of hard wood in standardized sizes and shapes.

V

Validity — A characteristic of a test that indicates that the test actually measures what it purports to measure.

W

Whole language approach — Strategy for promoting literacy by surrounding children with high-quality oral and print language.
Work sampling system — Samuel Meisel's alternative method of gathering reliable information about young children, using a combination of observations, checklists, portfolios, and summary reports.
Work time — In the cognitively oriented curriculum, the large block of time during which children engage in self-selected activities.

Y

You-message — Thomas Gordon's term for a response to a child's behavior that focuses on the child's character (usually in negative terms) rather than on how the adult feels.

Z

Zone of proximal development (ZPD) — In Vygotsky's theory, this zone represents tasks a child cannot yet do by herself but which she can accomplish with the support of an older child or adult.

Key Questions

CHAPTER 1

1. If you were given "three wishes" to bring about changes for young children and their families, what would they be? Share these with others in your class. From a combined list, develop several child and family issues that you think child advocates might address.

2. Visit an early childhood program in your community and share this information with other members of your class who have visited different programs. Classify the programs according to their characteristics; for instance, purpose, setting, ages of children served, and source of support. Does your community have a variety of programs? Which types of programs predominate? What family needs are met by these programs?

3. Visit a local Head Start program. What benefits do you see for the children? Talk to a staff member and find out what services are provided for the children and their families.

4. Suppose you were asked by the parent of a young child, "How do I find a good child care program?" What would you answer? How can you help a parent recognize quality indicators?

5. Projections for the future, as we have discussed, indicate an increased need for good early childhood programs. What changes do you think are needed to bring about improvements for children and for early childhood professionals?

CHAPTER 2

1. Observe several children of the same age. These might be children you work with and know well or children that you are observing for the first time. What traits do they share? How are they similar? Can you draw some conclusions about children of that particular age?

2. As you observe children, identify a child who appears to be self-confident. How does the child express this confidence? Do you see a difference between this child and another who seems less assured?

3. Observe a group of young children at play. Look for examples of the various types of play discussed in this chapter. Do you see a relationship between age and type of play?

4. Think about the same children you observed earlier for KEY QUESTION #1 and describe what makes each of them unique. How do they differ? Do you have any indications about what factors underlie these differences?

5. If you are able, observe an early childhood program in which a child with special needs is integrated. Observe and talk to one of the teachers. What special accommodations have been made for this child? How does the child interact with the other children in the class? How is the child's independence encouraged? Does the child participate in a few, some, or all activities?

CHAPTER 3

1. Think of your own family history. How has your family changed over the past two (or three or four) generations? Consider maternal employment, divorce, closeness to extended family, and other factors. Compare your family with that of other members of your class.

2. Sometimes the needs of families conflict with those of the program. Which elements of the early childhood program could pose a potential conflict? How might these be resolved? Read "Ethics Case Studies: The Working Mother" in *Young Children,* November 1987, page 16, for insight into the suggestions of professionals to resolve such a conflict.

3. Visit an early childhood program. What evidence of communication with parents do you see? Look at bulletin boards, notes, pictures, and other written material. What kind of interaction do you notice between parents and teachers? What "messages" about the school's concern for parents do parents get from this communication?

4. Ask several parents whose children are enrolled in an early childhood program about their contacts with the teachers and the program. What is their overall attitude about contact between home and school? Do they feel it is important or not important . . . positive or negative . . . present or absent . . . supportive or lacking in support? What do they expect from the teachers? Do they feel communication between parents and teachers is important for their children?

5. How can parental involvement benefit the early childhood program? List some concrete ways in which parents might contribute to the program.

CHAPTER 4

1. Review the four levels of early childhood educators suggested by NAEYC. What are the advantages of such a hierarchy? What are the disadvantages? Since these levels are not extensively used at this time, what needs to happen for wider adoption of such a system?

2. Obtain the requirements for the CDA credentialing process (from your instructor or from the Council for Early Childhood Professional Recognition, 1718 Connecticut Ave. NW, Washington, DC 20077). Compare these to the ones required by the program in which you are enrolled. What are the points of similarity and the differences?

3. What are the advantages of belonging to a professional early childhood organization? Review several issues of professional journals such as *Young Children* or *Childhood Education* to gain a sense of what organizations such as NAEYC or ACEI have to offer.

4. Talk to several teachers of young children. What do they view as the most rewarding parts of their job? What most frustrates them? Compare their answers with your own goals and expectations.

5. Professional organizations such as NAEYC have been active in advocating improved working conditions and status for those who work with young children. Review the "Public Policy Report" and "Washington Update" in several issues of *Young Children* to see what kinds of issues are being discussed.

CHAPTER 5

1. Historic events have a great impact on our view of children and how we treat them. What social and political events have taken place during your life that have had an impact on young children and their education? Also ask this question of a relative or friend who was born in an earlier era.

2. Observe an early childhood program. What evidence do you see of the influence of one or more theorists, for instance, Piaget, Erikson, or the behaviorists? Ask one of the teachers if he or she draws on any particular human development theories and compare to your observation.

3. What was your earliest school experience? How does it compare to the type of programs you see for young children today?

4. If one is available, observe a Montessori school in your community. How does it differ from other early childhood programs you have seen? How is it similar? What elements of Maria Montessori's original program do you see?

5. Visit a Head Start program in your community. Which family services and education experiences provided by this program might contribute to the types of long-range positive effects found by the research?

CHAPTER 6

1. Review a lesson plan that contains specific objectives. Do you see a relationship between the objectives and the planned activities? How do the objectives give direction to the teachers who carry out the activities?

2. With a fellow student, spend about 15 minutes observing the same child. Each of you write an anecdotal observation involving this child for the exact same period of time. Now compare your two observations. Do they describe the same behaviors, activities, and interactions? Do they convey the same "picture" of this child? If the two observations differ in a significant way, why is this? Are there some subjective elements in either observation that might contribute to this difference?

3. Design a checklist of 10 items to assess social development of a group of preschoolers. How did you decide on which items to include? What resources did you use to put this checklist together? If possible, observe a group of preschoolers and apply this checklist to several of the children.

4. Have you been tested with a standardized instrument? Recall how you felt about the testing situation and the questions asked. What emotional impact did the test have on you? How might young children feel about being tested? What can a tester do to help children perform to their best ability?

5. Given the information from this chapter about the values and potential misuses of evaluation procedures, develop a set of criteria that might guide you, as an early childhood professional, in using assessments in the most effective way. What do you consider to be the three most important benefits of such testing? What should you avoid?

CHAPTER 7

1. Talk to two or three children who are four or five years old. Ask them what they like about their class-

room and playground. Are the features they mention ones that you consider particularly interesting and noteworthy? What do their answers tell you about these children's interests, attitudes, and needs in relation to the environment?

2. Spend some time in an early childhood classroom and attune yourself to the environment. What do you like? What do you dislike? How would it feel to work all day in this setting? What changes could make this a more pleasant or accommodating environment for adults?

3. Observe a group of children in an outdoor environment. What kinds of activities are the children involved in? Which developmental needs are being met? If you see little involvement in activities that promote one, or several, areas of development (for instance, social, language, cognitive), what changes or additions could be made to bring these about?

4. Browse through one of the many catalogs in which early childhood materials and equipment are advertised. Evaluate several of the items in the catalog according to the criteria outlined in this chapter for selecting equipment and materials. What conclusions can you draw about selecting developmentally appropriate items for young children?

5. If you have access to a computer and early childhood software, try out one early childhood activity on the computer. After you have mastered the activity, evaluate the software according to the criteria presented in this chapter. What do you think young children will learn from the activity? What feature(s) do you think might be appealing, unappealing, or frustrating to preschoolers?

CHAPTER 8

1. Visit an early childhood program and look at its daily schedule. What elements are included? Does the schedule seem developmentally appropriate by taking into account the needs of the children? Does it provide the kind of balance discussed in this chapter? Would you change anything in this schedule? Why or why not?

2. Consider the issue of child-initiated vs. teacher-initiated activity. Do you agree with the author that there should be ample time for children to make decisions and exercise independence or do you think more teacher control is important? Note that not everyone agrees on this question. Discuss this question with others in your class and consider both sides of the issue.

3. You probably know children like Rita who spend most of their day in a child care center. How are the needs of these children met? How do they differ from a child like David? In what ways can the schedule take the children's needs into consideration?

4. What are your memories of your earliest school experiences? What kinds of activities were involved? Can you glean from your recollections what type of curriculum your preschool or day care or kindergarten or first grade teacher might have been following?

5. What are some of the unique features of your community? Which of these would be of interest to young children? Think of several ways in which your community can be the basis for relevant learning for preschoolers.

CHAPTER 9

1. Which of your friends or acquaintances do you consider to be creative? What creative characteristics do they possess? Do they fit the definition of creativity presented in this chapter? How do they use creativity in ways other than the conventional sense (for instance, art or music expression)?

2. Observe a group of children. What expressions of creativity do you observe? What factors in the environment or in the teachers' behavior encourage or discourage creativity? Does any child stand out as particularly creative in this group? What characteristics does this child possess? Is your criterion for identifying a creative child different from one used to identify a creative adult?

3. Look at children's artwork. Do you see an age progression from scribbles to shapes to representational pictures?

4. Make a finger painting or collage with materials typically found in an early childhood program. How does this activity make you feel? What benefits can children gain from such activities? Do the same with a music activity, for instance, using rhythm instruments or dancing freely to music, and answer the same questions.

5. Watch a children's television program, for instance, a cartoon. What messages does this program convey to children? Does it promote stereotypes? If a child watches programs such as this one frequently, how might such viewing affect creativity?

CHAPTER 10

1. Observe preschoolers of various ages at play. What differences in physical development do you see as a function of age? What do these abilities tell you about appropriate activities and expectations?

2. If you were asked to plan a physical fitness program for a group of preschoolers, what would you include? Would you plan different activities for three-year-olds than for five-year-olds?

3. Select two different manipulative materials. What do you think children can potentially learn from each of them? Now spend 10 minutes using each manipulative. Would you add any items to your lists of what children can learn?

4. Adults generally use their senses of sight and hearing far more than their other senses. Think about how and when you use information from the various senses. Does this suggest activities for young children that could enhance their sensory learning?

5. Plan a cooking activity for preschoolers. How can this activity reinforce nutrition education concepts?

CHAPTER 11

1. Consider the people in the class for which you are reading this book. In how many different ways can you classify these individuals? Think of as many categories as possible. What does this exercise tell you about cognitive skill development in young children?

2. Observe a young child for about 20 minutes. How does this child use cognitive skills? Note the many ways in which this child uses her or his thinking abilities, including evidence of problem solving, symbolic representation, memory, classification, seriation, time and space concepts, and number concepts.

3. In this chapter we have considered only math and science as activities in which children use cognitive processes. How is cognition a part of other areas in the early childhood curriculum?

4. Think of a science class you have taken. What topics from this class might be appropriate concepts for young children? How do you modify information that you, as an adult have learned, to be appropriate for young children?

5. What do children learn from the study of animals and plants?

CHAPTER 12

1. Listen to a young child's spontaneous language usage. What components of language do you note? Consider the child's understanding of the meaning of language as well as the child's grasp of language rules.

2. Talk to someone you know who learned English as a second language. What are this person's recollections about this learning process? What was most difficult and what was easiest? What strategies or techniques were most helpful in this learning process? Talk with others in your class and compare the findings of those whose friends learned English at an early age and those who learned it later in life.

3. Observe a teacher of young children engage in spontaneous conversation with children. What techniques does she or he use? How are the children encouraged to interact with each other as well as with the teacher? Did you hear examples of language play or humor?

4. Read a book written for preschool-aged children. Does this book appeal to you? Do you think it will appeal to children? Evaluate this book using the criteria outlined in Figure 12-1.

5. Examine some samples of children's artwork. Do you see examples of mock writing? Are there letters included? Are there any recognizable words written in invented spelling by the child?

CHAPTER 13

1. As we discuss in this chapter, becoming socialized into society is a complex process. Which early childhood activities and teacher behaviors do you think contribute to this goal?

2. What is your earliest recollection of a friendship? Can you recall why this friendship developed? How long did it last? What was special about this particular friend? What feelings does your recollection of this friendship evoke right now?

3. Observe a group of young children during a time when they can self-select activities. Note with whom they interact. How many of the children interact primarily with peers of the same sex? How many interact with peers of the opposite sex? Estimate the proportion of same-sex and cross-sex interactions.

4. Look around an early childhood classroom to assess how it promotes positive (or negative) attitudes toward other people in relation to sex, race, culture, or disability. What recommendations can you make for setting up a nonbiased classroom?

5. Try one of the cooperative games listed in this chapter with a group of young children. What was their reaction?

CHAPTER 14

1. Observe children arriving at school with their parents. What differences in the way they leave their parents do you note?

2. A three-year-old in your class consistently refuses to go to sleep during nap, but then almost always falls asleep later in the afternoon. What strategies might you use in such a situation?

3. Ask three teachers what rules they set for the young children in their class. Are there commonalities among the rules listed by the different teachers? Are there differences? Which rules seem reasonable and understandable to preschoolers? Do any of the rules seem inappropriate?

4. Observe a preschool class during transitions between activities. What strategies does the teacher use? Do these strategies reflect a sense of preparedness and forethought? Did the transitions go smoothly or were there some problems? How could these transitions be improved?

5. You are going to take a group of children on the first field trip of the year. How will you and the other staff members prepare for this trip? How will you prepare the children?

CHAPTER 15

1. List the behaviors you think are desirable in young children. Then make a list of the characteristics you like to see in adults. Now compare the two lists. Are the qualities on your two lists similar? Do you see a link between your expectations of children's behaviors and the outcomes you find desirable in adults?

2. Consider the three philosophies of guidance discussed in this chapter. Does one appeal to you more than the others? Why? Are there specific features in the approaches that you think would be effective as you work with children?

3. Observe a teacher at work with young children. What guidance techniques do you see this teacher using? Can you relate these techniques to any particular theory? Is this teacher's approach based on one theory or does it seem to be eclectic?

4. Why is it important to consider the underlying cause of a child's misbehavior? Consider the consequences for a child who is continually berated or punished for a behavior that she is not able to control.

5. Observe a group of children and note any aggressive behavior. What was the nature of the aggression? How did the aggressive child act? How did the victim of the aggression react? What did the teacher do? Was the teacher's action or reaction effective? Why or why not?

CHAPTER 16

1. What have been the most stressful events in your life? What were your reactions? How did you cope? What feelings did you experience? Can you think of a stressor in your life that has had a positive effect on you?

2. Talk to a teacher of young children and ask her what types of family stressors are experienced by the children in her class. How do these stressors affect the children? How does the teacher help the children deal with their stress?

3. Check what the procedures are for reporting suspected child abuse and neglect in your local community. Which agency or agencies should be contacted? What procedure will be set in motion by such a report? What is the involvement of the person who makes the report?

4. Review several children's books, such as those listed in Figure 16-4, that deal with sensitive issues. How do these books address such topics as loss, divorce, or fear? Could a young child identify with the characters? Do the books offer alternatives to the child who is experiencing a similar stressor?

5. Observe a self-protection program presentation for young children. What concepts are being presented? Are these concepts appropriate for the cognitive and emotional abilities of young children? What do you think young children might learn from this program? Do you see any drawbacks or potential problems from this program?

Name Index

Subject Index

Note: Numerals in *italics* refer to figures and illustrations.